Theories of Human Development

INTEGRATIVE PERSPECTIVES

Dale E. Goldhaber
University of Vermont

MAYFIELD PUBLISHING COMPANY
Mountain View, California
London • Toronto

To Jeanne

Library of Congress Cataloging-in-Publication Data

Goldhaber, Dale.
   Theories of human development : integrative perspectives / Dale E. Goldhaber
     p. cm.
   Includes bibliographical references and index.
   ISBN 1-55934-759-7
   1. Developmental psychology. I. Title
BF713
                           99-045104

Manufactured in the United States of America
10   9   8   7   6   5   4

Mayfield Publishing Company
1280 Villa Street
Mountain View, California 94041

Sponsoring editor, Franklin C. Graham; production editor, April Wells-Hayes; manuscript editor, Tom Briggs; design manager and cover designer, Susan Breitbard; text designer, Joan Greenfield; illustrations, Lotus Art; manufacturing manager, Randy Hurst. The text was set in 9/12 Stone Serif by TBH Typecast, Inc., and printed on 45# Highland Plus by Malloy Lithographing, Inc.

Brief Contents

Contents

Preface

Like most textbook authors, I wrote *Theories of Human Development* because I was unable to find just the right book for my course, in this case a seminar on theories of human development. I felt that the presentation of theories in other texts made them seem dated and set in stone. The presentations often made it difficult for my students to recognize the shared assumptions that different theories often have and the close link that exists between theory and method. Ironically, at the same time, these discussions also made it difficult for students to realize that, even though some theories do share common assumptions, there are nevertheless fundamental differences—differences so significant that it raises questions as to their comparability. Finally, I was frustrated that other texts did not provide a very adequate discussion of newer, emerging perspectives in developmental theory. So I now have a text that meets my needs, and I hope it meets yours too.

My seminar includes both advanced undergraduate and graduate students, and the text is written for both levels. It is equally appropriate for use across the wide variety of academic disciplines and departments for which a course on theories of human development is an essential part of the curriculum.

This book's organization reflects the *world view perspective* first introduced by the philosopher Stephen Pepper and brought to the attention of developmentalists through a series of articles by Willis Overton and Hayne Reese dating back to 1970. The three world views relevant to developmentalists are mechanism, organicism, and contextualism. Within each world view, it is possible to identify a "family of theories." Like all families, these share a common heritage (that is, world view), and, like all families, there are differences between relatives. The value of a world view approach is that it helps the reader identify, within each world view, the common threads that run between theories. It also helps the reader recognize that these world views present three fundamentally different theoretical images of human behavior and human development. A major purpose of the text is to help the reader understand the implicit and explicit assumptions of the three world views, why these three world views are so distinct, and in what ways it is possible to see the three as complementing each other.

Theories of Human Development is organized into four parts. Part I begins with a general discussion of the nature and value of theories and an introduction to Pepper's metaphoric concept of world views. I make the argument that the three world views are best appreciated as complementary to each other in that theories in each can be seen as addressing one of the three fundamental questions that a complete description of human development must address. These three questions are, How do we differ from each other? Why do we change over time? and What determines the particular content of our individual lives? The first question is a question of variability and is most closely related to mechanism. The second question is a question of sequential patterns of change over time and is most closely related to organicism. The third question is a question of the role played by particular sociohistorical contexts in the definition of both structure and function and is most closely related to contextualism.

Three chapters follow the introduction. Each chapter deals with one of Pepper's three developmental perspectives or world views. Each begins with a short discussion of Pepper's metaphoric image of that world view and is followed by a discussion of the implications of this world view for a theory of human development. Following the discussion of theoretical implications, the next section within each of these three chapters discusses the methodological implications of that particular perspective. There is a close correspondence between method and theory, and these sections highlight that correspondence.

Part II focuses on the mechanistic world view and is divided into four chapters—a chapter on learning theory, on social learning (now social cognitive) theory, on information processing theory, and on behavior genetic theory. Each chapter offers a discussion of the particulars of that theory and why it is reflective of a mechanist world view. The close link between theoretical assumptions and methodological strategies is also discussed. Examples of both exemplary and historically significant work within each of the four theories is discussed and, when appropriate, comparisons between theories within the mechanistic world view are also presented.

The issue of comparisons between theories within a particular world view is especially relevant to the mechanistic world view because the reductionist assumptions of the view make it possible to have theories that contradict each other but which at the same time are equally consistent with the world view. For example, the nature/nurture debate largely exists within the mechanistic world view because the view allows one to partition variance and therefore to treat antecedents as independent variables. Differences in the statistical assumptions relating to this partitioning lead to differences in how much variance is seen as accounted for by nature and how much by nurture. In other words, although radical behaviorism and behavior genetic theory are about as far apart on the nature/nurture issue as one can get, they both are nevertheless excellent examples of theories within a mechanistic world view.

Part III reviews theories within the organismic world view and is also arranged in four chapters—a chapter on the developmental psychobiological perspective, on Piagetian theory, on neo-Piagetian perspectives, and on the psychodynamic models of both Freud and Erikson. The chapter on psychobiological perspectives includes the historical work of both Gesell and McGraw as well as the current work of Thelen. The chapter on Piaget presents his theory as it evolved over the course of his career rather than in the more traditional format of the four developmental periods. I believe that presenting his work as it evolved helps the reader better appreciate the fact that theories are always living things. The chronological approach also makes it easier to include a discussion of the revisions he made to his theory after 1960, as the four periods were already well defined by 1960. The vitality of Piaget's work is also highlighted by a separate discussion on neo-Piagetian perspectives, notably the work of Fischer, Labouvie-Vief, and Damon. The discussion of Freud emphasizes the fact that in many cases he was the first to ask the questions that are of importance to developmentalists today. The discussion of Erikson emphasizes the truly life span scope of his work.

Part IV reviews theories within the contextualist world view and is divided into three chapters—a chapter on life span cohort models, a chapter on co-constructivist and sociocultural models, and a chapter on postmodern perspectives. Contextualism as a world view—in contrast to the treatment of context as a category of antecedent variables—forces us to consider the most fundamental question about theories of human development, namely, Is such a thing as an objective, universal theory of human development even possible? The question reflects the debate about the interplay of one's views of development and the sociohistorical context in which these views are formed. In the extreme, such arguments claim that developmental theory is little more than an apologia for the prevailing social and political forces within a society and as such can have little, if any, scientific value or validity.

The text concludes with an epilogue, which returns to the issues raised in the prologue—in particular, the issue of the comparability of theories within each of Pepper's three world views and about the "complementariness" of theories across the three views. The concluding point is that ultimately we may be better served by seeking a basis for the synthesis of the three world views than by debating their relative merits.

Acknowledgments

No one really writes a book alone. Although I am responsible for these words and for any errors they might hold, there are others who have made the task possible. I want to thank my colleagues Jeanne Goldhaber, Larry Shelton, Jill Tarule, and Jackie Weinstock for reading sections of the manuscript and for giving of their time to discuss with me the intricacies of particular theories. I owe a debt of gratitude to both Willis Overton and Hayne Reese for being the first to bring Pepper's work to the attention of developmentalists, and ultimately I owe a debt of gratitude to the people whose work is discussed on these pages. Their efforts have made the study and teaching of human development across the life span a much more meaningful and exciting experience for me.

The following individuals merit thanks for their thoughtful reviews of the manuscript: Kathleen M. Gallotti, Carleton College; Karen Hooker, Oregon State University; Marianne McGrath, University of Michigan at Flint; Cynthia J. Schmiege, University of Idaho; Laurie A. Sullivan-Hunter, Francis Marion University; and L. Eugene Thomas, University of Connecticut.

Thanks are also due to Tom Briggs for his careful editing, and to those at Mayfield Publishing Company who helped this book become a reality: Frank Graham, April Wells-Hayes, Marty Granahan, Susan Breitbard, Jay Bauer, and Mary Johnson.

1

Prologue

A *prologue* is a preliminary act or course of action foreshadowing greater events. On this optimistic note, let me begin our discussion of theoretical perspectives on human development. This short, introductory chapter has two purposes. The first is to examine theories in general—what they are, how they are developed, how they are validated. This general discussion will serve as a frame of reference for my second purpose —to provide a short introduction to three theoretical perspectives or *world views*. Each of the currently viable theories of human development reflects the theoretical assumptions of one of these three world views.

What Theories Are

Each of us, in our own way, is a human development theorist. We come up with theories all the time about all sorts of things we are trying to explain. For the most part, these personal theories seem directed at identifying simple cause-and-effect links, more generally referred to as *functional relationships*. In some cases the cause might be identified as some external condition or consequence; in other cases the cause is presumed to be some internal state. Saying that a child's improved performance in school is due to a new teacher in the classroom is an example of the first case. Saying that a child's aggressive behavior toward a new sibling is due to feelings of jealousy is an example of the second.

However, deciding whether a cause is internal or external is not always easy. Perhaps for the first child, school improvement reflects an increased desire to do well rather than any specific actions on the part of the new teacher. Perhaps for the second child, the reason for the jealousy is that the arrival of the new baby has resulted in a decrease in parental attention. Perhaps the internal and external reasons are so enmeshed that even to speak of them as distinct misrepresents the situation.

Because our personal theories aren't always testable in any formal or systematic manner, there may be no certain way to determine which of these explanations is the

1

most reasonable. Therefore, it is probably more appropriate to call them hunches or guesses rather than theories. We can reserve the term *theory* for the more formal statements about human development that are the work of *developmentalists*.[1]

Hunches do have one thing in common with theories. In both cases we aren't content simply to observe, collect, and store bits and pieces of data. We want to do something with these data; we want to act upon the data in such a way that the result is a greater understanding of our topic of interest. In both cases we want to know *why*. The distinction, then, between our personal hunches and scientific theories isn't one of motive or interest. It is one of method. Because of the way that theories are constructed, they are much more likely than our hunches to help us understand the world around us and our place in that world. The benefits of theories also provide the basis for judging a theory's scientific worth, that is, its integrity and usefulness.

Integrity is a measure of how well a theory holds together. It reflects both the evidence available to support the theory and the degree to which the different elements of the theory are integrated in a logically consistent manner. The *usefulness* of a theory is just that: Does this theory help us understand a phenomenon? Does it help us predict? Does it help us integrate diverse bits of knowledge? Does it lead to some desirable course of action or outcome?

The Value of Theories

So what do theories of human development actually help us do? First, they offer a systematic means to understand the phenomena that define our existence. They provide a means to categorize data, make comparisons, and identify patterns. Second, theories of human development enable us to generalize about these specific understandings. As such, they are economical—they allow us to use less to deal with more. They also provide a basis for recognizing the link among seemingly distinct events, as well as the independence of seemingly related events. Third, these theories provide a basis for decision making, a means to choose to do one thing rather than another. In so doing, they allow us to exercise a degree of control over the forces that directly or indirectly affect our lives. Fourth, these theories provide a means for predicting future events. Even if we can't control all the events in our lives, if we know what is likely to happen tomorrow or next month or next year, at least we can begin to make the appropriate preparations or accommodations. Finally, the answers that these theories provide help us define the next question to ask, the next theoretical topic to pursue.

---

[1] I will use the term *developmentalists* to refer to all those who study the course and process of human development. This is a more general term than *developmental psychologist*, and it reflects the fact that, although many developmentalists are psychologists by training and inclination, others represent disciplines as diverse as education, medicine, sociology, human development, family studies, and human ecology, to name a few.

The Validity of Theories

These five values also form the basis by which we can judge theories' integrity and usefulness (Horowitz, 1987; Howard, 1985). First, for a theory to claim to be scientific, it must be testable. That is, it must make possible the creation of a testable set of predictions and/or explanations. Furthermore, these predictions and explanations must ultimately be *empirical* in nature. That is, the data generated and the methods used to generate and analyze the data must be such that others can verify the data or even replicate the process. If others can't obtain at least similar results by repeating the process, then there is no way to confirm or refute the validity of the specific assumptions of the theory, and therefore the usefulness of the theory itself. What actually constitutes an acceptable method or acceptable data, however, varies greatly between theories (Overton & Reese, 1973) and is a topic of considerable debate among developmentalists. But within each theory there is some method, which leads to some behavior or behaviors, that allows us to conclude that the theory has some degree of validity.

Testability is not the only criterion by which theories can be evaluated. A second criterion is that the theory must be able to organize and interpret, in some systematic fashion, a broad range of data. The broader the range, the more useful the theory. For example, being able to explain the behavior of 3-year-olds is good; being able to explain the behavior of 3-, 4-, and 5-year-olds is better. In the same vein a theory that explains a variety of seemingly distinct phenomena is better than one that explains events only within one domain. For instance, a theory that explains the behavior of children in settings as diverse as the home, the school, and the playground is more useful than a theory that explains the behavior of children in only one of these settings. And, of course, a theory that explains how behavior changes over the course of a life span is more useful than one that explains behavior only at any one point in that life span.

A third criterion for evaluating the validity of theories is their generativity. A good theory is one that not only successfully explains whatever it is trying to explain but also leads others to both new areas of inquiry and new interpretations of existing data or theory. For example, my theory of children's behavior in diverse settings might prompt someone to investigate whether the theory is equally effective in explaining the behavior of adults. Or it might prompt a sociologist to determine whether the theory is equally effective in explaining the relationships among groups of people. Maybe what started as an attempt to explain the behavior of children ends up being a way to better understand why racial and ethnic tensions exist in society.

A fourth criterion for evaluating theories involves precision: the more precise the theory's predictions, the more useful the theory. A theory predicting that an earthquake is likely to occur within the next 90 days is good; one that predicts that the quake will occur next Friday at noon is better. Knowing when the event is most likely to occur provides a greater basis for action.

These four criteria—testability, organization, generativity, and precision—are commonly accepted across the broad ranges of theoretical perspectives. Even though different theoretical perspectives offer different definitions of what constitutes an acceptable measure of each criterion, they nevertheless agree that these four criteria define a theory's integrity and usefulness. But the fact that the four are often defined differently may significantly limit the degree to which the relative value of various theories can be directly compared.

Constructing Theories

How do we go about constructing a theory of human development so that it will meet these criteria? Theory building and testing involve a series of steps that collectively define the *scientific method* (Achenbach, 1978; Wolman, 1981). The steps in the series are observe, ask, test, analyze, and interpret. When the steps are sequenced from observe to interpret, the process is described as *inductive* because we are going from the particular "up to" the general. When the steps are sequenced from the general to the particular, the process is described as *deductive* because we are going from the general "down to" the particular. Different theoretical perspectives tend to favor one or the other approach, but in fact there is really a chicken-and-egg relationship between the two (Kurtines, Azmitia, & Gewirtz, 1992). That is, developmentalists do not observe randomly; rather, something guides their actions or prompts them to ask a question about a particular topic or in a particular manner. At the same time, developmentalists are not "armchair philosophers"; that is, they don't construct logical, abstract systems without first having in mind some behavior or event that the theory helps explain.

Observation is just that. It is noticing something, being amazed or intrigued by something, even finding something troubling or upsetting—such as an isolated behavior, a sequence of behaviors, interactions between two or more people, or a shift in cultural patterns. The behaviors might occur simultaneously, they might happen in close temporal or spatial proximity, or they might be separated by significant time and/or distance. Developmentalists are particularly interested in this last instance, because they focus on the ways people change over time. But, again, the observations are not likely to be random. There is almost certainly a reason we find one behavior change novel and intriguing and another banal. Some idea, however implicit, is certainly guiding our observations.

Once we have made an observation, we need to state it in the testable form of a *hypothesis*. A hypothesis restates the observation in the form of an "if-then" statement or prediction. Restating the observation in this form allows it to be tested. Here are some examples:

If quality of work among adults is related to salary, *then* increasing the salary of workers will lead to an increase in the quality of their work.

If traumatic early life experiences limit life satisfaction, *then* a therapy designed to help individuals restructure their early experiences in a less traumatic fashion will lead to higher levels of life satisfaction.

If a certain level of cognitive development is a prerequisite for successful school performance, *then* individuals who do not yet possess this level of cognition will not do well academically.

If the structure of a society limits opportunities for some in that society, *then* changing its structure will lead to greater social justice and equality.

If there is a relationship between height and popularity during adolescence, *then* knowing an individual's height will allow us to predict his or her popularity with peers.

Notice that in this last case the hypothesis does not predict a direction to the effect. It simply hypothesizes that a relationship exists. We will have to collect the data to see if there is a relationship and, if so, whether it is the taller or the shorter kids who are the most popular. By contrast, in the first four examples a direction is predicted: More pay will lead to higher-quality work, therapy will improve traumatized peoples' satisfaction with life, and so on. Both types of hypotheses are acceptable, but hypotheses that predict a direction to the results are preferred because they are more precise.

To be of any value, a hypothesis must be testable. In other words, some method must be devised to obtain the data necessary to determine if there is a relationship between height and popularity; or between salary and work quality; or between early life experience, therapeutic intervention, and life satisfaction; or between social structure and human potential. The data itself doesn't answer the question, but it does provide the basis upon which the validity of the hypotheses can be tested.

Methods of data collection vary greatly depending on the specifics of the hypotheses and the theoretical perspective in which the hypotheses are generated. Some methods are easier and more direct than others. For example, it is certainly easier to obtain reliable data about height than about a concept as complex as popularity or social structure. Some tests take place under highly controlled laboratory conditions; others, in naturally occurring settings. Some data is based on systematic observation; other data, on the narratives of individuals. However the data is collected, regardless of the actual procedures used, the data must be collected in such a way that others can verify its existence. This is an issue not of possible fraud (although this sometimes happens in science), but of replicability. Theoretical statements based on data that isn't ultimately replicable are of little or no value.

Once verifiable data is collected, it needs to be analyzed. As is true of data collection, methods of data analysis are highly varied and again reflect the nature of the hypotheses, the nature of the data collected, and the theoretical perspective of the developmentalist. The data might be subjected to a highly quantified statistical analysis to determine the probability of the observed relationship occurring by chance alone. Or it might be subjected to a logical analysis to see if the pattern of the data is consistent with certain theoretical expectations. Or it might be analyzed to detect the presence of certain themes, orientations, or topics. In each case the analysis is intended to determine if the data collected allows one to confirm or reject the original hypotheses.

Finally, the analyzed data has to be interpreted within some larger theoretical context. Interpretation attempts to answer questions like these: What does it suggest about human nature that the quality of our work is highly contingent on the level of rewards received for that work? How is it possible that events occurring during the early years of childhood can affect our behavior as adults? The process is usually abstract and, to a degree, speculative. For some theories the interpretation is limited to the specifics of the situation from which the data was obtained; for others the goal is to extrapolate to the greatest degree possible. In either case the interpretive process tries

to identify how a given behavior pattern relates to other behavior patterns, to particular life circumstances, and/or to some form of psychological process or structure. In
effect, the interpretive process is looking for the common forms or patterns that allow
the data to be understood within some larger context. How much larger this context
can be—and in particular, whether it is possible to argue that the findings have a universal quality to them—is a topic of much theoretical debate.

If the entire sequence of steps in the scientific method has been performed correctly, we now have one or more answers that we didn't have before. But the sequence
gives us more than answers. It also provides us with new questions, questions that
weren't recognizable before this new piece of the puzzle was identified. And so the
process repeats itself, with each answer providing us with both a greater understanding of and more questions about the way things are.

Before we examine specific developmental theories, it is important to note that
theories are *not* dogma. Dogma implies an absoluteness that theories cannot and do
not claim. Rather, theories are estimates or best guesses. Whereas dogma tends to be
static, theories are dynamic. They are modified as new evidence requires it; a sufficient
amount of contradictory evidence may even cause a once-promising theory to be
rejected as essentially valueless. None of the theories that we will examine is unchang-
ing. Theorists as eminent as Sigmund Freud, B. F. Skinner, and Jean Piaget changed
their views during their long professional careers, and even after their deaths their theories continue to change as a result of further research.

Three Developmental Perspectives

The discussion of theories and their value, evaluation, and construction to this point
has been very general. Except for some of the examples, the discussion would be
appropriate as a general introduction to a book on theory in many scientific disciplines. But this is, after all, a book about human development theories, and having
now laid the foundation, it's time to start building the structure.

Theories of human development try to explain why it is that we are the way we
are and why it is that, whatever we are, it seems to change over time. Different theories
approach this task in different ways. They differ in terms of the most important
aspects of behavior to study, the ways specific behaviors are linked to one another, the
presumed causes of the behavior, and the explanations as to how behavior changes. Of
equal importance is the fact that theories also differ in terms of the methods each uses
to study human development. Therefore a book about theories must also be a book
about methodology, because at least within the social sciences, theories and methods
are closely intertwined. In fact, it is this closeness between method and theory that
sometimes makes it very difficult, if not impossible, to directly compare the validity of
various theories (Gholson & Barker, 1985; Overton, 1991).

Theories do not stand in isolation to one another. Because individual theories typically share certain basic assumptions with other theories, it is possible to group theories in terms of shared basic assumptions. These shared assumptions reflect a common
theoretical perspective or world view. Theoretical perspective or world view implies a

level of analysis broader than any one specific theory (Reese & Overton, 1970). It concerns the particular theoretical and methodological assumptions that different groups or families of theorists use in the construction of their individual theories.

Theories that share a world view may differ on the particulars and may even be in opposition on some points, but they still share a set of basic assumptions or building blocks that each has used in arriving at its conclusions. The three developmental perspectives or world views that are most relevant to developmentalists are the *mechanistic world view,* the *organismic world view,* and the *contextualist world view.*

Pepper's Metaphoric Explanatory Framework

Stephen Pepper's (1961) work provides perhaps the most complete explanation of a world view approach to the analysis of theory. Pepper was a philosopher of science whose work is generally seen (Kendler, 1986; Overton & Reese, 1973; Reese & Overton, 1970) as providing the clearest differentiation of the three world views.[2]

Pepper's interest was not specific to theories of human development, but rather addressed, more generally and abstractly, what he referred to as the discovery of truth and the justification of human values. His approach to this process of discovery was through the use of metaphors—the machine in the case of mechanism, the living organism in the case of organicism, and the historical act in the case of contextualism. Metaphors are "as if" mechanisms. As such, they offer figurative rather than literal equivalents to the phenomena they are trying to explain.

Through metaphor Pepper sought to use something more familiar to help us understand something less familiar. In this sense the machine, the living organism, and the historical act are seen as being more familiar (we have a greater understanding of each) than our understanding of human development. Saying, for example, that it is possible to understand human behavior by arguing that we function *as if* we were machines does not in any sense imply that we are machines. It implies only that an understanding of one may give us insights into the understanding of the other. The failure to keep this distinction in mind often leads to inappropriate criticisms of theories, an especially common problem in the case of mechanism.

Mechanistic, organismic, and contextual world views differ from one another in terms of how they answer three basic questions; Table 1.1 summarizes the differences —and the similarities. On some of the questions, two of the three views overlap. But it is the unique patterns across all three questions that define the unique approach of each to the study of human development (Overton, 1984, 1991, 1994; Pepper, 1961; Reese, 1991; Reese & Overton, 1970).

The first question concerns beliefs about the universality of human development: Is the data on human development, in the main, an accurate reflection of development for all times and in all places, or is development so situation-specific that it is

---

[2] Pepper actually discusses four world views in his book. The fourth is formism, which uses the root metaphor of similarity. In essence, formism argues that things that seem to be alike are alike. No theory of human development is based on this notion, and so this world view will not be discussed further.

TABLE 1.1

Comparison of Pepper's Three World Views

World View	Generalizability	Types of Acceptable Causes	Level of Analysis
Mechanism	Universal	Efficient, material	Reductionist
Organicism	Universal	Efficient, material, formal, final	Holistic
Contextualism	Situation-specific	Efficient, material, formal	Holistic

impossible to generalize across time and place? Both mechanists and organicists believe that there are universal laws (although they differ sharply as to what those laws are); contextualists, true to their name and their metaphor, do not.

The second question concerns the causes of human development: What causes us to be the way we are, and what causes us to change? Consistent with their machine metaphor, mechanists accept only causes that are efficient and material in nature. *Efficient causes* are those that are external to the individual. They are things that happen to the person, and presumably the person's behavior is then a reflection of that antecedent event. Antecedents such as a particular pattern of reinforcement, a specific parenting style, or a certain educational technique are examples of efficient causes. *Material causes* refer to specific, internal components that make up the individual. When information processing theorists refer to an individual's memory capacity, or when behavior geneticists refer to specific genes, they are both describing material causes. In the first case the individual's behavior is said to be a reflection of his or her ability to remember things; in the second case the behavior is due to the action of a particular gene in the regulation of some ability.

Organicists accept both efficient and material causes as partial explanations of behavior but place the most emphasis on two other types of cause—formal cause and final cause. *Formal cause* refers to the influence of the interaction of the parts of a system. Living organisms are, in this sense, seen as more than simply the sum of their parts. Thus, a quality such as intelligence does not reflect the actions of any one component, but rather represents the synergistic interaction of many components. It is the particular form of the relationship between the components that is seen as the cause of the behavior. Organicists refer to *final causes* as a way to help them comprehend the fact that there must be a reason development seems, at least to the organicists, to be a unidirectional process. For instance, we walk before we run, we talk before we write, and we react to others before we are able to initiate independent action.

Contextualists appear most comfortable with efficient, material, and formal causes. But they have little use for final causes because they believe that development is always specific to historical time and social place. Furthermore, because they believe in the power of time and place, the meaning and influence of any particular efficient, material, or formal cause is also specific to time and place.

The third question concerns how causes relate to one another. Mechanists believe that it is possible to separate causes and to determine the relative influence of each. As such, they are *reductionistic* in their theorizing, a characteristic they share with theorists in many other scientific disciplines. Both organismic and contextualistic theories are *holistic;* causes acquire meaning—that is, become causes—only when they interact with other causes.

Mutual Exclusivity

The fact that each of these three world views rests on such a unique foundation led Pepper to conclude that the three are mutually exclusive. He argued that we cannot pick and choose pieces of each view to combine into an eclectic theory as we might do if we were selecting dinner items at a cafeteria. Rather, they come as a package deal, a "prix fixe" meal. If we accept the package of theoretical assumptions of one, we are rejecting those of the other two—at least as it concerns any particular theoretical developmental question. To do otherwise would be to create a theory that is internally inconsistent and therefore of limited explanatory value.

This issue of mutual exclusivity is very important because it implies that theories from one world view cannot be directly evaluated against or translated into theories from another. To do so would be akin to comparing the proverbial apples and oranges. This doesn't mean that we *can't* compare them; after all, we have been doing precisely that. Rather, it means that we can't directly test or determine the relative validity of one when compared to the other. A couple of examples of this distinctiveness might help clarify this issue.

Mechanism's machine metaphor implies that it is possible to understand human behavior as if it functions like a machine. The metaphoric implication is *not* that humans are machines, but rather that we can apply our understanding of the functioning of machines to gain insight into the functioning of humans. For example, one of the defining characteristics of a machine is that it is reactive. It remains at rest unless acted upon by some external force. Extending the metaphor to humans implies that an examination of the efficient and material factors that appear to influence human behavior is our best strategy for gaining a full understanding of that behavior. For mechanists human behavior is a reaction to the influence of efficient and material causes.

Organicism's metaphor of the living organism leads to a different type of explanation. Organisms are alive, they initiate activity, and they are self-directed. For organicists, they are more than the sum of their parts. They are certainly influenced by both efficient and material factors, but their responses to situations primarily reflect their interpretation of the situation rather than the specifics of the situation itself. That is, rather than reacting to the situation as it is structured, organicists argue, we actively construct meaning to the situation and then respond to that situation on the basis of this constructed knowledge.

Consider a second example: Organicists argue that a set of universal rules really does govern human behavior. In particular, they believe that the course of development involves a process of becoming increasingly adaptive in dealing with life situations. For the organicist, if development occurs, it will always do so in the direction of increasing adaptiveness over a broad period of time. By contrast, contextualists argue that there is no set of universal rules. They believe that the particular patterns of development that one might observe are specific to a historical time and a social place. As such, if the contextualist described development as adaptive, this would constitute a historical statement specific to a particular time and place rather than a universal statement appropriate to all times and all places. Change the specific circumstances associated with a particular historical time and social place, and the course of development would no longer appear as adaptive. Clearly, again, we can't have it both ways. There either is or there isn't a set of universals that regulates the course of development.

This is not a very satisfying state of affairs. We might argue that, even if theories within each world view are based on different assumptions, it still should be possible to find a method that would allow us to test which set of assumptions is best supported. Why couldn't we merely devise some experimental procedure to test whether human behavior is ultimately reactive or active in nature or whether there really are some universals regulating the course of human development. A reasonable proposal —but unfortunately one that is not yet workable, because the three world views differ not only in terms of their basic assumptions but also, to a large degree, in terms of the nature of the methods and the types of evidence each considers to be a valid test of a given theory. No matter how the experiment was designed, it would inevitably be more consistent with one world view or another. The data such an experiment would generate and the techniques used to interpret that data would therefore be more acceptable to adherents of one world view than the other two.

Mechanists, for example, design experiments based on the theoretical assumption that the effect of each variable that influences behavior can be measured independently of the effects of other variables. Organicists, on the other hand, being holistic, believe that variables gain significance only when they function in combination with other variables. Isolate a variable, and its significance is removed. Contextualists, in contrast to both mechanists and organicists, and consistent with their nonuniversal assumptions, limit their interpretations of their research to the setting from which it was drawn. Organicists would not accept data from an experiment that isolated variables, and mechanists would not do so from one that didn't; both would want to generalize their findings beyond the setting in which they were gathered. But contextualists would argue there is no justification for such a generalization.

Resolving the Impasse

Is there no way to get beyond this impasse? The answer is yes and no. Attempts have been made to integrate the perspectives, but usually these are little more than arguments that one perspective can be subsumed within another. Such arguments are typically made by members of the "subsuming" perspective. Needless to say, the "subsumed" perspective is rarely in agreement. In such cases the typical argument is that one of the world views is simply a special case of another and therefore need not be seen as standing alone, on equal footing. Organicists, for example, have argued that mechanism is such a special case; mechanists, in turn, have argued similarly with respect to contextualism. Aside from the merits of these claims, it is important to recognize that they are based on the assumption that each of the world views is trying to explain the same phenomena—that is, that the three are in direct competition with one another.

There is a second possible way to consider the relationship among the three perspectives. Each may be attempting to explain distinct aspects of behavior and development—that is, to explain complementary rather than identical phenomena. In particular, we might argue that organismic theory is largely concerned with an idealized image of developmental patterns that serve to define us as a species. From such a perspective organicists would, and do, concern themselves with questions about how we are all like one another, irrespective of the specifics of our sociohistorical contexts. From a second perspective we might argue that mechanism is largely concerned with those factors that create variability among individuals. As such, mechanists would be, and are, interested in defining those mechanisms that describe the processes by which we each become unique individuals.

The complementariness of these two perspectives should be clear—one helps explain why we are alike, the other how we are different. But the picture is not yet complete, because neither organicism nor mechanism addresses the specifics of our particular sociohistorical experiences. This specificity is the contextualists' level of analysis. Because contextualism is not concerned with identifying universal patterns, it is able to focus on the particular events that form our everyday experiences. It is only when all three world views are considered do we have the potential for a full understanding of both the processes and the products of the human condition. Unfortunately we have no strategy to link the three levels of analysis. Rather, each continues to function on its own, trying to answer its particular questions on development across the life span.

This impasse is not, however, such a terrible state of affairs. The work within each perspective has helped us understand particular aspects of development even if this understanding remains incomplete. Furthermore, the problem is certainly not unique to the study of human development. Physicists, for example, have been debating for centuries whether light is best conceptualized as a wave or a particle. In the case of human development, someone ultimately will come up with a broad enough conceptualization that the three perspectives can be incorporated within it. Pepper's world views are a step in that direction because they make it possible to group particular theories of human development that share a common set of core assumptions into families of theories.

We now turn to Part I of the text, a detailed discussion of the three world views introduced in Chapter 1. As you read the chapters in Part I, keep in mind the differences in the basic assumptions made by each of the three world views. Again, it is the differences in these basic assumptions that often are reflected in their respective methodologies and in debates as to their comparability.

Human Development in Perspective

The three chapters in Part I examine each of the three world views in greater detail. The goal in each of these three chapters is to provide you a fuller understanding of that world view than has been possible in the introductory chapter and to show the close relationship between the theoretical assumptions of a particular world view and the research strategies that have been designed to test those assumptions. The issue of the relationship between theory and method is very important because world views differ not only in terms of theory but in terms of methods as well. Parts II, III, and IV of the book then examine, respectively, the family of theories that constitute the mechanistic, organismic, and contextualist world views.

2

How We Are—
The Mechanistic World View

The first of the three perspectives relevant to developmental theory is Pepper's (1961) mechanistic world view. Historically this perspective has formed the backbone for the physical and natural sciences and for psychology, at least as the latter is pursued in the United States. For psychology in general and human development in particular, mechanism has an interesting status. Few developmentalists would label themselves as mechanists even though, at least at the methodological level, many follow a research program consistent with this perspective. Instead, they prefer to identify themselves using terms more specific to their particular theoretical interest within mechanism. Four of these approaches will be covered in Part II: learning theory, social cognitive theory, information processing theory, and developmental behavior genetic theory.

This preference for specificity probably reflects two things. First, because mechanism is defined as much by its approach to research as by the perspective itself, often less emphasis is placed on general discussions of theory. Second, the conflicts among the various theories of the mechanistic world view are perhaps greater than in organicism and contextualism. As such, these theorists may be reluctant to use the same label as some one with whom they have significant theoretical differences. This greater theoretical conflict within mechanism is partly a reflection of the fact that the basic assumptions of this world view make it possible to embrace, equally, theoretical perspectives as diverse as radical behaviorism—an approach almost exclusively interested in efficient causes—and developmental behavior genetics—an approach almost exclusively interested in material causes.

It may seem strange to include developmental behavior geneticists in this grouping, especially because people typically equate mechanism with behaviorism and learning theory. Although behaviorists, learning theorists, and information processing theorists are indeed mechanistic in their theorizing, it is important to remember that the defining characteristic of mechanism is not solely a focus on the external environment as the source of behavioral change (the behaviorists' orientation). Rather, we must acknowledge the even broader and more fundamental belief of mechanism that it is possible to tease apart the various factors that influence behavioral change and, having done so, to assign an independent relative level of importance to each.

Behaviorists and developmental behavior geneticists both share this belief. Where they differ is in the relative weight each assigns to the influence of environmental and genetic factors. It is this difference that defines the current form of the nature/nurture debate. Ironically the two groups are able to argue virtually opposite positions on the issue only because they do share a common perspective on how one should study behavior and behavioral change (Wahlsten, 1990).

Pepper's Analysis

Recall that Pepper's (1961) metaphor for the mechanistic perspective is the machine. As with all metaphorical analyses, Pepper is not saying that people are literally machines (nor are mechanists, I hasten to remind you). Rather, he is arguing that understanding the way machines operate can shed light on our understanding of the way humans operate.

There are, of course, all sorts of machines, from the very simple to the incredibly complex. Some machines, like those you might find on an assembly line, have hundreds of moving parts. Other machines, like computers, have virtually none. For Pepper the nature of the machine really isn't the issue. His argument is that there is a set of properties common to all machines, and these properties are metaphorically useful, from a mechanistic perspective, in our understanding of human development.

Primary Qualities

For Pepper, a description of the function of any machine requires a description of the machine's *primary qualities*—those elements of the machine that define how it operates. Pepper uses a simple lever to illustrate his analysis, but again, it is important to recognize that any other machine would yield the same pattern of relations.

The primary qualities of the lever consist of nothing but a board resting on a fulcrum. Downward force applied to one end results in an upward force at the other end. If this simple machine sounds familiar, it's probably because in childhood we all gain an intuitive understanding of its physics—it's a teeter-totter (or seesaw). If we were talking instead about a nondigital wristwatch, the primary qualities would include the gears and springs and a description of how a change in one component is reflected in a change in the other components.

Pepper makes three generalizations about the primary qualities that describe teeter-totters, wristwatches, and all other machines. First, each of the components of a machine (the board and the fulcrum, the gears and the springs, etc.) exists independent of the others, and this existence can be expressed in precise quantitative terms. The board, for example, can be described as having a particular weight and length, and the springs of the watch as having a specific tension. The board and the spring would still be a board and a spring even if they were parts of some other machines. They and all the other parts are the basic elements of each machine; they define the machine. The machine, then, is reducible to its parts and is nothing more than the sum of these parts. Understand that it is nothing more because it does not *need* to be anything more. That is, the metaphor is not meant to lessen us but rather to describe a level of analysis that mechanists believe is fully adequate to describe all that we are.

Second, each of the machine's elements exists in a particular relationship to the other elements of the machine. Knowing each element's location makes it possible to define that element in relationship to all the other elements comprised in the machine. Only when we know the location of all the elements (and therefore the relationship of each to the others) can we describe the precise mode of functioning of the machine. The lever, for example, will operate differently if the fulcrum is off center than if it is in the middle of the board.

Third, the components function in an exact quantitative relationship to one another. For instance, if we know the location of the fulcrum relative to the board and the amount of force being exerted on one end of the board, then we also know the force that would be needed on the other end of the board to balance it. The machine is considered a closed system in that knowing some things about the system make perfect prediction about some other aspect of the system theoretically possible. It also means that the relationship among the components can be expressed mathematically. As Pepper describes the relationship:

> It is an absolute mechanism. In such a universe almost anything might have been different, because almost everything is independent of almost everything else. If this atom had happened to be somewhere else at another time (and there is no necessary reason why it might not have been), then it would not have been hit by that atom.
> . . . But since this atom did happen to be at this place at this time and had been obeying the law of inertia, it was inevitable that the collision should have occurred. There is this strange polarity of accident and necessity in discrete mechanism, which is understandable as soon as it is realized that the accidental comes from the conception of the independence of the details, and the necessity from the inevitability of the events being just what it is since there is not reason to be found for it being anything else. (pp. 196–197)

Secondary Qualities

Pepper argues further that, from a mechanistic perspective, machines also exhibit a set of *secondary qualities*. Secondary qualities are as much a part of machines as are primary qualities, but they are not essential for a given machine to operate. For the teeter-totter, for example, these secondary qualities could include its color or movement or the sounds it makes as it operates; for humans, secondary qualities are those that relate to mental phenomena—such as sensations, perceptions, feelings, hopes, and dreams. Because none of these elements is involved in the efficient functioning of the machine, the mechanist isn't particularly interested in them. They are not seen as amenable to scientific analysis, and therefore they have no relevance to an understanding of the efficient operation of the machine.

A mechanist would certainly recognize that other scholars (e.g., those in the humanities) might be interested in hopes and dreams or in the images conveyed by the motion of the teeter-totter or the ticking of the watch. These other scholars might even argue, for example, that the ceaseless ticking of the watch is a much more meaningful image of the passage of time than the working of some gears and springs. But this analysis, the mechanist would counter, is literary, not scientific. The literary analysis would be seen as focusing not on real events (i.e., the primary qualities) but on epiphenomena (i.e., the secondary qualities).

The status of secondary qualities is an issue that differentiates the three world views. As will become clearer, what is largely a nuisance for the mechanist is, for both the organicist and the contextualist, an essential piece of the puzzle that is human development.

Mechanism as a Developmental Perspective

What do teeter-totters (and other machines, including computers) have to do with people and their development—besides the obvious fact that both have their ups and downs? Pepper's mechanistic world view reflects what was the dominant theoretical perspective in psychology for much of this century (approximately the 1920s through the 1960s) and what still represents a major family of theories examining behavioral change. Notice that I use the term *behavioral change* rather than *development* when discussing mechanism. The reason is that, for most mechanists, development has the status of a secondary quality whereas behavioral change is a primary quality—that is, it is observable and measurable and can be directly linked to other elements of the system.

Although any machine could be used to illustrate the concept of development as a mechanistic process, two specific machines—the telephone switchboard and the computer—are the ones most frequently used. The telephone switchboard is a simple mechanism in which inputs and outputs are connected. When someone dials a phone number, a signal is sent to the switchboard, the switchboard connects the incoming signal to an outgoing line, and the phone rings at the other end. This is essentially a process of linking stimuli with responses—and much of the research within the mechanistic tradition involves the linking of stimuli with responses.

The introduction of the computer has added another dimension to mechanistic accounts of behavioral change. Unlike the switchboard, which simply makes connections, the computer takes input (stimuli) and does something to it; that is, it processes information. What the computer does depends as much, if not more, on the nature of the program that is processing the input as on the nature of the input itself. Eventually, output (responses) emerges.

Mechanists who pursue an information processing approach to the study of behavior and behavioral change (Klahr, 1980; Siegler, 1991; Siegler & Shipley, 1987) believe that the computer provides them with a powerful means to go beyond the investigation of simple stimulus-and-response associations. They claim that the computer holds the promise of defining the mechanisms that account for complex as well as simple behaviors and for material as well as efficient causes.

Differences among theorists within the mechanist world view are usually a matter of machine preference. Some theorists, implicitly at least, pursue strategies more consistent with the switchboard metaphor in that they are primarily interested in the associations between external stimuli and response. They care little about the nature of the mechanism that intervenes between the two observable events. Other theorists, who are at least as interested in the role of the intervening mechanisms on the response as they are in the stimuli, frame their analyses in terms of the computer metaphor.

The specifics of each of these members of the mechanistic theoretical family—radical behaviorism, learning theory, social learning theory, social cognitive theory, information processing theory, developmental behavior genetic theory—will be discussed in Part II. For now, let us identify the threads that run through all of these mechanistic theories. These common threads reflect the belief that the best strategy for ultimately understanding why we are the way we are involves (1) viewing behavior as a response to discrete, antecedent events, (2) seeing observation and interpretation as separate and distinct, (3) describing causal agents as acting independently of one another, (4) classifying all behavior at all ages as consisting of the same basic elements, and (5) concluding that all behavior, theoretically at least, is lawful and therefore fully predictable.

Mechanists argue that this image of human behavior, based on the metaphor of the machine, offers four distinct advantages to the study of human development when compared to the organismic and contextual perspectives. These advantages are (1) the separation of observation and theory, (2) the discovery of universal laws, (3) the independence of antecedent variables, and (4) the integration of human development with other scientific disciplines.

The Separation of Observation and Theory

Basic to all theory within the mechanistic world view is the notion that observation and theory are distinct. Observations (facts) are not theories or value-laden comments; rather, they represent objective, factual reporting of events occurring within a spatio-temporal universe. As Kitchener (1983) puts it,

> Scientists, according to this view, simply open their eyes and directly (non-inferentially) observe what is directly and immediately present to their senses. No interpretation of inferences beyond what is immediately given (the data) is involved in observing something, and to allow such theoretical interpretations into one's observations (or data language) would be to contaminate a neutral observation (or observation report). (p. 5)

So what is it that is directly and immediately "present" to the mechanist? It is behavior. The mechanist observes behavior and changes in behavior. This is the objective data; this is what is locatable in time and space.

Just as the primary qualities of the board and fulcrum can be described in quantitative terms, so, too, can our behavior. To the mechanist our behavior is seen as demonstrating a variety of quantifiable characteristics, including (1) *frequency* (how often we do something), (2) *amplitude* (how hard we try), (3) *latency* (how long it takes us to respond), and (4) *accuracy* (how closely our behavior matches a model or standard).

Once objective behavior data has been collected, theory becomes the process of offering a plausible and testable explanation for the observed behaviors. These theoretical interpretations take two forms. In one case, they link one or more primary qualities of behavior to specific antecedent conditions. For example, the child is said to behave in a particular way because of the way the parent behaves; the adult works harder because the company links productivity to salary increases. In the other case, when it is less obvious what the functional relationship is between behavior and the environment, or even whether such a functional relationship exists, internal mechanisms are hypothesized as a mediating link in the chain between antecedent cause and subsequent behavior. These internal, mediating events are not seen as causing the behavior in the sense that they are the antecedent condition, or *efficient cause*. Rather, they are seen as serving as the *material cause* in the sense that they are the physiological, neurological, or genetic substrates that make the behavior possible (Overton & Reese, 1973). In either case, a direct link is posited between the cause (efficient or material) and the effect.

Debates among the family of mechanist theories are disagreements about the correct interpretation of these antecedent neutral observations (Kitchener, 1983). Skinnerians, for example, see no need to even go beyond the observations. They believe that the observation of functional relationships—that is, the relationship of a behavior and one or more efficient environmental circumstances—is all that is needed to eventually provide a full accounting of behavioral change (Baer, Wolf, & Risley, 1987; Bijou, 1989). Perhaps for this reason, Skinnerians are referred to as radical behaviorists (Zuriff, 1985). Developmental behavior genetic theorists and information processing theorists, on the other hand, each place as much emphasis (if not more) on material as efficient causes. For these theorists, behavior is much too complex to be explained solely by reference to the external environment. It is also necessary to talk about the materials or parts of the individual.

Secondary qualities (feelings, motives, aspirations, etc.), because they can't be directly observed or reliably inferred, measured, or located in a spatiotemporal universe, are of little interest to the mechanist. Mechanists aren't claiming that we don't experience these things. Rather, they are arguing that they are best studied and ultimately understood by focusing on behavioral change and on the efficient and material antecedents of that change.

As mentioned previously, this shunting of secondary qualities to the realm of poets and painters does not sit well with either organicists or contextualists. For their own reasons each believes that what mechanists call secondary qualities and assign the status of epiphenomena are, in fact, equally important data for a complete understanding of human development. Fundamental differences in opinion, such as on the status of secondary qualities, help explain why there is no direct way to test the validity of the three world views. The basis for any such comparison would necessarily rest on a set of assumptions and measurement techniques that would invariably be seen as favoring a given perspective or being more consistent with one perspective than another. This doesn't mean that we *can't* compare theories from different world views by describing their similarities and differences. But it does mean that directly testing theories from one world view against those from another is problematic.

The Discovery of Universal Laws

Mechanists believe that a second advantage of their perspective is that it allows for the discovery of universal laws. In particular, they argue that all behavior, from the simplest to the seemingly most complex, is regulated by the same factors (Kendler, 1992; Klahr, 1989). They can make this argument because the mechanistic world view favors a *reductionist* perspective. That is, it argues that *all* behaviors, complex and simple, comprise the same basic elements. They differ only in the number of elements present in each and in the arrangement of those elements. As such, if we understand the forces that regulate the elementary behaviors of the infant, we also, theoretically, understand the complex behavior patterns of the adult. Therefore, not surprisingly, more mechanistically oriented research and theorizing has been directed toward the study of infants and children than the study of adults.

Mechanists are not arguing that there is no difference between infants and adults. They are not even arguing that everything that the adult will become is already present in some form in the infant. Rather, they are claiming that the differences are best appreciated as one of degree rather than one of kind. Degree is a quantitative measure; kind is a qualitative measure. That is, we can directly compare things that differ quantitatively, but we cannot directly compare things that differ qualitatively. This issue— the conceptualization of human development as a quantitative or a qualitative process —is one of the major points of distinction between the three world views. Mechanists see the process as quantitative, while organicists and contextualists see it as primarily qualitative.

The Independence of Antecedent Conditions

Closely related to the importance of reductionism in mechanism is the importance of the independence of antecedent conditions (Kendler, 1992; Reese & Overton, 1970). Antecedent conditions are seen as the causes of behavior, as the elements of the behavioral machine. In the same sense that the elements of our teeter-totter each exhibit certain primary qualities that solely reflect that element, so do antecedent conditions as well. The influence of each antecedent either is directly observable in actual behavior or is seen as initiating a chain of internal events that results in observable behavior or behavioral change.

Antecedents that are directly observable are efficient causes. The behavior of others can serve as an efficient cause, as can characteristics of the physical environment (Wachs, 1992). Those that are not directly observable but that nevertheless are linked to external events are material causes. For instance, genetic material is seen as a material cause; so, too, are the computerlike components that define us as an information processing machine. Mechanists differ on the relative importance of efficient and material antecedents, but they agree that, for either to be seen as a causal agent, its influence must be independently linked to some behavior or behavioral change.

For mechanists, there can be any number of antecedents. The antecedents can each exert an effect directly or in interaction with other antecedents. In either case, because they are seen as independent of one another, their degree of influence relative to one another can be determined. In fact, the methodology of the mechanist is based on this assumption. When mechanists conduct controlled experiments and then submit the obtained data to some type of an analysis of the *variability* (i.e., the spread or range of the data collected) found in the data, they are attempting to determine the degree of influence each antecedent exerts on the behavior relative to other antecedents.

The Integration of Human Development with Other Scientific Disciplines

A final value mechanists see in their approach to the study of behavior and behavioral change is that the approach is consistent with a belief in the unity of science (Zuriff, 1985). Proponents of the unity-of-science position argue that all phenomena, irrespective of the particular discipline from which they are studied, are governed by a common set of explanatory mechanisms, typically mechanistic in structure.

From this unity-of-science position, human development is seen as a discipline no different from disciplines such as physics or chemistry in that, in all three cases, the same basic assumptions are made about the pursuit of knowledge. The only difference is that each discipline is interested in a different subject matter.

The unity-of-science position has one very significant impact on the study of behavior and behavioral change. In order not to violate the notion that objects at rest remain at rest until acted upon, mechanists question the role that intentionality plays in determining a person's behavior. In this sense, the mechanistic world view argues that an individual's behavior is best represented as either passive or responsive rather than active.[1] For example, Bijou (1989), arguing from a Skinnerian perspective on behavioral change, says that

> progressions in development were considered to depend on opportunities and circumstances provided by the individual's physical make-up (developmental level, health status, handicapping conditions) and the physical and social environment, past and present. And increments in development were brought about by *respondent* or Pavlovian processes that involve responses controlled by antecedent stimulation and by *operant* processes wherein responses are controlled by consequences. (p. 63)

Mechanism's insistence on viewing humans as passive or responsive rather than active or self-directing organisms is often misunderstood to mean that mechanists view humans as passive, as lacking the capacity for intentional behavior. But this is *not* what mechanism is claiming. Rather, mechanists are arguing that, because a concept such as intentionality cannot be defined as either efficient or material in nature, it is at best a secondary quality. Therefore it cannot be a proper object of study.

---

[1] Some mechanistic theorists, particularly information processing theorists and developmental behavior genetic theorists, do use the term *active* to describe some behaviors. However, they do so with reference to material as opposed to efficient causes and, as such, use the term very differently than do either organicists or contextualists. In these latter two cases "active" implies something beyond or independent of either efficient or material antecedent cause. For the sake of parsimony, I will follow the organicist/contextualist convention rather than the mechanist argument and reserve the use of *active* for discussions of organicism and contextualism.

The Study of Behavioral Change from a Mechanistic World View

Because mechanism in human development is based on the same set of universal assumptions as are found in other scientific disciplines, its methods, not surprisingly, parallel those found in those other sciences. These research strategies reflect the mechanist's argument that (1) behavior is a response to antecedent material or efficient events, (2) these antecedents exert their influence independent of one another, and (3) complex behaviors are best understood by reducing them to their constituent elementary components.

From this perspective the ability to understand means the ability to predict. The ability to predict requires the ability to document cause-and-effect relationships. And the ability to document cause-and-effect relationships requires the ability to independently assess antecedent factors. How this assessment process occurs usually reflects two factors: (1) whether the focus is on efficient and/or material antecedents and (2) whether the goal is understanding the average behavior of groups or the specific behavior of individuals. These distinctions reflect how different theories within the mechanist world view translate commonly held theoretical assumptions into specific research practices.

Given this set of assumptions, the primary research task of the mechanist is to explain the way in which antecedent forces act on human behavior to change it. Antecedent forces are described as the *independent variable(s)*, and behavior is described as the *dependent variable*. The relationship is linear, with the independent variable seen as the cause and the dependent variable as the effect. It is in this sense that behavior is portrayed as passive or responsive rather than active.

Independent variables can be either efficient or material. Efficient causes are described by Pepper as accidental in that they bear no necessary association to the dependent variable. Nothing is preordained. But once an association is established, the relationship is lawful and therefore predictable. Efficient causes come from our social and physical environments.

Material causes are not accidental. Genes and information processing variables such as memory capacity or processing speed, in the mechanistic world view, are good examples of material causes. Each is seen as having a direct, measurable influence on behavior and behavioral change.

Methods of Group Data Collection

The common research strategy for all theories within the mechanistic world view is the use of highly controlled experimental designs to collect behavioral data. For most of these theories, some sort of statistical procedure is then used to analyze the data. Information processing theorists (Klahr, 1980; Siegler, 1991; Siegler & Shipley, 1987) also use computer modeling methods to simulate the information processing structures and strategies believed to be regulating individual behavior. Radical behaviorists generally do not use statistical analysis because they prefer single-subject to group experiments. The research designs of the behavior geneticists are more likely to explore the already existing similarity of behavioral measures between individuals of different degrees of genetic relatedness (Plomin, Reiss, Hetherington, & Howe, 1994; Rowe, 1994; Scarr, 1992).

Because mechanists believe that variables exert their influence independent of one another, it is crucial in their work that they be able to determine the influence of each variable. It is equally crucial, given their belief in universal laws of behavior, that their findings for the research sample be generalizable to the larger population. For example, if the researcher is interested in the effects of mothers and fathers on sons' behavior, the experiment would need to be designed such that it would be possible to determine the influence of fathers independent of the influence of mothers. Furthermore, because the researcher's interest is not merely the fathers and mothers in the research sample, the sample would need to be representative of the larger population of mothers and fathers.

Ideally, the entire population of interest would participate in the experiment, but for obvious practical reasons, this is rarely possible. Instead, the researcher obtains a sample and then, through statistical analysis, determines how typical of the larger group the obtained results are. Because the ultimate focus of interest is the entire population rather than the sample itself, the representativeness of the sample to the population becomes an important element in mechanistic research. Sometimes, samples are drawn randomly from the target population. Other times, samples are stratified in such a way that it is possible to ensure that the sample contains the same range of diversity as is found in the population.

The research design seen as most likely to yield data consistent with the assumptions of a mechanistic world view involves the random assignment of treatment conditions to randomly selected individuals. The treatment conditions are the independent variables. Most mechanists accomplish this goal of control through randomization, assigning different individuals to different treatment conditions. The analysis of data collected in this manner involves *between-subjects* comparisons, or comparisons between the average score of the subjects in one group and the average scores of the subjects in another group. Actual research designs are usually more complex than a simple two-group comparison, but in all cases the logic of the process is the same.

For mechanists primarily interested in efficient causes, the antecedents are different environmental circumstances, such as school characteristics or teaching strategies. For mechanists primarily interested in material causes, the antecedents are individual characteristics, such as particular genetic characteristics.

Radical behaviorists, and to some degree information processing theorists, also make use of *single-subject* designs. In this case, individuals are presented with a sequence of treatment conditions (often randomly assigned as to sequence), and the analysis involves comparisons for each individual in terms of the different treatments. This is called a *within-subject* comparison because it involves different responses of the same individual to different antecedents. For both between-subjects and within-subjects comparisons, the basic logic is the same: Treatment conditions are independently assessed for their influence on behavior.

For example, if we were interested in conducting a between-subjects study of the effects of type of reward and type of instructional method on learning, we would randomly assign a sample of individuals to each of the possible combinations of reward and instruction used in the experiment. Both independent variables—reward and instructional method—are efficient causes. That is, the linking of a particular reward or instructional method with a particular individual is accidental or random. This assurance of randomness is important because statistical tests are designed to determine the likelihood of the pattern of results occurring by chance alone. If we wanted to conduct the same study using a single-subjects approach, we would sequence and pair the conditions in such a way that we could then later determine the relative impact of each reward and each instructional method on behavior.

From a methodological standpoint the random assignment of individuals to one or more efficient independent variables is the ideal expression of the mechanistic perspective. In some situations, however, this ideal is neither possible nor desirable. For one thing, ethical issues appropriately limit both the range and the assignment of efficient antecedents. No responsible researcher would assign an individual to a treatment condition that might prove harmful or that would violate basic human rights. Certainly no one would suggest to a group of prospective parents that they be randomly assigned a parenting strategy so that a researcher could study the effects of different parenting strategies on children's behavior in the most methodologically rigorous manner. In a situation like this, the variables (i.e., parenting behaviors) are efficient but clearly not under the control of the researcher.

The second limiting situation concerns material causes. Individuals can't be randomly assigned to a gender, or to a new set of genes, or to a lot of such things. With respect to material causes, you are what you are. For the mechanistic researcher this means looking for naturally occurring incidents of material independent variables. If, for example, we wanted to determine whether there was a relationship between genetics and academic achievement, we would have no option but to see if there was a relationship between degree of genetic relatedness and similarity of academic achievement. Were the grade point averages of siblings more similar than the grade point averages of cousins? Were the grade point averages of cousins more similar than the grade point averages of unrelated individuals? Was there a greater similarity between the academic achievement of children and their biological parents than between those same children and their adoptive parents?

From a practical standpoint research in the mechanist world view (or any other world view for that matter) rarely is "pure"—that is, it seldom completely meets the theoretical expectations. In reality, sampling procedures may not be as random as they should be; practical matters might limit sample size and composition; random assignment to treatment conditions might not be fully feasible; and it might not be possible to control for all potential influences on the behavior(s) in question. These complications do not prevent one from doing research, but they do make analysis and interpretation that much more difficult. Mechanists believe, however, that their methods of data analysis enable them to resolve some of these problems encountered in data collection.

Methods of Group Data Analysis

Once data is collected, it needs to be analyzed. For all mechanists except the radical behaviorists, this means some sort of statistical analysis. Statistical analysis allows the researcher to test the hypothesis that there is a causal relationship between one or more independent and dependent variables. Accomplishing this goal requires two things: (1) separating the influences of each of the independent variables from one another and from any other factors that have not been adequately controlled and then (2) demonstrating that the probability of the observed relationship between the independent variable and the behavior occurring by chance alone is so low as to reject the possibility of a chance relationship and accept the possibility of a causal relationship. Let me take each of these two tasks in turn.

Mechanism assumes that behavior is the sum of the influences of a number of variables, each acting independently of the others. But we cannot observe these independent effects simply by observing the behavior. All that is observable is the sum or cumulative impact of all of the variables. So how do we disentangle the variables? Unfortunately it can't be done literally. We can't unravel ourselves the way we can the rows of a sweater. Instead, we have to do it statistically.

For a statistical analysis to be valid, we have to assume that we can represent mathematically the influences of the independent variables on the dependent variables. In other words, we have to believe that the rules that govern the treatment of mathematical entities can be applied to the study of behavior. The relationship is again metaphorical. Mechanists are not saying that people are numbers; rather, they are saying that our understanding of mathematical relationships can help us to understand human relationships. Mechanists have no problem with this assumption; organicists and contextualists, as we will see, aren't so convinced.

For the mechanist, the independent variables are treated as distinct terms in a mathematical expression. The formula looks like this:

$$a + b + c = X$$

In this equation, a, b, and c are the independent variables (the influences) and X is the dependent variable (the behavior). Theoretically the number of terms in the equation should equal all the variables that influence the behavior in question (and would most likely be greater than three). However, because it would be impossible to include all of the variables that influence any particular behavior, we limit our equations to a manageable number of variables. We nevertheless acknowledge that still other variables influence the behavior by including an *error term* in the equation. The error term represents all the other possible influences on a particular behavior that we don't yet understand or that we have not been able to control for in our experimental design. So now our equation looks like this:

$$a + b + c + \text{error} = X$$

How do we solve the equation for a or b or c when all we know is X? That is, how do we determine the influence of each independent variable when all we actually have is data on the dependent variable? We solve the problem the same way we solve a math problem of the same form—by rearranging the terms in order to isolate one of them at a time. To solve for a, the equation would look like this:

$$a = X - (b + c + \text{error})$$

But how is it possible to accomplish this empirically? Mechanists are able to isolate variables because of the way they design their experiments. In particular, the assignment of individuals to different combinations of treatment conditions makes it possible, statistically, to determine the *amount of variance* (i.e., degree of influence) attributable to each variable, as well as the amount of variance attributable to error.

Consider the between-subjects experiment mentioned previously. The experiment was designed to test the influence of reward conditions and instructional techniques on learning. To simplify the example, we will assume that only two types of rewards (monetary compensation and interpersonal recognition) and two types of instructional techniques (rote learning versus discovery learning) are used. There could be more than two levels of each variable, and more than two variables, but this wouldn't change the logic of the analysis; it would only increase the complexity. Let us further assume that 40 individuals participate in the experiment.

I design my experiment such that I have four distinct groups, each with 10 people. Group 1 receives monetary reward and rote learning, group 2 receives monetary reward and discovery learning, group 3 receives interpersonal recognition and rote learning, and group 4 receives interpersonal recognition and discovery learning. I conduct my experiment, and then I give the identical test to each of the 40 participants to see what they have learned. What they have learned is the X in my equation. So how do I get to my (in this case) a and b and "error."

First, I obtain the average learning score for each of the four groups of 10 people. Let's assume that the average score for group 1 is 60, for group 2 is 80, for group 3 is 70, and for group 4 is 90. To determine the amount of variance accounted for by type of reward, I then average the average learning scores of groups 1 and 2 ($\frac{60+80}{2} = 70$) and compare this number to the average of the average learning scores of groups 3 and 4 ($\frac{70+90}{2} = 80$).

I now know that, irrespective of instructional technique, people appear to learn better if they are rewarded by interpersonal recognition than if they receive monetary compensation. In essence, I have isolated one variable from the others, not by moving it to the other side of the equation or by literally unraveling the variables but by mathematically eliminating the differential effect of the other variable through the use of averages. I would do the same thing to determine the influence of instructional methods, but in this case I would compare the averages of groups 1 and 3 ($\frac{60+70}{2} = 65$) with those of groups 2 and 4 ($\frac{80+90}{2} = 85$). Having now isolated the other variable, I can say that it looks as if people learn better if they use discovery learning techniques than if they use rote learning techniques.

This process of averaging across groups is the statistical process by which mechanists meet their theoretical claim of the independence of variables. In practice, the process is more complicated than this and involves more comparisons. But, again, if you understand the logic of this simple example, you can understand the logic of the more complicated instances—such as when there is evidence for a statistically significant interaction between two or more variables. Such interactions imply that the impact of one variable is dependent on the nature of a second variable.

Identifying a difference in the values for each of the two variables does not end the analysis process. Having partitioned the variance, I now need to determine the likelihood or probability that the relationship between the cause and the effect may be due to chance alone—that is, that there is no lawful, predictable relationship. This is where my error variable comes into play.

My design controls for reward condition and instructional method. Each person got only one of each, which is what allowed me to obtain my averages. But there are certainly variables other than these two that influence learning, and the experimental design doesn't control for any of them. Because these other factors aren't controlled, they can exert their influence on any person in any one or more of the groups. There is really no way to know because they aren't controlled. I know that some error is present because, within the four groups, there were differences in the scores of the 10 people in each group. If only my two variables were influencing learning, the scores of the 10 people in any one group should have been identical. Because they aren't, other factors are influencing the people's behavior.

In effect, I now have to determine the relative influence of my between-group variance and my within-group variance. Statistically, I do this by determining if the magnitude of the difference in the learning scores between the two levels of each of the two independent variables less the influence of the error variable is statistically significant. In other words, even considering the fact that there is within-group variability in each of the four groups, is the magnitude of the difference in the average learning scores between the rote and the discovery groups or the monetary and the recognition groups still large enough that the probability of the differences simply occurring by chance is very low.

Estimates of probability are the means through which the mechanist demonstrates the lawfulness of behavior. Because we can't test everyone on every variable, we have no direct empirical way to demonstrate that behavior is lawful. Instead, the mechanist has to be satisfied with the statement that the pattern of results from the sample means that the probability of a lawful relationship existing within an entire population is high enough to let a reasonable person draw such a conclusion. In general, if the experimenter can show, through statistical analysis, that the probability of the findings occurring by chance alone is less that 5%, then she or he can conclude that a functional relationship exists between the independent variable (the factor believed to cause the behavior) and the dependent variable (the effect of the actions of the independent variable). The choice of 5% as the cutoff is somewhat arbitrary and is more historical than logical in origin. But it is the generally accepted standard for statistical significance within the social sciences, particularly psychology. Most researchers see the 5% criterion as representing a reasonable balance between being so restrictive that no relationship is seen as lawful and concluding that everything has a lawful relationship to everything else.

Actually determining the probability of the obtained results occurring by chance alone is done by reference to a table of probability values. Two factors—the obtained results and the sample size—determine how the table is used and therefore whether the findings are likely to be statistically significant. The larger the sample size, the smaller the magnitude of the difference needed to obtain statistical significance.

This relationship of sample size and research results is consistent with the mechanistic model. Remember that the theoretical goal of the research is to make a universal statement concerning the entire population. Therefore, the closer the sample size is to the entire population, the less the chance of sampling error and therefore the greater the likelihood that the obtained sample results will accurately reflect the relationship present in the entire population.

Methods of Single-Subject Data Collection and Analysis

The Skinnerians, often referred to as the *radical behaviorists,* do not do experiments involving groups of individuals. Rather, they follow a single-subject procedure, in which the experiment involves only one individual. The Skinnerians prefer this strategy for two reasons (Perone, 1994). The first is that, because both sample size and the power of the independent variable influence the probability of finding statistical significance, the Skinnerians believe that group experiments always run the risk of a weak independent variable being found to be statistically significant if the sample size is made large enough. Skinnerians seek to discover powerful independent variables, so they choose to use the smallest sample size possible—one. The second problem that Skinnerians find with group data is that, in averaging individual scores, they lose information, because a set of individual scores is now represented by just one group score. Skinnerians are interested in establishing causal relationships at the individual level, so averaging scores for the purposes of statistical analysis is seen as counterproductive.

Most mechanists establish experimental control by having different groups receive different treatments and then making comparisons across the groups. With a sample size of one, this is not possible. Instead, Skinnerians sequence the presentation of the independent variable(s). For example, consider an experiment in which I want to determine the influence of reward size on children's attending to the teacher. The reward in this case is the amount of time each child is allowed to spend at recess, and attending is defined as maintaining eye contact with the teacher. Because there are 10 children in the class, I am conducting 10 parallel experiments.

To see if there is a causal relationship between my independent and dependent variables, I first establish a base rate by simply observing the amount of attending for each child without providing any reward. Having established a baseline for each child, I then begin to reinforce the children at the end of each day based on their attending scores. If my hypothesis is correct—that is, if there is a functional relationship between reward size and attending—I should expect to see an increase in each child's attending score.

Let us assume that I do find what I expected to and that each child's attending score increases and is now consistently at a higher level than before. It looks as if I have documented a causal relationship, but to be sure, I now remove the rewards. In other words, I reverse the procedure. If the increase in attending behavior was due to the reward system, then removing the reward system should move the attending behavior back down toward the original baseline. If it does so, I can conclude with a good deal of certainty that the increase in attending behavior was caused by my reward system. In other words, I have introduced experimental control by varying the experimental conditions for each subject (no reward, then reward, then no reward again). Such a research design is referred to as an *A-B-A design.*

The reversal of the experimental conditions in the single-subject design serves the same functional purpose as the statistical significance test in the group design. Both

TABLE 2.1
Primary Characteristics of the Mechanistic World View

1. Belief that behavior and behavioral change are naturally occurring, universal, lawful phenomena

2. Belief that it is possible to use objective, neutral empirical research strategies to study these phenomena

3. Belief that behavior and behavioral change are caused by one or more material and/or efficient causes

4. Belief that the influence of each efficient and/or material cause can be known independent of all others

5. Belief that the process of behavioral change over time is best understood as a quantitative process involving the increasing complexity of a set of basic elements common to all age groups

are strategies for determining the likelihood that a causal relationship exists between the independent and the dependent variables. It is also possible to extend the procedures to consider more than one independent variable (multielement design) and more than one dependent variable (multiple baseline design), but in both cases the logic is the same as in my simple experiment.

The radical behaviorists' approach to the study of behavior focuses almost exclusively on the study of efficient rather than material causes. This is consistent with their atheoretical interpretation of mechanism. It isn't that they deny those elements that constitute the material causes for other mechanists. Rather, they don't believe that these material elements add any explanatory power to the study of behavior and behavioral change. It is the ultimate expression of reductionism within the mechanistic family of theories.

Summary of the Mechanistic World View

I will have much more to say about mechanism when I discuss its family of theories in Part II. But, for now, a couple of summary points are in order (see Table 2.1). First, mechanism's approach to the study of behavioral change is based on the fundamental theoretical belief that the process of understanding behavior is no different from the processes used to study any other natural phenomena. Second, given mechanism's inductive approach to theory building, strategies of data collection and data analysis are strongly emphasized. In fact, this emphasis is so great that for many mechanists the method, both of data collection and of data analysis, *is* the theory. More to the point, the method is what for mechanists defines a scientific approach to the study of behavior and behavioral change. Third, mechanism characterizes human behavior as a response to antecedent conditions originating in either the external physical or social environment (i.e., efficient causes) or the internal environment, loosely conceptualized in terms of genetic and neurological and/or cognitive dimensions (i.e., material causes). Fourth, mechanists believe that, even though any single behavior may have multiple determinants, it is nevertheless possible to understand the impact of each of these causes independent of the others. Finally, for mechanists, change in behavior over time is seen as a quantitative process. The adult differs from the child in terms of the number of basic units present and their arrangement relative to one another, the basic units stay the same.

3

Why We Are—
The Organismic World View

Sigmund Freud, Erik Erikson, Arnold Gesell, and Jean Piaget are surely four of the giants in the field of human development. Their work has set the tone for and sharpened the focus of much of the research on human development in recent decades, and it continues to be interpreted, debated, extended, and revised today. The work of all four theorists reflects an organismic world view.

Of the three world views on human development, the organismic is the one that proponents would argue takes the "purest" approach to the topic. They claim that organicism goes farther than the other two world views in distinguishing between development and other forms of behavioral change. According to supporters of the other two world views, what organicists call development is best appreciated as behavioral change taking place over longer rather than shorter periods of time (the mechanists) or as particular sets of actions rooted in particular sociohistorical contexts (the contextualists). In neither case is a unique set of theoretical propositions seen as necessary to explain the phenomenon. Organicists' assertion that development is a distinct phenomenon should become clearer after reviewing Pepper's (1961) analysis of this world view.

Pepper's Analysis

Pepper's root metaphor for the organismic perspective is the living organism. He admits to not liking the metaphor as much as that of the machine for the mechanists or the historical act for the contextualists, but he notes that no other image comes as close to highlighting the integrative core of the organismic world view. The choice, then, of the living organism serves to emphasize, for Pepper, the fact that the key element of the organismic view is the process through which elements are integrated to form a *synergistic whole*. In a synergistic whole, the integrated system, unlike the machine, is more than the sum of its parts. The whole creates forces that could never be understood even if one knew everything there was to know about each individual element of the system. Actually, from an organismic perspective, this last sentence is somewhat misleading because, for an organicist, the elements acquire their meaning only when they interact with other elements in the system. In other words, organicists are not reductionists.

Development as Integrative Change

Perhaps the most significant difference between the mechanistic and organismic world views,[1] as described by Pepper, concerns how change occurs. For mechanists, change comes about when an external force (efficient or material) acts upon an object that is inherently at rest. For organicists, behavioral change is inherent in the living organism itself rather than externally driven. Change is therefore one of the defining characteristics of living organisms. It is what they do. This distinction concerning the reason things change prompts organicists to view development as a unique form of change, one that has a discrete set of defining characteristics.

Development, then, in Pepper's organismic world view, consists of the continuing integration of *fragments* into ever larger wholes. As such, development is directional: One can develop but not "undevelop." Neither of the other two perspectives make such a directional argument. For both the mechanist and the contextualist, the forces that each sees as regulating change can go in either direction. Because neither conceptualizes development as a distinct phenomenon, this change is not a matter of "undeveloping." Rather, it is a matter of a new set of circumstances reversing the consequences of a previous set of circumstances. One reason for this theoretical difference is that both mechanism and contextualism focus their analyses on observable phenomena. By contrast, organicism focuses on what is seen as the underlying process regulating these observable phenomena.

One area in which this issue of "undeveloping" is often debated is with respect to some of the behavioral changes observed in the very elderly. On some experimental measures, these people respond in the same manner as do young children (Goldhaber, 1986). Does this imply that, because the two behaviors appear to be similar, the mechanisms governing them are identical? Given their argument that development is directional, the organicists would say no. They argue that, even though the behaviors appear similar, they nevertheless are governed by developmentally distinct mechanisms. The same logic would apply to the issue of behavioral regressions, a pattern often reported in the clinical literature.

---

[1] Most of the comparisons in this chapter will be to the mechanist world view, for two reasons. First, having already discussed mechanism, you are now in a better position to differentiate it from organicism than you are from contextualism. The next chapter, on contextualism, will therefore appropriately differentiate organicism from both mechanism and contextualism. Second, because contextualism does not make universal claims, making general comparisons to the other world view is usually neither appropriate nor even possible. For the contextualist, often the only generalization that holds is, "It depends."

The Dialectical Process

In Pepper's organismic world view, the process by which fragments become progressively integrated is best viewed as *dialectical* in nature. At any given level of integration, fragments stand in opposition to each other as thesis and antithesis. They integrate to form, at the next-higher level, a synthesis. The synthesis now becomes the fragment or thesis of the new level, which integrates with the antithesis of this level to form a new synthesis, and so on and so on and so on.

Pepper (1961) describes the process in quite dramatic fashion:

> A fragment restless in its isolation and abstractness is driven by its nexus to a fragment which is its exact opposite and contradictory. These opposed fragments are inevitably connected and inevitably hostile. Each needs and implies the other for its completion, and each is destructive of and contradictory to the other. Thesis and antithesis, they cannot get along without each other and they cannot abide each other. The conflict is finally resolved in an integration, a higher synthesis, which recognizes the claims of each fragment, "transcends" them and harmonizes them into a richer, more concrete whole. But presently the whole exhibits an "abstractness" of its own and seeks the whole from which it is abstracted. Its nexus drives it to its own peculiar opposite. These two richer fragments again imply and contradict each other, love and hate each other, demand and try to destroy each other, until a new and still higher and still more concrete synthesis is attained. (p. 291)

Because this dialectical process has direction, each new integration is different from the previous one. According to Pepper, each integration brings the organism that much closer to a theoretical idealized state in which all fragments are united and harmonized. Development, then, from an organismic perspective has both direction and, theoretically, an end point.

To attempt to explain such an integrating process from a mechanistic perspective, we need to make reference to some efficient or material cause that would be seen as making the integration occur. This is not true in organicism. Integration is what fragments do rather than what something does to them. The fragments, Pepper argues, do not exist as independent components, as they do in mechanism; rather, each presupposes the presence of the other—that is, each exists within a nexus. This nexus or organic whole is such that every element within it implies every other. Change one element, and you also change all the others. The nexus defines the organism. The organism is, if you will, its own efficient cause.

Although the developmental process in organicism is directional, its outcome or end point is not preordained. Many fragments or antitheses are available at each level for integration. Potentially there are many paths to Pepper's harmony, each distinct in content but common in the process by which it comes into being. Furthermore, there is no guarantee that any individual will ever reach his or her developmental end point. The only guarantee is directionality.

These two theoretical aspects of the organismic world view—its end point and its path or paths—generate a great deal of controversy. The notion of end point raises the question of the limits of human development (Beilin, 1992; Flavell, 1992; Kaplan, 1994). The issue of path or direction generates debate as to the ability of organismic theory to explain equally the diversity of life paths that are typical in our species (Furth, 1969; Gilligan, 1986; Wertsch, 1991; Wertsch, Tulviste, & Hagstrom, 1993). We will return to these issues in the next chapter and in Part III. For now, it is important simply to keep these issues in mind because they provoke questions about the limits of organismic theory.

Organicism as a Developmental Perspective

The process of human development from an organismic perspective is a much more complicated affair than it is from a mechanistic perspective for three reasons: (1) It is a process in which something is always happening, (2) this process is occurring on a unique plane or level of action, and (3) this process appears to have a particular structure and course. None of these three is seen as necessary to the mechanist or the contextualist. But to the organicist, they are essential. It is not that organicists enjoy making things difficult. Rather, it reflects organicists' beliefs as to what is necessary to adequately explain the process of human development.

Mechanists are induction theorists. They believe that the way one creates a theory about human behavior is to observe behavior and then make inferences based on these observations. This assumption is reflected in their rigorous experimental controls and elaborate statistical analyses. Theoretically at least, their research eventually will reach a point when they have made enough observations to explain fully why we act as we do. The implicit assumption in all this is that the information is "out there" in the observations. If we are careful and thorough and systematic enough, and if we use adequate experimental controls, we will ultimately identify all of the causes of behavioral change.

By contrast, organicists would argue that the trouble with mechanists is that they "look but they don't see." And the reason they don't see is that what they are looking for isn't "out there" but "in here." In other words, from an organismic perspective, the process of theory building about human development starts not with observation but with reflection. In particular, it starts with reflection on "what one must necessarily assume about the nature of the organism in order for it to have the behaviors that it does exhibit" (Overton, 1985, p. 16). For organicists, this assumptive process is a crucial step in theory building; they argue that only when you know what you are looking for is it possible to find it. So, what is it that organicists claim is "in here"?

A Process Occurring on a Unique Plane or Level of Action

Organismic theory is holistic. Organicists do not believe that the study of development can be reduced to the study of its components, because the components exist only in relationship to one another—that is, as a result of synthesis. For organicists, this synthesis means that the whole is greater than the sum of its parts. One important implication of this line of reasoning is that the organicist needs to define a unique level of action on which human development occurs, a level at which the actions of this synergistic whole can be represented. This unique level or plane is a systemic one; it has been defined in dialectical psychological terms (Goldhaber, 1986) by theorists such as Piaget, Freud, and Erikson, and in dialectical biological terms by Gesell and, more recently, the developmental psychobiologists. For organicists, the theoretical construction of this unique level of action is primarily a rational or "a priori" process rather than an empirical one. This plan of action serves as one of the elements that must be present when organicists consider what is necessary to explain the process of human development.

This unique psychological level is not reducible to individual, nondialectical biological factors (material causes) and/or specific sociohistorical factors (efficient causes), although both obviously influence activity on the psychological plane. There is no one-to-one correspondence between events on the psychological plane and those on the biological and sociohistorical planes. Rather, these latter two fragments provide the raw materials that, when mixed, lead to the emergence of a unique phenomenon with a unique set of defining characteristics.

Perhaps an analogy might be useful at this point. When we mix two molecules of hydrogen and one molecule of oxygen, we get the substance called water. Water has certain defining characteristics; for example, it feels "wet" to the touch, and it can extinguish certain types of fires. But where do these two properties—its wetness and extinguishability—come from? Is one contributed by the oxygen, and the other by the hydrogen? If so, which comes from which? Or do both come from one, with the other acting as some sort of filler or binder? If you stuck your hand in a bucket of hydrogen, would your hand feel wet? If oxygen came in contact with the fire, would the fire go out? The questions sound strange. Neither hydrogen nor oxygen alone feels wet, and adding oxygen to a fire would, of course, make the fire stronger, not weaker.

So where do these defining characteristics of water come from? They come from or emerge out of the interaction of the two elements. The emerging properties—wetness and extinguishability—are not reducible to either of the contributing elements but are the qualitatively distinct product of their interaction. This notion of properties emerging out of the interaction of elements is basic to an understanding of organismic theories. It is why organicists such as Piaget argue that psychological activity occurs on a unique, nonreducible level or plane of action.

Consistent with Pepper, it is important to recognize that emerging properties are not limited to hydrological and psychological phenomena. The logic holds equally well at any level of analysis within any domain. Any level of functioning of the biological system can be conceptualized as emerging from the interaction of fragments from lower levels. Vision, for example, is the property that emerges through the interaction of a visually stimulating environment with a number of biological organs residing in a variety of biological systems. Eliminate any one of the elements, and there would be no vision (i.e., we would not experience the sensation of seeing something), even though all the other elements in the system are functioning perfectly. Put another way, vision does not reside in any one organ but rather is the emerging consequence of the interaction of several organs. Our concepts of family or society are also emergent concepts, in that each emerges from the interaction of its respective elements. For instance, reduce the family to its members, and you no longer have a family; instead, you have a group of individuals.

Just as the synergistic interaction of hydrogen and oxygen leads to the emergence of a qualitatively unique phenomenon—water—with a set of characteristics distinct to it, so, too, does the emergence of the psychological exhibit a qualitatively unique set of characteristics or structures. The structures that define the psychological are active rather than passive. They don't simply respond, store, and process. They construct. In particular, they construct meaning. Because this process is an active rather than a passive one, it cannot be reduced to either efficient or material causes. Therefore, organicists introduce a third type of cause, *formal cause* (Overton, 1991). The concept of formal cause implies that the organization or structure of a thing (in this case, the psychological plane of action) exerts a degree of influence over its functioning. It is in this sense that Pepper talks about thesis and antithesis existing in relationship to each other. It is their structure, their form, that causes, in part, their search for integration.

Admittedly, there is something unsettling about this notion of a psychological plane of action. Whereas mechanists can point directly to behavioral causes and their effects, organicists can only know them indirectly. There is something tangible, something "point-outable" to the mechanist's argument of one person's behavior serving as the efficient cause of another's. We also know that genes are real—we have pictures of them. We may not fully understand their mode of action, but this is really more a technical than a conceptual limitation. Even the information processing theorists' references to such things as storage capacity and processing strategies have a tangible feel. We know they exist in the computer, so how big a leap of faith is it to assume that somewhere in the brain parallel structures must also exist?

But what are psychological structures? Where are they? Are they like the information processing theorists' structures? If we knew where to look in the brain, would we find the psychological plane of action? For that matter, from this conception of the emergence of qualitatively unique levels of action, where are vision or hearing? What about sensations? It is as if the organicist is saying that these things don't really exist, that there isn't some specific place in the brain where some sort of cerebral videotape or audiotape is playing. At first glance, the organicist seemingly has simply reestablished the mind/body dichotomy with an emphasis on the mind. Quite the contrary, say organicists (Damasio, 1994).

What organicists are saying is that vision or hearing or psychological functioning doesn't reside in one place but rather is the sensation we experience or the awareness we have as the result of interdependent, synergistic actions occurring at a variety of sites. The sensation or the awareness is the emergent property, and it can't be "located" in any one site because no one site alone creates it.

Ultimately the organicist's argument for a plane of psychological action is a logical one, confirmed through empirical study. And, like all logical analyses, the conclusion reached is a necessary one, given the elements of the logical analysis. In this case, the necessary conclusion is the positing of an abstraction, a psychological plane of action. For organicists, it could not be theoretically otherwise, because nothing else appears theoretically capable of explaining as well the patterns of behavior and behavioral change that occur over the life span.

An Active Process

Mechanists argue that behavior is best understood as a reaction or response to efficient and/or material causes. They are not claiming that we are robots. Rather, they are suggesting that a scientific study of behavior and behavioral change only allows for the inclusion of those things that can be objectively observed and directly inferred—that is, efficient and material causes. Organicists counter that this restriction is too limiting, that this reactive image is insufficient to account for the diversity and complexity of human development across the life span.

In particular, organicists argue that one of the characteristics of the organizational structures that emerge on the psychological plane of action is the ability to construct knowledge. This constructive process means that individuals' social and physical worlds are best appreciated not as imperfect copies of the real world but as attempts to attribute meaning to the events that form these social and physical worlds. Organicists don't deny the existence of a real world independent of our awareness of it. Rather, they suggest that our knowledge of the physical and social worlds is always a unique representation or construction of that real world. Because the process is active rather than passive, the construction will necessarily reflect both the nature of the psychological structures present at a particular point in the life span and the particulars of the experiences encountered (Reese & Overton, 1970).

Kegan (1982) describes this active constructive process in this way:

> What an organism does is organize and what a human organism organizes is meaning. Thus it is not that a person makes meaning, as much as that the activity of being a person is the activity of meaning-making. There is thus no feeling, no experience, no perception, no thought independent of a meaning-making context in which it *becomes* a feeling, an experience, a thought, a perception, because we *are* the meaning-making context. . . . The most fundamental thing we do with what happens to us is organize it. We literally make sense. Human being is the composing of meaning, including, of course, the occasional inability to compose meaning, which we often experience as the loss of our own composure. (p. 11)

In other words, behavior is a reflection of an active process of construction taking place within an organized set of psychological structures. One significant implication of this argument is that, theoretically, from an organismic world view, behavior can never be fully predictable.

Different theories within the organismic family of theories focus on different domains of construction. Piaget, for example, was concerned, in part, with children's knowledge construction of physical and logico-mathematical phenomena such as number and weight; Freud was concerned with individuals' knowledge constructions within their psychosexual worlds; and Erikson focused on individuals' knowledge constructions of self/other relationships. Even though the particular domains of interest differ, because the theorists shared a common theoretical perspective, the logic of their theorizing follows a parallel process.

A Directional Process

Organicists argue that our efforts to make meaning out of our experiences—that is, to construct knowledge—is a lifelong activity. It is as evident in the behavior of the infant as in that of the elder. However, the manner in which this constructive process occurs changes. Consistent with a dialectical process, the actions of the psychological structures result in this change. Each synthesis represents a new, qualitatively distinct level of structural organization within the psychological plane of action. Organicists argue that there is a specific progressive and irreversible pattern to these changes. It is this pattern of change that, to the organicist, is human development. It is why we are.

The most general description of this progressive and irreversible pattern of change is offered by Werner's (1957) *Orthogenetic Principle*. Werner believed that, whenever development occurs, it does so in a particular fashion. To paraphrase Werner, it always moves from a state of relative globality and lack of differentiation to a state of increasing differentiation, articulation, and hierarchical integration. This process systematically changes individuals' perspectives and therefore how they see themselves in relationship to objects in the physical world and people in the social world. For Werner a number of specific consequences resulted from this orthogenetic process:

> This increasing subject-object differentiation involves the corollary that the organism becomes increasingly less dominated by the immediate concrete situation; the person is less stimulus bound and less impelled by affective states. A consequence of this freedom is the clearer understanding of goals, the possibility of employing substitutive means and alternative ends. There is hence a greater capacity for delay and planned action. The person is better able to exercise choice and willfully arrange a situation. In short, he can manipulate the environment rather than passively respond to the environment. This freedom from the domination of the immediate situation also permits a more accurate assessment of others. The adult is more able than the child to distinguish between the motivational dynamics and the overt behavior of personalities. At developmentally higher levels, therefore, there is less of a tendency for the world to be interpreted solely in terms of one's own needs and an increasing appreciation of the needs of others and of group goals. (p. 127)

For Werner and other organicists, this developmental sequence is purposeful. That is, when observing the pattern of change, organicists believe that it is useful to posit a reason this pattern of change is as it is. The purpose is *adaptation.*

All of the increasingly differentiated and integrated actions described by Werner are therefore best understood as sequences of changes that occur as individuals attempt to adapt by maintaining dynamic equilibrium between changing physical and social environments and changing patterns of psychological structures. The process is reciprocal and interdependent—each simultaneously affects and is affected by the other.

Organicists typically document this developmental sequence in terms of developmental stages. Each stage reflects a temporary respite in the progression and defines a qualitatively unique level of meaning making or knowledge construction. The concept of developmental stages serves as a sort of regulatory mechanism, ensuring a degree of continuity and integration of behavior across a variety of behavioral domains (Wohlwill, 1973). The particular psychological structures that characterize each stage depend on the interests of the theorist. Piaget's stages, for example, are defined in terms of cognitive operations; Erikson's, in terms of relationships.

Organicists believe that this pattern of progressively more effective levels of adaptation does not occur by chance. To highlight this claim, they introduce a fourth type of cause, *final cause* (Overton, 1991), as a way to emphasize the directionality of development. Final causes are a heuristic device. No one is suggesting that what is yet to be is somehow causing that which is already happening. Clearly this is nonsensical. Rather, final causes serve to identify the theoretical end point of development and therefore the anchor point for the study of development from an organismic perspective. For the organicist, final causes are a way of reminding us that unless we first know where we are going, it's hard to find out how to get there.

The Study of Human Development from an Organismic World View

Because the theoretical assumptions of the organismic world view differ significantly from those of the mechanistic world view, it should be no surprise that the approach to research differs as well (Overton, 1991; Overton & Reese, 1973; Wohlwill, 1973, 1991). The shift is from a focus on identifying significant functional (i.e., cause-and-effect) relationships to a focus on (1) identifying the status of the organizational structure at any particular time and (2) assessing how that organization changes over time. Documentation, analysis, and explanation of developmental patterns replace prediction of behavior change.[2]

This shift from prediction to explanation reflects the basic theoretical assumptions of the organismic model. Organicism is a universal, idealized developmental model in that it defines both a process by which development occurs and an end point toward which development proceeds. Because these are the givens in the model, prediction is less relevant than in mechanism, which only defines a universal process. The organicist doesn't need to predict what will happen because the logical construction of the theory stipulates what must happen if development is to occur. Instead, the organicist needs to document what is happening and to ensure that what is observed is consis-

---

[2] There are also methodological differences with the contextualist world view, but these tend to be more a matter of interpretation and generalization of similar research strategies; both world views share a holistic point of view.

tent with the expectations of the model. When the expectations are not confirmed, the organicist needs either to identify situational factors that are distorting the developmental process or, ultimately, to revise the expectations because they are not being confirmed.

Highly controlled experimental procedures have less relevance in organismic research. Because organismic theory presumes that factors influence one another in an interdependent nexus, there is no logical reason to attempt to look at each element independent of the other. To attempt do so would be inconsistent with the perspective because organicists argue that factors acquire their influence only in interaction with one another. For organicists, the mechanist's efforts to partition variance is an endeavor that may have mathematical but not developmental validity.

Statistical analyses are less common in organismic research than in mechanism. Recall that statistical analysis requires the grouping of individual scores to obtain group means. Differences between these means are then analyzed to determine if they are statistically significant, that is, to determine the probability that chance alone can account for the degree of difference obtained. Organismic researchers are less likely to use group data because they are typically more interested in documenting changes in an individual's behavior over some period of time or similarities in an individual's behavior across different domains at some particular time. Furthermore, the types of behavioral information obtained by organicists in their research do not easily lend themselves to statistical analysis. Organicists' data tends to be more qualitative and structurally elaborate rather than the discrete, highly quantifiable behavioral data preferred by the mechanists.

For example, an organicist studying moral development would most likely interview individuals about their reasons for believing that some act was right or wrong. A mechanist studying moral development would more likely observe the frequency with which individuals transgress under different experimental conditions. Again, the issue is not which approach is correct. They are both correct to the degree that they are consistent with the theoretical assumptions of their respective world views. The more relevant issue is which approach is more useful, and the answer depends on the answer to the question "useful for what?"

When organicists do make use of experimental designs and statistical analyses, it is usually to study how material and efficient causes influence the course of development (Overton, 1991). In this sense, the organicist is studying how situational factors might influence the rate of development or the degree of integration in behavior across behavioral domains. Notice that the issue is not one of how material and efficient factors "cause" development to occur, but rather of how efficient and material factors influence the variability in developmental patterns among individuals.

The actual research strategies used by organicists can be grouped into two categories. The first involves detailed, clinical investigation of the psychological organization present at a particular time. Clinical in this sense does not necessarily refer to abnormal populations; instead, it refers more generically to an individual rather than group approach to research. Given a world view in which knowledge is seen as constructed, the clinical approach represents one way to understand both the content of these constructions and the process through which they are formed. The second research strategy involves attempts to document one or more behavioral sequences over some period of time.

Methods of Documenting Organizational Structure

The concept of developmental stages implies a broad regulatory mechanism influencing behavior in a variety of behavioral domains. There is the theoretical expectation of a correspondence in levels of functioning across these behavioral domains. A change in the level of functioning within any one domain presumably would be closely followed by parallel changes in other domains. Research strategies focusing on organizational structure are designed to document these correspondences across behavioral domains.

Documenting organizational structure is difficult. It requires the collection of behavioral data across a variety of behavioral domains and then a demonstration of correspondence in their levels. In particular, it requires a demonstration that individuals who function at a particular level within one behavioral domain function at a similar level within another. For example, if we note that a child can sort objects on two dimensions simultaneously (e.g., color and shape), should we expect that same level of coordinating dimensions to be evident in other behavioral domains as well, such as the child's ability to recognize that a parent can be both a mother and a doctor or both a father and a lawyer?

A frequent strategy for getting information about organizational structure is the *clinical interview*. The clinical interview is not, in this case, a technique for doing psychotherapy; rather, it is a strategy for probing the deep psychological structures influencing a person's behavior. The technique typically begins with some sort of probe question or task, and then, depending on the response to this probe, a series of questions follow.

Damon's (1977, 1983, 1988) studies of children's friendships provide a good example of the clinical interview. Damon first asked each child who his or her friends were and then why these were his or her friends. The follow-up questions reflected the child's initial answers. What followed was a series of hypothetical questions designed to probe the psychological structures influencing the child's understanding of the concept of friendship: Under what conditions did friendships form or end? How did the child distinguish between best friends and others? How might the child compare the way one deals with friends to the way one deals with parents or teachers or teammates? Damon's interest was not so much any specific answer, but rather the pattern that began to emerge when all of the responses were considered as a package.

The response patterns were then analyzed to see what pattern of organizational structures emerged. The structure of the friendships of children around the age of 5, for example, seem determined mostly by activity pattern. Friends are people you play with, and when you stop playing with them, they are no longer your friends. The structure of the friendships of preteens shows a very different pattern. These children's responses to the questions reveal a much more psychological notion of friendship. Friends understand each other; they share personal thoughts and feelings; they deserve special status and treatment; they help each other. Such friendships are not as easily made as in the case of 5-year-olds, nor are they as easily ended. These two patterns are each interpreted as reflecting how children construct an understanding of themselves in relationship to others, and how children construct this understanding is, in turn, seen as reflecting differences in the organization of the psychological structures present in 5-year-olds and 12-year-olds.

To determine if this sequence of self/other constructions reflected a more general pattern, Damon then investigated children's understanding of relationships in the social domains of gender role, justice, and authority. He was trying to determine if an organizational structure exists on the psychological plane of action that exerts a parallel influence on children's behavior across a variety of behavioral domains.

It is important to note that this issue of interdomain continuity is a highly controversial issue within the organismic world view (Case, 1992; Feldman, 1980; Fischer, Kenny, & Pipp, 1990). Few researchers find the high degree of continuity that this idealized version of the theory would predict. The controversy surrounds the reasons for this failure to find a high degree of continuity. We will examine the specifics of the arguments in Part III. For now, it is sufficient to remember that, like most issues within the organismic perspective, the arguments focus on what is *real* versus what is *apparent*. In other words, is there really a high degree of continuity, and we are simply having a problem documenting it? Or is there really not a high degree of continuity, and we need to revise our idealized image of the way developmental stages influence behavior?

In addition to the types of clinical interviews used by Damon and others, *correlation techniques* are also sometimes used to measure the degree of relationship that exists across behavioral domains. A correlation is a measure of a relationship. Two things are said to correlate to the extent that knowing something about one reduces our uncertainty about the other. For example, height and weight correlate. In general, the taller you are, the more you weigh, so knowing your height reduces our uncertainty about your weight. The magnitude of the correlation (reflected numerically in the range of 0.0 for no correlation to 1.0 for a perfect correlation) reflects the degree of relationship. A perfect correlation would mean that there is a precise one-to-one correspondence between height and weight. That is, a specific increase in height would be accompanied by a specific corresponding increase in weight.

Correlations can either be positive or negative. Height and weight demonstrate a positive correlation in that as one increases, so does the other. A negative or inverse correlation would show the opposite pattern. For example, there is a negative correlation between weight and most measures of health. In this case, the more you weigh relative to your height, the poorer your health. Notice that in neither case does the pattern of the correlation offer an explanation. Rather, correlations simply document relationships.

Correlations are done with group data and therefore are not as ideal a strategy for organicists because they mask intraindividual patterns. Nevertheless, they are useful in providing a general demonstration of the validity of the developmental stage concept.

Methods of Documenting Behavioral Sequences

Documentation of behavioral change over time is basic to the organismic world view. It validates the logical models and provides the evidence needed to modify the models when necessary. *Longitudinal research designs* are the classic organismic approach to this documentation process. Longitudinal research involves the repeated testing, assessment, and/or observation of one or more individuals over a period of time. The use of longitudinal designs is integral to each of the theories that compose the organismic theoretical family.

The longitudinal study might take place over a period of months or years or decades. For instance, a longitudinal study of early motor development might last less than a year. A longitudinal study of early language development or of the puberty transition might last a few years. A longitudinal study of marital satisfaction could last across all of adulthood. The presumed rate of change of the behaviors of interest would determine how frequently they were observed or measured. Someone looking at early motor development might observe very young infants on a weekly or even daily basis. Change occurs that fast in young infants. But calling a couple every week to see how their marriage is doing would make less sense. Although some weeks are better than others in any relationship, the health of a relationship is usually measured over longer intervals. Perhaps every two or three months would make more sense.

The types of behavioral measures used are also specific to the study. Observation would certainly be an integral part of a study of early motor or language development, but many couples might object to being systematically observed. For the couples, conducting periodic interviews might make more sense, perhaps combined with the request that each partner keep a diary or check sheet documenting specific aspects of the relationship. Physical measures would be a logical component of the puberty study. Some sort of structured task might be a component of the data collection for each of these groups. The young infants might be given objects to grasp to determine changes in coordination and grip. The young child might be asked to name objects to determine vocabulary or to describe situations to determine grammar and syntax. In some cases the actual task might change; in others it might remain the same. Certainly you wouldn't document motor development in a 7-month-old with a task that was easily accomplished two months earlier. Some form of the clinical interviews mentioned previously would likely be a part of many longitudinal studies.

Sample size and composition also vary with the purpose of the study. Practical considerations place limits on sample size, but the universalist assumptions of organicism generally mean that there is less need for large samples. Sample composition is a somewhat more relevant issue. But again, if the organicist is interested in universal behavior patterns—that is, ones common to all members of the species—then the representativeness of the sample is less of an issue than it is for mechanists. It is important to point out that this presumption of universality is not universally accepted. Contextualists, in particular, take serious exception to this claim (Gergen, 1994; Gilligan, 1982). Their reasoning will be made clear in the next chapter.

Data analysis is always a difficult task with longitudinal research. Depending on the length of the study and the frequency of data collection, a longitudinal study can generate a great deal of data. In addition, because the actual data collected at one time might well be different from the data collected at a later time, making comparisons across times is also difficult.

In some cases, the data might be presented in terms of developmental norms, in which case group averages could be calculated. For instance, the motor development study might document how many blocks the average 2-year-old can stack, or the language development study might document the average sentence length of 3-year-olds. The maturationally based research of Gesell (Ames, 1989; Gesell, 1949) and his colleagues followed this pattern. You will find Gesell's charts of normative motor development and gains in height and weight in virtually every pediatrician's office in this country.

In other cases the data might be analyzed for patterns of change over time. Here, the organicist would be looking for evidence confirming the changing structure of developmental stages. Kohlberg's (1984) longitudinal research of children's moral development documents a sequence of children's moral reasoning. The data consisted of children's explanations of moral dilemmas, and the data analysis involved detailed coding of these responses for moral level. When asked, for example, why it is wrong to steal, younger children typically respond in terms of the likelihood of being caught and punished; older children and adolescents are more likely to talk in terms of rules, group norms, and socially defined conventions. In Kohlberg's model the recognition of being part of a large social group and of having that group's norms regulate behavior is seen as developmentally more mature than regulating behavior by what individuals think they can get away with.

For obvious reasons longitudinal methods pose a number of practical problems. Researchers thus have adopted other strategies to gather similar information. Although these other strategies remove some of the practical problems of longitudinal research, especially the time problem, they present some of their own theoretical and practical issues.

One strategy is to use a *cross-sectional design*, which involves the testing, assessment, and/or observation of different groups of individuals measured at the same time. At first glance, the cross-sectional design would seem to provide the same information as the longitudinal. The difference is that, instead of periodically testing one group of individuals (e.g., every 5 years) over some extended period of time (e.g., a period of 50 years), 10 groups of individuals, each group differing in age from the other by 5 years, is tested at one time. The tradeoff would seem to be more subjects for less time. True enough, but there is a more serious theoretical issue involved. Because different groups of individuals are used in a cross-sectional study, there is no way to study intraindividual change. It is only possible to study interindividual change, to compare the average score of one age group to another. It is also not possible to document the pattern of change, the primary interest of organicists. As such, cross-sectional designs are best used as approximations or trial runs for longitudinal designs.

A second strategy is a *retrospective longitudinal study*, which involves gathering information from the past rather than waiting to gather it as the future unfolds. The major potential problem with this approach is the degree to which the researcher must rely on the recollections of individuals as the source of documentation. This problem is alleviated if independent sources of information such as school or family records are available, if the interval is short rather than long, and if the focus of study is less likely to be distorted by the passage of time and subsequent experiences. In other words, the more factual and descriptive the focus, the less likely retrospective approaches are to provide invalid information. Freud (1905) made extensive use of retrospective data in developing his theories of childhood sexuality.

TABLE 3.1

Primary Characteristics of the Organismic World View

1. Belief that development is best understood as a qualitative process involving the progressive, active construction and reconstruction of levels of organization

2. Belief that development is a universal, unidirectional process typical of all humans

3. Belief that there is an idealized end point toward which all development proceeds

4. Belief that individuals actively attribute meaning to their experiences

5. Belief that development proceeds through a series of syntheses, each leading to a greater potential for effective adaptation to life experiences

Summary of the Organismic World View

Organicism offers a rational, idealized, universal vision of human development across the life span (see Table 3.1). It views development as a sequential process of structural changes that lead to increasingly more effective modes of adaptation. This process is holistic in nature and is conceptualized as taking place on a distinct plane of systemic, integrated action (psychological or biological), a plane not directly reducible to either individual biological and/or sociohistorical forces. Individuals play an active role in this developmental process. Their efforts to make meaning out of their experiences are not simply an attempt to replicate on the psychological level what is first present on the physical or social levels. Rather, they reflect a deliberate effort to construct a unique knowledge of those experiences consistent with their developmental level.

Organicism's methodologies are consistent with its theoretical orientation. Instead of searching for causes external to a synergistic plane of action, the organicist attempts to document changes in patterns of organization and offers explanations for these changes consistent with the assumptions of the world view.

4

What We Are—
The Contextualist World View

The root metaphor for the mechanistic perspective is the machine. The implication is one of prediction and stability. Mechanists have a strong belief in the universality of laws governing behavior and the value of reductionism as a strategy for understanding natural phenomena. The root metaphor for the organismic perspective is the living organism. The implication is one of ordered change over time. Organicists, too, have a belief in universal patterns, but ones that are meaningful only at a holistic level of analysis.

The metaphor for the contextualist perspective is the historical act. Here, the implication is that just about anything goes. At least, that's the way organicists (Overton, 1984) and mechanists (Kendler, 1986) regard this third of Pepper's world views (1961). Actually, the facts of the matter aren't quite so extreme, but they are a considerable leap from the assumptions of the other two perspectives.

Pepper's Analysis

Pepper chooses the *historical act* as the root metaphor for contextualism. This choice is not meant to imply that contextualism is a world view rooted in the past but rather that the meaning of any behavioral event is dependent on the context in which it occurs. Pepper (1961) describes these acts as intrinsically complex, composed of interconnecting activities with continuously changing patterns. He likens these acts to the plot of a novel; he sees them as "literally the incidents of life" (p. 233).

The one feature of the contextualist metaphor that distinguishes it most clearly from both the mechanistic and organismic world views is its emphasis on *dispersiveness*. Unlike the universal assumptions characteristic of the other two perspectives, contextualism makes no universal claims. Rather than searching for an understanding of human development by attempting to identify abstract universal principles, the contextualist looks to the interdependency of the individual within a *sociohistorical context*. In particular, the contextualist scrutinizes what the person is doing and what meaning or meanings he or she ascribes to both these actions and the surrounding events.

Time and Place

For contextualists, this search for meaning is always specific to time and place. There is no sense that the patterns identified necessarily hold the same meanings for other times and in other places. As Pepper says, order may come out of disorder and return to disorder—or it may not. For the contextualist there are no permanent structures to discover. There are only temporary confluences of incidents, with each incident exhibiting a structure specific to its time and place. Clearly prediction does not occupy the same valued status in contextualism as it does in mechanism, nor direction the same valued status as it does in organicism.

Contextualism is a relative concept; that is, it must always be defined from the perspective of the individual in a given time and place. For this person context consists of the events that are experienced as they are given meaning by the person. The meaning ascribed by this person reflects his or her experienced past as this past is represented in the present, the present as it is experienced by him or her, and the anticipated future. There is a true interdependence between the individual and the events, because each functions to give meaning to the other. Therefore any attempt to look at only one or the other (i.e., to take something out of context) distorts the relationship and renders any conclusions about it meaningless.

This definition of contextualism places significant limits on the developmentalist's ability to study behavioral change or development, at least as the other two perspectives view the process of change. It means that an objective or third-party view of individuals is not possible and that no universal meaning or even sequence can be given to the events that make up a particular context. What something comes to mean in one context offers no guarantees about what it will mean in another, either for a different person or for the same person at a different time. For Pepper, then, the only things that do seem predictable within this perspective are change and novelty—that is, unpredictability. Something always happens; it's simply not possible to generalize about what this something is.

Quality and Texture

Even though it's not possible to ascribe universal meaning to the events that make up a person's context independent of the person, Pepper does offer a way to describe the structure of the events comprised in a context. He states that, at least within our experience (his qualifier of our experience reflects a desire to be consistent with the nonuniversal assumptions of the perspective), it is possible to say that all contexts exhibit both *quality* and *texture*. Quality refers to the intuited wholeness of an event, texture to the details and relations that make up this quality. One is not a substitute for the other or an explanation of the other. Rather, each provides a unique way of viewing a context. As Pepper explains:

We intuit the familiar character of home as we drive up to our door, and only occasionally ask ourselves what features distinguish this from hundreds of other houses we drive up to. We intuit objects as chairs, cups, cats, tulips, oaks, linnets, and only rarely wonder how we know these so quickly and surely. These intuitions are of the qualities of these textures, and the textures are rarely noticed except when we do notice intently, and then it is the qualities that are not noticed. (p. 239)

There are three aspects to the quality of a context: spread, change, and fusion. *Spread* concerns the temporal aspect of a context's quality. It marks the past, present, and future of the events that make up the context, as each is represented in the present by the individual. *Change* refers to the fact that each act alters the quality of an experience because it redefines both its temporal aspects (its spread) and the relationship among its components. For the contextualist, change is a constant, so attempts to talk about people or events as stable—for any period of time—are a fiction. *Fusion* is the integrating aspect of events. It reflects the degree to which we integrate or fuse the specific textures of the event into a more meaningful whole. By implication, events that have no fusion are not events.

The texture of an event also involves three aspects: strands, context, and reference. Pepper treats the first two, strands and context, together.[1] "A texture is made up of strands and it lies in a context" (p. 246). The distinction is one of perspective. We could talk about the members of a family as the *strands* of its texture, and we could describe the *context* of this texture as the community in which the family lives. If we change the perspective from the family to the father and talk about the various strands that define his texture, the family now becomes the context. It isn't the unit that defines its status; it is the relationship of the unit to all others. In other words, it's all a matter of context. *Reference* refers to the beginning and ending of the strands that compose a texture, the degree to which these origins are similar, and the likelihood of any of the strands being blocked.

Contextualism and Context

It is important to point out that Pepper's use of context within a contextualist world view differs significantly from how the term is used in mechanism. Contextualism asserts that elements cannot be analyzed out of context because, once they are taken out of context, they no longer have any meaning. In a more practical sense, for contextualists, the analyses of variance that are the hallmark of the mechanists methodology are questionable because such an analysis requires the teasing apart of variables. Tease apart the variables, and we lose their meaning, that is, their patterns of relationship. Put another way, the mechanists' reference to efficient causes as events in an

---

[1] Notice that Pepper is now using *context* in a second sense. The first, the part that contextualists are ultimately interested in, refers to the entire experience. This second usage refers to one aspect of an experience's texture.

individual's environment or context is a very different application of the term *context* than is meant by contextualists.

Organicists share contextualists' view of context as an interdependent nexus. But contrary to the contextualists, they also believe that there is a deeper, universal organization regulating the structure and sequencing of contexts. In effect, organicists are arguing that all contexts have a common set of defining qualities (even though the specifics of each may still be distinct), and it is these common qualities that interact with the developing individual. The result of this interaction process is universal developmental sequences. For contextualists, however, there is no external or deeper cause, no necessary set of elements common to all contexts, no universal meaning to a given event, and no necessary direction to the course of the life span. It is in this sense that Pepper describes contextualism as having a *horizontal cosmology,* or view of the universe, and both mechanism and organicism as having *vertical cosmologies.*

> In mechanism or organicism one has only to analyze in certain specified ways and one is bound, so it is believed, ultimately to get to the bottom of things or to the top of it. Contextualism justifies no such faith. There is no cosmological mode of analysis that guarantees the whole truth or an arrival at the ultimate nature of things. On the other hand, one does not need to hunt for a distant cosmological truth, since every present event gives it as fully as it can be given. All one has to do to get at the sort of thing the world is, is to realize, intuit, get the quality of whatever happens to be going on. The quality of blowing your nose is just as cosmic and ultimate as Newton's writing down his gravitational formula. The fact that his formula is much more useful to many more people doesn't make it any more real. (p. 251)

It is the character of the quality and texture of an event or historical act, as viewed by the participant, that defines his or her context. And it is this interdependence between event and individual, each defining and at the same time being defined by the other, that is the focus of interest for the contextualist. This interest, of necessity, must be pragmatic in focus because that is presumably all there is to study. There is no deeper structure and no expectation of predictability across either time or setting. There is not even a guarantee that the changes that do occur will be progressive in nature—that is, that can be described as moving in the direction of increasing maturity or gain along some defined dimension (Cavanaugh, 1991). There is simply what we are, *at that moment.* At face value, this perspective would hardly seem to merit any interest from developmentalists. As it turns out, however, the perspective has been gaining increasing interest (Reese, 1991).

Contextualism as a Developmental Perspective

Contextualism as a way of looking at things has actually been around for a long time. Pepper discusses its origins in the pragmatism of William James at the turn of the 20th century. Reese (1991) traces strands of the perspective back to the writings of the ancient Greek philosophers. Even though it has been around for a while, it has really only been in the past 25 years or so that contextualism has entered the vocabulary of the discipline of human development. It has not done so at the expense of the other two perspectives. Contrary to the arguments of contextualists such as Gergen (1980), rumors of the death of both mechanism and organicism have been greatly exaggerated. But contextualism has prompted developmentalists of all persuasions to rethink the limits of their models.

Several factors have contributed to contextualism's growing status among the disciplines that study human development. All reflect an increasing uncomfortableness with the broad generalizations that have historically characterized theories of behavioral change and of development. One of these factors is the various attempts to show that the integrative element of Piaget's theory (i.e., the cross-domain similarities in developmental levels) is not well supported by research (Brainerd, 1993; Flavell, Miller, & Miller, 1993; Gallistel & Gelman, 1992; Gelman, Meck, & Markin, 1986). A second factor involves the renewed interest in a life span–centered rather than a child-centered view of development (Baltes, 1987; Goldhaber, 1979; Lerner & Kauffman, 1985; Schaie, 1994). When viewed from the perspective of an entire life span, one finds greater variability than is the case in a child-centered view. Third, the increasing interest in cross-cultural research (Cole, 1988, 1992) and the rediscovery of Vygotsky's work (Vygotsky, 1978; Wertsch, 1985; Wertsch & Kanner, 1992) have led to arguments that development may be highly culture specific, in terms of not only behavior but also the psychological structures underlying behaviors. Finally, the extension of postmodern thought from the humanities into the social sciences has raised questions about the justifications for the permanence of all social structures, especially those that serve to situate groups within the social order (Chandler, 1993, 1995; Gergen, 1994; Gilligan, 1986). Each of these factors will be discussed in more detail in Part IV.

A contextualist perspective offers four main contributions to the study of development. Each is not necessarily unique to contextualism, but collectively they do offer a unique view of the life course. These four are (1) an emphasis on the practical and the immediate, (2) individuals as active meaning makers in social settings, (3) the open-ended nature of human development, and (4) scientific inquiry as a fallible, human endeavor.

An Emphasis on the Practical and the Immediate

Contextualism, by definition, denies the existence of external cause, of the usefulness of trying to find the "bottom line" to development (Gergen, 1994). As such, there can be no interest in generating general laws of development or in pursuing abstract concepts. In fact, abstractions in contextualism are seen as reifications—that is, as giving a reality to things that are not real. But if laws and abstractions are out, then what is left to study?

The answer is, the practical and the immediate. Furthermore, contextualists argue, when this course of study is pursued, there almost automatically follows an increased concern with the problems and crises that individuals face. In Reese's (1991) words the task is to find "temporally effective answers" (p. 196).

It is not that developmentalists from the other two perspectives fail to have this applied focus—quite the contrary for many. However, when mechanists or organicists pursue applied issues, they do so because they choose to view certain topics or issues from an applied perspective. The contextualist has no choice. All there is, is the applied.

This emphasis on the practical and the immediate means that contextualists cannot be dispassionate observers of the universal human condition. After all, there is no universal human condition to observe. Rather, contextualists must be active participants and critics in the sociohistorical process that at any moment creates the human condition. As Wartofsky (1986) puts it:

> Theories of development, therefore, are neither neutral observer reports on the "objective facts" of development, nor are they, in themselves, the arbiters of what will count as development proper, i.e., of "normal" or "good" development. These norms are not simply instituted by theoretical fiat. Rather, they are affected by the social, cultural, political processes of child rearing, parenting, education, the media; by the whole range of artifacts which, in any given period, come to define the range and character of the accepted or approved modes of child activity or child development—the forms of dress, the codes of social behavior, the toys and games—in short, all those aspects of culture in which the norms are embodied, preserved, transmitted. Theorists of development do not have the power to determine these norms. But they do have the responsibility to engage in the criticisms of these norms, in society at large and in self-criticism of theories of development, i.e., of their own normative proposals. They are, moreover, responsible to recognize the historicity or situatedness of these norms and to come down on the right side. In this sense, the theory of child development, as a discipline, should be taken as a branch of social ethics or of critical social theory. (p. 125)

Individuals as Active Meaning Makers in Social Settings

All developmental world views look at persons in context. Mechanists do so in a reductionist way that allows them to disentangle independent variables. Organicists do so in a holistic way that allows them to make universal claims about sequence. For contextualists, however, the phrase *person in context* has a somewhat distinct meaning. Specifically, the person and the context are not two discrete entities interacting in some fashion; instead, they form one interdependent but ultimately temporary entity—each for a period of time influencing and being influenced by the other. Remove one and, in effect, you have removed the other. A focus on the person and not the context leads to no understanding of the person but rather to abstraction and reification. Go the other way—to the context and not the person—and you wind up in the same place.

For contextualists this interdependence means that development is best studied from a systems perspective (Bronfenbrenner, 1989; Ford & Lerner, 1992; Sameroff, 1994). As Sameroff (1989) explains it, such a systems approach is concerned with the relationships among elements in a system. It is the sum of the elements plus the sum of the relationships that allows us to say that the whole is greater than the sum of its parts and that the meaning of person and context is to be found in the relationships among the elements rather than solely in the elements themselves.

Systems exert a form of self-stabilization and self-reorganization. A change in any one element is likely to result in a change in all the other elements. The system is no longer as it was. The source of the change may be internal to the system, or, because systems are themselves always embedded in larger systems and abutting other systems, it may be in another system. The change may be incidental or intentional; contextualism makes no distinction between sources of change. If the change is too great, the system may become dysfunctional or even nonfunctional. We talk about family crises in this fashion. But on a more positive note such developmental changes would also be reflected in the successive reports that a person might give about his or her shifting understanding of a system such as a family when viewed from that unique perspective. The reports would document a sequence of meaning-making activities specific to that individual's experience within a particular sociohistorical context.

The Open-Ended Nature of Human Development

One of the ways in which contextualism differs most from the other two world views concerns the issue of direction in development. Proponents of the other two world views argue that prior events influence subsequent ones in a deliberate, limiting fashion and that it is possible to identify a continuous course of behavioral change (as the mechanists might refer to it) or sequence of developmental stages (as the organicists might refer to it). Contextualists make no such claim. In fact, they claim just the opposite. Consider the way Gergen (1980) puts it:

> In contrast to the stability account, we find little in the way of adult behavior patterns that is compellingly fashioned by early experience. And, with regard to the ordered change accounts, we find their applicability limited largely to early periods of physiological maturation. Explorations in adult developmental sequences largely support an aleatoric [uncertain or random] standpoint: developmental trajectories may be largely traced to the accidental composite of existing circumstances. This does not mean that the social world is essentially chaotic or that continuities may never be found in developmental trajectory. People may ensure that their environment remains reasonably well ordered at any time, or over time they may find a stable behavioral niche. However, precisely what patterns are maintained or changed over time is not recurrent in principle. (p. 37)

From a contextual perspective it is hard to overemphasize the significance of a statement like this. Gergen is arguing that not one but many developmental trajectories are possible. Furthermore, because no universal principles regulate the maintenance or change of patterns over time, there is no rational basis to argue that one pattern is in some way better, more mature, or more advanced than the other. Rather, each pattern must be considered for what it is, an interdependent system functioning within a specific sociohistorical context. It is, contextualists contend, an argument of liberation.

This argument of liberation has been very evident in the writings of many scholars, including that of Gilligan (1982, 1986) and her colleagues concerning gender differences. Gilligan's main point is that universalist theoretical perspectives make it possible to come to value one developmental pattern over another. In particular, such universal theorizing has often led to the conclusion that the developmental pattern typically associated with males is preferable to the pattern associated with females. In her own words:

> The quality of embeddedness in social interaction and personal relationships that characterizes women's lives in contrast to men's, however, becomes not only a descriptive difference but also a developmental liability when the milestones of child-hood and adolescent development in the psychological literature are markers of increasing separation. Women's failure to separate then becomes by definition a fail-ure to develop. (Gilligan, 1982, pp. 8–9)

The very same issue exists with respect to cross-cultural studies of developmental patterns. There is, from a contextualist perspective, no basis to argue the value of one culture's accomplishments over another, the level of civilization of one culture over another, or anything else for that matter. Each culture and the members of that cul-ture can only be considered as a unique expression of a system within a particular sociohistorical context. More to the point, as Cole (1988) notes, the contextualist per-spective eviscerates arguments that claim to show, for example, that the developmen-tal level of the adults in a "primitive" culture is essentially on a par with that of the children in a "modern" culture. Because terms such as *primitive* and *modern* lose their meaning in a contextualist perspective, so, too, do the value judgments based on such terms.

Contextualists believe that this argument of liberation is equally relevant when considering what they see as the paternalistic interpretations made across both socio-economic and racial-ethnic groups within a society. This is particularly true when it comes to those in power making decisions "in the best interests" of those who are effectively disenfranchised in a society (Jackson, 1993). It is even relevant to a recon-sideration of our current beliefs about facilitating development. Kessen (1990) argues that a contextualist perspective forces us to reconsider our common belief that mod-ern child-rearing practices are more progressive, or more developmentally appropriate, than those found in our past. Blank (1989) raises a similar caution with respect to old age. He argues that, when considered from a contextualist perspective, our prescrip-tions for successful aging are, in fact, actually little more than alternative descriptions, each holding an equal potential for successful aging.

Scientific Inquiry as a Human Endeavor

The fourth contribution reflects a debate not so much about developmental patterns themselves as about the scientific process that discovers or creates these patterns. The key question is whether it is actually possible to step out of context and objectively and dispassionately observe the human condition. Contextualists argue that develop-mentalists are no less mortal than anyone else and so are as prone as anyone to see things through the lens of the contexts they occupy. Therefore, our "truths" about development are obtained not by objective, dispassionate discovery but rather by a sociohistorically embedded process of creation. Gergen (1985) argues that the terms in which the world is understood are social artifacts, products of historically situated interchanges among people. Furthermore, the process of understanding is not automatically driven by the forces of nature but results from an active, cooperative enterprise of persons in relationship.

This contextualist perspective on the study of human development directs our attention to the social, political, moral, and economic institutions that sustain and are supported by current assumptions about human activity. It is only through such a reflective examination, contextualists argue, that developmentalists, as well as all other scientists, can become fully aware first of the values that are implicit in our theorizing and then of both the potential and actual consequences—both positive and negative—of our value-based statements (Ingleby, 1986; Labouvie-Vief & Chandler, 1978).

Such a reflective process is not seen as freeing us from our values. Rather, such a process will better help us appreciate how our values have helped shape the research questions we ask, the types of information we seek, the methods we use to answer these questions, and the types of explanations we use to interpret our answers. In this sense it is certainly worth remembering Wartofsky's (1986) claim that the discipline of human development should be recognized as a branch of social ethics.

The Study of Human Development from a Contextualist World View

How is it possible to study human development from a contextualist world view? If there is no deep structure to uncover, no guarantee of predictability across time and place, and no common sequence to piece together, what's left to find? As you might expect from a world view that prides itself on its dispersiveness, developmentalists under the contextualist banner pursue a range of methodologies—from techniques that do not differ from those used by mechanists and organicists to those that are highly subjective and qualitative in tone.

This distinction between those methods shared with mechanism and organicism and those unique to contextualism is not a matter of one being better than the other. Rather, it is a theoretical issue of the degree to which methods used within the other two world views can also prove useful within contextualism (Houts, 1991). Contextualists whose orientations reflect the psychological side of the discipline of human development appear most comfortable adapting methods from the other two world views. Contextualists from the sociological and anthropological sides of the discipline of human development favor methods not found within the other two world views. Houts explains the distinction:

> Such a search for the causes of development does not have to aspire to the discovery of universal causes, nor does it need to reject the important role of the laboratory experiment in identifying those factors of the organism and the environment that reliably produce certain developmental outcomes. Once one abandons the positivist expectation and requirement for universal laws of development, one is still left with

the task of identifying those nonuniversal "laws" that describe more local regularities between developmental outcomes and the factors that produce them. Such a weak form of contextualism amounts to specifying the scope of research findings obtained from traditional methods, but it does not require one to abandon those methods altogether. In this sense, contextualism in developmental theory adds up to a recognition that social scientists must be modest in their claims, but it does not, as strong contextualists would have it, entail abandoning the project of making causal claims in favor of merely telling coherent stories. (p. 49)

Irrespective of the origin of these methodologies, they share three basic assumptions. First, the intent of contextualist methods is to identify sociohistorically or contextually based information rather than to discover some universal truth. This is a rejection of the belief common to both mechanism and organicism that the purpose of scientific inquiry is the discovery of universal patterns and/or processes. This should not be surprising given that, to the contextualist, there is no universal truth but only sociohistorically situated information.

Second, the goal of contextualist methods is a better understanding of the person in context rather than the person out of context. If we take the person out of context—that is, methodologically speaking, if we control for other variables—then the meaning of the person's actions are lost since that meaning only exists within a context.

Third, contextualist methods are not value neutral—there is a reason one question rather than another is asked. To the contextualist, understanding the reason one question rather than another is asked in the first place is an important step in understanding the answers that are eventually found.

Cohort analysis and *pattern analysis* are the two most common methodologies used by contextualists that mechanists and organicists also find useful. Cohort analyses are used by life span researchers interested in identifying different developmental patterns reflective of sociohistorical context. Pattern analyses include a variety of techniques designed to identify the links or correlations among the elements of a system or context.

Ethnographic analysis and *narrative analysis* are the two most common methodologies relatively unique to contextualism. Ethnographic analyses examine cross-cultural patterns of human development while narrative analyses attempt to get at the subjective experience of the person in context.

Cohort Analysis

A *cohort* is a group of individuals who share a common characteristic, such as date of birth or age of entry into college or time of entry into the military. Cohorts can also be defined in terms of a shared experience, such as having lived through a natural disaster. The purpose of a cohort analysis is to determine the long-term, cumulative impact of the slice of history experienced as a result of the group's shared characteristic or experience. What, for example, is the long-term impact of starting college when you are 48 compared to when you are 18? What is the long-term impact of living amidst the destruction caused by a war? What are the consequences of growing up in a time when good nutrition and sanitation are readily available compared to a time when they are not?

Cohort analyses are an extension of the cross-sectional and longitudinal methodologies typically associated with the organismic perspective. The method is primarily intended to provide a means to differentiate *age-graded* from *historical-graded* influences on the course of development (Baltes, 1987; Schaie, 1994). Age-graded influences are those seen as having a close relationship to chronological age. The sequence and rate of motor development is a good example of an age-graded influence. Although the sequence and rate are not identical for every child, there is a clear relationship between the two. Knowing a child's chronological age enables a better-than-chance prediction about the child's level of motor development. The relationship is seen as strong enough that significant deviations—such as being too early or, even more so, being too late—are considered to have possible clinical significance. Notice that nothing is explained in this process. Rather, all that can be said is that, whatever the reason, the process occurs in an orderly enough fashion and rate that it can be linked to chronological age.

Historical-graded influences are those specific to time and place. These influences would not be easily predicted simply by knowing a person's chronological age. The reason for this difficulty in prediction based on chronological age alone is that the life experiences of different groups of individuals (i.e., cohorts) may be or have been so different as to prevent generalizations across different cohorts. In other words, the developmental pattern identified may be specific to time and place. The recognition of the importance of historical-graded influences has grown as developmentalists have extended their interests from topics specific to child development to those of the entire life span (Goldhaber, 1979, 1986). It is the impact of these historical-graded influences that is of most interest to contextualists.

In a practical sense cohort analyses involve the comparison of data obtained longitudinally with that obtained cross-sectionally. If there are no historical-graded influences—that is, if there are no cohort effects—then the data obtained from the two methods should overlap. For example, suppose the data from two groups of 50-year-olds, one group born in 1900 and tested in 1950 and the other born in 1940 and tested in 1990, overlaps. Then the particular life experiences unique to each cohort—in terms of both what they experienced and when they experienced it—apparently would have no differential influence on their views of the world as measured in the study. The only factor influencing their test scores therefore would seem to be their chronological ages. But most cohort analyses present a different picture, one suggesting that cohort does make a significant difference in the lives of individuals (Baltes, 1987; Elder, 1974, 1995; Schaie, 1965, 1994). It is these differences that are of most interest to contextualists pursuing cohort analyses, because such an approach documents the impact of the life events unique to individuals exposed to particular sociohistorical contexts. These life experiences likely would include educational achievement, exposure to technology, general health and nutrition, economic status, political activities, and work opportunities, to name a few.

A cohort analysis offers a way to highlight the developmental significance of these different contexts. In its most complete form the method requires the collection of longitudinal data from several distinct cohorts. Once the data is collected, the relative influence of age-graded and history-graded factors are determined by making the appropriate comparisons between the data obtained from different groups at different times.

Contextualists argue that cohort analyses caution us to be very careful in our generalizations about development. What seems to be true for one cohort may not be true for another, and as such, the contextualist argues, claims for universal developmental patterns may be unwarranted. Ironically, a cohort analysis even cautions us to be careful about assuming cohort effects. Just as there is no theoretical basis, from a contextualist perspective, to assume sociohistorical stability over time, there is also no theoretical basis to necessarily assume discontinuity in sociohistorical contexts over time. Some historical intervals within particular cultures have been characterized by rapid change, while other intervals and settings could be said to show virtually no change. In the first instance we would expect significant cohort effects; in the second we would not.

Pattern Analysis

Every context describes a pattern of interrelationships—the strands that define the texture and the quality that then emerges. One effective way to depict this rich tapestry is through the various methods of data analysis that search for relationships among and between the elements of the context. These methods range from the simple correlational techniques discussed in the previous chapter to complex factorial and systems analyses. What they all have in common, however, is the fact that they are all looking for patterns of relationships. Therefore they are an appropriate methodology within the contextualist perspective (Wohlwill, 1973).

Correlation is a measure of a relationship. As noted previously, two things are said to correlate to the extent that knowing something about one reduces our uncertainty about the other. For the contextualist correlation techniques are a way to identify the strands within a particular context. Simple correlations determine the degree of relationship between two strands. However, because it is hard to imagine a context with only two strands, contextualists turn to more powerful techniques of pattern analysis.

The logic of the process does not change as the number of strands increases; only the complexity of the calculations and the completeness of the resulting picture do so. Multiple correlation techniques allow us to examine simultaneously the effects of many different strands on a particular behavior. *Cross-lagged panel correlation* (Achenbach, 1978) is a form of multiple correlation analysis that looks at patterns of relationships across time. Such transactional analyses help explain how patterns embedded in sociohistorically defined contexts shift over time. The scale of time and place need not be grand. Such analyses have been very useful in assessing the changing dynamics of parent-child relationships (Patterson, 1986) and in assessing the likelihood that the presence of risk factors in a given setting can lead to developmental delays or later problems if no change in the context occurs (Sameroff, 1975, 1994).

Still another variation on the search for relationships is *factor analysis*. Factor analysis is particularly useful when the number of variables being correlated is so large as to make the process of analysis and interpretation unwieldly. Instead of trying to make sense out of the many correlations, researchers use statistical procedures to identify specific correlations that, in effect, themselves correlate with one another. These groups of correlations are then lumped together and treated as one factor. The factors that emerge from such an analysis provide insight into the dynamics of the context from which the factors were drawn. And, as is true of cross-lagged panel analysis, changes in factor patterns over time offer one means of understanding the nature of the forces influencing the dynamics of individuals and settings that make up that context.

Before moving on to the next two methods of analysis (ethnographic and narrative), it is important to again note how the use of the two methodologies just discussed differs in contextualism when compared to their use in either mechanism or organicism. It is a difference based on how the analyzed data is interpreted rather than how it is gathered or analyzed (Ford & Lerner, 1992). With respect to gathering and analyzing, the procedures do not differ from those found in the other world views. Variables are controlled and partitioned, and hypothetical constructs (e.g., factors) are abstracted from the data. It is the cautiousness of the interpretations that distinguishes the use of these methods in a contextualist perspective from their use in the mechanistic and organismic perspectives. For contextualists the interpretations are always specific to time and place, and they are seen as relevant and therefore useful to that time and place. But no further claims are made.

Ethnographic Analysis

Ethnographic analysis provides a means to understand how a particular cultural context influences the behavior of the members of that culture and, in turn, how the actions of the members of that culture or community maintain the stability of the culture (Cole, 1996a; Patton, 1990). Although the stereotype for such analyses is that of the anthropologist in a setting distant in both time and place from her or his own, ethnographic analyses can just as easily be done within one's own culture.

Whatever the setting, ethnographic analysis involves prolonged, active contact of the ethnographer within the culture. The goal, ideally, is to become so immersed in the culture that the ethnographer begins to understand the people and events that define the context from the same perspective as the members of the culture themselves.

The ethnographer is likely to collect all sorts of information, both quantitative and qualitative. An important element of this data gathering process is that the tools and techniques used to obtain the information are ones appropriate to the community. As Cole (1988) notes, failure to use culturally appropriate tools and techniques can lead to an inaccurate and often negative picture of the abilities of the people in the community. The problem arises when one fails to realize that, from a contextualist perspective, not only are skills and abilities culture specific, but so, too, are the techniques appropriate for their assessment.

Ethnographic information reflects both the actual physical conditions of the culture or community and the behaviors, rituals, laws, attitudes, and beliefs of its members. For example, observations would be made of the interactions of community members, and discussions held about contacts with those from outside the community. In addition, strategies of problem solving and conflict resolution would be noted, educational practices observed, and family dynamics and rituals recorded.

What finally emerges is a holistic picture of the culture, usually more descriptive than interpretive in nature (Podolefsky, 1994). The description is not presented as objective—that is, value free—because, from a contextualist perspective, there can be no such thing. Rather, the description is presented as an accurate picture through the eyes of a member of that community. Clearly the degree to which the ethnographer successfully immerses him- or herself in the community will have a significant bearing on any claims of descriptive accuracy.

Ethnographic analysis is a means to document one of the basic assumptions of a contextualist perspective—that contexts can only be understood from within rather than from without. Whenever we attempt to do so from without, either by using assessments not found in the culture or by making assumptions not appropriate to the culture, we fail, contextualists argue, to grasp both the meaning that the culture holds for its members and the means by which that meaning maintains its integrity.

Narrative Analysis

Narrative analysis also provides a means to understand from within, but its focus is even more circumscribed than that of ethnographic analysis. Whereas ethnography tries to provide a descriptive understanding of a culture or community, narrative analysis attempts to provide an interpretive understanding of the way people weave life experiences into coherent stories or narratives (Lightfoot, 1992).

The weaving of life experiences into a coherent sense of self and of place is, of course, a highly subjective enterprise. This subjectivity would be problematic for the other two world views because there would be no way to verify what an individual "really" means or to identify what events "really" are causing that person's actions. But from a contextualist perspective, there is no "really" beyond that expressed through the person's narrative. Therefore this subjectivity is not a problem—it is simply what there is (Cohler, 1982). As noted previously, this distinction is not meant to imply that contextualists deny that there is a "real world" out there, but only that the meaning of the events in that world are best understood as social constructions.

Because the focus in narrative analysis is on the voice of the participant, the researcher makes less of an attempt to become a participant observer. Clearly the narrative researcher wants to establish the kind of relationship that will allow the stories told to be the ones the person wants and needs to tell. However, there is no presumption on the part of the researcher that if he or she were to stay in the context long enough, he or she would be able to tell the same story. This limitation reflects the highly subjective nature of personal narrative. But it also reflects the fact that narrative analyses often are done with groups that differ significantly in age or social circumstances from that of the researcher (Brown & Gilligan, 1992; Scheibe, 1994).

Narrative analysis involves more than simply recording another's stories. It also involves an active process of interpretation. Because interpretation is by nature value laden, the narrative researcher must be very clear as to what those values are and how they are to be reflected in the analysis of the narratives. In some cases, the values drive the process. Patton (1990) notes, for example, that those pursuing narrative analysis from a feminist perspective presume the importance of gender in human relationships and societal processes and so orient the study in that direction. Someone considering the same narrative from a Marxist political or economic orientation would take a materialist perspective that presumes the centrality of class conflict in understanding community and societal structures and dynamics. Presumably the two orientations would lead to different interpretations. Such a difference would be a problem for mechanists and organicists because there would be no way to identify the "real" pattern. But for the contextualist, there would be no problem, only two possible interpretations of the same situation when viewed from two different perspectives.

The work of Brown and Gilligan (1992) provides a good illustration of this interpretive process. Their interest was the personal meanings young females give to their experiences as they make the transition into adolescence. The data comprised a series of interviews with each adolescent over the puberty years. Once recorded, each interview was heard four times, from four different frames of reference.

> The first time through the interview, we listen to the story the person tells: the geography of the psychological landscape, the plot. Our goal is to get a sense of what is happening, to follow the unfolding of events, to listen to the drama. . . . The second time through the interview text, we listen for "self"—for the voice of the "I" speaking in this relationship. We find this listening for the voice of the other to be crucial. It brings us into relationship with the person, in part by ensuring that the sound of her voice enters our psyche and in part by discovering how she speaks of herself before we speak of her. . . . In the third and fourth listenings, we attend to the ways people talk about relationships—how they experience themselves in the relational landscape of human life. . . . As resisting listeners, therefore, we make an effort to distinguish when relationships are narrowed and distorted by gender stereotypes or used as opportunities for distancing, abuse, subordination, invalidation, or other forms of psychological violation, physical violence, and oppression, and when relationships are healthy, joyous, encouraging, freeing and empowering. (pp. 27, 29)

Through this process Brown and Gilligan try to capture the different meanings of the adolescent transition as experienced by these young women. The primary goal is not to identify antecedents or to discovery universal patterns but simply to attempt to understand the transition as it is experienced for this cohort in this setting. For Brown and Gilligan this understanding focuses on how, from their perspective, societal restrictions on openness and directness for young women in our society can make the transition to adolescence a sometimes painful experience for them. Their goals were both to document the process so that others could understand it better and, by extension, to suggest the nature of the social forces that sometimes can serve to restrict or limit the development of women. Given the applied nature of a contextualist perspective, this is as it should be.

TABLE 4.1
Primary Characteristics of the Contextualist World View

1. Belief that the study of human development always reflects the sociohistorical perspective of the researcher

2. Belief that the meaning of an event is best defined from the perspective of the individual experiencing that event

3. Belief that explanations and interpretations of human development are always situated in and restricted to any particular sociohistorical context

4. Belief that human development is an open-ended phenomenon, with no necessary theoretically implied directions, patterns, or limits

5. Belief that there is a moral and ethical imperative in the study of human development that is directed toward a "politics of liberation"

Summary of the Contextualist World View

Contextualism offers a distinct perspective on human development, one limited to time and place (see Table 4.1). It does not claim the grand "truths" of either mechanism or organicism, but rather seeks to describe subjective individual experience situated within specific sociohistorical settings. Contextualists argue that, because individual experiences most often are holistic in nature, methods of analysis must be as well. Contextualists tend to be particularly critical of reductionist analyses leading to abstractions, and even when using methods common to the other two perspectives, they are careful to qualify and limit their conclusions as to time and place. Perhaps because of their emphasis on context, contextualists tend to be especially sensitive to the intentional and/or unintentional political and socioeconomic ramifications of developmental theories. This sensitivity is reflected both in their concern with the sociohistorical origins of the hypotheses tested by developmentalists and in their belief that the proper purpose of research is in fostering equality and social justice.

Part I—Summing Up

Developmental theories deal with "big" questions (and, by implication, world views deal with even "bigger" ones). Their usefulness is not so much in predicting or understanding a particular behavior on a particular day from a particular person as in predicting or understanding patterns of behavior over many days (or longer) from many people. To accomplish this task, developmentalists have searched for anchors to hold fast their observations. These anchors are Pepper's metaphors—the machine, the living organism, and the historical act.

What is perhaps most significant about these three metaphors is their respective sources. Images of machines are drawn from the physical and natural sciences, images of living organisms from the life sciences, and images of the historical act from the humanities. Each of these three rich intellectual traditions is used to construct a distinct perspective from which to view behavior and development and a distinct set of strategies from which to analyze it. These differences are defined in terms of whether human development is best understood from a reductionist or a holistic perspective and whether human development is a universal process or one best defined by the particulars of time and place. From these basic differences comes the question of where to look for and what to accept as the causes of our development.

These three world views stand in a unique tension to one another. Each offers a distinct explanation for the phenomena that are of interest to developmentalists. The developmentalist must either select one as a general guide or argue that some aspects of development are consistent with the assumptions of one world view while other aspects are consistent with another. Neither is an ideal choice. The first limits the frame of reference, and the second raises questions about a most basic tenet of science —namely, that there is an orderliness to natural phenomena. Furthermore, the differences in methodologies that follow from these three distinct world views make direct evaluative comparisons at best difficult and at times impossible. What is proof for one is usually not for the others.

It is not that we *can't* make comparisons among the three. We certainly can in terms of any of the four criteria for evaluating a theory: testability, organization, generativity, and precision. We can talk about these four criteria with respect to each of the three world views and, as we will see in subsequent chapters, with respect to each theory within a particular world view. We can certainly talk about the research strategies that theorists for each world view use to test their hypotheses, about how they each organize their findings, and about the process each uses to generate new hypotheses and interpretations. It is when we start asking evaluative questions across the three world views, however, that we run into problems. Is mechanism more precise than organicism? Is contextualism more generative than organicism? Is mechanism more testable (i.e., more scientific) than contextualism? Is organicism more organized and logically coherent than contextualism? These are all perfectly reasonable questions to ask. Indeed, we will never have a fully integrated theory of human development until we have the answers to them. The problem is that at the moment we don't have a way of asking these comparative questions that is equally consistent with and therefore acceptable to the basic theoretical assumptions of each world view.

Given these fundamental theoretical differences among the three world views, it is perhaps not surprising that each has tended to focus on different aspects of development, that is, to ask different questions about why we are the way we are. For the most part, mechanists ask questions about the variability that exists both within and between populations. These are questions about the processes that make each of us unique. To answer these questions, mechanists choose to use a fine-grained level of analysis, one intended to search for and identify what they see as the basic building blocks of human development. Organicists ask questions about pattern and sequence over time. These are questions about what we share by virtue of being members of the same species. To answer these questions, organicists pursue research strategies reflecting their belief that the individual, functioning as an integrated system, is the most basic level of analysis possible. Finally, contextualists ask questions about the situated experiences of our lives, about the here and now. These are questions about the reality of the day-to-day experiences that define the "what" of our lives. Like the organicist's, the contextualist's questions are answerable only at a holistic level. But now the basic level is not the person but the person in context. And because the basic level is the person in context, whatever discoveries the contextualist makes are seen as limited to that context.

This distinctiveness is not such a terrible state of affairs. Each world view helps us understand different aspects of our actions and conceptualizations. Each helps us recognize that the process of human development is not one-dimensional but multidimensional. By having to consider simultaneously three distinct images, we are forced to consider what we are as a species, what we have been, and what we someday may be. We are forced to consider why things are as they are and what we must do to make them different. We are forced to ask ourselves who we are and who we want to be. We are even forced to consider whether we even have much of a say in this matter. These are big questions, theoretical questions. And without these three theoretical world views on human development, each offering a different perspective from which to view human development, we couldn't even begin to figure out a way to answer any of them, much less find a mutually acceptable way to integrate them.

We turn now to Part II of the text, a detailed discussion of four models within the mechanistic perspective. In one sense mechanism is the most interesting of the three world views in that there is perhaps more disagreement among the four models than is true of the models within either organicism or contextualism. The disputes are largely methodological and statistical in nature, an appropriate circumstance given the fact that mechanism is a world view defined as much by its methods as by its assumptions.

The Mechanistic Perspective

Part II presents four theories representative of the mechanistic perspective: learning theory, social learning theory, information processing theory, and developmental behavior genetic theory. Of the four, learning theory is probably the one that historically has been seen as the model of a theory in the mechanistic tradition. Learning theory, which has also been referred to as stimulus-response theory, behavior theory, and conditioning theory, is associated with some of the most historically significant figures in the field of psychology: John Watson, Clark Hull, Edward Tolman, and B. F. Skinner. Through much of the 20th century, it was the dominant theory within the mechanistic tradition, although more recently, information processing theory has probably assumed this distinction.

Whereas learning theory is associated with the names of many individuals, social learning theory is associated with the name of one individual, Albert Bandura. Bandura's work is an extension of learning theory. It examines the degree to which the acquisition and demonstration of social behaviors and social cognitions can be explained in terms of the same principles of association that define learning theory. Bandura's work has made it clear that understanding the consequences of another's behavior can have as significant an influence on our own behavior as can experiencing these consequences directly.

Information processing theory has updated the machine metaphor in mechanism from the telephone switchboard to the computer. In so doing, the theory has made it possible to consider the role that both material and efficient causes play in determining behavior and behavioral change. In particular, information processing theory has made it easier to consider the role that such factors as memory capacity, rehearsal and retrieval strategies, and processing speed and strategy play in regulating our behavior and in changing that behavior.

Developmental behavior genetic theory focuses on the role that genetics plays in the regulation of behavior. The theory does this by trying to separate the influence of heredity from the influence of environment. Discussions of the relative influence of heredity and environment are, of course, highly controversial. Not surprisingly, proponents of developmental behavior genetic theory are often subjected to strong political and social criticisms in addition to the more conventional critiques leveled at all theorists of human development.

Not withstanding the important differences among these four theories, it is important to remember as you read the next four chapters that these four theories are all mechanistic. This means that all four share a belief that predictable and lawful antecedent forces influence our behavior, that we can best understand these forces by examining the influence of each independent of all others, and that the theoretical interpretation of this data is independent of the ways in which it is gathered. It is equally important to remember that all four of these perspectives are primarily concerned with understanding the variability that exists within and between populations—that is, in identifying those variables that make us each a unique individual.

5

Learning Theory

"There is no question that the ability to form associations (i.e., learn) is at the heart of any set of developmental mechanisms." This statement by Frances Horowitz defines the place of the study of learning in the larger study of human development. The statement is perhaps less noteworthy for its content than for its date—1987—a time in the evolution of developmental theories when some had already relegated the study of learning to the history rather than the theory books and had replaced it with studies of both information processing and social learning theory. But Horowitz is claiming that the issues raised first by Pavlov and Watson and later by Skinner and by the stimulus-response (S-R) psychologists still have relevance for the study of human development. We investigate this claim by (1) reviewing the contributions of the pioneers in behavioral theory and (2) by considering the current place of the study of learning in the study of human development.

Learning theory concerns the fundamental processes by which things become associated with one another. This process is seen as taking one of two forms. In the case in which an initially neutral stimulus acquires the response-eliciting powers of another stimulus, the process is referred to as *classical* or *Pavlovian conditioning*. In the case in which an association is formed between a response and its consequences, the process is referred to as *operant* or *instrumental conditioning*.

The Origins of Learning Theory

The origins of learning theory date to the work of the Russian physiologist Ivan Pavlov (1849–1936) and the American psychologist John Watson (1878–1958). Neither Pavlov nor Watson was the first to recognize some key aspects of learning—they have always been obvious to anyone who has ever tried to influence the behavior of another. Parents in ancient Greece were no doubt as aware of the value of a little honey to keep their child happy in the agora as modern parents are of the value of ice cream in the supermarket. But Watson (1913, 1914, 1930) and Pavlov (1927) each made contributions to learning theory significant enough that they are seen as ushering in the modern study of learning and, by extension, the modern study of behavioral change or development.

Pavlov's Contribution

Pavlov's (1927) actual interest was not learning but the physiology of gastric secretions. Nevertheless, his procedures and findings were adopted by psychologists who were trying to establish a natural science base for psychology. For our purposes, Pavlov's most famous experiment involved the conditioning of the salivary response in dogs.

Dogs salivate at the smell of food. In Pavlov's terms the dogs exhibit an *unconditioned response* to an *unconditioned stimulus*. The "un" part refers to the fact that the response appears to be built in or reflexive. That is, it seems to be present very early in a dog's life and doesn't seem to need any deliberate environmental intervention to establish it.

Pavlov quickly discovered that if another stimulus, such as the ringing of a bell, was paired with the smell of the food, it, too, came to elicit the salivary response, even in the absence of the smell of the food. In other words the association of the sound of the bell with the smell of the food had resulted in the extension of the response-eliciting power from the smell of the food to the sound of the bell. The sound of the bell had become a *conditioned stimulus* and the salivary response—now to the sound of the bell—was a *conditioned response*. The change in the dog's behavior, from doing nothing to salivating in response to the sound of the bell, indicated that the dog had made an association; that is, the dog had learned.

This process is by no means unique to dogs. The same process is equally evident in the behavior of very young infants, who soon begin to extend sucking motions from the nipple in the mouth to the mere sight of the nipple and soon thereafter even to the preparations preceding nursing (Papousek & Papousek, 1984). In this case the sucking actions in response to the presence of the nipple in the mouth are an unconditioned response to the sensation of the nipple, the unconditioned stimulus. Sucking movements at the sight of the breast or bottle are a conditioned response to what has become a conditioned stimulus.

There is nothing particularly special about the sound of a bell or the sight of a nipple that makes it possible for each to become a conditioned stimulus. Any number of sensory or motor impressions could acquire the same response-eliciting power. All that needs to happen is for the initially neutral stimulus (i.e., one incapable of eliciting the response of interest) to be paired with the unconditioned stimulus in an appropriate manner for it to acquire response-eliciting powers. In other words, what makes a conditioned stimulus a conditioned stimulus is not some property inherent in that stimulus, but rather its association with a stimulus already possessing response-eliciting power.

Watson's Contribution

Pavlov's work might have remained of little interest to American psychologists were it not for the work of Watson (1913, 1914, 1930), who is generally credited with being the founder of modern behaviorism (Horowitz, 1987, 1992; Reese, 1986). Watson used Pavlov's conditioning work as the foundation for a behavioral or natural science of psychology.

Prior to Watson, most psychological work was introspective in nature. Some sort of stimulus would be presented to a subject, and the subject would then be asked to introspect, or "look within," to describe the experience or sensation. The verbal report was then used by the introspective psychologists to form a descriptive picture of the workings of the mind. Watson (1913) thought this was all nonsense!

> The time has come when psychology must discard all reference to consciousness; when it need no longer delude itself into thinking that it is making mental states the object of observation. . . . There is no longer any guarantee that we all mean the same thing when we use terms now current in psychology. Take the case of sensation. A sensation is defined in terms of its attributes. One psychologist will state with readiness that the attributes of a visual sensation are quality, extension, duration, and intensity. Another will add clearness. Still another that of order. I doubt if any one psychologist can draw up a set of statements describing what he means by sensation which will be agreed to by three other psychologists of differing training. (pp. 163–164)

For Watson this inability to agree on the basic subject matter of psychology was a reflection of the then-accepted methodology—introspective reports. Furthermore, this lack of agreement prevented psychology from being accepted as a natural science. To remedy the situation, Watson proposed that observed behavior replace introspective reports as the basic subject matter of psychology. Watson (1913) put the matter rather directly:

> The psychology which I should attempt to build up would take as a starting point, first, the observable fact that organisms, man and animal alike, do adjust themselves to their environment by means of heredity and habit equipments. These adjustments may be very adequate or they may be so inadequate that the organism barely maintains its existence; secondly, that certain stimuli lead the organism to make the responses. In a system of psychology completely worked out, given the response the stimuli can be predicted; given the stimuli the response can be predicted. Such a set of statements is crass and raw in the extreme, as all such generalizations must be. Yet they are hardly more raw and less realizable than the ones which appear in the psychology texts of the day. (p. 167)

The S-R (stimulus-response) psychology that Watson established and championed is mechanistic in the purest sense. It is objective and observable. It is studied through the use of controlled experiments. It defines behavior as the functional unit of the natural science of psychology and suggests that all complex behaviors are ultimately reducible to these basic functional behavioral units. It argues that the development of these complex behavior patterns occurs through the simple associative processes that define both classical and operant conditioning. It views the organism as passive or at rest in the same sense that Newtonian physics views a body at rest until acted upon by some external force. It claims that these associative processes govern the learning of all species, including humans. And it states that the process of development is essentially governed by the rules of learning. For Watson, development is learning.

Watson's own research focused on the classical conditioning of emotional responses. His most famous subject was "little Albert," an 11-month-old child whom Watson used to demonstrate the classical conditioning of emotional responses. Like most children his age, Albert showed a great curiosity toward most things. One of these was a white mouse that, when presented to Albert, he would reach for eagerly. Once this preference for the mouse had been well documented, Watson successfully established a fear response to the initially positive stimulus by striking a steel bar hanging just behind Albert with a hammer. Watson observed that the infant "jumped violently and fell forward, burying his face in the mattress" (1930, p. 160).[1] Over a period of several weeks, Watson continued the pairing until, again in Watson's words, "The instant the rat was shown the baby began to cry. Almost instantly he turned sharply to the left, fell over, raised himself on all fours and began to crawl away so rapidly that he was caught with difficulty before he reached the edge of the mattress" (1930, p. 161). Watson had established a conditioned emotional response to what was previously a non-noxious stimulus—the now estranged mouse.

The experiment included a second element that was crucial to Watson's methodology. He attempted to generalize the fear response to other neutral but similar objects. For example, he noted that a rabbit now also elicited the fear reaction, as did a dog, a fur coat, and a ball of wool. In other words, the classically conditioned emotional response generalized to other, similar objects, objects that had never been paired with the unconditioned stimulus. *Generalization* and its counterpoint, *discrimination,* of both stimuli and responses play a key role in both classical and operant conditioning because they help explain particular patterns of response acquisition.

Interestingly enough, another important element of conditioning experiments, *extinction,* never occurred in the little Albert study. Extinction procedures reduce or eliminate the strength of the initial association by repeatedly presenting the now-conditioned stimulus without its periodic pairing with the unconditioned stimulus. The fact that extinction can be demonstrated indicates that associations, once formed, are not permanent but need to be maintained to be effective. As the story goes about Albert's fear response not being extinguished, Albert's mother, who was an employee in the hospital where Watson was conducting his experiment, apparently was initially unaware of the specifics of Watson's work; once she found out, she swiftly removed Albert from the study.

---

[1] Obviously we would view such an experimental procedure today as not only unethical but probably abusive as well. My discussion of the experiment should in no way be construed as condoning the procedure. It is only meant to illustrate Watson's typical procedure. It may be of some comfort that later studies of Watson's original data (Harris, 1979) suggest that he may have overstated the effectiveness of his conditioning procedures.

Watson was as much a promoter of S-R psychology as he was a student of it. His most famous claim was that, given 100 healthy babies, he could, through the use of conditioning techniques, make them into "doctor, lawyer, artist, merchant-chief and yes, even beggar-man and thief, regardless of his talents, penchants, tendencies, abilities, vocations, and race of his ancestors" (1930, p. 104). Here, too, he admits going beyond the facts but claims that others holding different views do the same. Through this statement and other, similar ones, Watson was taking an extreme environmental position, arguing for the primacy of efficient causes.

Watson did not deny the role of heredity, however. He saw heredity as the definer of species-specific physical structures. He simply argued that, within the broad range of behaviors that define a species, the judicious use of conditioning techniques could produce his 100 workers and more. Fortunately, given his cavalier treatment of Albert, no one took him up on his offer. In fact, his tenure as an academic psychologist was rather short-lived. Apparently, his brashness extended beyond his words, for he was dismissed from his post at Johns Hopkins for divorcing and then remarrying, behavior unbecoming an academic in those days. Watson spent the rest of his working life as a successful advertising executive, using his knowledge of learning to get people in the 1930s and 1940s to buy all sorts of unnecessary but appropriately associated items.

Although Watson's tenure as an academic psychologist was comparatively brief, his impact has been significant. He redefined the subject matter of psychology from introspection to behavior, and he established the conditioning paradigm as the primary strategy for studying behavior and behavioral change. In doing so, he established a legitimate claim for a mechanistically defined psychology to be considered a member of the natural sciences.

Watson was also one of the first psychologists to offer practical child-rearing advice based on a specific theoretical bias. In Watson's view this bias favored a very Spartan approach to child rearing, one that cautioned parents against establishing strong emotional bonds. Watson's vision seemed to favor creating strong, unemotional children who could successfully function in what Watson saw as a cold, cruel world.

Watson's recommendations went far beyond what his research could legitimately support. To say that conditioning experiences have a strong influence on children does not necessarily translate into an argument that one ought not to establish strong emotional associations. We could as easily argue that strong emotional ties would better serve children as they enter such a world. Stevenson (1983) offers an interesting explanation as to why Watson's views on psychology as a natural science and why his child-rearing techniques were so influential in the 1930s and 1940s.

Watson's efforts to better humanity through scientific methods had an irresistible appeal for Americans, both lay people and professionals. His extreme environmentalism offered a hopeful, optimistic, egalitarian view of human behavior. By denying biologically based differences in intelligence and other abilities, and by describing ways in which consistent, objective and attentive parents could rear bright and independent children, Watson projected an image of scientific psychology that was of immediate applicability. Child rearing became simply a matter of habit training. (p. 217)

Modern Learning Theory

Although S-R learning theory didn't die with Watson's dismissal from academia, it did begin to branch in two distinct directions (Reese, 1986). With the first direction the emphasis was on the mechanistic methodology of learning theory. This line can be traced through the work of the experimental psychologists Clack Hull (1943) and Kenneth Spence (1956) to the work of experimental child psychologists such as Charles Spiker (1966) and, more recently, to the work of developmental psychologists such as Tracy Kendler (1986, 1995).

For these and other researchers, the focus gradually shifted from the research findings of classical conditioning studies to the actual methods through which these findings were obtained. These methods were no longer seen as solely associated with conditioning studies, but rather, more generally, as the methodology through which a mechanistically oriented approach to behavioral change could be pursued. For want of a better term, this direction evolved into a methodological learning theory.

With the second direction the focus remained on the findings of research studies, but in this case the studies involved operant rather than classical conditioning. This second branch, referred to as *radical behaviorism,* is most closely associated with the work of B. F. Skinner (1938, 1953, 1971, 1974) and, more recently, Donald Baer and Sidney Bijou (Baer, 1970, 1973, 1976; Bijou, 1989; Bijou & Baer, 1978). Radical behaviorism focuses exclusively on operant learning techniques.

Proponents of both methodological learning theory and radical behaviorism are interested in investigating the variables that influence the formation of associations (i.e., of learning). In both cases, the belief, consistent with a mechanistic model, is that associations (classical or operant) are the basic elements that explain the establishment and maintenance of behaviors. Behaviors are best appreciated as complex sets of simple associations, in the same sense that a house can be thought of as the complex arrangement of bricks and mortar and other basic elements (Gagne, 1968). Researchers in each case have tended to study the development of associations within highly controlled settings using "simple" organisms such as laboratory mice, pigeons, and young children (Horowitz, 1987). Here, the word *simple* is not meant in a pejorative sense, but rather in the sense that behavioral researchers view these creatures as bringing less experiential baggage to the laboratory setting. These simple organisms therefore serve as a reasonable approximation to a naive organism—that is, one who enters the learning setting without any prior learning experiences that might serve to confound the results (Cantor, 1986).

Methodological Learning Theory

A review of the rich research history of methodological learning theory is beyond the scope of this text. But one issue is worth discussing, because this issue illustrates why what was once a theoretical learning theory is now a methodological learning theory (Stevenson, 1983). The issue concerns the attempts to explain how it is possible for different individuals to give different responses to exactly the same stimulus conditions—

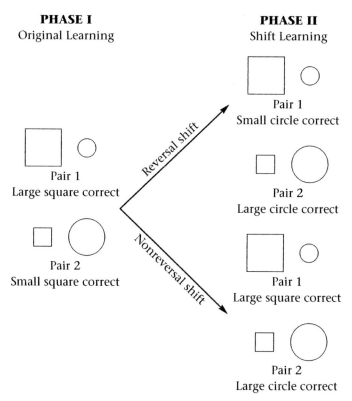

FIGURE 5.1
The Reversal-Nonreversal Shift Procedure

a finding that, according to a strict S-R theory relying strictly on efficient causal mechanisms, would be impossible.

The issue is often illustrated in terms of children's ability to learn to correctly discriminate between different objects, a skill that, for the methodological learning theorists, serves as an operational definition of the ability to abstract. Let us first examine the task, then the results, and finally the interpretation and its significance for our purposes.

The task is known as a *reversal-nonreversal shift procedure.* There are a number of variations of the task, but the basic procedure is illustrated in Figure 5.1.

A child is told that she will be presented with two pairs of objects, with each pair presented separately. The task is to learn which member of each pair the experimenter has already determined is the "correct" one. The pairs are designed to differ on two dimensions. For example, if the dimensions are size and shape, pair 1 might consist of a large square and a small circle, and pair 2 of a large circle and a small square. The decision as to the correct object in each pair is arbitrary and controlled across subjects. For one quarter of the sample, the large object in each pair is always correct, for one quarter it is the small object, for one quarter it is the circle, and for one quarter it is the square. The left-right relationship of the objects is controlled so that the child won't conclude that the reason an object is correct is that it's always on the left or on the right.

Each time a pair is presented, the child is asked to pick the correct one and is then reinforced or receives verbal confirmation for the correct response. If the incorrect choice is made, no reinforcement is given or the child is told that she picked the incorrect object. The task is not a particularly difficult one for children age 4 and above, and they soon reach a level of 100% reinforcement—that is, they successfully identify the correct member of each pair.

But then things change. Specifically, for half the children, the correct choice is reversed. The children are not informed of the change, but rather discover it on the next presentation when the response that had consistently been positively reinforced now receives no positive reinforcement. For instance, if they had learned that the large one was always correct, now it is the small one; if they had learned that the circle was always correct, now it is the square; and so on. This change is known as a reversal shift. Meanwhile, the other half of the group receives a nonreversal shift. Thus, if circle had been correct, now it is either small or large; if large had been correct, now it is either circle or square; and so on. The experiment continues until the child learns to consistently pick the new correct object. The question of interest is how long (defined as the number of trials needed to reach proficiency) it takes the child to learn the new contingency.

When we look at the results of such experiments, an interesting pattern emerges. Laboratory animals (at least the ones capable of performing the task) and preschool-age children find it easier to make a nonreversal shift; school-age and older children find it easier to make a reversal shift. That is, it takes more trials for the preschoolers to switch from small to large or from circle to square than it does for them to switch from circle to small or from square to large. By contrast, older children and adults have an easier time switching from large to small or from circle to square than they do from large to circle or from square to small. Why? In particular, why should the older children do better on the reversal task when they had been consistently reinforced for initially making exactly the opposite choice? Why shouldn't they also have an easier time with the nonreversal shift, given that the new choice already has some positive value by being paired with the initially correct answer on half of the trials?

The findings from reversal-nonreversal shift studies and from prior earlier studies dealing with similar issues (Kuenne, 1946) posed a significant problem for S-R learning theories. These theories, as they developed in the 1930s and 1940s as an extension of Watson's original arguments, offered explanations for behavior in terms of external stimulus conditions. The models seemed to work well at the time, but typically the research subjects were laboratory animals, and the tasks simple in nature. As humans were increasingly used as research subjects and as the tasks became increasingly more complex, explaining behavior simply in terms of stimulus and response associations became problematic.

Straight S-R learning theory offers a plausible explanation for the success of the preschoolers and the lab animals. Think of it this way: Four stimulus qualities were present on each trial—large, small, circle, and square. Assuming that large was designated as the correct cue and that the presentations of the stimuli were fully counter-balanced, then by the time the child had reached criterion on the initial discrimina-tion, "large" had been reinforced 100% of the time, "circle" and "square" each 50% of the time, and "small" never. The strength of the association between response and reinforcement was therefore greatest for large, smallest for small, and in between for circle and square. What, then, happens when the correct choice is changed?

Once the child realized that the initially correct choice was no longer correct, S-R theory predicted that she would make the response with the next highest association value. If her shift was from large to circle and she picked circle, then she was all set. If she picked square, it would not be reinforced, of course, and she would then try her next highest association, which was circle and which, once selected, would be rein-forced. It should now be clear why the reversal shift is the most difficult to make. Hav-ing initially been reinforced for choosing large, the weakest association, and therefore the least likely response, would be to small.

In explaining the behavior of preschoolers, the theory did fine. Consistent with mechanism's reactive view of the individual, the preschooler's behavior could be ade-quately predicted and therefore adequately explained by referring only to external, efficient, antecedent events. But what about the older kids? They were the ones who found it easier to do the thing that the theory predicted would be the last thing they should have done.

Accounting for the behavior of the older children required a fundamental change in S-R learning theories. The theory went from an S-R theory to an S-O-R theory. The "O" in this case stands for *organism* and reflects an awareness of the significance of internal factors as regulators of behavior. These internal factors were conceptualized as structures and are consistent with mechanism's use of material causes of behavior. The internal structures serve to mediate between the external stimulus and the external response. In other words, instead of an external stimulus eliciting an external response, it now elicited an internal response, which, in turn, elicited an internal stim-ulus. It was this internal stimulus that finally elicited the external response.

These mediating mechanisms are themselves also said to be acquired and then internalized through a process of learning. In the case of the reversal shifts, the media-tor was the ability to dimensionalize stimuli—that is, to recognize that large and small can be viewed not merely as distinct stimuli but as points along a continuum of size as well. The same statement is equally true of the dimension of shape. Thus, more often than not, the mediator was seen as verbal in nature.

Given the presence of these mediators, the theory was now able to explain why the older children did so much better on the reversal shifts. The explanation concerns how the initial stimuli were perceived. For the young children, the objects were viewed in terms of their absolute stimulus values (large, small, circle, square) and the appro-priate reinforcement value associated with each. But for the older children, the stimuli were perceived in a relational sense. It is as if they were saying to themselves that shape is the correct dimension and circle is the correct value. Put another way, for the older children shape as the relevant dimension was reinforced 100% of the time and size only 50% of the time. Under these circumstances, once the reinforcement values were reversed, the associative strengths were such that they would stay with shape but switch to the other value—in this example, the square. For the older children to make a nonreversal shift, they would need to extinguish their association to both the correct value and the correct dimension before they could begin to develop an association to the new value of the new dimension.

This acknowledgment of internal mediators opened a Pandora's box for S-R learning theorists. As the age of the subjects continued to increase, the tasks became more complex, and the experimental designs and analyses became more rigorous and precise, S-R learning theorists began to rely more and more on various sorts of internal or cognitive mediators to help explain why there was no clear and obvious relationship between the stimuli presented to children and their responses. And as explanations for behavior became as material as they were efficient in nature, the value of S-R learning theory declined. S-R learning theory perhaps reached its zenith in the late 1960s and early 1970s, but since then, the "cognitive revolution" has displaced it. The *cognitive revolution* refers to (1) a switch by some developmentalists to organismically based theories such as Piaget's and (2) a switch by others to information processing theories within the mechanistic tradition.

It is important to recognize, however, that even though S-R learning theory no longer fills a central theoretical role in the study of behavioral change, it continues to play an important role—and perhaps the key role—in the methodological study of behavioral change. The dominant research strategy within mechanism continues to be laboratory-based, highly controlled experiments, and the dominant analysis techniques continue to be strategies that partition variance into distinct and independent categories. These are methods that evolved out of the work of the early S-R learning theorists. Again, quoting Stevenson (1983):

> It is important to realize that it is the theories that have been susceptible to attack, not the data about children's learning. An important aspect of the behaviorists' movement was its emphasis on explicitness in experimental design and interpretation of data. This emphasis proved to be instrumental in its own demise. . . . Paradoxically, it appears that the enduring contributions of the laboratory based, experimentally oriented stimulus-response psychologists are methodological, rather than theoretical. Sophisticated in experimental design, statistical analysis, and philosophy of science, these psychologists produced methods so powerful and capable of producing clear results that their theories crumbled as much in the face of the evidence they produced themselves as from criticisms of opposing theories. (p. 231)

Radical Behaviorism

Radical behaviorism also involves both a method and a theory, both of which are alive and well. However, because of the nature of their methodology, radical behaviorists tend to occupy a "parallel universe" within the mechanistic tradition in psychology (Horowitz, 1987). We are unlikely to find studies in this tradition published in such mainstream developmental journals as *Child Development* or *Developmental Psychology* or the *Journal of Experimental Child Psychology*. These three journals tend to publish papers using research strategies more consistent with methodological learning theory —that is, controlled group experiments whose results are analyzed by the use of inferential statistical techniques. Reports on research studies using radical methodologies can be found in sources such as the *Journal of the Experimental Analysis of Behavior* and the *Journal of Applied Behavioral Analysis.*

BASIC CHARACTERISTICS AND METHODOLOGIES   Radical behaviorism is, of course, most closely associated with the work of B. F. Skinner (1904–1990) on operant conditioning. It is radical in two senses. First, Skinner believed that it is possible to explain all behavior by reference to external events—in particular, to the consequences that occur as a result of one's behavior. As such, radical behaviorism is a theory that limits itself to explanations based only on efficient causes.

It is not true (although often claimed) that Skinner denied the existence of such internal states as feelings, emotions, and thought (Todd & Morris, 1992). But he did argue that these internal states are not the causes of our behavior but one of its results. As such, attempting to study such internal phenomena will add nothing to our understanding of behavior and behavioral change, but rather will only create what he referred to as "explanatory fictions." As he explained in an interview (Evans, 1968):

> As I see it, psychology is concerned with establishing relations between the behavior of an organism and the forces acting upon it. Now, the organism must be there, I don't really believe in the empty organism. That wasn't my phrase. But the relationship that psychology discovers sets the problem which the physiologist must solve by filling in the gaps. The variables we study are separated in time and space, and something happens in between. . . . If I can't give a clean cut statement of a relationship between behavior and antecedent variables, it is no help to me to speculate about something inside the organism which will fill the gap. . . . I don't think inferred concepts adequately make up for things lacking in a behavioral analysis. We need a complete account at the external level. After all, the organism cannot initiate anything unless you assume it is capable of whimsical changes. As a determinist, I must assume that the organism is simply mediating the relationship between the forces acting upon it and its own output, and these are the kinds of relationships I'm anxious to formulate. (pp. 21–22, 23)

The second radical aspect of radical behaviorism concerns its methodology. Unlike the methodological learning theorists, radical behaviorists do not average data across subjects to obtain group averages; they do not give different treatments to different group as a strategy of experimental control; and therefore they do not use inferential statistics to determine the probability that the group data is representative of the population from which it is drawn. Instead, they use a research strategy know as a *single-subject design* (Perone, 1994; Sidman, 1960).

In single-subject designs experimental control is established by changing the experimental conditions for each subject and then observing the corresponding changes in the subject's behavior. For example, consider a study in which a child is asked to learn a simple discrimination task. The task involves learning to push a red button when the red light goes on and a green button when the green light goes on. Each correct response is followed by a positive reinforcement. In relatively short order, the child will learn the task and will reach a 100% success rate.

How is it possible to demonstrate that the reason for the child's successful behavior is that he has learned the contingent relationship between the lights, his responses, and the reinforcements? In a group design different groups would be exposed to different experimental conditions. Several children would be in the experimental group, and each would have the same learning experience as our single subject. Several more children would serve as the control group, and they would not get any reinforcement for pushing the red or the green button. A comparison of the average learning scores for the two groups (the average number of times each group pressed the red button when the red light went on and the green button when the green light went on) would permit a conclusion as to the probability that the reason, presumably, the experimental group did better than the control group was that members were reinforced for each correct response while the control group was not.

In a single-subject design each subject serves as his own control group. Once the child successfully learned the task, the experimenter would attempt to extinguish the response by stopping the reinforcement. If the child learned the task because he was reinforced for his correct responses, then stopping the reinforcement should extinguish the response. This reversal procedure is the way that experimental control is maintained in single-subject designs. In fact, to be doubly sure that the treatment condition (i.e., the reinforcement) was the reason for the child's behavior, the experimenter would then attempt to reestablish the association by again reinforcing the correct responses once the extinction process was completed. This sequence of reinforce-extinguish-reinforce, known as an *A-B-A design,* is the standard research methodology of the radical behaviorists. (There are more complicated variations of the basic design, but they all follow the same logic.)

To understand why the radical behaviorists favor individual over group designs, we must recognize that their theoretical goal is somewhat different from that of the early learning theorists. Skinner saw the goal of behavioral science as the study of the prediction and control of individual behavior. By contrast, for the early learning theorists, the goal was the discovery of the general laws of learning. The two goals are not contradictory, but they do imply a different research strategy. The discovery of general laws implies the formulation of assumptions about populations based on behavioral samples drawn from that population. Controlling and predicting individual behavior implies the documentation of the effectiveness of specific response contingencies for any one individual. Making generalizations about the population as a whole is at best a secondary consideration.

In fact, Skinner argued that the use of large samples and group averages was a "cop-out" because one could obtain statistical significance even with a weak effect if the sample was large enough. Additionally, a focus on group averages could serve to blur the preciseness of any one individual's learning curve. It is not that radical behaviorists study only one individual. Of course they include many subjects for any one experiment. But they don't average the findings, and they don't talk about the average number of reinforcers necessary to achieve learning. Rather, each individual serves as a parallel experiment, with the results from each analyzed separately rather than as part of some group.

It is interesting to note that, even though the use of single-subject designs has kept most radical behavioral research out of the methodological mainstream, it has been warmly welcomed in some parts of the clinical intervention community. A great deal of applied single-subject research is focused on clinical and developmentally disabled populations. In these cases, the focus is on meeting the needs of a particular individual rather than documenting some general law. In effect, in these settings, the single-subject research design becomes the case study.

THE OPERANT CONDITIONING PARADIGM Because Skinner believed that prediction and control were largely a function of the consequences of our actions, his research focused on how different response contingencies influence behavioral performance. Perhaps the best way to get a handle on the scope and significance of Skinner's work is first to review his major findings and positions on method and theory and then to consider more recent extensions of his work.

Operant conditioning involves the establishment of an association between a response and its consequences. Unlike in classical conditioning, in which a stimulus (conditioned or unconditioned) *elicits* a response (conditioned or unconditioned), in operant conditioning the response is said to be *emitted*. The distinction is important because it highlights the difference in the nature of the two associations. In classical conditioning the association is between the stimulus and the response; in operant conditioning the association is between the response and its consequences.

Skinner studied operant conditioning by using a "Skinner box," a term he neither coined nor liked (Richelle, 1993). It refers to a cagelike apparatus consisting solely of a lever or some other device that can be used to make a response, some sort of apparatus for delivering a reinforcement into a receptacle in the box, and possibly a light or other signaling device for informing the organism when it was appropriate to make a response (i.e., when the making of an appropriate response would lead to reinforcement). The signaling device should not be confused with the conditioned or unconditioned stimulus in classical conditioning. In classical conditioning, the stimulus elicits the response; the organism has little choice in the matter. In operant conditioning the signal is said to inform the organism when a response will produce a particular consequence. The decision to make the response is not under the control of the stimulus but rather is said to remain under the control of the past reinforcement history of the organism.

In a typical experiment a pigeon or laboratory rat (Skinner never used human subjects in his work although certainly others have in theirs) would be placed in the Skinner box. The animal might have been previously deprived of food because such deprivation increases the likelihood of the animal doing something in the box. Because the only thing to do in the box is press the lever in the case of the rat or peck at a disk in the case of the pigeon, sooner or later the animal does so and is reinforced, usually by a pellet of food in the receptacle. After some interval the animal is likely to repeat the response, and again a food pellet appears. At this point there is very little in the animal's behavior to suggest that an association has formed. The animal doesn't look in the receptacle following the response and may not even notice the food pellet in the receptacle until some time after the response is made. Over time, however, there is both an increase in the rate of responding and, following a response, an almost immediate look into the receptacle. The animal has formed an operant association between its behavior and the consequences of that behavior.

In this example the response required to receive a reinforcement is a simple one. In many cases, however, especially that of humans, the desired response is more complex. In fact, it may be so complex that the likelihood of it being emitted is close to zero. In these cases the experimenter would attempt to *shape* the response through a process of *successive approximations*. Initially any response even vaguely resembling the desired one would be reinforced. Then, gradually, the reinforcements would become more selective. Closer and closer approximations to the desired response would be required for reinforcement to result. Eventually only the desired response receives reinforcement.

Behaviors acquired through operant conditioning can show both *stimulus generalization* and *response generalization*. When a response shows stimulus generalization, it is emitted in response to stimuli similar to the original. When it demonstrates response generalization, behaviors similar to the original are made in the "expectation" that they, too, might lead to reinforcement.

The experimental procedures can be more complex than this. For instance, there might be more than one bar to press or disk to peck, or one or more stimulus signal(s) to indicate the appropriate time to make a response. Or associations might be "chained" so that the consequences of one response also serve as the signal to make a second, different response, and the consequences of this second response serve as the signal for a third response, and so on. Skinner believed that complex behaviors would ultimately be explained as combinations and chains of these simple responses.

Because the focus of this operant conditioning research is on the association of a response with its consequences, most of Skinner's research concerned how changes in response consequences result in a change in the response itself—in particular, a change in the frequency of responding. This research focused on two issues: (1) the nature of the consequence and (2) its pattern of presentation, typically referred to as its *schedule of reinforcement*.

TYPES OF RESPONSE CONSEQUENCES   Skinner found four types of consequences to a response: positive and negative reinforcers, punishment, and extinction. *Positive reinforcement* is the presentation of a desired consequence following a response. Because the consequence is desired, positive reinforcement leads to an increase in the frequency of the behavior being emitted and therefore being reinforced. *Negative reinforcement* also leads to an increase in desired behavior, but it does so because the response leads to the removal of a noxious or aversive stimulus rather than the presentation of a desired consequence. The rewards parents might give a child for earning high grades would be an example of a positive reinforcement if it resulted in continued grade improvement. Getting parents to stop "harassing" you for poor grades by getting better grades would be a form of negative reinforcement if it resulted in continued grade improvement.

It is important to keep in mind that negative in this sense refers to the nature not of the consequence but of the situation. In both cases there is an increase in grades. In the first case it occurs because of the possibility of gaining a positive consequence (a reward for the good grades); in the second case it occurs because of the possibility of ending a negative situation (getting your parents off your back).

It is also important not to assume that a consequence is positive or negative simply on the basis of its nature. As Nye (1996) notes, a parent's display of affection toward an adolescent may be seen by the parent as a positive reinforcement but by the adolescent as a noxious stimulus, especially when it occurs in front of friends. In other words, one can say that a consequence is a reinforcer (positive or negative) only if it leads to an increase in the frequency of the associated behavior. If it fails to do so, it is not a reinforcer no matter how appealing or desirable it might seem to others. In this regard it is also important to note that reinforcers can either be primary or secondary. *Primary reinforcers* are consequences such as food, water, and the elimination of pain. *Secondary reinforcers* acquire their reinforcing value by being associated with primary reinforcers. Skinner believed that secondary reinforcers serve as the main mechanism through which most human behavior is acquired and maintained.

The third type of response consequence is *punishment.* Whereas reinforcement leads to an increase in behavior, punishment leads to a decrease in behavior. It does so because the consequence resulting from the behavior is undesirable. Punishment can be of two forms: (1) The presentation of a noxious consequence results from a response; or (2) the removal of a positive situation results from a response. Spanking would be an example of the first form of punishment, because it involves the presentation of a noxious consequence. Losing your allowance would be an example of the second, because it involves the removal of something desired. As is true of reinforcement, a punishment is a punishment only if it leads to a decrease in behavior. If, for some unfathomable reason, a teen liked to lose his allowance, then what would be a punishment for most of us would be a reinforcement for this strange lad. Punishments can also be primary or secondary in nature.

The fourth response consequence is actually no consequence. When a response no longer produces a reinforcement, the association will gradually end. This is known as *extinction.* The length of time it takes for a response to be extinguished, or the number of unreinforced responses an organism will continue to make, is a measure of the strength of the association between the response and its consequences.

Extinction should not be confused with punishment. Although both might seem to accomplish the same purpose—response elimination—they are nevertheless quite different. Whereas extinction ends the association, punishment only inhibits the response. The association between response and consequence is still present when a response is punished; only its expression is halted. Remove the punishment and the response reappears. This is why Skinner never viewed punishment as a very effective way to control behavior and recommended against its use in schools, families, and other social settings (Skinner, 1971). He favored the positive reinforcement of a competing response as a way to deal with inappropriate behavior. In other words, rather than punishing a child for hitting a sibling, the parent would be better advised to positively reinforce appropriate behavior toward the sibling.

PATTERNS OF RESPONSE CONSEQUENCES   The previous discussion focused on the types of responses that Skinner studied. Clearly different types of consequences lead to different types of responses. Equally important to the issue of type of consequence is the pattern of its presentation—that is, when and how often a consequence is presented following a response. Skinner found that ideal response contingencies—ones that produced the highest response frequency—differed in terms of whether the association is being established or maintained.

When an association between response and consequence is first being formed, response consequences should be immediate and continuous. A *continuous reinforcement schedule* ensures that the association is formed between the desired response and the consequence.

Once an association has been established, a high response level can be maintained or even increased by switching from a continuous to a *partial reinforcement schedule.* Partial reinforcement schedules are of two types: (1) ratio schedules, which offer reinforcements based on a certain frequency of responses made, and (2) interval schedules, which offer reinforcements based on a certain time interval. Both ratio and interval schedules can be variable or fixed. A *fixed-interval schedule* means that the reinforcement occurs after the same interval of time has passed since the last reinforcement no matter how many responses have been made in the interim. A *fixed-ratio schedule* means that reinforcement occurs every 5th or 10th or, more generally, every "nth" response. A *variable-interval schedule* means that the time interval before the next reinforcement changes from reinforcement to reinforcement. A *variable-ratio schedule* means that the number of responses necessary for a response to occur changes from reinforcement to reinforcement. Variable-ratio and -interval schedules do have an average frequency or interval. That is, on average, reinforcement for a variable-interval schedule might be given every 1 minute or 5 minutes (or whatever) even though any one interval may be as short as 1 second or as long as 10 minutes. Similarly, on average, reinforcement for a variable-ratio schedule might be every 5 responses or 10 or 50 (or whatever) even though any one ratio might range from as few as 2 responses to as many as 100.

Each type of reinforcement schedule produces a distinct response pattern. Skinner found that variable-ratio schedules produce the highest rate of responding and the strongest associations, measured by the number of responses made to extinction. Fixed-interval schedules produce a "scalloped" response pattern; that is, response frequency increases as the time to the next reinforcement decreases.

THE IMPACT OF RADICAL BEHAVIORISM   Skinner's experimental work on reinforcement types and patterns took place early in his long career. This research was the focus of his two major early works, *The Behavior of Organisms* (1938) and *Schedules of Reinforcement* (Ferster & Skinner, 1957), as well as numerous papers. In the research for both books, animals were used exclusively as the laboratory subjects, and neither book made specific reference to issues of human development. From Skinner's mechanistic perspective this is as it should have been. If there are general laws of learning, then they would hold as true for humans as they do for rats and pigeons. Because the lives of laboratory animals clearly are more controllable than those of humans, they are the more appropriate means to the end of identifying the factors that allow for the prediction and control of behavior. Similarly, because radical behaviorists see no value in hypothetical constructs such as a concept of development, there is no reason to pursue such a topic. For Skinner, the study of behavior change is the study of development.

Beginning in the late 1940s, Skinner's attention began to shift from laboratory research with animals to a concern for the implications of his work for both human behavior and human culture. In a series of books and articles that continued almost to his death in 1990 (Skinner, 1948/1976, 1953, 1971, 1974, 1978, 1984, 1987, 1989), Skinner expressed concern that a failure to heed radical behaviorism's message that our behavior is a function of the external consequences of that behavior, and is not autonomous or self-directed, places humankind at risk. Skinner believed that unless we are willing and able to recognize the real causes of our behavior (at least as he saw them to be, efficient causes), we will never be in a position to do anything to significantly improve the human condition.

This shift in focus from basic animal research to social commentary can be marked by the publication of *Walden Two* (1948/1976), Skinner's utopian novel about a just and humane society based on behavioral principles. *Walden Two* was followed by *Science and Human Behavior* (1953), perhaps his clearest statement of the implications of his work. The central point that Skinner made in these and subsequent publications is that we should be as welcoming of a scientific approach to the study of human behavior as we are of a scientific approach to the study of medicine and technology. Once we do so, the same strides that have been made in the fields of medicine and technology will also be made in the field of human behavior.

Skinner's seemingly modest extension of his findings met with active and frequent criticisms. He was accused of wanting to introduce some type of "thought police" into society, of wanting to use punitive measures to regulate behavior, and of wanting to take away people's freedom and right to self-control (Delprato & Midgley, 1992; Todd & Morris, 1992). None of these charges was true. Skinner believed that positive rather than punitive consequences are the most effective way to influence behavior and that a recognition of the real factors (i.e., external contingencies) that regulate our individual behavior is the best way to ensure a degree of self-control over this behavior. To behave otherwise, he argued, is counterproductive on both the individual and societal levels. In this regard, it is worth noting Skinner's closing remarks in *Science and Human Behavior* (1953). The words remind us that radical behaviorism was not Skinner's invention but rather his discovery. As such, attacking the messenger, as his critics did, does nothing to deny the implications of the message—if the message is accurate.

> Even so, the conception of the individual which emerges from a scientific analysis is distasteful to most of those who have been strongly affected by democratic philosophies. . . . it has always been the unfortunate task of science to dispossess cherished beliefs regarding the place of man in the universe. It is easy to understand why men so frequently flatter themselves—why they characterize the world in ways which reinforce them by providing escape from the consequences of criticism or other forms of punishment. But although flattery temporarily strengthens behavior, it is questionable whether it has any ultimate survival value. If science does not confirm the assumptions of freedom, initiative, and responsibility in the behavior of the individual, the assumptions will not ultimately be effective either as motivating devices or as goals in the design of culture. We may not give them up easily, and we may, in fact, find it difficult to control ourselves or others until alternative principles have been developed.

But the change will probably be made. It does not follow that newer concepts will necessarily be less acceptable. We may console ourselves with the reflection that science is, after all, a cumulative progress in knowledge which is due to man alone, and that the highest human dignity may be to accept the facts of human behavior regardless of their momentary implications. (p. 449)

Richelle (1993), reflecting on Skinner's argument, makes the analogy between the resistance Skinner's notions have received and the resistance Joseph Lister received from the medical establishment of the 19th century when he urged physicians and surgeons to wash their hands as a way to control the spread of infection: "It just sounded too simple, and not worthy of serious physicians' attention. Happily enough, that simple message eventually got through and the practice was adopted" (p. 23).

EXTENSIONS OF RADICAL BEHAVIORISM   Although Skinner never used humans as research subjects, others working within the radical behaviorist tradition certainly have done so. The leap from pigeon to person is an easy one to make because radical behaviorism, consistent with its mechanistic perspective, presumes that the laws governing the formation of associations are universal. As such, questions relating to stimulus and response discrimination and generalization in one species, as well as those pertaining to schedules of reinforcement, are also relevant in the study of another species. Gewirtz (Gewirtz & Pelaez-Nogueras, 1992) notes that these common variables include changes in the environment, in terms of both discriminating stimuli and response consequences; the cumulative impact of one's reinforcement history; and the contextual variables that affect the relationship between stimuli and behavior. For example, in Gewirtz's research with infants, he reports that a number of variables have been identified as influencing infant behavior.

> Such varied stimuli as infant feed formula or sucrose water, auditory, olfactory, visual, tactile and kinesthetic stimuli, including stimuli with social characteristics such as mother picking up her child, vocalizing, smiling or touching her child, have been found to function as reinforcers for particular infant responses, including head turning, high-amplitude sucking, tracking, orienting, kicking, smiling, reaching, touching, vocalizing, protesting and crying. (p. 1412)

At the preschool level, radical behaviorists report that the use of *behavior modification* techniques have been found to increase young children's attention to educational tasks, productivity and assignment completion, and achievement test scores. At the same time, these techniques have been found to decrease rates of disruptive and aggressive behavior (Greenwood, Carta, Hart, Camps, et al., 1992). These particular preschool findings are part of a large-scale, ongoing research and intervention project known as the Juniper Gardens Children's Project. In addition to directly intervening with children, the project has been successful in changing children's behavior by changing the context in which they function—that is, by changing the discriminative stimuli to which they respond. Project staff, for example, were able to increase school children's active participation in class (defined as asking and answering questions, completing assignments on time, etc.) by changing the way in which the teacher engaged the children. Changing the teacher's behavior led to an increased rate of responding on the part of the children, which, in turn, led to a higher level of positive reinforcement.

In evaluating their efforts over the more than 25-year-life of the project, the Juniper Garden's staff report that

> this work has contributed substantially to the development of procedures for intervening in the lives of children in impoverished communities and the methodology for validating their effectiveness. The work now spanning the themes of consequences, antecedents, functional situational factors, and behavioral development illustrates the trend in applied behavioral analysis toward greater sophistication both in the use of more complex methods for studying interactive and developmental systems and in addressing issues of general concern in psychology (e.g., ecology and risk). (pp. 1471–1472)

Note that one of the most significant findings of this research is the observation that operant techniques can be used to address complex human issues. This finding stands in contrast to the frequent criticism that the utility of a radical behaviorist approach is limited to the study of simple organisms making simple responses. Examples of more recent work within the radical behaviorist tradition include research on improving academic performance (Enright & Axelrod, 1995; Greenwood, Finney, Terry, & Arreaga-Mayer, 1993), helping individuals with special needs (DeMario & Crowley, 1994; McClannahan & Krantz, 1993), and reducing workplace injuries (Carter, 1992).

A more general treatment of applied behavioral analysis is provided in a series of papers by Sidney Bijou and Donald Baer (Baer, 1970, 1973, 1976; Baer, Wolf, & Risley, 1987; Bijou, 1979, 1989; Bijou & Baer, 1978). They see development as a progressive change in the interactions between the behavior of individuals and the events in their environments. These complex interactions take place over the lifetime of the individual, simultaneously involving the interplay of many setting and response contingencies. At a practical level unraveling such a complex web would be very difficult. Nevertheless, this complexity is nothing more than the cumulative effect of chaining, shaping, and combining many individual response contingencies.

According to Bijou and Baer, as development proceeds, new responses are acquired, and new associations between existing responses and new consequences are made. From this perspective the meaning of objects in the stimulus environment is a function of one's previous reinforcement history with that or similar objects ("objects" in this sense refers to both social and nonsocial sources). Because the meaning of an object is inherent not in the object but in terms of one's experiences with that object, the specifics of one's development are seen as a highly individualized process, varying across individuals and across cultures. As Bijou (1989) explains this interactive process:

> For a crawling child, a chair is an object to avoid; for a child learning to stand upright, it is an object with which to pull oneself up; for a child with locomotor skills, it is an object to sit at a table; for an agile child, it is an object to stand on to reach the proverbial cookie jar. (p. 66)

In one of his papers, Baer (1970) offers an explanation of how this cumulative interaction history defines the developmental course of an individual. He refers to this concept as an "age-irrelevant" concept of development. Arguing from a radical behaviorist perspective, he says that chronological age, a common milestone within the organismic tradition, serves to hinder rather than enhance our understanding of behavioral change. In particular, he argues that developmental norms incorrectly give the impression of a normal and typical rate of development—that is, the ages at which one would expect children to demonstrate a particular skill or skill level. Baer argues that there is nothing normative about developmental norms. If anything, these norms simply indicate the behavioral outcomes of an "inefficient" natural environment.

Instead of these inefficient natural situations, Baer advocates more systematic and deliberate behavioral intervention strategies to accelerate the rate of behavioral change as compared to that associated with developmental norms. Baer believes two things are accomplished by such a strategy: (1) Children gain new skills at a more efficient rate, and (2) the demonstration that a child can perform a skill "sooner" than the norms would lead one to expect raises questions about the relevance of behavioral norms in particular and developmental theories based on those norms in general. For Bijou and Baer, as for all radical behaviorists, the only regulators of the course and rate of development are the patterns and types of response contingencies operational within a particular social setting. Change the contingencies, and you change development. To the radical behaviorists it is that simple.

Learning Theory in Perspective

Although there are important differences between what we now recognize as methodological learning theory and radical behaviorism, it is nevertheless important to remember their common heritage in the works of Pavlov and Watson. It is also important to remember their equal commitment to a mechanistic world view. There are significant differences between the two, particularly related to research strategies and explanatory constructs, but these differences are best appreciated as variations on a theme because the two approaches share a common set of assumptions about behavior and behavioral change.

It is also important to remember the unique place that learning theory's methodology occupies within the mechanistic world view. Few if any mechanists today are very interested in reversal-nonreversal shifts or other topics that debate the necessity of the "O" in S-O-R theory. The cognitive revolution in human development has, for now, answered this question for all but the radical behaviorists. The legacy of learning theory, however, is its methodology. Mechanists may well differ on theoretical points and on the relative importance of efficient and material causes. But they are able to have these debates because they all share a methodology that evolved from the early work of the learning theorists.

6

Bandura's Social Cognitive Theory

The work of Albert Bandura (b. 1925) is important for two reasons. First, and foremost, it represents a well-defined and well-supported view of child development within the mechanistic tradition. Bandura's methodology is consistently mechanistic, his focus is on understanding interindividual variability and his approach is reductionist. Second, the evolution of Bandura's theory (Bandura, 1977, 1986; Bandura & Walters, 1959, 1963) provides an excellent example of how, since the 1970s, the wider acceptance of information processing approaches within the mechanistic world view has made it possible to accommodate mentalistic concepts such as the concept of self and memory rehearsal strategies within descriptions and explanations of behavior and behavioral change. Even the name of the theory has changed. What began as "social learning theory" in 1963 had become "social cognitive theory" by 1986.[1]

All theory grows out of a desire to explain something that has yet to be explained or to explain something better than current accounts. Bandura's work is no exception. His initial efforts (Evans, 1989) were motivated by the desire (1) to provide a more rigorous and behavioral explanation for aggressive behavior than was available from psychodynamic theories such as Freud's and (2) to offer an explanation for the development of novel behavior—a type of behavior, Bandura argued, that was not easily explained by the more traditional Skinnerian radical behaviorism. Bandura's concern with socially relevant topics such as aggressive behavior is a hallmark of his work. Even though the theory has undergone revision over the years, scholarly interest in social issues has remained strong. In particular, the theory has generated a good deal of current work on topics ranging from health maintenance (Aas, Klepp, Laberg, & Edvad, 1995; Strecher, Seijts, Kok, & Latham, 1995; Zimmerman, Sprecher, Langer, & Holloway, 1995), to social gerontology (McDougall, 1995), to school restructuring (Zimmerman, Bandura, & Martinez-Pons, 1995), and employee relations (Solberg, Good, & Fischer, 1995; Waung, 1995).

---

[1] Bandura is not the only individual to have used the term *social learning* (or *cognitive*) *theory*. The work of Julian Rotter (1954, 1966, 1982) is also significant and should be read for a full treatment of the social learning approach. However, because Rotter's work was less focused on issues of development, I will restrict my discussion to Bandura's work.

Bandura's fundamental notion is that behavioral change is largely a social process, one that occurs in the context of our interactions with others. The results of such social experiences are reflected in virtually all behavioral domains, including gender-role development (Bussey & Bandura, 1992), parent-child and peer relationships (Patterson, 1986), and moral development (Bandura, 1988). This focus on the social context of behavioral change is shared by both organicists and contextualists. What distinguishes Bandura's work is his preference to pursue the study of behavioral change from a mechanistic perspective.

Although most of Bandura's research has been with children, he nevertheless believes that these social learning mechanisms have equal relevance across the entire life span. This life span focus is certainly consistent with mechanism because, within that world view, change is seen as a quantitative process. As such, the mechanisms of social learning that Bandura has identified through his work with children would hold, according to the theory, equal relevance for other age groups.

Bandura's notion of learning as primarily a social interactive process is as central to his theory today as it was originally. What has changed is his explanation of the mechanisms by which this social learning occurs. This change has been evolutionary rather than revolutionary. Successive versions of the theory have not rejected earlier notions so much as they have altered their mode of operation as new elements were added. In particular, these revisions have given an increasingly important role to internal cognitive processes as mediators of the relationship between social experiences and behavioral responses. A review of Bandura's major works will clarify this evolutionary process. It will also again document the fact that theories are best recognized and appreciated as dynamic rather than static entities.

Adolescent Aggression (1959)

Bandura's first important work, *Adolescent Aggression* (Bandura & Walters, 1959), was written in collaboration with Richard Walters. In their preface, they describe the work as an "account of an empirical study primarily designed to identify the child-training factors and family interrelationships that contribute to the development of anti-social behavior in adolescent boys" (p. vii).

Adolescent Aggression is important in the study of developmental theory because, at least in the United States, it serves as a significant marker in the shift from an organismically based psychoanalytic approach to the study of children and families to a more mechanistically based behavioral approach. This shift, which began in the 1940s and 1950s, marked the emergence of what those who favored such a shift viewed as a scientific approach to the study of development. Robert Sears, a significant figure in this transitional process (Sears, Maccoby, & Levin, 1957), noted that "the long centuries of pure, unverified speculation about the influence of a child's rearing on his personality seem to have ended at last. For this problem, as for so many others, the day of theory based empirical investigation has come" (p. iii).

The hallmark of this transition was the use of hypotheses and methods consistent with a mechanistic perspective—in particular, the conditioning paradigms of the learning theorists. The shift freed this scientific psychology from a reliance on mentalistic concepts that, mechanists argued, could not be directly linked to external, antecedent events. This shift also made it possible to bring the study of children and families into the mainstream of what traditionally had been a very animal-based approach to research and theory. Previously, because of their mechanistic orientation, American psychologists had been less likely to conduct research with children and families than their colleagues in such fields as education, child and family studies, home economics, and pediatrics.

Bandura and Walters' actual study consisted of a comparison between two sets of families—those having an adolescent with a history of aggressive antisocial behavior and those that did not. The methodology involved separate interviews with each father, mother, and son. The sons were also administered a projective test designed to assess their reactions to socially deviant behavior. Although these interview methods were not particularly behavioral (actually, they were ones that most psychoanalytically oriented theorists would still be comfortable with), the data analyses did make use of statistical procedures. In particular, the results were rated using a variety of numeric scales, averaged for each rating for each of the two groups and then tested for evidence of statistically significant differences between the two groups. Finally, a series of correlational analyses were done to document the interaction patterns among the father, mother, and son within each family.

The analyses focused on the emotional quality of the mother-son and father-son relationships for each of the two groups. In particular, it compared (1) the degree to which parents were seen as supportive of their son's dependency overtures to each parent, (2) differences in the two groups of boys' acceptance or rejection by peers and teachers, (3) the parents' degree of tolerance for aggressive behavior expressed toward themselves and others, (4) the parents' attitudes toward and tolerance of sexually related behaviors such as modesty, masturbation, and sex play, (5) the parents' efforts to restrict their sons' behavior, and (6) the actual parenting techniques that the fathers and mothers used to socialize their sons.

Bandura and Walters found that the aggressive boys were more antagonistic toward authority figures and less involved with peers. They tended to avoid situations that required them to be emotionally dependent on others. They expressed fewer feelings of guilt over either their aggressiveness or their expressions of sexuality, which were also more overt than in the control adolescent group.

In their relationships with parents, the aggressive adolescents expressed feelings of rejection from both parents. They did manage to maintain good relations with their mothers, but they were particularly critical of their fathers. Although the aggressive adolescents might have thought that their behavior would give them the autonomy and respect they were seeking from their fathers and other authority figures, they actually accomplished the opposite. Their behavior only resulted in more alienation and more direct control from those who they already distrusted and resented. Bandura and Walters concluded that, in many respects, the aggressive adolescents were like small children whose impulses are held in check by external rather than internal restraints.

Bandura and Walters explained their findings by arguing that the parents of the nonaggressive adolescents were much more effective in fostering an internalized sense of social control. They did this by establishing and maintaining a close, emotionally supportive relationship with their son and by using discipline techniques that focused on the quality of the parent-child relationship rather than ridicule, physical punishment, and loss of privileges. They were more likely to place high expectations on their sons and were more consistent in their demands and expectations. By contrast, the parents of the aggressive adolescents actually placed fewer demands on their sons, but perhaps because of the poor quality of the parent-adolescent relationship, even these were rejected.

Bandura and Walters' theoretical interpretation of their findings is clearly rooted in classical and instrumental learning theories. The socialization process is seen as involving the development of acceptable habitual-response patterns. These socially acceptable habits arise as a result of the association of drive-related motives and reinforcement. For the most part, these drives or motives are seen as secondary in nature. They acquire their motivating properties by being paired with primary drives like hunger or pain reduction, drives that reflect the physiological functioning of the individual. The desire to be nurtured by a parent, a secondary drive in this scheme, acquires its motivating power by pairing nurturance (e.g., being held and cuddled) with primary drive reduction (e.g., infant nursing). Gradually the child comes to do those things that meet the child's secondary needs. Those things are the behaviors that the parents are willing to reinforce. In other words, the child becomes socialized.

Bandura and Walters argued that the effectiveness of these secondary rewards are a direct function of the reinforcing value of the parent. Not surprisingly, therefore, the fathers of the aggressive adolescents were relatively ineffective in socializing their sons; that is, they were relatively ineffective in establishing their value as secondary reinforcers. Also not surprisingly, their sons were aggressive. The fathers modeled aggressive behavior, and their inconsistent parenting techniques, in effect, served as a partial reinforcement schedule for their sons' aggressive behavior—a reinforcement schedule highly resistant to extinction.

The analysis of adolescent aggression in terms of instrumental and classical conditioning theory clearly identified Bandura and Walters as, in 1959, traditional learning theorists. Their theoretical analysis would have been equally appropriate had they been discussing the shaping of Skinner's pigeon pecking behavior or Pavlov's salivating dogs. Nevertheless, two items are present in the general discussion that, in hindsight, proved very important to future developments in social cognitive (learning) theory: (1) their reference to the modeling value of the fathers' aggressive behavior and (2) their discussion of the role of high expectancies as a partial component of effective socialization practices. The importance of modeling became the focus of the 1963 book; the topic of high expectations, by 1986, became the core component of the role of self-efficacy in the socialization process.

Social Learning and Personality Development *(1963)*

Bandura's next major work appeared in 1963. It was again co-authored with Richard Walters and was titled *Social Learning and Personality Development*. Rather than a single study, this book was a review of many studies, each concerned with some aspect of children's imitation. In contrast to the 1959 text, this one is more firmly rooted in instrumental than in classical conditioning. However, it is a form of instrumental conditioning that extends the paradigm significantly beyond Skinner's limits.

There was a reason Skinner chose to shape pecking behavior rather than tap dancing in pigeons: Pigeons don't tap-dance. But because they do peck, at just about anything, it was possible for Skinner to demonstrate the validity of instrumental conditioning. He was able to demonstrate the power of different reinforcement schedules, the effect of techniques for stimulus and response generalization and discrimination, and the influence of punishment. But to offer these demonstrations, there first needed to be a behavior to modify; that is, the pigeon needed to peck.

For Bandura, the fact that instrumental conditioning couldn't offer much hope for tap-dancing pigeons or, more generally, for the expression of novel behaviors, was the reason Skinner's theory was limited and therefore in need of extension. The extension involved *imitative learning*. Even while staying within the theoretical limits of instrumental conditioning, Bandura offered a radically distinct set of conditions under which new behaviors can be acquired and existing ones modified. The revision concerned the role of reinforcement.

In Skinnerian instrumental conditioning, direct reinforcement of the organism's behavior is necessary if an association is to be made between the response and its consequence. Bandura argued that, in humans at least, this association need not be direct. Rather, modeling can also provide both a means of acquiring novel behaviors and a more efficient means of shaping current behaviors without the use of direct reinforcement. He referred to this type of learning as *observational learning* and suggested that the modeling of new behaviors might actually be more dependent on the child's observation of the response consequences to a model than on direct experience of those consequences. He referred to such indirect consequences as *vicarious reinforcement*. By introducing the concept of vicarious reinforcement, Bandura was stating explicitly that human learning was primarily a social experience. Learning theory therefore became social learning theory.[2]

Social learning theory involves the imitation of both real and symbolic models. Symbolic models can be presented either orally or pictorially. They can be characters in a book or a movie; they can be portrayed as real people, as cartoon figures, or as some other sort of caricature. This interest in the potential of symbolic models to influence behavior on a large scale led Bandura in 1963, well before most other critics, to express serious concern about the potential negative impact of television viewing. The potential influence of symbolic modeling, especially through television viewing, continues to be a major concern to Bandura (Evans, 1989), as well as to other social learning theorists (Huston, Wright, Alvarez, & Truglio, 1995; Leibert, Sparfkin, & Davidson, 1982).

Bandura believed that socialization through modeling occurs in three ways. The first involves the power of modeling to elicit novel responses in the observer; the second focuses on the role of modeling as an inhibitor or disinhibitor of previously

---

[2] This transition in Bandura's thinking is another good example of mechanism's jettisoning of the theoretical constraints of an association-based learning theory while at the same time continuing to use its methodology.

acquired behaviors; and the third concerns the power of imitation to elicit similar but not identical forms of behavior.

Bandura acknowledged that it might not always be possible, practically speaking, to differentiate these three types of influence, because to do so would require a knowledge of the reinforcement history of the individual. Consistent with his mechanistic perspective, however, he did (and still does) believe that experimental controls and statistical procedures in laboratory research enable us to study these potential effects independent of one another. The applied research task then becomes translating the findings gained through laboratory research into meaningful social interventions. This issue of the application of basic research findings remains one of the defining features of Bandura's work.

Bandura's research strategy for the study of observational learning is straightforward. Children observe a model performing some behavior or behaviors, observe some consequence to the model as a result of those actions, and then at some later time are provided an opportunity to imitate (or not imitate) the behaviors previously observed. The data is then analyzed to determine if a statistically significant relationship exists between the child's behavior and that of the model.

The "Bobo" experiments (Bandura, Ross, & Ross, 1961; Bandura, Ross, & Ross, 1963a) are probably the most famous of this series of observational learning studies. Bobo was a 5-foot-tall inflatable clown weighted at the base so that if someone tried to push him down, he would quickly right himself. Bobo actually enjoys a unique status within social learning circles. Bandura says that when he gives lectures around the country, he often finds a Bobo doll waiting for him by the lectern. Some students have even asked him to autograph their own Bobo dolls (Evans, 1989).

It is worth reviewing one of the classic Bobo experiments in detail because it serves as a good illustration of most of the studies examining observational learning. The purpose of the 1963 Bobo study was to determine if preschool-age children are influenced by observing a model acting in a particular manner. There were 48 boys and 48 girls in the study. They were divided into three experimental and one control group, with an equal number of boys and girls in each group. One experimental group observed either a male or a female behave aggressively toward Bobo; a second experimental group observed the same sequence, but on film; and a third experimental group observed a film of a model dressed as a cartoon character acting in the same aggressive manner. The control group had no exposure to aggressive models.

Children in the live-model experimental group were individually brought into a room and asked to sit at a table. Some art materials were on the table, and the children were told that they could use the materials as they wished. After each child was settled, the adult model was then brought into the room and seated at a second table. The model's play area had a Tinkertoy set, a wooden mallet, and the infamous Bobo. The model began playing with the Tinkertoys but soon turned to Bobo. In the words of the experimenter, the model

> punched the Bobo doll . . . sat on the Bobo doll and punched it repeatedly in the nose . . . raised the Bobo doll and pummeled it on the head with the mallet . . . tossed the doll up in the air aggressively . . . and kicked it about the room. While engaging in

this physical assault, the model verbalized aggressive phrases such as sock him in the nose . . . hit him down . . . throw him in the air . . . and kick him. (pp. 4–5)[3]

The preschoolers in the film group saw the identical sequence on film, while the cartoon group saw a film of a person dressed as a cartoon cat performing the same assault on Bobo. The children in the control group were not exposed to any model. They only participated in the second phase of the experiment.

Once the observation session was completed, the children were moved to a second room and again told that they could play with the toys that were present in this setting. There were two types of toys in this second setting. A set of aggressive toys included a 3-foot-tall Bobo, a mallet, a pegboard, dart guns, and a tetherball hanging from the ceiling, with a face painted on the ball. The nonaggressive toys included a tea set, crayons and paper, dolls, stuffed animals, cars and trucks, and plastic farm animals. During the 20 minutes that the children were in this second setting, their behavior was observed for evidence of imitative and nonimitative aggression and nonaggression. Nonimitative aggression was defined as acts judged to be aggressive but not previously performed by the model.

The analysis of the imitative behavior showed that the preschoolers in all three experimental groups exhibited significantly more aggressive behavior than did the preschoolers in the control group. Furthermore, there was no statistical difference between the total amount of aggressive behavior exhibited in the three experimental groups. In other words, observing a symbolic model was as powerful an influence as observing a real one. Because the children in each group, as well as the observed models, were both male and female, it was also possible to examine the influence of gender on imitation of aggressive behavior. Boys were more likely than girls to demonstrate both imitative and nonimitative aggressive behavior. Similarly, male models acting aggressively were more likely to be imitated by children of either sex than were female models. The combination of a boy observing a male model acting aggressively was particularly powerful. These boys were 10 times more likely to demonstrate aggressive gun play than were girls who observed a female model.

Other studies by Bandura and his colleagues have demonstrated that observational learning is not limited to the modeling of aggressive behavior. Similar patterns were found, for example, with respect to incidental learning (Bandura & Huston, 1961), standards for self-reinforcement (Bandura & Kupers, 1964), and judgments of moral behavior (Bandura & McDonald, 1963).

Bandura also demonstrated that imitation was influenced by the response consequences of the model's behavior. Models who were reinforced for their behavior were much more likely to be imitated than were those who either were not reinforced or were punished (Bandura & Kupers, 1964; Bandura, Ross, & Ross, 1963b). By the same token, models seen as having high status were more likely to be imitated than were low-status models. Bandura also reported on a number of studies that document the

---

[3] It is not clear from the original studies whether informed consent was obtained from the parents of these children. Such a study replicated today would clearly require it.

influence of observer characteristics on observational learning. He noted that observer effects have been found for a variety of personality characteristics, such as self-esteem and dependency. In addition, imitation is more likely to occur when the observers see themselves as similar in some respects to the models they are observing.

The series of studies reported by Bandura in the 1963 book clearly demonstrated the power of observational learning to influence socialization processes. Vicarious reinforcement was shown to be at least as significant a determinant of the observer's behavior as was direct reinforcement for that behavior. The studies demonstrated that a wide variety of behaviors, including those reflecting gender-role and moral behavior, were capable of being acquired through the observation and vicarious reinforcement of socially sanctioned models, both live and symbolic. In this sense social learning theory was a significant extension of Skinner's operant learning theory.

Even though this early version of social learning theory shifted the focus from the influence of direct to indirect consequences, it retained the operant notion that behavior is largely determined by factors external to the individual. But having made such a shift, Bandura was faced with the question of how this was possible. What must the nature of the internal mechanism be to make such indirect learning possible? Bandura's 1977 book attempted to answer this question. The answer prompted a significant revision of the theory.

Social Learning Theory (1977)

A comparison of the first sentences in the 1963 and 1977 books indicates the nature of the changes that took place in Bandura's orientation between the publication of the two works. The 1963 opener extols the virtue of social learning principles as being "more capable of accounting for the development and modification of human behavior" (p. vii). Bandura begins the 1977 preface with the statement "In this book I have attempted to provide a unified theoretical framework for analyzing human thought and behavior" (p. vi). The difference between the two is the use of the phrase "human thought" in the 1977 preface.

The 1977 preface goes on to say that recent advances in the understanding of psychological processes—in particular, the ability of humans to use symbols to represent events, analyze conscious experiences, plan, create, imagine, and engage in forethought—require a major shift in the structure of social learning theory. The essence of this shift again involved the meaning of reinforcement. In Skinnerian operant conditioning, as in the 1963 book, there is a one-to-one correspondence between reinforcement and behavior. Changes in behavior were seen as a function of changes in reinforcement patterns, direct or vicarious. There was no need to talk about human thought or psychological processes, or any other mentalistic concepts for that matter, because such references were believed to add nothing to the explanation of the association between behavior and its consequences. By 1977, however, Bandura was arguing that this one-to-one link misrepresented the nature of the association being made between behavior and its consequences. In particular, he claimed that the meaning of the reinforcement was not self-evident, but rather was acquired through the processing of the information the reinforcement provided. In making these changes, Bandura was clearly acknowledging the influence of the cognitive revolution that was taking place within the discipline of psychology. As will be more fully discussed in Chapter 7, the emergence of computers provided an entirely new perspective from which to consider and conceptualize how our behavior is influenced by what goes on inside our heads.

A Skinnerian view of operant conditioning assumes that behavior is best studied and represented as under the control of external factors. Operant learning research models—in particular, the reinforcement-extinction-reinforcement (i.e., A-B-A) paradigms—are designed to document this assumption. But, Bandura now argued, behavior in the real world isn't that volatile. Human behavior often shows remarkable consistency in the face of seemingly drastic changes in reinforcement patterns. There must, Bandura insisted, be more to the process of understanding human behavior than the study of reinforcement contingencies. There must be a way to account for consistency as well as change.

The Introduction of Reciprocal Determinism

This new accounting involved what Bandura called a process of *reciprocal determinism* among three factors: (1) the person (portrayed primarily as an information processing mechanism), (2) the person's behavior, and (3) the environment. Each of these three was depicted as influencing and being influenced by the other two. Bandura pictured this reciprocal process as a series of conditional probabilities—the likelihood of one event determines the likelihood of another, which, in turn, changes the probability of the next component in a never-ending sequence.

The most radical element of this triad is the differentiation between the person and the person's behavior. This split is anathema to the radical behaviorism from which social learning theory emerged. It smacks of the "explanatory fictions" that Skinner cautioned against. But for Bandura the differentiation was necessary if there was to be a way to explain behavior and behavioral change as caused by factors other than merely external, efficient causes.

Within this triad the environment serves not only as the source of efficient causes for behavior but also as a source of data for the person's information processing mechanisms. Behavior becomes not simply something that acts on the environment but a source of data that is fed back to the person. The person therefore becomes both the generator of specific behaviors and the interpreter of the environment to which those behaviors are directed. Again, each influences and is influenced by the other. The logic of this interdependence is no different from what an organicist or a contextualist might envision except for the very significant fact that for Bandura, the mechanist, it was still possible to tease apart these reciprocal influences and examine the influence of each independent of the other two.

The Function of Response Consequences

To understand how Bandura's process of reciprocal determinism works, we first have to understand his shifting conceptualization of the role of reinforcement. Reinforcement, or more generally, the consequences of one's behavior, was now portrayed as having three distinct functions. Specifically, response consequences were seen as (1) imparting information, (2) serving as motivators through their incentive value, and (3) regulating behavior.

Bandura argued that behavior change does not occur through a process of people associating each specific act with its immediate consequence. Rather, people gather information from their response histories and, on the basis of this information, form hypotheses about the relationship between their acts and the consequences of those acts. In this new formulation, aggregates of discrete behaviors replace individual discrete behaviors as the significant unit of analysis. These aggregates serve as the basis for the generation of hypotheses about the relationship between behavior and its consequences.

Skinnerian operant conditioning assumes that the motive or reason for behavioral change is a function of its consequences. Each new behavior, then, is seen as being caused by the cumulative impact of previous reinforcements. In other words, the past is causing the present. But Bandura suggested that our symbolic capacities change this equation. We are motivated not so much by what has happened on previous occasions as by our symbolic representation of what we believe will happen on subsequent occasions. In Bandura's (1977) words:

> Anticipatory capacities enable humans to be motivated by prospective consequences. Past experiences create expectations that certain actions will bring valued benefits, that others will have no appreciable effects, and that still others will avert future trouble. By representing foreseeable outcomes symbolically, people can convert future consequences into current motivators of behaviors. (p. 18)

Because of the role now assigned to hypothesis testing, reinforcement is no longer seen as automatically leading to the formation of an association between the response and its consequences. Rather, reinforcers are reinforcing only to the extent that the individual is aware of the contingent relationship between behavior and its consequences. The link is not automatic but deliberate. It depends as much (if not more) on the symbolic abilities of the individual as it does on the nature of the reinforcement itself. In this sense, Bandura argued, rather than viewing the function of reinforcement as a strengthener of associations, it makes more sense to speak of reinforcement as a regulator of behavior through the consequences resulting from that behavior. That is, the primary role of reinforcement is in determining the probability that a response will be made on a particular occasion. It has little effect on the development of the actual association because this is a cognitively mediated process. The distinction is between, on the one hand, understanding that an association exists between a behavior and its consequences and, on the other, exercising this knowledge by making a contingent response.

Elements of the Observational Learning Process

Bandura claimed that these new views of the role of response consequences (i.e., vicarious reinforcement) required a redefinition of the nature of the observational learning process itself. Instead of viewing it as essentially a form of operant conditioning, Bandura now introduces a much more complicated elaboration of the relationship between the behavior of the model and that of the observer. The elaboration focuses on the role of the person in the reciprocal triad of person, behavior, and environment.

For Bandura social or observational learning is a process through which "observers acquire mainly symbolic representations of the modeled activities which serve as guides for appropriate performances" (1977, p. 24). As Figure 6.1 shows, the process is governed by four components: attentional processes, retention processes, motor reproduction processes, and motivational processes.

ATTENTIONAL PROCESSES   Attentional processes orient the person to both the specific characteristics of the observed behaviors and the characteristics of the model exhibiting these behaviors. Both of these factors determine the likelihood that the observer will even attend to the model's behavior, much less imitate it. This depiction of attentional process is similar to the 1963 discussion of the model's behavior and its consequence. Still relevant are the likelihood of being exposed to a particular model, the actual nature of the behaviors modeled, the degree of similarity between the model and the observer, the salience of the model's behavior to the observer, and the actual consequences of the model's behavior. Still relevant as well is the belief that models can be either real or symbolic.

In this new formulation, however, the salience of the characteristics of the modeled event has been lessened to the extent that the information processing capacities have been emphasized. Attending to models is now seen as a reflection of cognitively generated expectations of the likelihood of future outcomes resulting from the modeling of behavior, and not as a function of past reinforcement experiences. This distinction may appear somewhat chicken-and-egg-like (which came first, the chicken or the egg?), but Bandura points out that acting on the basis of belief about future outcomes and acting on the basis of experiences with past outcomes are often quite different. Assessments of future outcomes may be inconsistent to one degree or another with previous experience. This inconsistency may be in either a positive or a negative direction and, accordingly, could result in both unexpectedly desirable and undesirable outcomes.

RETENTION PROCESSES   Observing a model's behavior is of little consequence unless these observations are symbolized in some form and then retained in memory. Bandura says that two forms of symbolization—imaginal and verbal—account for most of the information retained in memory. Images are direct forms of symbolization. They can be produced through any of the sensory systems, although the visual system is probably the most relevant for humans. Bandura notes that imagery may be particularly relevant for infants and young children because their verbal symbol systems are not yet well developed.

This developmental distinction between the mechanisms regulating the imitation process in infants and young children and those in older individuals is not present in the 1963 book because a straight operant analysis places little emphasis on the developmental status of the individual. But having recognized the role of psychological processes in social learning, Bandura now acknowledges that individuals may differ

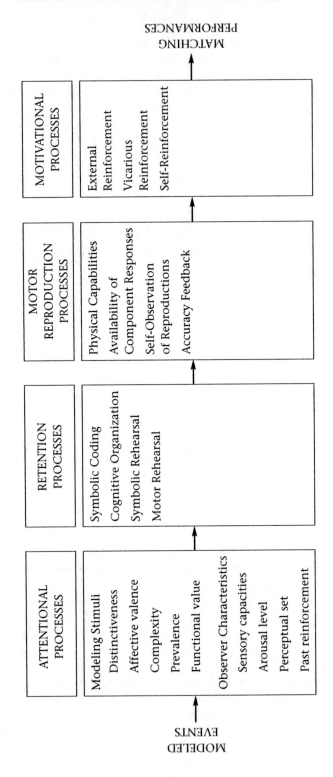

FIGURE 6.1 Bandura's Symbolic Representation Process   Source: Bandura, 1977, p. 23.

developmentally in terms of the maturity level of these processes. Developmental differences might also reflect the length of the interval between observing the behavior of a model and reproducing that behavior, the efficacy of different types of reinforcers, and the child's physical/motor ability to actually reproduce the behavior.

Closely related to how information is coded for retention is the issue of how it is stored in memory. Bandura notes that *rehearsal* is a significant component of the retention process, particularly with behaviors that are not easily displayed. He also believes that the use of cognitive symbols allows individuals to "pretest" unique solutions, problem-solving strategies, creative actions, and arguments concerning the validity of actions and thoughts. As with other aspects of his theory, Bandura believes that these rehearsal and pretest strategies are acquired through a social learning process—that is, by observing the external manifestations of such internal cognitive actions in the behavior of others.

MOTOR REPRODUCTION PROCESSES For social learning to occur, observed behavior not only must be attended to and then retained, but also must be reproduced. This aspect of the social learning process involves the ability to (1) recall the appropriate information from memory and then (2) cognitively organize it so that it matches the model's behavior. The observer also must have the physical and motor capabilities to actually provide a behavioral match of the model's behavior.

MOTIVATIONAL PROCESSES   Even if an observer is capable of acquiring, retaining, and demonstrating the behavior of a model, there still remains the issue of whether the behavior will, in fact, be modeled. As he did in the 1963 book, Bandura argues here that issues of performance are influenced by the degree to which observers value the model's behavior and see others as benefiting from imitating the model's behavior. However, Bandura (1977) adds that self-evaluations also play an increasingly important role in response motivation as individuals develop.

> At the highest level of development, individuals regulate their own behavior by self-evaluative and other self-produced consequences. After signs of progress and merited attainment become a source of personal satisfaction, knowledge that one has done well can function as a reward. (pp. 103–104)

Individuals make these self-evaluations by creating certain performance standards that serve as inducements for behavior and criteria against which behavior is judged. To do this, individuals first evaluate the observed behavior in terms of such dimensions as its quality, quantity, authenticity, ethicality, and deviancy. Next, having evaluated the observed behaviors, individuals compare the observed behaviors to a set of internalized standards. These standards may be unique to a particular individual or common to some group. These internalized standards typically involve judgments as to not only the adequacy of the behavior but also its significance to both the individual and others. Finally, individuals make judgments about whether the ability to imitate the behavior is within their grasp or depends on factors beyond their control.

Having evaluated the observed behavior and then judged it with reference to the set of internal standards, individuals then provide themselves an appropriate self-response or reinforcement. Bandura believes that such self-regulated processes are acquired in the same fashion as any other form of social learning. The only difference is that, in this case, standards of behavior rather than actual behaviors are being modeled. Bandura sees this self-regulative process as the means through which humans acquire and maintain a capacity for self-direction.

Self-reinforcement does not act independently of vicarious and external reinforcement. Because most behaviors are likely to involve more than one of these reinforcers, Bandura suggests that the likelihood of individuals behaving in a particular way reflects the relative strengths of the different reinforcement sources. This is especially true when the reinforcers are in conflict—that is, when the individual values the behavior and society does not, or vice versa. Bandura notes that one way individuals avoid such conflicts between personal and social values is by selecting associates who share similar standards of conduct.

In discussing the relative influences of external and internal reinforcers, Bandura makes special note of the impact of contradictory influences when moral or ethical concerns are involved. He is especially concerned about the potential for dehumanizing social influences to give people license to act toward others in immoral and unethical ways. He is particularly critical of those social values that make it possible to shift blame to the victim for some act against the victim (as is often the case in incidents of rape and spousal abuse), that foster the use of euphemistic language as a device for masking reprehensible acts (as is often the case in acts of war), and that allow individuals to be debased to some subhuman status as a pretext for harmful action against them (as is often the case in racial discrimination). Bandura believes that these same social learning forces can, of course, be used to humanize rather than dehumanize, but he is not sanguine about such a prospect. In particular, Bandura (1977) notes that

> many conditions of contemporary life are conducive to dehumanizing behavior. Bureaucratization, automation, urbanization, and high social mobility lead people to relate to each other in anonymous, impersonal ways. In addition, social practices that divide people into in-group and out-group members produce human estrangement that fosters dehumanization. Strangers can be more easily cast as unfeeling beings than can personal acquaintances. (pp. 157–158)

Summary of the Shift from 1963 to 1977

The shift in focus from 1963 to 1977 is striking. Bandura moved even farther away from his earlier emphasis on a conception of social learning consistent with operant learning principles. Now there is much more reciprocal determinism, or interaction, between individuals and their environments. Particularly significant in the 1977 revision is the recognition that the meaning individuals attach to their behavior, as well as to the behavior of models, is inherent not within those behaviors, but rather within the individual's cognitive representations of those behaviors.

Bandura also now believes that this increasing emphasis on reciprocal determinism has implications for the Skinnerian debate about whether we are really free agents or simply the sum total of our reinforcement histories. This issue was not pursued in the 1963 book because that earlier version of the theory was more closely tied to the environmental deterministic assumptions of operant learning theory. But now, with the recognition of the person as a causal agent, the issue becomes relevant. Bandura recognizes that, for philosophers, freedom and determinism are often seen as antithetical. But now, Bandura (1977) argues, when the two are defined in terms of options and rights, there is no incompatibility.

> From this perspective, freedom is not conceived negatively as the absence of influences or simply the lack of external constraints. Rather, it is defined positively in terms of the skills at one's command and the exercise of self-influence which choice of action requires. Given the same environmental constraints, individuals who have many behavioral options and are adept at regulating their own behavior will experience greater freedom than will individuals whose personal resources are limited. (p. 203)

The degree to which individuals can exercise freedom or self-direction is seen as a measure of their self-efficacy, a concept that will become the focus of the 1986 revision of the theory.

The changes made in the 1977 revision also have implications as to how individuals are seen as defining and directing the course of their development. Characterizations of the individual as passive are now seen as incorrect. Even to describe them as merely responsive is an underestimation. Bandura's individuals seem to be doing a lot more than merely responding. They are forming hypotheses, selecting options, and making evaluations. And they are doing so within the constraints imposed by their biological structures (the machinery of their cognitive processing activity) and the experiences encountered within their social contexts. Those two parameters, one material and the other efficient, define the limits of the active organism within social learning theory.

By contrast, for the organicist there are fewer limits on personal action, not because context makes no difference but because of the organicist's greater belief in the ability of individuals to attribute meaning to the events of their lives. This ability reflects the importance that organicism places on the emerging properties of the developmental process. The emergence of a distinct psychological level or plane of action allows a greater distancing from the limits imposed by both biological and contextual factors than is true for Bandura. For Bandura the organism is active by virtue of being able to choose among options; for the organicist, the organism is active by virtue of being able first to construct and then to choose among those options.

Social Foundations of Thought and Action: A Social Cognitive Theory *(1986)*

Bandura's shift toward the view of cognitive processes as regulators of social learning took on even greater importance in the 1986 revision (Bandura, 1986) of his theory. The shift was so great that social learning theory now became social cognitive theory. The preface is again a good place to start. Bandura emphasizes the role of *self-direction* and the *capacity for forethought* as central determinants of human behavior. These two capabilities assume this importance because, Bandura now argues, "Most human behavior is directed towards goals and outcomes projected into the future." (1986, pp. xi–xii). The process of understanding the causes of our behavior has shifted from a focus on how we react to the past and present to how we cognitively represent the future. Again, a good part of this shift in emphasis almost certainly reflects the continuing growth of the influence of information processing approaches to the study of human development

The core of the 1986 social cognitive model continues to be the triadic reciprocal relationship among behavior, the person (defined in terms of the biological, cognitive, and other internal events that affect perception and action), and the external environment. Bandura's major revision is a further elaboration of the "person pole" of the reciprocal triad. Five basic capabilities are now defined as regulating the processes through which individuals form hypotheses, set standards and goals, make judgments and comparisons, and, more generally, regulate the reciprocal interactions among person, behavior, and environment. These five are symbolizing capability, forethought capability, vicarious capability, self-regulatory capability, and self-reflective capability.

Symbolizing Capability

Bandura talked about the significance of our ability to represent experience symbolically in 1977, but now he depicts it as a distinct psychological process. The form that the *symbolizing* process takes—that is, the nature of the actual symbols used for representations, the actual content that is represented symbolically, and the ways in which these representations are organized—are still all acquired through social learning experiences. But there is now a greater emphasis on the mechanism that makes these representations possible, namely, the circuitry of the brain. Consistent with his information processing perspective, Bandura believes that changes over time in symbolic processing ability are largely a matter of increasing capacity within a particular representational domain or forming a new representational domain to accommodate new types of social learning experiences.

Acquiring the ability to effectively use this "apparatus" is, in turn, largely a matter of observational learning. Children learn the specific linguistic symbols (i.e., words) used in a culture to represent objects and experiences, as well as the syntactic rules governing how these linguistic symbols are arranged to form sentences, from the speech they hear around them. Through social learning experiences, they also learn the culture-specific grammatical rules for such things as forming the plural. The same process occurs in the development of written language. Bandura (1989) sees parents as playing a pivotal role in the language acquisition process.

> Their instructive and corrective strategies include repetitive modeling of more advanced linguistic forms, restructuring and elaborating the child's constructions in modeled feedback, simplifying linguistic structures, varying the content around the

same structure, rephrasing utterances, prompting, questioning, informing, answering, labeling, pictorial structuring of what is being talked about, and accenting grammatically significant speech elements. (p. 12)

Vicarious Capability

Vicarious capability refers to our ability to learn through observing the actions of others. This is certainly not the first time Bandura has talked about this issue, but it is the first time that he has defined this capacity as a basic psychological process. Bandura continues to use the same four elements—attention, retention, production, and motivation—to define vicarious capacity. But now he devotes more attention to the origins of these four processes that compose the vicarious capability. He sees the development of these four processes as grounded in the reciprocal social interactions that occur between infants and their parents.

Bandura now argues that newborns enter the world with both a basic ability to produce behaviors and the capacity for imitation of simple and concrete acts. These two skills make possible the simple reciprocal interactions that characterize early infant-parent relationships. Parents imitate infant behavior, and vice versa. Through these exchanges the infant soon comes to recognize that imitation is an effective means of establishing and maintaining parental responsiveness. And parents quickly recognize that imitation is an effective means for elaborating the infant's behavioral repertoire. The four processes regulating the vicarious capacity gradually emerge out of these simple imitative exchanges.

The development of attentional process is fostered by the selective and frequently exaggerated imitative responses by parents to their infants' behavior. These parental actions help the infant to attend to particular behaviors and to do so for increasingly longer periods. These animated social interactions provide the vehicle for expanding the infant's interests and behavioral skills.

These early social interactions also help infants recognize their ability to symbolically represent experience and to use rehearsal strategies as a means to retain information. Representation and retention skills become further enhanced as children gradually acquire the ability to use verbal symbols as a means to represent experience. In addition, the use of symbolic representation allows children, for the first time, to code and retain not only specific actions but also different strategies for representing and organizing experiences.

For imitation to take place, the child must be able to translate what he or she has observed or what has been symbolically represented into specific actions. This requires both the physical skill to reproduce the specific behavior and the cognitive ability to use feedback in making successively closer approximations of the desired output. In both cases social modeling experiences are seen as providing the basis for the acquisition of the production skills.

For parents the social interactions with the child also fill a significant instructive role. It is one of the primary channels through which parents attempt to socialize their child in culturally accepted ways. Adherence to these cultural norms then serve as a major incentive or motivator for children to act in particular ways, ways consistent with the instructional efforts of their parents.

The development of gender role serves as a good illustration of how these processes operate. For Bandura observational learning is at the heart of learning to be male or female. To acquire socially accepted gender roles, children must learn to attend to the discriminating features of masculinity and femininity and to the contingent responses their behaviors generate when they behave in gender-related ways. They must learn the representational strategies that are used to categorize behaviors into gender-relevant forms, and they must learn the cognitive rehearsal strategies necessary to practice their developing sense of gender-typical behavior. They must then learn to use these representational strategies to generate new gender-relevant behaviors consistent with their symbolic representations of appropriate male and female behavior. They must also learn how to translate their gender-related symbolic representations into appropriate behavior.

Forethought Capability

Forethought is the ability to symbolically represent the future in the present. Having made such a representation, forethought can then serve as both a motivator and a director of action. The capacity for forethought is important because it frees individuals from having previous outcomes dictate new ones. Clearly Bandura believes that we learn from our experiences. But what we gain from these experiences, he says, is not the appropriateness of specific behaviors in particular situations, but rather information relevant to the formation of hypotheses about likely future outcomes. This is an important and useful distinction, because we live in changing and sometimes ambiguous environments. Rarely do new situations precisely mimic old ones.

Like the other capabilities the effective use of forethought is not automatic, but rather develops over time as a result of children's social experiences. Because young infants seem limited in their ability to link their actions with response consequences, they are not very able to act in expectation of the consequences of those actions—that is, to use forethought. This changes as infants acquire the ability to recognize both direct and vicarious contingent relationships. Parents, of course, play a key role in these discoveries, particularly in the way they exaggerate these links. As children develop the ability to represent experiences symbolically and to use rehearsal strategies to reflect on that information, they become able to infer likely future outcomes based on previous experience. These inference skills include the ability to integrate contradictory information, to differentiate relevant from irrelevant information, to form hypotheses consistent with symbolically represented experiences, and to generate novel behaviors consistent with these hypotheses. Bandura believes that these cognitive skills are acquired largely through direct instruction and observational learning.

Self-Regulatory Capability

The ultimate goal of socialization practices, at least within our culture, is the development of internal control mechanisms. As important as external systems, either direct or vicarious, might be in influencing behavior, in an open society they can never be as powerful as self-regulatory control mechanisms. Bandura argues that there are two distinct *self-regulatory processes*. One regulates motivational standards, and the other moral and social standards.

One of the ways that Bandura sees internal controls operating is through the self-monitoring of our efforts relative to our standards. We motivate ourselves to work up to our expectations and generate some degree of self-remorse when we fail to do so. Experiences, both direct and vicarious, serve to define and modify these standards, as well as the reasons we give for meeting or not meeting them. These explanations for performance often reflect our degree of *self-efficacy,* the sense that we can or cannot actually live up to the standards we have set for ourselves. It is the interaction between these two internal regulatory mechanisms—our beliefs that we are or are not capable of a particular act and our beliefs about the desirability and appropriateness of that act —that serves as the source of motivation. A person with a high sense of self-efficacy, having done poorly on a task, would be highly motivated to work hard to live up to personal expectations. Then, having met the task, he or she would be likely to raise the standard. By contrast, a person with a low sense of self-efficacy, having done poorly, would be more likely to lower the standard.

Not only do self-regulatory mechanisms serve to motivate behavior, they also provide a basis for judgments of self-satisfaction and a sense of self-worth. And, like standards for personal motivation, those regulating a sense of self-worth are acquired primarily through social learning experiences.

Parents, through both direct instruction and the modeling of socially appropriate behavior, provide the behavioral standard that children gradually internalize as the processes regulating vicarious and direct instruction mature. This process of moral development not only involves the cataloging of morally acceptable behaviors but also eventually comes to include the internalization of the standards used to judge the morality and social acceptability of new behaviors.

Self-Reflective Capability

For Bandura the central component of our capacity for *self-reflection* is the capability to make judgments as to our ability to exercise control over the events that affect our lives—that is, to exercise a degree of self-efficacy over our lives. Self-efficacy judgments are involved in decisions concerning choice of action, degree of persistence, and commitment, and in interpreting feedback from one's actions.

> If there is any characteristic that is distinctively human, it is the capacity for reflective self-consciousness. This enables people to analyze their experiences and to think about their own thought processes. By reflecting on their varied experiences and on what they know, they can derive generic knowledge about themselves and the world around them. People not only gain understanding through reflection, they evaluate and alter their own thinking by this means. In verifying thought through self-reflective means, they monitor their activities, act on them or predict occurrences from them, judge from the results the adequacy of their thoughts and change them accordingly. (Bandura, 1989, p. 41)

Bandura sees young children demonstrating little or no sense of self-efficacy. Adults, particularly parents, must initially serve this function. Gradually, as children have more experiences and acquire more effective ways to represent these experiences, they gain a sense of causal efficacy, that is, a recognition of the relationship between their behavior and its consequences. The form this causal sense takes depends to a large extent on how successful children are in their endeavors. "Infants who experience success in controlling environmental events become more attentive to their own behavior and more competent in learning new efficacious responses than do infants for whom the same environmental events occur regardless of how they behave" (Bandura, 1989, p. 43). Here, too, parents and other adults serve as important mediators of this developing contingency awareness.

Establishing a sense of causal efficacy is only part of the process, however. Children also need to develop the self-reflective cognitive processes that allow them to realize that they were the cause of that contingency. Language development plays a particularly important role in this process because it is the primary means through which we symbolically represent behavioral standards.

The sense of personal efficacy that is established within the family setting extends to other social domains and relationships as children grow older. Each new setting provides feedback about one's own behavior, as well as that of others. And each new comparison of the two provides additional information for assessing one's effectiveness in different settings. Bandura believes that peers play a particularly significant role in this process in that they serve both as models of behaviors and standards and as "the most informative points of reference for comparative efficacy appraisal and verification" (1989, p. 45).

In the same sense that peers provide an arena for the development of social efficacy skills, Bandura sees schools as serving the same function for children's sense of intellectual efficacy. This sense of intellectual efficacy is evident both in children's strategies to achieve intellectual competence and in their desire to do so. Bandura is quite specific about the characteristics of schools that foster a high sense of intellectual efficacy in their students and those that do not. He favors individualized instructional strategies that allow children to make individual comparisons of their present skills with personal standards. At the same time, Bandura is highly critical of educational practices that favor ability grouping, lockstep instruction, and competition between children. He believes that such inappropriate educational practices instill a low sense of intellectual efficacy, which, once established, is difficult to change.

Bandura sees personal efficacy as a dynamic rather than a static process. Although it is a significant regulator of behavior, motivation, and thought throughout the life span, its structure changes with age as new demands and opportunities are presented and as new capabilities and limitations are encountered. In adolescence individuals must respond to greater expectations for personal responsibility and to fuller exposure to the range of adult issues; in early and middle adulthood, to the demands of balancing marriage, family, and occupation; and in later adulthood, to the challenges of declining physical capacity. Bandura sees the ability to maintain a strong sense of self-efficacy in old age as one of the primary means through which the aged can prevent themselves from being trapped in a cycle of loss of vitality, leading to loss of interest, leading to loss of skills, leading to loss of social contacts, leading back to a still further loss of vitality.

Social Cognitive Theory in Perspective

Bandura's work is important. It presents an image of human learning rooted in our social experiences. It advances the view that we learn not only through our direct experiences but also through our observations of the behavior of others. It stresses the concept that this learning is a mediated process, based on our interpretations of both the consequences we experience from our actions and the consequences we observe of the actions of others.

Social cognitive theory offers an explanation of these mediating processes as being rooted in our ability to cognitively process information. In particular, this ability to interpret experience reflects the presence of five basic psychological capabilities, which, in turn, reflect the functioning of basic physiological processes. Although these physiological structures serve as the mechanism in which information processing occurs, the form this processing takes more likely reflects both socially acquired strategies for the organization, storage, and retrieval of experiences and socially acquired standards for evaluating behavior.

Social cognitive theory is a good representative of current theory making within the mechanistic world view. It provides a path by which internal mentalistic concepts first appear as external social experiences and through which mentalistic concepts are ultimately expressed as behavior. It effectively uses experimental controls and statistical procedures to isolate and independently assess antecedent variables. And it recognizes these antecedent variables and psychological processes as being equally functional at all points in the life span.

Although Bandura has progressively moved farther away from the specifics of both classical and instrumental learning theories, he nevertheless has consistently argued that the various regulators of behavior are all acquired through a process consistent with the laws of learning.

7

The Information Processing Perspective

The two mechanistic theories we have examined so far are each identified with specific individuals. Think of radical behaviorism, and Skinner immediately comes to mind; social cognitive theory could almost as easily be called Bandura's theory. But the information processing approach differs in several respects.

In the first place, it isn't a theory so much as it is a perspective. There isn't one, single coherent body of theoretical knowledge that makes a clear and relatively complete statement as to what information processing is all about. Rather, there are a number of statements, each dealing with some aspect of what constitutes information processing. Although these individual statements share some general assumptions, they each reflect somewhat different topics pursued by somewhat different methods. In the second place, there isn't one individual's work that defines the approach; rather, it represents the work of many individuals. Again, although the leading proponents of the information processing approach generally agree that human thought is the processing of information, there is no clear consensus as to how this processing occurs, what the specific defining elements are, or, of greater relevance for our purposes, how or even whether the ways in which information is processed changes over time.

This state of affairs almost certainly reflects the "youthfulness" of the information processing perspective. Only in the past 25 or 30 years has information processing come to be recognized as a perspective on the study of behavior and development. Its youthfulness, however, has not limited its acceptance. Within mechanism the information processing perspective has become the mainstream approach to the study of cognitive development, at least among American psychologists. In other words, the information processing perspective now occupies the position once held by learning theory.

This shift from the study of learning to the study of cognition is a good illustration of the current theoretical breadth of mechanism as a world view. When mechanism was synonymous with learning theory, the image was one of a world view only comfortable with the study of efficient causes; thus a mechanist was a behaviorist. This is no longer the case. Mechanists are as comfortable dealing with material causes as with efficient ones. In this sense they aren't different from either organicists or contextualists. It is their theoretical assumptions as to the relationships between efficient and material causes, and the distinct methodologies that these assumptions generate, that distinguish mechanism from either organicism or contextualism.

Origins of the Information Processing Perspective

An information processing perspective on human development traces its origin to three distinct circumstances: (1) the decline of learning theory in the 1950s and 1960s (Knapp, 1986; McShane, 1991), (2) the examination by mechanistic psychologists in the 1960s and 1970s of Piaget's theoretical arguments (Flavell, 1992; Gelman, 1972), and (3) the growing interest in computers, initially as an information processing device in the 1940s and 1950s and then as a metaphor for human thought (Attneave, 1959; Broadbent, 1957; Newell, Shaw, & Simon, 1958; Newell & Simon, 1972).

The Decline of Learning Theory

Learning theory as a theoretical perspective (as distinct from its methodological con-tributions) ran into trouble when it tried to extend its predictions from studies of ani-mals and very simple human reactions to more complex human behaviors. The problem was that predictions based solely on antecedent or efficient conditions, the defining characteristic of a learning theory based on simple conditioning models, were as often disconfirmed as they were confirmed. Predictions and explanations of more complex human behaviors that relied solely on antecedent or efficient causes were simply proving to be inadequate.

Learning theorists attempted to deal with this dilemma by positing the existence of internal mediational devices that might explain the discrepancy in the reversal-nonreversal shift data. Unfortunately these hypothetical constructs offered little in the way of additional explanatory or predictive power because they were conceptualized as merely the internalization of what were previously external regulators. It was not that learning theory denied that something happened between input and output. Clearly something did. Rather, it was that whatever that something was, it wasn't conceptual-ized as having an active effect on the input. It was merely a passive conveyance, in the same sense that the events that occur between your speaking into a telephone and someone on the other end listening to your message is a passive conveyance—that is, the output is fully predicted from the input. In both cases, the input is conveyed rather than processed. And, in the case of learning theory, that was the problem. As tasks seemingly as simple as a reversal-nonreversal shift procedure were showing, the output suggested that the input was not only being conveyed but being processed as well.

One significant attack on learning theory's claim for the primacy of antecedent causes was linguist Noam Chomsky's (1957) critique of Skinner's interpretation of lan-guage development. Chomsky argued convincingly that it was impossible to imagine a behavioral system relying solely on antecedent causes that could account for chil-dren's development of both vocabulary and syntactic structures, especially given that many of the early utterances of young children were novel in the sense that they had never been heard before and were often grammatically incorrect. In the first case there was nothing for the child to imitate, and in the second what parent would ever positively reinforce a child for saying "I goed to the store"?

The Examination of Piaget's Theory

The introduction of Piaget's organismic theory of cognitive development to American audiences (Flavell, 1963; Hunt, 1961) was a second impetus to the emergence of the information processing perspective. When Piaget's arguments were read by American researchers (who were primarily mechanistically oriented psychologists), a common first response was to question the theory by testing its limits—as these limits were interpreted within a mechanistic orientation. The result was a long series of "training studies" in the 1960s and 1970s that were designed to test Piaget's claims about what children of a particular age could and could not do. We will examine the theoretical significance of these training studies later in the text, but for now it is important to recognize these studies as helping shift the attention of American researchers away from the antecedent conditions of the learning theorists and more toward an investigation of the internal mechanisms that processed input.

These training studies, as well as other studies of Piaget's theory, led information processing theorists to define a set of internal regulatory mechanisms that differed in a number of ways from those proposed by Piaget. In particular, these researchers defined a set of internal mechanisms that were consistent with a mechanistic world view and that resembled the information processing mechanisms of a machine that was making its presence felt everywhere—the computer.

The Emergence of the Computer

The origin of the computer as the dominant metaphor for human thought within the mechanistic world view dates at least to the research conducted during World War II on communication, pattern recognition, mathematical attempts to reduce uncertainty in a system, and self-regulatory mechanisms. Computers as we know them did not yet exist, but certainly the logic on which computers would soon be built was becoming well defined. These early efforts and the work that followed were not primarily concerned with the modeling of behavior or behavioral change. Rather, they were focused on representing mathematically information in a mechanical system, on conceptualizing how information could flow or move through a system, on identifying how much information could be processed at any one time, and on deciding whether this processing is best represented as serial or parallel in nature (Eysenck & Keane, 1990). *Serial processing* implies that only one process is active at any one time; *parallel processing* implies that several processes can be active simultaneously. Only later did people begin to consider the possibility and the implications of conceptualizing the human mind as an information processing mechanism in the same sense that the computer was conceptualized as doing so.

These efforts to conceptualize human thought as an information processing mechanism, along with the decline of learning theory and the examination by mechanists of Piaget's theory, serve as the basis upon which our modern explanation of human behavior and development from an information processing perspective sits.

Commonly Held Assumptions of the Information Processing Approach

Although there is no *one* information processing perspective, there is a general consensus among scholars (Eysenck & Keane, 1990; Kail & Bisanz, 1992; Klahr, 1989; Massaro & Cowan, 1993; Palmer & Kimchi, 1986; Siegler, 1991) as to a set of four defining elements or core assumptions of the perspective.

Cognitive Activity as the Processing of Symbols

The first, and most fundamental, of these four core assumptions is that "children's mental activity can be described in terms of processes that manipulate symbols and symbol structures" (Klahr, 1989, p. 136). Or, as Siegler (1991) puts it more succinctly, "thinking *is* information processing" (p. 59). What is being expressed in these quotes is the belief that when we talk about knowing something, we are, in fact, talking about the mental events that have acted upon a particular sensory input. These sensory inputs are translated into some form(s) of symbolic representations. The representations are then acted upon or processed by one or more cognitive processes stored in one or more cognitive structures, and some form of output follows. Depending on the situation, the output might be in the form of behavior or in the form of the processed information being stored in long-term or permanent memory, or both.

The analogy to the functioning of a computer should be fairly obvious through this description. In both cases information is put into a system, the information is represented symbolically, it is then acted upon by one or more internal processors, and finally, it is expressed in some form of output. The processing is considered active in the sense that predictions about the output cannot be determined solely by knowledge of the input but must also take into consideration what has happened to that input.

It's important to note that, in most information processing accounts of human cognitive activity, the discussions of modes of representation and processing are characterized as functional rather than literal in nature. No one is suggesting that the human brain literally functions like a computer. In fact, solid neurological evidence (Greenough, Black, & Wallace, 1987) suggests that the two are quite distinct in their actual modes of operation. Rather, what these theorists are arguing is that, whatever the actual biological and neurochemical mechanisms at work in the brain, the product of their actions is consistent with our growing understanding of how computers operate. As such, the argument goes, the more we learn about computers, the more potential insight we can gain into the functional activity of the brain.

Cognitive Activity as the Functioning of a Few Basic Elements

The second core assumption of an information processing perspective is that a relatively small number of cognitive processes underlie all cognitive activity (Kail &

Bisanz, 1992). As such, a complex cognitive activity such as reading a book or solving an algebraic equation can be best understood as reflecting the actions of a number of more specific subprocesses. Working in concert, these subprocesses produce the output that we describe as reading or multiplication, inference or problem solving, categorization or seriation, and so on. The number of these subprocesses, the degree to which any one is active with respect to a particular type of information, and their exact nature are hotly debated among information processing theorists. But the belief that this is the best way to represent cognitive activity seems to be generally accepted. In effect, this belief implies a cognitive architecture that depicts the form and the constraints that regulate the operations of the cognitive system. This image of a limited number of processes being responsible for a wide variety of outputs is, of course, consistent with the way computers operate, as well as with the importance placed on reductionism within mechanism.

Higher-Order Cognition as a Coordinated Process

The third core assumption (which is essentially a corollary of the second) is that the cognitive processes relevant to a particular type of information operate in concert with one another. What we might describe or be consciously aware of as a higher-order cognitive activity (e.g., reading or mathematics) is, in fact, the coordinated activity of a set of smaller subprocesses. We are not necessarily aware of the individual actions of these subprocesses, nor would they necessarily be meaningful even if we were. It is only their joint product that is meaningful. The particular higher-order activities that have typically been studied tend to be drawn from topics in mathematics, logic, and reading. This should not be surprising given the fact that these subject matter domains are often conceptualized in terms of subprocesses and therefore are consistent with the computer metaphor.

Some information processing theorists (Palmer & Kimchi, 1986) refer to the higher-order products of this coordinated activity as an "emergent property" in that the nature of the higher-level activity is distinct from that of the lower-level activities. It is important to note that this use of the term *emergent properties* is different from its use in organicism. For information processors what emerges from subprocess interactions is a unique product; for organicists what emerges from stage transitions is a unique process. This distinction again highlights one of the major theoretical differences between world views—namely, whether change is best conceptualized as a quantitative or a qualitative process. The emergence of a unique product in a quantitative sense refers to a novel arrangement and/or a number of basic elements; the emergence of a unique process in a qualitative sense refers to a fundamental change in the very elements that regulate human activity.

Cognitive Change Through Self-Modification

The fourth core assumption is perhaps the one most relevant to the issue of human development. This assumption is that cognitive development occurs via self-modification of the information processing system (Klahr, 1989). As Siegler (1991) describes this process, outcomes generated by the child's own activities change the way the child processes information in the future. With respect to his research on children's problem solving strategies, he finds that

> the use of various strategies creates increasing knowledge concerning the effectiveness of each strategy, the difficulty of the problems that the strategies are used to solve, and which strategies work best with which problems. This knowledge, in turn, changes the strategies that are used and the answers that are generated. (p. 59)

This image of cognitive development as essentially an internal process of self-modification does not mean that the external environment plays no part in the process. Obviously it provides much of the input for the process. The manner in which the information is represented, stored, and processed reflects, to a significant degree, the specifics of the task itself. It is for this reason that task analysis is such an important element of an information processing approach to the study of behavior and behavioral change. Nevertheless, the focus on internal self-modification is meant to convey the image of change coming about through a gradual and continuous modification of the mechanisms of information processing rather than simply the continuing accumulation of new experiences. It is not that the actual mechanisms change. It is that, with experience, children and adults become better both at using these mechanisms effectively and at recognizing which subprocesses or routines are most appropriate to use for which tasks.

Basic Elements of an Information Processing System

An information processing account of behavior and behavioral change is primarily interested in explaining the events that occur between input and output. To accomplish this task, emphasis has been placed on the human equivalent of both a computer's hardware and its software. In human terms, the hardware becomes the cognitive structures that store the information, and the software becomes the cognitive processes that act on the information.

As Figure 7.1 shows, three types or levels of processing structures have been used to explain how information enters the system, is processed, and either emerges as output or is put into long-term memory (Atkinson & Shiffrin, 1968). The first are the *sensory registers* through which data enters the systems and is represented as information; the second, a *short-term working memory (STWM)* where information is actively processed; and the third, a *long-term memory (LTM)* structure where information is stored.

To make the computer analogy more specific, think of the sensory registers as equivalent to the computer keyboard or scanner (or other input device), STWM as equivalent to a computer's RAM (random access memory), and LTM as equivalent to a computer hard disk. As is also the case with computers, STWM is seen as having a much smaller capacity than LTM and, unlike the information in LTM, which is stored permanently, information resides in STWM for a limited amount of time.

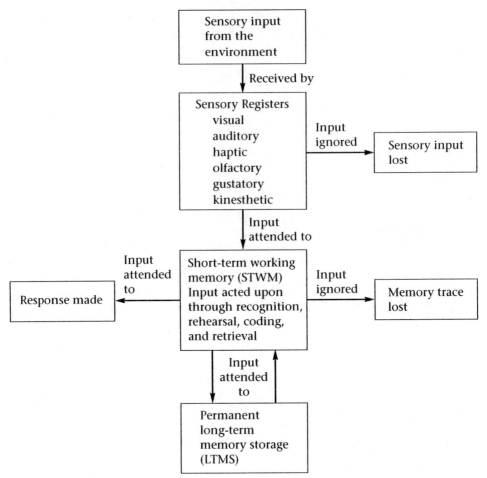

FIGURE 7.1
Basic Components of an Information Processing System.
Source: Adapted from Atkinson & Shiffrin, 1968, p. 333.

Research within the information processing perspective has focused both on the characteristics of the structures at each of the three processing levels (sensory, short-term, and long-term) and on the particular processes that act on the information present at each level. One issue that is a topic of continuing debate is whether cognitive structures and processes are generic to all information or specific to particular types of information (Siegler, 1989; Sternberg, 1989).

Keep in mind as you read these descriptions of the components of an information processing system that information processing theorists are making a functional rather than a literal comparison between the way computers operate and the way we think. They are suggesting that, whatever the actual mechanisms operating in the brain, at the functional level, they appear similar enough to the way computers work that our understanding of the operation of a computer can help us understand the operation of the brain.

The Level of Sensory Registers

For there to be output, there must first be input. Sensory stimulation must enter the human cognitive system through one or more of our senses. We must at least be able to see it or hear it, smell it or taste it, or feel it. To accomplish this sensory awareness, the sensory receptor in one or more organs must be stimulated by sensory data. The receptor(s) will translate that data into a neural impulse, which will travel along the appropriate sensory nerve to the brain. In computer language this process involves the *encoding* of the information.

Information processing theorists have focused their study of encoding on the identification of the processes that regulate what sensory data we attend to. Clearly there is a great deal more going on in our worlds than we can process at any one time. So what determines what is attended to and what is not attended to? Do we attend to different things as we get older? Do the processes that regulate this selective attention change over time? How much of the process seems "hard-wired" into the cognitive system, and how much of it is acquired through experience?

Infants show remarkable sensory abilities—abilities far more mature than that demonstrated by either their cognitive processing system or their motor output system (Kail & Pellegrino, 1985; McShane, 1991; Siegler, 1991). In fact, for all practical purposes, by one year of age, the sensory capabilities of infants are little different from those of adults. Very young infants, for example, demonstrate excellent sensory discrimination ability in all senses. They can differentiate similar sounds, visual images, and smells. They have clear visual preferences, generally preferring objects that are moderately discrepant from ones seen repeatedly. They also prefer to look at a human face rather than a stimulus with the same visual features but arranged in a nonsymmetrical fashion. They have a clear and strong orienting reflex, attend to moving objects, and show intersensory coordination. They have good depth perception, although it is unclear if this perception translates into appropriate avoidance behavior (Siegler, 1991). They even demonstrate both shape and size constancy, an important skill because the actual sensory stimulation we receive is never stable and constant but always in flux.

Given the high level of sensory functioning evident even in very young infants and the fact that these abilities reach maturity so early in life, most information processing theorists believe that these skills are both hard-wired and nondevelopmental in nature. That is, our evolutionary heritage has ensured that these skills are part of our basic structure.

The Level of Short-Term Working Memory (STWM)

As obviously important as the sensory system is for information processing, its role is largely that of translating sensory stimulation into a form that can be read by the system and then passing that information along to STWM. This is where the real action occurs.

In a computer RAM is where all information processing occurs. It is here that the instructions that make up individual software programs reside; it is here that basic operations hard-wired into the operating system function. RAM gets information both by retrieving it from permanent memory and by receiving it as input from the keyboard or other input device. STWM serves the same function in the human cognitive system.

Whereas the sensory system is well developed at birth and soon thereafter reaches maturity, STWM develops more slowly. Information processors believe that it is this difference that explains much of the discrepancy between what children are capable of sensing and what they are capable of understanding. Young children can see a printed page as well as you or I. However, their ability to understand that letters combine to form words, words to form sentences, sentences to form paragraphs, and paragraphs to form a whole message is a very different matter.

For information to be acted upon within STWM, it must first be recognized as meaningful and then be processed. Both activities have received considerable attention from information processing theorists (Kail & Pellegrino, 1985). Recognition is the first step. In some cases, recognition is a simple process of matching the new representation to one held in LTM. This is a process of *identity*. But, more often than not, the sensory system has to deal with representations that are not exact matches to those already in memory. In this case the system must make a judgment of *equivalency*, as when comparing the same letters written in a variety of different sizes and styles, or a judgment of *relevance*, as when deciding whether new information bears some relationship to old information.

Recognition strategies for simple physical stimuli such as geometric shapes and patterns, the ability to retrieve information from memory, and the ability to form simple stimulus-response associations appear to be present at birth. They are part of the hardware of the system (Siegler, 1991). Other, more sophisticated processing strategies develop more slowly. These include strategies for searching for missing objects, for rehearsing items in STWM so they will not fade from memory, and for organizing information in such a way as to make it easier to remember or act upon. Techniques such as these are general in that they can be applied to all types of representations. Others are more specific to particular representations. Counting, for example, is a process that only works on representations of quantity.

Research on children's use of strategies shows a relatively common developmental pattern. As described by Siegler (1991),

> although many particulars vary with the strategy, certain features characterize the development of all strategies. When children first acquire a memory strategy, they use it in only some of the situations where it is applicable. They limit it to materials where the strategy is easy to use and to situations that are relatively undemanding. They also are quite rigid in applying the strategy and often fail to adapt to changing task demands. All of this changes with development. Older children and children more experienced in using a strategy more actively initiate it; use it in more diverse situations, including ones that make the strategy difficult to execute; use higher qual-

ity versions of the strategy; and become more flexible in tailoring the strategy to the particulars of the situation. (p. 182)

How do information processing theorists explain this developmental pattern? The answer involves both hardware and software dimensions. Interestingly the one item that you might think would change the most actually changes the least. This item is STWM capacity (McShane, 1991). Many studies conducted over a long period of time seem to point to the capacity of STWM as being approximately seven meaningful units or "chunks" at any one time, irrespective of the age of the individual.

A *chunk* can be a single item, such as a number or a letter, or it can be a number of things that bear some meaningful relationship to one another. In this sense, it would be much easier to remember a long-distance phone number than a string of 10 digits even though the phone number would also have 10 digits. The difference is that, in the case of the phone number, the 10 digits are put into three chunks and therefore become much easier to remember. The same logic would hold for remembering words. Trying to remember a group of 15 words is difficult. It becomes much easier, however, if the words bear some relationship to each other, as would be the case if five were names of cars, five were names of fruits, and five were names of vegetables. Having first grouped the words into shared categories, the task becomes one of remembering the contents of three sets or chunks, each with five members.

The ability to group discrete items into meaningful units explains a significant part of the improvement in STWM functioning over time. Much research has been directed at identifying those variables that influence an individual's ability to identify meaningful relations between objects and at developing techniques (i.e., memory processing strategies) for fostering chunking skills.

Although the number of meaningful units that can be processed in STWM at any one time does not itself increase, the speed with which this processing takes place does (Kail & Bisanz, 1992). This increase appears to be a function of the structure of STWM itself, rather than of the use of a particular information processing strategy, because the rate of increase, as measured by changes in reaction time, is very similar across different subject matter domains. Tasks as distinct as addition, visual search, and name retrieval show the same developmental function.

Information processing efficiency is also a function of the particular strategies that individuals use. Strategies that allow more effective chunking, that identify the most direct path to problem solution, and that provide for more complete and efficient retrieval of information from LTM all aid in the efficiency of STWM operation and all show a developmental pattern. This process is further aided as children become more aware of the cognitive mechanisms they use to process information. This awareness, known as *metacognition,* also improves over time. Finally, information processing efficiency improves as well-practiced strategies come to require less deliberate mental effort, thereby freeing capacity for other tasks. This last transition is known as *automatization.*

Automatization is a particularly important information processing skill because it does not seem to require any STWM to operate. Simply "knowing" the right answer to a problem without having to consciously make an effort to solve it is an example of an automatic process. In this case, all that is required is the "automatic" retrieval of a past problem solution from LTM. The person wouldn't be able to say how he or she went about retrieving the correct answer, because automatic processes are assumed to be nonconscious. Reading a manuscript for content and spotting a spelling or grammatical error is another example of automatization. The task was not to look for spelling errors but at the same time as the processes relevant to the intended task were operating, so too was an additional, automatic task.

The Level of Long-Term Memory (LTM)

LTM differs from STWM in two very significant ways: (1) It appears to be permanent, and (2) its capacity seems virtually limitless. There is no evidence, empirical or theoretical, that suggests a finite capacity limit for LTM, however large it might be. Compare this to the serious capacity limits of STWM, even when effective chunking strategies are used.

LTM storage is an active rather than a static or passive process. That is, information, once placed in LTM, does not merely sit there as some sort of "photographic" representation of some event; it changes as new knowledge and procedures enter and as new strategies of organizing and retrieving information are acquired. Active in this sense does not imply a conscious or deliberate effort on the part of the individual. Rather, it simply reflects the fact that what we know factually and what we know procedurally change over time.

This active notion is generally used to explain why we find it so difficult to recall events that occurred before 3 or 4 years of age. The information may in fact be there, but the ways that we originally coded the information may be so different from the processes we now use that we simply have no effective way of retrieving the information. A similar phenomenon occurs with computers for which older disk-operating systems are incompatible with newer ones. Here, too, the information is still in storage; the problem is that there are no processes available for recalling it.

This issue of active memory is also relevant to the topic of children as witnesses in legal proceedings and the debate about the accuracy of "repressed" memories (McShane, 1991). The issue in such court cases is the accuracy of events, usually traumatic in nature, recalled after a period of many years. Is the memory now recalled one that is an accurate recollection of the original, repressed event, or has the memory been influenced by subsequent events and by new efforts to recall it? The recognition of LTM as an active structure should make us very cautious in using young children as witnesses in some circumstances and in accepting the accuracy of repressed memories without the presence of independent collaboration.

Within the information processing perspective, research relating to LTM has focused both on changes in the organization of representations in long-term storage and on the ease of retrieval of representations from storage. The two topics are closely related because ease of retrieval is partly a function of how the different representations of a particular experience are related to one another.

With age there appears to be a greater tendency for representations to be stored in a more systematic or relational manner. The more links between the representations of a particular experience, the more likely the recall of one will prompt the recall of others (Smith, Sera, & Gattuso, 1988). The fact that recall seems to work in this fashion provides an important insight into how representations are actually stored in LTM. In all likelihood, rather than a symbolic representation of some event being stored as a single meaningful unit, each meaningful element of a particular episode is stored separately. For example, for any given experience, there might be one storage site for the visual elements of that experience, another for the auditory ones, another for the emotional impact of the experience, and still another for the cognitive impact. The individual representations are obviously connected in some fashion, but equally likely is the fact that each representation is linked to others with which it shares some common property. This linking of similar impressions is presumed to be reflected in the fact that recalling one memory often also stimulates the recall of others not necessarily related to the original event.

One further issue with respect to the long-term storage of representations is the actual form in which these associations are held. The conventional wisdom among information processors has been that, because representations of events bear some meaningful relationship to the events they represent, there is no need to be concerned about the actual manner in which the storage occurs (i.e., the focus is on the functional rather than the structural aspects of long-term memory storage).

However, one group of information processors, who take a more neurological or structural approach to information processing, offer a different argument. These individuals (Eysenck & Keane, 1990; Karmiloff-Smith, 1992; Plunkett & Sinha, 1992) favor a *connectionist* or *parallel distributed processing model* of information storage. Unlike conventional models in which symbols stored in LTM represent experiences or events, in connectionist models fragments or subsymbols are what is actually stored. Unlike the elements mentioned previously, these subsymbol representations do not bear a meaningful relationship to the original event. It is only when subsymbols are combined with other subsymbols that the representation becomes meaningful. Consider a very simple illustration, the storage of the letter *A*. According to traditional information processing models, a symbol representing the letter is stored in long-term memory. But connectionists would argue that what is actually stored are three distinct subsymbols or units, each corresponding to the three lines or strokes needed to form the letter. Each subsymbol bears no meaning to the letter. It is only when they are combined that the letter is recalled from memory. There is an obvious advantage of efficiency to a connectionist account. With respect to the alphabet, for example, the storage of 26 specific symbols is replaced by the storage of a handful of lines and shapes.

Traditional and connectionist accounts of long-term memory storage do not contradict each other so much as they present two alternatives ways of conceptualizing memory storage. A preference for one or the other reflects, to a large degree, the extent to which an information processing theorist believes that accounts of memory storage should reflect, as consistently as possible, our best understanding of the actual structure and functioning of the brain. Traditionalists believe it is unnecessary so long as they are able to accurately predict and explain behavior using only functional levels of explanations. Connectionists believe that functional theories should always correspond to our best understanding of the structures we are attempting to model. The difference is a good example of how theoretical interpretations can differ as to what is the most appropriate level of analysis to best understand some topic.

Three Research Programs
Within the Information Processing Perspective

Now that we have a general sense of the basic assumptions and mechanisms that define an information processing perspective, it will be worthwhile to examine how individual researchers actually study behavioral change from this perspective. The three researchers considered here pursue different topics from different approaches. Robert Siegler is interested in procedural knowledge, Katherine Nelson in children's semantic organization of episodic events, and Robert Sternberg in the cognitive mechanisms that account for intelligent behavior. But in each case the work reflects four basic assumptions of the information processing perspective: (1) cognitive representations of experience, (2) a limited number of mechanisms combining to produce complex behavior, (3) a search for independent efficient and material antecedents, and (4) change occurring primarily as a result of self-modification.

Siegler's Information Processing Approach to Children's Problem Solving

The first example is drawn from the work of Robert Siegler. Siegler and his colleagues (Siegler, 1981, 1983, 1988a, 1988b, 1989, 1995; Siegler & Crowley, 1991, 1994; Siegler & Robinson, 1982; Siegler & Shipley, 1987) have for many years been examining the ways that children develop and use strategies in their problem-solving activities. This work has focused on children's learning in a number of distinct subject matter domains including mathematics, reading, spelling, time telling, and science. Based on these studies, Siegler has proposed a general model to explain the sequence of events involved as children progress from having little or no skill in a domain to being proficient at the task. His focus has been on the learning of preschool and young school-age children, but the implications of his work extend beyond this particular age range.

Siegler's study of children's early learning of addition serves as a good illustration of his overall approach. His interest is in documenting and explaining how children come to use particular strategies in trying to solve addition problems and how the likelihood of any particular strategy changes as the child becomes more skilled at adding numbers together.

Siegler noted that, when young children are first learning to add single-digit numbers, they use a variety of strategies to arrive at an answer. Sometimes they use their fingers; other times they do not. Sometimes they merely guess; other times they are able to retrieve an answer from memory without any apparent effort; still other times they use one of a variety of counting strategies. These counting strategies might include counting from one to reach the sum, counting from the first number by adding the second number to it, or counting from the larger number by adding the smaller number to it. If, for example, the problem was adding 2 + 7, the first of these three counting strategies would have the child count 1, 2, 3, 4, 5, 6, 7, 8, 9; the second would have the child count 2, 3, 4, 5, 6, 7, 8, 9; and the third would have the child count 7, 8, 9. All three counting strategies, if done correctly, will lead to the same correct answer. But there are differences among the three in terms of the ease of execution (the number of numbers that actually have to be counted) and the likelihood of an error being made (the number of points at which a counting mistake could be made).

In analyzing these different strategies using a technique he referred to as the *microgenetic method,* Siegler developed a model of children's procedural knowledge as it applies to mathematics learning. The microgenetic method involves a systematic and intensive analysis of some behavior(s) covering the entire period from initial learning to stable task proficiency. The number of behavioral observations made is proportional to the rate of change: the faster the rate of change, the greater the density of the observations. Unlike typical statistical procedures that focus on group averages, microgenetic analyses are subjected to intense trial-by-trial analysis, with the goal of inferring the processes that give rise to different types of change (Siegler, 1991). Siegler notes that different strategies take different amounts of time to complete and produce different error rates. Furthermore, he finds that, although there is a progression over time in children's preferred mode of solution, it is not a simple process. At almost all points in the sequence of becoming fully proficient at these addition problems, different children used different strategies, and, equally important from an information processing perspective, each child used a variety of strategies—sometimes a less efficient one after having previously used a more efficient one. The issue for Siegler (1991) was how best to explain this variability.

> This variability could not be explained entirely as a result of more knowledgeable children using more advanced approaches, such as retrieval. There was some relation between knowledge and use of the more advanced strategies, but it was far from perfect. The child who used retrieval on the greatest percentage of trials ranked seventh among eight children in percentage correct. The child who produced the highest percentage correct was only fourth highest in percentage use of retrieval. This was not an isolated finding. There were exceptions to even the most regular relations in the study; the extensive data collected on each subject made it difficult to dismiss these exceptions as random occurrences or reflections of measurement error. Such results as this and other microgenetic studies indicate that theoretical accounts need to explain the variability as well as the consistencies that characterize performance and change. (p. 612)

The theoretical account that Siegler devised to explain these behavioral patterns is known as the *distributions of associations model.* The model proposes that a set of cognitive processes operates on internal representations of a problem or task to determine the child's selection of a strategy to use in attempting to solve a problem. In particular, with respect to simple addition tasks, the representations are associations between specific problems and specific answers. For each problem there are associations not only between the problem and the correct answer but between the problem and incorrect ones as well. The strength of these associations is specific to a particular child and is a function of both the child's previous use of each problem-answer combination and the feedback received on each occurrence. For very difficult problems and/or for unfamiliar problems, the different answer probabilities would each be initially quite low and therefore about equal; that is, the distribution would be flat. For frequently encountered problems, one answer would have a higher association than others, in which case the distribution is said to be peaked.

The model predicts that the child will first attempt to use the most efficient strategy possible (efficiency as defined by solution time and error probability). In almost all cases, this means that the first strategy used will be retrieval of an answer stored in LTM. The model hypothesizes that two factors influence the retrieval effort: (1) a confidence criterion and (2) a search length. The confidence criterion determines how certain the child has to be of the correctness of the answer before stating the answer. The search length determines how many times the child will attempt to retrieve a correct answer before going on to another strategy (assuming that the retrieved answer(s) is incorrect). Both of these parameters reflect the child's previous problem-solving experiences and the child's confidence in his or her ability to solve the problem correctly. The probability of an answer being retrieved on any one occurrence is a function of that answer's association strength. The higher the association, the more likely it is to be retrieved and, if the association strength is higher than the confidence interval, to be stated. If, however, a retrieval strategy does not produce a correct answer within the number of searches proscribed, the child falls back on a second but less efficient strategy.

Siegler describes this second strategy as an *elaboration of the representation*. Elaboration involves the use of some prop or prompt that might aid in retrieving the correct answer. If the problem involved the calculation of 2 + 3, an elaboration might be holding up two fingers from one hand and three from the other. Having elaborated the representation, the child would try once more to retrieve an answer. The particular answer retrieved would again be a function of its association strength.

If this second strategy doesn't produce a correct answer, then a third alternative is used—a problem-solving strategy or algorithm. This strategy could be any of the ones mentioned earlier in the chapter. Having chosen a strategy, the child uses it to come up with an answer. In all likelihood, the choice of a strategy follows the same distribution-of-associations patterns as is true of answer selection.

Perhaps the most significant aspect of Siegler's model from a developmental perspective is his argument that the model is self-modifying. Each answer statement changes the magnitude of that association between the problem and the answer, as well as those between all other associations. Similarly, the use of any particular algorithm changes both its association and those of the others. To Siegler this gradual and continuing process of change illustrates how development occurs. The fact that it might occur over short intervals in some instances and over long ones in others is of little consequence to Siegler because he believes the process to be the same in both cases. This conclusion is, of course, different from what an organismic theorist would argue. For organicists, short- and long-term changes are seen as reflecting different processes—learning and development, respectively.

One important element of Siegler's attempts to validate his distribution-of-associations model is his use of a computer simulation of the model to produce the same response patterns as were found empirically with children. Within the information processing perspective, such simulations are an important element of theory building that lend support to the argument for a functional (but not necessarily structural) equivalence between the operations of the brain and the computer.

The computer simulation involves writing a program that mimics the children's behavior by telling the computer how to respond to each problem presented to it. In particular, it instructs the computer to respond in the same sequential manner as the child (i.e., retrieval, elaboration, and algorithm), to retrieve an answer or algorithm based on its strength of association to the problem, and to modify these associations on the basis of feedback as to the correctness of the computer-generated answer. Consistent with the basic assumptions of the information processing perspective, Siegler has been able to demonstrate that a small set of simple computer instructions is sufficient to generate the same range and pattern of responses from the computer as is reflected in the behavior of the children. Of particular importance to Siegler is the fact that the simulation also demonstrated self-modifying characteristics. Specifically each problem solution resulted in a change in the association values of the problem-solution pairs and therefore the increasing probability of the correct answer being retrieved on subsequent trials.

The distribution-of-associations model does a good job of accurately predicting children's behavior given the various strategies that are available for any given task. In fact, Siegler argues that the model holds true across a wide variety of tasks. The only domain-specific components would be the particular strategies—for example, counting from one for addition problems and sounding out letters to form words for reading tasks.

Siegler's recent work has shifted toward an analysis of how children discover new strategies to add to their response repertoire. This is obviously an important issue because one characteristic of development is the use of more effective and efficient strategies to solve problems and complete tasks, both new and old.

Siegler believes that one key element in children's acquiring new problem-solving strategies is their ability to form a *goal sketch* of the problem. A goal sketch is a general sense of what an appropriate problem-solving strategy needs to look like. For addition problems the goal sketch would involve the recognition that the answer needs to be a number larger than either of the two numbers being added.[1] Notice that the sketch doesn't define how the number should be added or what the actual answer should be. It is, as the name implies, only a sketch.

By giving direction to children's problem-solving efforts, goal sketches appear to be instrumental both in children's combining elements of current strategies to form newer, more efficient ones and in their discovery of new problem-solving elements. In other words, goal sketches provide a conceptual framework in which the multiple strategies associated with a particular type of problem are tested, compared, and adopted or discarded.

Goal sketches and problem-solving strategies appear to have a sort of "leapfrog" relationship. As the distribution of associations for strategies changes with experience, goal sketches are also modified. As the goal sketch is modified, a broader conceptualization of the problem (perhaps this time including problems with zero) follows. The new sketch, in turn, allows for the generation of new strategies. Because newer sketches typically move in the directions of greater breadth and abstraction, they may help explain why, as they get older, children become better able to recognize the

---

[1] This sketch would not hold in the case that one of the numbers being added is a zero, but such problems are usually not introduced to children who are learning how to add. Older children presumably would have a goal sketch that accounted for a zero in the problem.

appropriateness of using a strategy derived from one context in a distinct but conceptually similar context. For example, goal sketches may be involved in school-age children's eventual recognition of the conceptual and procedural relationships among addition, subtraction, multiplication, and division.

Nelson's Information Processing Approach to Children's Event Knowledge

Siegler's work is concerned with children's development and use of problem-solving strategies, a type of procedural knowledge. Katherine Nelson's work (Nelson, 1986, 1993a, 1993b) has a different focus. Nelson is concerned with a type of semantic knowledge—in particular, with children's development and use of patterns of representations that allow the sequencing of events into meaningful wholes, or *scripts*.

Scripts (Schank & Abelson, 1977) are cognitive representations of ordered sequences of action that are held in LTM. They specify actors, actions, and props and are made up of slots and requirements as to what can fill a slot. The slot filler requirements allow for both specific and default entries. For example, a script concerning a trip to the supermarket would specify a sequence of permissible and nonpermissible actions, props, and actors. Buying vegetables would be a permissible action; buying a new car would not be (although it probably soon will be, given the evolution of the supermarket). Encountering a checkout clerk would be permissible; encountering a grizzly bear would not be. The checkout person could be a particular individual with a name, or it could merely be someone filling that role or slot. The script does not refer to any particular trip but rather describes a generic trip to the supermarket. Unlike a conceptually structured semantic network, which is organized in terms of some defining characteristic of the objects that make up the concept (e.g., warm-blooded animals), scripts are organized sequentially. It is permissible to pick up vegetables before going to the checkout counter; it is not permissible to do the reverse.

Scripts serve an important developmental function. By providing a means to cognitively represent a generic event sequence, scripts make it possible to both predict and plan for future encounters, to guide actions within a familiar setting, and to both interpret and participate in the narratives of others about script-related events. It is also likely that, given their generic nature, scripts play an important role in the subsequent development of the ability to process truly abstract representations.

Nelson's research has focused on four fundamental questions about the development of scripts: (1) How do children go about integrating discrete episodic representations of events occurring at a particular time and a particular place into more generalized and integrated representations of event patterns that cut across time and place? (2) How do these early generalized event representations change as children gain additional experiences? (3) What factors, both internal and external, seem to regulate the process? and (4) What are the implications of this research for a more general understanding of the course of cognitive development, especially in terms of children's organization of knowledge?

To answer these questions, Nelson has relied on three research strategies. The first involves detailed longitudinal analyses of individual children's language narratives. The goal of such an approach is to identify early evidence of the use of scripts and to trace how this use changes as children grow older. This type of methodology is similar to Siegler's microgenetic method in that, in both cases, a very detailed and extended analysis is made of an individual child's actions. The second method involves parents' reports of children's narrative language and the nature of their interactions with their children. The third method involves controlled research studies in which the relationship between specific antecedent conditions and the children's actions are studied.

Probably the most interesting and developmentally significant finding to emerge from Nelson's studies of early script development is that there is evidence of episode integration in the earliest indications of children's memory functioning. This finding is contrary to the seemingly commonsense notion that very young children would first be able to remember only discrete episodic events and only later would acquire the representation skills to integrate these episodes into scripts. In fact, Nelson's work suggests that even a single episode prompts a representation not so much of the particulars of that experience but of its pattern, that is, its script. These early scripts are, of course, very simple in structure and limited in scope. But Nelson notes that over time children develop an increasing ability to use general role slots, embed action sequences within higher-order acts, differentiate between required and optional acts, and identify both boundary events and goals. In Nelson's (1986) words:

> The attribution of a general structure does not negate the possibility of a specific representation of an episode; however, the generalization of an experience appears to be a natural product of the child's mind. There is evidence that such a generalization is formed on the basis of only one experience of an event, although factors such as what adults say about the event before, during and after it is experienced may influence the degree to which this is the case. (p. 232)

Nelson's findings indicate that both internal and external factors influence the development of scripted memory. She notes that a number of processes, apparently hard-wired into the system, operate on all forms of representation. These processes include the ability to detect patterns, form associations, and note the co-occurrences of events, as well as to order, infer, and form higher-order organizational structures. The fact that simple examples of these basic elements are reflected in the actions and subsequently the language of very young children suggests that the changes in these processes are best appreciated as quantitative in nature. That is, they are most likely already present at birth although they are in no way fully functional so early in life. As Nelson (1993b) explains it:

> Indeed, the data overwhelmingly support the conclusion that the *basic* ways of structuring, representing, and interpreting reality are continuous from early childhood into adulthood. Spontaneous recounts such as this one are highly consistent in showing that young children, in both their script recounts and their specific memory recounts, tell their stories in a sequence that accurately reflects the sequence of the experience itself, and that has the same boundaries that seem natural to adult listeners. Indeed, experimental research with children as young as 11 months indicates that mapping an accurate sequence of events is part of the human cognitive capacity at least by the first birthday. (pp. 366–367)

Nelson further notes that structural hard-wiring is a necessary but not sufficient condition for script formation. Because scripts are representations of the knowledge of the generic sequencing of events, there also needs to be experience with events. These social experiences, especially those with parents, influence the forms in which events are scripted. In particular, these social interactions determine how specific episodes are structured into meaningful representations of sequence.

Parents serve to *scaffold*, or help support, their young children's experiences. Parents scaffold their children's learning by helping to structure the context-specific forms in which events are sequenced and in the elaboration of these forms. Parents scaffold through the types of questions they ask; through the degree to which they talk about past, present, and future events; through the information they provide to fill in the gaps in children's memory; and through the narratives they offer about shared events. Nelson (1993a) summarizes the interplay of internal and external regulators of children's memory development:

> What the child brings to the social construction process is the capacity for holding in mind a sequence of events, involving self and others, temporally and causally arranged. This capacity is applied to both generic scripts and specific episodes. The social construction process then builds on these skeletal event sequences. Parents and others may talk about what is going to happen, what is happening, and what has happened in different ways. Parents seem to assume that the child will experience, is experiencing, or has experienced, the same event in the same way as the parent, and can interpret what the parent is telling her about it. (p. 17)

Sternberg's Information Processing Approach to Intelligence

Both Siegler's work and Nelson's work focus on specific aspects of cognitive competence. Siegler is interested in how children select and apply specific problem-solving strategies in mathematics and related areas. Nelson is interested in how children organize and integrate their representations of episodic events in long-term memory.

Robert Sternberg's interest is much broader. His *triarchic theory of intelligence* (Sternberg, 1984, 1985, 1988a, 1988b, 1990) offers an explanation of the cognitive mechanisms that individuals use to adapt to the everyday demands of life and, in turn, the way these everyday events further define the structure and operation of these cognitive structures and operations.

For Sternberg intelligence reflects the operation of three elements or, as he refers to them, subtheories. As Figure 7.2 shows, the *componential subtheory* concerns the cognitive mechanisms through which we process information; the *experiential subtheory* concerns the various adaptation strategies we use to adjust to novel situations; and the *contextual subtheory* concerns our ability to identify environments in which we can function effectively. For the purposes of this chapter, Sternberg's discussion of the componential subtheory, the cognitive structures and operations used to process information, is most relevant. However, it is not possible to fully understand these mechanisms without first recognizing the other two aspects of the theory, so we will start with an overview of the whole theory and then focus on the information processing aspects.

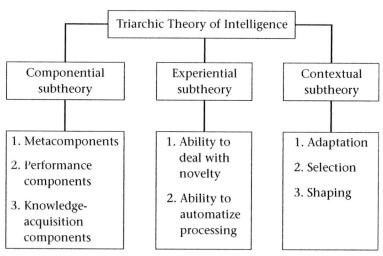

FIGURE 7.2
Sternberg's Triarchic Theory.
Source: Sternberg, 1985, p. 320.

For Sternberg intelligence is not aimless or random mental activity. Rather, it is activity purposefully directed toward the pursuit of three global goals: (1) adaptation to the environment, (2) shaping of an environment, and (3) selection of an environment. Adaptation involves efforts to establish the best fit possible between oneself and the environment. When adaptation is not successful enough, individuals choose either to select a different environment that might offer the potential of a better fit or to shape the current environment in ways that might increase the likelihood of a good fit. This behavior defines the contextual subtheory of the triarchic theory and makes clear that measures of intelligence must always be both contextually specific and purposive in nature. In Sternberg's (1985) words:

> This view of intelligence has one strong and perhaps unsettling implication for the nature of intelligence across individuals and groups. It implies that what is required for adaptation, selection, and shaping may differ across persons and groups, as well as across environments; intelligence is not quite the same thing from one person (or group) to another, nor is it exactly the same thing across environments. Nor is intelligence likely to be the same thing at different points in the life span, as what is required for contextual fit will almost certainly differ, say, both for children versus adults and for adults of one age level versus adults of another age level. The contextual aspect of intelligence, therefore, is ideographic in nature. (pp. 46–47)

Although intelligent behavior is purposive and contextually defined, Sternberg argues that not all tasks or settings are equally appropriate as potential measures of intelligence. Rather, situations requiring the use of one or both of two skills—the ability to deal with novel types of tasks and situational demands and the ability to automatize the processing of information—are most appropriate for this measurement. This concern with novelty and automatization defines the experiential subtheory of the triarchic theory. In effect, it reflects a narrowing of the contextual subtheory to those particular tasks or situations that provide for the most appropriate measure of intelligence.

Why the focus on novelty and automatization? Contextually defined novel tasks are seen as measurements of the limit of an individual's understanding and ability. As such, they are seen as measures of insightful behavior, a particularly effective adaptation strategy. Tasks or situations may be novel in terms of comprehending the nature of the task or solving the task. Sternberg argues that both provide valid measures of intelligence. Interestingly Sternberg has found (Sternberg & Clinkenbeard, 1995; Sternberg & Zhang, 1995) that gifted children's uniqueness is particularly evident on tasks requiring insightful behavior. In fact, for Sternberg, it is this aspect of intelligence that distinguishes the truly gifted from the rest of us mere mortals.

Automatization reflects our ability to deal with complex tasks, especially ones that have so many distinct components, such as reading. Attempting to deal with all of the components at a conscious level—sounding out letters, forming words, putting words together into sentences, interpreting meaning, integrating new and old information— would be overwhelming. Like the fabled centipede thinking about how to walk, we would, figuratively speaking, trip all over ourselves. Automatization allows us to focus on higher-order task elements such as meaning and lets elements such as syntax and grammar "take care of themselves."

Sternberg's third subtheory, the componential subtheory, specifies the information processing mechanisms or components underlying intelligent behavior. A *component* is defined as an elementary information process that operates on an internal representation of objects or symbols. Sternberg identifies three types of components: metacomponents, performance components, and knowledge acquisition components.

Metacomponents are "higher order, executive processes used to plan what one is going to do, to monitor it while one is doing it, and to evaluate it after it is done" (Sternberg, 1990, pp. 268–269). In other words, metacomponents involve the selection both of strategies and of mental representations for use on a particular task. Sternberg notes that effective problem solvers differ from others in terms of these dimensions, often spending as much time (if not more) comprehending the task as they do solving it. On the other hand, individuals demonstrating some sort of significant cognitive disability are most likely to demonstrate this deficit on tasks that do measure executive processing (Spear-Swerling & Sternberg, 1994; Williams & Sternberg, 1993).

Performance components are lower-order processes that execute the instructions of the metacomponents. Some performance components, such as inference, encoding, and comparison, are global in that they can be used in a variety of tasks. Other performance components, such as counting, are more specific to particular types of tasks.

Knowledge acquisition components are the processes used in gaining new information. Sternberg has identified three types of knowledge acquisition components: selective encoding, selective combination, and selective comparison.

Selective encoding involves the sifting out of relevant from irrelevant information with respect to a particular task or situation. *Selective combination* involves combining selectively encoded information in such a way as to form an integrated, plausible whole. *Selective comparison* involves relating new information to previously acquired information; it may also involve new ways of integrating two or more previously stored representations.

The three elements of the componential subtheory function in a particular relationship to one another. At the heart of the system are the metacomponents, which activate and receive feedback from the other two components. The other two components activate and receive feedback from each other indirectly via the metacomponents. For example, once the metacomponents have comprehended the task, they designate specific performance components to operate on the task. Depending on the feedback from the performance components to the metacomponents, the metacomponents might continue the process, designate new performance components to operate, and/or activate knowledge acquisition components to identify new performance strategies. The task may also demand a greater capacity than is available in the metacomponents, in which case the task may be stopped and a new task pursued.

Just as the three elements of the componential subtheory function in a particular relationship to one another, so, too, do the three subtheories themselves. Sternberg (1990) describes the relationship:

> The components of intelligence are posited to be universal to intelligence: Thus, the components that contribute to intelligent performance in one culture do so in all others as well. Moreover, the importance of dealing with novelty and automatization of information processing to intelligence are posited to be universal. But the manifestations of these components in experience are posited to be relative to cultural context. What constitutes adaptive thought or behavior in one culture is not necessarily adaptive in another culture. Moreover, thoughts and actions that would shape behavior in appropriate ways in one context might not shape them in appropriate ways in another context. Finally, the environment one selects will depend largely upon the environments available to one and the fit of one's cognitive abilities, motivations, values, and affects to the available alternative. (pp. 282–283)

Sternberg's description of the interplay of the three subtheories nicely illustrates the triarchic theory as an example of the information processing approach. The theory argues for the universality of basic information processes, recognizes the importance of both material and efficient causes, and is comfortable breaking down or reducing these processes to their individual components.

The Information Processing Approach in Perspective

The information processing approach represents a major advance over the learning theory that it has effectively replaced as the mainstream of research within the mechanistic tradition. By forging more plausible theoretical links between material and efficient causes, the information processing approach has been able to offer hypotheses to explain the complex human behaviors that had eluded learning theory. Rather than having to resort to defining material causes as the internalization of external, efficient antecedent causes, information processing's reliance on the computer metaphor has allowed theorists to identify internal, material causes independent of external, efficient causes.

Although information processing differs significantly from learning theory, it is still a perspective within the mechanistic world view and as such adheres to the same assumptions that define all mechanistic approaches. Information processing appears to make little if any distinction between learning and development—that is, between long-term and short-term behavioral change—and views change largely from a quantitative perspective. In this sense, individuals differ in terms of such factors as how much or how fast or how soon or how long rather than in terms of simply how. Finally, the perspective is reductionist; that is, complex actions are best appreciated as the integrated functioning of independent, simpler processing units.

The emergence of the information processing perspective has had, and will continue to have, profound effects on how we think of ourselves as purposive individuals and how we establish and maintain such purposive skills through our educational systems.

8

The Developmental Behavior Genetic Perspective

Views of human development are always subjects of debate. Some, such as Skinner's radical behaviorism, have been highly controversial. But none has generated the often extreme, even passionate scientific, political, and social debates as has the developmental behavior genetic perspective—debates even to the point of whether such a line of inquiry should be allowed within a democratic society.

In one sense it is a strange debate. No one is surprised to find that genetically related individuals are more like one another in terms of height or hair color than are randomly selected individuals. Yet, when the measure is some aspect of intelligence or personality, the situation changes drastically. Our psychological being is said, by some, to be more distant from or less influenced by or perhaps even independent of our genes. But is it? Is the "cause" of our personality different from the "cause" of our height? Is this the mind/body question reincarnated? To understand the furor that the developmental behavior genetic perspective generates, and to separate the rhetoric from the reality of the model, we will begin with a brief history lesson.

A Brief History Lesson

The debate that is at the heart of the developmental behavior genetic perspective involves the nature/nurture issue. For much of history, this debate was largely philosophical, reflecting the logical arguments of those who pursued such interests. So, to the English philosopher John Locke (1632–1704), a strong adherent of the nurture position, it seemed obvious that we come into the world as a tabula rasa (blank slate) and that what becomes of us reflects what gets written on the slate. But to the French philosopher Jean-Jacques Rousseau (1712–1778), an adherent of the nature position, it was just as obvious that we come into the world with inherited qualities and traits that have the potential to make us good or bad. And so it went back and forth for generations, with each side mustering what it viewed as clearly self-evident logical arguments to support its position.

The basis for the nature/nurture argument began to change in the late 1800s with the publication of Charles Darwin's (1859) theory of evolution and Gregor Mendel's (1866) research on plant breeding. Together, these two lines of inquiry established the notion that some unit of heredity passes from generation to generation, and in so doing, they also established a scientifically plausible base for the genetic argument as to why children resemble their parents.

Contemporaries of these two men, most notably Darwin's cousin Francis Galton (1822–1911), extended Darwin's arguments to include not only the anatomical elements that were of interest to Darwin but behavioral ones as well. In effect, Galton argued, we acquire not only such physical features as hair and eye color from previous generations but also all of the mental and psychological qualities that lead some to positions of eminence and others to positions not so lofty. This extension of evolutionary theory came to be known as *social Darwinism*. For Galton and many of his contemporaries, it was an easy leap of logic to extend their notions from individuals to nations. Thus, just as some people were more naturally fit than others, so, too, were some nations. Such notions served as one rationale to justify the colonialism pursued so actively by England and other European nations in the 19th or 20th centuries. In the United States social Darwinism served as the rationale by which many then reputable psychologists advocated the passage of restrictive immigration policies during the late 19th and early 20th centuries (Pastore, 1984).

This line of reasoning and social policy, often referred to as the Eugenics Movement, remained popular through the 1920s and 1930s. It was the counterpoint to Watson's behaviorism. But the movement quickly lost its momentum and its scientific appeal with the rise of the Nazis in the 1930s. The Nazi's pseudoscientific justifications for the superiority of some groups over others, the passage of laws in Germany based on such nonsense, and finally the Holocaust itself led just about any one who had an interest in the study of the genetics of behavior to keep a very low profile indeed (Mann, 1994).

Following World War II and the discovery of the scope of Nazi atrocities under the guise of genetic superiority, the focus of the nature/nurture debate moved in two different directions. The first was a call to move beyond the debate by studying how heredity and environment work together or interact, rather than focusing on how much each independently contributes to behavior (Anastasi, 1958). The second, more political and social in orientation, seemed simply to deny the role of genetics. This trend was reflected in the large-scale social programs begun in the 1960s and designed to end poverty, discrimination, and other causes of human oppression in our society. These attempts at social engineering reflected a strong belief in the power of the environment to redress past circumstances and injustices. This rationale led to the establishment of Project Head Start and the Office of Economic Opportunity, among other initiatives, and was clearly reflected in the slogans—the War on Poverty, the Great Society—that identified the movement.

But the nature/nurture debate did not end here. In recent decades there has been a renewed interest in defining the distinct role that heredity plays in the expression of behavior and behavioral change. This resurgence reflected three factors. The first was the renewal of the debate as to the power of large-scale social intervention projects to significantly alter the lives of the least fortunate in our society (Gould, 1996; Jencks,

1972; Jensen, 1969; Kozol, 1991; Schorr, 1988). The fact that we have not yet won the war on poverty has raised the question in many minds as to whether such a war is winnable, at least through the mechanism of large-scale social interventions. The second factor prompting this renewed interest in the debate has been the amazing discoveries being made in the fields of molecular genetics and developmental biology—from understanding the nature of DNA itself (Crick, 1981; Watson, 1968) to pinpointing its role in the development and regulation of specific biological structures and functions (Edelman, 1988; Jacob & Monod, 1961). The third factor, and the focus of this chapter, has been a renewed interest in the original nature/nurture question—namely, in identifying the role that genetics and environment each play in defining specific psychological characteristics. This third factor is the one addressed by a developmental behavior genetic perspective (Plomin, 1986, 1993; Plomin & Daniels, 1987; Scarr, 1992, 1993; Scarr & McCartney, 1983).

Basic Assumptions
of a Developmental Behavior Genetic Perspective

As was true for the information processing perspective, there is no one theorist who defines the developmental behavior genetic perspective. Rather, a group of individuals whose work, sometimes published independently and sometimes in collaboration, can serve as the source from which to abstract a set of basic assumptions.

The theoretical arguments of the developmental behavior genetic perspective rest on two points, both of which are consistent with the defining features of a mechanistic world view. The first is that method and theory are independent. Method simply documents what is "really out there," and theory provides a matrix in which to connect the discrete observations. The second point is that any measurable phenomenon has one or more causes, each acting independently on that phenomenon.

It is important to recognize that, for both organismic and contextualist theorists, these two points are seen not as givens but as assumptions. For organicists and contextualists, given the deductive nature of their respective theory building, method follows from theory. Therefore what is found is often a function of how it is sought. But for mechanists such as the behavior geneticists, because method and theory are seen as independent of each other, what is found is seen as a reflection not of how it is sought but of what there is to be found. And for behavior geneticists what is to be found is the degree to which behavior is a function of genetics and the degree to which it is a function of the environment.

Why do these issues of the relationship of method and theory and the independence of antecedents make such a difference, particularly with respect to the developmental behavior genetic perspective? They make a difference because of the highly charged subject matter of developmental behavior genetics. Asking questions about the relative influence of heredity and environment on a characteristic such as intelligence in a society that continues to debate what "equality" really means is, to say the least, controversial. If, in asking such questions, the possibility exists that the answers we get have as much, if not more, to do with the way the questions are asked as they do with the answers to be found, then we have a very relevant issue indeed.

So how do developmental behavior geneticists ask their questions? Consistent with a mechanistic world view, they study behavior and behavior change by partitioning *variance*—that is, by teasing apart the different independent variables (both efficient and material) that are believed to be influencing the behavior of interest. Variance is simply the range or spread of scores that would be obtained from a sample of individuals on any type of behavioral measure. Developmental behavior geneticists are primarily interested in determining, from an evolutionary perspective, the relative influence of heredity and environment (i.e., how much variance each accounts for) in the distribution of scores within a population on what are viewed as stable, polygenetic psychological traits. This interest is specific both to any one age period and to changes in the heredity/environment ratio across the life span. Let us address each of these points in turn.

Focus on an Evolutionary Perspective

Developmental behavior geneticists are interested in the variability of psychological traits within a population and the way this distribution changes across generations. They have taken an evolutionary perspective as a way to understand this intergenerational process. An evolutionary perspective emphasizes two basic concepts—genetic variation and natural selection (Scarr, 1993).

> Selection acts at the level of individual phenotypes (not genes), who more or less contribute to the next generation, and thereby *indirectly* affect gene distributions. If there were no genetic variation, there could be no evolution. Evolutionary theory's central principle is that gene frequencies in breeding populations change from generation to generation because environments differentially affect individuals' reproductive success. The next generation more closely resembles the successful breeders and nurturers of the preceding generation, because their genes are more frequent in the offspring generation. Generational changes in the gene distribution lead to changes in behavioral phenotype distributions across species histories. . . . Variation in behavioral development depends, then, on genotype distributions, environmental opportunities, and the timing of experience. (Scarr, 1993, p. 1334)

From this quote it might seem as if developmental behavior geneticists' emphasis on heredity is inappropriate. Because variance in behavioral development depends as much on environmental opportunities as it does on genotype distributions, one might argue that we should concern ourselves less with genes and more with environmental opportunities. This argument is certainly logical, but developmental behavior geneticists add an additional factor to the mix that, from their perspective, places a significant damper on this environmental optimism. The additional factor is the concept of the *average expectable environment*.

Average expectable environment is a threshold concept. It reflects the fact that, for there to be sufficient variability to ensure the survival of the species (i.e., intergenerational continuity), there must at least be a level of the environment that is "normal" for that species. Normal in this sense means that the environment provides enough support to ensure sufficient variability so as to maintain reproductive viability. Environments that are below normal in this sense restrict genetic variability and therefore restrict the reproductive viability of the species. To take a clearly extreme example, an environment without oxygen would, to say the least, reduce the phenotypic variability within the population (we would all be dead) and therefore would certainly compromise our reproductive viability (there wouldn't be any).

The concept of average expectable environment provides an additional rationale for environmental intervention in situations in which the environment is seen as less than average. In this sense developmental behavior geneticists share a call to action with other, more environmentally oriented, mechanists (and organicists and contextualists, for that matter). It is on the other side of the threshold that the developmental behavior geneticists part company with the environmentalists.

Efforts to improve the quality of the environment beyond or above the average expectable level are seen as having little if any significance. What have been described as "good-enough parents" are just that—good enough to ensure sufficient variability in the population so as to maintain reproductive viability and therefore species evolutionary adaptiveness (Goldsmith, 1993, 1994; Plomin, 1986, 1993; Rowe, 1994; Scarr, 1992, 1993; Scarr & Ricciuti, 1991). Developmental behavior geneticists see this notion as a positive because, they argue, it relieves parents of the need to try to be superparents. As Scarr (1992) puts it, "Children's outcomes do not depend on whether parents take children to the ball game or to a museum so much as they depend on genetic transmission, on plentiful opportunities, on having a good enough environment that supports children's development to become themselves" (p. 15).

Suffice it to say for now that the concept of the good-enough parent does not sit well with developmentalists from other perspectives for two reasons (Baumrind, 1993; Jackson, 1993). First, they are concerned that the concept of the good-enough parent could be used as a rationale by those who oppose environmental intervention programs for not meeting the needs of low-income families. These individuals might argue that even in these families the parenting is good enough to ensure the viability of the species (Fraser, 1995; Herrnstein, 1994). Second, they are concerned that the concept of the good-enough parent fails to recognize the important contributions that different parenting strategies make to children's welfare, even when the family setting is above the threshold.

With respect to the first issue, these critics raise a legitimate concern, because genetic arguments are often made by opponents of social intervention programs. With respect to the second, the critics' argument is somewhat misdirected, because Scarr and her colleagues' models are only addressing issues of intergenerational reproductive viability, not the more immediate parent-and-child concerns that are the source of most parents' hopes, fears, and efforts, as well as the interest of many developmentalists.

This distinction between an interest in intergenerational reproductive viability and more immediate concerns is both important and often misunderstood. Developmental behavior geneticists take a very long-range, evolutionary view, longer than most other developmentalists. They are not saying that parents and teachers, and everyone else for that matter, don't make a difference. Obviously they do. But the differences that parents, teachers, and everyone else do make may not be very relevant in explaining the variability that is of interest to behavior geneticists. Think of it this way: It will make a great deal of difference to an adult's life if she spends her adult years as a physician or a stockbroker. It will almost certainly make a difference in terms of her parenting, her social relationships, and perhaps even the chosen professions of her children. But it may not make any difference in terms of the long-term reproductive viability of our species. Being a physician or a stockbroker would seem to be equally effective means through which to play one's part in preserving the species. It should not then be very surprising that the behavior geneticists place so much emphasis on the role of genetics. At their evolutionary level of analysis, they see genes as the relevant explanation of variability.

The more intriguing question, then, involves what happens at the interface of these two levels of analysis. If they aren't completely independent of each other, then maybe in some way, to some degree, generations of physicians just might make the world a different place than generations of stockbrokers. And if this is the case, then what does this imply about social policy? In particular, what does it suggest about the ways in which we ensure our future. Rowe (1994) offers an interesting take on this question:

> Understanding that for most individuals IQ score does represent mainly genetic differences, with a pound of unshared environment and several ounces of measurement error, does not mean that IQ tests should necessarily be used either in the selection of individuals for jobs or in the placement of children in special classes for the educationally retarded. Such decisions must reflect our values and goals as a society. Nonetheless, any reasonable choice of policy alternatives must acknowledge that ignoring IQ differences has potential costs for economic productivity, as mentioned earlier, and that variation in rearing has limited effects. Let us not, as social scientists, sell the "snake oil" of unrealistic expectations for changing educational performance merely by placing children in schools with Olympic-sized swimming pools and with a cadre of well-educated teachers. Nature develops via nurture, but we must be modest about our control over children's fates while making our best efforts to secure their futures. (p. 127)

A Focus on Polygenetic Inheritance

Developmental behavior geneticists are primarily interested in those behavioral phenotypes that are *polygenetic* in origin—that is, that are caused by the combined influence of many different genes. This places the approach in contrast to *molecular genetics*, which is more typically interested in the actions of individual genes on either some physical or physiological outcome.

A focus on the cumulative impact of many individual genes allows developmental behavior geneticists to use statistical techniques to partition variance into the different factors identified by their model as potentially influencing the behavioral phenotype. The application of statistical techniques to the study of genetic effects is possible because, even though any single gene demonstrates little variability in its expression, the impact of several genes considered simultaneously disproportionately increases the number of potential outcomes or phenotypes. The more outcomes, the greater the potential variability. And the greater the potential variability, the more appropriate the use of statistical measures to test for the causes of that variability (McClearn, 1993; McClearn, Plomin, Gora-Mazlak, & Crabbe, 1991; Plomin, 1986; Plomin, Owen, & McGuffin, 1994).

Not only is the focus of the developmental behavior geneticists restricted to polygenetic influences, but it is further restricted in terms of which polygenetic influences are studied and which behavioral phenotypes are investigated. McClearn (1993) notes that the model

applies to those genes that contribute to individual differences among individuals within a species, not those that contribute to differences between species. There are undoubtedly many genes that all human beings have in common in an invariant allelic state. A subset of these will also be shared with other primates, and a subset of those with other mammals, and so on. Those genes for which allelic genes are compatible with life provide the genetic base for individuality. Estimates of the number of these segregating genes in human beings typically range from 50,000 to 100,000. (p. 35)

Of these segregating genes, developmental behavior geneticists are only interested in those that affect stable behavioral traits. Rowe (1994) describes traits as the "enduring themes" of our lives. They are the foundation from which specific behaviors emerge. The specific behaviors may change over time and across place, but the presumption is, for example, that the person who scores high on a test of intelligence will always exhibit behaviors that are distinct from someone who scores low on the test. What these actual behaviors may be with respect to a comparison of 5-year-olds will certainly be different from those appropriate to a comparison of 50-year-olds, but the basis for the expression of the trait of intelligence is said, by the developmental behavior geneticists, to remain constant. The smart 5-year-old will also be the smart 50-year-old. In addition to intelligence (Scarr, 1991; Scarr & McCartney, 1983; Scarr & Weinberg, 1994), other traits of interest to developmental behavior geneticists include some forms of psychopathology (Gottesman, 1993; McGuffin & Katz, 1993) and some measures of personality—in particular, measures of extroversion, agreeableness, conscientiousness, emotional stability, and intellectual openness (Rowe, 1994).

A Focus on Differentiating Genetic and Environmental Influence

The ultimate concern of the developmental behavior geneticists is how this intergenerational, polygenetic process is reflected in the behavioral phenotypes of individuals. Consistent with mechanism's assumption of the independence of causal events, developmental behavior geneticists view this behavioral phenotype as an additive function of the influence of heredity and the influence of environment. As such, the equation would read, "Behavioral phenotypic variance = Percent of variance accounted for by genetics + Percent of variance accounted for by the environment."

From this relationship, it should be clear why solving for the influence of heredity or environment within a mechanistic world view is done by arithmetically rearranging the terms and why something that leads to a change in the degree to which either heredity or environment contributes to any particular behavioral phenotype therefore must change the relative contribution of the other factor as well.

This second point is an important one because it implies that any variability estimates must always be restricted to the populations from which they are drawn. Such estimates are not universal statements. Consider this example: Five hundred years ago, probably most if not all of the variability explaining visual acuity was genetic. In other words, you either inherited good eyesight or you didn't. Today, this statement is no longer true. The availability of prescription eyeglasses means that your visual acuity is as much a reflection of an environmental variable—glasses—as it is a genetic one. The glasses don't change your eyes; they change your eyesight. As was the case 500 years ago, your poor eyesight will still get passed on to the next generation. But what is not the case any more is that you will be at a distinct disadvantage in hunting for your supper.

Developmental behavior geneticists further divide both genetic and environmental variance into two distinct categories, add two more terms relating to the relationship between the two, and, for good measure, also add an error term to the equation.

Genetic variance is further partitioned into additive and nonadditive components. The distinction reflects how different forms or alleles of a gene at a particular site or locus on a chromosome interact. *Additive genetic variance* is seen as linear. Consider a gene that can have three genotypes—AA, Aa, or aa. In a quantitative sense assume that large "A" carries a value of 1 and small "a" carries a value of 0. As such, the three phenotypes possible are 2 for genotype AA, 1 for genotype Aa, and 0 for genotype aa. The relationship is linear. That is, there is a one-to-one correspondence between the genotype and the behavioral characteristic it regulates. This same linear logic is used in the consideration of the phenotypic expression of polygenetic traits.

Nonadditive genetic variance has a nonlinear relationship to the phenotype. It takes one of two forms. *Dominance* is the one we are most familiar with. In the preceding example, if large "A" is dominant over small "a," then even though genotypes AA and Aa would have different quantitative values, they would both express the same phenotype. In other words, for this example, assuming genetic dominance, there would still be three distinct genotypes (AA, Aa, aa) but now only two distinct phenotypes.

The other nonadditive cause of genetic variance is *epistasis*. Epistasis refers to the fact that the phenotypic expression of a particular gene may be influenced by the presence or absence of a particular allelic form of a different gene or genes at different loci on the same chromosome.

Environmental variance can be partitioned into shared and nonshared variance. *Shared environmental variance* refers to those aspects of the environment that are seen as influencing each person in that environment to the same degree. Shared environmental variance usually is described with reference to situations, experiences, or people that members of a family have in common. Because these elements are common to all members of the family, their impact on phenotypic variance is seen as equal for all family members. *Nonshared environmental variance* is the other component of environmental variance. It represents all the events, situations, and people that are experienced in a unique fashion by each member of a family. Shared environmental variance makes family members more like one another; nonshared environmental variance makes them less similar.

In addition to the further partitioning of heredity and environment, developmental behavior geneticists also talk about gene-environment correlations and about gene-environment interactions.

Gene-environment correlations reflect the fact that certain genotypes are more likely to be found in particular environments than others. Therefore, knowing a person's genotypes reduces, to some degree, the uncertainty about the particular environment that person occupies. A child's demonstrated musical talent, for example, might be seen as (1) a reflection of having inherited a set of genes from the parents that would influence musical ability and (2) a reflection of the fact that this child is more likely than other children to grow up in an environment rich in music. In effect, the parents have given this child two advantages—a set of genes fostering musical ability and a set of environmental circumstances fostering musical ability. A correlation therefore exists between the genetic component and the environmental component.

Gene-environment correlations are almost always positive. That is, both the genetic influence and the environmental influence work in the same direction. In this example, both serve to enhance the child's musical ability. Although it is possible to consider a negative gene-environment correlation, the evidence is that such events are extremely rare.

Gene-environment interactions also presume a relationship between genetics and environment, but the form of the relationship is specific to the particular genetic and environmental elements involved in the interaction. The influence of the genetic component only acquires meaning in the presence of a particular environmental circumstance, and vice versa. Gene-environment interactions are a highly controversial topic within developmental behavior genetics (Wahlsten, 1990, and replies). Those working with human populations rarely report such interactions (Plomin & Daniels, 1987; Plomin, Owens, & McGuffin, 1994); those working with animal populations are much more likely to report them (Gottlieb, 1995). This difference is often discussed in terms of both the types of research that are possible with each population and the particular statistics one uses to search for gene-environment interactions.

The last element in the full equation is *error variance,* the "everything else" term in the equation. It is seen as accounting for all other sources of variance in the distribution. This additional variance might be due to other unknown factors and to imperfect experimental controls or methods of data collection.

Given all these additional factors, the full developmental behavior genetic equation for partitioning genetic and environmental variables now looks like this:

$$V_{bp} = V_{ga} + V_{gna} + V_{es} + V_{ens} + V_{gecorr} + V_{geint} + V_{err}$$

where V_{bp} is the variance in the behavioral phenotypes in population, V_{ga} is additive genetic variance, V_{gna} is nonadditive genetic variance, V_{es} is shared environmental variance, V_{ens} is nonshared environmental variance, V_{gecorr} is the variance attributable to the correlation between genetics and environment, V_{geint} is the variance attributable to the interaction of genetics and environment, and V_{err} is error variance.

Ideally, consistent with the assumptions of the mechanistic model, research designs would make it possible to test for the influence of each of these variables independent of the others. This is not practical in developmental behavior genetic research or in any other approach within the mechanistic perspective.

In the case of developmental behavior genetics, it is difficult, given our knowledge of genetics, to differentiate additive and nonadditive genetic effects. Behavior geneticists argue that this is not as much of a problem as it might seem because, at least for nonadditive genetic effects due to dominance, the direction of effects would be the same as for additive genetic effect (Plomin, McClearn, Smith, Vignetti, Chorney, et al., 1994; Plomin, Owens, et al., 1994). However, that still leaves open the question of epistatic nonadditive genetic effects.

The model is able to differentiate between shared and nonshared environmental effects, but more environmentally oriented developmentalists argue that the behavior geneticists' conception of the environment leads to a serious underestimation of its impact on development (Wachs, 1983, 1992, 1993). Finally, there is the question of gene-environment interactions. There continues to be a significant debate as to the frequency of such interactions in human populations. The fact that such interactions are frequently reported in the animal behavior genetic literature (see below) only adds to the debate.

These methodological and statistical limitations are important, but they do not—and should not—stop research. As any empirically oriented developmentalist, from any perspective, will note, it is only through research that our models become more comprehensive, sophisticated, and accurate. The next section discusses the two primary research strategies used by developmental behavior geneticists.

Methods of Data Collection and Analysis

Developmental behavior geneticists search for evidence of genetic contributions to variability in behavioral phenotypes using both animal and human populations. For obvious reasons, the particular strategies used for data collection and analysis differ for each population.

Animal Research Methods

Studies using animal populations focus on selective breeding experiments. Successive generations for any particular species are crossbred and inbred so that each succeeding generation is more likely to demonstrate a particular skill or a particular level of a skill. After a sufficient number of inbred generations, the resulting population is virtually genetically homogeneous. Given the additive assumptions of the mechanistic world view, comparing two distinct homogeneous populations on a common task is seen, within the model, as an unambiguous test for the influence of genetics on the variability of the behavioral phenotype of interest. Conversely a comparison of two different environments on two subsamples of an identical genetic strain is seen, within the model, as an unambiguous test of the influence of the environment on the variability of the behavioral phenotype in question.

Because animal studies allow for rigorous experimental control, analysis of variance–type statistics are used to test the hypotheses of genetic and/or environmental influence. Furthermore, as already noted, because animal studies can use more extreme breeding, rearing, and testing conditions, gene-environment interactions are more likely to be reported than is the case with human studies. Reports of these interactions are sometimes used by more environmentally oriented developmentalists (Chiszar & Gollin, 1990; Hirsch, 1990; Scott, 1987; Wahlsten, 1990) to call into question those human studies that rarely report interactions. The human researchers respond by arguing that these animal interactions exist only because those studies go way beyond the borders of average expectable environments and therefore have little value in terms of understanding the role of genetics in maintaining the evolutionary viability of a species (Crow, 1990; Plomin, 1990).

Human Research Methods

Because the ethics of human behavioral genetic research do not allow for selective breeding or deliberate exposure to extreme environmental circumstances, behavior geneticists must rely on comparisons between genetically different individuals in normally existing environments. Because of these methodological restrictions, data analysis of human studies usually involves some form of correlational analysis.

Like analysis of variance techniques, correlational analysis also looks for the probability of particular patterns of correlation occurring by chance. Both approaches allow for complex comparisons and the partitioning of variance. The major difference between the two approaches is that, because analysis of variance techniques are based on random assignment to treatment groups and highly controlled experimental procedures, it is theoretically possible to make causal arguments based on the outcome of the data analysis. Correlational studies do not allow for such controls, so these conclusions are limited to statements about relationship rather than statements about cause and effect. Nevertheless, the frequently repeated patterns of association found by developmental behavior geneticists working with human populations often lead them, at least implicitly, to argue that these correlations do, in fact, reflect the role that genetics and/or environment play in causing the variability in the behavioral phenotype of interest.

Human behavior genetic studies typically use one of two research strategies. The first method involves comparisons between individuals of different degrees of genetic relatedness or kinship, particularly between *monozygotic (MZ)* and *dizygotic (DZ)* twins; the second involves comparisons of adopted and biological children in the same family. It is worthwhile to examine both the methodologies and representative findings of the two approaches because this is the information that serves as the base for developmental behavior geneticists' theoretical arguments.

KINSHIP STUDIES   Kinship studies are based on the fact that individuals differing in degree of family relatedness also differ in degree of genetic similarity. The finding of a correlation between relatives (compared to nonrelatives) on some behavioral measure, when all other factors are statistically controlled, suggests a genetic influence. And the finding of a greater correlation between close, when compared to distant, relatives is seen as stronger evidence yet for a genetic contribution to the variability of the behavioral phenotype of interest.

Most kinship studies have compared MZ and DZ twins. MZ twins are genetically identical and are, on average, twice as similar genetically as DZ twins (who are about as similar genetically as nontwin siblings). As such, if genetics is the only factor influencing the distribution of scores on a particular behavioral phenotype, the model predicts that the magnitude of the correlation coefficient will be twice as large for MZ twins as it is for DZ twins (1.0 compared to 0.5). If genetics does not influence the distribution, there will be no reason to expect a difference in the two correlation coefficients. The statistical analysis of the difference between these two coefficients (MZ compared to DZ) is one measure of "h^2" or *heritability.* Coefficients in between these two extremes suggest the influence of other factors in addition to genetics, and the task then becomes determining how much variance each of these factors accounts for in the distribution.

A study by Plomin and his colleagues (Plomin, Reiss, Hetherington, & Howe, 1994) on genetic contributions to measures of the family environment is a good illustration of the use of kinship as a measure of heritability. Plomin was interested in determining how much variability genetics accounts for in measures of family interaction styles. His sample consisted of both MZ and DZ twins, nontwin sibling pairs in nondivorced families, and siblings from stepparent families. The stepparent group represented an additional way to measure genetic variability, because half-siblings would, on average, be expected to share only 25% of their genes compared to 50% for full siblings and DZ twins and 100% for MZ twins. The siblings were all in their teens. The goal of the study was to assess the genetic influence on three aspects of parent-child interaction—positivity, negativity, and control. Plomin defined *positivity* as a complex domain that includes warmth, support, empathy, rapport, and the degree of mutual involvement in enjoyable activities. He defined *negativity* as the frequency and intensity of disputes in a relationship, as well as feelings of anger. *Control* referred to a measure of the degree to which parents either monitored or at least were aware of their children's positive and negative activities. To measure these dimensions, the researchers had the parents and children complete a variety of questionnaires designed to assess the nature of the parent-child and the sibling-sibling interactions.

The data analysis focused on the degree of similarity between siblings in their responses. If genetics plays a factor in these reports, we would expect that the correlations between ratings (i.e., their degree of similarity) would be highest for the MZ twins, next highest for the DZ twins and full siblings and then for the half-siblings, and finally lowest for genetically unrelated individuals. Given the magnitude of the study, a full discussion of the results is beyond our means. In general, however, the closer the degree of genetic relatedness, the more similar the reporting of the perception of the parent-child relationship.

In interpreting his findings, Plomin argues that the results do not imply genetic determinism so much as they do genetic influence. The distinction involves how much of the variance is accounted for by measures of genetic variability. Plomin sees this genetic influence as reflecting one of two possibilities. In the first case, the correlation patterns could reflect the fact that the more similar two individuals are genetically, the more they tend to act alike, and therefore the more likely their parents are to treat them alike. And the more likely the parents are to treat them alike, the more likely the children are to see themselves as being treated similarly by the parents. A second possibility is that there may simply be a greater similarity in the perceptions of MZ as compared to DZ twins. In this case, the actual parental behavior need not be more similar; only the children's perception of that behavior need be more similar. Both explanations account for the correlation patterns found, and as is true of most topics, more research is needed to determine which of these two explanations is the more plausible.

Whatever the outcome, both interpretations place strong emphasis on the role that nonshared environmental variance plays in determining behavioral variability. For developmental behavior geneticists, evidence for nonshared environment variability is important because such variability is seen as more a reflection of genetics than of environment. This is the case because, if it turns out that there is a great deal of variability among people sharing the same environment, then the explanation for this variability can't, the argument goes, be the environment because it's the same for everybody. If the environment can't explain the variability, what's left? For the developmental behavior geneticist, what is left is the variability attributable to genetics.

One particularly intriguing finding from kinship studies (McCartney, Harris, & Bernieri, 1990; Plomin, 1986; Plomin, Emde, Braungart, Campos, & Corley, 1993; Plomin, Pedersen, Lichtenstein, & McClearn, 1994) is the suggestion that heritability estimates may, for some measures, actually increase as kinship pairs become older. This hypothesis is based on the assumption that, because shared environmental variance decreases as siblings leave their families of origin and establish independent lives, nonshared environmental variance (which may be correlated with genetic variance) increases. We will discuss the implications of this possible developmental pattern later in the chapter. For now, simply keep in mind the notion that heritability estimates may have a developmental dimension.

ADOPTION STUDIES   Kinship studies of heritability have an inherent flaw. Not only do family members such as twins, other siblings, and parent-child pairs share genes, they also share environments. Within the model the adoption design is seen as eliminating this confounding because genes and environment are now distinct. In the "ideal" adoption design, MZ twins who have been separated at birth and placed in different adopted homes are later found and tested. Because they have been living in different environments, any resemblances between them (i.e., any correlations of their scores on measures of behavioral phenotypes) are presumed to be due to their shared genotype. By the same token, given the additive assumptions of the model, genetically unrelated individuals who have been adopted into the same family will resemble one another to the extent that the environment has an influence on the behavioral phenotypes being measured. This design becomes even more powerful when one or both biological parents of the children placed for adoption at birth are identified and located. In this case the difference in the magnitude of the correlations between the "child–adopted parent" and the "child–biological parent" is seen as a clear test of the relative influence of heredity and environment.

Although the logic of the adoption design is compelling, like all research designs from all perspectives, it is not without its problems—problems that adherents of the model see as qualifiers and that opponents of the model see as nullifiers. The two major issues concern the degree of similarity of adoptive placements and the likelihood of sample bias in the later location of children placed for adoption at birth.

If the likelihood of a child being placed for adoption in any one home is as likely as in any other, then the environments are uncorrelated, and any similarity between the children can be claimed as genetic in origin. But one home is not as good as another. Adoption agencies are picky, and they are looking for what they consider to be good homes. This may be especially true when they are forced to separate twins and place them in different settings. As such, these adoptive homes share certain qualities, and so the environment must also be taken into consideration if similarities are found between, for example, MZ twins separated at birth and placed in two different homes. Such placement confounding does not negate the value of the adoption design, but it does, as developmental behavior geneticists acknowledge, qualify it.

The potential sample bias involved in locating twins separated at birth offers another qualifier. There is very striking evidence about the similarity between twins separated at birth and later reunited as adults (Bouchard, 1994). However, what is still an open question is how representative this sample of strikingly similar twins is to the entire population of twins separated at birth, particularly those who have not been reunited (Reiss, 1993; Rose, Kaprio, Williams, Viken, & Obremski, 1990). Again, such issues should not be seen as negating behavior genetic research so much as qualifying it—in the same tradition that all research must be seen as qualified by practical constraints.

The adoption studies of Scarr and Weinberg (Scarr & Weinberg, 1983, 1994) serve as a good illustration of the value of the adoption design to developmental behavior geneticists. The studies have been going on for over two decades and include not only comparisons between adopted and nonadopted children in the same home but also comparisons between adopted children and both their biological and adopted parents. The studies involve the testing of parents and children, both biological and adopted, on a variety of cognitive and personality "paper-and-pencil"-type assessments and then comparing the different parent-child-sibling combinations. The 1983 paper reported on two studies, one involving transracial adoption and the other white-only adoptions. The 1994 paper reports on a followup to the second sample.

In the transracial sample, two-thirds of the children were placed for adoption in the first year of life, and the remaining third after 12 months. Because many of the adopting families had adopted more than one child and because these children were from genetically unrelated families, even more elaborate comparisons were possible. The children in the transracial study ranged in age from 4 to 18 years at the time of testing, making it possible, Scarr and Weinberg argued, to gauge the cumulative impact of genetic and environmental factors on development.

Two findings are noteworthy from the studies. The first, consistent with the findings from kinship and other adoption studies (Rowe, 1994; Wadsworth, DeFries,

Fulker, & Plomin, 1995) is that the correlation coefficients for IQ were higher for genetically related ("adopted child–biological parent") than nongenetically related ("adopted child–adopting parent") pairs. Further confirming the pattern was the fact that the "adopting parent–own biological child" correlations were higher than the "adopting parent–adopted child" correlations. In fact, the two possible biological parent–child comparisons were equally high, and both were higher than the adopting parent–adopted child correlation—even though the adopted child had lived almost his or her entire life with the adopting parent.

At the same time as Scarr and Weinberg reported that the correlations reflecting the influence of genetic variability were high, they also reported what may seem a contradictory second finding. Even though the correlations were higher across genetic than environmental pairs, the actual average IQ scores of the adopted children were closer to the mean IQ score of their adopted parent than they were to the actual average IQ scores of their biological parents. That is, even though we would be better able to predict the rank order of the adopted children's scores by knowing their biological parents' rather than their adopted parents' score, we would be better able to predict the actual IQ scores from knowing the adopted parents' IQ scores.

This seeming contradiction is not a contradiction at all; rather, it reflects what correlations actually measure. Correlations measure similarities in *rank ordering*. Scarr and Weinberg's reporting of the higher correlations between biological parent–child pairs means that there was a greater similarity in the rank ordering of the IQ scores between the biological parents and their biological offspring (even if that offspring had been adopted soon after birth) than between the adopted parents and their adopted children. But a measure of rank order says little about the magnitude of the actual scores that make up the ranking. The adoptions did have a significant influence on the adopted children's IQ scores, which were considerably higher than the scores of their biological parents (and presumably their own scores if they had remained with their biological parents). The scores were still not as high as those of the adopting parents' own biological children, but the difference between the two sets of children's IQ scores was considerably less than the difference between the scores of the adopted children and their biological mothers. This is why the correlations were as they were. Rank ordering is insensitive to the size of the interval between the ranks.

Because the children in the second study were at least all in their teens at the time of the second testing, it was possible for Scarr and Weinberg to see if the correlation coefficients between biologically nonrelated siblings living in the same house had changed over time. Such a change, depending on the direction, could indicate the power of the shared environment. They report that, by the late teen years, the correlations on both aptitude and achievement tests for the biological siblings were "modest but statistically different from zero" and that the nonbiological siblings correlations were "virtually unrelated."

They interpret this finding as reflecting the relatively small and time-limited impact of variance due to the shared environment. The shared environment seems to have an influence on the variability of behavioral phenotypes as long as individuals remain in that environment. However, once they become old enough to leave home and establish their own lives, the influence of the shared environment wanes, suggesting, say Scarr and Weinberg, that the shared environment has no permanent impact

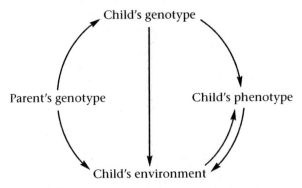

FIGURE 8.1
Scarr and McCartney's Gene-Environment Effects
Model.

on one's developmental status. As shared environmental variance decreases, non-shared environmental variance increases. And, as nonshared environmental variance increases, so, too, does the magnitude of the gene-environment correlation coefficient. And as the gene-environment correlation coefficient increases, so, too, Scarr and Weinberg argue, does the presumed role of genetics in defining the life course.

The data obtained through kinship and adoption studies has led developmental behavior geneticists to make a number of theoretical generalizations about the relative influence of heredity and environment across the life span on the variability of behavioral phenotypes within populations. The next section reviews these theoretical statements.

Developmental Behavior Genetic Theory

There is no such thing as developmental behavior genetic theory per se. This is probably due to the relative newness of this most recent revival of interest in behavior genetics. As is true for the information processors, no one voice has yet emerged to speak for the perspective. Nevertheless, the work of Sandra Scarr (Scarr, 1991, 1992, 1993; Scarr & McCartney, 1983; Scarr & Ricciuti, 1991; Scarr & Weinberg, 1983, 1994) and of Robert Plomin (Plomin, 1986, 1990, 1993, 1994; Plomin & Daniels, 1987; Plomin & DeFries, 1983; Plomin, Owen, et al., 1994; Plomin, Pedersen, et al., 1994; Plomin, Reiss, et al., 1994) probably best reflect the current theoretical thinking within the developmental behavior genetic perspective.

Scarr's Theoretical Perspective

Scarr's theoretical argument is that genes drive experience and, as such, development. It was originally proposed in a 1983 paper, co-authored with Kathleen McCartney, and has been elaborated in subsequent publications. The model is presented in Figure 8.1.

The direction of the arrows indicates the directions of influence of both environmental and genetic components. What is significant to note is how genes, both directly and indirectly, are depicted as having a larger influence on the child's development than does the environment.

The model attempts to answer two questions: (1) How do genotypes and environment combine to produce human development? and (2) How do genetic and environmental differences combine to produce variation in development? As Scarr and McCartney (1983) note:

> A theory of behavioral development must explain the origin of new psychological structures. Because there is no evidence that new adaptations can arise out of the environment without maturational changes in the organism, genotype must be the source of new structures. . . . We propose that development is indeed the result of nature *and* nurture but that genes drive experience. Genes are components in a system that organizes the organism's experience to the world. The organism's abilities to experience the world change with development and are individually variable. A good theory of the environment can only be one in which experience is guided by genotypes that both push and restrain experiences. (pp. 424–425)

Scarr and McCartney base this argument on what they see as clear logical and empirical grounds. The logical claim is that, because genotype precedes environment, environment must be responsive to it rather than vice versa. Empirically they note the consistently high correlations found between scores on virtually any measure of developmental status and degree of genetic relatedness.

Scarr and McCartney see genes pushing the nonshared rather than the shared environment—that is, the environment actually experienced or grasped by the individual rather than the environment to which the individual is exposed. The push is reflected in the pattern of gene-environment correlations across the life span. They argue that this correlation takes three distinct forms—passive, evocative, and active— with each exerting its maximum impact at a different point in the life span.

Passive gene-environment effects are the ones best documented and the ones most common early in the life span. Passive gene-environment correlations occur because parents typically provide a rearing environment that is correlated with the genotype of the child. As noted previously, the parent who is seen as passing along a set of genes favoring musical ability is also the parent most likely to provide an environment supporting the development of musical ability.

Evocative gene-environment effects occur because different genotypes elicit or evoke different responses from others in that child's environment. Responses to the persons shape development in ways that correlate with the child's genotype. As Scarr and McCartney (1983) note, "It is quite likely that the smiley, active babies receive more social stimulation than sober, passive infants" (p. 427).

Active gene-environment effects involve what Scarr and McCartney refer to as *niche picking*. People are seen as picking out environments in which they feel comfortable. These environments or niches feel comfortable because there is a good fit between the characteristics of the person and the characteristics of the environment. Characteristics of the person are reflections of genotype, so there is a correlation between genotype and environment. Scarr and McCartney see these active gene-environment effects as the most powerful of the three and the ones that provide the most direct expression of the genotype in experience.

Passive correlations are seen as most common during the early years because young children have relatively little intentional influence on the course of their development. Scarr argues that, as children become more intentional and, eventually, less directly influenced by their parents' actions, active gene-environment effects increase in importance. Evocative gene-environment effects are seen as constant across the life span although there are certainly changes in the characteristics of the child that evoke responses in others. Because active gene-environment effects are seen as increasing over the course of the life span and because such effects are seen as the most direct expression of the genotype, one clear prediction from the theory is that heritability coefficients should increase over the life span. The prediction has received support from longitudinal studies of middle-aged MZ and DZ twins, both reared apart and reared together (Plomin, Pedersen, et al., 1994).

Finally, for Scarr, placing a greater importance on the role of genetics in defining human experience also casts a new light on the role of the environment.

> If genotypes are the driving force behind development and the determinants of what environments are experienced, does this mean that environments themselves have no effect? Certainly environments are necessary for development and have effects on the average level of development, but they may or may not cause variations among individuals. We argue like McCall that nature has not left essential human development at the mercy of experiences that may or may not be encountered; rather, the only necessary experiences are ones that are generally available to the species. Differences in experience, per se, therefore, cannot be the major cause of variation among individuals. The major features of human development are programmed genetically and require experiences that are encountered by the vast majority of humankind in the course of living. Phenotypic variation among individuals relies on experiential differences that are determined by genetic differences rather than on differences among environmental effects that occur randomly. (Scarr & McCartney, 1983, pp. 428–429)

Plomin's Theoretical Perspective

Plomin's theoretical arguments are presented as sets of hypotheses or principles, the most detailed versions of which appear in his 1986 publication *Development, Genetics and Psychology* and his 1994 book *Genes and Experience*. In both instances, the statements are conclusions Plomin has drawn from his review of the developmental behavior genetic research. Not surprisingly, given their overlapping research efforts, his conclusions are similar to Scarr's.

His first research-based generalization is that heredity is a significant determinant of the variability in behavioral phenotypes at all ages and in most behavioral domains. Plomin (1989) explains:

> Genetic influence sometimes accounts for as much as 50% of the observed variance. The relationship between genes and behavior is remarkably strong—perhaps unparalleled in the behavioral sciences, where observed relationships between independent

and dependent variables often account for only 1% of the variance and rarely more than 10%. (p. 325)

Plomin's second generalization is that, when heritability estimates change over the life span, they increase. That is, based on both kinship and adoption studies, correlations increase as individuals age. Plomin believes that this shift is contrary to the predictions of most other developmentalists, who believe that individuals become more diverse over time because their environments become more diverse. Plomin's argument is the opposite: Environments become more diverse because individuals become more diverse.

Plomin's third generalization serves as a partial explanation for the pattern noted in the second generalization. Genetics plays an increasingly significant role in individual variability because most environmental influences are of the nonshared rather than the shared variety. As such, this variability increasingly reflects the correlation between genes and the nonshared environment. In particular, the pattern of correlation changes reflects the fact that, with age, passive gene-environment correlations are replaced with active gene-environment correlations, a conclusion identical to Scarr's.

Plomin's last generalization is perhaps the most interesting. Rather than reflecting what developmental behavior geneticists have reported, it reflects what Plomin believes they will report in the future. He predicts that specific genes will be found that affect experience. This is a significant departure from developmental behavior geneticists' present focus on polygenetic effects. He believes that the significant advances in molecular genetics will allow researchers to do away with the indirect measures of genetic influence now available through kinship and adoption studies and instead seek to identify a set of DNA markers of genes that accounts for a substantial portion of the genetic variance on measures of behavioral phenotypes. It is important to note that this claim of a one-to-one correspondence between genes and phenotypes, behavioral or otherwise, is not shared by all molecular geneticists, a point that will become clearer after reading the chapter on the developmental psychobiology perspective in Part III.

Developmental Behavior Genetics in Perspective

There is nothing particularly noteworthy or original or controversial about claiming that our genes are a factor in our development. There is nothing particularly astonishing about further claiming that this is as true in the last years of life as it is in the first years of life. It is hard to imagine how one could argue otherwise. What, then, is so controversial about the claims of the developmental behavior geneticists? As is true of most things, it depends on how one views the nature/nurture debate.

In particular, it depends on the assumptions one makes about the course of human development, about the best way to study that process, and about the most appropriate conclusions one can draw based on those studies. This is why, within the mechanistic perspective, the nature/nurture debate is largely a methodological and statistical debate concerning control groups and measurement instruments, sample sizes and selection criteria, and ways of partitioning variance. And it is why, from the organismic and contextualist perspectives, it is a debate about the basic assumptions of world views—namely, about reductionism, universality, and the independence of antecedent conditions. Put another way, the nature/nurture debate is a debate that can only exist within a mechanistic world view because only in mechanism can one argue that it is theoretically legitimate to reduce complex behaviors to sets of independent efficient and material antecedent causes.

If the debate about the role of genetics were largely an academic one, confined to error variance, control groups, and theoretical musings, probably it would not generate the intensity of debate that it does. There is something more at issue here, and that something more is the implications of the claims made by the developmental behavior geneticists. The implications speak to all of our social policies, which is why the debate is more than merely academic in tone.

The assumptions of the developmental behavior genetic model and the data generated within those assumptions force us to think about limits—in particular, limits in the degree to which we can significantly influence human behavior. If, for example, environments that have generally been thought of as offering very limited developmental opportunities are now to be thought of as "good enough" to fit into the "average expectable" category, what does that imply about the moral and empirical grounds for spending significant amounts of money on those settings?

Developmental behavior geneticists force us to think about how best to judge ourselves. Theirs is an emphasis on variance, on how people stand in relationship to one another. This is not an unimportant issue. A large part of our educational experiences has been spent determining such rankings. But, at the same time, we could be just as concerned with an individual's improvement over time as we are with that person's relative standing at any particular time. We could be just as concerned with an individual's actual skill level as we are with his or her ranking relative to others. In the final analysis the potential importance of the developmental behavior genetic perspective may depend on how we choose to view ourselves.

Part II—Summing Up

Several different theories have been presented in Part II. This is a good time to briefly review the defining characteristics of each, to see in what sense each is a reflection of a mechanistic world view, to see how each reflects the criteria for good theories presented in Chapter 1, and finally to see how each explains why we are the way we are.

We first examined two theories based on classical and operant conditioning models. In both instances the belief was that, ultimately, what were seen as the laws governing simple associations would also be able to account for more complex phenomena. In the case of learning theory, the evidence did not support the original optimism, and as a theoretical perspective, it has relatively little influence today. Its legacy has been a methodology for studying behavioral events that is perhaps the defining feature of all research within a mechanistic world view. In the case of radical behaviorism, we have an approach to the study of behavior and behavioral change that not only is still active within the research community but has established for itself a significant place within the clinical and educational communities as well. Each places primary emphasis on the study of efficient causes as the best way to ultimately understand behavior.

Bandura's early social learning theory, based as it was on Skinner's operant learning model, shared this emphasis on efficient causes. But as is true of most good theories, Bandura's evolved in the direction of the information processing models that became increasingly common explanations of behavior. In Bandura's case, his social cognitive model describes a set of both material and efficient variables that are seen as explaining how both direct and indirect learning experiences are used by individuals as they simultaneously generate new behaviors and generate internal standards for evaluating these behaviors.

Information processing models have replaced learning models in the same way that the computer has replaced the telephone as the embodiment of the machine metaphor within a mechanistic world view. Computers act on information; telephones merely convey it from one place to another. The significance of this distinction is that the adoption of the computer has allowed information processing theorists to argue that they now have an independent means by which to hypothesize the presence and action of internal, material causes of behavior. Bandura's social cognitive theory and information processing theory both represent, within the mechanistic world view, theories strongly drawing on both efficient and material causes.

Developmental behavior genetic models focus almost exclusively on material causes—to wit, genes. Behavior geneticists don't deny that efficient causes influence behavior any more than Watson denied the role of material ones. It is just that, in both cases, the questions each chose to ask placed heavy emphasis on one or the other. Behavior geneticists study what for them is the distinct role of genetics, a seemingly limiting factor on our behavior, and they do so in a society whose political values and rhetoric stress the future as limitless. This is, of course, a recipe for strong debate and argument. And it will almost certainly continue to be as long as questions of genetic differences are equated, rightly or wrongly, with attempts to demonstrate the superiority of one group over another.

Notwithstanding the significant differences that do exist among these theoretical perspectives, it is important to remember that they share a common set of fundamental assumptions about how to study and interpret behavior and behavioral change. These are all members of the mechanistic world view family of theories. They all share a belief that, ultimately, it is possible to discover the set of universal laws that regulate our actions. They all share the belief that these laws exist independent of our efforts to know them and that they are best conceptualized as a set of forces that influence how we behave. These forces, both material and efficient in nature, are seen by mechanists as the building blocks that are used to create the infinite variety and complexity of our behaviors. Finally, because it is these basic building blocks that combine and recombine in various ways over the life span to generate behavior, it is best to represent behavioral change as a quantitative rather than a qualitative process.

How do theories within the mechanistic world view reflect the criteria against which theories are typically viewed? First, all of these theories are highly *testable*. They are each designed to make specific predictions about outcomes given a knowledge about particular efficient and material antecedents.

Second, they each offer a highly *organized* and *integrated* set of empirically testable theoretical assumptions that ultimately are seen as being capable of explaining a broad range of behavioral phenomena. Much of this organization is reflected in the highly structured, highly controlled research strategies preferred by mechanists. As noted previously, it is ironic that a world view that views method and theory as independent is so much defined by a shared approach to its methodology. At the same time, it is this shared approach that allows mechanists to debate with one another the relative merits of their theoretical arguments. The centrality of method in the organization of these theories is also evident in the fact that their debates often turn more on arguments about the appropriateness of methodological and statistical procedures than they do on the appropriateness of theoretical assumptions.

Third, all of these theories are highly *generative*. They each actively search for new aspects of behavior to study, for new ways to conceptualize what we already know, and for new ways to apply this knowledge.

Finally, one of the defining characteristics of all theories within the mechanistic world view is their high level of *precision*. Perhaps because of their approach to the study of behavior, mechanists have always preferred to examine discrete pieces of behavior rather than the broader strokes more common to organicism and contextualism. This is as it should be in a world view that is inductive rather than deductive in focus. These theories share the belief that the best strategy for discovering these universal laws is to approach the task in the same way we would approach putting a puzzle together—one piece at a time.

So, what does it mean to be a developmentalist within a mechanistic world view. It means being interested in identifying the efficient and material variables that influence behavior and behavioral change over the life span—in particular, those variables that appear to have the potential to influence this change over longer rather than shorter periods of time.

We now turn in Part III to a review of four organismic perspectives. The first, the developmental psychobiological perspective, is concerned with how biological structures interact with the environment to influence developmental patterns. The second, Piaget's constructivist theory, is the single most comprehensive account we have today of how we go about making sense out of our encounters with our world. But because even a theory as comprehensive as Piaget's is an incomplete representation of the process of development, we also examine three neo-Piagetian accounts of development. Finally, we review the work of two other very well known developmental theories, Erikson's psychosocial stage theory and Freud's psychosexual theory.

PART III

The Organismic Perspective

The next four chapters review models, theories, and perspectives consistent with an organismic perspective. As you will recall, an organismic perspective uses the living organism as its metaphor (Pepper, 1961). Organicists' reference to living organisms stands in clear contrast to the mechanists' reference to the machine (Reese & Overton, 1970). Living organisms are conceptualized as active; machines, as passive. The significance of the difference is in terms of what types of causes each model emphasizes and how psychological development is portrayed. For organicists psychological activity reflects the synergistic interactions of a biological organism within a sociohistorical context. In this sense psychological activity, to the organismic theorist, is reducible neither to biological activity nor to context, but it is still influenced by each.

As is true of mechanism, organicism is a universalist perspective. Organismic theorists believe that the underlying patterns they are discovering are not, in contrast to the contextualists, specific to time and place, but rather reflect some of the underlying characteristics that define us as a species. However, in contrast to the mechanists, the particular patterns of interest to organicists are the ones that make us similar to one another rather than ones that make us different from one another. It is worth pointing out again that this distinction in focus between how we are alike and how we are different is not a contest as to which is correct. Nor, of course, should there be a contest between claims of universality and claims of situality. Each is correct; each offers a piece of the puzzle that is human development; and, ultimately, as the larger picture is beginning to emerge, each is being recognized for its contribution. Nevertheless, each world view tends to focus on one piece of this puzzle, and so direct comparisons, and even translations of concepts and findings, are difficult.

Trying to characterize a world view as broad as organicism is no easy task. The writings of one scholar, however, do come close to capturing the organismic concept that the process of development involves the formation of systematic, orderly sequences. This individual is Heinz Werner. In his *Orthogenetic Principle of Development* Werner (1957) states that "whenever development occurs it proceeds from a state of relative globality and lack of differentiation to a state of increasing differentiation, articulation and hierarchical integration" (p. 126).

Werner's orthogenetic principle offers a sketch of the process of development as seen from an organismic perspective. It suggests that the process of development is characterized by (1) a decreasing dominance of the immediate, concrete situation over the individual, (2) a decreasing influence of affective states, and (3) a greater capacity to differentiate means and ends. Werner's fully developed individual is one who exhibits a capacity for delay and planned action and an ability to actively and deliberately reflect on and exercise choice in a given situation. For Werner the successful outcome of this process is an individual who demonstrates "less of a tendency for the world to be interpreted solely in terms of one's own needs and an increasing appreciation of the needs of others and of group goals" (p. 127). Not all organismic theorists place Werner's value judgment about the outcome of the development process at the core of their work, but all do describe a process that is essentially parallel to that of Werner, a process that distinguishes the child in the world from the adult in the world.

Part III contains four chapters. The first, Chapter 9, deals with the developmental psychobiological perspective. Developmental psychobiologists come closest to attempting to fully integrate, often in a literal sense, the psychological and the biological. For these theorists any distinction between what is psychological and what is biological is arbitrary and therefore of questionable value. Like other organismic theorists

(Johnston, 1987), the developmental psychobiologists are very critical of explanatory mechanisms that dichotomize phenomena in terms of heredity and environment or learning and maturation. Given this psychobiological orientation, not surprisingly, most work in this tradition has focused on early developmental events, particularly those related to motor development. The developmental psychobiologists argue that the patterns uncovered through work on early motor development hold the promise of providing insights into other developmental domains during other developmental periods or stages. Keep in mind the arguments of the developmental behavior geneticists discussed in Chapter 8 as you read Chapter 9. In both cases the focus is on the relationship between events defined at the biological level and those defined at the psychological level. But the respective strategies for understanding this relationship are fundamentally very different. Understanding this difference will help you get a clearer picture of the underlying theoretical assumptions of each approach.

Chapter 10 focuses on Jean Piaget's developmental theory. The depth and breadth of his work was remarkable. He wrote more books than most people probably ever read, and trying to capture the flavor of such a monumental accomplishment in the space of a chapter is no easy task. Rather than touching on each of the topics Piaget and his colleagues pursued, we will focus on the cumulative impact of the interplay of a set of invariant functional processes and a sequence of stage-specific cognitive structures. The result of this interplay, according to Piaget, is the construction of increasingly more effective strategies of establishing and maintaining a dynamic equilibrium between individuals and their surroundings.

A theory as important as Piaget's certainly has its revisionists and its critics. The revisionists are those organismic theorists who, while staying within the perspective, nevertheless either fault Piaget for particular aspects of his work or attempt to extend the theory beyond Piaget's original limits. These individuals are the focus of Chapter 11. For the most part, these theorists either have raised issues with Piaget's claims of the relative uniformity of the developmental process across different developmental domains or have attempted to look more carefully at the changes that occur during the adult years with respect to Piaget's cognition structures.

In the first case the issue concerns Piaget's concept of *horizontal decalage* (Goldhaber, 1981). Decalage refers to the unevenness in development across particular developmental domains. For example, it might seem that a child's ability to recognize that the number of objects in a group is not affected by their spatial arrangement or that the amount of clay in a lump is not affected by the shape of that lump should occur at about the same age because they require the same logical processes. But the two discoveries do not, in fact, occur at the same time. Piaget recognized these asymmetries but did not assign much significance to them. The neo-Piagetians think that such decalages are important enough to warrant revision of what they see as Piaget's somewhat idealized vision of development.

In the second case the revisions are really more in the form of extensions to the theory. Piaget did not pursue the study of development beyond adolescence, and most people have the impression that he believed that the formal operational cognitive structures (the fourth of his four developmental stages), which emerge during adolescence, serve as the basis for mature thought. In fact, he did acknowledge in his later works that the development of cognitive structures is, theoretically, a never-ending process, but he didn't pursue the issue. Efforts to consider adult development from a neo-Piagetian perspective usually have focused on the ways in which the cumulative impact of adult experiences "temper" the purely logical, abstract cognitive structures that characterize formal operational thought. Put another way, these extensions of Piaget's work examine the developmental consequences of coming to recognize that what is possible is not necessarily what is probable.

A word also needs to be said about mechanistic and contextualist critiques of Piaget's theory even though these concerns will not be included in Chapter 11. For reasons that should now be clear, I believe that such "cross–world view" critiques are problematic because different world views are based on distinct and seemingly contradictory beliefs. For example, researchers working within the mechanistic world view often report that they are able to show that a child can do something much sooner than Piaget would have predicted. Such a demonstration is an important discovery, but it probably has less to say about Piaget's theory than might first appear to be the case.

The issue is, of course, one of methodology. Because the procedure used to produce the younger child's behavior is typically very different from the technique Piaget would have used with the older child, there is really no way to determine if the two seemingly identical behaviors are reflective of the same cognitive structures and mechanisms. In some cases not only the methods but even the behaviors used to measure the phenomena are different. Again, it is not a question of one being right and the other being wrong. Both researchers have documented a behavior of interest and importance, and both findings are valuable because they provide insight into why we are the way we are. But the issue is the degree to which the two findings are comparable.

Chapter 12 looks at the work of Erik Erikson and Sigmund Freud. Neither individual's work is at the forefront of developmental research today, and neither has the stature of Piaget. Both are usually relegated to that section of introductory human development texts entitled "the historical roots of human development." This is unfortunate. Although few today accept Freud's literal explanation of infant attachment or parent-child identification as valid, the figurative elements of his work nevertheless continue to guide work in many areas, especially in the areas of attachment and parent-child socialization (Emde, 1992).

Erikson's work, although often more literary than psych-ological in nature, nevertheless is one of the few truly life span conceptions available within any of the three world views. In particular, Erikson's work continues to provide guidance in the areas of adolescent and young-adult identity and intimacy and in the area of the development of wisdom during later adulthood.

One final note about the organismic models to be reviewed in Part III: These models are not in conflict with one another, as was the case with the mechanistic models discussed in Part II. The models don't always agree on the fine points, but generally they differ more on the details and the implications than on the basics. The explanation for this difference between the mechanistic and the organismic models is actually rather straightforward. Because mechanistic models allow for dichotomies such as nature and nurture, their structure allows for debates between those who favor one element of the dichotomy over the other. This is the case when comparing developmental behavior genetic theories with radical behavioral theories. But organismic models are holistic and synergistic. That is, parts have meaning only when they are in relationship to each other, so there can be no dichotomies. Because all organismic models share this basic assumption and because all agree on the parts, there can be none of the fundamental arguments characteristic of the mechanistic models.

9

The Developmental Psychobiological Perspective

Whatever else we may be, we are biological organisms. However, theories of human development have always had a difficult time trying to incorporate this fact into their accounts of our psychological existence. The reasons for this difficulty range from philosophical debates about what it means to be human to more mundane debates about academic turf. As you might imagine, the proposed solutions have ranged from one extreme to the other. At one extreme are arguments claiming that what is psychological is, in fact, only what is biological, and so psychological explanations are redundant and unnecessary. At the other extreme are arguments claiming that, in effect, we have bodies and brains but they really don't have any more to do with our behavior and thoughts than providing a place to house them.

A *developmental psychobiological perspective* offers what might be considered a middle ground. Consistent with an organismic world view, developmental psychobiological arguments do not dichotomize the biological and psychological. Rather, they see them as interdependent planes of action, each reflecting the products of the unique interaction of a biological organism within a particular level of the environment (Gottlieb, 1983).

The plan of this chapter is rather straightforward. We will first review the major assumptions of a developmental psychobiological perspective and then examine three theories within this tradition. The first two theories, those of Arnold Gesell (1948; Gesell & Ilg, 1949) and Myrtle McGraw (Dalton & Bergenn, 1995), perhaps today have more historical value than anything else. But they do provide a frame of reference in which to better appreciate the contemporary evolution of the developmental psychobiological perspective, particularly in the work of Esther Thelen (Thelen, 1989a, 1989b, 1995; Thelen & Adolp, 1992; Thelen, Kelso, & Fogel, 1987; Thelen & Smith, 1994) and her colleagues on dynamic systems theory. Thelen's work will also provide a means to consider the contributions of Nobel laureate Gerald Edelman (Edelman, 1988, 1992) to our understanding of human development. Whereas Gesell, McGraw, and Thelen focus on early motor development, Edelman is concerned both with how the brain develops before birth and with how it changes over the course of a lifetime.

Basic Assumptions
of a Developmental Psychobiological Perspective

Perhaps the most important thing to recognize about a developmental psychobiological perspective is that it makes no distinction between activities of the organism that could be considered biological and activities that could be considered psychological. For the psychobiologists what is psychological is simply the activity that occurs at one particular level or plane of action of the organism. In this sense, what we consider to be psychological phenomena are the emergent properties or consequences of the biological organism functioning within a particular context (Michel & Moore, 1995). Even though the psychological is seen as emerging out of this biological-social interaction, it can't be reduced to either. The psychological encompasses a distinct and unique level of analysis. No amount of understanding at another level will provide a full understanding of the activity at this level. The primary interest of developmental psychobiologists is how the nature of this psychological phenomena changes over time.

Planes of Action

A key element in this conception of development is the concept of distinct levels of functioning or planes of action in an organism. The concept has its modern origin in the writing of Theodore C. Schneirla (1957, 1966) and its clearest expression in the writing of Gilbert Gottlieb (1991, 1992).

Gottlieb argues that it is useful to consider an organism as existing simultaneously at a number of different levels or planes of action—from the level of the gene, to the level of the cell, to that of organs and then organ systems, and finally to the level of the individual. Each level or plane of action can be characterized by a particular type of activity. This activity reflects the reciprocal interactions of the structures found at that level and the environment in which these structures function. Environment is specific to level. For example, whereas the psychological environment is typically framed in terms of the people and events we encounter, the environment of the cell would be defined in terms of the composition of the intercellular fluid and so on.

Interactions take place not only horizontally within levels but vertically across levels as well. It is possible to think of this vertical interaction between planes of action in two ways: (1) in terms of the emergence of new levels and (2) in terms of the interplay between levels. Both occur at all points in the life span. Although it is easiest to recognize this process when considering prenatal development, the emergence of new levels or stages of psychological function across the life span is an equally appropriate example.

For example, the activity of genes is the synthesis of amino acids. How successfully this process proceeds depends on the structure of the genes in interaction with the elements that define the environment at that level of analysis. In turn, amino acids in interaction with their level of environment, produce proteins; proteins in interaction produce cells; cells in interaction produce tissue; tissue in interaction produces organs; organs in interaction produce organ systems; and organ systems in interaction

Bidirectional Influences

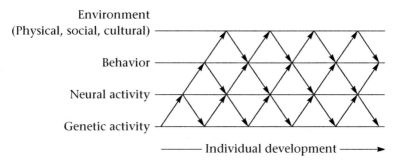

FIGURE 9.1
Gottlieb's Bidirectional Model.
Source: Gottlieb, 1992, p. 186.

produce the organism. Given such a mechanism, the relationship between two nonadjacent levels is always indirect rather than direct, because the manner and degree of influence are always mediated by both the structures and the functions present at intermediate levels. In this sense, rather than providing a blueprint of development, genes can be said to offer at best a rough sketch. It is this process of new, larger, more structurally complex levels emerging out of the interactions of lower levels that is the defining element of the process of development as an *epigenetic* process.

Once a new level emerges, its influence on lower levels is bidirectional and indirect rather than linear and one-way. Just as actions at lower levels influence actions at higher levels of organization, so, too, do actions at the higher levels influence those at lower levels. Genes, for example, clearly influence structure and function at higher levels of organization. But, of equal importance, activity that occurs at higher levels in turn influences which genes are active at any particular time.

Gottlieb refers to these bidirectional interactions as a process of *co-action* (see Figure 9.1). The term is meant to emphasize the fact that changes in structure or the emergence of new structures are always a product of the particular relationship between the elements rather than the elements themselves. This notion of co-action is especially easy to recognize when considering the behavior of individual cells early in prenatal development.

Although each cell has the identical genetic material, at some point early in the prenatal sequence, cells begin to specialize or differentiate into particular forms. But different cells carry the same genetic information, and individual cells don't come with instructions specifying their fate. So how does the cell know to become, say, a part of the arm rather than a part of the leg?

Gottlieb points to a large body of research demonstrating that one major determinant of individual cell differentiation is the relationship of that cell to other cells. Somehow the location of individual cells in relationship to others and in relationship to their location within the developing embryo sets the differentiation mechanism in motion. No one is quite sure how the process works, but clearly the regulator is not solely within the individual cell. We know this because if a cell is transplanted to a different region of the embryo early in the differentiation process, the cell assumes the differentiated structure of its new neighbors. But if it is transplanted after the process has begun, the cell structure continues to differentiate as it would have had it not been transplanted (Gottlieb, 1992; Michel & Moore, 1995)

A further way to appreciate the bidirectional, co-actional nature of development is to compare the developmental psychobiologist's concept of the *norm of reaction* with the developmental behavior geneticist's concept of *reaction range*. Although the two concepts sound the same, they are, in fact, based on very different theoretical assumptions. The behavior geneticist's reaction range is a measure of the range of expression for any given genotype given the range of environments to which it might be exposed. In effect, in this conceptualization, genotype sets the range, and environment determines the actual value within that range. The psychobiologist's norm of reaction does not give a priori status to either genotype or environment. Neither sets a range in which the other is free to operate. Rather, the co-actional relationship means that it is virtually impossible to determine the phenotypic expression or even range of expression of a gene or group of genes without first defining the environment in which those genes will operate to synthesize one or more amino acids. In this sense norm of reaction is a much more potentially optimistic but a much less definable view of human potential than is reaction range.

Characteristics of Development

Even though from a developmental psychobiological perspective higher levels cannot be reduced to lower ones, all levels or planes of activity, biological and psychological, are seen as adhering to the same set of defining characteristics (Anderson, 1957; Michel & Moore, 1995). The first characteristic is that change at any level is *irreversible*. That is, development is a progressive event. Even when later actions or behaviors appear to mimic earlier ones, the presumption of irreversibility dictates that the mechanisms prompting the new actions or behaviors are not the same as those of the earlier ones.

A second defining characteristic is that developing systems are *active*. Organisms at all levels of functioning are structured in such a way that input is acted upon rather than simply stored. The organism does something to this input to make it more useful or more meaningful. This act of organizing helps the organism be more effective in adapting to changing environmental demands. At the same time, as organisms change, so do their actions and, as such, their potential for impacting the environment. This reciprocal give and take—environment acting on the organism, organism acting on the environment—helps to establish a dynamic equilibrium between any level of the organism and the environment effective at that level.

A third defining characteristic is that organisms *develop*. The cumulative impact of the interactions between organisms and environments leads to progressive adaptations, which periodically require structural reorganizations at any particular level of functioning of the organism. The nature of these progressive reorganizations is best described as *emergent*. Rather than the specifics of the sequence being packaged as a type of blueprint in one of the already existing components of the system, the new form of organization reflects the interaction of the components with each other and with their relevant environment.

Successive reorganizations are typically referred to as *stages*. Successive reorganizations do not eliminate earlier modes of action, but rather incorporate them into the newer, more complex and more adaptive stage. The earlier modes of action are therefore still available to the organism. In this sense, stages reflect what Sameroff (1989) refers to as the "resolution of a cascade of dialectic contradictions between physical status, cognitive development and social roles" (p. 227).

The consequence of these successive stages of reorganization is a more capable and adaptive level of organization. There is, however, a down side to this progression. The tradeoff for efficiency and effectiveness appears to be flexibility. Because of the integrated nature of systems at any level of organization, the more the system moves in one direction, the less able it becomes to move in another.

If these basic assumptions sound familiar, they should. They are really nothing more than what was said in Chapter 3 about organismic models in general. This commonality (or redundancy) across perspectives within the organismic world view again reflects the fact that organismic theories differ not so much in assumptions as they do in their areas of specialization. For Piaget and the neo-Piagetians, it is cognitive development. For Freud, Erikson, and other psychodynamic theorists, it is social development. And for developmental psychobiologists, it is biological structures and their expression, particularly as they are reflected in terms of motor development. It is this sense of commonality that shows the relation of theories within the organismic world view to be quite different from what exists within the mechanistic model.

Gesell's Maturation Theory of Human Development

We turn now to an examination of the work of Arnold Gesell (1880–1961), the first of the three theorists featured in this chapter. One could argue that Gesell might just as easily fit in the chapter on developmental behavior genetics as in this one. The issue of where to place Gesell's theory reflects the concept of *maturation,* or at least Gesell's use of the term.

For Gesell maturation—the orderly, sequential nature of development—presumes some mechanism controlling the process. Furthermore, given its regularity, Gesell felt that the mechanism had to be regulated by some sort of predefined plan—in particular, a plan that more closely resembled a blueprint than a rough sketch. The unfolding nature of this plan is well reflected in Gesell's (1948) description of the maturational process.

> Growth is a step-by-step miracle—a gradual and not a sudden apocalypse. Each step is only made possible by the step that preceded. First the blade, then the ear; after that the full corn in the ear. As with a plant, so with a child. His mind grows by natural stages. The eyes take the lead, the hands follow. The baby grasps with his palm before he grasps with his finger tips. He creeps before he walks, cries before he laughs, babbles before he talks, builds a tower before a wall, a wall before a bridge, draws a circle

before a square, a square before a diamond. Such sequences are part of the order of nature. (p. 8)

Gesell saw human development as this "order of nature"—a sequence of changes or maturations regulated by a genetically defined timetable. As such, Gesell saw genetics as having a direct effect on behavior rather than the indirect influence discussed earlier in the chapter. Nevertheless, two other aspects of Gesell's work lead me to place him in this chapter: (1) his focus on the universal rather than the particular characteristics of development and (2) his interest in the interactive mechanisms through which this maturationally timed process is expressed. In essence, although Gesell saw the control mechanism as genetic, the process he describes is clearly organismic in character.

A Biographical Sketch

Gesell began his professional career as an educator (Thelen & Adolp, 1992). He initially taught high school but soon became interested in issues surrounding the placement and education of children with special needs. This interest led, in 1911, to an appointment at Yale University as director of the Yale Clinic of Child Development, a position he retained until his mandatory retirement in 1948. Gesell's growing interest in the physical and physiological bases of development led him also to pursue a medical degree at Yale. He completed this degree in 1915.

Gesell's interests in education, medicine, and development prompted a long and distinguished career in documenting and interpreting the universality of developmental milestones. His work pioneered new approaches to the observation and recording of children's behavior, providing a scientific base for a greater recognition of developmental assessment in well-child pediatric practice. The work also served as the basis for a very successful series of parent-oriented child development books and has prompted an active and at times even raging debate (Ames, 1989; Bear & Modlin, 1987; Gesell Institute, 1987; Meisels, 1987; Porwancher & deLisi, 1993) over the timing of children's entry into formal education and, more specifically, their introduction to formal educational practices.

Ironically Yale shut down the Child Study Clinic shortly after Gesell's retirement, in spite of the fact that the clinic continued to enjoy a worldwide reputation. Yale's actions in 1950 probably reflected the theoretical shift away from biologically based models and toward the learning theories that were making their mark in the 1950s and 1960s. The Gesell Institute continues today under private sponsorship. The renewed interest in genetic and psychobiological accounts of behavior and development has led to a renewed interest in Gesell's work at many institutions. Yale, for example, recently established an endowed chair honoring Gesell (Thelen & Adolp, 1992).

Basic Elements of Gesell's Maturational Model

Gesell viewed the sequence of psychological development as conforming to what he saw as the same set of universal laws as all other form of sequential change. He was not alone in this view. The idea that the sequence of ontogenetic development recapitulates or repeats the sequence of phylogenetic and cultural development for humans was a common one for developmentalists of his era to hold (Gottlieb, 1992). And it is a notion that continues to be a topic of debate and discussion today (Gould, 1996). At one extreme is the argument that there are no parallels between the development of the individual and the development of either the species or the culture. Any seeming parallels are at best coincidence. At the other extreme is the argument that the parallels are so strong that it is possible to compare the relative developmental status of cultures in the same way that one can compare the developmental status of individuals. Needless to say, such claims of the developmental comparability of cultures are highly controversial and are generally not well accepted today (Cole, 1996a).[1]

Gesell did believe that ultimately one set of explanatory mechanisms will be shown to be equally true not only for psychological and biological development but also for the development of the species through evolution and the development of groups within a species through cultural change. From this perspective Gesell argued that his findings on motor development in infancy also held the keys to our understanding of cognitive and social development at all stages of the life span and, by the same token, our understanding of the larger issues of culture and evolution.

The key element in Gesell's maturational theory was biological structure—in particular, the structure of the nervous system. Gesell believed that behavior was a direct expression of the structure of the nervous system. Changes in the structural organization of the nervous system invariably led to corresponding changes in psychological functioning. Structure always preceded function; the reverse was never true.

The control of this maturational unfolding of successive layers of structural organization of the nervous system was seen as genetic. The role of the environment was to support and nurture, to be in tune with these internal mechanisms. When the child was ready for new experiences, the environment had to be ready to provide them. This notion of *readiness* is at the heart of the debates over Gesell's views about education and his belief in the appropriateness of assessing children's readiness for academic instruction.

Gesell's belief in development as a maturational process naturally led him to favor a longitudinal approach to the study of behavioral change. It could hardly be otherwise for someone who saw the regulation of development as internal and the role of the environment as supportive. Gesell's methodology was ingenious for his time, and except for obvious improvements in technology, it is just as appropriate today for the noninteractive assessment of developmental status.

Infants in his longitudinal sample visited his lab at regular intervals. They were presented with a variety of objects to see how they would respond to each and how

---

[1] Be careful not to confuse this issue of recapitulation with the prior discussion of the characteristics of development from a psychobiological perspective. The recapitulation argument is one of parallels: Is there an inevitable and parallel sequence of change across all levels of analysis? Is it as appropriate to talk about an "infant culture" as it is an "infant child"? The characteristics of the psychobiological perspective reflect a process restricted solely to ontogenetic development at both the biological and psychological levels. No assumption is made as to the relevance of ontogenetic patterns to either species evolution or cultural change.

these response patterns changed over time. Observations were done both directly with trained observers and indirectly through motion picture analysis. The motion pictures were viewed virtually frame by frame to detect response patterns and changes in those patterns. Gesell also collected information on children's behavior through parent interviews and observation of parent-child interaction patterns.

One of Gesell's more enduring legacies are the developmental norm charts and "typical day" descriptions that grew out of these longitudinal observations. They appear in most child development texts and are found on the wall in virtually every pediatrician's office. There is a precision to these normative descriptions of behavior that today borders on caricature. Rather than the broad strokes that other organicists use to depict sequential change, Gesell painted with a very fine brush indeed. And, as is often the case when people write normative descriptions, there is in Gesell's observations the sense that they are perhaps as much prescription as they are description. Consider these typical examples of normative descriptions. The first describes part of the typical day of a 2½-year-old.

> The luncheon at noon is usually his largest meal. He likes to feed himself for at least half of the meal, during which he selects the food which he most prefers. He may assert his self-dependence by asking his mother to leave the room, but he calls her back and accepts her help for the last half of the meal, reverting again to self-help for dessert. He is toileted, and often has a bowel movement at this time. . . . The scheduled nap may begin at about 12:30, but usually he consumes an hour or more in self-activity before going to sleep. He likes to have the side of the bed down and he may get in and out of bed two or three times. He talks a great deal to himself during this pre-nap period. He may finally fall off to sleep after he has been tucked in by his mother. (Gesell & Ilg, 1949, p. 181)

A 3-year-old's typical day has the same flavor.

> The routines of the day do not have to be rushed. He makes comfortable transitions and adaptations. He feels his own increasing independence and demands that his afternoon nap at 1 o'clock should be a "play nap." This is a relaxation and rest period. He utilizes it for that purpose. He gets in and out of bed a few times and he may finally fall asleep without further aid from his mother. He is content to "play" at napping from one to two hours. If he should not fall asleep, he presents himself to his mother as if to say, "Time is up." . . . He goes to the toilet again on suggestion at 3 o'clock. He needs very little help in his toileting. . . . He likes to go on excursions to a friend's house in the afternoon. He plays best out of doors. (Gesell & Ilg, 1949, p. 205)

The child-rearing advice that Gesell offered based on his longitudinal work (Gesell, 1940; Gesell & Ilg, 1943, 1946) stood in stark contrast to the advice that John Watson (Watson, 1928) had been offering. Watson's very regimented behavioral approach to child rearing stressed the importance of the environment, primarily in the form of the parent, as the shaper of development. Watson claimed that children fed on a schedule would soon learn to become well-socialized individuals. Gesell offered virtually the opposite advice: Children should be fed when they are hungry, napped when they are tired, and nurtured without the slightest concern for the "spoiling" and "sentimentality" that Watson was so concerned about. No wonder Gesell's books sold so well. They offered parents a more relaxed approach to child rearing, one that, in effect, let them off the hook as long as they provided an appropriately responsive environment for their children.

Gesell's Developmental Principles

Toward the end of his career, Gesell integrated his observational findings into a set of developmental principles (Ames, 1989; Gesell, 1948, 1952). He believed that these principles held for all developmental processes at all ages and at all levels of organization.

His first principle, the *principle of developmental direction,* is a summary of his observations of the course of motor development in infants and young children. It dictates that, at least with respect to motor development, accomplishments move in a predictable direction along three gradients. The first gradient, *cephalo to caudal,* indicates that infants gain control of muscle groups first near the head and then, in turn, the shoulders, the trunk, and eventually the legs. In a similar fashion muscle groups mature in a *proximal-to-distal* manner, with infants able to control their arms before their fingers. More generally, muscles near the trunk mature sooner than those in the extremities. Finally, muscle development also shows an *ulnar-to-radial* direction. That is, with respect to the hand, infants develop the ability to grasp with the fingers pressing against the palm before they are able to develop a pincer grasp in which the fingers and the thumb work opposite to each other. More generally, this first principle emphasizes Gesell's belief that development occurs in a predictable, predetermined sequential fashion.

Gesell's second principle, the *principle of reciprocal interweaving,* highlights the fact that development does not occur in a linear fashion. Rather, the course of development more closely resembles a helix or spring. Moving up the helix does confirm the directional nature of development, but there are continuous shifts from left to right and back again. Gesell believed that these complementary shifts at the psychological level reflected the same basic mechanisms as are found in the regulation of excitatory and inhibitory responses at the level of the nervous system. With regard to infant motor development, for example, stages of flexion alternate with stages of extension, adduction with abduction, and bilateral with unilateral.

Gesell's third principle, the *principle of functional asymmetry,* seems almost a contradiction of the second. Whereas the second asserted that mature development involves the progressive integration of seemingly contradictory poles, this third principle holds that in some cases asymmetry rather than symmetry is the preferred, more adaptive, developmental outcome. Handedness is a good example. Our handedness does not become more reciprocal as we age but maintains a clear preference for the left or the right.

Gesell's fourth principle, the *principle of individuating maturation,* highlights two important elements of his theory. The first is that even though development is ultimately an interactive process between endogenous and exogenous factors, it is the former that regulates the process. The environment supports and modifies, but it creates neither the norms nor the sequence. Second, this sequence has a distinct quality to it, moving in the direction of increasing differentiation. That is, the initial actions of the infant are global in nature; only later do they become more specific to one part of the body. Because Gesell believed that the developmental patterns revealed through the study of motor development hold equally true for other developmental domains, it is reasonable to presume that he would hold the same differentiating view with respect to other domains such as emotion or cognition.

Gesell's fifth principle, the *principle of self-regulatory fluctuation*, essentially restates the second principle but on a larger plane. Rather than talking about the relationship between particular elements of a motor pattern, as might be the case in a discussion of the sequence of steps in learning to walk, Gesell is here arguing that this reciprocal pattern also exists at a broader level. In general, stages of relative equilibrium alternate with stages of relative disequilibrium, focus on self alternates with a focus on other, and stages of expansiveness alternate with stages of inwardness. This Ping-Pong-like process seems to be serving the purpose of helping children adjust to the developmental changes that they encounter. As children continue to develop, these complementary pulls become integrated or woven together at increasingly more complex levels of organization. This depiction of development as fluctuations between competing poles is a common one in organismic models (Kegan, 1982). It is well illustrated in Gesell's (1949) explanation of the typical behavior of 2½-year-old children.

> Why does he go to such extremes? It is because his command of *yes* and *no;* of *come* and *go; run* and *stop; give* and *take; grasp* and *release; push* and *pull; assault* and *retreat* is so evenly balanced. Life is charged with double alternatives. Every pathway in the culture is a two-way street to him, because he is most inexperienced. . . . His action system likewise is a two-way system, with almost equally inviting alternatives, because he is so immature. His equilibrium is unstably balanced, because his inhibitory mechanisms are very incomplete. (p. 178)

Thelen and Adolp (1992) argue that, in the final analysis, Gesell's work has generated little contemporary research because his view of development as genetically determined left little for others to do except continue to record the course of maturation—an activity not likely to arouse much enthusiasm among contemporary developmentalists. At the same time, however, they also note that his determinism notwithstanding, Gesell's work does provide a foundation for an interactive view of development, one in which both function and structure work to influence the emergence of new developmental stages.

> Gesell understood as well as any the dynamics of development: the totality of the organism, the cyclic phases of equilibrium and disequilibrium, the participation of infants in their own change, the self righting tendencies of the organism. Yet he doggedly assigned the intricacies of development to a single cause. (Thelen & Adolp, 1992, p. 376)

If, as current psychobiological accounts do, you consider the patterns that Gesell so carefully documented as coming not from a single cause but from the interaction of many, then you have the basis for modern work in developmental psychobiology. You also have Gesell's most important legacy.

McGraw's Growth Theory of Human Development

Myrtle McGraw (1899–1988) was a contemporary of Gesell. She did her early work at Columbia and then completed her academic career at Briarcliff College. Both Gesell and McGraw published their major works in the 1930s and 1940s (McGraw, 1935, 1939, 1940, 1942, 1946). There was clearly a rivalry between the two, and it is probably accurate to say that Gesell got the best of it—at least in the sense of theoretical impact and public visibility at the time. Gesell was older and more established, and he was male (a not unimportant issue in academia in that era). His work was typically seen at the opposite pole as Watson in the very visible debate over the importance of maturation versus learning in development. At a time, then, when dichotomies were the primary approach to developmental theory, McGraw's middle-ground notions received comparatively little attention. The move away from dichotomous conceptions of development, by developmental psychobiologists in particular and organicists in general, probably explains why McGraw's ideas are now being revisited (Bergenn, Dalton, & Lipsitt, 1992; Dalton & Bergenn, 1995).

There was actually very little contact between McGraw and Gesell in spite of the fact that both were pursuing the same issues using similar methodologies. McGraw frequently cited Gesell in her work, although the same cannot be said for Gesell. McGraw notes that she did once visit Gesell's lab at Yale, but according to her, he had no interest in talking to so junior a researcher. In fact, ironically, McGraw credits Gesell's disinterest as a defining moment in her theoretical work.

> Unintentionally, but in the long run, Gesell did me a favor. I was shown the Yale laboratory but he gave me the brush off on the request to stay for instruction. So I returned to the medical center empty handed. I was on my own. Not knowing what to do next for hours on end, I spent hours on hours in the delivery room and the laboratory just looking at babies, always asking what can they teach me? (McGraw, quoted in Dalton & Bergenn, 1995, p. 52)

Basic Elements of McGraw's Growth Model

At first, watching these babies, McGraw made the same sort of normative observations that Gesell pursued so successfully. However, she began to be increasingly curious about the process through which their new behaviors emerged. In particular, she began to wonder if Gesell might be wrong in arguing that structural development must always precede function. She began to seriously consider two possible alternatives: (1) a child's action might influence the further development of the very structure influencing that action, and (2) the functioning of one aspect of behavior might also influence the structural development of another.

These two hypotheses were significant. Gesell was arguing, in effect, that because structure always preceded function, it was structure that always determined capacity—that is, the limits as to what the individual was capable of doing. McGraw was suggesting that the issue may not be so clear-cut, that what a person does now may, in part, ultimately determine what the person will be fully capable of doing later.

For McGraw the study of development became the study of the interplay of structure and function and the way this interplay results in the emergence of new behaviors. McGraw's emphasis on new behaviors was partly an attempt to clearly differentiate her views from those of both Watson and Gesell. McGraw believed that because most behaviorists, including Watson, studied relatively mature organisms, they were not studying development (i.e., an emergent process) so much as the factors that regulate the rearrangement of already present behaviors. With reference to Gesell, she believed that his insistence on defining development as a predetermined maturational process prevented him from recognizing what she saw as the emergent nature of development.

Given her emphasis on emergence, it is not surprising that McGraw's research was longitudinal and focused on very young infants. In this regard, her most famous work was her study of Johnny and Jimmy. Johnny and Jimmy were believed to be identical twins.[2] At the tender age of 21 days, Johnny began to receive a regimen of deliberate interventions that was to continue, on virtually a daily basis, for the first two years of his life. He was encouraged to move his limbs and even to crawl. He was held erect to exercise his stepping reflex and stimulate his spinal muscles. And the reflexes present in most young infants were stimulated on a regular basis. As Johnny got older and new behaviors emerged, these were reinforced, extended, and exercised. When he began to creep, he was given the chance to do so not only on a level surface but also on one of increasing steepness. When be began to walk, he was given a specially constructed pair of roller skates to help foster his sense of balance and to exercise muscle groups not normally used by infants. He was also placed in a water tank and encouraged to exercise his swimming movements. As his motor skills improved, he was given opportunities to lift and build with large cubes and then to climb on them.

In the meantime, Jimmy spent his days (both were brought to McGraw's lab every day by their parents) in a crib. Aside from routine interactions around feeding, diapering, and so on, McGraw noted that his opportunities for activity were relatively limited.[3]

The results of the study were striking. McGraw reported that Johnny was scaling slopes of "unbelievable steepness" before the age of 1. By 15 months, he was able to roller skate with some proficiency and swim underwater a distance of 12–15 feet. His climbing abilities were beyond those of any child his age.

Toward the end of the second year, however, Jimmy apparently had had enough of being the "control group" and became increasingly unwilling to hang around in his crib while Johnny got to do all the seemingly fun stuff (who could blame him?). Therefore, McGraw decided to provide Jimmy with intensive intervention in all of the same

---

[2] It was eventually determined that they were, in fact, fraternal rather than identical twins. From a methodological perspective this made comparisons between them more difficult, but it does not negate the significance of the findings from McGraw's intervention.

[3] As noted in previous chapters, for ethical reasons, research such as this would never be allowed today, for either Johnny or Jimmy. At the time, however, it was seen as a perfectly reasonable thing to do.

activities as Johnny. She reported that Jimmy also improved rapidly but never reached the same level of competence in these activities as his brother. Shortly after their second birthday, the experiment ended. Follow-ups of the children were made on a regular basis for several years; McGraw gave this summary of the follow-up evaluations:

> In certain acts, such as tricycling, neither Johnny nor Jimmy exhibited loss of skill, even after practice was terminated. In others, such as skating and climbing inclines, there was a marked change. . . . When all activities are considered, it is safe to say that in so far as quality of performance goes, Johnny has consistently exhibited greater motor coordination and an ability to handle his muscles with ease and grace. Jimmy has consistently exhibited greater linguistic facility. Johnny has also shown greater fortitude in performing difficult feats, such as jumping. (McGraw, in Dalton & Bergenn, 1995, pp. 113–114)

It is hard to put into words the impact that McGraw's co-twin study had and how that impact made its interpretation that much more difficult. This was an era when the nature/nurture question was in the public eye and when the belief in science's ability to solve human problems was perhaps at its zenith. McGraw's finding that Johnny's significant initial advantage was relatively short-lived was generally interpreted by the media and by professionals as proof of the relative importance of maturation over learning. The findings were seen as further confirmation of the findings from a similar but less intensive co-twin study conducted by Gesell. As seemed true for McGraw, Gesell's trained twin showed an initial advantage that was short-lived and easily compensated for by a briefer intervention at a later time with the control twin. In both studies the initial advantage was seen as a "hot house" phenomena. That is, the intervention was seen at best as accelerating the rate of development to a level that would have been achieved anyway had a more normative developmental path been followed. In other words, the claim was, it doesn't make much difference how you go about doing it, you still end up with the same level of development. This issue of how best to interpret the reported fade of gains from early intervention efforts has continued to be a significant topic of debate, most notably concerning issues of early educational intervention (Bryant, 1994; Goldhaber, 1979).

McGraw's Developmental Principles

So how did McGraw interpret her findings, and how does this interpretation reflect her more general views on the psychobiological nature of development? McGraw suggested that three factors must be considered when viewing the long-term stability of early intervention efforts and, by extension, the role of early experience on later development. She describes the first as the degree of *fixity* the behavior pattern has obtained when practice is discontinued. Fixity refers to the structural state of the organism both when the time practice begins and when it is completed. More generally, fixity reflects the notion of *critical periods* in development, a point we will return to shortly.

Her second factor concerns the degree to which physical changes in the developing child facilitate or hinder subsequent expression of the initial behavior. McGraw notes, for example, that Johnny and later Jimmy showed remarkable ability to scale a slope as steep as 60 degrees—a feat that most older children have difficulty accomplishing. But both twins lost this skill over time, largely because of their changing body proportions.

> The center of gravity in the infant's body is relatively higher and his legs are relatively shorter. It is therefore possible for him to get his chest, and therefore his center of gravity, nearer to the slide without raising his pelvic girdle too high. . . . The difficulties of older children are manifest by slipping or a deficient gripping power in the toes and in managing their long legs. (McGraw, 1939, p. 5)

McGraw's third explanation for change over time in the impact of early intervention concerns changes in children's attitudes. In effect, this third explanation parallels the second. In both cases subsequent developmental events—changes in body proportion and now changes in the way children view an event—serve to facilitate or inhibit the expression of earlier behaviors. As McGraw (1939) puts it:

> A child who is just beginning to walk may leap off a tall pedestal without hesitancy because he has not developed adequate powers of height discrimination to appreciate all the possibilities in the situation. A little later, when his powers of discrimination have advanced, he squats and refuses to jump. Again it must be emphasized that his behavior has changed not because of an unfortunate personal experience but because of development in another aspect of his behavior. (p. 10)

Gesell would have interpreted these findings as confirming a maturationist argument. McGraw offered a different explanation. She argued that her findings showed that (1) it was indeed possible to significantly alter typical behavior patterns and (2) the long-term permanence of such changes reflected the interplay of a number of developmental systems. In other words, for Johnny and for Jimmy, their loss of early motor skills says more about what did and did not happen *following* the intervention than it did about what did and did not happen *during* the intervention. The same argument is typically used in explaining the long-term outcomes of intervention studies today as well.

In trying to draw some more general conclusions from her twin study, as well as her other work, McGraw drew heavily on the work of George Coghill (Coghill, 1933, 1936), an eminent embryologist whose work is still cited in psychobiological sources. Coghill was interested in two things: (1) the role that the movements of the embryo play in influencing its structural development and (2) the impact of the timing of embryological events on the emergence of both structure and function.

Coghill's embryological research led him to claim that movements of the immature embryo, often in response to position shifts, serve as one element in determining the integration of the sensory and neuromuscular systems. Furthermore, the pattern of early neurological growth appeared to be one of "overdevelopment" of nerve fibers. Which of these too numerous connections between nerve cells subsequently faded and which were strengthened again, in part, reflected functional activity. Finally, his studies of cells transplanted to different areas of the developing embryo led him to conclude that the timing of developmental events was a significant determinant of development outcome; that is, there were critical periods in development.

A believer in the idea that the principles of development held across all forms and levels of development, McGraw applied Coghill's ideas to the interpretation of her own work. First, she extended the concept of critical period to highlight the interdependence of different aspects of development. From this perspective a critical period became the optimal time for a particular developmental intervention—optimal in the sense of the relative levels of maturity of the different developmental domains influencing that behavior.

Second, McGraw believed that development was a bidirectional process in which function and structure mutually influenced each other. For McGraw the fact that development appears to occur in a systemic, sequential manner was not due to some built-in plan, but rather to the regularities of the interactions between structure and function, particularly as they occur in prenatal and early postnatal life. Introduce an atypical event such as her intervention during a critical period and the course of development can be changed. In the same sense that a particular cell will develop into a particular organ unless that cell is moved early in the sequence to a new location, so, too, will postnatal development occur in a most likely pattern unless the "most likely" events are changed.

Third, McGraw believed that the expression of any behavior reflected the interdependence of all behavioral systems in interaction with a responsive environment. As noted previously, children's willingness to engage in any behavior was not simply a function of their physical ability to perform that behavior; it was equally a function of other factors such as attitudes and perceptions. An effective intervention would be one that considers all behavioral domains. She portrayed this interdependence as a weaving, so that behavioral patterns emerged only when strands were combined to form a particular pattern. The strands were aspects not merely of the developing child but of her context as well.

> A watch in the visual field is just as much an integral part of reaching and prehension as is the flexor-extensor movement of the hand. Although retaining their own identity, these factors unite in the formation of a behavior pattern which is distinct from the summation of its parts. While the watch, the eyes and the arms may remain as constant ingredients in the activity, as the behavior pattern matures, it becomes more apparent that the interrelation has materially altered. The form and design of that interrelation has changed. These changes are the signs of development. (McGraw, 1935, p. 303)

Thelen's Dynamic Systems Theory of Development

The work of Gesell and McGraw laid dormant for many years following the 1940s. Gesell's documentation of the sequence of motor development and his maturational explanations seemed so complete that there appeared little else to do with the topic. And McGraw's influence was even smaller. Although her views differed from Gesell's, she nevertheless tended to get lumped together with him. Because Gesell's work was so much more prominent, McGraw seemed doomed to "footnote status." This remained the case through much of the 1950s and 1960s with behavior theory's emphasis on learning over maturation.

However, as the cognitive revolution took hold with the rediscovery of Piaget (Flavell, 1963; Hunt, 1961), as information processing models began to replace learning or association models (Klahr & Siegler, 1978), and as new discoveries about the working of the brain seemed to be made on an almost daily basis (Tobach, Aronson, & Shaw, 1971), things again changed. Motor development once more became a topic of both empirical and theoretical interest, and the questions first asked by both Gesell and McGraw once more were being raised. This time, however, the approach reflected a true developmental psychobiological perspective, one that moved beyond the dichotomies of earlier times—dichotomies that distinguished nature from nurture, learning from maturation, and performance from competence. The best example of this more recent approach is the work of Esther Thelen and her colleagues (Thelen, 1989a, 1989b, 1995; Thelen & Adolp, 1992; Thelen & Smith, 1994; Thelen et al., 1987) at Indiana University on a *dynamic systems theory* approach to motor development in particular and human development in general.

Thelen's work is motivated by the same question that McGraw and indeed most organicists ask: Where does behavior come from? Gesell argued for a predefined genetic blueprint. McGraw, although more interactive in her theorizing, still gave primary emphasis to structure over function. Thelen suggests a more interactive explanation. She notes that claims about the instructions for new behavior being "out there"—residing either in genes or in the environment—ultimately face a regressive logical impasse (see also Oyama, 1985). That is, once we ask where the instructions come from, we then are forced to asked where the instructions for the instructions come from, and on and on.

Basic Elements of Thelen's Dynamic Systems Model

Thelen's alternative solution involves the systems principles used to explain the organization of biological systems. In biological systems, Thelen suggests, pattern and order can emerge from the process of the interactions of the components of a complex system without the need for explicit instructions (Thelen et al., 1987). Therefore, to understand the function of any complex behavior pattern such as walking, Thelen's primary interest, or cognition or socialization, one looks to the mix of the components. It is the task-defined interactions that are the causes of behavior. Development, from this perspective, becomes a self-defining and self-structuring process.

> Activity in the world, real time activity, makes development happen in our theory, but this is not learning in the usual sense and it is not a denial of evolutionary history. The heterogeneous processes of real brains, with their multiple convergent and divergent connections, are the intrinsic dynamics from which activity emerges. The nature of these heterogeneous components, their initial state and couplings, will determine the direction that development can take. But we are not nativists; development does

not unfold according to some prespecified plan. There is no plan! We posit that development, change, is caused by the interacting influences of heterogeneous components, each with its own take on the world. (Thelen & Smith, 1994, p. 338)

This shift, from identifying an ultimate cause to looking at interactions, is perhaps the most important element of Thelen's approach. It is particularly relevant within organismic models because arguments about universal sequences seem to beg for some sort of ultimate regulator of the sequence. How else, the argument typically goes, could such a regular and seemingly universal pattern be explained if not by reference to some regulatory mechanism. And, the argument continues, if there is some predefined, regulatory mechanism, then what is left to distinguish the organicist's formal cause from the mechanist's material cause?

Thelen's argument is that such regularity need not presume a regulating mechanism, but instead, is as easily explained by the inevitable outcomes of components in interaction with one another. No one component has primacy over another. Each is equally important in producing the outcome even if, mechanistically speaking, one element seems to contribute significantly more of the variance than another to the mix.

When viewed from this organismic perspective, Thelen's dynamic systems theory places great emphasis on formal causes, less on efficient and material causes, and relatively little on final causes, because there is nothing in the model that presumes an inevitable direction toward which development is proceeding. In this sense, development to Thelen is, like evolution, an opportunistic process.

Consider, as an example, the developmental course of one motor pattern in very young infants. Newborns exhibit a stepping reflex. That is, when supported in an upright position with their feet touching the floor, they "walk." Their motor patterns are virtually identical to what will be the case many months later when they are able to walk unsupported. But around 2 months of age, this reflex disappears. According to traditional explanations going back to McGraw and Gesell, this stepping reflex was controlled by lower centers in the brain. These areas became inhibited as higher-brain control was established, particularly those higher-brain functions that regulated volitional behavior, such as independent walking. Thelen suggests another explanation. She notes that even though the stepping reflex disappears around 2 months, infants continue to demonstrate motor patterns identical to walking when they are lying on their backs. The fact that the behavior continues in one posture (supine) but not the other (vertical) suggests to Thelen that the traditional explanation is insufficient. Something more complex is going on.

Consistent with a dynamic systems perspective, Thelen notes that changes in a seemingly irrelevant factor—namely, weight—probably best explain why the stepping behavior continues when infants are on their backs but not when they are held erect. Weight gain during the first year is mostly in the form of fat rather than muscle. The stepping behavior was disappearing at around 2 months because the legs were simply getting too heavy to lift, an issue less relevant when the infants were on their backs. The weight gain also proved less relevant when infants were held in a waist-high tank of water. The stepping movements "reappeared" at 6 or 7 months (an age when such movements are not typically present) when infants were held erect with their feet placed on a moving treadmill. The introduction of the treadmill changed the organization of the components such that the result was the emergence of walking. But, Thelen argues, the weight gain alone does not explain the change in stepping behavior. Rather, the weight gain in interaction with other elements changed the stepping behavior. This distinction is neither trivial nor merely a matter of semantics. The reappearance of the stepping behavior on the treadmill and in the waist-high water makes this point clear. No one component caused the walking behavior. Rather, the presence or absence of the behavior reflected the product of the interaction of a number of components, each at a particular level of developmental maturity.

This brief discussion of early stepping behavior provides a concrete example of the more general principles of dynamic systems theory. The theory is based on the notion that when individual elements or components interact, the state of each serves to restrict the expression of the other in such a way that a pattern or form of organization emerges from the interaction. Change one of the components, and you change the interaction and therefore the form that emerges. For humans the number of components is, of course, very large. They exist at a variety of levels, from the molecular to the environmental, so we are dealing with a very complex system. Nevertheless, as complex as the system is, the interaction of these components organizes the system in such a way that patterns of behavior emerge.

The patterns that emerge are neither random nor infinite. There is a potential range of expression for each component, and the status of each component exerts a limiting influence on the expression of all other components. Limiters are referred to as *attractors* in the system; these attractors define a preferred state or level of equilibrium of the system. For example, the preferred state of a pendulum is a resting state. Disturbances to the system will make the pendulum move, but over time it will return to its preferred state. The preferred state reflects the interaction of all the elements of the system. Change one element, such as removing friction from the pendulum system, and you change the preferred state.

Humans are not pendulums, however. Whereas the attractor state for a pendulum in a friction environment is a point, for humans, like all biologically active systems, stability is dynamic rather than static. There is an attractor range rather than an attractor point. Furthermore, the interactions for some behaviors produce more stable configurations than for others. The logic of the adult or the coordinated movement of the school-age child seem so stable as to appear fixed or prewired. But to Thelen they are not prewired; instead, they reflect the interaction of elements with very strong attractors. But they are not perfect. There can be circumstances in which the most logical of adults are left without a major premise to their name and in which even the most coordinated of 9-year-olds look like clumsy oafs. In general, the stability of a behavioral state is a function of its cumulative history, its current status, the social and physical context in which it functions, and the intentional state of the actor (Thelen, 1995). The intentional state of the actor reflects the desire of the individual to accomplish a particular task. This motivation serves as the initial impetus for the individual to define the situation and, in so doing, to call into action the elements seen as necessary for problem solving. Once the elements are defined, their product reflects the emergent property of their interactions.

How, then, do systems change, especially ones that appear so stable? Systems change as one or more elements in the system change. Thelen uses the example of the gaits of a horse to illustrate her point. For a given speed of the horse, there is a preferred gait. *Preferred* in this sense does not mean predetermined. Rather, it simply means that a particular gait is a dynamic attractor because it permits the most efficient energy expenditure at that particular speed. Here efficient energy expenditure is the adaptive element of the system. Change the speed of the horse, and the gait changes from a walk to a trot to a canter to a gallop. Why does the gait change? Because a change in one or more components of the system has resulted in a new pattern of organization characterized by a new attractor state, that is, a different gait. The phase shifts between gaits are loosely analogous to stage transitions during development. In both instances periods of relative stability are interspersed with transitional periods characterized by increasing variability and a loss of pattern. Thelen and Smith (1994) describe the process:

> In a dynamic analysis of developmental processes at whatever level and in any domain, we identify a collective variable that expresses the behavioral change over time. This collective variable, by definition, is a compression of these asynchronous and nonlinear systems. Over different points in time, the system stability is determined by the cooperative interactions of the subsystems and therefore by the status of the subsystem *at the time the behavior is assembled.* . . . In no sense are any of the components logically causal in determining the developmental change because all components and contexts determine the system's product. . . . In this developmental model, there are many potential *control parameters* engendering change, and the task of the developmentalists is to discover these motors of change. (pp. 84–85, italics in original)

Dynamic Systems Theory Methodology

The strategy for studying the development of a dynamic system follows logically from the characteristics of the model (Thelen & Ulrich, 1991). The first step is to identify the *collective variable* or behavior of interest. For Thelen this is typically some aspect of walking, but it could be any behavior as long as the behavior exhibits the characteristics of both stability and change over time. Identifying such behaviors is not necessarily an easy task, because there first has to be a basis for arguing that new behaviors represent the same set of dynamic forces as did the previous behavior. This problem of the comparability of behaviors over time is not unique to dynamic systems theory but is, in fact, a problem inherent in any developmental analysis from any perspective. If anything, one value of a dynamic systems approach is to make the problem more visible and, in so doing, more likely to be appropriately resolved.

Having identified a collective variable, the next task is to acquire some information about its preferred attractor states—that is, how the behavior is typically expressed at different ages. Thelen believes that cross-sectional research strategies are useful for this purpose because the goal at this point is simply to get a picture of the states of the behavior, and not an understanding of the forces that contribute to both its stability and its change.

Gaining information about preferred attractor states indicates the frequency at which different behaviors appear at different ages. But it does not provide information about the developmental course of those behaviors. To obtain this information, longitudinal data needs to be collected. The frequency of sampling depends on the normative data obtained from the cross-sectional research. Behaviors that are changing rapidly would be sampled more frequently than behaviors that have a slow rate of change. The tradeoff for this denser sampling is that the total time period needed to sample the transition from one steady state to another would probably be less. Whereas the cross-sectional data provides an indication of what to use as reference points, the longitudinal data provides a map as to how each individual gets from point A to point B.

Figure 9.2 illustrates what such a dynamic systems longitudinal analysis might reveal. In this ontogenetic landscape for locomotion, Thelen has plotted how the simple reflexes present at birth develop into the more complex, differentiated, and voluntary means of locomotion available to older infants and toddlers. The relative significance of each of the motor patterns at each age is reflected by the depth of the trough. Note that walking, being the most adaptive means of locomotion, has the deepest trough; that is, it is the most stable pattern.

Thelen believes that one particular advantage of this longitudinal dynamic systems analysis is the identification of *transition points*. Transition points are indicated by a greater degree of variability in measures of individual performance or by an increase in the amount of recovery time needed following a disturbance to the preferred attractor range. Therefore, in this model, variability, rather than being something that needs to be reduced or ideally eliminated through more rigorous experimental controls, becomes the most meaningful measure of the process of development.

Once a clear picture of the stable and transition states of the collective variable is obtained, the next task is to identify the role that different components or parameters play in the system. This requires a mapping of the trajectories of each of the possible control parameters of the system. In the case of motor development, Thelen and Ulrich (1991) suggest that likely candidates to map would include changes in body proportion, sensory or perceptual capabilities, practice, muscle strength, and motivational variables. The transitions in motor patterns depicted in Figure 9.2 would reflect changes in these parameters. In the case of cognitive change, likely control parameters might include memory capacity, perceptual ability, knowledge base, and social or motivational factors. The goal of this component analysis would be to see how the trajectories of the component match up to or correlate with transitions in the collective variable.

Having identified a correlation between changes in the status of the collective variables and one or more control parameters, the next step is to verify experimentally whether the correlation is, in fact, causal. In other words, the experimental goal is to induce a developmental change by causing a change in the control parameter. If there is a causal link, then changes in the control parameter should result in either an increase in the variability of the collective variable or a longer recovery time.

In presenting this methodology, Thelen and Ulrich (1991) point out that the intent of the analysis is not to continue the process until the "real" causal level is identified. They stress that a dynamic systems approach is not a reductionist approach.

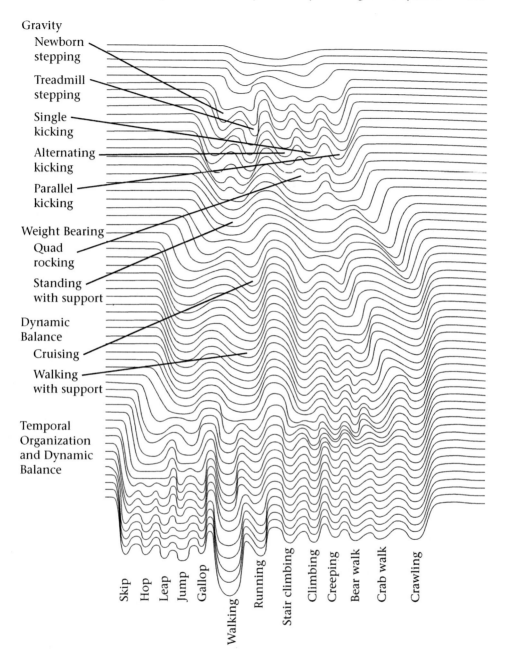

FIGURE 9.2
Ontogenetic Landscape for Locomotion.
Source: Thelen, 1994, p. 124.

Although such an analysis can be carried out at any level of the system, once a collective variable has been identified, its causes can only be its immediate control parameters. Behavior is not reducible to brain structure, nor brain structure to DNA. Each level of analysis involves a unique emergent property of the system, a property not reducible to some single ultimate cause.

Thelen recognizes that such an approach to research is complex and difficult. But it is not an approach that necessarily requires large samples. Consistent with an organismic perspective, she argues that it is as possible to understand this dynamic, emergent process by studying a few children as it is by studying many children. Such an argument presumes a universal quality to the process and an interest in how we are the same rather than how we are different.

The Significance of Edelman's Work to Dynamic Systems Theory

One essential element of Thelen's dynamic systems theory is her explanation of the bidirectional influence between events at different levels of the system—in particular, between the behavioral level and the level of the functioning of the brain and nervous system. This bidirectional element is essential because, unless a psychobiological model can show a mechanism through which function (i.e., the behavioral activity of the individual) influences structure (i.e., the anatomy of the brain and nervous systems), then psychobiological models have nothing more to offer than more traditional "primary source" accounts of development. According to such traditional accounts, best exemplified in Gesell's work and, for that matter, in the work of the developmental behavior geneticists, structural status precedes and therefore must determine and/or limit functional status. In support of her bidirectional arguments, Thelen draws heavily on Gerald Edelman's (Edelman, 1988, 1992; Sporns & Edelman, 1993) *theory of neuronal group selection.*

Edelman's theory of neuronal group selection provides a mechanism by which biological components self-structure themselves and through which structure and function are interdependent. The mechanism is evident in Edelman's explanation of how new structures are formed during prenatal development and how experience throughout the life span serves to influence the connection patterns existing between groups of nerve cells at the same and at different levels of the brain.

Edelman's view of prenatal development concerns the same basic issue as Coghill's many years earlier. For both, the basic embryological question is how it is possible for a highly differentiated organism to form if the genetic material in each cell is identical. Edelman's answer is based on two things: (1) the characteristics of cells and (2) the nature of their relationships to each other.

Edelman argues that cells exhibit five characteristics that help make it possible for differentiation to take place. These five characteristics are their capacity (1) to divide, (2) to migrate from one location to another, (3) to die, (4) to adhere to other cells, and (5) to differentiate into specialized structures and functions. These five characteristics operate in an interdependent fashion with three elements of each cell's environment: (1) the cell's location, (2) the activities of other cells at that location, and (3) the qualities of the context in which this process occurs. These three elements of a cell's environment determine what genetic material within each cell will become active and, as a result, determine the ultimate fate of that cell. At the same time, the migration of individual cells affects which cells will come in contact with and adhere to each other, progressively forming larger and larger structures and influencing which genetic material in that cell will be expressed. (It is important to remember that even though each cell contains the same genetic material, not all that material is active at the same time.) Edelman's model offers a mechanism for determining which genetic material in a cell becomes active and therefore how the cell will differentiate. As Edelman (1992) describes the process:

> Cells express genes in time and place to govern morphoregulatory molecules, which in turn control cell movements and cell-to-cell adhesion. These actions place groups of cells in proximity, allowing them to exchange further inductive signals. These alter the expression of homeotic genes, which then alter the expression of other genes. The key players in this topobiological cascade are the cells which move, die, divide, release inductive signals or morphogens, link to form new sheets, and repeat variants of the process. Genes control the whole business indirectly by governing which morphoregulatory or homeotic product will be expressed. But the actual microscopic fate of a cell is determined by epigenetic events that depend on developmental histories unique to each individual cell in the embryo. (p. 62)

Edelman argues that his epigenetic view of cell differentiation helps explain why the brain is structured the way it is and why it functions the way it does. He notes that the brain is "wired" in such a way that, rather than there being a seemingly logical one-to-one correspondence between sensory and motor inputs and specific regions of the brain, there are actually multiple pathways both within and across levels of the brain. The initial development of these pathways is highly individualistic and reflects the fact that particular patterns of cell adhesion occur during prenatal development. What happens to these neural networks following birth is, to a large degree, a function of the sensory and motor inputs that they receive. In other words, Edelman says, there is a clear bidirectional interdependent relationship between the structure of the brain at the level of intercell connectivity and the functioning of the organism. In particular, experience is seen as strengthening the connections between specific groups of neurons—hence Edelman's description of his theory as a theory of neuronal group selection. More to the point, rather than individual cells being the functional units in the brain and in some fashion having a one-to-one correspondence to sensory and motor input, it is groups of cells that serve this function. And they do so in a dynamic, epigenetic manner.

Edelman's research has helped to describe how this epigenetic process occurs. During prenatal development, the connections that are formed as a function of cell adhesion and genetically regulated cell differentiation create what Edelman refers to as the *primary repertoire*. This repertoire consists of millions of neuron groups, collections of hundreds or even thousands of cells that have strong connections to one another and that share a functional property relating to some sensory or motor input.

Almost from its initial formation, the primary repertoire undergoes a continuous process of modification as sensory and motor inputs selectively strengthen the synaptic connections between neuronal groups. According to Edelman, this modification process creates a *secondary repertoire*. As inputs change over time, so, too, do the strengths of the neuronal group connections. For example, crawling as an activity generates a wide range of sensory and motor inputs to the brain. These inputs converge simultaneously on different areas of the brain, stimulating a variety of neuronal groups. Because different neuronal groups are linked, their coordinated, simultaneous firings serve to strengthen the connections among them. As development proceeds and as new behavior patterns replace older ones, new connections are strengthened while older ones begin to fade. The neural connections that support crawling are, for example, eventually replaced by those that support walking (as reflected in Figure 9.2).

The dynamic systems process that Edelman describes at the neurological level is the same as what Thelen describes at the psychological level. Consistent with a psychobiological perspective, the same mechanisms can be seen operating at different levels of the organism even though the specific emergent products of these mechanisms are unique to the components that define that plane of action. At both levels new structures emerge out of the particular organization that exists among components. For Edelman the components are the cells and their links to one another. For Thelen the components are the physical and contextual elements that regulate an activity such as treadmill stepping and, by extension, all psychological phenomena.

Development, then, for both Edelman and Thelen, is always a "real time" phenomenon in which the status of the organism at any level of functioning is, to some degree, always changing as a result of changing inputs to the system. In this sense, for the developmental psychobiologist, stages are best appreciated as periods of "relative" stability.

Both Thelen's and Edelman's work highlights developmental psychobiologists' basic argument that attempts to dichotomize development are wrong. That is, attempts to differentiate the psychological from the biological, to differentiate genes from experience, and to differentiate thought from action are all counterproductive because they invariably lead to an incorrect image of the process of development. For these theorists development is a synergistic, interactive process—a process in which emergent forms are fully explainable from a knowledge of the components. From a psychobiological perspective there is no need to search for an ultimate regulatory structure because human systems are dynamic and self-organizing. Thelen (1995) puts it this way:

> What motor studies have shown us, however, is that each component in the developing system is both cause and effect. What is the ultimate "cause" if task motivates behavior while behavior enables new tasks; if biomechanical factors both limit movement and facilitate it; if diversity is the stuff of change, yet small differences have large effects; or if individuals must solve "phylogenetic" movement problems themselves, within their own limits of strength, energy and motivation? At what point then can researchers partition causality into genes versus environment, structure versus function, or competence versus performance? (p. 94)

Like any work in progress, Thelen's dynamic systems theory is an incomplete picture of the process of development. Its focus has been the motor development of very young children, and only by extension does it claim to offer a picture of development at all stages and within all domains. Nevertheless, it does offer an image that integrates the biological with the psychological, that provides a bidirectional mechanism for change, and that portrays development as a dynamic, emergent process. In these regards dynamic systems theory offers a developmental model consistent with an organismic world view.

Developmental Psychobiological Models in Perspective

Developmental psychobiological models reflect the growing impact of the contact between the biological and the psychological sciences within an organismic world view. In this sense these models occupy a niche parallel to developmental behavior genetic models within a mechanistic world view.

Developmental psychobiological models, by seeking tangible links between structure and function, go beyond the metaphorical or inferential links that exist in other theories within the organismic world view. Even Piaget's work, which talks most explicitly about cognitive structures , never goes beyond a "it is as if" description of those structures. Certainly for Piaget and his contemporaries, the depth of the available knowledge about neurological development was so limited as to make arguments about tangible links very difficult, if not impossible. Even today, the fact that the demonstration of these tangible links is limited to early infant development reflects how much we still have to learn about the relationship between structure and function. Nevertheless, the writings of Thelen and other developmental psychobiologists convey a clear sense of optimism that further research will eventually uncover similar tangible links at other points of the life span. It is intriguing to speculate on how such discoveries will change the nature of theory within an organismic world view.

10

Piaget's Constructivist Theory

Picture this scene: A 4-year-old child and an adult are sitting at a table. On the table are two glasses of the same size. The adult fills each glass to the same level with water and then asks the child if there is the same amount of water in each glass. The child says yes. Then the adult puts a third glass on the table, one that is taller and thinner than the other two. Telling the child to watch, the adult pours the water from one of the two original glasses into the third glass. The child is again asked if the amount of water in the two glasses is the same. The child now says no. When asked why, she says, "Because this one is taller," and points to the level of water in the third glass. The water in the third glass is now poured back into its original container and the question is asked once more. This time the child says they are the same and points to the level of the water in the two identical glasses.

A second child replaces the first; this one is about 10 years of age. The same series of questions is asked. For all three comparisons, this child says that there is the same amount of water in the two glasses. The adult suggests to the child that perhaps he is wrong, that the little girl who was here previously said that the amount of water differed when they were in different-shaped glasses. The 10-year-old says something to the effect that she must have been "one really dumb kid" and then gives you a look suggesting that maybe you are not playing with a full deck, either.

But the adult persists: "How do you *know*? Don't you need to measure the amounts of water to be sure."

"No," the child says, "you don't need to measure the water because there *has* to be the same amount of water in the two glasses, because you didn't add any and you didn't take any away."

"But look," the adult argues, "look how much higher the water level is in the third glass."

"Yes," the child acknowledges in what is beginning to sound like a slightly patronizing tone, "the water level is higher, but it is just as much thinner as it is higher."

What is happening here? Do we simply have a "really dumb" 4-year-old? Why is the 10-year-old's tone becoming increasingly patronizing? Why is he beginning to think that the adult isn't much smarter than the 4-year-old? Actually, the 4-year-old isn't dumb and the 10-year-old isn't ill-mannered. According to Piaget's theory their respective reactions to the *conservation-of-liquid* task are typical and reflect different developmental levels—levels that differ in terms of how children go about constructing knowledge by acting on the experiences they encounter. In both cases the children are giving answers that they believe to be correct, and in both cases their respective answers reflect a systematic and deliberate attempt to understand the problem that has been presented to them. Understanding why these two children give such different answers to this and similar problems was Piaget's lifework. For Piaget and other Piagetians, the different responses are not simply a matter of learning or of maturation. Neither direct instruction nor time alone is sufficient to have the 4-year-old respond as the 10-year-old. Something more complex is involved, and this complexity is the stuff of Piaget's theory. Probably no single theorist has had more influence on our modern conception of human development than Jean Piaget (1896–1980). The magnitude and the significance (some would say genius) of his work have become a primary focal point of scholarship within the field—both for those who support his work and for those who try to disprove it.

It is somewhat ironic that Piaget's work has come to have such a profound influence on human development, because this was not, directly at least, his interest. His actual interest was in a field of philosophy known as genetic epistemology. Piaget, the genetic epistemologist, was interested in how we come to know something. This knowledge could be about the physical properties of objects, about the procedures we might use to accomplish some task, about social norms or moral values, or about the logical processes involved in knowing concepts such as number or space or time. Because Piaget chose an empirical rather than an armchair approach to attempt to answer these philosophical questions, he needed to find a source of information. Children were the obvious answer because the process of development is, in fact, a process of coming to know. But, consistent with an organismic perspective, Piaget's interest was in discovering developmental patterns common to all children rather than noting differences in the individual behaviors of different children. In this sense Piaget's study of children represented an attempt to identify not the variability among children but the developmental patterns of the generic child or, as he preferred to call it, the "epistemic subject" (Beilin, 1989).

Piaget's Developmental Perspective

Piaget's theory concerns the cumulative impact of the interactions between subjects and objects or, as it is sometimes phrased, between the knower and the known. The subject (the knower) is the individual and the object (the known) is something the subject acts upon in some way. The object can be something in the real world, such as another person or some physical object, or it can be something reflected on within the subject's consciousness. In this latter case the reflected object might be thoughts about the spatial or numeric relationship between a set of objects or, in the case of our 10-year-old, the reason there has to be the same amount of water in the two different-shaped glasses.

To begin to understand Piaget's perspective, it will help to keep four points in mind. First, there is a cumulative dimension to these subject/object interactions. That is, each subsequent interaction is in some way and to some degree different because of the one that preceded it. The course of this cumulative impact defines Piaget's developmental sequence, a sequence typically described in terms of four developmental periods.

Second, it is difficult, if not impossible, to clearly distinguish actions on objects in the real world from actions on objects in consciousness. In other words, we can't think about the quantity of water in glasses unless either there are glasses actually present or we have the cognitive competence to represent mentally such a physical event. There is an interdependent relationship between the two.

Third, we come to know something only by acting upon it. The infant comes to know the rattle by shaking it and mouthing it; the preschooler comes to know the rules of social exchange by interacting with peers; the adolescent comes to know the solution to the chemistry problem by systematically trying out all of the logically possible combinations of the chemical compounds. Again reflecting the interdependent nature of the theory, being able to know something is therefore influenced both by the means available to us to act upon the object and by the nature of the object itself. The infant's actions are more limited than those of the adolescent. The infant's immature motor skills, for example, limit how that rattle can be manipulated and therefore what knowledge can be gained from the interaction to a much greater degree than the adolescent's.

Finally, if to know something means to act upon it, then knowledge is never a perfect carbon copy of reality. Rather, it must always be, to some degree, an approximation of it—an approximation constructed by the child (i.e., the subject). To be sure, this approximation increasingly comes to resemble objective reality as individuals become more competent, but it will never be an exact copy because the people's actions partly define the interactions. This is why Piaget's theory is thought of as a *constructivist theory*.

Origins of Piaget's Constructivist Theory

Jean Piaget was born in 1896 in Neuchatel, Switzerland, and spent almost all of his life in Geneva, Switzerland. He held various professorships and directorships in his distinguished career, the most important of which, with respect to the development of his theory, was as director of the International Center for Genetic Epistemology at the University of Geneva. Scholars from many disciplines would join Piaget at the Center each year to study some particular aspect of cognitive development. Throughout the academic year Piaget and the group would meet regularly to discuss and debate their findings. At the end of each academic year, Piaget would take the data collected over the year, as well as the substance of these discussions, to a cabin high in the Swiss Alps. There, each summer, he would convert the work done under his direction into one or more books or monographs summarizing the findings of the year and, in so doing, further extend the scope of his theory. These summers were very productive, resulting in over 40 books currently available in English, plus many that have never been translated from his native French, and even more shorter publications. But the importance of this work lies not so much in its scale as in its uniqueness and vision.

Piaget's vision of how we come to know something traces back to his very early work—work not with young children but with a very different subject, mollusks. And it was early work, given that Piaget was something of a prodigy. He wrote his first scholarly paper at the age of 10. Several papers on mollusks followed, and on the basis of this work, he was offered the position of curator of natural history at a museum in Geneva. However, he had to decline the offer because, unknown to the museum, he was only 11 at the time. He continued his work with mollusks through his doctorate, but larger questions were always at the heart of his work, questions that pertained not merely to mollusks but more generally to the patterns and structures he noticed through his study. In particular, he was interested in the nature of the logic and the forces that accounted for the things he observed (Cowan, 1978).

Trying to resolve the dilemma of how best to integrate his interest in the issues of logic and meaning that were the domain of the philosophers with the precision of the methods of the natural sciences led Piaget away from zoology and toward psychology, a seeming compromise. After a short flirtation with psychoanalysis, Piaget in 1920 took a position in Henri Simon's laboratory in Paris. Simon was an early collaborator with Alfred Binet on his test of intelligence, the test we now know as the IQ test. Piaget's job was to standardize some items originally developed in English and now being reworked for a French-speaking population.

The IQ test, of course, is a measure of content, with the score based on the number of correct answers. But Piaget noticed something far more interesting than the actual answers the children gave. He noticed the reasons they offered for the answers they gave. Although the reasoning behind the answer was not an element of the IQ test, to Piaget the information was fascinating, especially when he observed certain patterns of reasoning common to many of the children, even when they gave incorrect answers (Harris, 1997). It is this interest in the reasoning behind the answers that has come to be the defining element of Piaget's *clinical method*. It was through the clinical method that Piaget finally had a means to empirically study the types of epistemological questions that were most of interest to him—questions about how we come to construct meaning out of our everyday experiences.

Causal Factors in Piaget's Theory

How does this all happen? If our ability to understand the meaning of something isn't packaged in our genes and if it isn't simply acquired through some sort of learning process, how do we construct knowledge? To understand Piaget's answers to these questions, you first must remember that Piaget is an organismic theorist. This means that his theory is based on the belief that the process of development is holistic. Elements do not exist in isolation but only function in an interdependent fashion with all other elements. Second, you must remember that organismic models are *dialectical*. Change occurs through a continuing and cumulative sequence of syntheses, each serving to integrate elements existing at a lower level. Finally, you must remember that the driving force for this process of development is internal rather than external to the organism. That is, development is best understood by considering formal rather than either efficient or material causes.

For Piaget the defining formal element of development—the driving force—is the process of *equilibration*. Consistent with the organismic belief that distinctions between the biological and the psychological are at best arbitrary and at worst misleading, Piaget saw one factor regulating the activity of all living species, both plant and animal, at all levels. This was the process of equilibration—namely, the effort by the organism to exist in harmony with its environment. Any threat to this harmony is seen as a source of disequilibrium. With respect to psychological issues, Piaget believed that disequilibrium results from some sort of cognitive conflict. The conflict may be between the subject and an external object or the subject and an internal object. The young child who calls all four-legged animals dogs will soon enough encounter a four-legged animal that another person calls a cow. This new piece of information is discrepant with the child's existing understanding. A state of disequilibrium results, and efforts are made to reestablish an equilibrium. Adolescents often have a view of social relationships that, at the same time, allows for a great degree of autonomy and a great degree of commitment. At some point, they are likely to reflect on the fact that these two notions are, in fact, mutually exclusive. Realizing that you can't have your cake and eat it, too, is another type of cognitive conflict, and again efforts are made to reestablish an equilibrium.

But for Piaget reestablishing an equilibrium is not a *homeostatic* process. That is, the equilibration process does not function solely to return the organism to its original state in the sense of our bodies changing blood pressure or heart rate back to some ideal level. For Piaget, equilibration is a dynamic rather than a static process, in which stability can come about only through change (i.e., development), and not through a static balancing mechanism. Ironically we develop (i.e., change) because of our efforts to maintain stability (i.e., stay the same).

It is important to note that although Piaget saw equilibration as the most powerful driver of development, it was not the only force he recognized. He argued that three other factors are significant as well. In this sense, that the three serve to define what is possible in terms of development, they are all necessary but not sufficient conditions for explaining development (Piaget & Inhelder, 1969). Maturation, a material cause, is the first causal factor. The process of maturation, for Piaget, reflects the genetic element influencing development. Piaget saw the process of maturation, particularly in terms of the nervous system, as setting a significant upper limit on development. The second and third causal factors, experience with the social world and experience with the physical world, are both efficient causes. Even though we come to know something by acting upon it, our ability to do so is, in part, a function of the thing we are trying to act upon. The infant will certainly have an easier time coming to know a rattle than an automobile because there is a better fit between her skills and the nature of the rattle than of the car. Similarly certain types of social situations are easier to comprehend than others. The infant will have a much easier time defining herself in terms of a parent than in terms of a whole peer group.

Although Piaget certainly acknowledged the importance of maturation, physical experience, and social experience, he never pursued their impact to the same degree as he did with equilibration. This appears true for two reasons. First, these three factors help explain variability between individuals, a topic of less interest to Piaget than his concern for what we have in common as a species. Second, consistent with an organismic perspective, Piaget saw equilibration as a more basic causal mechanism than the other three—more basic in the sense that the impact of the other three can only be interpreted with respect to individuals' efforts to maintain a degree of dynamic equilibrium.

The Two Sides of Piaget's Constructivist Theory

Understanding the mechanisms that make equilibration possible requires an understanding of the two "sides" of Piaget's theory. One side concerns function, and the other structure. The two are interdependent, and to even talk about them separately is, in a sense, to misrepresent them as distinct.

The Functional Side

The functional side of the theory concerns a set of *invariant functions,* invariant in the sense that their purposes do not change over the course of development. At each point in the developmental sequence, the same functions are present, operating in the same manner and for the same purposes. Piaget identified two functional invariants—*adaptation* and *organization.* Together, they serve as the means through which individuals attempt to maintain a dynamic equilibrium.

ADAPTATION   Adaptation concerns the patterns of interaction between the individual and the physical and social environment. It consists of two complementary processes—*assimilation* and *accommodation.* Each experience we encounter, large or small, is interpreted or given meaning in terms of the knowledge we bring to the situation. The child whose contact with four-legged creatures has been limited to dogs will most likely assume that the new four-legged creature he has discovered is also a dog. This is an act of assimilation—that is, interpreting new experiences in the context of previous knowledge. It is a "conservative" effort in the sense that we try to maintain equilibrium by interpreting the new in terms of the old. But, in fact, not all four-legged creatures are dogs, and someone has just told this child that this four-legged creature is called a cow. This new piece of information creates a degree of disequilibrium because it cannot simply be assimilated into existing knowledge. To resolve the cognitive conflict, an accommodation must be made. That is, the child has to make a change in light of this new information.

Both assimilation and accommodation are acts of transformation. When a new experience is given meaning by being assimilated into previous knowledge, the experience is to some degree and in some manner transformed so that it is meaningful in terms of the old information. But the very act of assimilation also requires a transformation in terms of accommodation, because the child is now different by virtue of having incorporated the new experience. The degree of accommodation would, of course, depend on how discrepant the new experience is from the old, but in all instances some degree of change is involved. Again, the organism maintains a dynamic equilibrium by being able to change, by being able to establish new balance points.

All experiences involve both an element of assimilation and an element of accommodation, although not necessarily to the same degree in each situation. Piaget viewed play as the closest to a pure example of assimilation and imitation as the closest to a pure act of accommodation. In play the child directs all efforts toward making the world as the child wishes it to be; in imitation the child directs all efforts toward becoming a carbon copy of the model.

The degree to which we are able to assimilate and accommodate is a measure of our ability to adapt. The more previous experience we bring to a situation, the better we are able to assimilate a new experience and to maintain a degree of equilibrium. The degree to which we are able to change in light of new situations (i.e., accommodate) is a measure of the degree to which we can establish a new level of equilibrium. Not surprisingly, given this line of reasoning, a correlate of maturity is greater adaptability. In fact, one could argue that a reasonable definition of maturity is the ability to adapt.

ORGANIZATION   Assimilation and accommodation do not happen in a piecemeal fashion. Consistent with an organismic perspective, efforts to adapt are interconnected in a systematic fashion. That is, they are organized. It is organization that is the second of Piaget's two functional invariants. The tendency of organisms to organize is as much a formal characteristic of species as is their tendency to adapt. Each species organizes in ways consistent with its makeup and experiences, but the function is evident in all species. As humans we compare and contrast experiences; we sequence events, quantify them, group them in various ways and at various levels, show preferences, and invent signs and symbols to represent experience, to name just some of the ways that we organize our experiences. The degree to which we are able to effectively organize information is a measure equally of our ability to maintain a dynamic equilibrium and of our ability to assimilate and accommodate to specific experiences.

The Structural Side

If Piaget's theory was only about functional invariants and equilibration, then it could as easily be seen as mechanistic as organismic, because function provides no mechanism for qualitative change, a defining characteristic of organismic theory. This is where the other side of the theory comes in—the focus on structure.

Developmental level is a measure of the state of the cognitive structures available to the individual. Over time, these structures change in such a way that new structures evolve out of older ones. This evolution is not a quantitative process, however, because the new structures demonstrate properties that the older ones did not have. Our 10-year-old knew the two glasses contained the same amount of water because he was able to perform the cognitive activity that proved they were the same. To him they *had* to be the same. It was this sense of logical necessity that led him to argue that there was no need to empirically test the amounts of water in the two glasses and that led him to question the adult's view of the world. Our 4-year-old did not have such structures, and as such there was no logical contradiction in her mind that a constant amount of water when placed in some glasses is more than it is in others. So, she was able to see them as the same, then as different, and then as the same without the slightest degree of cognitive conflict.

The two children are operating from different sets of cognitive structures. Notice that the significant issue is not one of right and wrong. Rather, the issue is understanding the nature of the cognitive structures that led to the 4-year-old saying one thing and the 10-year-old another. The particular value of Piaget's clinical method is that it allows the investigator to go beyond the answer and to look at the reasoning behind the answer. In all children, at all ages, there is reasoning because there are structures. The difference, across developmental levels, is the nature of the structures. Different types of structures define different developmental levels.

PIAGET'S FOUR DEVELOPMENTAL PERIODS   Piaget identified four developmental periods, each defined by a particular form of logic reflecting a particular type of cognitive structure. The four are (1) the *sensorimotor period,* which is most typical of children up to the age of 18 to 24 months; (2) the *preoperational period,* which is most typical of children as young as 2 and as old as 6 or 7; (3) the *concrete operational period,* which is most typical of children as young as 6 or 7 and as old as 11 to 13; and (4) the *formal operational period,* which begins to be evident in the logic of adolescents and continues throughout the adult years. The cognitive structures of the infant are described as *schemes.* As children move through the preschool years, a second level of structure, *cognitive operations,* emerges. By the time children reach the school years, a third level of structure, the *cognitive grouping,* becomes evident in their actions. The cognitive grouping continues to evolve across the adolescent years, enabling older children to become increasingly able to deal with abstractions.

We will examine the specifics of each period later in the chapter, but for now it is important to note five general characteristics of Piaget's developmental periods. First, age norms are much less relevant than sequence. When a child first shows evidence of entering a period and how long behavior consistent with that period continues is not, to Piaget, highly significant. Such variability is most likely a function of the particular circumstances of an individual's life. Second, there is no rule stating that everyone's development will continue through the formal operational period. Again, circumstance dictates variability. Third, this variability is a function of circumstance, and not some quality inherent to the individual. For Piaget all members of the species are capable of full development, and the fact that not everyone exhibits such development is not to be taken as evidence of what is, to Piaget, a characteristic of the species. Fourth, when development occurs, it always does so in the sequence described here. It has to be this way because newer structures build on and incorporate elements of older ones. Fifth, the elements associated with the structures characteristic of each period are integrated. A developmental period is not simply a loose collection of skills across a variety of subject matter areas or domains; it is a level of functioning that is reflected across different domains. The degree of synchrony across domains is a major point of debate. Most critics attribute a greater expectation of synchrony (Brainerd, 1993) than Piaget ever did, but there is still the clear expectation that, increasingly toward the end rather than the onset of a developmental period, the level of functioning in one domain is predictive of and similar to that in another (Goldhaber, 1981, 1982).

SCHEMES   Each developmental period is characterized by a unique set of cognitive structures. The cognitive structures of the infant are described as schemes, or generalized action patterns. Looking, reaching, grasping, and mouthing, for example, are all schemes typical of the infant. Notice that the scheme is not simply the actual grasping of the rattle or the ball, but rather more generally an integration of all of the elements involved in making such an action possible. These elements can be used with respect to more than one scheme. For Piaget much of infant development actually involves the child coming to construct such an understanding. It is this flexibility of schemes as action patterns that makes them effective adaptive mechanisms and that indicates, to Piaget, that infants are able to construct knowledge through their ability to modify schemes to fit particular situations. Schemes provide the first means through which infants come to know their worlds. They are the means through which new experiences are assimilated and new accommodations, often in the form of new schemes, are made.

COGNITIVE OPERATIONS   Cognitive operations begin to emerge during the preschool years as young children become better able to mentally represent their experiences and then to act on those representations—as opposed to acting directly on the experience itself. In this sense a cognitive operation is an action on a mental representation. Whereas physical actions of the infant involved actions such as mouthing, grasping, pushing, and pulling, the cognitive actions of the preschooler might involve ordering, sorting, classifying, and quantifying. Notice that operations are potentially a more adaptive mechanism because the child is less restricted by the specifics of the physical or social environment. In the case of preschoolers, this is not a huge advantage because their ability to use cognitive operations is somewhat limited. Nevertheless, the beginnings of the shift toward reflection as a more adaptive mechanism are clearly evident.

GROUPINGS   Neither the physical action schemes of the infant nor the cognitive operations that begin to appear during the preschool years exists in isolation of each other. Rather, Piaget argues, within each developmental period individual actions become increasingly integrated to form a *structure of the whole*. The structure has the form of a grouping in which each of the elements is interrelated with all the others. It is important to note that the child is not aware of any of this, at least not until well into the school years, but children's behavior patterns clearly indicated to Piaget that such groupings are developing.

The integrity of the grouping has a developmental dimension. That is, for the infant and the preschooler, these structures of the whole are fragmentary and incomplete. It is not until children reach the period of concrete operations that there is clear evidence of these structures functioning in a complete and integrated manner.

For Piaget a grouping has four interrelated logical properties. First, the grouping demonstrates *combinativity*, the logical understanding that any two elements in a set may be combined to form a third element of the same set. Combinative logic is evident when school-age children observe that, given a bunch of roses and a bunch of daisies, there are more flowers than there are either roses or daisies. Combinativity is an essential element of all hierarchical classifications, because the larger category has been formed by combining two smaller categories.

A second property of a grouping is *associativity*. The rules of logic dictate that acts of combinativity can only be carried out on two elements of a set at any one time. However, any but the simplest sets will contain more than two elements. How, then, is it possible to combine all of them? The child who also demonstrates associativity recognizes, at least implicitly, that the combining of objects in a set can be a cumulative process, one in which increasingly larger sets are combined to eventually reach the broadest set. Furthermore, this child realizes that the order in which these associations are made is irrelevant because eventually all members of the set will be combined with all others to form the general category.

The third property of a grouping is *identity*, the basic notion that things stay the same unless changed. Our 10-year-old's explanation for the amount of water being the same "because you didn't add any and you didn't take any away" is an example of identity. In other words, the water maintained its identity, at least with respect to its amount.

The fourth property of a grouping is *reversibility*. Reversibility is the opposite of combinativity. Not only is it possible to combine smaller elements to form a larger one (combinativity), it is equally possible to disassemble larger sets to form smaller elements. Reversals can be done through *negation,* as in the case of arithmetic problems when children realize that it is possible to "undo" a problem by reversing or negating the original operation (i.e., 3 + 5 = 8, and therefore 8 − 5 = 3, etc.). Reversibility can also come about in the form of *reciprocity.* In the water problem the 10-year-old was demonstrating reciprocity when he noted the relation of the changes in the height of the water and its width. One change doesn't literally negate the other in the sense that it undoes it, but it does compensate for it; that is, there is a reciprocal relationship between the two.

All of the elements of the grouping are interrelated into a general structure. Each can be defined in relation to the others in the same sense as in the relationship of combinativity and reversibility. It is this wholeness that is the defining element of mature thought for Piaget. It is this sense of wholeness that allows our 10-year-old to say that "there *has* to be" the same amount of water in the two different-shaped glasses.

Schemes, operations, and groupings are the three elements of Piaget's structural side of his theory; adaptation and organization are the functional elements. The interaction of the two—structure and function—serve to maintain a dynamic equilibrium. Each new assimilation changes, to some degree, cognitive structure. Changes in structure make possible new assimilations and new forms of accommodation. The process is continuous, although certain types of syntheses (i.e., the developmental periods) define the nature of these interactions at different points of the child's development.

The Evolution of Piaget's Constructivist Theory

As is true of most theorists whose work spans many years, Piaget's ideas evolved as his ongoing research suggested new perspectives, emphases, and interpretations. Covering an interval of more than six decades, Piaget's work led him to identify the functional and structural elements of his theory, delineate the characteristics of his four developmental periods, clarify the role of the four causal factors in regulating the process of development, and toward the end of his career, reemphasize the equilibration process as the core element of development. Perhaps the best way to appreciate these remarkable accomplishments is by examining the four phases of his work. By looking at the evolution of his theory chronologically, it is possible to see both the cognitive conflicts and the syntheses that ultimately led to the theory as we know it today (Beilin, 1989, 1992; Chapman, 1988; Gruber & Voneche, 1996).

Phase I: Approximately 1923–1932[1]

This first phase of Piaget's work is reflected in five major publications, *The Language and Thought of the Child* (Piaget, 1974b [1923]), *Judgment and Reasoning in the Child* (Piaget, 1966 [1924]), *The Child's Conception of the World* (Piaget, 1979 [1926]), *The Child's Conception of Physical Causality* (Piaget, 1960 [1927]), and *The Moral Judgment of the Child* (Piaget, 1965 [1932]). These early works focused on three topics: (1) children's use of language, (2) their understanding of the rules or invariants that define our physical world, and (3) their understanding of the rules that define our social relationships. The common theme in all of these works is an examination of the transition from the prelogical thought of the preschooler to the logical thought of the school-age child.

In *The Language and Thought of the Child*, Piaget attempts to categorize the changes that occur in children's use of language from the preschool years to adolescence. He is particularly interested in how children use language to serve their own purposes, in terms of explanations, arguments, and questions. Of the many findings from this early study, one of the most significant and enduring is the sequence of conversation styles that Piaget identified. The language of the preschool-age child is most often *egocentric* in structure whereas that of older children is described by Piaget as *socialized speech.* The difference between the two is that preschoolers have considerable difficulty in recognizing that others do not view either their actions or their words from the same perspective as they do. It is as if these young children are working on the premise that "you know everything that I know." As Piaget (1974) described these early language patterns:

> When a child utters phrases belonging to the first group, he does not bother to know to whom he is speaking nor whether he is being listened to. He talks either for himself or for the pleasure of associating anyone who happens to be there with the activity of the moment. This talk is egocentric, partly because the child speaks only about himself, but chiefly because he does not attempt to place himself at the point of view of his hearer. (p. 32)

As preschoolers move into the school years, these monologues give way to true communication. Comments are stated with reference to the listener, and the listener

---

[1] The dates for each of the four phases reflect the publication dates for the books reflective of that phase. In most cases the actual work may have begun earlier.

is selected by the child as the focus of the comments. Comments are modified in light of responses from the listener, and both questions and answers are appropriate to the situation.

In *Judgment and Reasoning in the Child,* Piaget continues his investigation of children's language use between the ages of 3 and 11. Here the focus is on children's use of language to express causality. Piaget finds that even children as old as 6 or 7 have trouble with causal terms, often incorrectly using a term such as *because* to associate two events that have no necessary causal relationship. When presented with the unfinished sentence "I lost my pen because," one 6-year-old replies, "I'm not writing any more." To the stem "I had a bath because," a 7-year-old answers, "afterwards I am clean" (Piaget, 1966, p. 17). In both cases the two elements of the sentence have a relationship to each other, but it is not causal. As in the cases of communication, younger children have considerable difficulty recognizing the appropriate form of the subject-object relationship and therefore have difficulty in forming an appropriate response.

This difficulty for preschoolers, or, as Piaget referred to them, *prelogical,* is also evident in their seeming lack of awareness of contradictory statement. When, for example, Piaget asks children how many brothers and sisters they have, each gives the appropriate number. But when then asked how many brothers or sisters one of their siblings has, they typically give a number that is smaller by one. In other words, they can see their brothers and sisters in terms of themselves but they have difficulty seeing themselves in terms of their brothers and sisters. To Piaget such data indicate that reversible mental structures have yet to develop. Because these prelogical children lack reversibility, what would be an obvious cognitive conflict to an older child (the two sibling questions must produce the same response) is no more a contradiction for these younger children than is functioning on the implicit assumption that the amount of water in a glass is partly determined by the shape of the glass.

The significance of these two early studies is not so much the specific behavior identified, but rather that they served for Piaget as a first clear indication of the influence of a larger developmental pattern, a pattern reflecting the logical and integrated structure of children's cognitive operations. In both studies there is an indication of the adaptive value of being able to fully differentiate self from other, a skill not evident in Piaget's samples until about the age of 7 or even 8. These early studies also reflect two other foundations of the theory. The responses of these young children are very unlikely to be ones that they have learned from adults. Instead, they have been constructed by the children themselves. Furthermore, these early constructions reflect the developmental level of the children's cognitive structures interacting with their respective physical and social worlds. Although Piaget did not yet discuss this pattern in terms of qualitatively distinct developmental periods, the foundation for such later conclusions is already evident.

Piaget's next two books, *The Child's Conception of Physical Causality* and *The Child's Conception of the World,* focus on children's construction of knowledge within several topics or domains. In the first book the emphasis is on children's understanding of such natural phenomena as the wind and the clouds, water currents, flotation, and shadows, and on the operation of machinery such as bicycles and engines. In the second book the focus is on dreams, the nature of thought, the origin of names, and the origin of physical objects such as the planets, trees, and mountains.

Piaget's interest in how children construct knowledge in different domains is a defining element of his work throughout his career. It reflects an interest in how the nature of the content of different phenomena hinder children's assimilation of the information in that domain. It also reflects his interest in how capable children are of using particular cognitive operations to integrate information across different domains. As his later work would make clearer, this type of higher-level abstraction isn't very common before at least the adolescent years, and even then it is sometimes more the exception than the rule.

In both books Piaget's approach is the clinical method. All interviews start with a common thread, and, as in the case in a therapeutic setting, what follows reflects the responses of the client, or in this case, the child. The flexibility of the method also allows the researcher to challenge the child's answer either by noting inconsistencies in the response or by comparing the response to that given by another child. The child's efforts to resolve the discrepancy often provide a deeper insight into the child's level and mode of understanding. Piaget's (1979) interviews with a 5- and an 11-year-old concerning the origin of dreams provide a good example of the technique.

> (Metr 5.9 years) Where does the dream come from? *I think you sleep so well that you dream.* Does it come from us or outside? *From outside.* . . . When you are in bed and you dream, where is the dream? *In my bed, under the blanket. I don't really know. If it was in my stomach, the bones would be in the way and I shouldn't see it.* Is the dream in your head? *It is I that am in the dream: it isn't in my head. When you dream, you don't know that you are in bed. You know that you are walking. You are in the dream.* (p. 113)

> (Vics age 11.1 years) Where do dreams come from? *You dream with your head. It is in your head.* It isn't in front? *It's as if you could see it.* Is there anything in front of you? *Nothing.* What is there in your head? *Thoughts.* Do the eyes see anything in the head? *No.* (p. 119)

It is useful to contrast this clinical approach with that used within the mechanistic model. Here the goal is to vary the method and look for a constant pattern of response—constant in the sense that particular period-related properties are found in the responses of all the children. In contrast, the mechanist attempts to hold the method constant in order to detect the variability presumed inherent in the sample. Both methods are equally appropriate to their respective goals. For the mechanist the goal is to see how we differ; for the organicist it is to see how we are the same.

The findings of these two books show some common themes in terms of children's understanding about elements in both the physical world and their psychological worlds. In general, children younger than age 6 or 7 have difficulty differentiating their view of self and their view of their reality.[2] As such, these young children show an animistic characteristic in their thought. They believe that psychological qualities

---

[2] As always, it is important to remember that references to chronological age are somewhat arbitrary. Sequence is the more important consideration. Children from another country or culture or children of today certainly might show very different age norms. This is not a challenge to the theory as long as the longitudinal sequences predicted by Piaget are evident in these other children's behavior.

of the self such as feelings and awareness can also be attributed to objects and forces in the physical world. It is through the cognitive conflicts that such a view of reality eventually prompts that the child comes to make the necessary accommodations during the school years. In the larger sense this sequence is consistent with Werner's orthogenetic sequence of undifferentiated-differentiated-integrated. Piaget's young children have only begun to differentiate themselves from their objective reality.

In the last chapter of *The Child's Conception of Physical Causality*, Piaget (1960) draws some general conclusions about the growth of logic in children based on his findings from all four of the early volumes:

> This explains why the thought of the children we questioned was so lacking in logic. We were able, within each sphere, to establish special stages, but it would be extremely difficult to establish inclusive stages for the reason that during these early years the child is still very incoherent. At the age when the child is still very animistic, artificialist, or dynamic in his way of thinking on some points, he has already ceased to be so in others. He does not reap the benefits of a progress in all the domains where this progress is bound eventually to make itself felt. Corresponding stages are at varying levels, because the influence of one belief upon another takes place unconsciously and not thanks to a conscious and deliberate generalization. Thus child thought is in no way organized. (p. 292)

It is possible in looking at this conclusion to detect the origins of the structure of groupings and the concept of structures of the whole.

Piaget's last book in this first phase, *The Moral Judgment of the Child*, shifts the focus away from the physical world and toward the social world. Instead of asking about children's understanding of physical reality, he now asks them about their understanding of social reality. And he does so in a particularly ingenious way, one very appropriate to the social reality of Swiss children at that time—he watches them playing marbles. Actually, he not only watches them play but also plays the game with them and then asks them questions about how the game came to be played as is was, whether the rules could be changed, who could change them, and how it would be done. In effect, by watching children play marbles, Piaget is attempting to understand how they construct the concepts of fairness and rules and, by extension, a moral code.

Piaget's decision to pursue the topic of moral development by observing peer interactions rather than some type of parent-child interaction is itself a significant indicator of his view of the origins of the construction of moral knowledge. His choice reflects his belief about how the structure of parent-child and peer-peer interactions each make some forms of knowledge construction more likely and others less likely. The distinction concerns the significance of status in relationships and the way that status influences what can be gained from an experience. Given the greater power that adults hold over children, the rules, demands, rewards, encouragements, and so on that come from adults are, to Piaget, most likely poorly understood by children. To the young child, they are seen as arbitrary because the child has limited means to engage in the types of interactions necessary to fully appreciate the presumably logical basis of adults' actions toward children. The young child possesses neither the power necessary to logically challenge the adult's dictates nor the level of cognitive structures necessary to fully comprehend the adult's decision-making process.

But with peers it is different. By definition peers are on the same level, so they share the same degree of power and the same level of cognitive structures. The logic of the young child may be less "rational" than that of the adult, but it is still more "challengeable." It is the cognitive conflict that these challenges prompt that, for Piaget, is the basis for children's construction (as contrasted to children's acceptance from adults) of a moral code. The code begins as rules specific to particular games and then gradually broadens to a more abstract view of the self in relation to others and to society.

Piaget documents a developmental sequence of marble play that in many ways parallels his findings concerning children's understanding of the physical world. Very young children, under the age of 2, play with the marbles but don't show any understanding of their use in terms of the game of marbles. The infants' interests are in the objects as ends rather than as means. Preschoolers' play is reminiscent of their collective monologues. They use the marbles in ways related to the ways of the older children they observed, but there is no indication of their understanding of the rules or purpose of the game or of taking turns or competing to win. By the school years children are able to play the game in a social fashion. They are able to take turns, follow the rules of the game, and understand that one person will win the game. It is not until adolescence, however, that children can reflect on the rules and structure of the game while not playing the game.

Not surprisingly, children's understanding of the rules of the game corresponds with their play patterns. Preschoolers have an idiosyncratic view of the rules. Piaget notes that it is hard for them to recognize that rules do not always correspond to their desires. For them a rule is what they want it to be, and as such it is something easily changed. To the extent that each child plays in a parallel fashion, these individualized rule systems produce little conflict. For the school-age children, however, a rule is a rule, and everyone has to act accordingly. Perhaps because the adolescents are finally able to think about the game out of context, they are able to recognize that the rules of the game can be anything that the participants agree upon and can therefore be changed by the participants.

Interestingly, in Piaget's (1965) conclusion to the studies in this volume (he also examines children's understanding of lying and punishments), he makes a rare reference to educational practice. Not surprisingly, given the value he places on peer relations as the basis for moral reasoning, he is not very sympathetic to traditional top-down approaches to education and is clearly more supportive of the approaches being advocated by John Dewey at that time.

> It is, as we said in connection with Durkheim, absurd and even immoral to wish to impose upon the child a fully worked-out system of discipline when the social life of children amongst themselves is sufficiently developed to give rise to a discipline infinitely nearer to that inner submission which is the mark of adult morality. It is idle, again, to try and transform the child's mind from outside, when his own taste for active research and his desire for cooperation suffice to ensure a normal intellectual development. The adult must therefore be a collaborator and not a master, from this double point of view, moral and rational. But conversely, it would be unwise to rely upon biological "nature" alone to ensure the dual progress of conscience and intelligence, when we realize to what extent all moral and all logical norms are the result

of cooperation. Let us therefore try to create in the school a place where individual experimentation and reflection carried out in common come to each other's aid and balance one another. (p. 404)

Phase II: Approximately 1936–1945

The focus of the second phase of Piaget's work began in the same way as it has for many other developmentalists, and for Piaget it had the same monumental impact: He became a parent. Piaget's three children were born in 1925, 1927, and 1931. The three volumes associated with phase II are based to a large extent on Piaget's observations of his three children during their first three years. The three books are *The Origin of Intelligence in Children* (Piaget, 1952b [1936]), *The Construction of Reality in the Child* (Piaget, 1954 [1937]), and *Play, Dreams and Imitation in Childhood* (Piaget, 1962 [1945]). The first two volumes concern development during the first two years of life, Piaget's sensorimotor period. The third examines the transition from sensorimotor to preoperational thought.

Piaget's studies of his three children led him to recognize the role of action in the development of logical thought. Because all of the children in the phase I work were verbal, Piaget's initial assumption was that there is a close link between language and thought—even perhaps a causal one, with language development serving to foster the development of logical cognitive operations such as reversibility.

But young infants do not have verbal language. They express themselves not through words but through actions. And it was an examination of the course of these actions over the first two years that led Piaget to better appreciate their significance in the development of thought. A major conclusion of this second phase is that the logical cognitive operations that act upon mental representations have their origins in the sensorimotor physical actions of infants acting on the objects and people in their physical and social environments.

The work of this second phase also meant an extension of the clinical method. The reliance on questioning typical of the earlier work would clearly no longer be effective. Now Piaget, in addition to his interviews, used the manipulation of objects as a means to gain a deeper understanding of the meaning of the children's behavior.

THE SIX STAGES OF THE SENSORIMOTOR PERIOD   Taken together, the first two books describe a six-step sequence of knowledge construction occurring during the first two years of life. This sequence concerns both the ways infants interact with their environment and the consequences of these interaction patterns in terms of infants' early constructions of the concepts of objects, space, and causality. For Piaget it is through these early interactions that infants begin to construct a distinction between themselves and their immediate environment and, in so doing, begin the process of coming to be psychological as well as biological beings.

Stage 1: Birth to 6 Weeks   Infants are born with a set of reflexes that serve as the first means through which interactions with the world are possible. They suck, they grasp, they cry, to name just three. Of these the sucking reflex is the most important because it is the mechanism through which nourishment is obtained and, at least in humans, through which many social contacts are made.

From the moment of birth, newborns are able to assimilate the physical touch of the nipple to their scheme of sucking. As Piaget observed his children nursing over the first few weeks of life, however, he noticed significant changes in these action schemes —changes that reflected the workings of the functional invariants of adaptation and organization. The infants' search for the nipple gradually becomes more efficient, indicating that they are able to make accommodations to the sucking scheme in response to their contact with their mother's breast. Piaget also observed that the sucking scheme begins to differentiate. When newborns are hungry, sucking is directed only at the nipple, but when not, they seem willing to suck on virtually anything.

Piaget attributes great significance to the fact that infants' sucking activity is not limited to feeding situations. In the same way that all biological organs need to function to remain viable, infants need to act on their environment to exercise or use their newly developing capabilities. It is this need to exercise schemes (and subsequently cognitive operations) that illustrates the organicist's belief that humans are active rather than passive organisms.

Stage 2: 6 Weeks to 4–5 Months During the first few weeks of life, Piaget sees behavior as largely reflexive in nature. To be sure, there are some modifications of the reflexes, but each functions largely intact and independent of the others. By the second month this pattern begins to change. A new pattern, which Piaget refers to as a *primary circular reaction,* first emerges. These primary circular reactions are efforts to repeat an event that has initially occurred by chance. Thumb sucking is the classic example. Given the body proportions of newborns and the fact that they spend so much time on their stomachs, it is quite likely that a thumb will be positioned touching or in the mouth. The placement of the thumb prompts sucking. Given young infants' very limited voluntary motor control, it is also likely that the thumb will slip out of the mouth. What Piaget observed are efforts to reposition the thumb back in the mouth—hence the circularity of the pattern. The pattern emerges not all at once but over a period of weeks, with a clear but gradual increase in the skill necessary to get the thumb to the mouth and, once inside, to keep it there.

Theoretically, this seemingly simple accomplishment is very important. To Piaget it demonstrates a mechanism through which new schemes emerge out of the integration of earlier ones. In this case two independent reflexes—sucking and motor activity —become integrated to produce a new action pattern, thumb sucking. In Piaget's terms each scheme is assimilated to the other, and as each comes to be recognized in terms of the other, appropriate accommodations are also made. Movement of the hand, for example, is accommodated to the position of the mouth. Closure of the mouth is accommodated to the position of the thumb in the mouth. Chapman (1988) in his review of Piaget's theory notes that the emergence of circular reactions is not limited to thumb sucking.

> Besides sucking, Piaget observed the development of primary circular reactions and the first acquired adaptations for seeing, hearing, phonation, and prehension. Thus, he observed his children developing beyond mere orientation reflexes to patterns of

looking in order to see, listening in order to hear, grasping for the sake of grasping, and so on. Just as the activity of sucking incorporated movements of the arm and hand, these other activities began to incorporate each other into their respective patterns. Seeing incorporates hearing as children come to orient themselves visually in the direction of something heard, and so forth. (p. 83)

The new integrated schemes emerging during stage 2 more generally reflect the young infants' efforts at adaptation. These adaptations, in turn, reflect the role of the function of organization, because reflexive schemes cannot be integrated unless there is some mechanism that allows each to be organized or defined in terms of the other. These adaptations also reflect the constructive nature of development, because new schemes are built by putting together simpler ones.

Stage 3: 4–5 Months to 9 Months   Piaget reports that this third stage marks a major shift in the infant's focus. Until now the focus has been on exercising schemes and attempting to repeat events that focused on the infant. There appears to be little awareness of or interest in the environment surrounding the infant. But this all changes as a new level of circular reaction, *secondary circular reaction,* makes its first appearance. The structure of secondary reactions is the same as the primary (both still begin as a result of a chance event) with the important exception that the focus now is on repeating an interesting event external to the infant. Furthermore, whereas the focus of the primary reactions is on maintaining a pleasurable sensation such as sucking, now the focus seems to be on repeating the consequences of that action. Piaget (1952) provides wonderful examples of his daughter Lucienne at 6 months of age and Jacqueline at 9 months.

> She looks at a wooden Pierrot which I have hung before her and with which she has rarely played. Lucienne at first tries to grasp it. But the movement she makes in holding out her hand shakes the Pierrot before she has touched it. Lucienne at once shakes her legs and feet in a regular and rapid rhythm in order to maintain the swinging of the object.
>
> Jacqueline too shakes while holding a celluloid rattle in the form of a parrot. She smiles when the noise is slight, is anxious when it is too loud and knows very well how to graduate the phenomenon. She progressively increases the noise until she is too frightened and then returns to the soft sounds. Furthermore, when the rattle is struck at one of the ends, she shakes the parrot by turning it in another direction and thus knows how to reestablish the noise. (pp. 166–167)

These actions by Lucienne and Jacqueline indicate an ability to make accommodations in response to events external to them, and they suggest an interest in the consequences of their actions rather than the actions themselves. Piaget also notices in these behaviors the first indication of the infant's ability to differentiate means from ends, and as such to engage in goal-directed behavior. But there is an important qualifier to this goal-directed behavior: It appears only able to function to reproduce an interesting event initiated fortuitously. The infant is not yet able to generate a goal and then act accordingly to make it happen. This milestone is still a few weeks away.

Stage 4: 9 Months to 12 Months   In stage 2 infants demonstrate an ability to integrate schemes focused on the body. Primary circular reactions are the consequence. In Stage 4 infants for the first time demonstrate the ability to coordinate schemes focused on external objects. The result is the first true indication of goal-directed behavior and the first true indication of the concept of *object permanence,* the first clear indication that development has proceeded to the point at which the infant is able to differentiate self from the external environment. Object permanence also signifies that infants have developed a conservation of shape and size. Infants now are able to realize that the same object viewed from two different perspectives is still the same object. Together, these two accomplishments signal for Piaget the first evidence of true intelligent behavior—that is, intentionally goal-directed behavior that serves some adaptive purpose. Again, Piaget's (1952) examples are very illustrative of both the means/ends differentiation and the concept of object permanence:

> Laurent too uses my hand as an intermediate to make me resume the activities which interest him. For example, I tap my cheek with my left index finger, then I drum on my glasses (he laughs). Afterwards I pull my hand halfway between his eye and my face. He looks at my glasses, then at my hands, and ends by gently pushing my hand toward my face. . . . Laurent uses as means an element of the whole which he has just observed and an element which can be assimilated to his own activity. The other person's hand is comparable to that of the subject and the child simply prolongs its action. (p. 224)

The important thing to note in this example is that Laurent's interest is not in getting his father's hand to the face. That is only the means to the further goal of wanting his father to tap his cheek and drum on his glasses.

> Laurent lifts a cushion in order to look for a cigar case. When the object is entirely hidden, the child lifts the screen with hesitation, but when one end of the case appears, Laurent removes the cushion with one hand and with the other tries to extricate the objective. The act of lifting the screen is therefore entirely separate from that of grasping the desired object and constitutes an autonomous "means" no doubt derived from earlier analogous acts. (p. 222)

In both examples there is a clear differentiation of means from ends and therefore evidence of goal-directed behavior. But an additional accomplishment can be seen in the second example. In the first the goal is evident while the means are being pursued; in the second it isn't. The cigar case is hidden entirely. What, then, is regulating the removal of the pillow if the cigar case is not evident? For Piaget the answer is that Laurent has now become able to construct a mental representation of the goal object, and it is this representation of the object rather than the object itself that is directing the removal of the pillow. This representational ability has great adaptive significance because for the first time infants' efforts are not limited by what is present in their sensory and motor fields. This is certainly not to suggest that by 12 months infants are as adaptive as adults, but it does indicate that a major milestone has been reached in their development.

Stage 5: 12 Months to 18 Months   Until now, the accomplishments of the infant have been essentially conservative. They have primarily served to make things recur, those focused either on the infant (primary circular reactions) or in the external environment (secondary circular reactions). By the first birthday, however, Piaget identifies a third type of circular reaction emerging—a *tertiary circular reaction.* Rather than simply trying to make an interesting event reoccur, tertiary circular reactions have a "mad scientist" quality about them. Infants are now trying out different means with different ends simply to see what happens. They are now trying not merely to repeat the event but to figure out ways to vary the outcome. In effect, now that they have discovered that there is an objective reality independent of their sensory and motor awareness, they seem quite determined to learn as much as they can about it. This exploration is driven by a need to reestablish a new equilibrium now that the infant and the world have become differentiated. In the process new knowledge is constructed. Consider these examples of Jacqueline:

> In her bath, Jacqueline [at thirteen months] engages in many experiments with celluloid toys floating on the water. . . . not only does she drop her toys from a height to see the water splash or displace them with her hand in order to make them swim, but she pushes them halfway down in order to see them rise to the surface.
>
> [A few months later] she notices the drops of water which fall from the thermometer when she holds it in the air and shakes it. She then tries different combinations to splash from a distance. She brandishes the thermometer and stops suddenly, or makes it catapult.
>
> Between the ages of a year and a year and a half, she amuses herself by filling with water pails, flasks, watering cans etc. and studying the falling of water. She also learns to carry the water carefully without spilling it and by holding the basin horizontally.
>
> She entertains herself by filling her sponge with water and pressing it against her chest or above the water; by filling the sponge at the faucet; by running the water from the faucet; by running the water from the faucet along her arm, etc. (1952, p. 273)

Clearly Jacqueline is now interested in more than simply repeating an interesting event. She is involved in what Piaget refers to as creating new means through active exploration, an activity he aptly labels as *groping*. For Piaget the gropings of this fifth stage help infants differentiate the properties of objects from the properties of their actions on the objects and, in so doing, recognize that a property of objects is that they also can have causal qualities.

Stage 6: 18 Months to 24 Months   Until now, all the infants' efforts to construct knowledge have involved direct action on objects. The focus of the effort changed as infants became aware of the external environment and then as they were able to differentiate self from other. But even in stage 5 the construction of knowledge is still an act of groping, of seeing what happens if the infant does this and then that. But this pattern changes during this last stage of the sensorimotor period. For the first time Piaget finds evidence that infants are no longer restricted to constructing knowledge through direct action; they are now also able to construct knowledge by acting on mental representations of these actions. An example should prove helpful.

Piaget describes a sequence of experiments with Lucienne in which a watch is put inside a matchbox and Lucienne turns the box over to retrieve the watch. Piaget then reduces the size of the opening, and through trial and error Lucienne figures out how to get her finger into the opening to grab hold of the watch chain and retrieve the watch. Now Piaget further reduces the opening so that there is no longer any room for even Lucienne's tiny fingers. She nevertheless tries to use her fingers and fails. What happens next is significant.

> A pause follows during which Lucienne manifests a very curious reaction bearing witness to the fact that she not only tries to think out the situation and to represent to herself through mental combination the operations to be performed, but also to the role played by imitation in the genesis of representations. Lucienne mimics the opening of the slit.
>
> She looks at the slit with great attention: then, several times in succession, she opens and shuts her mouth, at first slightly then wider and wider! Apparently, Lucienne understands the existence of a cavity adjacent to the slit and wished to enlarge the cavity. The attempt at representation which she thus furnishes is expressed plastically, that is to say, due to inability to think out the situation in words or clear visual images she uses a simple motor indication as "signifier" or symbol.
>
> Soon after this phase of plastic reflection, Lucienne unhesitatingly puts her finger in the slit and, instead of trying as before to reach the chain, she pulls so as to enlarge the opening. She succeeds and grasps the chain. (1952, pp. 337–338)

It is important not to underestimate the significance of this change because it represents a major shift as to the level at which knowledge is constructed—a shift from functioning on objects to functioning on representations of those objects. In the example it is Lucienne's "very curious reaction" that indicates the shift. Rather than trying different actions directly on the objects, she appears to do nothing, but of course she is not doing nothing. She is thinking about what possible actions on the box might get the chain out. Her immediate success at getting the watch out of the box is, for Piaget, confirmation of her representational thought. The transition to the level of representational thought does not occur automatically, but rather reflects the cumulative influence of infants' increasing sophisticated interactions with the environment.

THE TRANSITION FROM THE SENSORIMOTOR TO THE PREOPERATIONAL PERIOD   The third book representative of phase II, *Play, Dreams and Imitation in Childhood*, focuses on the transition from the sensorimotor to the preoperational period of cognitive development. As mentioned previously, Piaget saw imitation as the "purest" form of accommodation possible and play as the "purest" form of assimilation. It is useful to note in this regard that Piaget viewed intelligence (defined as adaptation) as a balance between the two. Although Piaget traces the development of both imitation and play through the entire sensorimotor period, his primary interest is in discussing the form each takes as children move from a sensorimotor to a preoperational level of cognition. The form each takes during this transition time (typically

20–30 months of age) serves, for Piaget, as evidence of young children's emerging skill at having mental representations rather than physical actions serve as the primary regulator of their behavior.

With respect to imitation, the emergence of *deferred imitation* during sensorimotor stage 6 is the most significant event in this sequence. Deferred imitation is, as the name implies, behavior that reproduces a previously observed event. The key phrase is "previously observed" because, to demonstrate such imitation, the mental image of the model's behavior has to be stored in memory. It is these mental images of the original acts, rather than the acts themselves, that regulate their reproduction in behavior.

The evolution of children's play shows a similar pattern. In this case, however, children use familiar objects as symbols to represent props in their make-believe activities. So, for example, the child who puts her book under her head and pretends to sleep is pretending that the book is a pillow. What is guiding her activity is not the properties of the book as book (it is reasonable to assume that by the age of 2 most children are very familiar with the typical use of a book as something to read). Rather, it is her newly emerging ability to mentally represent the object as something she wants it to be rather than something it actually is. The book stands for or represents what she wants it to be—in this case a pillow. She has assimilated the book to her now mental rather than sensorimotor scheme of pretending to sleep.

In the final pages of *Play, Dreams and Imitation in Children,* Piaget offers a very brief synthesis of the work in his first two phases. He now clearly differentiates three developmental periods—the sensorimotor, preoperational, and concrete operational—and discusses how the events within each serve as the necessary prerequisites to the next. By the concrete operational period, play with its emphasis on assimilation and imitation with its emphasis on accommodation become integrated to form the structural basis for reversible, intelligent thought. In Piaget's (1962) words:

> This coordination in permanent equilibrium constitutes operational thought. . . . The characteristic feature of operations is their reversibility, and reversibility can only be explained as the product of equilibrium between assimilation and accommodation. Accommodation by itself is essentially irreversible, since it depends on a one-way modification of reality. . . . Assimilation by itself is also irreversible for without correlative accommodation its object is distorted to suit the activity of the subject. . . . When there is equilibrium between assimilation and accommodation, however, the former is decentered in accordance with the transformations of reality, while the latter has to take into account earlier and later states. Equilibrium between the two tendencies thus ensures reversibility, and thereby produces the operation of reversible action. (p. 289)

In all of the activities summarized by the quote and reflected in Piaget's writing, what emerges is an image of development as a repetitive sequence of differentiating what is initially undifferentiated and then integrating the now distinct pieces. Each of these constructive acts leaves the child just that much more adaptive because each piece of the puzzle, whether at the level of sensorimotor acts or mental representation, is now more likely seen in relation to all the other pieces.

Phase III: Approximately 1941–1960

In this third period in his career, Piaget focuses on the development of representational thought from the preoperational through the concrete operational to the formal operational periods. It differs from phase I, which covered some of the same age range, in that now the focus is on delineating the structural characteristics of each of these three developmental periods. The major works published during this phase include *The Child's Conception of Number* (Piaget, 1952a [1941]), *The Child's Conception of Space* (Piaget & Inhelder, 1956), *The Child's Conception of Time* (Piaget, 1971b [1946]), *The Development of Physical Quantities in the Child: Conservation and Atomism* (Piaget, 1974a [1941]), *The Early Growth of Logic in the Child: Classification and Seriation* (Inhelder & Piaget, 1964 [1959]), and *The Growth of Logical Thinking from Childhood to Adolescence* (Inhelder & Piaget, 1958 [1955]).

The six stages of the sensorimotor period form an interesting parallel to the developmental events of the next three periods, examined during phase III. During the sensorimotor period schemes become integrated, means and ends become differentiated, and behavior becomes goal-directed and intentional. The two major developmental milestones that occur—object permanence and mental representation—are "products" that emerge out of the functional activity of the infant. Both milestones are constructed because they are the most efficient ways for infants to maintain a dynamic equilibrium. In the case of object permanence, infants' differing actions on the same objects and the same actions on differing objects lead, intuitively at least, to the construction of the object as an independent reality. Similarly, the active experimentation of creating new means and ends that follows leads, again intuitively, to a shift from the level of acting on objects to acting on representations of objects.

The culminating event of the sensorimotor period—acting on mental representations—is now the beginning event for the next three developmental periods. What happens is a parallel sequence, but instead of it occurring on objects, it occurs with respect to representations of objects. It also ends, potentially, with a milestone that frees the individual from the limits of the real world. In this latter case, however, the leap is not from acting on objects to acting on representations of objects, but from acting on mental representations of concrete objects to acting on mental representations, period (Piaget & Inhelder, 1969).

All of the studies included in these phase III works serve to document these developments at the level of mental representations. They include studies examining children's ability to use number, to classify and seriate, to understand the physical properties of objects, and to use logic and reasoning to form hypotheses and reason deductively. As is true of all of Piaget's work, these studies serve two purposes: (1) They document children's developmental progress within each of the subject matter domains, and (2) they provide evidence for the more general patterns of cognitive development that are at the heart of Piaget's constructivist epistemology.

The constraints of space prevent a discussion of all of the topics addressed during phase III. Instead, we will focus on three topics that illustrate the approach Piaget used, the developmental patterns he documented, and the theoretical implications he drew from the data: (1) the conservation studies, (2) the classification studies, and (3) the studies on the development of propositional logic. The first two focus on the transition from preoperational to concrete operational thought, and the third, on the transition from concrete operational to formal operational thought.

One common element of these three, as well as of all the other topics pursued during phase III, is a further revision to the clinical method. The method in phase I relied almost completely on language. In phase II Piaget shifted to objects because infants have very limited language skills at best. In phase III the two approaches are combined. Children are now presented with tasks involving concrete objects, are asked to do something with the objects, and at the same time are queried about their actions, their predictions and conclusions, and the reasoning behind their actions.

THE CONSERVATION STUDIES   Conservation is about invariance. It is about the ability to recognize the logical necessity of certain dimensions (e.g., continuous quantity, number, area, length, weight, or volume) remaining constant or invariant in spite of some sort of transformation being performed on them.[3] Piaget studied the development of a number of conservations. The example at the beginning of this chapter is an illustration of a conservation-of-liquid task. The issue is whether each child recognizes the logical fact that the amount of liquid must remain constant irrespective of the shape or the number of containers that hold it.

Conservation of liquid is a type of task involving conservation of continuous quantity. Conservation of continuous quantity can also be demonstrated with a solid. In this case, instead of pouring water from one glass to another, the typical task involves changing the shape of one of two balls of clay or of breaking up one ball of clay into several smaller balls. The parallel between the two tasks should be obvious.

As was the case for the conservation-of-liquid task, the procedure in all the conservation experiments takes the same form. The child is initially asked if the two examples are the same—is there the same amount of water or clay, the same number of coins, and so on? The child then observes the transformation, and the question is asked again—is there more, less, or the same amount, number, distance, and so on as before? The child's second answer is now probed to identify the logical (or seemingly illogical) basis for the answer. And additional variations of the task may be done to obtain further insight into the child's solution strategies. Figure 10.1 illustrates these procedures.

Each type of conservation task probes for an understanding of a particular dimension. Conservation of number involves the ability to recognize that the number of objects in a group remains constant irrespective of the spatial arrangements of those objects. The typical task involves showing a child two rows of coins. Each row has the same number of coins, and the coins are all spaced the same distance from each other. Then one of the rows is rearranged. The space between each coin might be increased or decreased, or the coins might be arranged in a circle.

---

[3] It is important to note that conservation is not a phenomenon specific to the preoperational/ concrete operational shift. Given the definition of conservation as the recognition of invariance, the demonstration of object permanence by the infant is also a form of conservation.

Step 1 – *Interviewer shows . . .*

two identical glasses with the same amount of water and asks the child to confirm that there is the same amount of water in glass A as in glass B (for the conservation-of-liquid task).

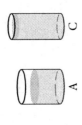

two balls having equal amounts of clay and asks the child to confirm there are the same amounts of clay in ball A as in ball B (for the conservation-of-substance task).

two rows of coins and asks the child to confirm that the number of coins in row A is the same as in row B (for the conservation-of-number task).

A ○○○○○○○
B ○○○○○○○

Step 2 – *Interviewer tells the child to "watch what I am going to do" and then . . . .*

pours the water from glass B into C, a different-sized glass.

flattens ball B into the shape of a pancake.

rearranges the coins in row B so that they are farther apart from each other than those in row A.

A ○○○○○
B ○ ○ ○ ○ ○

Step 3 – *Interviewer asks the child,*

"Now, is there the same amount of water in glass C as in glass A? Does one have more or does one have less? Why?"

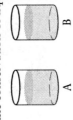

"Now, does the pancake have the same amount of clay as the ball, or does one have more, or does one have less? Why?"

"Now, does row B have the same number of coins as row A; does one have more, or does one have less? Why?"

A ○○○○○
B ○ ○ ○ ○ ○

FIGURE 10.1 Piaget's Conservation Procedure.

Piaget tested for the conservation of length, the recognition that a unit of distance is constant, by showing children two rods of the same length, placed parallel so that the ends of one rod matched those of the other. Then one rod is moved forward so that it is "ahead" of the other, and the child is asked if they are still the same length. Conservation-of-length tasks can also involve asking children to build towers of the same height but starting from different levels off the floor or asking them to compare two heights using a rod equal to the length measured or using a shorter rod. In effect, Piaget is asking if children understand what they are doing when they use a ruler to measure something.

Conservations of time, distance, and speed all involve children observing the actions of trains on parallel tracks. All three dimensions are varied to see how well the child is able to disentangle the relationships. That is, are children able to recognize that the distance traveled is independent of the amount of time it takes to travel the distance, and are they able to recognize that one train is going faster if it starts and stops at the same time as another but nevertheless has traveled farther?

Two things are important to note about Piaget's conservation studies. The first is that not all conservations are achieved at the same age. The second is that even though they are not all achieved at the same age, they show a remarkable similarity in their developmental course.

Typically, conservation of number is achieved by most children around 5 or 6 years of age. Conservations of mass, area, and length follow at about 7 or 8 years of age. Conservation of weight isn't commonly demonstrated until about 9 or 10 years of age, and finally, conservation of volume makes its appearance at around 11 or 12. Furthermore, the same type of conservation using one material may be attained sooner than when using another.

Piaget offers two explanations for this pattern, which he referred to as *horizontal decalage*. In some cases, he argues, conservations build on each other. Conservation of volume, for example, because it involves the coordination of the dimensions of length and width, presupposes that the conservation of length has been successfully constructed. Similarly, the conservation of weight presupposes the conservation of substance. In other cases some materials or transformations of materials are more resistant to being assimilated than others. For example, children who are just beginning to demonstrate conservation of liquid are much more likely to give a conserving answer when the water is poured into 2 glasses than when it is poured into 10.

Irrespective of the particular conservation, Piaget notes a common three-step sequence. Initially, young children give nonconserving responses and explanations. They may say, "Now there is more"; they may say, "Now there is less"; and they may show very little predictability or consistency across variation of the task. What seems to be driving their behavior are the particulars of the task before them at that moment. Furthermore, when they give an explanation for their answers, it is empirical rather than logical. They will point to some aspect of the display—the height of the liquid, the number of clay balls, and so on—as the explanation for their answer.

In the second, or transition, step, the children are able to give a conserving response when the transition is small but fail to give one when it is great. One child in Piaget's conservation-of-liquid studies had no trouble recognizing that the amount of liquid would remain the same if it was poured into two glasses, but he ran into trouble when the liquid was poured into three glasses.

> *No, in three there is more.* And if you pour the three back into that one how far up will it come? (He points to a level higher than the original glass.) And if we pour the three glasses into four glasses and then pour it all back into the big one, how far will it come up? (He points to a still higher level.) And with five? (He shows a still higher level.) And with six? *There wouldn't be enough room in the glass.* (Piaget, 1952a, p. 14)

By the third step children not only consistently give conserving responses irrespective of the transformation but are also able to give a logically consistent explanation for their answer. Their explanations reflect their ability either to mentally reverse the operation ("If you poured it back into the original glass, it would still be the same as the other glass"), to conserve the identity of the original amount ("You didn't add any and you didn't take any away"), or to compensate for the changes ("This glass is higher but it is also thinner").

Piaget's goal in these conservation tasks is not simply to document children's growing ability with respect to each of these tasks but, more broadly, to show a more general developmental pattern emerging across several domains. The pattern is the gradual replacement of responses based on the appearance of things by responses based on the logically necessary relationships existing among the elements of the task. It is children's ability to use logic as the basis of their problem solving that allows them to differentiate the relevant from the irrelevant transformations. It is their logic that allows them to shift their focus of attention from the static images present during each variation of the task to the transformation involved in going from one variation to another. It is, even more broadly, the demonstration of these logically consistent answers that gives Piaget reason to argue for the emergence, during the period of cognitive operations, of a group of integrated logical cognitive operations.

THE CLASSIFICATION STUDIES   Piaget's studies of the development of classification skills reflect the same interest in understanding children's ability to use logical operations as does his interest in the conservation tasks. In the case of the classification studies, however, the focus is on children's ability to recognize the defining properties of objects, not their ability to disregard irrelevant transformations.

The ability to classify presumes, at least implicitly, the ability to recognize both the intensive and the extensive properties that define a class. The *intensive* properties of a class are its defining elements, the one or more elements shared by all members of that class. For example, the intensive properties of simple physical objects include their color, size, shape, and weight. The *extensive* properties of a class reflect the recognition of all of the members of that class. That is, the ability to recognize the extensive properties of a class reflects the ability to recognize the relevant intensive property in all objects, present or not, irrespective of the other defining properties of those objects. In other words, it is the ability to realize that if "red" is the defining intensive property of a class, then all red objects, irrespective of size, shape, weight, or whatever, are in fact members of the class.

True classification ability requires that the child be able to recognize both the intensive and the extensive properties in a collection and effectively act on that recognition—that is, to put all the objects that belong to the same group together. To determine how children acquire these skills, Piaget examined their ability to do simple classification, class inclusion tasks, hierarchical classification, and multiple classification, and to understand the concepts of "all" and "some."

As is true of the other cognitive accomplishments at the level of acting on mental representations, Piaget sees classification skills as first emerging at the level of acting directly on objects during the sensorimotor period.

> A child may be given a familiar object: immediately he recognizes its possible uses; the object is assimilated to the habitual schemata of rocking, shaking, striking, throwing to the ground, etc. If the object is completely new to him, he may try a number of schemata in succession, as if he is trying to understand the nature of the strange object by determining whether it is for rocking, or for rattling, or rubbing etc. We have here a sort of practical classification, somewhat reminiscent of the later definition by use. But this rudimentary classification is realized only in the course of successive trials and does not give rise to a number of simultaneous collections. (Inhelder & Piaget, 1964, p. 13)

In effect, infants' early classification behavior is defined by the moment and is reflective of the particular objects in view. There is little evidence of intensiveness other than on an idiosyncratic level, no evidence of extensiveness, and no evidence of consistency across time and objects.

For children just entering the preoperational period, Piaget notes a type of classification, which he referred to as *graphic collections* rather than true classifications. For these children, typically 2 to 4 years of age, their groupings of objects often reflect the spatial continuity of the objects as they are presented to the child. In one study involving geometric shapes and colors, Piaget reports a child as first placing a blue triangle next to another and then continuing with a blue square.

> The blue square is followed by a yellow triangle (a change from the criterion of color to that of form) and then by red, yellow and blue squares. Since the last square is preceded by a yellow one, the child places a yellow one after it (probably guided by symmetry). This induces him to choose six more triangles, first two red then two yellow, and finally two blue. (Inhelder & Piaget, 1964, p. 23)

A similar pattern was noted with nongeometric objects. In this case objects are grouped together because they are often associated with each other (e.g., babies and cribs, houses and trees, children and bicycles) rather than because they share a common defining property.

If the logic reflective of the graphic collections of the young child seems parallel to that of nonconserving children, it is more than merely coincidence. Piaget presumes a loose synchrony across all of the different tasks he used to document cognitive development. After all, in all cases, he is arguing that the same set of emerging cognitive operations is reflected in each of these particular experimental procedures.

Piaget notes a significant shift in children's classification skills by 4 to 7 years of age. Now, when children are given groups of objects differing in color, shape, size, and so on, they are partially able to group the objects in terms of their intensive properties, but children rarely exhaust the possibilities. In other words, children are not very sensitive to the extensive dimension of classification. Furthermore, their success occurs largely through trial and error. The fact that they are using trial and error as a problem-solving strategy is significant for Piaget because it suggests that the children are not yet fully acting on the objects in terms of a fully defined mental representation of the relationships between them.

Piaget refers to these groupings of the 4- to 7-year-olds as *nongraphic collections* rather than true classifications. They are nongraphic in the sense that they are no longer based on their physical contiguity in the placements or their general associations of use. But they are still not true classifications because they do not yet fulfill the dual definition of intention and extension. Piaget believes that the reason for the difficulty reflects children's limited ability to differentiate the concepts of "all" and "some."

To test this hypothesis, Piaget conducted a series of studies with children from 4 to 7 years old involving *class inclusion* tasks. Class inclusion concerns the awareness of the relationship between classes—in particular, the fact that classes can be organized hierarchically. Consider a display in which several types of flowers and several types of animals are presented. A simple classification would be to put each of the specific types of flowers in distinct groups (roses with roses, daisies with daisies, etc.) and to do the same with the animals. The question now is whether the children recognize the fact that each of the types of flowers can also be grouped into the larger, more general class of flowers, that each of the types of animals can also be grouped into the larger, more general class of animals, and that these two larger classes can, in turn, be further combined into an even broader class of living things. To answer the question, Piaget asked children such things as "Are all the flowers daisies?" and "Are all the daisies flowers?" and "Are there more roses or flowers?" To answer the questions correctly, children had to be able to understand the difference between "all" and "some."

Piaget believes that 4- to 7-year-olds have problems with class inclusion tasks because they tend to define "some" in absolute rather than relative terms. For these children "some" means a small number rather than a subset (which could, in fact, be a very large number) of a larger group. Furthermore, although children of this age are able to combine classes into more general ones, they don't seem able to recognize the relationship between their actions. Having made the large group, they no longer seem able to recognize that it is made up of two smaller ones. The parallel to the conservation tasks is again obvious because in both cases the children's limitation reflects a lack of reversibility in their thought.

Piaget found that, by the age of 7 or 8, children demonstrate clear classification ability. Their sorting reflects both intension and extension, they have little difficulty with class inclusion problems, and they soon become able even to deal with multiple classification problems—problems involving the classification of objects on two or more dimensions simultaneously. Furthermore, the fact that they are able to correctly place newly introduced objects into their sorts even after the sorting of the original group has been completed indicates that their skill is based not so much on the perceptual image of the objects as on a logically generated concept of the defining properties of a class. Put another way, the child of 9 or 10, having made the transition from preoperational to concrete operational thought, is now operating on the basis of the interdependent grouping of the logical operations of combinativity, associativity, identity, and reversibility.

THE DEVELOPMENT OF PROPOSITIONAL LOGIC   Piaget's studies on conservation and classification document the transition from preoperational to concrete operational thought. They demonstrate young children's growing ability to systematically use logical operations—in particular, their growing ability to compare and contrast simultaneously rather than successively. It is this simultaneity or reversibility in their thinking that allows them to recognize that the glass is both taller and thinner in the conservation task and that the flowers are part of both the smaller group of roses and the larger group of living things.

Clearly, these accomplishments are major advances over the skills of the preschooler. However, concrete operation is not, to Piaget, fully mature thought because it still shows one major limitation. Concrete operational children's ability to use logical thought is restricted to real, concrete situations. They are still not able to logically consider situations contrary to fact or their experience or situations hypothetical in nature. Ask the 8-year-old what would happen if people had eight fingers on each hand rather than five, and the likely response would be "But people don't have eight fingers on each hand, they only have five!"

Piaget's studies of the transition to formal operational thought were done in collaboration with his long-time colleague Barbel Inhelder (Inhelder & Piaget, 1958). They focus on children 12 to 14 years of age and generally document children's growing ability to differentiate "form" from "content" in their thinking. That is, during early adolescence children begin to demonstrate the ability to use their logical operations to act on the relationships that exist among the elements of an argument irrespective of the particular content of those elements. In other words, the real now becomes a special case of the possible. Inhelder and Piaget (1958) describe the difference this way:

> But how can we explain the adolescent's new capacity to orient himself toward what is abstract and not immediately present (seen from the outside by the observer comparing him to a child) but which (seen from within) is an indispensable instrument in his adaptation to the social adult framework, and as a result his most immediate and most deeply experienced concern. . . . Formal thinking is both thinking about thought (propositional logic is a second-order operational system which operates on propositions whose truths, in turn, depend on class, relational, and numerical operations) and a reversal of relations between what is real and what is possible (the empirically given comes to be inserted as a particular sector of the total set of possible

combinations). . . . The adolescent's theory construction shows both that he has become capable of reflective thinking and that his thought makes it possible for him to escape the concrete present toward the realm of the abstract and the possible (pp. 341–342)

One of the particular studies documenting this transition was Piaget and Inhelder's study of the development of propositional logic in young adolescents. Propositional logic is "if-then" logic. It is the ability to form and then systematically test all the logically possible hypotheses related to a particular task. Note that the ability to do this is not based on some sort of trial-and-error process, but rather on the young adolescent's ability to mentally act on the logically possible relationships—a subset of which will, upon examination, prove to be the empirically correct ones. (If this new skill sounds somewhat parallel to the distinction between stages 5 and 6 of the sensorimotor period, you're beginning to understand the theory.) One of the actual tasks Inhelder and Piaget used to test for the development of propositional logic was the pendulum task.

The task is simple enough. The child or adolescent is presented with a weight suspended by a string. Her task is to determine what controls the rate of oscillation of the pendulum (i.e., how fast it swings). To solve the problem, she is given different lengths of string and different weights to attach to the string. She is also instructed on how to release the pendulum from different heights and how to use different degrees of force to get the pendulum moving.

Preoperational children are not able to solve the task and rarely are able even to explain their actions. As we might expect of children who have very limited ability to classify and seriate, their behavior is not systematic.

Concrete operational children's actions are described as systematic but incomplete. A child may discover the correct answer (the only relevant variable is the length of the string), but because he is unlikely to test all of the logically possible combinations, he is not able to isolate the relevant variable. Consider the progress of this 8-year-old who, after several trials in which he has varied the length of the string, finally says:

> The less high it is (i.e., the shorter the string), the faster it goes. The suspended weight, on the other hand, gives rise to incoherent relationships: With the big ones, it falls better, it goes faster. It's not that one (500 gram weight), it's this one (100 gram weight) that goes slower. But after a new trial, he says in reference to the 100 gram weight: It goes faster. What do you have to do for it to go faster? Put on two weights. Or else? Don't put on any: it goes faster when it's lighter. As for the dropping point: If you let go very low down, it goes very fast and It goes very fast if you let go high up. (But in this second case he had also shortened the string.) (1958, p. 70)

The adolescent's performance is different. She is now able systematically to isolate the variables and then test each independent of the others. She is able to do this because she is able to generate all of the logically possible combinations, test each one independent of the others, and then draw logically correct conclusions based on a comparison of the performance of the pendulum across all of the test conditions.

She at first believes that each of the four factors is influential. She studies different weights with the same string length but doesn't notice any appreciable change: *This doesn't change the rhythm.* Then she varies the length of the string with the same 200 gram weight and finds that *when the string is small, the swing is faster.* Finally, she varies the dropping point and the impetus with the same medium length string and the same 200 gram weight, concluding for each one of the two factors: *Nothing has changed.* (1958, pp. 75–76)

The significance of this change from concrete to formal operational thought is less in terms of what the child can do and more in terms of what the child can do it on. Concrete operational children are able to demonstrate the same systematic behavior in classifying objects. They are sensitive to both the intensive and the extensive properties of sets. They are able to solve multiple classification problems because they can work on two dimensions simultaneously. But they are able to do this only because they are acting on real objects. Their operational skills are concrete and reflect the content of the task. Formal operational adolescents can do the same things, but now on the possible forms of the relationships. No matter that some of these forms will prove incorrect when applied to the content. The fact that they can be logically generated means that they exist for these adolescents and therefore can be acted upon. It is in this sense that Piaget describes the thought of the adolescent as "taking flight" and reality now being seen as a special case of the possible or hypothetical.

The sum of the formal operational studies provided Piaget the basis to argue that formal operational thought is characterized by a set of 16 *binary operations* that define all of the logically possible operations that can be applied to any situation in the physical or social world. By freeing thought from content, the adolescent achieves a degree of flexibility of thought that is highly adaptive. Presumably the adolescent now has all the mental competence necessary to deal with any and all problems and tasks encountered in either the real or the hypothetical world. Piaget is not suggesting (nor, for that matter, would anyone else over the age of 15) that the adolescent now has all of the competence necessary to successfully engage in any and all adult tasks. Such maturity of thought is a longer and slower process and is not often fully achieved. But he is suggesting that with the emergence of formal operational thought, the adolescent has all the mental operations necessary to begin, and logically to accomplish, the process of becoming mature. Ironically, for Piaget, this process of maturing will require the adolescent to recognize that there is more to adult thought than the ability to generate logically possible hypotheses.

> But the focal point of the decentering process is the entrance into the occupational world or the beginning of serious professional training. The adolescent becomes an adult when he undertakes a real job. It is then that he is transformed from an idealistic reformer into an achiever. In other words, the job leads thinking away from the dangers of formalism back into reality. (1958, p. 346)

Piaget's studies of formal operational thought completed phase III of his work. During this phase he defined the structural characteristics of the preoperational period, the concrete operational period, and the formal operational period. Furthermore, he demonstrated how the progression across these three developmental phases paralleled, at the level of acting on mental representations, the progression of the six sensorimotor stages acting on real objects. The structure of his theory was now complete. The elements that most people think of when they think of Piaget's theory were now defined.

But Piaget was not finished. Having completed the structural elements of his theory, he returned in the latter years of his life to a reconsideration of the functional elements of the theory. It was a task that continued to his death in 1980 at the age of 84.

Phase IV: Approximately 1960–1980

By age 65 most people are ready to retire. By age 65 Piaget was ready to revise his theory by redefining the balance between its structural and functional elements. He did so through a number of books, some published posthumously. These books include *Genetic Epistemology* (Piaget, 1970), *Biology and Knowledge* (Piaget, 1971a [1967]), *The Grasp of Consciousness* (Piaget, 1976 [1974]), *Success and Understanding* (Piaget, 1978 [1974]), *Experiments in Contradiction* (Piaget, 1980b [1974]), *Adaptation and Intelligence* (Piaget, 1980a [1974]), and *The Equilibration of Cognitive Structures* (Piaget, 1985 [1975]).

The work of phases II and III focused on the structural aspects of the theory. They defined in detail the characteristics of thought at each stage within each of the four periods of cognitive development. Less emphasis was placed, during these phases, on the mechanisms of change—that is, on how new structures emerge. Piaget certainly talked about the role of the functional invariants in this process of emergence, and he clearly saw the process as ultimately serving the overarching goal of maintaining a dynamic equilibrium. But he did not concern himself as much with the specifics of this process as he did with the specifics of the structures constructed. Given his biological background, he saw the necessity first to fully describe what would then later need to be explained. In phase IV he returned to the issue of the explanation, a task he had loosely pursued in the original phase of his work when he studied the role of egocentrism in young children's thought.

The main issue that Piaget pursued in phase IV is that of how new structures emerge out of older ones. The issue gained importance at this point in his work because, having completed the taxonomy of the four developmental periods, he was in a better position to recognize that one of the implications of the course of development he had charted was that its emphasis on the development of a sense of logical necessity seemed to place some unnecessary restrictions on the course of development.

A sense of logical necessity reflects the activity of logical operations functioning in an integrated manner. The reason our 10-year-old at the beginning of this chapter gives the experimenter such a dubious look when asked if the amount of water was still the same is that he knows it has to be the same. It is this "has-to-be-ness" that reflects the logic of the child's thought. This growing sense of necessity allows the school-age child and then the adolescent and finally the adult to construct an understanding of reality that is a close enough approximation to it that the person can function effectively within it. But, Piaget now argues, at the same time that necessity provides a more effective means to maintain a dynamic equilibrium, there is a limitation to this powerful logic. By devoting too much attention to the study of how children decide what must be, the theory placed too little emphasis on the study of how children decide what could be. In other words, much of Piaget's later work on the study of children's understanding of possibility was meant to serve as a counterbalance to his earlier studies of children's understanding of necessity. The later work does not contradict the earlier work so much as it extends it by putting it in a still broader context.

One way to understand this new emphasis is to consider it as a shift from a focus on assimilation to a focus on accommodation. The work of phases II and III focused on the growing ability of the child to act first upon objects and then on their representations of those objects. This ability reflected the status of the child's cognitive structures, and as such, it can be seen as reflecting the role of assimilation in development. The meaning of experience is always defined in terms of the developmental level of the cognitive structures. Although accommodation was an equally important element in this process, during those phases its role received less attention. But that all changed.

Each new level of cognition now became recognized as defining not only how objects and events would come to have meaning (the assimilatory side of the process) but also, and equally important, what new procedures would come to act on objects and events (the accommodatory side of the process) as a result of the emergence of these new structures. Piaget argued that the presence of new procedures reflects the possibilities of thought inherent in the new structure.

He documents the development of new procedures, as always, by using very simple tasks. The common element of these tasks is that they allow the child to identify not one solution but many. One of the tasks involves showing children a picture with two things (e.g., a house and a tree) and then asking them how many different ways there are to get from one to another. In another task children were shown an object half hidden and asked what the shape or the color of the nonvisible portion could be.

The results from these studies are interesting in two ways. As might be expected, the *types* of possibilities offered corresponded to the developmental level of the child. In some ways, though, the more interesting finding was that the *number* of possibilities offered did as well. The older the child, the more possible solutions offered. The interesting thing about this second finding is that, at the same time that children are becoming more competent in logically determining what *must* be, they are also becoming more competent in generating more notions about what *could* be. By the formal operational stage, adolescents who could effectively use propositional logic to determine the necessary combinations that determine the swing of a pendulum or similar problems also recognized that, in fact, the color or the shape of the hidden portion of the object could be anything; the possibilities were infinite.

The results of his studies of possibility led Piaget to revise his perspective on the place of logical operations in his theory. Rather than being the defining element of mature thought, necessity now was seen as a special case of possibility. Furthermore, the equilibration process was now portrayed as a sequence of new structures allowing for new possibilities, which, in turn, are translated into new procedures. These new procedures allow for new interactions with the physical and social environment, which inevitably leads to new disequilibriums, the resolution of which leads to the emergence of new structures—and then the cycle repeats itself. Beilin (1992), in his review of the phase IV work, notes that three significant changes in the theory came about as a result of the work Piaget did on possibility during the last years of his life:

> The new theory, with its emphasis on possibility and on procedures, places much greater emphasis than the past theory on the functional aspects of development in accounting for the origins of mental structures, first by stressing procedures that accompany the use of existing structures, or the use of capabilities achieved by the use of newly constructed structures. Second, the motive force and instruments of change are in the mechanisms that exploit new possibilities in the form of capacities created by structures. Further significance of the change in the theory is that it stresses that there is no end in development, in that each development represents new possibilities. Such possibilities can never be fully realized in that new contexts continually create the need for new solutions and new procedures. (p. 12)

It is important to recognize that the work of phase IV did not in any way negate the earlier findings, especially those of phases II and III. The four-period sequence still describes the course of cognitive development. However, in the same sense that the emergence of formal operational thought made the real a special case of the hypothetical, the findings of phase IV made the necessary a special case of the possible. In so doing, Piaget laid the groundwork for a view of development holding the possibility of stages beyond formal operations (an issue we will consider in the next chapter).

Piaget's Constructivist Theory in Perspective

There is so much to this theory that trying to put it in perspective is difficult. However, the defining aspect of the theory—the one element that holds all the others in place—is Piaget's lifelong interest in how we come to construct knowledge, that is, how we attach meaning to the objects, people, and events that define our individual realities. It is a process fueled by a need common to all organic forms at all levels of organization. It is the need to maintain an equilibrium between self and surroundings.

The developmental theory Piaget constructed in pursuit of this interest is a classic organismic theory. It depicts psychological development as distinct from but nevertheless continuous with biological development. It describes a dialectical process through which qualitatively unique structures emerge, as opposed to being copies of external reality or the outcome of maturational change. It makes clear that there is a direction to development but no necessary rate or end point. It provides a view of intelligence as the ability to adapt effectively rather than as a repository of information. It makes clear that the construction of knowledge is an act of transformation, first on objects and then on their representations. It is the act of transformation that indicates the active, reflective role of the organism. It prompts us to consider the parallels that perhaps exist between the development of an individual and the development of a scientific discipline.

Let us close this chapter with a quote by Piaget that is reprinted in Ginsburg and Opper's (1969) book on his theory. Piaget's intent in the quote was to offer a perspective on the goals of education, but it can also equally well be read as a commentary on his own work. The statement was made in the early 1930s, so I hope you will overlook his reference only to men rather than to men and women.

> The principle goal of education is to create men who are capable of doing new things, not just of repeating what other generations have done—men who are creative, inventive and discoverers. The second goal of education is to form minds which can be critical, can verify, and not accept everything they are offered. The great danger of today is of slogans, collective opinions, ready-made trends of thoughts. We have to be able to resist individually, to criticize, to distinguish between what is proven and what is not. So we need pupils who are active, who learn early to find out by themselves, partly by their own spontaneous activity and partly through material we set up for them; who learn early to tell what is verifiable and what is simply the first idea to come to them. (p. 232)

11

Neo-Piagetian Perspectives

No theory, even one as broad and powerful as Piaget's, is without its critics, modifiers, and elaboraters. In the case of Piaget, the scale and scope of his work continues to generate a great deal of scholarship examining both the theory and its implications.[1] The work of three individuals is highlighted in this chapter. Each, working within an organismic perspective, is pursuing work that both revises and extends Piaget's original work. Kurt Fischer (Fischer & Granott, 1995; Fischer, Knight, & Van Paris, 1993; Fischer & Rose, 1994), the first of the three, has done so by pursuing a more fine-grained analysis of developmental sequences than did Piaget. His work gives greater emphasis to the place of individual variability in theoretical accounts of cognitive development. Gisela Labouvie-Vief (Labouvie-Vief, 1994; Labouvie-Vief, Chiodo, Goguen, Diehl, & Orwoll, 1995; Labouvie-Vief, Orwoll, & Manion, 1995) has focused her work on an examination of the developmental patterns characterizing the adult years, a period of the life span not discussed by Piaget. Her findings suggest that adult life is more than the simple extension of formal operations to new subject matter domains. Finally, William Damon's (1996) work focuses on the social context of moral development in children and adolescents, a topic Piaget pursued only to a limited degree early in his career.

It should be pointed out before we look at the work of these three individuals that none of them has simply continued the line of Piaget's work into new areas or refined it in old ones. Rather, each, by critically evaluating Piaget's arguments, has redefined particular elements of the original theory and, in so doing, has prompted us to recon-

---

[1] Although there are problems with evaluating work in one world view from the perspective of another, there are several critiques of Piaget's work done by both mechanists and contextualists. For those interested in examining mechanistic critiques of Piaget's theory, a good place to start would be with the works of Gelman, Meck, and Markin (1986), Brainerd (1993), Siegler (1996), and Flavell, Miller, and Miller (1993). For those interested in contextualist critiques of Piaget, a good place to start would be with the works of Broughton (1987b), Kessen (1990), Morss (1992), and Gergen (1995).

sider the legitimate domain of the theory and even of the boundaries of an organismic world view. In particular, these three researchers are exploring the boundaries between organismic and contextual world views and the ways in which organismic and contextualist perspectives might complement each other.

Fischer's Skill Theory

Kurt Fischer is interested in the variability that is evident in patterns of cognitive development. Contrary to Piaget, Fischer believes that the understanding of variability is as fundamental a topic of cognitive development as is the discovery of the developmental sequences common to all children. Fischer focused on two types of variability. The first is differences in the timing of children's accomplishments across tasks that are seen as requiring the same level of cognitive competence for solution. This is an issue of developmental synchrony. The second type of variability concerns differences between individuals in the particular steps that define their respective sequences of cognitive development. This is an issue of the universality of developmental patterns.

Piaget, of course, noted the presence of variability in his data, but it was never a major focus of his theory. Variability, or *decalage*,[2] as Piaget referred to it, was seen as reflecting the degree of "resistance" to assimilation presented by different objects. Decalage did influence when children first demonstrated particular cognitive competencies. However, because Piaget did not see decalage as influencing the sequence of these accomplishments, he paid relatively little attention to it. To understand the reasoning behind Piaget's decision, you have to remember that his primary interest was in epistemology, not psychology. The psychological study of children was the means to the larger goal of understanding how knowledge, in general, is constructed. His focus was therefore on the "epistemic" or generic child rather than the "psychological" child. Even if there was not perfect synchrony in the psychological child, there was presumed to be such synchrony in the epistemic one.

For Fischer, however, the focus is the psychological child, and to understand this child, Fischer believes that we have to understand all of the factors that influence his or her behavior. Understanding these factors requires a closer examination of the contexts in which development occurs, a shift that places less emphasis on the structural and more emphasis on the constructivist aspects of Piaget's theory (something Piaget himself began to do in his phase IV work). The result of this shift of focus is a move toward what Fischer (Mascolo, Pollack, & Fischer, 1997) refers to as an emphasis on *constructive epigenesis*.

---

[2] I am referring here to *horizontal* decalage. Piaget also talked about a vertical decalage. *Vertical* decalage referred to Piaget's observation that similar developmental processes reoccur at increasingly sophisticated cognitive levels. The parallels between developmental events at the sensorimotor and the representational levels are examples of vertical decalage.

Although, like Piaget, we retain a role of human agency in the construction of knowledge, the concept of constructive epigenesis differs from the Piagetian notion of equilibration. Like Piaget's notion of equilibrium, constructive epigenesis suggests that the individual is active in coordinating subsystems of activity into larger wholes. However, unlike Piaget, we argue for the inseparability and mutual interpenetration of the biogenetic, cognitive-behavioral, and sociocultural behavioral systems. The concept of constructive epigenesis is far more open-ended than the notion of equilibration, which places the major burden of development on processes that are universal, intrinsic, and autonomous to the individual. Because constructive epigenesis stresses the inseparability of the systems that create cognitive activity, this notion provides a framework for understanding alternative trajectories in development as a function of individual differences in biogenetic and sociocultural systems. This concept stands in opposition to views that predict universal sequences of stages that are incited by processes endogenous to the child. (pp. 45–46)

Fischer's concept of constructive epigenesis reflects the current status of a research agenda that has focused on children's developmental sequences within the subject matter domains of gender role development (Fischer, Hand, Watson, Van Parys, & Tucker, 1984; Fischer & Pipp, 1984; Fischer, Bullock, Rotenberg, & Raya, 1993), reading (Fischer, Knight, et al., 1993), mathematics (Fischer & Rose, 1994), abstract reasoning (Fischer, Hand, & Russell, 1984; Fischer, Kenny, & Pipp, 1990), and emotional development (Fischer, Shaver, & Carnochan, 1989, 1990).

Developmental Sequences Within Skill Theory

The developmental sequences that Fischer identified through this research differ from Piaget's in a fundamental way. Piaget's sequences are markers of the development of the individual; Fisher's sequences are markers of the development of *skills*. According to Fischer (Mascolo et al., 1997), skills refer to "cognitive control systems that function to organize and coordinate mental, emotional, and physical activity within specific contexts" (p. 38). Skills are not attributes of individuals but are always attributes of the person in context. As such, individuals function not at a particular skill level but rather at several simultaneously—each specific to a particular task in a particular context. From such a perspective, decalage is seen as the rule rather than the exception. A person's skill level for one task is not necessarily the same as it is for another task. Nevertheless, consistent with his neo-Piagetian perspective, Fischer argues that there is order in the developmental sequences compared across tasks.

Within a task domain, the *sequence of development* for a given assessment context can be predicted and explained in detail. Across domains, there is an upper limit on the complexity of skills that a person can show at any one time, the person's *optimal level*. This limit constitutes the highest developmental level that a person can produce consistently, and it is hypothesized to reflect a central information-processing limit. People commonly function below optimum, with optimum-level performance occurring primarily when the environment provides support for complex behavior. At certain points the optimum level changes relatively abruptly, showing stage-like develop-

ment. Ordinary performance below optimum, on the other hand, changes in a continuous, non-stage-like manner. (Fischer & Farrar, 1987, p. 647)

Much of Fischer and his colleagues' efforts have been devoted to identifying the
common patterns that characterize skill development within specific domains. This
work has led to the description of a developmental sequence common across skill
domains, identification of a set of transition rules that link steps in the sequence, and
documentation of both the role of context and the role of brain maturation in supporting skill development.

Fischer describes this developmental sequence as consisting of four *tiers*. Each tier
is, in turn, defined in terms of four distinct *levels*. The four tiers are the *reflex, sensorimotor, representational*, and *abstract*. The first two tiers correspond to Piaget's sensorimotor period, the representational tier to Piaget's preoperational and concrete operational periods, and the abstract tier to Piaget's formal operational period.

At the reflex and sensorimotor tiers, infants gradually acquire the skill to integrate
reflexes and then particular actions with objects or people. Preschoolers and school-
age children at the representational tier "can think of the concrete properties of things
independently of their immediate actions on those things, and they can use those representational skills to control their actions" (Fischer & Farrar, 1987, p. 648). Finally,
when adolescents reach the abstract tier, they become more able to think about intan-
gible properties independently of specific concrete people, objects, or events, and they
can use these abstract skills to control their concrete representations.

At the tier level of analysis, there is very little to distinguish Fischer from Piaget. In
both cases major developmental periods have been defined, and in both cases the
transition between levels is recognized as being relatively abrupt and discontinuous.
The particular contribution of Fischer's work, however, becomes clear when we consider his description of the four levels that characterize development within each tier.
Fischer's analysis of levels provides the finer-grained analysis that clarifies his argument that decalage is more the rule than the exception in development.

Fischer uses the visual images of a dot or point, a line connecting two points, a
square connecting four points, and a cube connecting eight points to depict his four
levels within each of the four tiers. Each image reflects a specific and parallel level of
functioning within a given tier. As such, it would be possible to talk about a child and
an adult functioning at the same level. However, the child might be doing so with
respect to her ability to represent the relationship between concrete experiences (the
representational tier) while the adult would be doing so with respect to his ability to
represent the relationship between abstractions (the abstract tier).

At the first level, the level of the single point, children and adults demonstrate the
skill to control specific actions.[3] Within the reflex tier the newborns exhibit the skill of
sucking or the skill of flexing the foot in response to some stimulus. At the sensorimotor tier this first-level action might involve the coordinated action of reaching for an

---

[3] It is worth noting that Fischer's developmental sequence documents developmental change at
least until age 30, a much longer age range than Piaget.

object in the infant's visual field. By the age of 2, the now representational child at level one can, for example, engage in a particular pretend play action such as bathing a baby doll. With the emergence of the abstract tier, level-one adolescents can construct singular abstract concepts such as honesty, trust, kindness, or justice. Perhaps the best way to appreciate the skill level typical of level one is to consider the significance of the word "or" in the previous sentence. The adolescent can construct any of these simple abstractions but can only deal with each one at a time. The same is true at the other three tiers.

Level-two skills at each tier are appropriately called *mappings*. Level-two skills demonstrate the ability to integrate and differentiate specific actions. The reflexive infant responds to the mother's voice by turning to look toward her face. The sensorimotor infant begins to babble by integrating the skills of audition and vocalization. The 4-year-old level-two representational child might engage in a role-play episode by having a father doll and a child doll interact. The level-two adolescent can map abstract concepts such as argument and evidence to see the role of each in knowledge construction. (Fischer & Rose, 1994). In all four examples of level-two functioning, the same skill is being demonstrated. The difference is the type of information that can successfully be, to use Piaget's term, assimilated.

By level three several skills are coordinated into systems. Fischer describes the reflexive tier level-three infant as being able simultaneously to coordinate looking at the mother's face, listening to her voice, and smiling at her. The result is the *greeting response*. To illustrate the greater complexity of level-three skills within the sensorimotor tier, Fischer describes the actions of a 13-month-old who

> moves a ball around, using what she sees to guide what she does and anticipating many of the consequences of moving the ball. When she does not know how to accomplish some desired goal, such as dropping the ball so that it falls into a small hole in a box, she experiments with different ways of holding and dropping it until she finds one that works. (Fischer & Rose, 1994, p. 43)

Level-three function at the representational tier is reflected in young school-age children's ability to recognize that individuals can occupy more than one social role at the same time (e.g., parent and professor or child and student) and that these individuals can relate to each other simultaneously in terms of all the possible social relationships defining these roles. This child would be able to recognize the complexities of having one's own child as a student in one's class.

Fischer's data suggests that level-three functioning within the abstract tier makes its appearance around the age of 18–20. Young adults now appear capable of, for example, recognizing the relationships among the arithmetic operations of addition, subtraction, multiplication, and division as the coordination of actions involving, on the one hand, combining or separating and, on the other, working with single numbers or multiples of a number.

If you have been doing your math, you might think there should be a total of 16 level-by-tier combinations and that the level-four skills within each tier should represent the last four elements in this sequence. But by Fischer's count there are only 13 such level-by-tier combinations because a level-four skill within each tier is also the level-one skill within the next tier (see Table 11.1).

Consider Fischer's explanation of this transition with respect to the reflex to sensorimotor shift.

> The fourth reflex level, appearing at 15 to 17 weeks, marks radical change to a new tier—the first level of sensorimotor development. Infants coordinate two or more systems of reflexes from the previous level to form a single action, marking the beginning of a new tier or cycle based on independent sensorimotor actions, which are generalizations based on the coordination of reflex systems. (Fischer & Rose, 1994, p. 42)

The transition from sensorimotor to representational tiers comes about through the coordination by 18- to 24-month-olds of two or more sensorimotor action schemes into a single mental representation. The child is now able to act on this single representation rather than having to rely on the actual objects, events, or people. The same process occurs with the representational-to-abstract-tier transition, only now it involves the construction of a single abstraction through the coordination of two or more concrete representational systems. Fischer gives the example of a 12-year-old who, in comparing the concrete actions of children acting "nice" and "mean" to each other, concludes that intentions, an abstraction, matter more than specific, concrete actions in judging people. Because Fischer's skill system is open-ended, level-four skills at the abstract tier would also be level-one skills at a fifth tier, although to date no research or theorizing has been pursued to identify such a lofty plane.

The Regulation of Skill Development

How does development occur within a skill hierarchy? How do skills transfer from one task to another within a particular level of a particular skill domain? How do skills grow from one level to another? How do skills generalize across domains? How do skills make the leap across tiers? And, of course, what regulates the process? Much of Fischer and his colleagues' (Fischer & Farrar, 1987; Fischer, Kenney, et al., 1990; Fischer & Pipp, 1984; Massaro & Cowan, 1993) work has been directed at providing answers to these questions.

Transitions across tasks at the same skill level within a domain and transitions across skill levels within a domain are explained through a series of at least five transition rules: *substitution, focusing, compounding, differentiation,* and *intercoordination.*[4] The first four explain transfers across tasks within a level; the fifth provides a mechanism for transfers across levels.

Substitution involves the transfer of a skill from one task to another. *Task* in this sense refers to particular activities that a child or adult might engage in. The substitution is between tasks that are at the same level within the same tier of a skill domain. Studies of children's social role development produced evidence of substitution when a young child was able to transfer her skill at having a doctor doll interact with a child patient doll (one task) to a doctor doll interacting with an adult patient doll (a second

---

[4] To date Fischer has identified five but makes clear that there are probably others that will eventually be identified.

TABLE 11.1
Fischer's Skill Theory

Level	Tier				Examples of Skills	Age[a]
	Reflex	Sensorimotor	Representational	Abstract		
Rf1: Single reflexes[b]	[A] or [B]				Single, simple species-specific action components (reflexes): With fixed posture: Infant looks at ball moving in front of face. Infant grasps cloth placed in hand.	3–4 weeks
Rf2: Reflex mappings[b]	[A — B]				Simple relations of a few reflexes: Hearing voice leads to looking at eyes. Infant extends arm toward ball that he or she sees.	7–8 weeks
Rf3: Reflex systems[b]	$\left[A_F^E \leftrightarrow B_F^E \right]$				Complex relations of subsets of reflexes: Looking at face and hearing voice evokes coordinated smiling, cooing, and nodding (greeting response). Infant opens hand while extending arm toward seen ball.	10–11 weeks
Rf4/S1: Single sensorimotor actions	$\left[\begin{array}{c} A_F^E \leftrightarrow B_F^E \\ \updownarrow \\ C_H^G \leftrightarrow D_H^G \end{array} \right] \equiv [I]$				Relations of reflex systems to produce a single, flexible sensorimotor action: Infant looks at ball as it moves through complex trajectory.	15–17 weeks

Level	Formula	Description	Age
		Infant opens hand while extending arm toward seen ball, and in middle of reach sometimes adjusts hand to changes in ball's trajectory.	
S2: Sensorimotor mappings	$[I - J]$	Simple relations of a few sensorimotor actions: Infant grasps ball in order to bring it in front of face to look at it. Infant uses looking at ball to finely guide reaching for it.	7–8 months
S3: Sensorimotor systems	$\left[I_N^M \leftrightarrow J_N^M\right]$	Complex relations of subsets of sensorimotor actions: Infant moves a rattle in different ways to see different parts of it. Infant imitates pronunciation of many single words.	11–13 months
S4/Rp1: Single representations	$\begin{bmatrix} I_N^M \leftrightarrow J_N^M \\ \Updownarrow \\ K_P^O \leftrightarrow L_P^O \end{bmatrix} \equiv [Q]$	Relations of action systems to produce concrete representations of objects, people, or events: Child pretends that doll is walking. Child says, "Doll walk."	18–24 months
Rp2: Representational mappings	$[Q - R]$	Simple relations of representations: Child pretends that two dolls are Mom and Dad interacting in parental roles. Child understands that self knows a secret and Dad does not know it.	3.5–4.5 years

TABLE 11.1 (Continued)

Level	Tier				Examples of Skills	Age[a]
	Reflex	Sensorimotor	Representational	Abstract		
Rp3: Representational systems			$\left[Q_v^U \leftrightarrow R_v^U\right]$		Complex relations of subsets of representations: Child pretends that two dolls are Mom and Dad as well as a doctor and a teacher simultaneously. Child understands that when water is poured from one glass to another, the amount of water stays the same.	6–7 years
Rp4/A1: Single abstractions			$\left[\begin{array}{l}Q_v^U \leftrightarrow R_v^U \\ S_x^w \leftrightarrow T_x^w\end{array}\right] \equiv [y]$		Relations of representational systems to produce abstractions (intangible concepts): Child understands addition as general operation of joining numbers. Child evaluates how parents demonstrate conformity. Child understands that honesty is a general quality of being truthful.	10–12 years
A2: Abstract mappings				$[y - z]$	Simple relations of abstractions: Person understands how addition and subtraction are opposite operations. Person integrates two social concepts of honesty and kindness into the complex concept of a social lie.	14–16 years

A3:
Abstract
systems
	$\left[y^e_{\mathfrak{D}} \leftrightarrow Z^e_{\mathfrak{D}} \right]$	Complex relations of subsets of abstractions:
		
		  Person understands how operations of addition and division are related through the ways the numbers are grouped and combined.
		
		  Person integrates several types of honesty and kindness in the complex concept of constructive criticism.
			18–20 years

A4:
Principles
	$\begin{bmatrix} y^e_{\mathfrak{D}} \leftrightarrow Z^e_{\mathfrak{D}} \\ \Updownarrow \\ \mathcal{A}^e_{\mathfrak{Z}} \leftrightarrow \mathcal{B}^e_{\mathfrak{Z}} \end{bmatrix}$	General principles for integrating systems of abstractions:
		
		  Person understands moral principle of justice.
		
		  Person understands principle of reflective judgment as basis of knowledge.
		
		  Person understands principle of evolution by natural selection.
			23–25 years

Note. In skill structures, each letter denotes a skill component, with each large letter designating a main component (set) and each subscript or superscript a subset of the main component. Thin letters designate components that are reflexes, in the sense of innate action components; bold letters designate sensorimotor actions, italic letters designate representations, and script letters designate abstractions. Lines connecting sets designate relations forming a mapping, single-line arrows designate relations forming a system, and double-line arrows designate relations forming a system of systems.

    [a]Ages given are modal ages at which a level first appears, based on research with middle-class North American or European children. They may differ across cultures and other social groups.

    [b]These levels are hypothesized, but to date there are too few data to test their existence unequivocally.

Source: Fischer and Rose, 1994, pp. 36–39.

task). The two interactions remain distinct. The adult role is substituted for the child role even though in both cases the interactions reflect representational mappings.

Focusing involves the sequences of related skills. The child might first have the doctor doll examine the patient and then have the nurse doll do the same. Unlike substitution these actions are related at least to the extent that they are sequenced.

Compounding involves the integration of skills. The doctor-patient and nurse-patient doll-play roles are now combined or compounded into a doctor-nurse-patient interaction. The doctor and nurse now jointly examine the patient, who responds appropriately to each.

Fischer argues that the fourth intralevel transition, differentiation, usually accompanies one of the other three. It is not so much a distinct transformation as it is the acquisition by the child or adult of a new perspective on the task. This interplay of compounding and differentiation is an excellent example of Werner's (1957) orthogenetic principle. Fischer describes the differentiations possible as a result of the compounding of the doctor-nurse-patient roles.

> In the uncompounded skills, a doctor can interact with a patient, or a nurse can interact with a patient. So long as these skills remain separate, many appropriate doctor, nurse, and patient behaviors will not be differentiated, even if the child also possesses a third uncompounded skill for the doctor/nurse relationship. The behavior of the doctor, for instance, will not include ways of (1) having the doctor interact with the patient to the exclusion of the nurse, (2) having the doctor interact with the nurse to the exclusion of the patient, or (3) having the doctor interact with the nurse and patient simultaneously. In the compound structure these behaviors can be differentiated, and as a result, all three roles become both clearer and richer. (Fischer & Pipp, 1984, pp. 64–65)

Intercoordination, the fifth transformation rule, explains how skills combine to move from one level to another. All of the examples given for the first four rules involved tasks reflecting the same set of social roles. A parallel set of examples might have involved the roles of parent and child. Intercoordination involves the merging of two or more skills in distinct tasks to form a larger intercoordinated unit—in this case a child's understanding of the intersections and the complementary nature of the multiple roles of doctor, parent, patient, and child. Given the low but persistent correlations that are found across tasks and even domains, Fischer (Fischer & Farrar, 1987) believes that similar transformation rules probably operate on the transfer of skills across these broader boundaries as well.

Fischer's analysis of levels within tiers and even transformations within levels has led him to the belief that even though there may be a great deal of uniformity in developmental sequence when measured at the levels of Piaget's interest, when measured at more micro levels, the evidence is that multiple pathways are possible. In all cases the same set of transformation rules apply, as do the level/tiers structure. But beyond that—at the level of the particular tasks within particular skill domains that define the person's life experience—variability is the rule rather than the exception.

The lattice or web, for Fischer, is the better image of the course of development than is the ladder (Biddle & Fischer, 1992).

Given this emphasis on variability across tasks and the proposed latticelike nature of the developmental sequence, making statements about an individual's developmental level are, to Fischer, relatively meaningless. For Fischer the more valid developmental measure is a person's *developmental range* for any given skill. For any individual on any given skill, the developmental range operates between a *functional skill level* and an *optimum skill level*.

The optimal level specifies the most complex skills that a person can consistently control under ideal conditions. For Fischer (Fischer & Rose, 1994) such ideal conditions include an alert state, familiarity with the context and the task, absence of interfering conditions, and adequate practice and support. Functional skill–level performance occurs when children and adults are deprived of such supports. It is the skill level demonstrated under spontaneous conditions. However, the discontinuous developmental spurts that characterize development between tiers happen only under conditions supporting optimal skill performance.

It is interesting to consider the possible implications of the fact that optimal conditions rarely exist when either children or adults are asked to demonstrate their competence on standardized tests. If Fischer is right, standardized test scores, at best, reflect the least we can do rather than the most. This wouldn't be a major problem if the "least" and the "most" were correlated (i.e., the higher one's "least" score, probably the higher one's "most" score), but Fischer does not suggest any such link. Knowing the least a person can do tells us little about what he or she could do under optimal conditions.

Fischer and his colleagues' most recent work (Fischer & Rose, 1994; Mascolo et al., 1997) has been directed at identifying those conditions that foster optimal performance level. This work has led him to look at both contextual issues and maturational ones. Fischer finds, for example, significant differences in skill level performance depending on (1) the amount of previous practice children are provided to learn a new skill, (2) the amount of feedback provided, (3) the availability of supportive and responsive mentors, and (4) the familiarity of the practice and test environments. None of these findings should be surprising; they are the product of good pedagogy.

Fischer's research on the links between brain maturation and developmental spurts is in many ways more intriguing than the context data. The findings are consistent with the arguments of the developmental psychobiologists discussed in Chapter 9. The basic premise is that periodic changes in brain structure correspond to periods of development in skills level across both levels and tiers. The brain changes involve the linking or networking of distinct areas in the brain. These neural coordinations allow a new integrated level of skill functioning that is reflected, at the behavioral level, in the coordinations that characterize skill shifts across both levels and across tiers.

Development thus moves through cycles of successive coordination among simpler networks to form more complex ones. Processes like the concurrent growth of synapses across cortical areas in infants can help induce these successive levels of coordination, as can other processes such as myelination of neurons to produce faster neural impulses and thus allow greater coordination. . . .

As our sketch of the 13 developmental levels indicates, each level requires a new type of control system to coordinate component skills, and each produces a cluster of discontinuities in behavioral growth. Our simple brain growth hypothesis is that each of these levels is founded in a broad-based brain growth spurt, which produces a new type of neural network and thus a new type of control system. The key new capacity at each level is the coordination of components to form a more complex control system incorporating previous skills; a key cortical region for that capacity for most levels is probably the frontal area, which seems to be specialized for holding information on line from various regions while other activities occur. (Fischer & Rose, 1994, pp. 22, 54)

Fischer's Skill Theory in Perspective

Fischer's work is a significant extension of and elaboration on Piaget's stage model. It provides a means to put some "flesh and bones" on Piaget's epistemic child. In so doing, variability within developmental sequences replaces synchrony within epistemological ones as the defining characteristic of development. Variability does not completely replace synchrony in Fischer's theory, but its new status does highlight the fact that one's level of analysis will often determine which will appear dominant. Fischer's work also provides a more tangible approach to the study of contextual variables and offers an intriguing hypothesis as to the links between brain maturation and cognitive development. Finally, it adds further fuel to that continuing debate as to the sequence of development—broad-based structural change then being reflected in particular task domains versus the continuing coordination of skills across tasks leading to the construction of new tiers or planes of functioning.

Labouvie-Vief's Perspective on Adult Development

As is true of most theories of human development, Piaget's theory is more a theory of child development than it is of life span human development. Piaget's fourth period of cognitive development, formal operations, makes its appearance not during the adult years but during adolescence. Even though the issues Piaget investigated during the latter years of his life laid the groundwork for the further development of cognitive operations beyond formal operations, he was never able to pursue this issue.

Gisela Labouvie-Vief's work (1980, 1992, 1994a, 1994b, 1996; Labouvie-Vief & Chandler, 1978; Labouvie-Vief, Chiodo, et al., 1995; Labouvie-Vief, Diehl, Chiodo, & Coyle, 1995; Labouvie-Vief & Hakim-Larson, 1989; Labouvie-Vief & Lawrence, 1985; Labouvie-Vief, Orwoll, et al., 1995) represents an extension of Piaget's theory into the adult years. Rather than accepting the notion that the abstract skills that make their first appearance during adolescence are the defining element of mature cognition, she has pursued the argument that, as is true of all of Piaget's stages, formal operations themselves become over the course of the adult years integrated into the tasks that define adult life. Put another way, just as infants come to use the reaching scheme to grasp an object only after they first practice reaching for its own sake, adults come to use their skills at abstraction for solving adult issues only after, as adolescents, they used their skills at abstraction simply to abstract.

Labouvie-Vief's work involves three interrelated themes: (1) the extension of Piaget's ideas into adulthood, (2) an analysis of Piaget's emphasis on the development of rational thought within the context of Western intellectual tradition, and (3) the implications of this emphasis on the intellectual development of men and women across the life span.

Labouvie-Vief's Neo-Piagetian Perspective on Adult Cognitive Development

Like most interpreters of Piaget, Labouvie-Vief sees Piaget's theory as depicting a process through which individuals construct meaning. This process occurs over a sequence of levels, each defined in terms of a particular set of cognitive structures. Each level affords the individual an increasingly effective means to maintain a sense of equilibrium between one's own constructed meanings and one's actual experience. The direction of this process is toward an increasingly objective and rational view of the world. This objectivity and rationality come about through a process of distancing—that is, a process of being increasingly able to stand back far enough from specific experiences to gain the necessary perspective to deal with them in the most adaptive fashion.

As Labouvie-Vief sees it, each step in the process can be viewed as an advancement in this distancing progression. The development of representational thought provides the 2-year-old the more adaptive opportunity to stand back and think about the best strategy for retrieving the toy from under the table rather than merely engaging in a sequence of trial-and-error efforts. The class inclusion skills of the school-age child provide her with the more adaptive opportunity to gain a better perspective on concrete experiences by recognizing the embeddedness of particular events within a larger context. Certainly, her growing understanding of geography reflects this process. The hypothetical/deductive abstract logic of the adolescent provides him with the more adaptive opportunity to stand back and recognize "what is" as only one possibility of "what could be". No doubt, such a process is behind many adolescents' efforts at self-improvement. This progression of levels of meaning making is seen as defining the way one interacts not only with problems of logic but also with all forms of endeavor, including the affective and the interpersonal.

THE RELATION BETWEEN DEVELOPMENT IN ADOLESCENCE AND IN ADULT-HOOD   So far, so good. Piaget's depiction of development does seem to offer a plausible account of the process through adolescence. But what about the years following adolescence? Here it does not seem to be as effective in explaining the data on cognition during the adult years. In fact, in seeming contradiction to the theory, the adult data has typically appeared to show that, rather than continued cognitive growth across the adult years, decline is more often the norm.

The data suggests that elders are less likely to deal with problems in an abstract manner. Even on simple conservation tasks, those typically accomplished by children age 9 or 10, elders over the age of 70 or 75 often fail to conserve. Furthermore, measures of *fluid intelligence* show a similar pattern of decline. Tests of fluid intelligence are considered to be measures of an individual's information processing or problem-solving ability. They are often contrasted to tests of *crystallized intelligence,* which show little pattern of decline. Tests of crystallized intelligence measure the ability to effectively use already acquired knowledge and skills.

How are such findings explained? Labouvie-Vief makes note of two explanations typically offered to account for this seeming pattern of apparent cognitive decline across the adult years. First, Piaget's organismic model may be a fine explanation of child development, but it has little to offer the study of adult development. In other words, progression may be the watchword of cognitive development through adolescence. But then an entirely different set of variables, presumably more mechanistic or contextualist in nature, comes to regulate cognitive behavior during the adult years.

The second common explanation of the decline in cognitive competence is that the decline might reflect a cohort or generational effect. Cohort analyses measure life circumstances particular to time and place. As such, findings that current cohorts of elders perform poorly on measures of cognitive competence may be more a statement of the early life conditions of those who are now age 70 and older than it is a statement of the inevitable decline in cognitive abilities with advancing age. Presumably, future cohorts would not show these declines because their early developmental experiences, particularly in terms of their health, nutritional, and educational experiences, would be better than those of cohorts from an earlier era.

Labouvie-Vief finds neither of these explanations very satisfying. She argues that it makes no theoretical sense for one world view to explain the events of one part of the life span and then, abruptly, for another view take over. Even cohort explanations, which do allow for the possibility of continued growth, are seen as inadequate because cognitive growth through the adult years is still seen as situational rather than universal.

The basic issue, then, for Labouvie-Vief is how best to understand the relationship between development through adolescence—Piaget's four developmental periods—and development during the adult years. Labouvie-Vief notes that the traditional interpretation of the four periods is a linear one. Individuals are seen as becoming increasingly able to effectively use logical strategies to distance themselves from the immediate situation and, in so doing, gain a better (i.e., more adaptive) perspective on a situation. The assumption is that this linear progression would continue throughout the adult years as adults presumably gain even more effective logical strategies to distance themselves even further from immediate situations. But according to the data, this isn't what happens. The data seems to imply that adults become less effective in using abstract logic, less effective in using their fluid intelligence.

Labouvie-Vief argues that the problem is not with the data but with its interpretation—particularly, its interpretation with respect to Piaget's theory. Development from a Piagetian perspective is best appreciated not in terms of the development and utilization of increasingly abstract logical structures but as a linear sequence of increasingly effective means of adapting to the demands of one's context. The misinterpretation of the theory comes about because, through adolescence, the use of increasingly logical abstract strategies is the most effective way to adapt to the demands children and adolescents encounter. But this is no longer the case during the adult years. Effective adaptation is not accomplished through the use of cognitive structures well suited to deal with the hypothetical. Rather, it comes about through the use of cognitive structures well suited to deal with the pragmatic nature of adult life. As Labouvie-Vief (1980) describes the distinction:

> While the theme of youth is flexibility, the hallmark of adulthood is commitment and responsibility. Careers must be started, intimacy bonds framed, children raised. In short, amidst a world of a multitude of possible logical alternatives, there is a need to adopt *one* course of action. This conscious commitment to one pathway and the deliberate disregard of other logical alternatives may indeed mark the onset of adult cognitive maturity.
>
> . . . Cognition becomes constrained by pragmatic necessities; strategic control of one's life, managing time, conserving energy. This phase may bring a relinquishment of the earlier emphasis on resolving contradiction; contradiction must be accepted as part and parcel of adult life, giving rise to a new form of "contradictive" cognition which accepts, and even thrives on, imperfection, compromise, and the necessity to fumble. (p. 153)

In effect, Labouvie-Vief is describing a process that is parallel to the one described by developmental psychobiologists such as Thelen. According to Thelen, during prenatal development the brain "overwires" itself, seemingly in preparation for all possible life contingencies. Because only some of these contingencies become reality, some neural connections are strengthened and become better integrated while others disappear. For Labouvie-Vief cognitive development through the formal operational period is functionally analogous to Thelen's period of prenatal development. Instead of overwired neuronal connections, however, we are now talking about "overwired" logical connections.

> The adaptive *potential* (i.e., necessary condition) of formal logic consists in the fact that it provides a mechanism by which all possibilities can be generated by permutations and recombinations. But only some of those will stand pragmatic tests, while others will need to be discarded. Thus again, logical growth provides a necessary but not sufficient condition for continued development. (Labouvie-Vief, 1982, p. 69)

Piagetian development then, according to Labouvie-Vief, is not some linear process moving toward perfection. Instead, it reflects a series of tradeoffs, with each tradeoff reflecting a particularly effective mode of adaptation given the context in which the individual is functioning.

The nature of this adaptive process is perhaps best reflected in the answer of an elder to a typical conservation task. The task presents the elder with two equal-sized pieces of paper, which are described as representing two pastures. In one pasture several small barns are placed together to form one large barn; in the other the same number (and size) of barns are spread across the pasture. The elder is asked if the same number of cows placed in each pasture would have the same amount of grass to eat. The "correct" or conserving answer is yes, because even though the barns are distributed differently on the two pastures, the amount of land covered is still the same. The elder says, "No." His explanation is instructive. Rather than giving a typical noncon-serving answer such as "There is less grass on the field with the spread out barns because the barns are in more places," he says, "No two fields ever grow grass the same way." It is the logic behind this elder's answer that, for Labouvie-Vief, reflects the argu-ment that progressive qualitative growth in cognition continues throughout the adult years and that this growth reflects an adaptation to the particular demands of adult life. That is, the elder's response is not one based solely on the logical requirements of the task, but rather reflects the life experience that this elder brings to the task. This is the difference. For adults, Labouvie-Vief argues, all tasks are situated within one's life experience—even conservation tasks.

Perhaps the best way to understand the particulars of Labouvie-Vief's argument is (1) to review her data and developmental sequence and (2) to consider her broader dis-cussions about Western intellectual thought and gender differences in cognition.

LABOUVIE-VIEF'S ADULT COGNITIVE STUDIES   Labouvie-Vief's research has examined four aspects of cognition during the adult years. In all four cases adults are asked to respond to open-ended questions or described situations; their responses are then coded as to developmental level. The four areas of research are emotional devel-opment (Labouvie-Vief, 1992; Labouvie-Vief & Hakim-Larson, 1989; Labouvie-Vief, Hakim-Larson, DeVoe, & Schoeberlein, 1989), changes in the sense of self during the adult years (Labouvie-Vief, Chiodo, et al., 1995; Labouvie-Vief, Diehl, et al., 1995), changes in memory strategies (Labouvie-Vief, 1992; Labouvie-Vief & Hakim-Larson, 1989), and changes in patterns of text interpretation (Labouvie-Vief & Hakim-Larson, 1989).

In the text interpretation tasks, for example, adolescents and adults are presented with described situations such as the following: "John is known to be a heavy drinker, especially when he goes to parties. Mary, John's wife, warns him that if he gets drunk one more time, she will leave him and take the children. Tonight, John is out late at an office party. John comes home drunk. Does Mary leave John? How certain are you of your answer?" This and the other questions in the task are designed so that they can be answered literally and logically on the basis of the story structure itself or in any of a number of ways based on one's psychological interpretation of the story structure. For the moment, suffice it to say that the adolescents in the sample tend to give the logi-cally consistent answer, (e.g., "Mary would leave John because she said she would if he came home drunk one more time and that's exactly what he did"), and older adults tend to give seemingly less logically consistent answers (e.g., "I know she said she would leave him but I'm not sure that she really would; it would depend on so many other things").

Labouvie-Vief sees the difference in the two modes of text interpretation as reflect-ing a difference in how individuals see themselves in relation to others. For the young adults, "information is seen as an outer given that one attempts to reproduce with a minimum of infusion of one's own self" (1992, p. 215). But the responses of the middle-age adults in her sample suggest a different frame of reference.

As the individual realizes that information is not independent of an interpreter—a self who reads and infuses herself or himself into a text—the individual turns more to the landscape of human motivations and intentions that determines how texts are generated and interpreted. Hence, these adults may become experts at the processing of information relating to subjective processes and inner dynamics. Although this processing style will result in deficits in tasks requiring more objective and formal ways of processing, it may be an advantage in ones that specifically require more psychological ones. (p. 215)

The memory task data shows a similar pattern. Adolescents and adults are asked to either recall or summarize a fable about a wolf who offers a crane a reward for removing a bone stuck in its throat. The crane complies, putting its head down the wolf's throat and pulling out the bone. When the crane asks for its reward, the wolf replies that the reward is that it is still alive. When college students are asked to either recall or summarize the fable, they give the same response—a highly detailed recollection. But for older adults, the two conditions, recall or summarization, produce very different responses. In the recall condition the elders do the same as the college students— they faithfully recall the details of the fable. But in the summary condition they focus on the broader, more metaphorical issues raised in the fable rather than its particulars. Labouvie-Vief (1989) illustrates this summarization difference by reporting the following response from an older adult:

> The moral of the story, as I understand it, was that people should not seek a reward for their well-doing, but to be content with having done a good deed. It also depicts a certain shrewdness, as noted by the wolf who sought help in time of need, but was unwilling to give of himself, even in a small way, to show any appreciation of the help he had received from the crane. Many times, people who do good deeds receive only a spiritual reward for their well-doing. (p. 83)

Labouvie-Vief points out that because summarization rather than literal recall seems to be the preferred mode of dealing with past events for older adults, their responses may be misinterpreted as reflecting memory declines. But given the fact that, under the recall condition, the older adults' responses are as detailed as the college students', the preference for summarization over recall reflects the same developmental shift as was noted in the text interpretation task. Specifically, it reflects a preference for always embedding the particular within a larger and often less abstract and less hypothetical context.

This developmental shift is equally evident in the emotional development and self-concept studies. Labouvie-Vief reports that, across the adult years, at least from the period of late adolescence through middle age, there is a shift in self-reports toward ones reflecting greater complexity and self-reflection. Young adult reports are characterized as reflecting "a goal-directed individual whose evaluations are guided by achievement-oriented and conventional goals, values and roles. Achievement of these goals and values is a frequent theme" (Labouvie-Vief, Chiodo, et al., 1995, p. 407). As adults move through the adult years, their self-reports become increasingly reflective, particularly in terms of the desire to pursue individual interests and considerations of the appropriateness of pursuing socially sanctioned values. These adults now seem to have a greater sense of and interest in the processes through which the value systems they so eagerly once pursued have been formed. In particular, they seem to have a greater appreciation for the historical and social processes that define social systems.

This pattern of increasing complexity and reflectiveness continues through middle age. Middle-age adults' self-reflections are described as existing at a complex psychological level. They reflect an awareness of the intricacies of reciprocal interactions. As an indication of this complexity, Labouvie-Vief reports one middle-aged adult as saying, "At this point in my life and my parents' lives, they are becoming dependent and I find myself reliving the above tensions of struggling to remain my adult self but getting pulled back to my 'younger' self as I have spent more time with them" (Labouvie-Vief, Chiodo, et al., 1995, p. 407).

In summarizing these findings, Labouvie-Vief (1996) argues that development across the adult years reflects an individual's ability to reunite the dualities of mind and self.

> Following our public ways of speaking, these languages become dualistically and oppositionally structured in early development when the individual is concerned with acquiring mastery of the rules and symbol systems of a culture. At this junction of the life span, knowledge comes to be understood as certain and structured by outer, objective processes. But in later life, many individuals discover—as have many contemporary philosophers—that so-called objective knowledge structures already embody a language of subjective processes that, though hidden from conscious view, has exerted a powerful influence. Out of this recognition the unique opportunity arises of reintegrating these languages of objective knowledge and subjective desire as they are allowed to engage in a dialectical interchange. (p. 110)

This reuniting process is particularly evident in Labouvie-Vief's discussion of her data on changes in emotional development across the adult years. She notes that the younger adults in her research tend to express emotions in ways consistent with social norms. But to accomplish this task, young adults need to distance themselves from themselves; that is, they need to dissociate their personal meanings of events from those that are more abstract and culturally sanctioned.

Older adults are more aware of this feeling of dissociation and are more concerned about its consequences. Labouvie-Vief describes their self-descriptions as more "inner and personal rather than outer and technical" (1992, p. 218). These middle-aged adults are much more aware of reconciling inner thoughts and outer behaviors, of "accepting impulses and thoughts that had previously seemed too overwhelming to accept" (1992, p. 218).

Techniques for controlling emotions show a parallel shift. Whereas young adults tend to eliminate emotional conflicts by intellectualizing them, middle-aged adults are much more likely to own their emotions and to recognize them as part of the complex system that defines them as individuals.

LABOUVIE-VIEF'S DEVELOPMENTAL SEQUENCE   Based on her data, Labouvie-Vief sees this reuniting of mind and self taking place over a five-step sequence (Labouvie-

Vief, Chiodo, et al., 1995; Labouvie-Vief, Hakim-Larson, et al., 1989). Table 11.2 presents this sequence with respect to adults' levels of self-representation.

At the *concrete-presystemic level* individuals are said to not yet be able to organize and integrate behavioral actions and psychological states into a coherent abstract system. Explanations of one's actions are more likely attributed to the influence of others such as parents or peers than personal states. At the *interpersonal-protosystemic level,* individuals' psychological and physical characteristics are described more in terms of immediate relationships and social networks.

Adolescence marks the emergence of an *institutional-intrasystemic level,* which appears to closely resemble Piaget's formal operational stage. The individual is now able to coordinate actions and states into coherent abstract systems, which tend to correspond to particular institutions in society such as marriage or the family. The result is that the adolescent and young adult is now able to function effectively within these abstract systems but has not yet constructed the means to reflect on how these abstract systems were constructed in the first place.

Labouvie-Vief's final two levels are the real extension of Piaget's theory in that they offer a further differentiation of the formal operational period. Again, from this perspective, the formal operations of the adolescent are merely the first of several steps in the maturing of psychological functioning at this particular developmental level. At the *contextual-intersystemic level* the language necessary to reflect on abstract systems makes its first appearance. Adults are now able to reflect on the dialectical tension between personal desire and institutional constraints.

> Focus is more on how context has shaped and transformed individual biography. Descriptions involve understanding of processes and contrasts over time, and psychological reasoning indicates the emergence of awareness of interpersonal dynamics and psychological mechanisms. Focus is less on a stable self and more on personal, psychological, and spiritual transformations. The self becomes viewed as a dynamic system subject to change and transformation. (Labouvie-Vief & Chiodo, 1995, p. 406)

In a sense, from Labouvie-Vief's description of intersystemic thought, one could argue that it represents the first time in the life span when individuals are truly able to construct a developmental perspective.

Labouvie-Vief describes the final step in the sequence as a *dynamic-intersubjective level.* Change and transformation continue to be the defining characteristics of this level, but what is added is a fuller recognition of the role played by inner psychological mechanisms in this continual process of change and transformation. There is a greater recognition and awareness of the role of unconscious processes and of the self in defining and interpreting historical change and contextual diversity. Experiences are viewed from the interpretive perspective of the self, or, as the elder in the conservation-of-area task put it, "No two fields ever grow the same amount of grass."

Adults who successfully accomplish the full sequence are ones whom Labouvie-Vief describes as recognizing thought as an individual, interpretive activity and, as such, the legitimacy of the existence of distinct perspectives on a subject. Given such a mature perspective, contradictions are not eliminated by designating one as right and

TABLE 11.2
Labouvie-Vief's Sequence of Self-Representation

Level	Description	Example[a]
0 (concrete-presystemic)	The language used is simple and concrete. Characteristics and physical traits are seen as global. Events are detailed in simple seriation. Action-oriented behaviors describe activities. No references to goals or psychological processes occur.	An engineer Physically-robust-strong 6 ft 280 lbs. I am nice. I'm tall. I am pretty. I have two sisters.
1 (interpersonal-protosystemic)	Simple evaluations are made that reflect the values of the immediate social group. Traits described are nondifferentiated. Individuals are described in terms of relationships (simple descriptors) and social networks. Emphasis is on features of the self or others that make for ingroup acceptance.	I like to fool around and make my friends laugh. I am outgoing and friendly. I love my family. I am fun to be with. I have lots of friends. I am involved in many clubs at school.
2 (institutional-intrasystemic)	Interpersonal descriptors indicate a clearer sense of the individual within the social group. Traits at this level indicate a more self-directed and goal-directed individual whose evaluations are guided by achievement-oriented and conventional goals, values, and roles. Achievement of these goals and values is a frequent theme.	I am family-oriented and active in my community. Effective as a mother. I am an empathic and committed friend. I have not been successful in my life. I work hard to support my children and really love them. Have tried, with some success, to develop the patience of my father and devotion of my mother.

3 (contextual-intersystemic)	Descriptions are critical of convention, involve an awareness of how traits change, and give a sense of individuals with their own value system. Institutional goals are reexamined and put into historical or psychological perspective. Descriptions involve references to processes and contrasts over time.	I am a singer, an actress, and a writer and want to use these talents more creatively than I do now. I get along well with all people, but need to develop more insight as to what motivates other people. Relearning who I am. I am adding new dimensions to my life in as many ways as possible.
4 (dynamic-intersubjective)	Roles and traits are described at a complex psychological level and reflect awareness of underlying, often unconscious, motivation and reciprocal interaction. Activities and goals are seen as subject to continual revision as one gains knowledge of oneself and others. Reference is to multiple dimensions of life history and an emphasis on process, becoming, and emergence.	I struggle with the concept of who I am and have been identified (all giving mother, self sufficient, religious) and I think, feeling the need to be more individualized woman with specific needs and desires. I work for profit now rather than for satisfaction, partly because of my (guilty) need to continue to support my family. At this point in my life and my parents lives, they are becoming dependant and I find myself reliving the above tensions of struggling to remain my adult self but getting pulled back to my "younger" self as I have spent more time with them.

[a] Errors in grammar and spelling reflect actual responses.

Source: Labouvie-Vief, Chiodo, et al., 1995, p. 407.

the other as wrong but rather are appreciated as offering the basis for furthering one's own perspective on a topic. Labouvie-Vief's developmental sequence is consistent with and supported by the findings of the work of both Perry (1970) and Kitchener and King (1981; Kitchener, King, Wood, & Davison, 1989).

Logos, Mythos, and Piaget

One of the major issues raised by Labouvie-Vief in her extension of Piaget's theory into the adult years is that, because most theories portray development as a linear, hierarchical process, the adult years inevitably come to be seen as a period of stability followed by a period of seemingly inevitable decline. Her argument, again, is that such a perspective misinterprets the meaning and significance of the behavior found in middle and old age. Her solution is to reconceptualize the developmental changes occurring across the life span in terms of increasingly adaptive strategies and away from unidimensional measures such as abstract reasoning.

Labouvie-Vief's interest in this issue is not limited to the particulars of contemporary developmental theory but rather extends to an examination of the origins of our images of development and maturity within Western intellectual thought, especially those images that equate maturity with increasing rationality and objectivity. She traces the origin of this equating of maturity and rationality to Plato and the ancient Greeks—in particular, to the tension between *logos* and *mythos*.

> Western intellectual tradition has brought us a separation of two aspects of mind and self. On the one hand, there is the realm of *logos*—the realm of logic and objectivity, of all that can be stated in terms of rational truths, of our hope that life can be reduced to laws that are mechanical and precise. On the other hand, there is the realm of *mythos*—the realm of all that is felt and organic, of that which is private and imaginative, of all that appeals to the inner world of emotions, of our tendency to leap out of the constraints of analytic precision and to seize the novel. (Labouvie-Vief, 1994a, p. 1)

Labouvie-Vief (1992) notes that this differentiation between logos and mythos first appeared around the time of Plato. Prior to that time, there is little indication that people thought of themselves as anything other than as one with their instincts. For them reality was permeated with magic and myth. From a developmental perspective, one could argue that these individuals saw themselves not as active organisms but as beings reacting to their surroundings. Even Greek myths seem to portray this image. Mortals usually appear as little more than puppets existing either for the amusement of their gods or as surrogate warriors on the gods' battlefields.

Plato was one of the first to equate maturity with reason and, in so doing, differentiate logos from mythos. The self was now seen as a distinct and causal agent. The new self was abstract rather than concrete, oriented toward thought rather than toward the imaginative and the mythic. As this notion of the self as an independent thinker evolved over the centuries, thinking became increasingly a process distinct from the thinker. That is, it came to be recognized as an "objective" and "rational" process, one leading inevitably to logical conclusions that mirrored increasingly an objective reality and decreasingly a subjective personal perspective. Such objectivity came to be seen as the ultimate criterion of maturity.

The result of this differentiation is that what Labouvie-Vief refers to as *context-sensitive* forms of knowledge came to be less valued that *context-free* forms of knowledge (Labouvie-Vief & Hakim-Larson, 1989). Context-sensitive forms of knowledge are reflected in imitation and intuition, the analogical and the figurative, the organic and the instinctual, and in processes of conflict and change. Context-free forms of knowledge are reflected in abstract understanding, rational analysis, and the mental and the voluntary, and in processes of stability and harmony. Labouvie-Vief argues that contemporary developmental theories focus on the development of context-free processes because, within Western intellectual traditions, context-free forms of knowledge have come to be seen as "better," as reflecting "greater maturity," as demonstrating "higher levels" of cognitive competence than have context-sensitive forms of knowledge.

Labouvie-Vief sees this valuing of context-free forms of knowledge as serving a useful purpose with respect to our understanding of child development because development during this period does require that "more state-dependent, organic, and private modes of experience give way to ones that are more abstract and collective." She goes on to say that she does not believe the same is true with respect to the adult years.

> The adaptive advantage of this process of dissociation and hierarchic organization in earlier development is the acquisition of culturally relevant symbol systems and language systems. These systems permit the novice adult to categorize experience in a stable and reliable manner. In adulthood, however, this hierarchical structure becomes a liability. The devaluation of inner and personal experience, on which the success of childhood development largely depends, can result in structures that are limited, closed, and rigidified in adulthood. More mature cognitive development is aimed an organization that reacknowledges the importance of private ways of knowing. (Labouvie-Vief & Hakim-Larson, 1989, p. 73)

Given this equating of rationality with maturity within Western intellectual thought, it is possible to consider Labouvie-Vief's extension of Piaget's theory as not only an extension of the theory itself but, more broadly, as an attempt to replace a *vertical model* of development with a *lateral model* of development. Whereas vertical models are relevant for the acquisition of culturally appropriate forms of self-regulation, lateral models are better suited for appreciating the interplay between, on the one hand, hypothetical/deductive modes of thought and, on the other, intuitive and mythical modes of thought. The result of such an integration is reflected in Labouvie-Vief's latter periods of adult thought. In general, such integration allows adults to recognize the importance of individuals' perspectives in making judgments about validity and in enabling them to deal with the practicalities of adult life.

For Labouvie-Vief, Piaget is unique among developmental theorists because there are elements in his theory that relate to both context-free and context-sensitive forms of knowledge. That is, at least the theory did initially. It is, after all, Piaget who studied play, dreams, and imitation in childhood; who investigated private speech; and who asked young children about shadows and clouds and things alive and things dead. Mythos was as much a part of his investigations as was logos. But as Piaget's theory evolved, particularly during his second and third phases, the nature of his questions changed. His studies of concrete and formal operational children increasingly resemble a science textbook. Clearly, for Piaget, and consistent with the intellectual tradition he was a part of, increasing maturity is equated much more with logos than with mythos. Labouvie-Vief therefore sees her extension of his work as not simply examining forms of cognition during the adult years but also as serving the larger role of restoring Piaget's original balance to his theory and of presenting the theory as holding the key to a lateral model of development.

The Gendered Mind

The third theme evident in Labouvie-Vief's work concerns one of the consequences of the differentiation of logos and mythos in Western intellectual thought. Given this differentiation and the emphasis placed on logos in images of development, adults, according to Labouvie-Vief, must rediscover mythos and then reintegrate it with logos if they are to achieve full maturity in later life. This is a task that confronts all adults. But not all adults respond in the same way.

Labouvie-Vief's most recent work considers the implications of logos and mythos in terms of the development of men and women. She believes that both genders learn to place more emphasis on logos during their childhoods in response to the demands to acquire socially accepted forms of reasoning and behaving. However, the ease of accomplishing this task is not the same for men and women because, historically, logos as a form of knowing has been more closely associated with men's voices than with women's. This association of gender and ways of knowing has two significant implications: (1) Development through adolescence may be easier for men, but (2) the reintegration of logos and mythos in the middle years of adulthood may be more easily accomplished by women.[5]

Labouvie-Vief's argument rests on two presumptions: (1) Logos and mythos are to some degree associated with masculinity and femininity, and (2) full adult maturity, for both men and women, requires a reintegration of the two. The second presumption has already been reviewed because it is, in fact, Labouvie-Vief's extension of Piaget's theory into the adult years. This extension presumes that logos and mythos are equally significant ways of knowing very early in the life span, that logos comes to dominate as children and adolescents are required to construct socially appropriate forms of accommodation, and that mythos must be reintroduced later in life as personal perspective becomes an increasingly important element in maintaining equilibrium. It is really Labouvie-Vief's (1994b) first presumption, concerning the relationship of gender and ways of knowing, that now needs to be considered.

---

[5] It is important to recognize at this point the significant work of Carol Gilligan (1982; Gilligan, Murphy, & Tappan, 1990; Gilligan, Ward, Taylor, & Bardige, 1988) and her colleagues on the issue of gender and the construction of knowledge. I have chosen to pursue Labouvie-Vief's work on this topic rather than Gilligan's because Labouvie-Vief's discussions are more often integrated within Piagetian theory and are more fully articulated within an organismic, stage-based model. Gilligan's work is presented in Chapter 15, in the context of postmodern perspectives.

Not only has our tradition divided human functioning into two classes—the "lower," passive, organic and material as opposed to the "higher," active, abstract and spiritual-mental—but the two have also been attributed differently to each sex. At the same time, the "masculine" and the "feminine" have always carried very different cultural valuations. The man can derive a positive sense of self worth from his identification with agency-mind-spirit. But for the women, such positive self identity remains extremely problematic. Indeed, she is pressured to surrender her claim to consciousness and knowledge, a major source of positive self-identification. Thus her major source of identification remains negative, because she carries the devalued aspects of culture. (pp. 150–151)

In effect, then, as Piaget noted, the lives of young children are as defined by the world of mythos as by logos—and perhaps even more so because much of the thinking in early childhood is often described as "magical." But with the emergence of concrete operations and entry into the formal education system, boys experience a greater symmetry between culturally defined expectations for ways of knowing and culturally defined expectations for ways of expressing gender-related behaviors. Labouvie-Vief notes that one consequence of this gender-related pattern is that, even though there is no evidence of differences in ability level between boys and girls, the gap between their intellectual achievements and even their willingness to engage in intellectually challenging pursuits grows from childhood through the early adult years. She is quite clear as to the reason for this discrepancy.

That is, in identifying herself as "feminine," the woman does need to learn to surrender those attributes that are culturally labeled as "masculine," including her claim to knowledge and achievement. Interpersonally, and culturally, becoming feminine requires that the woman renounces her sense of agency and consciousness. Part of the self—the creator, thinker, questor—is experienced as monstrous, as outside of the self, and the woman attempts to cut it off from awareness altogether, to banish it into the unconscious. Indeed, she learns to feel a profound sense of shame of her competence. Instead, she realizes herself as sweet, beautiful, and caring, while her agency is projected onto the man. (1994b, p. 154)

The consequences of this differentiation are significant. She reports (Labouvie-Vief, Orwoll, et al., 1995) evidence of differences in the likelihood of boys and girls attempting difficult tasks, in their interpretations of their successes and failures, and in their vulnerabilities to psychological disorders. In all instances the patterns reflect a belief in males that they are causal agents (i.e., a sense of self rooted in logos) and in females that they are not (i.e., a sense of self rooted in mythos).

Labouvie-Vief sees this pattern changing as men and women move into the middle years of adulthood. The cognitive changes evident in her contextual-intersystemic and then dynamic-intersubjective levels ultimately allow adults to situate abstract thought in a broader context, one that requires an examination of the perspective from which one's logic emerges. The personal therefore reemerges as a significant element in cognition—not, she is quick to point out, as an anything-goes process, but rather one that permits a recognition that *both* ways of knowing may be correct. In other words, the transition to middle age brings with it for men the "unearthing" of mythos and for women the "unearthing" of logos.

Although this unearthing process brings a greater balance to the lives of both men and women, Labouvie-Vief notes that it is not equally well received by both. Citing several studies of middle-aged adults (Gutman, 1987; Helson & Moane, 1987; Livson, 1981; Maas & Kuypers, 1974), she notes the women typically view this transition much more positively than do men. This is not surprising given that women now find themselves reengaging in culturally valued patterns whereas men find themselves reengaging in cultural patterns that they have often viewed as less valued. The shift is characterized as a move from confinement to openness, as a time of greater creativity and unconventional strivings, and as a move toward greater self-direction, self-awareness, and satisfaction. Developmentally the advantages of this shift are equally available to both men and women. But our cultural norms, Labouvie-Vief believes, make it more difficult for men to embrace these changes than for women. In particular, it requires men to become more comfortable with nurturance, affiliation, and emotion—images previously viewed as feminine and therefore, to some men, as measures of weakness.

Labouvie-Vief also notes that the pattern she describes is still the exception rather than the rule in the lives of most men and women. She believes this adult developmental trajectory leads to full maturity. But she recognizes as well that the cultural context for most men and women is not yet supportive enough of full development—a point reflective of Piaget's basic argument that development is not an inevitable process.

Labouvie-Vief's Theory of Adult Development in Perspective

Labouvie-Vief's work is significant for three reasons. First, it offers an extension of Piaget's theory into the adult years that maintains the basic elements of his theory in particular and an organismic world view in general. That is, it maintains the principle that development is an active process involving the construction of successively more adaptive levels of activity. To do so, she has reframed Piaget's developmental sequence as one of successive adaptations rather than one of successive levels of logical thought —a shift apparently consistent with Piaget's work during the latter years of his life. This reframing is an important accomplishment because most accounts of adult development have pictured the processes regulating adulthood as discontinuous with those regulating childhood. Labouvie-Vief's work offers an image of life span development as a continuous process.

It seems only logical that a theory that defines mature thought as the ability to situate abstract reasoning within one's personal context should also examine the context in which theories themselves evolve and exist. In this sense, Labouvie-Vief's placement of the evolution of developmental theories—particularly Piaget's—within the larger context of Western intellectual thought is also significant. The effort serves to highlight the interconnectedness of all human endeavor. In particular, it reminds us that theories don't emerge from a void, but instead are efforts to explain what is of interest to the theorist.

Labouvie-Vief's most recent work on gender represents another extension of Piaget's theory—in this case to domains of little interest to Piaget. There is virtually nothing in Piaget's work that speaks to issues of gender. This should not be surprising given his interest in what he saw as universal patterns of development (ones typical of all members of a species) and his disinterest in factors influencing variability in these patterns. Labouvie-Vief's work on gender does offer an explanation of why there is gender-related variability in the development of cognitive competence. In the larger sense her work on gender offers a glimpse into the possible interplay of mechanistic and contextualist factors influencing interpersonal variability and organismic factors influencing intrapersonal development. In this sense her theory serves as a good illustration of how theories from different world views can come to complement one another.

Damon's Moral Goals Model

William Damon's work (Colby & Damon, 1995; Damon, 1977, 1984, 1988, 1995, 1996, 1997; Damon & Colby, 1987; Damon & Hart, 1988) focuses on moral development. More specifically, it concerns the processes through which individuals acquire and maintain the "broad interests and commitments that emanate from values, principles, and reactions" (Damon, 1996, p. 202) that reflect moral concerns. His work, an extension and elaboration of the work Piaget (1965) did on moral judgment early in his career, illustrates an approach to the study of moral development that is also reflected in the work of Lawrence Kohlberg (1984; Kohlberg & Ryncarz, 1990) Robert Selman (1971, 1990), James Youniss (Davidson & Youniss, 1991; Youniss & Damon, 1992; Youniss & Yates, 1997), and Elliot Turiel (Kim & Turiel, 1996; Laupa, Turiel, & Cowan, 1995; Turiel, 1980).

Damon's work has itself followed a life span perspective. His early research focused on children's understanding of such moral issues as friendship, equity, and authority. This was followed by work looking at children's concepts of self-understanding, and more recently, his work has focused on moral development during the adult years, particularly in terms of the study of what he refers to as "extraordinary moral commitment." He has pursued these topics at both an academic and an applied level. In fact, his most recent work has raised issues about how, as a society, we raise and educate our children and how we form and maintain our sense of community.

Damon's Extension of Piaget's View of Moral Development

Piaget's studies of moral judgment were done early in his career and have received less attention from developmentalists than has his later work on the construction of logico-mathematical thought. The moral judgment work is best known in terms of Piaget's observations of children playing the game of marbles. The point of the observations, as well as his related work, was to document the course of children's moral reasoning. His findings led him to argue that moral judgments are constructed in the same manner as any other concept. In this and other circumstances, efforts to resolve cognitive disequilibrium lead to new levels of cognitive organizations.

With respect to moral judgments, these organizations concern issues of fairness and equity. Such notions, in turn, were seen by Piaget as eventually helping adults form concepts of society based on a sense of *constructed mutuality* rather than a sense of *assigned rules*.

Central to these constructions is the role of peer interactions. It is through peer interactions that children and eventually adults come to understand both the skills for and the necessity of justifying one's own position and of listening to the positions of others. Piaget contrasted peer interactions with those of adult-child relationships. In the latter the inequality of power and experience actually is seen as hindering the construction of moral judgments because these relationships of inequality make justification and listening more difficult.

> He [Piaget] proposed that relationships of unilateral authority generated respect for the view's espoused by the authoritative figure. However, such respect lacked a grounding in communicative understanding, because it was not open to development in the classic Piagetian meaning of that concept. This is because construction is one-sided with the result that the child cannot accommodate adequately to the authority figure's initiatives. While children understand that adults bring points of view to interactions, and while children try to grasp adults' views, they end up failing to comprehend adults' perspectives and distort the views toward their own schemes. (Youniss & Damon, 1992, p. 272)

Piaget's interest in the development of moral judgment in children was far more than an academic pursuit. As was true of many European intellectuals following the end of World War I, Piaget was committed to finding ways of establishing a more just society through education—one less vulnerable to the authoritarianism and nationalism that fueled World War I. This perspective is clearly evident in Piaget's statement on educational reform, which appears at the end of Chapter 10. It is interesting to speculate on what the world might be like today had Piaget and others been more effective in getting governments to institute educational and social policies emphasizing a morality based on mutual respect.

Damon's efforts to expand on this early work of Piaget reflects three primary goals. The first is to dispel the image of Piaget's theory of development as an overly intellectualized, highly abstract, socially isolated sequence. The second is to further elaborate on the issues of moral judgment that Piaget identified, particularly in terms of the role peers and adults play in the process. The third is to place greater emphasis on the dissemination and application of his findings to real-world issues.

Damon's Early Studies of Children's Moral Development

Damon's early work is summarized in *The Social World of the Child* (1977). The book reviews his studies in the areas of children's developing understanding of the concepts of fairness and social justice, friendship, legitimacy and obedience to authority, and social conventions and rules. As these topics suggest, the work provides a basis to differentiate the development of moral understanding in domains defined by interactions among peers and those involving interactions between individuals in nonequal roles such as that of parent and child or teacher and student.

A similar method is used to investigate each of these topics. For each topic children are initially presented with one or more "moral dilemmas" and asked to explain the reasoning behind their proposed solutions. In this sense the method draws on Piaget's clinical interview methodology. With respect to the topic of positive justice (i.e., fairness and social equity), children are given some hypothetical situations and then asked how rewards should be distributed.

For example, young children (ages 4 and 5) are asked about how two friends might share an uneven number of toys. Older children (ages 7–12) are presented a dilemma in which a group of children make bracelets to sell. Some children make more than others, and some of the bracelets are better made than others. How should the proceeds of the sale be distributed among the children? A second longitudinal study follows some of the children in the original group with respect to their responses to these hypothetical dilemmas; a third study tests whether children's arguments for what others should do are, in fact, the same actions they themselves would take. In particular, in the third study, groups of children actually participate in a bracelet-making activity and are then asked to decide how to divide the rewards they receive for making the bracelets. To "guarantee" a dilemma for the children in the third study, one of the four children in each of the experimental groups is younger than the other three. Once the group completes its work, the three older children are then asked to decide how to distribute the rewards; that is, they are asked to decide what is fair.

The studies on legitimacy and obedience follow a similar three-step sequence. In this case, however, the issue is why a child should obey a parent. Specifically the issue concerns a child who wants very much to go with his (or her—the story reflected the gender of the child) friends to a picnic, but his mother says that he first must clean his room. The problem is that his friends are leaving right now, and if he stays to clean his room—that is, if he obeys his mother—he will miss out on the picnic. The second study follows the children longitudinally to see if their responses and the reasons for the responses change over time; the third study examines how children actually deal with issues of authority. In the third study children are assigned to basketball teams and told they are competing for prizes based on the number of free throws each team makes. After the children on each team complete a "warm-up" session in which each gets to observe the skill level of the other members of the team, the children are asked to pick a captain whose job is to decide how often each child gets to take shots during the allotted time period. At "half-time" the children are again individually interviewed to see how each feels about the captain's strategy. A final interview is done after the game. In all of the interviews for both the room-cleaning and the basketball tasks, the questions are designed to elicit the same information: On what basis do children make decisions about who should be given the authority to do something, and what is the rationale for obeying that person?

It is useful to compare Damon's findings with respect to children's understanding of positive justice and obedience to authority, because the comparison provides insights into how children see themselves in relationship to peers and in relationship to both adults and others in positions of authority. For both studies the cross-sectional and longitudinal phases yield similar developmental patterns. The most striking differences are with respect to the "real life" study in each domain.

POSITIVE JUSTICE SEQUENCE   The positive justice studies document a six-step developmental sequence over the age range of 4 through 9. At the two lowest levels, most commonly found with the youngest children in the study, fairness tends to be confused with personal desire. The difference between these first two levels is that, in the second, children do recognize a need to offer some explanation for their seemingly "selfish" distribution of rewards. The explanations, however, have little relevance to the task. A child might say that she should get more because she is wearing a blue sweater or that chocolate is her favorite candy. The issue for these young children is that their ability to recognize and appreciate the claims of others is still very limited—hardly surprising for 4- and 5-year-olds.

By the time the children reach age 6 or 7, their justifications change significantly. Now children initially argue that everyone should get the same reward irrespective of merit. Fairness is synonymous with equality, even to the point of some children saying that if an amount of money could not be divided equally among the participants, then the remainder should be "given back." Children's rationales for this strict equality often reflect beliefs about politeness or issues about conflict. As one 6-year-old put it when asked about some children getting more money than others: "Because then we would start fussin'. Like, say I have four and you have seven, then we would start fighting" (Damon, 1977, p. 81).

Slightly later, merit becomes a more significant issue. The difference appears to reflect children's growing understanding of the concept of *reciprocity*. For the first time in the sequence, children's notions of equity take on an interpersonal quality. No longer is absoluteness of either extreme the rule. Instead, people who are seen as deserving more should get more. The concept of merit now reflects beliefs about effort or success, as well as reciprocity of exchange. Kids who do the most or the best should receive the most: "If I am nice to you, you need to be nice to me." There is very much of a "bottom line" mentality to these children's reasoning. Issues of mitigating circumstances do not yet enter the picture.

By age 8, Damon's children begin to recognize that issues of fairness and positive justice can reflect a broad range of considerations. In addition to merit, need is now considered. Judgments are more likely to be based on considerations of individuals than considerations of acts. Initially, all considerations are taken into account; later, however, children come to recognize that only those considerations of need and merit relevant to the situation should be considered in determining how much reward each child should receive. Damon notes that, by this point in the sequence, children are able to differentiate a moral from a practical orientation to a social issue. They seem to understand that not all issues of distribution demand total equality; some can also be decided simply in terms of who is most deserving. Damon is quick to point out that this level of reasoning, while a significant improvement from the 4-year-old's, still has limitations. In the first place, even 8- and 9-year-olds have difficulty talking about notions of fairness and positive justice in more general terms, in terms of situations not involving them. Furthermore, there does not yet appear to be much evidence of universal standards of justice, ones that would be used as the basis for resolving all issues of equity.

What happens when children's beliefs are put to the test? Are they as equitable in their distribution of rewards when they are among the recipients? The three older children in each bracelet-making group were asked how they would distribute the 10 candy bars among the four participants (the younger child in each group was not part of the distribution discussion) and why they would do so. The results showed that children's reasoning in real situations was either at the same level as their reasoning in the hypothetical sessions or below the hypothetical reasoning. Rarely was it above. Damon's (1977) explanation for the discrepancy is useful because it provides insight into his perception of the factors that influence the development of social judgments in both children and adults.

> It is the interaction of the child's self-interest with his social judgment, rather than developmental relations between theoretical and active thought, that often accounts for lags between hypothetical and real-life social reasoning. . . . The direction of the lag between the two types of reasoning is determined by the way in which self-interest is best served in the particular social area considered. Self-interest can act either as an instigator or a retardant for advanced social judgment, depending on the type of social problem that the child encounters. (pp. 110–111)

AUTHORITY SEQUENCE   As is true for positive justice, 4-year-olds have difficulty in differentiating personal desires from issues of obedience to authority. In the case of the child who wants to go to a picnic with his friends but his mother insists that he first clean his room, 4-year-olds resolve the issue by denying that a conflict exists. In other words, they argue that the mother will do what the child wants or that the child will do what the mother wants. They seem to have great difficulty in recognizing the simultaneous existence of competing claims.

By age 5, children do recognize authority as an independent force but tend to see its only purpose as opposing their wishes. As such, obedience is largely a matter of the likelihood of detection and the potential severity of punishment. One 5-year-old notes that the boy shouldn't go to the picnic because his mother will punish him. But when the child is told that the mother is taking a nap, that the front door is open, and that she wouldn't find out about his going to the picnic, he says, "If he was going to the picnic and his mother was cleaning then he should run down the stairs and out the door so that his mother can't see him" (Damon, 1977, p. 185).

In these first two steps in the sequence, there is no indication in the children's responses that authority figures have an inherent right to be obeyed. Self-interest is the only criterion for action, with the only difference between the two being a concern about detection and punishment in the second step. But by the age of 5 or 6, this changes. For the first time children talk about obeying a parent because that is what one is supposed to do with parents. The rationale is still given in terms of detection and punishment, but for the first time the rationale is framed in terms of expectations and obligations of social roles rather than simply in terms of personal desire.

By the fourth step in the sequence (see Table 11.3 for a complete description of the sequence), the previous merging of "might" with "right" is transformed into a true recognition of reciprocity—children should obey their parents because their parents can help them. One 7-year-old explains that the child should obey his mother and not

TABLE 11.3
Damon's Authority Sequence

Level 0-A	Authority is legitimized by attributes that link the authority figure with the self, either by establishing affectional bonds between authority figure and self or by establishing identification between authority figure and self. The basis for obedience is a primitive association between authority's commands and the self's desires.
Level 0-B	Authority is legitimized by physical attributes of persons—size, sex, dress, and so on. The specific attributes selected are those which the subject considers to be descriptive of persons in command. These legitimizing attributes may be used in a fluctuating manner, since they are not linked logically to the functioning of authority. The subject recognizes the potential conflict between authority's commands and the self's wishes, and thinks about obedience in a pragmatic fashion: commands are followed as a means of achieving desires, or to avoid actions contrary to desires.
Level 1-A	Authority is legitimized by attributes which enable authority figure to enforce his commands (physical strength, social or physical power, and so on). Obedience is based upon subject's respect for authority figure's social or physical power, which is invested with an aura of omnipotence and omniscience.
Level 1-B	Authority is legitimized by attributes that reflect special talent or ability, and that make the authority figure a superior person in the eyes of the subject. This special talent or ability is no longer associated simply with power, but is rather indicative of the authority figure's ability to accomplish changes that subordinates cannot. Obedience is based on reciprocal exchange: one obeys because authority figure takes care of him, because authority figure has helped him in the past, or because authority figure otherwise "deserves" his obedience.
Level 2-A	Authority is legitimized by prior training or experience related to the process of commanding. Authority figure therefore is seen as a person who is able to lead and command better than subordinates. Obedience is based on subject's respect for this specific leadership ability and on the belief that this superior leadership ability implies a concern for the welfare and the rights of subordinates.
Level 2-B	Authority is legitimized by the coordination of a variety of attributes with specific situational factors. Subject believes that a person might possess attributes which enable him to command well in one situation but not in another. Authority, therefore, is seen as a shared consensual relation between parties, adopted temporarily by one person for the welfare of all. Obedience is seen as a cooperative effort which is situation-specific rather than a general response to a superior person.

Source: Damon, 1977, pp. 178–179.

go to the picnic "because if you were sick and asked for a glass of water she would do it for you. But if you won't do something for her she won't do it for you" (Damon, 1977, p. 191). Still missing, of course, from this rationale is any recognition of a sense of obligation as extending beyond the particulars of interactions—parents help their sick children even when those children have not been particularly delightful.

In the final two steps in the sequence, typical of 8- or 9-year-olds, Damon notes that for the first time children begin to recognize and understand that obedience and authority have a legitimacy based in training and experience: One should listen to the captain of the team because she knows more about the game. By extension, if she doesn't know more, there is no reason to listen to her or to let her be the captain, for that matter.

As is true in the case of positive justice, children are now also able to differentiate pragmatic from moral considerations: One might want to obey the captain even if she doesn't know anything if not doing so might lead to some sort of punishment. Even here, though, children are quick to point out that they obey the captain only to avoid the negative consequences, not because they think the captain is right (and therefore deserving of obedience). This differentiation of the pragmatic from the moral is important because it provides the criterion for recognizing the legitimacy and, by extension, the logic of a social order. But now the order is no longer absolute or arbitrary; rather, it is one in which individuals participate willingly because everyone presumably benefits from it. Everyone benefits because those in positions of authority are there by virtue of their knowledge and experience and their willingness to help others acquire similar knowledge and experience.

How do these hypothetical views of authority transfer to real-life situations—in this case one involving the choice of a team captain and a willingness to follow the captain's directives? Damon's data indicates that here the relationship between children's hypothetical and real judgments is closer than it is with respect to issues of equity and positive justice. Perhaps most interesting is the finding that children scoring higher on the authority sequence are *less* likely to nominate themselves for captain than are children who scored lower. Damon (1977) notes that self-interest may also be an issue here but that its role is now different.

> It is clear therefore, that in authority and positive justice rationale self-interest plays widely different roles. In an authority problem, a child's self-interest is not in conflict with the interest of others (at least in relation to issues of authority). Rather, everyone's self-interest is at stake in the relationship, and the chief area of disagreement is how the welfare of all parties is best served. To the extent that such disagreement derives directly from conflicting conceptions of the authority relation, it is a function of developmental differences between different children's authority knowledge. Thus, even in this sense, self-interest (and the issue of how it is best obtained) is an intrinsic part of children's developing conceptions of authority. In a justice problem, on the other hand, a child often sees his or her self-interest as directly opposed to fairness. This is particularly true at children's higher levels of positive justice knowledge, and it places the child in a state of conflict, since fairness, rather than self-interest, is the crux of justice. (pp. 223–224)

THE DEVELOPMENTAL SIGNIFICANCE OF DAMON'S EARLY WORK Damon's findings with respect to children's understanding of positive justice and obedience to authority both support and extend Piaget's own findings. Clearly there is a developmental progression in children's understanding of these two moral issues, and the nature of the progression is better described in qualitative than quantitative terms. That is, children do not simply become more or less in terms of some dimension across the age range. Rather, they progressively construct new understandings of the relationship of the elements relevant to each moral issue. However, the progression is not as uniform as Piaget's work might lead us to believe. Like Fischer, Damon finds only a loose consistency across developmental domains. Damon argues that a lack of uniformity across domains reflects both children's still-limited ability to abstract general principles and their differences in resolving issues of positive justice and obedience to authority. In particular, this early work clarifies the significance of the differences in the social interactions that exist among peers and those that exist between individuals of different levels of authority, training, and expertise.

Damon (1984) has used both the data and the theory concerning this distinction between social interactions of equals and unequals, particularly in terms of fostering dialogue and reflection, to serve as a basis to argue for more peer education in our schools. He believes that educational strategies incorporating both peer collaboration and peer tutoring increase the likelihood that children (1) will be better motivated to learn, (2) will be more likely to reflect on their knowledge, (3) will develop more effective interpersonal communication skills, and (4) will discover a "process for generating ideas and solutions with equals in an atmosphere of mutual respect. This, in turn, can foster an orientation toward kindness and fairness in interpersonal relationships" (Damon, 1984, p. 335).

Damon's Studies of Self-Understanding

Damon (Damon & Hart, 1988), in collaboration with Daniel Hart, followed up the original studies of children's social constructions of positive justice and obedience to authority with a series of studies on children's development of an understanding of themselves as unique individuals. The studies involve children between the ages of 4 and 17 and include both cross-sectional and longitudinal approaches. The children come from communities in the United States and the Commonwealth of Puerto Rico. The method is again the clinical interview, in this case asking children questions about how they defined and evaluated themselves (e.g., "What are you like? What are you especially proud of about yourself?"), about their images of themselves in the past and future (e.g., "Do you think you will be the same or different when you are an adult? What do you want to be like?"), about their sense of agency (e.g., "How did you get to be the way you are? How did that make you the kind of person that you are?"), and about their sense of distinctiveness (e.g., "Do you think there is anyone exactly like you? What makes you different from anyone that you know?") (Damon & Hart, 1988, pp. 81–82).

Consistent with his earlier work, Damon finds that children's development of self-understanding is not a unitary dimension. In this case two distinct dimensions are evident, and although the two show a similar developmental progression, they do not reflect a single developmental dimension.

Damon's two dimensions of self-understanding are the *self-as-subject* and the *self-as-object*. Damon traces this differentiation of the concept of self to the work of both William James (1961 [1892]) and Herbert Mead (1934). The self-as-object reflects a "third-person" or "me" perspective. This dimension includes all the elements that define the self as a unique configuration of personal attributes and includes such things as physical attributes, social and personality characteristics, and psychological feelings and awareness. The self-as-subject reflects a "first-person" or "I" perspective. Whereas the self-as-object can be known by others, the self-as-subject is a wholly subjective dimension. It can only be known by the individual.

> The essence of the "I" is its subjectivity. This translates into an awareness of several core features of individuality, among which are: (1) an awareness of one's own agency over life events; (2) an awareness of the uniqueness of one's life experiences; (3) an awareness of one's personal continuity; and (4) an awareness of one's own awareness. (Damon & Hart, 1988, p. 6)

Damon and Hart find evidence for a developmental progression within each of the components that define the two dimensions (self-as-object and self-as-subject) of self-understanding. With respect to the four components defining the self-as-object (the physical self, social self, active self, and psychological self), a four-step sequence is identified spanning early childhood through late adolescence. A parallel four-step sequence is identified for the three components defining the self-as-subject (continuity, distinctiveness, and agency).

THE SELF-AS-OBJECT DEVELOPMENTAL SEQUENCE   Damon and Hart find that young children's view of themselves in the third person is very categorical. Simple, factual descriptions of self in terms of each of the four components define this level of self-understanding. These young children understand themselves to be someone, for example, having a particular eye and hair color, having particular likes and interests, occupying a particular role in the family, and demonstrating particular behavioral patterns.

By the early school years these simple taxonomic categories are integrated into comparative assessments. The specific elements by which the self is understood remain the same, but now they are viewed in a relative rather than an absolute perspective. Whereas the preschooler might have said, "I am a fast runner," she is now, a few years later, more likely to say, "I am one of the fastest runners in my class."

As children approach puberty and early adolescence, a further transformation becomes evident. The categorical assessments are still evident, but now they have become integrated into a social context. The issue is no longer one of being the fastest runner, but of how that status affects one's relationship to the other children in the class. Finally, by late adolescence, a fourth level emerges, one that shows a greater evidence of integration between the four components than had been seen earlier. Damon and Hart (1988) describe this new level:

> Categories of the self-as-object are organized through systemic beliefs and life plans. Characteristics of the self draw their meaning for one's identity through such beliefs and plans, which may include philosophical or moral belief systems, ideological choices, or any variety of personal goals. The priority of the belief or plan creates a new coherence in self-understanding, because self defining categories are selected and related to one another only in a manner consistent with the belief or plan. At this level, therefore, a consciously systematic conception of self is first achieved. (p. 67)

THE SELF-AS-SUBJECT DEVELOPMENTAL SEQUENCE   As is true for the self-as-object sequence, the self-as-subject sequence reflects four levels spanning early childhood through late adolescence. Unlike the self-as-object sequence, however, Damon and Hart report less evidence of integration across the components in late adolescence. As such, they present the sequences for the three components (continuity, distinctiveness, and agency) separately.

Preschoolers seem not to have much understanding of themselves as agents of change. This doesn't mean that they are not; rather, it means only that they are not very aware of themselves as doing so. Forces external to the self are seen as regulating personal actions. But this begins to change during the early school years, when personal effort is seen as the reason for one's accomplishments. And puberty brings with it an increasing recognition of the role others play in one's sense of personal agency. Children now seem better able to appreciate the role of the interpersonal context in influencing one's actions. Finally, by late adolescence, an awareness of one's own sense of agency reflects both a reflected plan as to how one wants to act and an awareness of the role of others. As one adolescent put it:

> Well, I decided to be kind to people because I've seen lots of kids hurt other people's feelings for no reason, and it's not right or fair. Nobody should try to hurt another person's feelings or be mean to them. (Damon & Hart, 1988, p. 71)

Children's understanding of self-as-subject in terms of their sense of continuity shows a similar pattern of change. Continuity of self is initially defined in terms of categorical qualities: You will still be you in the future because you will still have the same color hair or will still have your bike or a sister. By the school years this continuity of characteristics evolves into a sense of continuity defined in terms of capabilities and characteristics. Level three marks the emergence of an understanding of how the interpersonal context influences one's sense of personal continuity: You continue to be who you are in part because others continue to treat you as you are. Finally, by late adolescence, individuals seem to acquire a developmental perspective. That is, they now seem able to understand themselves not as a static entity but as a changing one. This change reflects the cumulative impact of actions by both the self and others.

Understanding the self as a distinct entity also shows a parallel developmental course. Distinctiveness is initially expressed in terms of physical characteristics, possessions, preferences, behaviors, and so on. This becomes integrated into a comparative frame of reference by the early school years. As children approach puberty, psychological qualities are increasingly recognized as contributing to one's uniqueness —how you think and feel become as important as what you are wearing and how you behave. By late adolescence distinctiveness also becomes defined in terms of unique interpretations and orientations.

REAL-LIFE CORRELATES OF SELF-UNDERSTANDING   The nature of the subject matter of these studies did not allow for a real-life test of the developmental sequences, as is true for the positive justice and obedience to authority studies. But Damon and Hart did examine the relationship between level of self-understanding and adolescent mental health issues. In particular, they first compared level of self-understanding in a sample of adolescent females who were anorexic against a nonanorexic sample and then did a parallel study involving conduct disorders in adolescent males. With respect to the anorexic comparison, anorexic females were found to score developmentally lower on measures of agency. The anorexic females are much less likely than the controls to see themselves as having some degree of influence over themselves. Rather, they are more likely to attribute their circumstances to external, concrete factors—family or fate.

> Within such an immature conceptual framework, the sights on which any agentic efforts would be set would necessarily be physicalistic or possibly action oriented. Fixed regimens to effect such goals would be rigidly adhered to as though coming from another source, such that the girl herself had no choice over them. (Damon & Hart, 1988, p. 152)

With respect to adolescent males exhibiting conduct disorders, Damon finds that these males are much less likely to think of themselves in a relative perspective and much less likely to have a future image of themselves. And, as is true of the anorexic group, these males seem to have little insight into their present circumstances, especially in terms of the role they might have played in defining those circumstances. As a result of this pattern, these adolescent males feel less inhibited by social context. As such, they act out, the consequences of which only further estrange them from social contact with others.

Damon is quick to point out that he is not arguing that either anorexia or conduct disorders are caused by immature self-understanding. Both situations are more complicated. But he does believe that understanding individuals' developmental levels provides insights into how they view their own situations and therefore into the possible design of intervention strategies.

Social Influence and Moral Change

Damon's studies with children and adolescents has made it clear to him that even though moral development cannot be imposed by outside forces, social influence is nevertheless necessary to foster the construction of moral knowledge. Damon bases this conclusion on the positive role peers play in prompting children to reflect on their moral reasoning. But, somewhat contrary to Piagetian reasoning, Damon sees situations involving peer agreement rather than peer conflict as the most likely to prompt shifts in the level of children's moral reasoning. A Piagetian would argue that we can expect peer conflict to prompt a greater degree of disequilibrium, an essential prerequisite to change. These findings have prompted Damon to look more carefully at the types of social influence most likely to foster moral change.

In trying to better understand why peer agreement rather than peer conflict is most effective in fostering growth in moral reasoning, Damon has made use of a *substitution-of-goals model*. The goals of interest to Damon are moral ones, and he defines these as efforts to establish and maintain a "just" or "benevolent" state of affairs (Damon, 1996). The model is based on the work of the Russian developmentalist Lev Vygotsky (1896–1934) (1978; Vygotsky & Luria, 1993). Vygotsky's theory will be examined in Chapter 14 because it falls within a contextualist world view. For now it is important only to recognize that, as is true of other neo-Piagetian applications, Damon's extension of Piaget's work provides evidence of the value of better understanding how images of development from different world views can serve to complement each other. In this case the value is in better understanding the role social context plays in fostering developmental change. In discussing Vygotsky's work, Damon notes that

> its advantage over a Piagetian framework is that it provides for the incorporation of a new system of motives developed in communication with others, rather than merely for the acquisition of new knowledge. It also assumes that new perspectives are shaped cooperatively (or co-constructed) in the course of many negotiations between persons. This means that all new ideas must owe their shape to some interaction between external guidance and internal belief. (Damon & Colby, 1987, p. 10)

Damon's most recent work (in collaboration with Anne Colby) has extended his interest in fostering moral change by examining the role that negotiation plays in restructuring the goals of a group of adults whom Damon describes as "morally exemplary individuals." The moral development of these individuals reflects a "best case" scenario of a substitution-of-goals model.

These adults, few of whose names would be recognized by others, come from all walks of life but share a set of characteristics that Damon believes identify morally exemplary individuals. These characteristics include a sustained commitment to moral principles, a willingness to risk personal well-being, a talent for inspiring others, and a dedicated responsiveness to the needs of others. Although the particulars of the lives of these individuals differ, Damon does note certain common elements. In all cases the development of these morally exemplary lives reflected the interaction of personal qualities with particular social contexts. It was a matter of the right person being in the right place at the right time. These morally exemplary individuals share three common personal qualities: (1) a sense of certainty, (2) a sense of positivity, and (3) a unity of self and moral goals (Colby & Damon, 1995). These individuals also have in common a very clear sense about the correctness of their beliefs, irrespective of the reactions of others. They are able as well to maintain an optimistic view of their work, in spite of obstacles. Finally, their strong moral beliefs form the core element of their personal identities—what they believe is who they are.

> The close relationship of personal and moral goals that we saw in our exemplars means that they do not see their moral choices as an exercise in self-sacrifice. To the contrary, they see their moral goals as a means of attaining their personal ones, and vice-versa. This can only be possible when moral goals and personal goals are in synchrony, perhaps even identical. Our exemplars have been invulnerable to the debilitating psychological effects of privation because all they have needed for personal success is the productive pursuit of their moral mission. Their hopes for themselves and their own destinies are largely defined by their moral goals. In the end, it is this unity between self and morality that makes them exceptional. (Colby & Damon, 1995, p. 362)

Damon is quick to point out that although these individuals are exemplary, they are not aberrations. That is, their lives may reflect an extreme point on a developmental progression of moral reasoning, but it is the same progression that the rest of us pursue. Presumably, under the right set of circumstances, we could all be exemplary. Perhaps this is why Damon's current work (1995, 1997) focuses on the prerequisites for the establishment of moral communities in our society.

For all of us, exemplary or not, Damon believes that mature moral reasoning comes about only when personal interests and moral goals become one, a finding noted in his work with children, adolescents, and adults. What starts out in young children as a conflict between "what I want" and "what is fair" can only be resolved through a continuing form of social dialogue and negotiation that supports (1) active participation by all parties, (2) a receptivity to direction and feedback, (3) exposure to differing opinions and goals in an affirming environment, (4) guidance that provides a bridge from mismatch to match of goals, and (5) the adoption of broader goals that can be integrated into an individual's personal framework (Damon, 1996). Ultimately, the individual must come to recognize that what is fair must also be what he or she wants. For his exemplary adults the fusion appears total, but for the rest of us, Damon argues, it is only partial. As a result, most adults retain a gap between their moral judgments and their moral conduct. The role, then, of a just society is to provide the social supports necessary to foster a correspondence between individuals' developing sense of moral reasoning and the conduct of their day-to-day lives.

Damon's Moral Goals Model in Perspective

The significance of Damon's work has been noted throughout this discussion. Perhaps only two points need to be added here, each in reference to his work as an extension and revision of Piaget's original work on moral development.

First, Damon's work provides a much clearer base for understanding the interplay between thought and action. Although Piaget certainly talked about the importance of social context on individual development, it was never his primary interest. As such, his work provides little guidance as to how social forces influence developmental level. Damon's work, at least with respect to the development of moral reasoning, provides a very clear picture of the interplay that is necessary between the individual and society for development to continue and, ideally, to become exemplary.

Second, Damon's work provides further evidence that development is not a unitary process moving across all domains at the same rate, but one reflecting several loosely connected domains. For example, although one's levels of logico-mathematical thought correlates with level of moral reasoning, the correlations are far from perfect. Piaget did note these "discrepancies" through his concepts of vertical and horizontal decalage, but again, he did not pursue them because issues of variability were not his primary focus. By examining the interplay of contextual factors influencing variability with organismic factors influencing change over time, Damon is able to present a much fuller picture of moral development than was Piaget.

12

The Psychodynamic Models of Freud and Erikson

The works of Sigmund Freud (1856–1939) and Erik Erikson (1902–1994) occupy interesting places within theories of life span human development. Seemingly every year, for example, several books are published showing beyond a shadow of a doubt why Freud's work is of little value to the study of human development. The fact that this has now been happening for many years suggests that perhaps there is more to Freud's work than first meets the eye. After all, if Freud's work is of such little value, why is it still around to be picked on every year? Perhaps, at the least, Freud understood very clearly some of the fundamental questions that a theory of human development must address—even if his answers to these questions continue to generate so much controversy.

Erikson's theory, which derives from Freud's, is less controversial but still has never enjoyed the focus or status of other developmental theorists such as Piaget (although, to be fair, I should point out that both Freud and Erikson enjoy considerable status within psychotherapeutic circles). Like Gesell, Erikson is often relegated to the opening chapters of introductory child development texts, where his stages are discussed and then usually ignored. As is true for Freud, this is unfortunate because the very scale and scope of Erikson's ideas—a scale that does make their testability very difficult—is an excellent model of the interdisciplinary approach that is needed to establish a full perspective on development across the life span.

It is important to note that Freud's and Erikson's respective developmental theories form only a portion of their writings. In both cases a significant portion of their work is also devoted to issues related to psychotherapy and to issues that touch on historical, sociological, anthropological, religious, and even political topics.

Freud's Psychosexual Theory of Development

Freud's work contains an interesting parallel to Piaget's. As was true of Piaget, Freud was never particularly interested in children or in issues of normal development. But both Freud and Piaget came to the study of human development, particularly child development, as a way to answer other questions. For Piaget these questions were epistemological in nature and concerned what it means to know something. Because children are in the process of coming to know things, it made sense for them to serve as the "means" to his larger "end." For Freud these questions were psychotherapeutic in nature and concerned how best to treat his adult patients. It soon became apparent to Freud that his adult patients' problems stemmed from what he saw as their traumatic childhood experiences, so the study of children's development again served as a "means" to a larger "end."

> All the wishes, instinctual impulses, modes of reaction and attitudes of childhood are still demonstrably present in maturity and in appropriate circumstances can emerge once more. They are not destroyed but merely overlaid—to use the spatial mode of description which psycho-analytic psychology has been obliged to adopt. Thus it is part of the nature of the mental past that, unlike the historic past, it is not absorbed by its derivatives; it persists (whether actual or only potentially) alongside what has proceeded from it. The proof of this assertion lies in the fact that the dreams of normal people revive their childhood characters every night and reduce the whole mental life to an infantile level. The same return to infantilism (regression) appears in the neuroses and psychoses, whose peculiarities may to a great extent be described as psychical archaisms. (Freud, 1913, in Strachey, 1955, vol. 16, p. 184)

Lives are never perfectly parallel, however. Whereas the questions that defined Piaget's lifework began to emerge when he was still a child studying with mollusks, for Freud they came much later and partly as a result of the anti-Semitism that blocked other opportunities for scientific inquiry.

A Biographical Sketch

Sigmund Freud was born in 1856 in Freiberg, a city in what is now the Czech Republic, but at the age of 4 moved with his family to Vienna. He did well in school, earning high marks in a broad range of subjects. This eclectic quality to his interests was a hallmark of his work throughout his life. He initially hoped for a career in politics or the law, but as Stevens notes, "Such possibilities for a Viennese Jew of modest means were limited" (1983b, p. 19). He decided instead on medicine and completed his degree in 1882 with a particular interest in the anatomy of the nervous system.

Freud's goal was to make research in neurology his lifework. But this would have required an academic appointment, and again, "such possibilities" were not available. Because Freud did not have the financial means to support his own research, and because he was now married and planning for a family, he turned to clinical work as a means of making a living.

At that time the treatment of what was then referred to as "nervous diseases" was very primitive, relying heavily on electrotherapy (the passing of mild electric currents through the body). Freud was not impressed with this approach to therapy because of its limited effectiveness and its lack of scientific rationale for its use. He turned instead to hypnosis, a technique he had first encountered while studying in Paris with Jean

Charcot, an early advocate for the use of hypnosis in the treatment of hysteria. Freud's particular responsibility while studying with Charcot was differentiating paralyses believed to be organic in origin from those seen as hysterical (i.e., psychological) in origin. This work appears to have been a significant experience for Freud because it furthered his belief that many psychological disorders may not have an organic base, a common assumption at that time.

Freud's early clinical work was based on the use of hypnosis. The use of hypnosis helped him recognize that some things come into a person's consciousness only when that person is in an altered state. This realization, in turn, helped him to differentiate the role of conscious from unconscious thought. However, he still found the technique limiting in that what the patient recalled was largely a reflection of what the therapist prompted him or her to recall. Little was volunteered by the patient under hypnosis. Freud wanted a less intrusive and less directive means into his patients' psyches. He found it through his work with a Viennese colleague and friend, Joseph Breuer. The technique, which we know as *free association,* is linked with the stereotype of the therapist quietly sitting on a chair behind a patient lying on a couch. But it allowed patients to talk freely about whatever comes into their consciousness—about dreams and any other issues that the therapist's usually subtle and indirect questions might provoke in patients' memories.

What Freud soon discovered when he analyzed his patients' free associations was that what his patients talked about the most was sex, particularly in terms of their earliest childhood recollections. To say the least, this revelation changed everything. Freud's initial efforts to present to his colleagues the notion that psychological disorders do not necessarily have an organic base and that adult psychopathology has its roots in childhood experiences was difficult enough. But to further suggest that these early childhood experiences were sexual in nature was more than even the most open-minded in what was then very proper Vienna could bear. His ideas were met with anger, scorn, and ridicule, and he was professionally isolated.

Freud, however, apparently had a very strong ego. For most of us, the intensity and breadth of the criticism he received would have been enough to halt our pursuits; for Freud it seems to have intensified them. He continued with his practice of psychiatry and his writing and lecturing. His first major works on his theory were *The Interpretation of Dreams* (1950 [1900]) and *Three Essays on the Theory of Sexuality* (1905). Although the traditional medical establishment had little regard for these early works, they did serve to bring together a "Vienna circle" of individuals interested in Freud's ideas. Among the more notable of this group were Carl Jung and Alfred Adler. Both eventually moved away from Freud's ideas—a particularly painful separation for Freud —but their work nevertheless bears the imprint of this early association.

Gradually, Freud's work gained international fame, although it wasn't until 1909 that he received an honorary doctorate for his pioneering work, from Clark University in the United States. As his work gained international fame, his contributions also finally became recognized by the medical establishment in Vienna. In the early 1920s he was granted a full professorship at the University of Vienna. In the following years, however, the rise of Nazism in central Europe, as well as the beginning of a long and difficult battle with cancer of the jaw, prevented Freud from enjoying this long-deserved recognition. At the urging of many who feared for his safety under the Nazis, Freud left Vienna and resettled in London in 1938. He died in 1939.

The most complete set of his work is represented in the twenty-four volume set of his collected works edited by Strachey (1953–1966). The most complete biography of his life is by Jones (1961).

The Basic Elements of Freud's Theory

To appreciate Freud's view of development, we need first to consider the elements that he saw as regulating psychological functioning and then to understand how these elements evolve—that is, their developmental sequence. As is true of all theory, the elements of Freud's theory reflect the major intellectual movements active during its creation. In the case of Freud, these ideas reflect the influence of Darwin's theory of evolution and the then-current research in physics dealing with thermodynamics (i.e., the activity of energy in closed systems).

Darwin's fundamental notion of the preservation of the species implied the existence of a drive or motive force that regulates the behavior of the members of a species —namely, that species always act in ways that increase their chances of survival across generations. There is nothing intentional or necessarily conscious about this force from the organism's perspective. But as he observed the behavior of different species, Darwin found it necessary to posit such a mechanism to explain the behavior of these species.

At the same time that Darwin's notions were receiving attention in biological circles, extensions of Newton's theories about the conservation of energy were receiving attention in physics circles. Newton's laws of thermodynamics offer an explanation of the "behavior" of energy in a closed system. In particular, Newton argued that energy is never gained or lost in such a closed system but is simply transformed.

Together these two fundamental concepts, one concerning motivation and the other concerning conservation, appear to be the frame of reference Freud used in trying to make sense out of his patients' behavior and symptoms. As Freud saw it, from this frame of reference, all adult behavior, normal or abnormal, can be traced back to events in childhood. In fact, in his later writings on religion (Freud, 1975) and society (Freud, 1951), he even argued that, by extension, the institutions we create to structure our lives also ultimately reflect the early life experiences of individuals.

The energy in Freud's system is a psychic energy, usually referred to as the *libido*. The libido is the energy produced from the functioning of biological systems. Freud saw the source of this energy as instinctual rather than acquired. It reflected the biological imperative of the organism to have its basic needs met. For Freud an organism's sexual needs were the most important of these needs because meeting one's sexual needs is the only way to preserve the species. Keep in mind, however, that Freud argued that one does not meet one's sexual needs simply or exclusively through sexual intercourse. More generally, at all developmental levels, meeting one's sexual needs involves having pleasurable experiences. It is only with maturity that these pleasurable activities become equated with sexual intercourse and therefore the preservation of the species. Consider how Freud describes the relationship between the sexuality of the child and that of the adult:

> To suppose that children have no sexual life—sexual excitations and needs and a kind of satisfaction—but suddenly acquire it between the ages of twelve and fourteen, would (quite apart from any observations) be as improbable, and indeed senseless, biologically as to suppose that they brought no genitals with them into the world and only grew them at the time of puberty. What *does* awaken in them at this time is the reproductive function, which makes use for its purposes of physical and mental material already present. You are committing the error of confusing sexuality and reproduction and by so doing you are blocking your path to an understanding of sexuality, the perversions and the neuroses. (Freud, 1917, in Strachey, 1963, vol. 16, p. 311, italics in original)

Activities are pleasurable because they reduce tension. In this sense Freud's model is sometimes referred to as a *drive reduction model.*

Not only are instincts not learned, they are for the most part also unknown to the individual. For Freud much of human activity occurs at the *unconscious* rather than the *conscious* level. That is, individuals have little understanding of the real forces motivating their behavior. Over time there is a shift toward more conscious activity, but as will become clearer, individuals never reach a point at which unconscious actions become irrelevant—quite the opposite, in fact. For Freud the process of achieving sexual maturity—defined in the broadest sense—is the core element of the process of development. All other aspects of development, to one degree or another, in one manner or another, reflect the status of one's sexual maturity. And, most importantly given the clinical emphasis of psychoanalysis, all adult psychological problems are traceable to the events and experiences that form one's process of sexual maturity. It is this process that defines Freud's *psychosexual developmental sequence.*

Freud's Psychosexual Developmental Sequence

Freud's psychosexual developmental sequence involves five stages: the oral, anal, phallic, latency, and genital.[1] Each stage is associated with a particular part of the anatomy, an *erogenous zone* in Freud's terms, because Freud believed that the libido focuses on that part of the anatomy at that particular point in development. The concentration of the libido at that body area creates an increase in tension that needs to be reduced. Tension reduction is experienced as pleasure, and as such, the process is

---

[1] It is important to remember that, as is true for all stage theories, the chronological age markers are only approximations. The important element of Freud's stages is the sequence, not the age of occurrence.

motivated by this effort toward tension reduction. Furthermore, skills acquired and relationships established over the course of development occur in the service of this tension reduction.

STAGE 1: THE ORAL STAGE (THE FIRST YEAR OF LIFE) It is not difficult to appreciate why Freud saw activity related to the mouth as the first erogenous site. Everything young infants touch eventually ends up in their mouths. Sucking, biting, teething, mouthing, and gumming all seem to bring young infants great pleasure, that is, to reduce tension.

But these acts of incorporation, to Freud, have more than a biological purpose. They also have a psychological purpose in that they are the first experiences the infant has of taking in or incorporating into the self things that are initially external to the self. For the moment these things are simply sources of nourishment or exercises in self-stimulation. But to Freud these early activities nevertheless serve as the foundation upon which attitudes, values, and social roles eventually will be incorporated.

These pleasurable activities associated with the mouth are not done in isolation. Someone, usually the parent, is providing a breast or bottle or other object to suck or mouth or bite. By virtue of being associated with these pleasurable acts, the parent (or whoever) also acquires some tension-reducing properties. The association is essentially a process of classical conditioning. For Freud it is the mechanism through which others first come to have value in the child's eyes.

But not all activity associated with the mouth is pleasurable. Teething can be painful. The clear displeasure expressed by a mother when her infant bites down during breast-feeding is sensed by the infant as a feeling of anxiety. A delay of gratification (i.e., the infant not being fed when hungry or not having an object to mouth) increases tension in the oral region to a point at which the child senses it as discomfort. In other words, for Freud, one of life's early lessons to be learned is that each erogenous zone is a site of pain as well as pleasure. The task, then, for the individual becomes one of learning how to maximize the pleasure and minimize the pain. How successful infants are at this task and how they accomplish it define, to a significant degree, the character of future developmental accomplishments. In the extreme it also begins to define the likelihood of future needs for psychotherapy. In particular, Freud believed that individuals would become *fixated* at a particular developmental stage if the resolution of the issues associated with that stage were too extreme. In other words, infants who have every one of their needs met or are continually frustrated in their efforts to obtain satisfaction are most likely to become fixated at the oral stage. Such a fixation at the oral stage would be reflected in a preoccupation with the mouth at some later point in development. Presumably adults who are always chewing, biting, eating (or not eating), or sucking something are demonstrating the effects of an incomplete resolution of the oral stage.

What determines how well and in what fashion this most basic of life's lessons is learned? What is regulating the process? For the young infant the process is regulated solely by what Freud referred to as the *id*. The id is a psychological structure residing in the infant's unconscious whose sole purpose is to bring about the reduction of tension and the immediate gratification of all needs. Freud paints a very colorful picture of its nature. He describes it as a "cauldron full of seething excitations," filled with energy but having no organization. Its only function is "striving to bring about the satisfaction of the instinctual needs subject to the observance of the pleasure principle." Neither the laws of logic nor the laws of contradiction seem to apply to the id; it has no sense of time. Ideas that enter the id appear to have no chronological arrangement but simply exist in the past.

> The id of course knows no judgments of value: no good and evil, no morality. The economic or, if you prefer, the quantitative factor, which is intimately linked to the pleasure principle, dominates all its processes. Instinctual cathexes seeking discharge —that, in our view, is all there is to the id. (Freud, 1933, in Strachey, 1964, vol. 22, p. 74)

No wonder Freud thought that the best way to understand the functioning of the id was through the analysis of dreams.

From a developmental perspective a structure such as the id is not a very functional structure. Admittedly, the infant wants what he wants when he wants it, but he is not in a very good position to do much about it. He must rely on the goodwill of others. And because, fortunately, few parents see their sole purpose in life as immediately meeting their infants' every need, the infant soon discovers the necessity of having to deal with reality. In other words, the socialization process begins.

STAGE 2: THE ANAL STAGE (AGE 2 TO 3)   Sometime during the second year, the libido shifts its focus from the mouth to the anus, and activities relating to elimination and retention of bodily wastes become the focus of reducing tension and seeking pleasure. The basic issue—increasing pleasure, eliminating tension—remains the same as it is during the oral stage, but it is now played out in a more complicated fashion. Maturation of the sphincter muscles gives children the opportunity to exercise a degree of control over their bowel and bladder functions. At the same time, there is increasing pressure, from society in general and from parents in particular, to become toilet trained. Clearly, the regulation of behavior solely through the id will no longer suffice because the child is increasingly being asked to behave in ways that do not lead to immediate gratification.

The conflict the toddler confronts is a first lesson in the balancing of power and control. Holding on to feces and urine brings a corresponding increase of tension but also, upon elimination, a greater sense of pleasure and parental approval. In addition, holding on is one of the first ways that toddlers exercise their sense of power. They can hold on and defy their parents, or, at the appropriate time and place, they can comply. Eliminating wastes immediately brings the least buildup of tension and the least immediate pleasure but also, increasingly, parental rebuke.[2] Freud paints a vivid image of the dilemma:

---

[2] There are, of course, significant differences across cultures in the age that toilet training begins and the degree of deliberateness by which it is done. It is worth noting that 19th-century Vienna's views on toilet training were particularly harsh. Training was begun before the first birthday, and "accidents" were not well accepted. Not surprisingly, Freud saw many of his adult patients' symptoms as reflecting this extreme approach to toilet training.

Children who are making use of the susceptibility to erotogenic stimulation of the anal zone betray themselves by holding back their stool till its accumulation brings about violent muscular contractions and, as it passes through the anus, is able to produce powerful stimulation of the mucous membrane. In so doing it must no doubt cause not only painful but highly pleasurable sensations. One of the clearest signs of subsequent eccentricity or nervousness is to be seen when a baby obstinately refuses to empty his bowels when he is put on the pot—that is, when his nurse wants him to —and holds back that function till he himself chooses to exercise it. (Freud, 1905, in Strachey, 1953, vol. 7, p. 186)

The successful resolution of such an important social demand cannot rest solely on the id. The id is not rational or logical; it cares for nothing other than its own pursuit of pleasure. The id cannot be socialized. What now emerges, therefore, probably as a result of these struggles (Freud was never very specific as to the actual mechanism), is a second psychological structure, the *ego*. The ego is an extension of the id, deriving its energy from the id and serving as the mediator between the wishes of the id and the external world. Unlike the id, which operates on the pleasure principle, the ego operates on the *reality principle*. Because of this, the functioning of the ego is based not entirely in the unconscious but in a second area of the psyche, the preconscious. Whereas events in the unconscious can never directly be known, those in the preconscious can, with reflection, be made apparent.

The ego's goal is the same as the id's, but its strategy differs. Because it is a rational mechanism, it is able to recognize, for example, that deferring gratification may at times be the better solution because the buildup of tension may eventually lead to greater tension reduction and therefore to greater ultimate pleasure. Because the ego is based in reality, it is able to decide which possible strategy might be most likely to lead to a desired end. Certainly, this would be true as children come to learn to deal with their parents. "For the ego, perception plays the part which in the id falls to instinct. The ego represents what might be called reason and common sense, in contrast to the id, which contains the passions" (Freud, 1923, in Strachey, 1961, vol. 19, p. 25).

Because the events of the anal stage are the first instance of intentional conflicts concerning power and control between parent and child, Freud saw the resolution of this stage as having significant long-term consequences in terms of personality development. We recognize this impact today in terms such as *anal-expressive, anal-retentive,* and *anal-aggressive,* which are part of our everyday vocabulary. Whether it is possible, as Freud claimed, to trace such qualities as messiness or stinginess to the outcome of one's toilet training, we nevertheless recognize these behavioral patterns in adults.

STAGE 3: THE PHALLIC STAGE (AGE 3 TO 5) Development up to this age is, according to Freud, essentially gender neutral. That is, boys and girls experience the same issues in the same forms with the same possible range and types of resolutions. As children enter the preschool years, however, this pattern changes. The focus of the libido shifts from the anus to the genitals, and for the first time gender-related anatomical differences become significant—so significant that Freud described the developmental events of this stage separately for boys and girls.

Although the particulars differ by gender during the phallic stage, the core issue is nevertheless the same for both boys and girls. This issue is developing an appropriate sex-role identification in terms of a relationship to the mother and to the father. Freud believed that the shift in the libido to the genitals in general and to the pleasure derived from self-stimulation of the genitals in particular led both boys and girls to pursue a love relationship with the opposite-sex parent. It is this love relationship that sets the stage for the conflict that, if resolved successfully, results in what to Freud is an appropriate sex-role identification.

It is this *oedipal* interest that gives this stage its other commonly used name—the oedipal stage. The name of the stage refers to the tragedy in Greek mythology of Oedipus. Abandoned to die at birth, Oedipus is found by strangers and raised as their own son. When grown, Oedipus returns to his homeland, slays the king, and marries the queen. Only then does he learn that he was abandoned at birth to prevent fulfillment of the prophesy that he would someday kill his father and marry his mother. The king he has killed and the queen he has married are, of course, his father and mother. Realizing what he has done, Oedipus gouges out his eyes and spends the rest of his life wandering the earth.

For preschool boys the oedipal experience is not nearly as tragic, but in many ways it is as dramatic. Freud believed that the preschool boy falls in love with his mother, perhaps even proclaiming his desire to marry her when he grows up. There is, of course, a problem with this plan. His mother is already married, and to make matters worse, she is married to his father.[3] The son therefore begins to compete with the father for the mother's attention and affection. The son might be affectionate to the mother in ways similar to what he sees his father doing, and he might demand to sleep in the parents' bed at night. However, it soon becomes apparent to the son that his father is more powerful and that he cannot win the battle. Unconsciously he comes to fear that the father will cut off his penis, clearly leaving the child at a disadvantage in terms of his desires for the mother. Freud refers to such fears as *castration anxiety* and argues that one of the reasons the son comes to this conclusion is the likelihood that the son may have seen or at least know that girls do not have a penis. In other words, Freud is arguing that the preschool boy thinks that perhaps girls once had penises and that they were castrated—perhaps for having similar incestuous thoughts.

The resolution of the oedipal complex for the preschool boy is to *identify* with the father. Through this sex-role identification, the son resolves the fear of castration and, by becoming more like the father, comes to believe that he will continue to be viewed positively by his mother.

As is true of the other stages, the success of the resolution of the oedipal complex for the son has lifelong implications, particularly in terms of his ability to compete with other adult males and to establish intimate relationships. Freud believed this to be especially true when the son's oedipal feelings toward the mother and his self-

---

[3] An obvious question at this point is, What about single parents? Freud does not pursue the matter, presumably because such circumstances were rare in his experience. But the question is an intriguing one, nevertheless. It is certainly true that the absence of a same-sex parent or parent-substitute is often seen as a possible impediment to sex-role identification. At the very least, it suggests that sex-role socialization in single-parent families may follow a different pattern, with the possibility of an altered outcome.

stimulation of the genitals are dealt with harshly. Although self-stimulation is a common enough activity in young children, the Viennese of Freud's time dealt with it in highly threatening and punitive ways. It's no wonder that Freud made the association between his adult patients' symptoms and free associations and his understanding of their early childhood experiences.

Freud's explanation for sex-role identification in preschool girls follows a similar logic, but, as Freud acknowledged, the argument was never as clear. The preschool girl, upon discovering that boys have a penis and she doesn't, develops what Freud referred to as *penis envy*. Freud believed that young girls saw themselves as less valued or worthy because they didn't have something that boys had. Furthermore, because their mother also did not have a penis, they somehow come to blame their mothers for their predicament. This perception of lower worth begins to change when the girl becomes increasingly aware of the attention she is receiving from her father (again, Freud does not deal with the situation of a single-parent family). But the increasing awareness of attention from her father also means an increasing awareness of her mother as a competitor. As is true for boys, the girl soon realizes that she is not nearly as powerful a competitor for her father's attention and affection as her mother is. Therefore, she also comes to realize that her best chance for winning her father's continuing affections is to identify with (i.e., model herself after) her mother.

For Freud the dilemma in this explanation, a dilemma he never was able to successfully resolve, is the motivation for the girl's identification with her mother. In the case of the boy, the motivation is clear—it is a fear of the loss of his penis. But, having no penis, the girl seemingly has nothing left to lose. So why does she nevertheless stop seeing her mother as a rival and begin to see her as a role model?

Sex-role identification brings with it not only a resolution of oedipal conflicts but also a change in the psychic structure of the child. Just as the ego emerged from the id as a way to cope with conflicts arising through the power struggles of toilet training, now the *superego* arises out of the ego to deal with the child's acceptance of the expectations of others as a regulator of his or her behavior. The superego resides in a third level of the psyche, the *conscious level*. Events at this level of the psyche are clearly knowable to the individual. Figure 12.1 illustrates how Freud saw the relationship among the id, ego, and superego.

The role of the superego is not simply to serve as a third way to gain the pleasures irrationally demanded by the id. Rather, the superego serves to remind the child of what society says should be done; that is, it is the child's conscience. It is worth noting Freud's suggestion that because the motivation to identify with the same-sex parent may be less in girls (i.e., they have less to fear because they cannot be castrated), their level of conscience development may also be less. This assumption is clearly one of the focal points of the criticisms leveled against psychoanalytic theory, particularly from feminist critics.

The superego has a second role as the source of the *ego ideal,* an idealized image we each carry of what we should be like. Sex-role identification provides such an ego ideal. Children who have successfully resolved their oedipal passions now want to grow up to be just like their father or their mother. But, as Freud makes clear, the emergence of the superego serves a larger purpose than simply aiding the preschooler's identification.

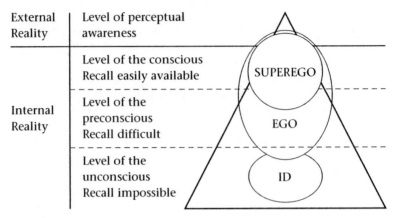

FIGURE 12.1
Freud's Representation of the Mind
Source: Muuss, 1996, p. 23.

It is easy to show that the ego ideal answers to everything that is expected of the higher nature of man. As a substitute for a longing for the father, it contains the germ from which all religion evolves. The self-judgment which declares that the ego falls short of its ideal produces the religious sense of humility to which the believer appeals in his longing. As a child grows up, the role of the father is carried on by teachers and others in authority; their injunctions and prohibitions remain powerful in the ego ideal and continue, in the form of conscience, to exercise the moral censorship. The tension between the demands of conscience and the actual performances of the ego is experienced as a sense of guilt. Social feelings rest on identifications with other people, on the basis of having the same ego ideal. (Freud, 1923, in Strachey, 1962, vol. 22, p. 37)

STAGE 4: THE LATENCY STAGE (AGE 5 TO PUBERTY)   Freud saw little happening during middle childhood that was of psychosexual developmental significance. No erogenous zone is defined as the focus of the libido; no major developmental achievement such as occurred in the previous stage happens now. In fact, not only does no new element emerge, but Freud suggests that the opposite actually may occur, that earlier psychosexual events are forgotten.

> The majority of experiences and mental impulses before the start of the latency period now fall victim to infantile amnesia—the forgetting which veils our earliest youth from us and makes us strangers to it. The task is set us in every psycho-analysis of bringing this forgotten period back into memory. It is impossible to avoid a suspicion that the beginnings of sexual life which are included in that period have provided the motive for its being forgotten—that this forgetting, in fact, is an outcome of repression. (Freud, 1917, in Strachey, 1963, vol. 16, p. 326)

Because earlier psychosexual conflicts are now repressed, school-age children seem to Freud to be little concerned about issues of sexuality. Instead, they focus their energies on building same-sex peer relations, on strengthening their ties with their parents, and on meeting the social and intellectual demands imposed by schools and other social institutions. These activities are seen by Freud as strengthening intellectual and motor competencies and, because children are increasingly modifying their behavior to meet socially accepted patterns, as furthering the organization of the superego.

It should be noted that being less concerned about psychosexual issues is not necessarily the same as being less likely to engage in sexual activity. As they move into puberty, children commonly engage in various forms of sexual activity, involving both the self and others. The issue is the motive for such behavior. Freud seems to be suggesting that such behavior is motivated not by the libido but, more likely, by peer group pressures. As such, these sexual behaviors were of less interest to him than those occurring at earlier ages because he saw them as having less psychosexual significance.

STAGE 5: THE GENITAL STAGE (FROM ADOLESCENCE ONWARD) The libido reemerges full force in adolescence, and again, its focus is on the genitals. In a sense adolescence marks a reappearance of the oedipal conflict, but now, rather than the child competing with the parent, the adolescent resolves the conflict by transferring his or her love interest from the opposite-sex parent to a sexual partner. In the more general sense this transference not only finally resolves the original oedipal issue itself but, more generally, allows sons and daughters to finally see themselves as independent adults—if not necessarily their parents' equals, then at least their colleagues. Furthermore, because expressions of sexuality are, for the first time, socially acceptable, the adolescent is less likely to feel guilt or shame over his or her thoughts and behaviors than was the case previously. Perhaps because of this greater acceptance, the adolescent's sexual focus gradually shifts from a focus on self to a focus on others. This shift marks, for Freud, the onset of mature sexuality, in which the sexual instinct is now subordinated to the reproductive function. In this sense Freud depicts mature sexual activity as altruistic; that is, the focus of mature sexual activity is now not solely the pursuit of pleasure but also, through reproduction, preservation of the species.

The ease of establishing mature, adult sexuality is to a large extent a function of the resolution of the first three psychosexual stages. The degree to which the adolescent and young adult are comfortable competing with others for sexual partners, the degree to which each is able to enter into an intimate relationship without seeing it as in some sense incestuous, the degree to which each is able to view adult sexual thoughts and behaviors as healthy rather than shameful acts—all reflect the resolution of the first three stages. In Freud's view no one escapes unscathed. But the more important question is whether the resolution of the first three stages allows the adolescent and young adult to establish an intimate adult sexual relationship. Failure to do so is often reflected in sexual behaviors focused on the mouth or anus, activities that Freud viewed as sexual perversions. And neurosis occurs when *all* sexual behaviors are repressed. Individuals then express a variety of *defense mechanisms* as an unconscious way of not having to deal with the issue.

It is somewhat strange that Freud never pursued the topic of adolescent and young-adult sexuality to the same degree that he did the first three psychosexual stages. The most plausible reason is that he believed that the psychosexual events of the first five years of life so defined all subsequent life events that there was really nothing unique left to study. It was actually his daughter, Anna Freud (1936, 1958), a respected psychoanalyst in her own right, who wrote more extensively on the developmental significance of this stage.

Freud's Theory in Perspective

Say what you will about Freud, but if one measure of a theory's worth is its generativity, then Freud made an important contribution to our understanding of human development. Certainly, his theory has many flaws. It is sexist; it is rooted in a 19th-century Victorian sensibility; it is imprecise; and, ultimately, in many ways it is untestable. No matter what the behavior in question, psychoanalysis seems to have an explanation for it. It is debatable whether a theory that purports to explain everything is actually able to explain anything.

But it is equally true that Freud identified many issues that continue today to be core elements of developmental research and theory (Emde, 1992). He was one of the first to formally define the concept of a developmental stage and then to offer an explanation of how the events of prior developmental stages influence those of subsequent stages. The role of early experience remains a major topic of current debate. The debate may no longer be couched in psychosexual terms, but it continues to form the empirical base for our national debates on the value and timing of early intervention programs.

Freud was also one of the first to formally recognize the developmental significance of early parent-child attachments and separation, a line of inquiry that continued through the work of John Bowlby (1969), Mary Ainsworth (1982, 1989), and a significant number of contemporary developmentalists. Current debates about the appropriateness of young children in day care settings and, by extension, the appropriateness of mothers of young children working rather than staying home with their children can certainly trace their lineage back to Freud.[4]

Freud's view of development is equally reflected in what are generally referred to as permissive approaches to child rearing. Permissive approaches are based on the assumption that preventing young children from having what they want and/or need when they want and/or need it serves to frustrate the child and that this frustration can have long-term negative developmental consequences. In terms of child-rearing advice, Benjamin Spock's (1992) classic work is perhaps the clearest expression of this view, but a visit to any local bookstore will reveal many others offering essentially the same message. It is, by the way, a message that is roundly criticized by those holding contrary views; these critics claim that it leads to various forms of rebellion and antisocial behavior among adolescents and youth.

---

[4] A related legacy is that, unfortunately, the debates are about mothers rather than parents. In Freud's view fathers seem to be virtually absent during the oral and anal stages and only serve to terrify their sons during the phallic stage. Freud's emphasis on the role of women has clouded our recognition that social welfare and work policies should be directed at fathers as well as mothers.

Freud's work also serves as one of the earliest discussions of the development of sex-role identification. Current evidence indicates that Freud's oedipal notions are probably not the basis upon which boys and girls form an initial sexual identity of themselves. Current evidence suggests that it occurs sooner than Freud's phallic stage and does not involve the type of same-sex parent-child conflict depicted by Freud. Nevertheless, even though Freud may not have had the right answer, he was asking the right question.

Finally, Freud established psychoanalytic theory as a distinct intellectual tradition. Psychoanalytic writing today differs in several ways from Freud's original notions, particularly in terms of the origin of the ego, and has several distinct and sometimes contradictory branches. But it still rests on a foundation established by Freud. Freud's work has also prompted several efforts to integrate psychosexual theory with the other dominant organismic theory, Piaget's cognitive-developmental theory. There is an appealing logic to such an integration because Freud focused on the affective and unconscious dimensions of development whereas Piaget focused on the cognitive and reflective dimensions. Three excellent efforts at this integration can be found in the work of Wolff (1960), Greenspan (1979), and Furth (1987).

Erikson's Theory of Psychosocial Development

It is certainly possible to think of Erik Erikson (1902–1994) as a neo-Freudian. As he pointed out many times in his writing, his work is very much in the psychoanalytic tradition established by Freud. To view Erikson as a neo-Freudian, however, would be somewhat misleading, because Erikson's work extended Freud's concepts to such a degree that they are really best appreciated as original contributions that can and should stand on their own merits.

Erikson's writings span more than half a century, producing several books (Erikson, 1950, 1958, 1964, 1968, 1969, 1977, 1980, 1982; Erikson, Erikson, & Kivnick, 1986) and numerous articles. Of all of these, *Childhood and Society,* published in 1950, continues to be his most significant and enduring single contribution.

Perhaps more so than for most theorists, it is important to first know something about Erikson's life in order to fully appreciate his contributions to the study of human development. For it is the events of his life that provided him the perspectives necessary to so significantly broaden Freud's original concepts.

A Biographical Sketch

Erikson was born in Germany to Danish parents in 1902. His parents soon divorced, and he was raised by his mother and her second husband, a German pediatrician. Strangely enough for one of the most significant developmentalists of our time, his formal education ended at the high school level. While in high school, his interests tended toward art, history, and language. Following high school he more or less wandered through several major European cities, eventually finding himself, at the age of 25, in Vienna (Stevens, 1983a), where he took a teaching position at a progressive elementary school. The school had been established by Anna Freud, Sigmund Freud's daughter, to apply psychoanalytic concepts to educational practice. Many of the families in the school were either patients or colleagues of Anna Freud. Erikson became interested in psychoanalysis and soon joined the Vienna circle of analysts. By this time Sigmund Freud was in his 70s and severely hampered by cancer of the jaw. They apparently had little contact with each other, and it was actually Anna Freud and the other analysts in the group who were Erikson's first teachers and colleagues.

Erikson stayed in Vienna until the early 1930s. By this time Hitler's rise to political power and the corresponding rise in ethnic, racial, and religious intolerance in Austria, particularly in the form of anti-Semitisim, made it clear to all the members of the Vienna circle that they would have to leave Vienna.

Erikson moved to Boston in 1933, where he began working as that city's first analyst (Coles, 1970) and as a researcher at the Harvard Psychological Clinic. In 1938 he accepted a similar position at Yale. It was during his tenure at Yale that he did his cultural study of the Sioux, a Native American tribe living in the Dakotas. Erikson's study of the Sioux was one of the first indications of his desire to broaden his psychoanalytic perspective beyond the more traditional conventions of treating patients. This stretching was no doubt strongly influenced by the wide range of colleagues from several disciplines, particularly anthropology, whom he encountered both at Harvard and at Yale —especially those interested in the study of Freud's psychoanalytic notions about the development of civilizations. In addition, both settings provided him access to children and adults who were in need of his clinical services, as well as those he saw through his growing role as teacher and researcher. It is this widening of interests and opportunities that soon led to his revision of Freud's work away from a focus on psychosexual issues and toward one emphasizing psychosocial issues.

In 1939 Erikson and his family moved to California where he accepted an academic position at Berkeley. Again, new opportunities presented themselves, this time in the form of becoming part of the now famous series of longitudinal studies of children begun at Berkeley in the 1930s. This work gave him additional contact with psychologists, sociologists, and anthropologists and exposed him to populations that allowed him to continue the study of normal development and to pursue his clinical work. One of Erikson's last works (Erikson, Erikson, & Kivnick, 1986) was actually a followup of the original sample. He also performed work for the government related to U.S. involvement in World War II, analyzing German propaganda in general and Hitler's speeches in particular.

It was also during his stay at Berkeley that Erikson pursued his study of the Yurok, a Native American tribe living in Oregon. The study of both the Sioux and the Yurok played a significant role in his reinterpretation of psychoanalytic thought in terms of a more psychosocial foundation. In particular, these experiences helped Erikson to recognize that behaviors which under traditional psychoanalytic doctrine might be seen as evidence of pathology were, in fact, evidence of strengths within a particular cultural setting. As Erikson put it:

The interesting thing was that all of the childhood problems which we had begun to take seriously on the basis of pathological developments in our own culture, the Indians talked about spontaneously and most seriously without any prodding. They referred to our stages as the decisive steps in the making of a good Sioux Indian or a good Yurok Indian. What we describe clinically as orality or anality, the Indians evaluated and emphasized according to whether these characteristics would serve to develop the kind of person the culture considered "good." And "good" meant whatever seemed "virtuous" in a "strong" man or woman in that culture. I think this contributed eventually to my imagery of basic human strengths. (in Evans, 1967, p. 62)

Erikson resigned from Berkeley in 1950 rather than sign a loyalty oath stating that he was not a member of the Communist party. He was, in fact, not a member of the party, but he refused to sign it (as did many other Berkeley faculty) as a matter of principle. His letter of resignation reflects his profound concern with the significant elements that define one's true identity as opposed to activities that merely "save face." As Erikson explained, the development of personal identity is the core element of his theory.

My field includes the study of hysteria private and public, in "personality" and "culture." It includes the study of the tremendous waste in human energy which proceeds from irrational fear and from irrational gestures which are part of what we call "history." I would find it difficult to ask my subject of investigation (people) and my students to work with me, if I were to participate without protest in a vague, fearful, and somewhat vindictive gesture designed to ban an evil in some magic way—an evil which must be met with much more searching and concerted effort. (in Coles, 1970, p. 150)

Erikson returned east, accepting a clinical and teaching position at the Austen Riggs Center in western Massachusetts and, in addition, a professorship at Harvard in 1960. He continued to revise and refine psychoanalytic theory, particularly in terms of his view of life span human development, throughout the rest of his life. After his retirement from Harvard, he returned to California and increasingly wrote about issues concerning aging. When his physical health began to decline, he once again returned east for his final years. He died in 1994.

There are, of course, many links between a person's life history and his or her world views. In Erikson's case two themes seem most significant. The first is the greater diversity of experiences, settings, and contacts experienced by Erikson than Freud, which certainly provided the basis for his broadening of psychoanalytic theory. The second, which follows an interesting parallel to Piaget's life, is the events relating to World War II. As was the case for Piaget with respect to World War I, Erikson's interest in identity as the defining element of the individual and of the cultural events that foster a positive resolution of the identity crisis was clearly influenced by his observations of how easily so many Europeans were taken in by Hitler's message. Erikson seemed very interested in the same issue as Piaget—namely, the social conditions that make it possible for people to resist "ready-made slogans" and "be able to think for themselves."

Erikson's work touches on many themes, ranging from issues relating to clinical practice to the analysis of cultures and from discussions of Freud to the study of individual lives. Although all of these, to one degree or another, relate to issues of life span human development, it is primarily his stage theory that is the focus of this discussion.

To fully appreciate Erikson's stage-based concept of development, it is necessary to understand four things: (1) the ways Erikson's model differs from Freud's, (2) his rather eclectic methodology, (3) the epigenetic nature of his conception of development, and (4) the issues that define each of his eight stages of psychosocial development. Let us take each in turn.

Erikson's Revision of Freud's Developmental Model

In one sense Erikson's model differs little from Freud's. Id, ego, and superego remain. Organ modes (i.e., oral, anal, phallic, and genital) still define the developmental stages through childhood. Development is still seen as a process of resolving competing forces. The resolution of early developmental stages is still seen as having a profound effect on subsequent development. Nevertheless, Erikson's model is very different.

Because of the variety of his own life experiences, Erikson differentiated the form of psychoanalytic theory from its content. In so doing, he redefined psychoanalytic theory in a culturally relevant manner. That is, the universal elements of the theory, its organismic core, remain the same, but the way this core is expressed becomes culture specific.

Erikson believed that Freud was unable to recognize the distinction between the form and content of his theory because of the cultural context in which Freud lived. Erikson explains:

> One cannot emphasize enough how many things Freud took for granted—all the values, facts, and conditions of the pre–World War I bourgeoisie *within* which he wanted to bring about change. To us, all of these have now become dated circumstances made fluid by progress as well as war and revolution. . . . Freud belonged to a period of history which came to an end with his generation. He worked as an erstwhile physiologist in a setting in which the stability and cultural dominance of the upper middle class in Europe was taken for granted. It was not quite as possible to see the social and cultural relativity of psychological phenomena in his time. (in Evans, 1967, pp. 92–93)

By making the theory culturally relative, what was originally a psychosexual theory of the clash of instinctual energies playing out against the neutral backdrop of the environment becomes a psychosocial theory of the tensions of integrating self and other played out within a particular sociohistorical context. The ego replaces the id and superego as the primary focus of interest. The search for a personal identity—something taken for granted by Freud and therefore never considered as an issue—becomes the focus of development. Because the content of development assumes a culturally defined form, notions of normality and abnormality change. Now they need to be defined within the cultural context rather than as absolutes. Now there are many more ways to behave and still be normal. And because the search for identity is a lifelong process, the theory is one of life span development rather than child development. Now, rather than the adult years simply being the playing-out of the resolution of childhood psychosexual conflicts, adulthood also becomes a time of confronting new issues. Now, rather than the focus turning inward to probe the unconscious, it turns outward to probe the social circumstances, particularly in terms of relationships, that define conscious experience.

Erikson's Methodology

Given the breadth of Erikson's interests, especially in terms of the interplay between the individual and society, it should not surprise anyone that his methodology involved more than an armchair and a couch. In fact, Erikson's approach to the study of development probably bears more similarity to Piaget's approach than it does to Freud's.

As was true of Piaget, Erikson's approach is primarily that of participant observer. However, whereas Piaget restricted his observations to children, either individually or in small group settings, Erikson's observations take place at many levels. Clinical cases are reported throughout his writings, but so are observations of healthy children, such as the observations he made while at Berkeley of the types of block structures most commonly made by boys and girls.

Given his psychosocial focus, many of Erikson's studies are of cultures, both ones he observed directly as in the case of the Sioux and the Yurok and also ones he analyzed indirectly through the literature and the artifacts he saw as typifying that culture. His observations (1950) of "mom" within American culture and of Hitler's youth, for example, each represent attempts to understand the identity of a culture by examining what he saw as some of its more defining elements.

In his essay entitled "Hitler's Youth" in *Childhood and Society*, Erikson attempts to understand how it is that someone as evil as Adolf Hitler could assume the power that he did in a society that prided itself on its modernity, its culture, and its sophistication. Erikson begins by examining the images Hitler used to portray German society in *Mein Kampf*. He discusses a passage in which Hitler speaks of his own childhood years —of a mother devoting herself to the care of the house, of a father who was a faithful civil servant, of eternal loving care, of a town gilded by the light of German martyrdom. Erikson's (1950) analysis of the passage is illustrative of his method.

> The sentence structure, the tone quality, indicate that we are to hear a fairy tale; and indeed we shall analyze it as part of a modern attempt to create a myth. But a myth, old or modern, is not a lie. It is useless to show that it has no basis in fact; nor to claim that its fiction is fake and nonsense. A myth blends historic fact and significant fiction in such a way that it "rings true" to an area or an era, causing pious wonderment and burning ambition. The people affected will not question truth or logic; the few who cannot help doubting will find their reason paralyzed. To study a myth critically, therefore, means to analyze its images and themes in their relation to the culture area affected. (p. 285)

The rest of his essay on Hitler then turns to an analysis of German culture, that is, of the German identity at that time. In Erikson's eyes this identity reflects the humbling defeat in World War I, the humiliation of the terms of the subsequent armistice, and the ease with which most Germans were willing to blame their self-made plight on Jews and other minorities.

The influence of anthropology on his method and theory is evident in Erikson's analysis of German society, as well as in his other cultural studies. In general, Erikson appears more comfortable than most developmentalists in using the methodologies of all the behavioral and social sciences to pursue his theoretical interests. This broad-based approach, for Erikson, is as it should be because a full understanding of development must consider the somatic interest of the biologist, the interest in the ego of the psychologist, and the interest in the social processes relevant to the social scientist—a combination Erikson refers to as *triple bookkeeping*. As he puts it, "Our thinking is dominated by this trichotomy because only through the inventive methodologies of these disciplines do we have knowledge at all" (1950, p. 33).

One place this triple bookkeeping is most evident is in Erikson's *psychohistorical* studies. Psychohistory attempts to provide an in-depth analysis of an individual through that person's writings and deeds. Much as the analyst probes the patient's psyche through recall and reflection and through the analysis of dreams and other mental products, the psychohistorian probes the individual through that person's public documents. Naturally, such psychohistories must be of prominent individuals, those who have left a rich legacy. Erikson's psychohistories of Martin Luther (1958) and Mahatma Gandhi (1969) are today recognized as classics in this genre.

Erikson's Epigenetic Model of Development

Organismic theorists like Erikson and Piaget are more discoverers than they are inventors. They are similar to Darwin, who did not invent evolution but rather discovered certain patterns that lent support to the notion that species evolve from each other. Discovery is usually not a random process, however. It is a process guided by one or more hypotheses, and what is discovered serves to confirm or refute the hypothesis.[5] For organismic theorists these hypotheses are about formal causes. For Erikson this formal cause is *epigenesis*.

Erikson's epigenetic model is based on the same logic as is found in the work of the developmental psychobiologists and of Piaget. It is a notion of postnatal development that derives its form from the study of prenatal development. Namely, it posits that there is—at a general, species-specific level—a universal developmental pattern that is defined in terms of the sequence and the timing of the emergence of new structures. Furthermore, as parts emerge, they interact and integrate with other parts, even-

---

[5] In all fairness, it should be pointed out that a common criticism of organismic theory, particularly from mechanists, is that what organismic theorists discover has more to do with what they are looking for than it does with what they find. Again, the different interpretation of the same process reflects the significant differences in the basic assumptions of the two world views.

tually forming a functional whole. Finally, variability across individuals in the interpretation and significance of these common developmental patterns reflects issues specific to culture, time, and place. For Erikson the universality refers to those things that
must happen, and the variability to those things that *may* happen.

For Erikson these universal patterns refer to the organ modes that Freud originally
used to define psychosexual development. The organ modes are *incorporation, retention, elimination, intrusion,* and *inclusion.* To Erikson the mouth is primarily an organ of
incorporation, the anus and urethra both retain and eliminate, the phallus intrudes,
and the vagina includes.[6] However, in Erikson's hands these organ modes now assume
a more generic quality.

> But these modes also comprise basic configurations that dominate the interplay of a
> mammalian organism and its parts with another organism and its parts, as well as
> with the world of things. The zones and their modes, therefore, are the focus of some
> prime concerns of any culture's child-training systems, even as they remain, in their
> further development, central to the culture's "way of life." (Erikson, 1997, p. 34)

The first five of Erikson's eight developmental stages correspond to Freud's stages.
For each there is a correspondence to an organ or zone and to a mode of action associated with that organ. Because the last three stages are original to Erikson, they have no
such zone or mode associations. Nevertheless, in all eight instances the basic issues of
sequence, timing, and integration are the same.

Erikson's developmental sequence is most typically presented as a progression of
the eight psychosocial stages, each corresponding to a particular age period and involving a particular developmental crisis. Erikson's use of the term *crisis* is meant to convey
a radical turning point or change in perspective rather than some sort of catastrophe.
In this sense crises are a necessary and healthy component of the process of development and convey the same theoretical intent as Piaget's concept of disequilibrium.

In most cases the progression is diagrammed as moving from one corner of a 64-
square matrix diagonally to the opposite corner. In one corner is the psychosocial crisis of trust versus mistrust encountered during infancy. Tracing a diagonal course
through the next six crises to the opposite corner, we arrive at the psychosocial crisis
of ego integrity versus despair encountered during old age. The eight stages presented
diagonally certainly form the heart of Erikson's epigenetic scheme, because they

---

[6] It is important to make reference to the issue of sexism in Erikson's writing. Certainly, all of his
writing portrays gender roles in very traditional forms. Men are portrayed as in search of identity, and
women as mothers and often little else. The starkness of these contrasts is more evident in his early than
his later writing. This shift probably reflects three events. First, as he continued his move from the psychosexual to the psychosocial, the significance of organ modes became more generic. Anatomy no
longer was destiny. Second, as the roles of men and women changed over Erikson's lifetime, so, too, did
his understanding of the meaning of gender in the twentieth century. Third, the contribution of his
wife, Joan Erikson, to his writing became increasingly evident in his later works. As would only be fitting for an organismic theorist, these three events probably had a synergistic influence. As such, interpreting Erikson from a literal perspective shows him to be very much the sexist, but from a broader
perspective the issue is less clear-cut.

clearly indicate the major issue that individuals must resolve at each point in the life span for what Erikson considers "healthy" development to occur.

Each psychosocial crisis involves the resolution of a basic issue necessary for full, mature development to occur. In all cases successful resolution reflects a balance between the two extremes of the conflict. For infants, for example, the goal is a healthy sense of trust. To Erikson a healthy sense of trust involves a balance allowing the infant to feel comfortable enough to trust the parent and the environment (and, by extension, the self) without so much trust that the infant becomes vulnerable to exploitation or exposure to risk and danger. Successful resolution of each stage creates a *basic strength* (hope in the case of the infant) whereas failure to successfully resolve the crisis leads to a *basic antipathy* (withdrawal in the case of the infant). The interactions of each stage involve a *radius of significant relations*. This radius broadens as the sequence progresses. For the infant Erikson sees the radius as involving only mother and child. But by early childhood it grows to include the family; by the young-adult years it incorporates "partners in friendship, sex, competition and cooperation"; and by old age it has fully expanded to "my kind."

Erikson argues that more occurs and more is at stake at each stage than the resolution of the immediate crisis. The individual is also learning a larger lesson about the culture. The infant, for example, by developing a sense of trust or mutuality with the parents is also learning something about the patterns of her culture because the response modes of the parents reflect the values of the culture she is about to enter. Cultures, in this case, differ in terms of their beliefs about indulging infants. Cultures that are more indulgent in their child-rearing beliefs, that give the infant more to incorporate in a manner and pace consistent with the infant's inner timetable, foster a different sense of trust and mutuality than cultures that are brisk and relatively harsh in their child rearing. It isn't that one culture creates more trust than another. Rather, the infant is getting a first lesson in coming to understanding what can be expected in her culture.

The diagonal in Erikson's epigenetic chart occupies only 8 of the 64 squares, however (see Figure 12.2). For Erikson they are the most important 8 squares because they correspond to the primary psychosocial crises of each age. But it is important to recognize that the other 56 squares also have significance. Events also occur in each of these squares, and a full appreciation of Erikson's schemes requires an understanding of these events as well.

Although Erikson never fully developed all 64 squares in the chart, he made it clear in many of his writings that, in some form, each psychosocial issue exists at each of the eight age periods. That is, although the issue of identity is most dominant during adolescence, it is not fully resolved by the end of that period, no matter how successful the interaction of parent and child. Nor, for that matter, does it make its first appearance during adolescence. As the child moves through the life span and his or her radius of significant relations is continuously broadened, each new level requires a reestablishment of that sense of identity. Successful resolutions at earlier levels make the task at each new level easier, but the process is never automatic. By the same token, difficult or incomplete earlier resolutions make subsequent ones more difficult, even to the extent that, at some point, one may no longer be able to extend one's radius

	1	2	3	4	5	6	7	8
I Infancy	Trust vs. mistrust				Unipolarity vs. premature self-differentiation			
II Early Childhood		Autonomy vs. shame, doubt			Bipolarity vs. autism			
III Play Age			Initiative vs. guilt		Play identification vs. (Oedipal) fantasy identities			
IV School Age				Industry vs. inferiority	Work identification vs. identity foreclosure			
V Adolescence	Time perspective vs. time diffusion	Self-certainty vs. identity consciousness	Role experimentation vs. negative identity	Anticipation of achievement vs. work paralysis	Identity vs. identity diffusion	Sexual identity vs. bisexual diffusion	Leadership polarization vs. authority diffusion	Ideological polarization vs. diffusion of ideals
VI Young Adult					Solidarity vs. social isolation	Intimacy vs. isolation		
VII Adulthood							Generativity vs. self-absorption	
VIII Mature Age								Integrity vs. disgust, despair

FIGURE 12.2
Erikson's Epigenetic Stage Model.   Source: Erikson, 1959/1980, p. 129.

because of a lack of identity. Development is arrested, and some form of psychoanalytic clinical intervention is required.

One factor that has a significant impact on the likelihood of a successful resolution of a particular psychosocial crisis is the timing of the occurrence of that event. Again, drawing on analogies from embryology, Erikson argues that successful development requires not only a particular sequence of events but also the occurrence of each event at the right time. This notion is most clearly elaborated in the case of identity, the psychosocial crisis of adolescence.

Adolescents, according to Erikson, need a sufficient amount of time to experiment with identities, a period he refers to as a *psychosocial moratorium,* before they can resolve the crisis and reach a state of *identity achievement.* Too short a moratorium, or the absence of one altogether, leads to *identity foreclosure,* in which are achieved only the outward trappings of a role rather than a deep understanding of the full implications of that role. An overextended moratorium can lead to a sense of *identity diffusion,* an inability to acquire any personal sense of identity. Clearly both foreclosure and diffusion make the resolution of subsequent psychosocial crises just that more difficult, if not impossible. How, for example, can one establish a sense of intimacy with another person if one lacks any clear sense of oneself as a person?

Before examining the eight stages in greater detail, it is important to note that Erikson does not posit a particular mechanism by which this epigenetic process occurs. He does discuss the role of play or playful engagement at all ages as the means through which the ego "attempts to bring into synchronization the bodily and the social processes of which one is a part even while one is a self" (1950, p. 184). But for the most part, he seems comfortable painting this idea in very broad strokes. Unlike the psychobiologists, who look very carefully at the interplay of neurons and neural networks; unlike Piaget, who developed a very complicated and formal logic to explain changes in children's level of cognition; and unlike Freud, who used drive reduction as his driving force; Erikson seems comfortable simply referring to the constant interplay of biological, psychological, and social forces as propelling his developmental sequence.

Erikson's Eight Stages

For most of his writing, Erikson presented his stage sequence in chronological order, birth to death. In his last writing on the topic (1982), he reversed the order, largely to emphasize the growing importance of old age in our society. In the same sense that cultural changes prompted him to revise a psychosexual theory into a psychosocial theory and to reevaluate the status women were assigned in his writing, he was now recognizing the dramatic shifts occurring in our culture as the percentage of elders in the population continues to increase.

In spite of Erikson's 1982 presentation of the stages, we will follow the original presentation, primarily because it makes a clearer case for his developmental model. Nevertheless, as Erikson was finding out in his own life, it is useful to remember that "in old age all qualities of the past assume new values that we may well study in their own right and not just in their antecedents—be they healthy or pathological" (Erikson, 1982, p. 64).

STAGE 1: INFANTS—TRUST VS. MISTRUST Each psychosocial crisis occurs because there is a radical shift in perspective between child and surroundings. It is hard to imagine a more radical shift than birth. To Erikson the child is thrust out of a seemingly safe and predictable world into one that, at first estimation, is neither. The task of the infant is to learn to reasonably trust this new environment and, if successful, to acquire the basic virtue of *hope.*

Acquiring a sense of trust revolves around activities of *incorporation.* The infant takes in nourishment not only through the mouth (Freud's oral focus) but, more generally, through all his sensory modalities. Ideally, a pattern of predictability or mutuality is established between infant and parent. The more predictable the parent's behavior in terms of the infant, the easier it is for him to recognize the correspondence between his needs and the parent's responsiveness. The more predictable the infant's behavior, the easier it is for the parent to respond in an appropriate fashion. The interactions lead to a sense on the part of the infant that not only is the world a predictable and therefore safe place but, by extension, so is he.

> The general state of trust, furthermore, implies not only that one has learned to rely on the sameness and continuity of the outer providers, but also that one may trust oneself and the capacity of one's own organs to cope with urges; and that one is able to consider oneself trustworthy enough so that providers will not need to be on guard lest they be nipped. (Erikson, 1950, p. 220)

Successful resolution of this stage is a healthy sense of trust. Unsuccessful resolutions reflect the extremes. At one extreme a sense of mistrust, in self and others, results from a failure to establish a degree of predictability or mutuality between infant and parent. The world is seen as unpredictable and unsafe, and rather than the strength of hope emerging, the antipathy of *withdrawal* is seen. In Erikson's description such withdrawal, when extreme, leads to disengagement, to a refusal to be comforted, and even to a refusal to be fed. When dealing with withdrawn adults, Erikson (1968) notes that the most difficult part of the therapeutic process is gaining the confidence of the person, to get him or her to trust the therapist enough to be willing to engage in the healing process. At the other extreme Erikson views too much trust as equally debilitating because it opens the person to exploitation by others.

As is true for all stages, a healthy sense of trust is a necessary prerequisite for further successful development. To the degree that resolution is not successful, subsequent development becomes that much more difficult. The infant who does not trust the environment is less likely to explore that environment. The infant who does not trust herself is less likely to initiate activity.

STAGE 2: TODDLERS—AUTONOMY VS. SHAME AND DOUBT Like most observers of child development, Erikson sees the period of approximately 18–36 months as a time when great leaps in the child's accomplishments confront increasing efforts on the part of parents to socialize their child. It is thus a time of finding a balance between *holding on* and *letting go.* A successful resolution of the crisis is a healthy *sense of autonomy;* failure to successfully resolve the conflict leads to a *sense of shame and doubt.* A healthy sense of autonomy leads to the *basic strength of will;* shame and doubt, on the other hand, lead to the antipathies of *compulsion* and *impulsivity*. The radius of significant relations now extends from the mother to *parental persons*.

For Freud this second stage is the anal stage. It centers on the bowel and bladder and issues of toilet training, and therefore on issues of retention and elimination. For Erikson the issue is broader, more generic. It is not solely one of the anxious and eager parent coaxing and urging and perhaps even shaming the child into using the "potty." Rather, it is one of the young child exerting a sense of "I" and "me" and "mine."

> At the same time, the child is apt to both hoard things and to discard them, to cling to treasured objects and to throw them out of the window of houses and vehicles. All of these seemingly contradictory tendencies, then, we include under the formula of retentive-eliminative mode. . . .
>
> Thus, "to hold" can become a destructive and cruel retaining or restraining, and it can become a pattern of care: "to have and to hold." To "let go," too, can turn into an inimical letting loose of destructive forces, or it can become a relaxed "to let pass" and "to let be." (Erikson, 1980, pp. 70, 72)

Erikson sees culture in general and parents in particular now facing a difficult balancing act. Provide too much autonomy, and the toddler may not only come to face danger but, because of the "potential anarchy" of a still "untrained sense of discrimination," may also force situations that will lead to failure and therefore to a sense of doubt over her skills. Provide too little autonomy, and the toddler comes to feel constantly monitored; she becomes overly self-conscious and ashamed of trying to do any independent action. She develops what Erikson refers to as a *precocious conscience*. Cultures, of course, differ in where this balance point sits. Erikson is very clear about his sense of American culture when he refers to our ideal of "a mechanically trained, faultlessly functioning, and always clean, punctual, and deodorized body" (1968, p. 108). He is also very clear that such a deliberateness is at the root of much of the neurotic complusiveness evident in his adult patients.

The basic strength of *will*, the successful outcome of the resolution of this psychosocial crisis, reflects a balancing act of self-control. These children have acquired the foundation that allows them to know how to exert their will without being willful. They are learning to exercise good judgment and self-restraint without also feeling shame and doubt about what is being considered.

> This stage, therefore, can be decisive for the ratio between love and hate; for that between cooperation and willfulness, and for that between freedom of self-expression and its suppression. From a sense of *self-control without loss of self-esteem* comes a lasting sense of autonomy and pride; from a sense of muscular and anal impotence, of loss of self-control, and of parental overcontrol comes a lasting sense of shame and doubt. (Erikson, 1980, pp. 70–71)

STAGE 3: PRESCHOOLERS—INITIATIVE VS. GUILT A basic sense of trust provides infants with confidence in themselves and their environments. It is a necessary prerequisite to "test the waters" of the second stage—beginning the process of defining oneself as an autonomous individual. Having accomplished this initial differentiation of self from other, the psychosocial task now confronting the child is to use this autonomy. Having now discovered that she *can* do, she now considers what she *may* do. But, of course, at the same time that she is trying to figure out what she may do, so are all the other children in her world. Each intrudes into the space of the other, as well as into the space of the parent. And others' sometimes negative reactions to this intrusiveness leaves the child to wonder about the wisdom of her actions. Another radical change in perspective is thus precipitated.

Erikson talks of preschool-age children's newly acquired cognitive, social, and motor skills promoting them to "make" and "be on the make." In terms of locomotion, for example, children's skill level is now such that they no longer need to focus on simply getting from one place to another; they can do this with ease. So the question becomes one of the reason for getting from point A to point B.

Playing, being playful, and having playful encounters become the defining characteristics of children's activity during this third stage. Successful resolution of this stage is a healthy *sense of initiative;* failure leads to a *sense of guilt.* A sense of initiative fosters the basic virtue of *purpose;* its antipathy is *inhibition.* The radius of significant relations now extends from parents to the *basic family.* Erikson explains:

> The child begins to envisage goals for which his locomotion and cognition have prepared him. The child also thinks of being big and to identify with people whose work or whose personality he can understand and appreciate. "Purpose" involves the whole complex of elements. For example, when the child plays, it's not just a matter of practicing his will or practicing his ability to manipulate. He begins to have projects, as it were. It is during this period that it becomes incumbent upon the child to repress or redirect many fantasies which developed early in life. He begins to learn that he must work for things, and that even his secret wishes for omniscience and omnipotence must be attached to concrete things, or at least to things which can materialize. Paradoxically, he continues to feel guilty for his fantasies. (in Evans, 1967, p. 25)

For Freud early childhood was a time for establishing appropriate identities with each parent. Erikson gives much less attention to these issues as Freud originally presented them, noting instead that "play liberates the small individual for a dramatization in the microsphere of a vast number of imagined identifications and activities." (1982, p. 77). It is through play that the young child first tests out his ideas and fantasies in a safe setting. It is the first time when and place where the young child assumes one element (but obviously in a very immature manner) of adult roles—that is, deliberate decision making. Erikson believes that these early and playful decision-making exercises indicate the child's growing identification with adults ("I can now do what adults do").

But with the power to initiate also comes the fear of making the wrong decision. Guilt is therefore the potential negative resolution of this stage, particularly in the form of the child's superego raising concerns about what it is that he wants to do. In the extreme, overobedience and overconformity become evident as the child, feeling guilt over his self-initiated activities, retreats to the control of others. In a more conventional Freudian sense, this guilt would be over the child's wish to replace the same-sex parent and marry the opposite-sex parent. The corresponding castration fears would certainly be cause enough to instill guilt and to become overobedient. But to Erikson the issue and the resolution again become more generic. The issue is no longer framed in terms of the particulars of incestuous ideas but, more generally, in terms of all ideas. Successful resolution becomes a balance of "being on the make," but not to such a degree that one's actions come to be cruel and exploitive of others. Because the radius of significant relations still resides at the family level, parents' interactions with their child become a crucial element in the resolution of this third crisis. Erikson notes that it is important for parents at this time to establish a relationship of companionship, of shared activities, of "essential equality."

> Only a combination of early prevention and alleviation of hatred and guilt in the growing being, and the consequent handling of hatred in the free collaboration of people who feel *equal in worth although different in kind or function or age,* permits a peaceful cultivation of initiative, a true free sense of enterprise. And the word "enterprise" was deliberately chosen. For a comparative view of child training suggests that it is the prevalent economic ideal, or some of its modifications, which is transmitted to the child at this time when, in identification with his parent, he applies the dreams of early childhood to the as yet dim goals of an active adult life. (Erikson, 1980, pp. 86–87)

In essence, the successful parent of the preschool-age child manages to convey the message "Don't fear me, be like me."

STAGE 4: SCHOOL-AGE CHILDREN—INDUSTRY VS. INFERIORITY   Erikson's first three stages closely parallel Freud's. For each theorist the same fundamental issues are relevant; the difference is in terms of degree of literalness. For this fourth stage there is a more significant differentiation between the two. Freud saw the school years as a period of latency, as a pause between the oedipal resolution of the preschool years and the storms of adolescence to come. To Erikson, however, the school years are a time not of waiting but of developing a *basic sense of industry* and avoiding a *sense of inferiority.* If the child is successful, her sense of industry provides her with the *basic strength of competence;* if not, she ends up with its antipathy, *inertia.* Appropriately enough, Erikson now sees the radius of significant relations extending out to the *neighborhood* and *school.*

A sense of industry builds on the three prior accomplishments. Most immediately, what was previously simply an attempt on the part of the child to initiate activity now is extended into an effort to complete that initiated activity (i.e., to produce something). For most children this transition occurs after they enter a formal educational system. Entry into the school system prompts another radical shift in perspective as the child finds her products being compared, in some standardized fashion, with those of her classmates.

For Erikson this fourth stage is significant, in part, because it makes even clearer to the child, now between 6 and 12, the necessity of conforming to the expectations of the culture. Serious work now joins play as modes of expression.

> He has mastered the ambulatory field and organ modes. He has experienced a sense of finality regarding the fact that there is no workable future within the womb of the family, and thus becomes ready to apply himself to given skills and tasks, which go far beyond the mere playful expression of his organ modes or the pleasure of the function

of his limbs. He develops industry—i.e., he adjusts himself to the inorganic laws of the tool world. He can become an eager and absorbed unit of a productive situation. To bring a productive situation to completion is the aim which gradually supersedes the whims and wishes of his autonomous organism. (Erikson, 1950, p. 227)

Given that this is really the first point in the life span when the child finds herself being systematically compared to others, Erikson expresses significant concern about the child being ready to successfully enter the school, about the school system and the community being able to support the child's learning, and about teachers being nurturant and competent and able to recognize problems early enough to intervene effectively. The dangers are, on the one hand, that none of these necessary prerequisites occur and the child sees herself as failing and therefore inferior when compared to others, or, on the other hand, that she is so successful that her sense of self is defined solely in terms of meeting the expectations defined by others. In the latter case the danger is that always functioning to fulfill the expectations of others makes the child more vulnerable to the exploitation of others and does not prepare her for situations that require a degree of self-direction and self-regulation.

Erikson (1980) makes clear that a failure to successfully resolve this psychosocial crisis can have lasting and significant effects:

This is socially a most decisive stage: since industry involves doing things besides and with others, a first sense of *division of labor* and *equality of opportunity* develop at this time. When a child begins to feel that it is the color of his skin, the background of his parents, or the cost of his clothes rather than his wish and his will to learn which will decide his social worth, lasting harm may ensue for the *sense of identity*. (p. 93)

STAGE 5: ADOLESCENCE—IDENTITY VS. IDENTITY CONFUSION The radical shift in perspective ushering in adolescence involves two elements: (1) the rapid and remarkable changes occurring in physical status, including the onset of genital maturity, and (2) inquiries by society about what adolescents plan to do with their lives. Once again, the radius of significant relations expands. Now the radius also includes *peer groups* and *outgroups*.

Both of these issues prompt adolescents to think about who they are, or at least who they are becoming. A successful resolution of this psychosocial crisis leads to a *basic sense of identity*; failure to create such an image leads to a sense of *identity confusion*. Tipping the balance in the other direction leads to a sense of *overidentification*. Erikson believes that adolescents are vulnerable to overidentification when they are having trouble "keeping themselves together." Rather than constructing an identity, they "temporarily overidentify, to the point of apparent complete loss of identity, with the heroes of cliques and crowds" (Erikson, 1950, p. 228). Erikson believes that the intolerance that adolescents express toward anyone who is in some way different, who is not a member of their in-group, is often a reflection of the insecurity they feel in trying to decide who they are themselves.

A healthy sense of identity leads to the more general *basic strength of fidelity*; identity confusion creates its antipathy, *repudiation*. Fidelity implies an ideological acceptance, a recognition of the wisdom of the logic of one's own social system. Erikson suggests that repudiation can take one of two forms: (1) in the form of *diffidence,* when no commitment to any allegiance is made, or (2) in the form of *defiance,* when a commitment is made to a "negative identity." Erikson describes a negative identity as a commitment to "a combination of socially unacceptable and yet stubbornly affirmed identity elements" (1982, p. 73).

Of all of Erikson's stages, this one has probably received the most attention from both Erikson and others (e.g., Archer, 1992; Marcia, 1994; Waterman, 1994). This should not be surprising given that identity is the core element in Erikson's theory. Identity, for Erikson, is the emergent property of the interaction of the three elements in the triple-bookkeeping ledger. The fact that identity is the core element in his theory no doubt, in turn, reflects his rootedness in and valuing of democratic political systems, systems in which each person ideally has the opportunity to pursue and construct his or her own identity.

Erikson is particularly pointed in his writing about the importance of social systems providing adolescents enough time and opportunity to develop a healthy sense of identity. He is as critical of societies that rush adolescents into a premature closure of the identity process as he is of those that provide neither the guidance nor the opportunity to form an identity. The first circumstance is generally referred to as *identity foreclosure,* and the second as *identity diffusion.* Erikson believes that to prevent either of these two extremes, society must provide opportunities for adolescents to enter into a period of *psychosocial moratorium,* a time of exploring roles or identities without having to permanently commit to any.

It is useful to remember in closing this discussion on identity that adolescence is neither the first nor the last time in the life span when identity is an issue. As Erikson notes throughout his writings, each psychosocial issue exists in some form at each stage of life. As such, issues of identity have always been an element of the child's developmental makeup and will continue to be part of the adult's as well. In fact, it is not much of a stretch to recognize the issues of trust, autonomy, initiative, and industry (and those to come—intimacy, generativity, and ego integrity) as basically all issues of identity. The fact that each particular psychosocial issue is most dominant at one particular stage does not mean that it isn't relevant during the other seven stages as well.

STAGE 6: YOUNG ADULTHOOD—INTIMACY VS. ISOLATION   The sixth stage of intimacy marks the first of Erikson's three adult stages. These stages are original to Erikson rather than being reformulations of Freud's psychosexual stages.

> It is only as young people emerge from their identity struggles that their egos can master the sixth stage, that of intimacy. What we have said about genitality now gradually comes into play. Body and ego must now be masters of the organ modes and of the nuclear conflicts, in order to be able to face the fear of ego loss in situations which call for self-abandon: in orgasms and sexual union, in close friendships and in physical combat, in experiences of inspiration by teachers and of intuition from the recesses of the self. The avoidance of such experiences because of a fear of ego loss

may lead to a deep sense of isolation and consequent self-absorption. (Erikson, 1950, p. 229)

This description of the basic element in this sixth stage is significant because of how it contrasts to the event of the previous stage. The contrast, however, is not in terms of the actual events. Orgasm, friendship, and even inspiration by teachers are equally elements of adolescence. But in adolescence they play a different role. For the adolescent these and similar activities help to establish a definition of self. In a harsh sense the adolescent uses others for the purpose of constructing a personal identity. But in young adulthood the motivation is different. Now the goal is no longer to use others for a personal need, but rather to join with others in a shared experience, to enter into self-abandon without fear of abandoning the self—a sleight of hand Erikson believes the adolescent is not yet capable of accomplishing.

A successful resolution of this sixth stage is a *basic sense of intimacy;* failure to achieve a sense of intimacy leads to a sense of *isolation.* A sense of intimacy fosters the more general *basic strength of love;* failure to do so leads to the antipathy of *exclusivity.* The radius of significant relations now grows to include *partners in friendship, sex, competition,* and *cooperation.*

Achieving a sense of intimacy involves a fundamental transition in the way individuals see themselves—in particular from a definition of self involving "I" and "you" to a definition involving "we." This transition in perspective is prompted by society's expectation that individuals will form lasting partnerships. Individuals who are unable to achieve this synthesis remain in conflict with others or, as Erikson puts it, in a perpetual state of opposition or antagonism.

Erikson draws an interesting parallel between the issues of infancy and the issues of the young-adult years through his reference, in both cases, to the role of *mutuality.* In both cases the term refers to the give-and-take, to the joyful interplay between, on the one hand, parent and child and, on the other, two people in love. What was initially established at one radius of significant relationships now becomes reestablished at another. The parallel is not, of course, literal. The first is involuntary and involves a relationship between unequals in power whereas the second is voluntary and involves, by definition, the relationship of equals. But in both cases it is a relationship form involving a "mutuality of mates and partners in a shared identity," which serves the purpose of a "mutual verification through an experience of finding oneself, as one loses oneself, in another" (Erikson, 1964, p. 128).

STAGE 7: ADULTHOOD—GENERATIVITY VS. STAGNATION Each of Erikson's stages builds upon those that precede it, and each moves the individual more fully into the role of a mature, active participant in one's culture. Identity provides the individual the sense of self necessary to choose an adult role. Intimacy provides the individual the opportunity to join with another to better accomplish these selected adult roles. And now a *basic sense of generativity* provides individuals the perspective of considering the significance of their efforts beyond their own generation. Individuals who fail to develop a sense of generativity develop instead a *sense of stagnation. Care* is the basic strength that emerges from a sense of generativity; the antipathy is *rejectivity.* In

Erikson's words care is "the widening concern for what has been generated by love, necessity or accident; it overcomes the ambivalence adhering to irreversible obligations" (1964, p. 131). Erikson now describes the radius of significant relations as including *divided labor* and *shared housework.*

Parenthood is the quintessential form of expressing generativity, but it is not the only way to be generative. More generally, any efforts that demonstrate a sense of caring for the future are a measure of generativity. The crucial component is that, through their generative acts, adults are demonstrating a recognition of their responsibility to maintain their culture—in the form of a child, a student, an institution, an ethic or value, and so on—even beyond their time. The implicit aspect of this recognition is that the adults see themselves as part of this culture, an issue reflecting the degree of resolution of earlier stages. Erikson is quick to point out that simply having children is not a measure of generativity; rather, it is the degree to which adults modify their own lives to care for these children. Adults who are unable to care about the future beyond their own time, and who therefore stagnate, regress into a self-centered narcissism, according to Erikson. They tend to "indulge themselves as if they were their one and only child" (Erikson, 1982, p. 103).

STAGE 8: OLD AGE—EGO INTEGRITY VS. DESPAIR   At a point in the life span most often characterized in terms of loss of biological and psychological competence and loss of social status, Erikson sees the last psychosocial crisis as one of maintaining a *basic sense of ego integrity* and avoiding a *sense of despair.* Individuals who are able to establish a sense of ego integrity demonstrate the *basic strength of wisdom;* those who fail to do so, the antipathy of *disdain.* The radius of significant relationships now extends out to *my kind.*

Ego integrity is a measure of the ability to accept one's life as lived. This means acknowledging responsibility for one's own actions, both positive and negative. Ego integrity does not mean that elders do not recognize that if they had to do it over again, they would do it differently. Quite the contrary; but it does mean that they now recognize that, for the most part, they no longer have the time to do it over again. Wisdom in this sense, then, is the ability to recognize this inevitable fact of life.

Elders may not have the time to do it over again, but Erikson (1964) argues that they do have the opportunity to share the wisdom that is only possible at this point in the life span.

> Potency, performance, and adaptability decline; but if vigor of mind combines with the gift of responsible renunciation, some old people can envisage human problems in their entirety (which is what "integrity" means) and can represent to the coming generation a living example of the "closure" of a style of life. Only such integrity can balance the despair of the knowledge that a limited life is coming to a conscious conclusion, only such wholeness can transcend the petty disgust of feeling finished and passed by, and the despair of facing the period of relative helplessness which marks the end as it marked the beginning. (pp. 133–134)

Issues of aging and of successful aging became more central in Erikson's later writings. He was particularly concerned that at a time in our own society when the number of elders is increasing significantly, their value to this society seems actually to be decreasing. Unlike in other societies, Erikson saw elders in our society as having few, if any, meaningful roles. Few continue to work, and in many cases relocation reduces the continuity of family ties. But, most important, from Erikson's perspective, this loss of role means that their wisdom is less valued, and as their wisdom becomes less valued, their ability to establish a sense of ego integrity becomes more difficult. The possibility of despair therefore becomes greater, and with it a greater fear of one's own death. For Erikson acceptance of one's finality is possible only if one first has acquired a sense of ego integrity.

Erikson's Theory in Perspective

Like Freud's, Erikson's work sometimes seems so broad and general that it's hard to know how to judge it. Certainly, those who have attempted to translate his ideas into more empirical forms have faced this issue. Nevertheless, there is something enduring about Erikson's writings. One gets the sense that he was a keen observer of cultures, particularly our own. Admittedly these observations seem more relevant to the lives of men than women, but even this changes in his later writings as his concepts become more generic and less tied to traditional psychoanalysis.

Erikson has made four particularly significant contributions to our understanding of life span human development. The first is simply that the study of life span human development cannot reside solely within any one academic discipline. Erikson drew insight from the work of biologists, psychologists, sociologists, anthropologists, historians, and others. To him each particular perspective illuminated one facet of the whole picture. His triple bookkeeping is a useful reminder of the need for an interdisciplinary approach to the study of life span development.

Erikson's second contribution is in highlighting the fact that even though psychosocial crises are associated with particular age periods, the issue nevertheless exists in some form at all age periods. In other words, from his perspective, development is not best appreciated as a sequence of one issue or concern replacing another over time. Rather, development is the continual construction and reconstruction of the meaning and significance of a set of common topics or themes (trust, autonomy, initiative, etc.) across the entire life span. This is a concept similar to Piaget's vertical decalage, although Piaget never developed the idea to the extent that Erikson did.

Erikson's third contribution is in making Freud's original concepts culturally relative. Even if development as a sequential process is a universal characteristic of the species, the form of the expression of this sequence is dependent on culture. This transformation accomplishes two things. First, it makes the sequence more generic in form, emphasizing the psychosocial rather than the psychosexual. Second, by making the sequence culturally relative, it makes the assessment of healthy development always specific to time and place. What is a healthy expression in one setting may not be so in another. But, equally important, what is an unhealthy expression in one setting may be a healthy one in another.

Finally, Erikson is one of the first truly life span theorists. His work reminds us that development does not end with the accomplishments of childhood or even adolescence but continues across the entire life span.

Part III—Summing Up

The defining element of the organismic theories reviewed in Part III is their search for and identification of developmental sequences. In the case of psychobiologists such as Thelen, the focus has been on sequences of motor development; in the case of Piaget and, to a large extent, the neo-Piagetians, on sequences of knowledge construction; and in the case of both Freud and Erikson, on sequences of relationships.

The fact that in each case the process is one of discovery rather than one of invention highlights another defining element of these organismic theories, namely, the emphasis they each place on formal and in some cases even final causes of development. Canters follow trots, preoperational thought precedes concrete operational thought, and egos evolve from ids; it's never the other way around. For each of these organismic theorists, the search is for the universal, species-specific developmental sequences that we share and that define us as a unique species. The expression of these sequences may well be specific to time and place—both the neo-Piagetians and Erikson in particular remind us of this argument—but in all cases the underlying process is the same. The search for identity may have very different expressions among adolescents in India, Brazil, Sierra Leone, and Italy, but in all cases it is a search for identity. The timing of the emergence of new developmental levels may also vary across time and place, as might even the likelihood of the emergence of higher levels of functioning. But, as Werner reminds us early in Part III, if development does occur, it always does so in a sequence of undifferentiated to differentiated to integrated.

Sequence is not the only defining characteristic of theories within the organismic world view. These theories all see development as a qualitative rather than a quantitative process. To organicists new levels of functioning are not simply "souped up" versions of earlier levels; they are unique forms having distinct functional properties, which have emerged out of the interactions of all the elements present at the previous levels. The new forms are not reducible to earlier ones because they are qualitatively distinct wholes. It is these new forms (hence the focus on formal causes) that are seen as the primary regulator of behavior during a particular developmental period or stage. Efficient and material causes are also recognized as influencing that behavior, but only in the sense that they generate variations on a theme. And as is true of a musical composition that offers variations on a symphonic theme, in all cases the theme remains clearly visible.

Sequence implies direction, and for organicists such as Piaget, Freud, and Erikson, direction implies an idealized, theoretical end point to the process of development. No matter that none of us will ever see this end point, much less even come very close to it. No matter that this notion of a final cause is a "gimmick" in that no one really is suggesting that the future is literally determining the present. For most organismic theorists the notion of a final cause is the yardstick against which development can be measured. The yardstick is evident in Gesell's advice to parents as to how to best raise their children, in Piaget's beliefs as to the principal goals of education, and in Erikson's warnings of the dangers of identity foreclosure and identity diffusion. This is not to suggest that mechanists are any less concerned about such matters (or the contextual-ists for that matter, but we will get to them soon enough), but the concern of the mechanists has a different character to it. First, mechanists are more likely than organicists to distinguish the statements they make as behavioral scientists from those they make as concerned and informed citizens. Second, because formal causes play lit-tle role in mechanism, there is no yardstick that can be turned into a flagpole around which to rally. Put in still another way, mechanists seem most comfortable talking about what will and won't happen; organicists seem equally comfortable also talking about what should and shouldn't happen.

How do organismic theories reflect the four criteria of good theories identified in Chapter 1? That is, in what sense are these theories testable, organized, generative, and precise? The answer to this question serves as a good illustration of the problems involved in testing the relative merits of (as opposed to simply comparing) theories within one world view against those in another. Consider the issue of testability. For theories within a mechanistic world view, testability is measured by a theory's ability to predict, to say that if we do this, that will result. Such a criterion is clearly consistent with mechanism's emphasis on efficient and material causes. Such an emphasis means, theoretically at least, that 100% accuracy in prediction is possible.

But 100% predictability is not a theoretical expectation in an organismic world view. For organicists the measure of a theory is not its ability to predict so much as it is the theory's ability to explain. It is the difference between Skinner trying to determine the antecedents that cause behavior to occur and Piaget trying to understand how children's categorization strategies change over time. Skinner believed that his ability to control behavior also meant that he could predict it. Piaget didn't believe that he had much control over children's ability to sort and classify, but he did believe that through observation he had the ability to understand it. Again, testability means dif-ferent things in different world views. For theories within an organismic world view, measures of the testability of a theory are reflected in that theory's ability to explain the phenomena of interest to that theory.

Theories within an organismic world view tend to offer highly organized systems. This should not be surprising given the fact that these theories are all about identify-ing structures. Gesell and McGraw each offer a detailed set of developmental princi-ples. Thelen's "epigenetic landscapes" depicting the emergence and disappearance of different forms of locomotion offer insights into the organization of the psychobiolog-ical systems of the young child. Piaget's, Fischer's, Labouvie-Vief's, and Damon's sys-tems each offer equally detailed glimpses of how individuals organize their knowledge of the world. Freud's image of the psyche is no less detailed, even if most of it does seem to lie below the "water line." And finally, Erikson's matrix, though never com-pleted, offers a highly organized and detailed image of the meaning of each of the eight psychosocial tasks across his eight stages of the life span.

All of the theories presented in Part III have been and continue to be highly gen-erative. They constantly serve as the basis for new ideas, for the generation of new

hypotheses across all three world views. This is no less true when the goal is to disprove as it is to prove their theoretical claims. Piaget's theory is no less generative
when researchers try to find fault with his claims than it is when someone uses the theory to justify a new approach to education. Ironically, Freud's theory may be the most
generative of them all. As noted at the beginning of the chapter, year after year the
theory generates a host of studies showing that he couldn't possibly have been right.

One of the reasons that, year after year, Freud's theory generates so many studies
and remains a staple of theory textbooks may be that, as is true of organismic theories
in general, Freud drew his theory in broad, bold strokes. This is no less true of Erikson
or Piaget. From a mechanistic perspective these theories aren't very precise, but then
again, they were not meant to be. Piaget never intended to offer as precise an explanation for children's problem solving as the information processing theories do. Erikson
was uninterested in how much variance is accounted for by each of the entries in his
triple-bookkeeping ledger. In the tradeoff between scope and precision, organismic
models tend to place more emphasis on scope, and mechanistic models on precision.

So what does it mean to be a developmentalist within an organismic world view?
It means being interested in the identification and explanation of the psychological
forms of knowing that generate and regulate our actions at each point in the life span.
It also means being interested in identifying the reasons qualitatively distinct new
forms of knowing sequentially emerge at particular points in the life span.

We turn now to Part IV, an examination of three theoretical perspectives within the
contextualist world view. Life span cohort models look at the ways in which development is influenced by the slice of history a particular life span occupies. Sociocultural
perspectives look at ways in which development is influenced by the cultural context
in which it occurs. The postmodern perspective, the most recent development in theories about development, is certainly the most controversial of all in this book,
because if we accept the postmodern argument, there may not have been much reason
to read the chapters that preceded it.

PART IV

The Contextualist World View

By this point it should be very clear to you the various ways in which organismic and mechanistic models differ from each other. One is holistic; the other, reductionist. One places great emphasis on formal and final causes; the other, on efficient and material causes. One sees the process of development as a qualitative event; the other sees the process of change as a quantitative event. Clearly, the differences are great enough that we can appreciate Pepper's argument that there is no direct way to compare the claims made by each.

As different as organicism and mechanism are, however, they share one common element—an element necessary to understanding contextualism as a world view. Whatever the differences between organicism and mechanism and whatever the merits of their competing claims, both share a belief in knowable, universal patterns of behavior and development. Furthermore, both believe that these universals are not directly observable but can only be known indirectly through inferences based on the study of the behavior of humans and other species.

Why did Skinner spend so much time teaching pigeons to play Ping-Pong? Why did Piaget become so intrigued with watching children play marbles and asking them about what happens when water gets poured among different-shaped glasses? It was not because they were particularly interested in these tasks per se. Rather, it was because each believed that these tasks (and others serving parallel functions) are reasonably effective and efficient ways to pare away the outer layers and, ultimately, to distill the essence of the processes of behavioral change in the case of Skinner and the process of development in the case of Piaget. For Skinner and Piaget, and for all other mechanists and organicists, there is an essence to be discovered, a universal bottom line that once known will, theoretically at least, completely explain the process. Furthermore, it will be an explanation that will hold not just for the here and now but for all time and in all places. To scientists, this search for "truth" is their primary motivator.

But what if this assumption of *essentialism* is incorrect? What if there are no universal patterns to development? What if the laws of behavior are not universal but particular to time and place and even group, changing as circumstance dictates? Contextualism, as a world view, is based on just such an assumption—that is, that there are no universals. There is no essence to be discovered by systematically going deeper and deeper in the same way that one eventually gets to the heart of the artichoke by peeling away the outer leaves. What is at the surface is what there is to be found. A contextualist watching children play marbles would be doing so because she has an interest in children playing marbles. Whatever conclusions she might draw from her observations would be limited to this time and place and nothing more—but, the contextualist would be quick to argue, also nothing less. Is it no surprise, then, that Pepper's metaphor for the contextual world view is the historical act?

Within contextualism the historical act is an event occurring in everyday life, is defined temporally (i.e., it has a beginning and an end), and "consists of a conglomeration of factors, relations, and activities in a state of perpetual change" (Jaeger & Rosnow, 1988). The purpose of the study of such events is to discover what the events themselves say about the web of interactions that create and maintain the events and about the role of the individual within this matrix of interrelationships. There is no intention to generalize, to abstract, or to propose universal arguments based on the observation of the event. Because the focus is on events as they occur, contextualists are much more concerned with the actual content of people's lives (i.e., the "what" of development) than are either mechanists or organicists. In these latter two cases, because the focus is on universal processes, the actual content of behavior is relevant primarily because of what it says about the underlying process.

The significance of contextualism as a developmental perspective has grown considerably over the past 25 years or so. It has done so largely as people increasingly have come to question the appropriateness of models of human development based on concepts drawn from the physical and natural sciences and even to question the very concept of progress, the keystone of the modern age. Although each of these issues will be discussed in some detail in the coming chapters, it is important to discuss them briefly at this point because they are the bases of contextualism's critiques of both mechanism and organicism.

Contextualists question mechanism's claims of objectivity. The issue is not one of a deliberate distortion of the data. Rather, it involves the argument that, because the very nature of all human contact is interactive, the study of development is necessarily the study of subject-subject interactions, and not subject-object interactions, the essence of the physical and natural sciences. In other words, the astronomer can safely study the orbit of a planet without fear that the act of studying that orbit will in some way affect the orbit. The astronomer's method may affect the accuracy of the observations, but it will not affect the course of that orbit. That planet is going to go where it is going to go. But, argue contextualists, the same cannot be said for the study of development. The very act of studying a particular behavior itself partly defines what it is that is being observed. As such, contrary to the mechanist's claims that the behavior of subjects is independent of the method used to obtain it (because of the use of experimental and statistical controls), contextualists argue that the behavior of the subject is, in part, very much a reflection of the methods used to obtain it. And if the subject's behavior partially reflects the experimenter's behavior (i.e., the method used to obtain it), then it becomes important to examine the basis for the methodology itself. That is, it becomes necessary to examine the experimenter's biases.

> As scientists do not stand apart from their subjects, so too do they not stand above or beyond the cultural boundaries of their time. Their role in the scientific community is not one of disseminating the facts, but rather of participating in the construction of social knowledge. "Facts" do not represent absolute and static forms of an objective reality. What is "taken to be fact" is developed within historical and social contexts that also give rise to the investigative process itself. (Jaeger & Rosnow, 1988, p. 70)

For contextualists, the interdependent and subjective nature of all human interactions means that the search for an objective reality is an illusion. Research should instead focus on both practical and emancipatory issues. In this case, practical issues involve efforts to understand socially defined shared meaning, and emancipatory issues involve efforts to liberate the human spirit from the dependencies, powers, and constraints imposed by others (Teo, 1997).

Contextualists' concerns about organicism differ from their concerns about mechanism. In fact, to a significant degree, contextualists and organicists hold many theoretical assumptions in common. In particular, both favor a holistic, interactive view of development in which the individual actively participates in constructing the meaning of experiences and events. But there remains a fundamental difference between the two views. Organicism embraces a directional concept of development; contextualism does not. A directional concept presumes that there is an order to the process of development, and this order implies that later steps or stages are in some way better than earlier ones. "Better" in this sense usually means more integrated, and "more integrated" implies being better able to deal with or adapt to changing life events. Different organismic theories present this sequence in different ways and focus on different aspects of development. But there is no question that, for Piaget, functioning at the formal operational level is preferable to doing so at the sensorimotor level; or, for Erikson, that individuals who have achieved a sense of ego integrity are better off than those who haven't; or, for Freud, that individuals who function at the genital stage are psychologically healthier than those arrested at the oral stage.

The organicist's concept of development as a progression of stages, each in some way better than the previous, is, in turn, rooted in the larger social concept of progress itself. The concept of progress, as noted previously, is the keystone of the *modern age*. It is a notion that traces its origins at least back to the 18th century and is still the defining element of most of the social policy of industrialized nations. It is defined by two great ideas: (1) the utopian idea of progress and (2) the idealistic notion of the unity of thought (Chandler, 1993).

Reason, rationality, and science became the engines to achieve these dual goals. There was a "truth" to be known through objective methods; there were achievable ideals that could be reached through concentrated and deliberate human effort. The progress of a society toward some utopian ideal was seen as parallel to the progress (i.e., development) of the individual. Just as society is seen as moving toward an increasingly better state, so, too, is the individual. Even the course of biological evolution was seen (and still is seen by many) as showing the same progression. For many organismic theorists, social progress, biological evolution, and human development were all seen as reflecting this larger universal "truth" of directionality (Kessen, 1990).

To contextualists, and the larger *postmodern movement* of which they are a part, what others claim is progress is little more than change. Contextualists argue that events of the 20th century such as two world wars, the Holocaust, and ecological disasters are anything but measures of improvement. Furthermore, postmodernists argue that, where change has led to improvement, it has usually happened for one group at the expense of another. In effect, for postmodernists, progress is not a universal movement toward an ideal state but rather, at best, a Western construction that has benefited the ruling class of industrial nations to the detriment of all others. Even the very notion that change is inevitable and beneficial is suspect. What is wrong, contextualists ask, with a stable society maintaining its ways indefinitely?

If organismic theories are based on the premises of the modern age, and if, as contextualists claim, these premises are not universal but rather may be little more than self-serving devices, then are organismic theories little more than efforts to provide a rationalization for maintaining the status quo of those groups in favored positions within a society? Clearly, organicists would not subscribe to such a charge—either of their theory or their politics—and they do offer clear rebuttals to such charges (see, e.g., Chandler, 1993, 1995). But for contextualists, the close association of organicism with the social concept of progress is the reason organicism, as a model of development, is incorrect.

The next three chapters examine these contextual arguments in more detail. Chapter 13 focuses on life span cohort models of development (Baltes, 1979, 1987; Schaie, 1994). Cohorts are groups of individuals born during a particular period of time. Because different cohorts experience different historical events, or at least the same events at different developmental levels, comparisons among them are one means of looking at the impact of context on development. Cohort analysis is a powerful means of demonstrating the cumulative and differential impact of life experiences across the entire life span. Glen Elder's cohort studies (Elder, 1974, 1998; Elder & Rockwell, 1979) of the impact of the Great Depression of the 1930s is discussed in detail as an illustration of a life span cohort perspective.

The discussion of life span cohort models highlights the debate among developmentalists over the distinction between "context" and "contextualism." All models within all three world views talk about context effects. In this sense context becomes synonymous with external antecedent events or independent variables and is simply a category of efficient causes. If, for example, children learn to read better with method A than with method B, then the two methods define the children's contexts, and the variability in the children's behavior (i.e., differences in their reading scores) is said to reflect context. But contextualism is more than merely a source of variability. Variability presumes some central process or mechanism around which children's behavior differs. It assumes an essence. In the reading example, the process is the ability to learn to read and the effects of different teaching strategies. Contextualism presumes no essence, so the focus is on the interplay of events at the surface. There is no deep process to vary around, but simply different behaviors in different settings. The life span cohort perspective is a good place to examine this distinction because different theorists have interpreted the findings from these studies in both ways (Houts, 1991; Kendler, 1986; Lerner & Kauffman, 1985, 1986).

Chapter 14 reviews contextual models emphasizing socio-cultural perspectives. Debates about comparisons among cultures also revolve around issues of progress and modernism. The question becomes whether it is possible to compare the developmental level of different cultures in the same way that developmental levels of different individuals have been compared. The logic of the modern age suggests that such comparisons are possible because all individuals and groups of individuals are moving, presumably at different rates, toward some universal utopian state. Historically such comparisons have been used as rationalizations for one nation or cultural group to interfere in the affairs of another. From a contextualist perspective, of course, there is no justification for such interventions because one culture cannot be said to be more advanced than another. Different, yes; advanced, no. The particular focus of this chapter is on the developmental theory of Lev Vygotsky (Vygotsky, 1962, 1978; Vygotsky & Luria, 1993) and on the sociocultural research of Barbara Rogoff (1990, 1997; Rogoff & Chavajay, 1995).

Chapter 15, the last chapter in Part IV, examines postmodern or critical theories of human development. These theories are "critical" in the sense that one of their primary purposes is to criticize other models, particularly those within the mechanistic and organismic world views. In this sense these postmodern models attempt to *deconstruct* the assumptions underlying other models and therefore open them up to a full examination of their implications. From a contextualist perspective, theories in the other two world views are often seen as serving to maintain the status quo within a society. Not surprisingly, then, critical theories give special attention to how developmental models treat traditionally disenfranchised groups, particularly women and both racial and ethnic minorities. The work of Kenneth Gergen (1977, 1980, 1985, 1994, 1995) plays an important role in these critical analyses.

One caution to keep in mind as you read these three chapters on contextualism: Be mindful about the claims of both mechanists and organicists that contextualists have a tendency to "throw the baby out with the bath water." It might well be that industrialized nations have used the concept of progress as a rationalization to compare themselves favorably to other nations and therefore to feel justified in imposing their will on those nations. It may also be true that, for example, organismic models such as Piaget's incorporate a notion of progress or development. But does it follow that if the actions of industrialized nations are without justification, so, too, is Piaget's theory? And, does it follow that if politicians have applied developmental concepts for their own purposes, purposes quite removed from their original role, then the theory serves to maintain the political status quo and therefore should be abandoned? Each of you will arrive at your own answers to these questions (and there are good points to be made on both sides), but do keep them in mind because they are important questions to ask.

13

Life Span Cohort Perspectives

The life span cohort perspective prompts us to consider two fundamental issues in the study of human development. The first, which we touched on previously, is the distinction between *context* and *contextualism*. This issue is particularly relevant to a life span cohort perspective because, for the most part, these researchers use methodologies grounded in both mechanism and organicism. They argue that their efforts are nonetheless distinct because they have modified these methodologies to also consider the effects of historical time and social place (i.e., the impact of cohort) and because their interpretations do not make claims of universality but rather are situated in time and place. In any case, they do seem to be straddling a theoretical fence. To those on one side of the fence, their methodologies indicate that they are really investigating the same role of context on development as any other mechanist or organicist might study. For those on the other side of the fence, their interpretations indicate that they are really investigating the situated, nonuniversal influence of historical time and place on individuals' social and nonsocial interactions.

The second fundamental issue raised by this perspective is the distinction between *development* and *change.* One of the things that distinguishes almost all models within both mechanism and organicism is that their primary interest is the events marking the first parts of the life span. This is true for different reasons for different models, but in general the models in these two world views can best be appreciated as *growth models.* That is, they are primarily interested in changes that are seen as "positive," involving in one way or another the study of how we get better at things as we move from infancy through childhood and adolescence into the adult years. But then, with a few exceptions such as Erikson and Labouvie-Vief, the models seem to lose interest in us as adults. They do so because, for most of these models, by the time we reach our adult years, we are seen as having *developed.*

Fortunately (or unfortunately), we don't stay the same as we are at 18 or 20. So what about the rest of the life span? The answer to this question is what differentiates the life span cohort theorists from most mechanists and organicists. For life span cohort theorists, development is a lifelong process. For most other theorists, in contrast, development is a process essentially completed by the end of adolescence. What happens after adolescence is simply change and is therefore of relatively little interest to developmentalists. Consider how Bower (1979) puts it in summarizing his text on human development:

> This book has said nothing about the study of development in adulthood. There are many theories which would argue that psychological development continues through the life span. With respect, I feel that such claims do some violence to the idea of development. To be sure there are changes after 20 or so, but they are not changes resulting from gene expression, nor are they are age-linked, nor indeed are they at all universal. . . . I know of no evidence indicating genuine developmental change in the adult's basic view of the world, whether of the self, the social world or the physical world. (p. 432)

Bower's words may be more strident than those of others, but the sentiment is common. Flavell (1992), for example, has raised similar concerns. Again, keep in mind that neither Bower nor anyone else is saying that adults don't change—obviously we do. The issue is whether these changes reflect the same underlying structural changes that are seen as accounting for change during the first 20 or so years of life.

To contextualists, including the life span cohort theorists, what is of little interest to classic developmentalists is of great interest to them. Ridding themselves of what they would argue are the unnecessary and unsupported universal and structural theoretical constraints of both mechanism and organicism, they see themselves as being in a position to consider the hypothesis that all forms of change at all points of the life span may have theoretical developmental significance (Baltes, 1987, 1997; Labouvie-Vief & Chandler, 1978; Lerner, 1993; Lerner & Kauffman, 1985; Schaie, 1984, 1994). Furthermore, this broadening of the age range into the adult years has led life span cohort researchers to become interested in the events of our lives not simply as a means of identifying deeper structures (because to contextualists there aren't any) but as ends in themselves. It is in this sense that contextualists are interested in "what we are."

The Origin of Life Span Cohort Models

Life span cohort models have played an important role in developmental theories since the 1960s, but their roots go back much farther. Baltes (1979) reports on academic writing dating from the 18th century on development across the life span. He also notes that references to what, in effect, are a life span view of development can be found in the Bible and in many early literary works, including those of Shakespeare and Longfellow. This life span view is evident in these lines from Longfellow's poem "Age Is Opportunity."

> For age is opportunity no less
> Than youth itself, though in another dress.

And as the evening twilight fades away
The sky is filled with stars, invisible by day.

The more recent emergence of life span cohort models can be traced to three related developments: (1) the changing demographics of old age, (2) the aging of the participants in longitudinal studies begun in the 1920s and 1930s, and (3) the growing interest in multidisciplinary research.

Changing Population Demographics

Population demographics reflect the relationship between the birth rate and the death rate for any given period. If the birth rate is greater, the population is expanding; if it is less, the population is contracting; and if they are the same, the population is stable. Several factors can affect each. Since the early 1900s in the United States and most other industrialized nations, there has been both a gradual decline in the birth rate and, largely because of improvements in medicine, nutrition, and public health, a gradual increase in the average life expectancy. The result has been a shift in the population demographics. The average age of the population is moving upward. In fact, the fastest-growing segment of the population is now those over 80.

The result of all these demographic changes has been an increased awareness of elders in society and increasing questions about the social roles they can and should play. These questions have been given added weight because of so many elders entering retirement—a relatively recent phenomenon. The notion that after a certain age people need no longer work is new. It wasn't until the 1930s that this notion was even formally recognized with passage of the Social Security Act.

Retirement as a social role reflects the fact that a society has the financial resources to support nonworking older adults and the belief that these individuals have earned the right not to work. It is the wealth of a society that also is reflected in the birth rate, because historically those no longer able to work needed to rely on family members, most often their children, to provide for their needs. If society in general is now able to assume this responsibility, there is one less reason for large families.

All of these social and demographic changes also led to a renewed interest in gerontology as an academic discipline. If adults no longer have to work until they are physically incapacitated, then old age is no longer seen as simply a period of physical decline followed by death but rather as a time of renewal of previous interests and establishment of new ones. In short, old age becomes a period of the life span in which both gains and losses are evident (Baltes, 1987; Featherman, 1983; Neugarten, 1975). And understanding the antecedents of gains and losses in old age becomes an important issue in the study of one's entire life span. As Featherman (1983) observed:

> The gerontologists placed biological aging and behavioral changes in older adults within the context of cumulative life histories, linking contemporaneous changes with sequences and events over the entire life span. They became as concerned with the emergence of novel behaviors in their older subjects as they were with ones that could be construed as outgrowths of predisposing earlier ones. They observed large differences in the courses of aging and in behaviors among adults, and they sought

explanation of this variation in historical circumstances and in chance occurrences such as illness, accidents, and births of grandchildren that are more individualized in their impact. (p. 7)

The Maturing of Longitudinal Study Samples

At the same time that gerontologists were beginning to understand the new meanings of being old, some child development researchers were encountering a set of events that led to their discovery of new meanings of being young. These researchers were involved in a series of longitudinal studies of child development begun between 1900 and 1930. Many facets of these children's lives were studied and reported over the course of many years. As the studies continued through childhood into adolescence and eventually the adult years, these researchers found themselves no longer dealing with issues specific to the early years (Eichorn, 1973; Eichorn, Clausen, Haan, Honzik, & Mussen, 1981; Hunt & Eichorn, 1972).

Data collected when the individuals were in their early and middle adult years show that, for instance, correlations of chronological age with behavior (a frequent finding when the samples were in their childhoods) are less common and, when they are still found, less strong. Variability is greater among the samples as adults than as children. New behaviors and behavior patterns emerge in the adult years, ones not easily linked to early childhood experiences. Data on middle-aged adults indicates that by this point in the life span many adults, particularly women, feel less constrained by traditional social roles (Livson, 1981). All of these findings rekindled an interest in adult development and provoked significant theoretical questions about the links of early experience to later events. In particular, they raise questions about the role of contextual variables and about the stability of ability rankings across the life span. In general, the adult data from these longitudinal studies contradicts Bower's claim that little of developmental significance occurs after the age of 20 or so, especially given contextualism's broader definition of the term.

Multidisciplinary Approaches to the Life Span

Psychology might well claim ownership of the study of child development, but when it comes to the study of the life span, no clear claim is possible. Many academic disciplines—sociology, anthropology, history, economics, psychology, gerontology, and human development, to name a few—pursue issues related to adult development. Even as shifting demographics and ongoing longitudinal studies were raising new questions, an increasing interest in multidisciplinary approaches to the study of the life span was gaining momentum (Dannefer, 1984; Dannefer & Perlmutter, 1990; Elder, Modell, & Parke, 1993; Featherman, 1983). One significant consequence of this renewed interest in viewing the life span from a multidisciplinary perspective is that there is now a shift away from the classic "growth followed by decline" model of the life span. Viewing the life span from the vantage point of many disciplines again raises questions about (1) variability across the adult years, (2) the role of the individual in defining his or her life course, (3) the influence of historically situated life events, and (4) the emergence of novel behaviors in later life (Elder, 1998; Elder & Rockwell, 1979;

Ford & Lerner, 1992; Lerner, 1993). More to the point, life span models argue that a multidisciplinary perspective makes it easier to recognize that both gains and losses are part of all stages of the life span.

One particularly significant influence of a multidisciplinary perspective is the increasing interest paid to *cohort influences.* Cohort influences reflect the significance of historical time and social place. In traditional psychological research, cohort variables are often seen as "noise" in the system and as such are statistically controlled for (i.e., their influence is eliminated). This is reasonable given that the goal of such a traditional approach is to identify universal patterns that transcend time and place. But what is noise to some has become a primary focus to others. By changing the status of cohort influence, these multidisciplinary efforts have placed greater emphasis on the particular influence of events specific to different cohorts. The goal is not to be able to generalize across cohort but rather to understand the particular life experiences unique to each cohort.

Basic Elements of a Life Span Cohort Model

Many individuals would refer to themselves as life span (or life course) cohort theorists, but there is no life span cohort theory per se. Rather, as is the case for information processing models, several generally accepted elements or basic assumptions guide the work of most life span cohort theorists.

It is possible to identify three interrelated basic assumptions that underlie life span cohort models: (1) the "openness" of the process of development, (2) the placement of any developmental analysis in a particular historical time and social place, and (3) the ways in which the process of development can be characterized in such an open, situated system.

Development as an Open Process

The concept of development as an open process stands in contrast to the organicists' claims of the role of both formal and final causes. Both formal and final causes serve to restrict or direct the process of development in particular ways. Because formal cause is presumed to reflect structural aspects of the organism, the presence or absence of a particular structure (e.g., formal operations or the superego) strongly influences what the organism can and cannot do. In the case of final cause, a developmental sequence is presumed, one in which later stages are seen in some sense as more adaptive or more mature than earlier ones. But if we remove these two forms of cause from the theory, then we remove the restrictions that define them.[1]

---

[1] In fairness to organicists, it should be noted that neither formal nor final cause precludes openness in the sense of either the final level of development or the particular behaviors documenting that developmental level. In other words, even though Piaget, for example, argued that formal operational

The result, according to life span theorists, is an open ended co-evolving system—
a system that reflects the interplay of the continuing processes of organic and social
evolution (Dannefer, 1984; Dannefer & Perlmutter, 1990; Featherman, 1985). The fact
that these processes are ongoing means, to life span theorists, that any universal
claims as to the structure or direction of development are incorrect. It also means that,
because individuals structure their own social environments, we play an active role in
defining our own development.

Life span cohort theorists believe that this openness is particularly true for
humans. For one thing, we are born less mature than other species (i.e., we are more
open to experience). For another, the structure of our culture allows for each generation to build on the accomplishments of previous generations rather than simply
repeat a particular level of functioning, a pattern typical of other species. Notice how
Featherman (1985) describes this process of co-evolution, especially in terms of what
he sees as the potential consequences of the process.

> Put simply, the central idea of my thesis is that individual development is the out-
> come of a continuing evolutionary process in which *Homo sapiens* is adapted to its
> changing environment. That individuals develop or change systematically after birth
> (and perhaps over the entire course of life) is the result of a historical or evolutionary
> process expressed at the level of the species and realized as a consequence of *Homo*'s
> adaptive ascendancy within its niche through cooperative communal organization.
> Human social organization, itself a part of the individual's environment, is a funda-
> mental and proximate cause of neonatal development and other age-related changes
> over the life-span. Within this framework, processes commonly denoted as develop-
> ment and aging, and indeed even longevity itself, are cast as social products to be
> understood within the particular features of a specific societal and historical context.
> (p. 214)

Development as a Situated Process

For life span theorists, if the process of development is open in terms of both form and
level, and if it always reflects the co-evolution of organic and social processes, then the
social environment is seen as playing a more significant and defining role than they
claim is the case in organicism.[2] In particular, the sociohistorical context is seen as
defining not only the rate and final level of development but the very structure of the
life span itself. In particular, sociohistorical context defines the criteria through which

---

thought was the most mature thought demonstrated, he also argued that this observation says nothing
about the possibility of an even more advanced form of cognition becoming evident at some point in
the future evolution of a culture. By the same token, Piaget would make no restriction on the content of
the individual's cognition—that is, on what it is that the formal operations are acting upon.

[2] The social environment is also seen as a defining element in mechanistic models, but it is treated
in a reductionist manner. As such, although both mechanism and contextualism make strong reference
to environments, they do so through significantly different assumptions. For contextualists, environments are never reducible to individual elements but always exist as an integrated system or web.

status is conferred upon individuals within a society, the roles that individuals are expected to play at different points of the life span, notions of normality and abnormality, expectations as to age typical behavior, and even measures of wisdom and intelligence (Dannefer & Perlmutter, 1990; Featherman, 1985; Labouvie-Vief & Chandler, 1978; Lerner, 1993, 1996). In addition, context defines forms of both appropriate and inappropriate social interaction at all levels of the social structure, the degree to which the society supports social mobility, and the extent to which individuality is nurtured (Bronfenbrenner, 1989).

Consider, for example, the notion of developmental stages. For contextualists, to the extent that stages are seen as existing at all, they are primarily a reflection of sociohistorical context. Contextualists are quick to point out that both the number of stages and their boundaries are often arbitrary. They note that historically the life span was not nearly as segmented as it is now. Prior to the Industrial Revolution the life span was generally segmented into two stages: (1) a period from birth to middle childhood, which was essentially seen as the stage of childhood, and (2) the stage of adulthood. But as society changed, so did the structure of the life span. With industrialization, the need for a better educated work force and the corresponding decline in the family as the primary economic unit led to the greater segmentation of the life span (Aries, 1962).

Individual stages are also seen as situated in time and place rather than as universal. From this perspective adolescence is largely a 20th-century creation of highly industrialized, affluent societies. This is not to say that puberty is a recent phenomenon or that people were not teenagers but rather that the set of behavioral characteristics that define adolescence in modern America and in other industrialized nations is a recent construct. Extending this argument about the emergence of adolescence, Keniston (1971) suggested that we are beginning to witness a new developmental stage—youth—which takes place during the college and young adult years. According to Keniston, youth as a developmental stage exists only for those who have resolved most of the issues of adolescence but have not yet assumed the traditional adult roles of marriage, parenthood, and work. This new "space" in the life span is seen by Keniston as having a unique set of developmental tasks and issues. Note that, in the case of youth, the stage exists only among those who are able to go to college and therefore delay entry into the work force.

Still one more example of how context defines the structure of the life span is the changing developmental character of old age (Neugarten, 1975). As the average life span has increased and as social structures are providing new opportunities for elders, old age has become at least a two-step or -stage process. The "young-old" are seen as those who have entered retirement but, because of good health and adequate financial and social resources, are able to pursue all that the retirement years have to offer. The "frail elderly" then becomes a stage of the life span that is characterized by significant physical, social, and/or psychological decline. In this two-step process, the young-old are the new stage, because the image of old age historically has been more closely associated with the frail elderly.

Not surprisingly, this image of development as an open-ended and situated process has led many people to argue that there can be no justification for social hierarchies and the corresponding treatment of those in society who have less status and power. "Historically, the imagination of such alternative 'developmental possibilities' has been a powerful force for social movements including, as recent example, those of blacks, women and the elderly" (Dannefer, 1984, p. 109).

Development as a Successive Sequence

Contextualists talk about development as a sequential event, but they do so in a significantly different way from organicists. For contextualists the sequence is *successive;* for organicists it is *progressive.* The distinction is one of the relationship between the steps in the sequence. When the sequence is progressive, the implication is that each step builds on the previous one and is in some way an improvement—that there is progress. But when the sequence is successive, there is no such assumption of progress. Rather, a successive sequence is simply that, a sequence. There is no implication that later steps in the sequence are in some way necessarily an improvement over earlier ones. This notion of sequence as succession reflects two characteristics of the contextualist model. First, because there is no belief in a deep structure, there can be no basis to even consider the possibility that stages are progressive. Second, because behavior is always situated in time and place, each successive step in the sequence is a unique and temporary response in a sociohistorical context.

Contextualists argue that the organicist's progressive view of stages may even actually be more apparent than real. That is, it may reflect more what organicists have chosen to look at than what there is to see, and as such, it may say more about the process of theory building than the content on which the theory is based. Labouvie-Vief and Chandler (1978) make exactly this point in their discussion of changes in cognition across the life span.

> The extensive demonstration of a deficit in life-span intellectual development in this view may be the result of a lopsided growth of a field slanted toward formalistic content. The simple beauty of the resulting overarching idealistic system may thus be a result of not having identified a parsimonious and comprehensive development, but of selectively discarding behavioral content that defies ready synthesis under an idealistic teleology. (p. 202)

Labouvie-Vief and Chandler further argue that this problem is often compounded by the frequent correlations of chronological age and behavioral status that such a "selective discarding" is likely to produce. Rather than recognizing these correlations as at best reflecting situated relationships, they are seen as universal ones. In other words, "what is" comes to be seen as "what always is" and, even worse, as "what ought to be."

If developmental sequences are situated rather than universal and if they are successive rather than progressive, then is it possible to make any generalizations about them? Baltes (1979, 1987, 1997; Baltes, Reese, & Nesselroade, 1977), among others (Lerner, 1993, 1996; Lerner & Kauffman, 1985), argues that the answer is yes. Specifically, Baltes suggests that there are four ways to characterize developmental sequences within a life span cohort model.

The first characterization is that ontogenetic development is a lifelong process, and not one restricted to the early years of life. Rather than seeing adulthood as the playing out of issues and structures originating in the first 20 or so years of life, Baltes argues that new issues, problems, competencies, and challenges emerge at all points in the life span and that these events continually give new meaning, force, and direction to development at all points in the life span. These events reflect the continual interplay of biological and social forces and the reflective capacity of individuals to influence their own developmental trajectories. In this sense Baltes sees development as a reflection of the interplay of normative factors, non-normative situated factors (i.e., cohort factors), and idiosyncratic factors.

Baltes's second and third characterizations of the developmental sequence within contextualism is that it is both *multidimensional* and *multidirectional*. These two characterizations reflect Baltes's belief that development is best understood in terms of fine strokes rather than broad ones. Rather than involving a few general competencies such as intelligence or emotional maturity or sociability, development is a process involving many different specific competencies or dimensions. Furthermore, rather than all developmental dimensions following the same trajectory, each follows its own path, reflecting the particular contexts individuals find themselves occupying.

Baltes's fourth characterization, *plasticity*, refers to "within person variability and designates the potential that individuals have for different forms of behavior or development" (1987, p. 617). The concept of plasticity questions our limits as a species. It is a particularly appropriate question to ask within contextualism because this is a world view reluctant to make sweeping generalizations about what we are or are not capable of doing or becoming.

Baltes integrates these characterizations of life span development by concluding that the developmental sequence is ultimately best appreciated as a succession of balances of gains and losses. Each step in the life span involves some degree of gain and some degree of loss—for the young and for the old. The fact that we only think of gain when we think of the young and loss when we think of the old is a good illustration, contextualists would argue, of the selective discarding of behavioral content. Baltes does acknowledge that for present cohorts there is more gain and less loss early in life and just the opposite in later life. But he is also quick to point out that we should recognize this finding as a "what is" rather than a "what ought to be" statement. The fact that such patterns characterize current developmental trajectories should not be interpreted to mean that this will always be the case. In fact, one could interpret much of the history of human cultural evolution as stemming the losses of old age and increasing the opportunities for gains.

Life Span Cohort Methodology

In life span cohort models, if development is a situated phenomenon, then there needs to be a methodology by which researchers can understand the influence of the sociohistorical context. This methodology is *cohort analysis*. Cohort analysis was discussed briefly in Chapter 4, but because the technique is so central to life span research, it is worthwhile to examine the technique now in more detail.

Cohort analysis is an extension of longitudinal and cross-sectional research strategies. Its central value is as a way to correct for the biases that life span researchers argue are inherent in both longitudinal and cross-sectional designs. These biases are ones that prevent the measurement of the impact of the sociohistorical context.

As you should remember from previous chapters, longitudinal research designs involve the repeated testing of the same group of individuals over an extended period of time. The size of the group, the time frame of the study, the focus and frequency of the testing, and the length of the intervals between each testing reflect the intent of the study. What stays constant are the participants. With the exception of those who drop out of the study, the individuals tested at the end of the study are the same ones tested at the beginning and at each point in between.

Cross-sectional studies are based on the same logic. But instead of using the same group of individuals and testing them over a period of time, a cross-sectional design takes different groups of individuals (usually differing in terms of age) and tests them at the same time.

Under ideal circumstances and, for the moment, the theoretical assumption that the only thing determining a person's score on these tests is his or her age, then the data from a longitudinal study and the data from a cross-sectional study involving the same age range in each should be identical. In other words, the 10-year-olds in the longitudinal study should show the same test score as the 10-year-olds in the cross-sectional study, the 40-year-olds in the longitudinal study would give the same results as the 40-year-olds in the cross-sectional study, and so on. We would expect this because, if the only relevant variable is chronological age, then it would make no difference if the comparisons were between different people at the same time or the same people at different times. But the fact is, it does make a difference.

More often than not and for most measures, data obtained from longitudinal samples shows a different pattern than data obtained from cross-sectional samples. Cohort theorists (Baltes, 1997; Baltes et al., 1977; Schaie, 1965, 1984, 1994; Schaie & Strother, 1968) argue that this discrepancy reflects the presence of cohort effects. More to the point, it reflects the fact that even though there would be a group of individuals of the same chronological age in both the longitudinal and cross-sectional samples, these two groups would not necessarily have grown up and lived during the same sociohistorical period.

Cohort designs address this problem by making it possible to compare different samples such that the influence of cohort becomes evident. How this is done also reflects which side of the theoretical fence the researcher is working on.

Cohort Design Elements

Cohort designs reflect three elements: (1) a characteristic shared by a group of people, (2) a slice of history, and (3) a time of measurement.

COMMON GROUP MEMBERSHIP   The characteristic shared by a group of individuals is what defines the group as a particular cohort. Cohorts are most often described in terms of sharing a common point of entry into a specific environment, typically in terms of year of birth. But as Schaie (1984) has pointed out, anything can identify a group as a cohort. He notes that, in addition to sharing a common year or range of birth dates, cohorts could also be defined in terms of sharing common events such as entry into puberty or menopause, into the school system or retirement, or even a new community or job. Note that, for some of these examples, there is a significant correlation between chronological age and point of entry (e.g., birth), but in others (e.g., entry into graduate school), the correlation would be less. The relevance of the degree of the relationship between chronological age and cohort membership would depend on the interest of the researcher. If there is reason to believe that the focus of interest would theoretically have a close relationship to maturational aspects of development, then the common element defining the cohort would be chronological age. But if there is no reason to think such a relationship exists, then the cohort could show considerable variability with respect to chronological age even though members of the cohort did share the element defining its identity.

A SLICE OF HISTORY   Cohort analyses are interested in how specific cohorts react to context. "Context" in this sense is a time interval marking the passage of a particular cohort in a particular place through a particular period of time. The period of time would reflect the interest of the researcher. For example, someone interested in the transition to walking in infants might have a period lasting a few months. Someone interested in the transition to adolescence might have a period lasting five or six years. Someone interested in the sense of well-being during the adult years might have a period lasting decades. In other words, the issue isn't how long the period is, but whether it is long enough to measure the topic of interest.

A TIME OF MEASUREMENT   Time of measurement(s) is just that—it is when behaviors are sampled from the cohort(s) in question. Schaie (1994) argues that time of measurement can be thought of in two ways. In the first, time of measurement is simply some appropriate periodic interval to sample the behavior in question. The researcher interested in the transition to walking would sample behavior more frequently than would the one interested in the adolescent transition, and both would sample more often than the adult well-being researcher. In all three cases, however, the testing would occur at a regular interval so that changes could be noted. In general, it is safe to say that the shorter the slice of history, the more frequent the measurement periods.

Schaie's second use of time of measurement is more interesting. Rather than being some arbitrary calendar interval that serves to measure the cumulative impact of life events, Schaie argues that time of measurement can also correspond to discrete, historically significant periods or intervals. For instance, the introduction of technologies such as the telephone or television or personal computer have drastically changed the lives of people in the United States and in many other countries as well. The same argument can be made for medical advances such as the polio vaccine or effective and safe oral contraceptives. Political events such as a war or drastic change in government policy would also be a period effect. In all these examples, the defining element is that the event is significant and the onset is discrete. The effect of the event may not be discrete, however. As will become clear when we review Elder's work on the impact of the Depression of the 1930s, even though the Depression is long over, its effects on certain cohorts clearly is not.

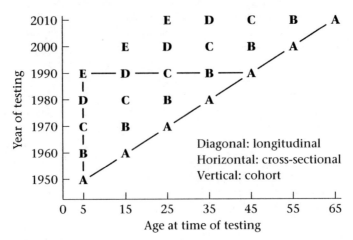

FIGURE 13.1
Cohort Research Design.

Cohort Analyses

The actual research design in a cohort analysis consists of data collection from a series of longitudinal (i.e., cohort) samples. Figure 13.1 shows this relationship in its most generic form. In the figure five successive longitudinal samples are represented as five diagonals (A series, B series, etc.). Each comparison involves the repeated testing of the same group of individuals over an extended period of time. Group A was first tested at the age of 5 in 1950 and then again every 10 years through the year 2010. Any horizontal comparison represents a cross-sectional comparison because individuals of different ages are being compared at the same time. So, for example, in 1990 it was possible to do a cross-sectional comparison of the 5-year-olds in group E, the 15-year-olds in group D, the 25-year-olds in group C, and so on.

The cohort comparison—the comparison of the impact of the sociohistorical context—involves a comparison of the verticals. It is a comparison of the same-age individuals at different times of measurement. For the first vertical, the cohort comparison involves a comparison of the group A 5-year-olds born in 1945 (and tested in 1950), the group B 5-year-olds born in 1955, the group C 5-year-olds born in 1965, and so on.

It is the next step in the cohort data analyses that determines what side of the theoretical fence the life span researcher is sitting on—the context or the contextual. The comparisons described in the previous paragraph all look at unique combinations of variables. From a contextual standpoint that is really as far as one can—or should—go because there are no universal principles that transcend time and place. That is, if development is a situated phenomenon, then the appropriate level of analysis is at comparison of unique combinations of factors—that is, at the level of the data points. But from a more mechanistic standpoint the same sort of main effects analysis of variance as was described in Chapter 2 can be performed. In this case context becomes another main effect and in this sense is no different from any environmental variable studied by a mechanist. That is, you would reduce the data points into separate components (years in cohort, time of measurement, and cohort) and test for the significance of each variable independent of the other two.

Which side of the fence you work from is not an issue of the right side and the wrong side but rather of which side best answers the question you are asking. If, for example, you are interested in how technological change, in general, influences populations, then you are asking a question about variability—and as such, a question best answered through a mechanistic approach. In this case, you would identify some population measure or measures that logically would be influenced by technological change and then try to draw some generalizations about how such changes influence the behavior within your population. But if you are specifically interested in how, for example, the introduction of television changed family interaction patterns, particularly in terms of mealtime routines, then you are asking a question that is situated in time and place and would seek the answer through a contextualist approach. This distinction should become clearer in the next section, which reviews a research paradigm well reflective of life span cohort models. The paradigm is Glen Elder's life course paradigm.

Elder's Life Course Paradigm

Elder's work (1994, 1995, 1998) focuses on how social change influences family structure and function and how, in turn, changes in families influence the life course of individuals. The frame of reference is multigenerational and covers the entire life span. Because the frame of reference is the entire life span, Elder's work serves as a good example of the importance of documenting the impact of social change at various point of the life span rather than at only one point.

Cohort comparisons are an important element in Elder's work because they allow an understanding of the impact of a particular set of social circumstances. Furthermore, because in the life course paradigm life events are always embedded within social systems and individual behavior always reflects the meaning that individuals ascribe to these social circumstances, the model is well grounded within a contextualist world view. That is, the model is holistic in structure and rooted in sociohistorical contexts.

Elder's classic work (1974) examined the impact of the Great Depression of the 1930s on families and individuals. Elder has investigated not only the immediate impact of the Depression but also how this initial impact was tempered, modified, or amplified by subsequent events such as World War II and the social changes following the war (Elder, 1986; Elder & Clipp, 1988; Elder & Hareven, 1993). Elder also has examined the impact of several other significant social changes, including the cultural revolution in China (Elder, 1998), the steep decline in farm property values (Elder, 1996), and the impact of urban poverty on families (Elder, Eccles, Ardelt, & Lord, 1995). As Elder (1994) describes the paradigm:

In concept, the life course generally refers to the interweave of age-graded trajectories, such as work careers and family pathways, that are subject to changing conditions and future options, and to short term transitions ranging from leaving school to retirement. . . . Transitions are always embedded in trajectories that give them distinctive form and meaning. In terms of theory, the life course has defined a common field of inquiry by providing a framework that guides research on matters of problem identification and conceptual development. These problems have much to do with the impact of changing societies on developing lives. (p. 5)

The Four Themes of the Life Course Paradigm

Elder identifies four themes as central to the life course paradigm: (1) the interplay of human lives and historical times, (2) the timing of lives, (3) the linking or interdependence of lives, and (4) human agency in choice making. It is the interplay of these four themes that defines the meanings of the events that individuals encounter over their life spans. It is important to recognize that, from a contextualist perspective, the four do not function independent of one another but rather represent four perspectives from which to consider the interdependent nature of life course.

THE INTERPLAY OF HUMAN LIVES AND HISTORICAL TIMES   The interplay of human lives and historical times is, in effect, a definition of a cohort effect. Elder sees different historical times as exposing individuals to different priorities, constraints, and options. Furthermore, because different cohorts will experience these particular historical pressures at different developmental levels, the impact that these events will have, in both the short term and the long term, can differ significantly.

However, Elder is not simply interested in demonstrating that historical events do make a difference in the lives of individuals. To do only that is to identify cohort as another main effect and, as such, place it within a mechanistic model. Elder's interest is more specific and bounded. Not only does he want to demonstrate that different cohorts experience historic events differently, but of greater relevance to his contextualist orientation, he wants to understand how the particular weave of a particular time and place is reflected in the behavior of individuals and families. Because historical acts are always specific to some time and place, Elder's primary goal is a search not for universal patterns but for a greater understanding of the playing out of events specific to historical times such as the Great Depression, war, or social revolution—that is, times of drastic social change.

THE TIMING OF LIVES   The continuing impact of historical events is not merely a function of developmental level. Its impact is also a function of the social roles prescribed by that society and, more specifically, how the individual is playing out each of these social roles. Such social timing defines (1) the social events (e.g., marriage, parenthood, and retirement) that constitute a social life within a particular sociohistorical context, (2) the timing of those events in terms of when they should occur, (3) the sequencing of those events in terms of the order in which they occur (e.g., the socially preferred order of marriage and parenthood), and (4) the socially accepted duration between events (e.g., social norms about the interval between marriage and the birth of a first child).

Because individuals develop along more than one trajectory, the synchrony between social trajectories is also reflected in the timing of lives. For example, the interplay between the adult trajectories of marriage, parenthood, and work—their goodness of fit, if you will—is a significant factor in the life course of most adults. Another example of such synchrony or asynchrony is the onset of physical maturation in young adolescents and the social expectations typical of that age group. Early and late maturers, both boys and girls, experience the puberty transition differently from those more "on time." These differences often have long-term as well as short-term consequences (Turkewitz & Devenny, 1993).

THE LINKING OF LIVES   Just as it is possible to consider the interdependence of different trajectories for any one individual, it is also possible (Elder would argue essential) to consider the interdependence of different individuals' lives.

> No principle of life course study is more central than the notion of interdependent lives. Human lives are typically embedded in social relationships with kin and friends across the life span. Social regulation and support occur in part through these relationships. Processes of this kind are expressed across the life cycle of socialization, behavioral exchange, and generational succession. The misfortune and the opportunity of adult children, as well as their personal problems, become intergenerational. (Elder, 1994, p. 6)

The concept of linked lives is most easily appreciated in terms of family relationships. Clearly events in the lives of parents have profound influences on the lives of their children, and vice versa. But the principle holds across all forms of relationships, whether the link is through kinship or the workplace or the community. And these links exist across the entire life spans of the individuals. The interdependence of lives is just as evident when parents are elderly and their children middle-aged as it is when parents are young adults and their children infants and toddlers.

HUMAN AGENCY   Elder believes that the life course is more than a sequence of historical events impinging on linked lives. The life course also reflects the principle of human agency. Human agency is evident in two ways. First, individuals make choices within the range of options and resources available. At the same time, however, the very notion of the options and resources available within a particular context are a reflection of how the individual conceptualizes that situation. This meaning-making aspect of human agency is therefore reflected both in a quantitative sense of how many options are envisioned and in a qualitative sense of the relative value and risk of the options envisioned. A situation that for one person holds few options and promises may for another be envisioned as offering the chances of a lifetime. No doubt one reason Elder has been so interested in periods of drastic social change is to see how personal choice and meaning making are affected by particular major transitions.

Elder's Research

Probably no piece of research better illustrates the integration of Elder's four themes than his studies of the impact of the Great Depression. The original work, *Children of the Great Depression,* published in 1974, followed a single cohort of children from the Oakland, California, area who were born between 1920 and 1922. By virtue of their years of birth, this cohort experienced childhood during a time of economic affluence and adolescence during a period of what was for many significant economic deprivation. They graduated from high school just as the economic outlook was beginning to brighten and just before the start of World War II. Many served in the military and at war's end entered their adult years during a period marked by remarkable economic growth, social stability, and, for veterans, ample opportunities for a free or low-cost education.

Elder wanted to know the impact that such a momentous and contrasting set of social events had on this cohort, in terms of both the specifics of their lives and their interpretations of these experiences. Although the 1974 study looked at only one cohort, subsequent work has examined the impact of the same set of historical events on cohorts with different birth dates.

Elder examined the impact of the Depression by looking at four distinct family groups within this cohort. Each group was defined in terms of socioeconomic status (middle class versus working class) and degree of economic loss (moderate versus significant). Elder focused on the actual ways that families in each of the four groups coped with their life changes and the impact these adaptations had on their children's perceptions of life events.

Economic loss in the deprived group was three to four times greater than in the nondeprived group. This was true in both social classes, although there were more deprived families in the working-class group. Because within this cohort the employment of women outside of the home was a rare event, loss of income was almost exclusively a reflection of changes in the father's employment status. Although most Oakland families were able to regain their pre-Depression economic status by 1941, the year the United States entered World War II, Elder found that the legacy of the Depression did not end with the return of economic sufficiency.

Families coped with economic loss both by reducing expenditures and by finding ways to acquire additional income. Families turned to public and private assistance, and they took in boarders when possible.[3] Mothers and children sought outside income, a significant move in an era when fathers saw themselves as the sole breadwinners in the family.

All of these role changes brought about significant changes in both family dynamics and individual psychological states. Fathers' psychological states were particularly affected because they saw themselves as failing in their primary roles as provider and head of the household. Ironically, at the same time that economic loss brought about

---

[3] Because individuals and families were often unable to maintain rent and mortgage payments, many lost their own housing and were forced to rent rooms in others' homes.

declines in fathers' psychological health and status, in some ways those of mothers and children actually increased. Because mothers assumed a greater financial role in the family and because adjusting to economic loss meant that most families had to resort to more labor-intensive strategies (e.g., growing food rather than buying it), both mothers and children assumed more meaningful and essential roles in the family.

With respect to older children and adolescents, Elder notes that many took jobs outside the family and so had more adultlike contact with nonfamily adults than would have been the case otherwise. The nature of these contacts followed what for the time were very traditional patterns (if anything, the Depression experience prompted gender roles to become more traditional and stereotypic). But in all cases these children and adolescents took a social leap into adulthood before they were ready to do so psychologically. As Elder (1974) describes the pattern:

> According to our analysis, the roles children performed in the economy of deprived families paralleled traditional sex differences in the division of labor, and oriented them toward adult ways. Economic hardship and jobs increased the desire to associate with adults, to "grow up" and become an adult. This adult orientation is congruent with other behavioral correlates of roles in the household economy, including the responsible use of money (as perceived by mothers), energetic or industrious behavior, dependability and domesticity among girls and the social independence of boys. (p. 82)

Although Elder believes that these behaviors were both a necessary and an appropriate response to the changes in family conditions, he nevertheless raises concerns about the long-term consequences of an accelerated coming of age. He notes, for example, that adolescents from deprived families saw themselves in much more negative terms than their peers and teachers saw them. This was especially true for girls.

Although all these changes were true of most families, Elder found that their significance differed across social class. Middle-class families were more affected by the perceived loss of social status that accompanied economic loss; working-class families, perhaps having less social status to concern themselves with, were more affected by the consequences of their actual loss of income. Elder notes that mothers' roles changed not only in terms of assuming added economic responsibilities but also in terms of mediating the link between fathers' loss of economic power and their children's perception of the accompanying loss of social status. The mother who reacted negatively to the father's changing economic status seemed to convey this displeasure to their children. The result was a significant loss of status for the father in their children's eyes.

Elder also points out that even though all families suffered some degree of economic deprivation, how families interpreted their situation was also a significant factor in how they responded to their changing circumstances. In some instances families came to see themselves as essentially passive victims of large social forces. Seeing the causes of their hardship as beyond their control also meant that they were equally likely to see effective coping strategies as beyond their control. In terms of economic, social, and psychological measures, these families suffered the greatest harm from the Depression. By contrast, families that accepted that they were not the cause of their troubles but still recognized that there were things they could do to cope with their cir-cumstance were much more effective in maintaining a degree of economic, social, and psychological stability.

The Depression did end by the end of the 1930s. World War II followed (some argue that it actually was the war itself that ended the Depression) and after that a remarkable decade of economic and social prosperity and stability for many Ameri-cans. How did the children of these Oakland families cope with these new life experi-ences? To what degree, if any, did the Depression leave a legacy? What form might that legacy take? The second half of *Children of the Great Depression* examined these issues.

In general, for men the war and the educational opportunities that followed meant that most of the Oakland sample, both deprived and nondeprived, acquired good educational experiences and good employment. In this sense the Depression had little negative impact on adult work experiences. But at another level Elder (1974) notes that there were significant differences in the meaning attached to work.

> In both the middle and working classes, boys from deprived families arrived at a
> firmer vocational commitment in late adolescence and were more likely to be judged
> mature in vocational interests than the offspring of non deprived parents. In adult-
> hood, they entered a stable career line at an earlier age, developed a more orderly
> career, and were more likely to have followed the occupation which they preferred in
> adolescence. Vocational maturity in crystallized interests established a positive link
> between family deprivation and occupational attainment, and at least partly offset the
> educational handicap of a deprived background. (pp. 200–201)

These differences in orientation to work were even evident when these men reached middle age. Issues of job security and reasonable income continued to be much more important to those from families suffering economic deprivation 30 years earlier than to those from relatively nondeprived families. Furthermore, leisure activi-ties meant little to these previously deprived men; home and work were their lives.

The legacy of the Depression was also significant for women, especially for those from deprived families. Elder found that these women were much more receptive to traditional women's roles as they were defined in the 1940s and 1950s. They married at an earlier age and were more involved in household routines. They were less likely to attend college, and if they did work, they were more likely to stop at marriage or the birth of a child. As was true of the men who showed little interest in activities outside of the home and family, for many of these women from deprived families, marriage and family were their lives.

To leave the story of the effects of the Depression at this point might give the impression that there were some significant "main effects" acting, in both the short and long term, on those who experienced it. The issue is, as Elder shows, clearly more complicated. By comparing the long- and short-term impact of the Depression on two other cohorts—one older and one younger than the Oakland sample—Elder demon-strates the contextual embeddedness that is reflected in his four themes.

Data from two other longitudinal samples also was available to Elder. The Terman sample involved children born between 1900 and 1920, and the Berkeley sample included children born between 1928 and 1929. Because of the differences in the birth dates of these three cohorts, they experienced the same set of events at different points in their lives (see Table 13.1). The older members of Terman's sample were trying to enter the job market during the depths of the Depression while the Berkeley children were in their early childhoods. The Terman sample also served in World War II, but unlike the Oakland sample their service interrupted already started adult lives. The Berkeley sample was too young to serve in World War II, but many did serve during the Korean War. All three samples experienced the same set of historical events, but they did so at different points in their lives and by assuming different roles in the family. It is only when we examine the differences in the experiences of the three cohorts that it becomes clear why contextualists are reluctant to generalize across time and place.

With respect to the timing of military service, Elder argues that the Oakland sample, by entering the military as they were making the transition from late adolescence to early adulthood, did so at just the "right time." That is, they entered before having established adult careers and at a time when they were still deciding on a life direction. As such, the military offered a dramatic break from the impact of the Depression. Furthermore, for those who were fortunate enough to return from the war, the educational benefits of the G.I. Bill allowed them the opportunity to act on their newly formed sense of adulthood.

In contrast, the consequences of military service for the older Terman cohort were very different. Because they had already entered the adult years by the start of the war, most had married, many were parents, and all had entered some sort of work or career path. For this cohort service was more a disruption than a transition point. The return to civilian life was marked not by opportunities to start adult roles but by efforts to put things back together again. The difference left a legacy. Elder describes the adult lives of the Terman men as punctuated by many difficulties: "They suffered more work instability, earned less income over time, experienced a higher rate of divorce, and were at greater risk of an accelerated decline in physical health by their fifties" (1998, p. 9). This adult life pattern for the Terman men seems even more remarkable when we consider the nature of the group. Unlike the Oakland and Berkeley samples, which represented a cross-section of the middle- and working-class community in Oakland, California, at that time, the Terman sample, established by Louis Terman (one of the early proponents of intelligence testing in the United States) was designed to study the development of gifted and very high-intelligence individuals. This sample represented the best of the best.

What about the Berkeley cohort, those who were young children during the Depression? Whereas members of the Oakland cohort were in their adolescence and were therefore actually able to play a meaningful role in helping their families deal with adversity, members of the younger Berkeley cohort were still at home, able to do little to alleviate their families' economic difficulties. But by being present in the home, this younger cohort was more likely to experience the impact of the family stresses accompanying the loss of income and family disruption. Elder reports that the Berkeley cohort had lower scores on measures of self-confidence during childhood and on measures of assertiveness, social competence, and aspirations during adolescence (Elder & Hareven, 1993). Elder believes that these differences reflect the opportunities provided the two cohorts to acquire a sense of human agency, one of his four themes.

TABLE 13.1

Age of Oakland and Berkeley Cohort Members by Historical Events

Date	Event	Age of Cohort Members	
		Oakland	Berkeley
1880–1900	Birth years of OGS parents		
1890–1910	Birth years of BGS parents		
1920–21		Birth	
1921–22	Depression		
1923	Great Berkeley Fire	2–3	
1923–29	General economic boom, growth of "debt pattern" way of life, cultural change in sexual mores	1–9	
1928–29			Birth
1929–30	Onset of Great Depression	9–10	1–2
1932–33	Depth of Great Depression	11–13	3–5
1933–36	Partial recovery, increasing cost of living, labor strikes	12–16	4–8
1937–38	Economic slump	16–18	8–10
1939–40	Incipient stage of wartime mobilization	18–20	10–12
1941–43	Major growth of war industries (shipyards, munitions plants, etc.) and military forces	20–23	12–15
1945	End of World War II	24–25	16–17
1946–49	Postwar economic growth	25–29	17–21
1950–53	Korean War and McCarthy era	30–33	22–25
1954–59	Civil rights era begins	34–39	26–31
1960–73	Civil rights mobilization, urban civil strife, Vietnam War	40–53	32–45
1974–	End of affluent age in postwar America: energy crisis, rising inflation	54–	46–

Source: Elder & Hareven, 1993, p. 15.

The older Oakland cohort was old enough to be able to do something to help the family cope with its economic losses. These opportunities provided a sense of purpose and meaning, and as such, a sense of self that emphasized human agency. The younger Berkeley cohort, being too young to engage in such purposeful activity, was left to experience the adversity without the opportunity to do much about it.

Elder's research is much too extensive to be fully reviewed in this discussion, but before we discuss how his work reflects his four themes, it is worthwhile mentioning one other cohort effect. The Depression studies suggest that in general the outcome for women was more favorable than for men, especially for women in the middle class. Because they were not viewed as breadwinners, their families' loss of income was not seen as a reflection on them. To the contrary, the opportunities that hardship and adversity provided for them to make a contribution to the family actually gave many of them a heightened sense of value and purpose. And this was further reinforced by the need for female labor during World War II. Unprecedented numbers of women joined the work force and often worked in heavy industrial roles previously reserved for men. The image of "Rosie the Riveter" is certainly one enduring image from that era.

The social forces of contemporary America are significantly different from those of the 1930s and 1940s. This is especially true in terms of the lives of women. Elder (1994) notes that, although there are similarities in the findings of his studies of the impact of the Depression in the 1930s and those of the drastic fall in farm prices in the 1980s, a major exception involved mothers.

> In the Iowa research, the mother's emotional distress represents a strong link between economic pressure and marital discord. By comparison, mothers in the Depression study were less prominent as a social and emotional link between hard times and the children's developmental experiences. Plausible explanations for this difference include historic trends in women's social roles, especially in the workplace. Women in the 1930s were far less deeply involved in the financial support and management of their families than are Iowa women in the 1990s. (p. 12)

Life Span Cohort Models in Perspective

The changing role of women is a good example of why contextualists are leery of making generalizations across sociohistorical contexts. The example also serves as a good illustration of the interdependence of Elder's four themes of the life course. These four themes, in turn, serve to highlight the focus of contextualist research and theory. In so doing, they illustrate how life span cohort models in particular and contextualism in general differ from both organicism and mechanism.

Elder's four themes are (1) the interplay of human lives and historical times, (2) the timing of life events, (3) the linking of lives, and (4) the role of human agency. Each human action can be understood as reflecting the interaction of these four themes. The themes serve to place human action in time and place, to emphasize the role of cultural values and beliefs, to acknowledge that all human endeavor reflects interpersonal and intergenerational contacts, and to highlight that ultimately the meaning of life events is as much assigned by the individual as by the sociohistorical context.

Given these four themes, it is not hard to appreciate why cohort theorists argue for a situated theory of human development. A situated theory does not seek abstractions or universals but rather tries to understand human effort within the particular contexts in which it occurs. Similarities across contexts will produce similarities in effort and outcome. However, for cohort theorists, as for all contextualists, such similarities are not the norm and therefore should not always be expected. Furthermore, even when similarities in setting are found, the specific life histories of the participants in each setting will always limit the degree of generalization possible. In other words, even though Elder finds some similarities between events in the Depression and in the more recent farm crisis in the Midwest, a full understanding of one does not provide a full understanding of the other. For each there are elements unique to it.

A failure to appreciate this caution often leads, contextualists argue, to the confusion of "is" and "ought." As mentioned earlier in the chapter, such confusion is a particularly serious problem for contextualists given the applied focus of their interests. They would argue that a failure to recognize that the relative status of different groups of individuals in a society is a reflection of the present structure of that society rather than some more universal, natural cause is often the reason inequities are perpetuated. By contrast, recognizing the situational embeddedness of human social structures makes it easier to recognize that the inequities that might exist in a society are not inevitable. It is this situated perspective on social issues that is one of the ways that contextualism as a world view is particularly useful.

The life span (or as Elder prefers to call it, the life course) cohort perspective serves two other useful purposes. First, it prompts us to consider our definitions of development—in particular, a definition of development that encompasses the events of an entire lifetime rather than just part of it. This is a significant theoretical and practical issue because effective social policy must be based on a sound theoretical base. Second, it helps remind us that the study of development is the study of the lives of people. This is not to suggest that organicism and mechanism are not interested in people. Obviously they are. But it does highlight that the quest for universal, and at times idealized, images of development tends to make us forget about the particulars—even the "messiness"—of individual lives. The life span cohort perspective's emphasis on lives embedded in a sociohistorical context may make it more difficult to generalize across particular contexts. But it does make it easier to appreciate the elements defining the lives of individuals within each of these contexts. In this sense the perspective does help us appreciate "what we are."

14

Vygotsky and the Sociocultural Perspective

The focus in the previous chapter was on a comparison of cohorts within a particular cultural setting. The work of Elder and other life span researchers concerns the cumulative impact across the life span of the intersection of specific life events (e.g., the Great Depression) experienced at specific points of the life span. The study of these intersections offers a way for life span researchers to understand the situated nature of development. How they understand it—that is, what research and data analysis strategies they use to interpret their data—distinguishes those who approach the issue of cohort from a mechanistic perspective from those who approach it from a contextualist perspective. For those, like Elder, whose perspective is contextualist, the goal is to understand the unique developmental experience of each successive cohort within a culture.

The *sociocultural perspective* asks a question similar to that of Elder. However, instead of looking at cohorts within cultures, sociocultural researchers take a step back so as to get the broader perspective of how the structure and function of particular cultures influence the structure and function of an individual's development within each culture (Cole, 1996a, 1996b; Wertsch & Kanner, 1992). It is a perspective that places great emphasis on the concept that individual development is always embedded within a cultural context. The perspective is therefore holistic and contextualist. It argues that there is neither a legitimate basis to directly compare cultures in terms of common criteria nor any necessary reason that developmental patterns across cultures should demonstrate the same universal patterns.

The Emergence of the Sociocultural Perspective

The sociocultural perspective has emerged over the past 30 years or so as a result of two interrelated factors: (1) an increasing dissatisfaction with cross-cultural research within the mechanistic and organismic traditions and (2) the translation into English of the writing of the Russian developmentalist Lev Vygotsky.

The Growing Dissatisfaction with Traditional Cross-Cultural Research

The first of these two factors was the increasing dissatisfaction with the cross-cultural research typical in the 1970s (Cole, 1988, 1992; Miller & Goodnow, 1995; Rogoff & Chavajay, 1995). These earlier studies reflected work within both the mechanistic and organismic traditions. In the mechanistic tradition culture was treated as an independent variable in the same sense that reinforcement schedule or characteristics of the model could be considered an independent variable. One or more dependent variables were identified, and the research issue became one of deciding if the children in culture A were in some way better, worse, or the same as the children in culture B. The research was truly cross-cultural in the sense that comparisons and even rankings were made across cultures.

In the organismic tradition most cross-cultural research attempted to demonstrate the universality of Piaget's developmental stages. In some cases the tasks were identical to those Piaget used with the children of Geneva; in others the task was modified so that it would be "culturally equivalent." In other words, instead of asking children about the amount of water in different-shaped glasses, or the amount of clay in different-shaped forms, or about ways to sort and classify geometric objects, the materials used would be ones common to that culture.

Both research strategies, the mechanistic and the organismic, rest on the assumption of the universality of developmental patterns. If we accept this assumption as true, then it is legitimate to make comparisons across and between cultures or to validate a theory by attempting to show that predictions from that theory hold equally well in different cultural settings.

Contextualists argue that the data generated through these two strategies is not a convincing argument for universality. The task of identifying "culturally equivalent" testing conditions became so problematic as to raise questions about the comparability of data obtained in different cultures. In fact, the only consistent conclusion that can be drawn from these earlier studies is that children's cognitive performance across cultures is best predicted by whether they have attended Western-style schools. In other words, these comparisons said less about the level of some ability (e.g., intelligence or concrete operations) than they did about the similarity of the experiences of these different children in different cultures. Contextualists argue that this should not be surprising because our tests of basic cognitive skills actually are little more than tests of the competencies that children are expected to learn in schools. To contextualists, what is ironic about these early cross-cultural studies is that they did a better job of showing the impact of one cultural setting (i.e., Western-style educational practices) than they did differences between different cultural settings (Rogoff & Chavajay, 1995). Ironic as well is the fact that skill on school tasks did not necessarily predict skill on nonschooled tasks. In fact, as researchers began to look closely at "everyday cognition," they found that individuals in different cultures were clearly more competent than the prior, schooling-linked studies had suggested. And as researchers increasingly began to look at measures of competency specific to a particular culture, the field began to shift away from comparisons of presumed universal, content-free cognitive competencies to ones embedded in time and place. As Rogoff and Chavajay (1995) note with respect to studies of memory:

Whereas less schooled individuals may have less practice in organizing isolated bits of information, people from all backgrounds may have similar needs to remember information that is embedded in a structured context and to use strategies that incorporate the existing organization, using meaningful relationships among items as an aid to recall. With contextually organized materials, there seem to be fewer cultural differences in memory performance, as the majority of memory problems for any individual involve material that is organized in a complex and meaningful fashion rather than lists of items that have been stripped of organization. (p. 862)

The findings on memory tasks, as well as on other tasks that traditionally have been used to study cognitive development in North American and European settings, led contextually oriented researchers to become disenchanted with the notion of identifying universal, context-free measures of development or even valid ways of making developmental comparisons across cultures. Increasingly the argument was made that the problem was not one of methodology but rather one of conceptualization. Context-free measures could not be found because there was no such thing to be found. As a result, the interest shifted toward examining development within rather than across settings. And as the approach increasingly came to focus on development within settings, the perspective stopped being cross-cultural and came to be known as sociocultural.

The Rediscovery of Vygotsky

If development was not universal but was always situated within a sociohistorical context, then a new theoretical framework was needed to guide this new perspective on development. This new perspective is increasingly coming to be recognized as that offered in the work of Lev Vygotsky (1896–1934). Although born in the same year as Piaget, Vygotsky's life was much shorter. After a long battle with tuberculosis, he finally succumbed in 1934. Because of his shortened life, his writing was not as prolific as Piaget's, and what was written was suppressed by the Soviet government for many years. Only since the 1960s has his work begun to appear in English (Vygotsky, 1962, 1978, 1997; Vygotsky & Luria, 1993), and only more recently have developmentalists begun to seriously consider the implications of his theoretical arguments (Kozulin, 1990; Moll, 1990; Tryphon & Voneche, 1996; van der Veer & Valsiner, 1991; Wertsch, 1985, 1991).

We will examine Vygotsky's work in great detail later in the chapter. For now, however, it is sufficient to know that Vygotsky's seminal idea was that development is a *co-constructed* rather than a constructed phenomenon. The difference between the two terms may seem trivial, but it is anything but. By proposing a co-constructed image of development, Vygotsky was arguing for the recognition of the particular structure of the culture as defining not only the content of an individual's development but also the very structures through which this content functions. For Vygotsky, what is *intramental* is first always *intermental*. That is, development always evolves out an individual's immersion in specific culturally defined activities, practices, and rituals. Because of this, the focus of analysis for Vygotsky is the *child in context*. It is only through the child's engagement in culturally defined practices that he or she gradually internalizes the psychological structures and dimensions relevant to that particular cultural setting.

Defining Elements of the Sociocultural Perspective

In her review of the sociocultural perspective, Rogoff (Rogoff & Chavajay, 1995) states that "the stance of sociocultural approaches to cognitive development is that the intellectual development of children is inherently involved with their participation in sociocultural activities" (p. 871). As such, an understanding of development requires an understanding of the cultural practices and institutions in which individuals participate. This emphasis on culture, in turn, directs the researcher to examine individual *activity,* because what a person does reflects the structures defining that culture.

Activity focuses on people engaged in socioculturally defined practices and rituals, using culturally defined tools and processes in culturally prescribed ways. These activities not only reflect existing cultural practices but also serve to transform these practices, because each succeeding generation or cohort within a culture constructs new tools and practices and redefines old ones. Activity differs from behavior in that activity is always defined in context whereas behavior is a property of the individual. Activity also differs from schemata in that activity exists at the intersocial level while schemata exist at the intrapsychological level.

The study of development within a sociocultural perspective, then, is the study of activity. Rogoff (Rogoff & Chavajay, 1995) describes this process as an "analysis of sociocultural activities [that] involves examination of the active and dynamic contributions from individuals, their social partners, and historical traditions and materials and their transformations as people engage in shared endeavors" (p. 871). A sociocultural perspective is therefore a multidisciplinary perspective involving psychologists, sociologists, anthropologists, linguists, historians, and others. This multidisciplinary perspective is necessary because individuals are always embedded within multifaceted social structures having both a cultural and a phylogenetic history (Bronfenbrenner, 1989). One interesting consequence of this multidisciplinary approach is that there is no one methodology associated with the sociocultural perspective. Unlike mechanism, in which there is a very close link between method and theory, here method is defined by the question asked. The only restriction is that the method must allow for a holistic analysis. Otherwise, the method may be one drawn from any discipline or one that reflects an integration of strategies across disciplines.

Finally, a sociocultural perspective does not assume generality across contexts. The goal is not to make comparisons across contexts but rather to understand development within a particular context. As Rogoff notes, one might focus on how individuals within a culture come to participate in the practices of that culture, how participation in one practice relates to participation in another, how cultural practices structure psychological structures, and how the activity of individuals transforms cultural practices.

Vygotsky's Cultural-Historical Theory of Development

A full understanding of the sociocultural perspective on human development requires first an understanding of Vygotsky's *cultural-historical theory.* It is Vygotsky's work that is the theoretical foundation of the sociocultural perspective.

A Short Biography

It is perhaps only fitting that the person whose name is virtually synonymous with contextualism should himself have lived through such a tumultuous period of history as describes Russia between the years of 1896 and 1934. It is no coincidence that Vygotsky's fundamental notion—that the structure of the sociohistorical context defines the structure of individual thought—was also the philosophical rationale for the Russian Revolution that was supposed to change Russia from an absolute monarchy to a utopian, egalitarian socialist state. History tells us that the course of Russian history since the 1917 revolution has been anything but toward a "workers' paradise." But in those heady early days surrounding the revolution itself, this powerful, idealistic notion influenced the thought of most Russian intellectuals, including Vygotsky.

Lev Semyonovich Vygotsky was born in 1896 in the small town of Orsha. Within a year his family moved to Gomel, a somewhat larger and more culturally active community. Both cities are in what is now Belorussia. Although information about his early life is sketchy, his major biographers (Kozulin, 1990; van der Veer & Valsiner, 1991; Wertsch, 1985) agree that his parents were well educated and relatively prosperous. His father was a banker and a manager of insurance companies. His mother was educated as a teacher but remained at home to raise Lev and his seven siblings. Music, literature, drama, and art were ever present qualities in the Vygodsky home.[1] Probably because of the family's prosperity, Vygotsky was educated at home by private tutors. By all accounts he was a remarkable child. His range of interests was broad and he excelled in his studies; today, we would certainly call him gifted.

The Vygodsky's were Jewish, and to be Jewish in tsarist Russia carried significant meaning. It meant that one was restricted to certain geographic areas to live, that certain occupations were unavailable outside of one's own community, and that opportunities for higher education were severely restricted. It meant as well that one was subject to pogroms—indiscriminate, unprovoked, and often brutal attacks on Jews and their homes and businesses by other Russians. During pogroms public officials, including the police, often looked the other way and were probably themselves participants in many. It is no wonder that, having grown up in such a discriminatory and at times brutal context, Vygotsky and most other Jews welcomed socialism (as did many other

---

[1] Vygotsky's family name was actually Vygodsky. He changed the spelling of his name as a young man because he believed that it more accurately reflected the regional origins of the family. To be more exact, Vygotsky believed that the family originated from the community of Vygotovo—hence, apparently, the decision to spell the name with a *t* rather than a *d*.

Russians, for that matter, whose lot wasn't appreciably better than that of the Jews under the tsar). Being a Jew and being a socialist, for most, soon became synonymous.

When Vygotsky completed his high school education, he applied for one of the 3% of the slots made available to Jews at Moscow University. He was admitted, but only by chance. Even though he had graduated with highest honors, Russian authorities had just changed the application process for Jews so that they were admitted through a lottery rather than by their exam grades. The purpose of such a change was to ensure that "the best and the brightest" didn't have the chance to become the leaders of their communities.

Vygotsky entered Moscow University in 1913 to study medicine. Within a month, however, he had changed his major to law and completed his degree in 1917. While he was studying at Moscow University, he also took courses in psychology, philosophy, literature, and history at Shanyavskii People's University. Wertsch (1985) describes this school as "an unofficial school that sprang up in 1911 after the Minister of Education had expelled most of the students and more than 100 of the faculty from Moscow University in a crackdown on antitsarist activity" (p. 6).

Surprisingly there is little information on the impact of the revolution on Vygotsky or on whether he participated in antitsarist activity. Following graduation he returned to Gomel to teach literature, logic, education, language, and psychology. He taught at a variety of schools and was actively involved in literary and drama groups. He read extensively during this seven-year period, particularly the great literature of the day and the leading texts in philosophy and psychology.

During this time he also established in Gomel a small psychology laboratory at a local teacher's college where, in addition to giving instruction on psychological methods to aspiring teachers, he conducted his own investigations of reflexive behavior and began work on a book based on his lectures at the college. The book has only recently been published in English (Vygotsky, 1997). His work at the college provided him an opportunity to work with children having special needs—in particular, blindness, deafness, and mental retardation. His work with these children was to prove very significant for his later efforts. He apparently never practiced law.

It is also important to note that, during this time in Gomel, tuberculosis struck his family. His younger brother Dodik died, and by 1920 his own condition was so serious that there were concerns for his life as well. After a spell in a sanitarium, his health returned, and he was able to resume his activities. But in that era tuberculosis was a fatal disease, and Vygotsky knew that his life would be short. Living with such a knowledge no doubt contributed to the frantic pace of the last 14 years of his life and his practice of only sketching the many elements and implications of his theorizing.

Up to this point in Vygotsky's life, little had occurred that either suggested a clear future direction for his efforts or indicated the brilliance that was soon to become so evident. All this was to change, however, in 1924 when Vygotsky was invited to deliver a paper in Leningrad at the Second Psychoneurological Conference, the foremost gathering of psychologists in Russia at that time. Luria (1979), who was to become a colleague and interpreter of Vygotsky's, describes the presentation as momentous:

> When Vygotsky got up to deliver his speech, he had no printed text from which to read, not even notes. Yet he spoke fluently, never seeming to stop and search his

memory for the next idea. Even had the content of his speech been pedestrian, his performance would have been notable for the persuasiveness of his style. But his speech was by no means pedestrian. Instead of choosing a minor theme, as might befit a young man of twenty-eight speaking for the first time to a gathering of the graybeards of his profession, Vygotsky chose the difficult theme of the relation between conditioned reflexes and man's conscious behavior. . . . Although he failed to convince everyone of the correctness of his view, it was clear that this man from a small provincial town in western Russia was an intellectual force who had to be listened to. (pp. 38–39)

One tangible way that this recognition was soon given was that Vygotsky was invited, largely on the basis of this presentation, to join the staff of the Psychology Institute in Moscow.

The last decade of his life was very productive. He soon developed a very loyal following of colleagues (most notably Alexander Luria and Aleksei Leont'ev) and students, and he wrote and lectured widely on his vision of development. By all accounts he was held in awe. This partly reflected his remarkable intellect and his skills at presenting information. But it also reflected the moment in Russia.

The early years following the revolution were a unique period of intellectual excitement and fervor. Despotic, autocratic rule had been eliminated, and a belief in the goodness and competence of common men and women had taken hold. Nothing was more important than making the new socialist state a reality. Vygotsky's ideals were an important element of this effort because he was offering an account of development at the psychological level that paralleled that of Marx and Engels at the economic and historical levels. Much of his writing during this last decade of his life was dedicated to a translation of Marxist's principles to developmental issues—in particular, to the concept of how the intramental begins as the intermental. These writings offered a theoretical explanation of how individuals can transform themselves through their personal labor. The form of this labor (socialist, capitalist, or feudal) was seen as structuring both society and one's psychological self. Change the conditions of labor, and you change society; change society, and you change the individual. This may not seem such a radical notion today, but in a time and place when status was conferred by birth and considered permanent and when those in power justified their rule by the claim that others were incapable of ruling themselves, it was indeed revolutionary.

It was not enough, however, for Vygotsky simply to serve as a major psychological theoretician of the revolution. He also assumed responsibility for many of the pressing social problems affecting the new socialist state, including widespread illiteracy, significant cultural differences among peoples who were now all to be Soviet, and an almost total lack of services for those less able to participate in the new society (Wertsch, 1985). In particular, much of Vygotsky's efforts were directed toward developing and implementing education interventions for children with special needs, a cause he first pursued while still in Gomel following his graduation from college.

During this last decade his bouts with tuberculosis became more frequent and severe. Rather than heeding his doctor's order to rest, he worked at an increasingly more frantic pace. He died on June 11, 1934, and is buried in Moscow.

Vygotsky's work was suppressed by the Stalinists for about 20 years following his death. Stalin's brutal regime, which had begun in the late 1920s, effectively put an end to an idealized notion of a workers' paradise. A tsar of the political left had come to replace a tsar of the political right. Vygotsky's "crime" was his concept of development —the idea that people can better themselves through their efforts. The idea was inconsistent with Stalin's ideology that the then illiterate masses in the rural regions of the (former) Soviet Union already had the same intellectual competence as people in Western nations. To suggest that any Soviet, irrespective of circumstance, was in some sense less than someone from another country, particularly in the West, was considered treasonous. The Stalinists simply repressed, usually brutally (Vygotsky's older brother David died in one of Stalin's labor camps), all sources that were inconsistent with the party line that the workers' paradise was already a reality.

Stalin died in 1953, and by 1956 Vygotsky's books again began to be published in Russia and eventually were translated into English and other languages. The interest in his work in the United States and elsewhere reflects both the growing interest in contextualist approaches to development and the continuing reevaluation of Piaget's universalist position.

Vygotsky's Theoretical Arguments

Vygotsky's cultural-historical theory is more in the form of a rough draft than a well-laid-out and empirically tested set of propositions. Given the events of his time, his always precarious health status, and his early death at the age of 38, this should not be surprising. What is surprising is that this rough sketch has come increasingly to be recognized among contextualists and others as offering such a conceptually rich source of ideas about human development.

Vygotsky's theory rests on a fundamental idea with three key components: To understand the developmental status of an individual first requires an understanding of the developmental history of that individual. To understand the developmental history of that individual first requires an understanding of the historical evolution of that individual's culture. And to understand the historical evolution of that individual's culture first requires an understanding of the phylogenetic evolution of that individual's species. All three levels of analysis—ontogenetic, historical, and phylogenetic —are best understood as developmental in nature, and an understanding of all three levels is necessary for a complete understanding of the process of development. All the particulars of his theory reflect his efforts to verify what he referred to as a "genetic" concept and to illuminate its implications. Probably the best way to examine these particulars is to first consider his phylogenetic-historical-ontogenetic argument and then to consider the theoretical implications of this developmental sequence.

VYGOTSKY'S GENETIC ANALYSIS   The first thing to understand about Vygotsky's *genetic analysis* is that the term is not meant to refer to genetics per se (i.e., chromosomes and mechanisms of inheritance). Rather, it is used in its more generic sense to refer to the origins of something. In this case Vygotsky is asking about the origins of mature human thought. Consider how he (Vygotsky & Luria, 1993) describes this search for origins.

The structure of our essays may be outlined as follows. The use and "invention" of tools by anthropoid apes brings to an end the organic stage of behavioral development in the evolutionary sequence and prepares the way for a transition of all development to a new path, creating thereby the *main psychological prerequisite of historical development in behavior.* Labor and, connected with it, the development of human speech and other psychological signs used by primitive man to gain control over behavior signify the beginning of cultural or historical behavior in the proper sense of the word. Finally, in child development, we clearly see a second line of development paralleling the processes of organic growth and maturation, that is, we see the cultural development of behavior based on the acquisition of skills and modes of cultural behavior and thinking (p. 37)

Phylogenetic Evolution—Ape to Human   What is it about apes that distinguishes their behavior from ours? This was the first question that Vygotsky asked in his genetic analysis because, as he notes, the difference between ape and human marks the transition from phylogenetic to historical evolution.

Vygotsky did not himself study apes but rather relied on the work of Wolfgang Kohler (1887–1967), a German psychologist who, between 1912 and 1920 on the Tenerife Islands, studied tool use in chimpanzees. Vygotsky, like most developmentalists of his time, saw phylogenetic evolution as a much more linear process than we do now. Vygotsky argued that the course of phylogenetic evolution could be appreciated as a sequence from species lower on the phylogenetic scale functioning at an instinctual level, to the later evolution of species who are also capable of both operant and classical conditioning, and finally, in the case of the apes, to the appearance of simple tool use and some forms of insight. Most of Kohler's work examined how chimps used tools to solve problems.

Kohler's work is quite extensive, but a few examples of his studies are sufficient for our purpose. In his most classic study chimps in a cage were shown a piece of fruit on the other side of the cage, attached to a rope. The chimps appeared to quickly and easily recognize the relation between the rope and the fruit, pulling the rope toward them in order to reach the fruit; that is, they used the rope as a tool. A second experiment again involved the chimps and a piece of fruit outside of the cage, with the chimps able to reach the fruit by using a stick inside of the cage. A still more dramatic example of chimp problem solving was the demonstration that chimps could even put sticks together (by placing the end of one into another) to make a stick long enough to reach a piece of fruit placed out of the range of any single stick. The chimps seemed equally adept at stacking boxes to reach a piece of fruit suspended from a high wire.

But there are limits to chimps' problem-solving skills, limits that Vygotsky saw as defining the phylogenetic boundary between ape and human. In the first place, the chimps are able to use objects as tools only so long as the object and the goal (i.e., the piece of fruit) are in the same perceptual field. There have to be boxes visually available to stack; the chimp will not go off in search of one. Furthermore, if another chimp is sitting on a box, the problem-solving chimp never goes to get it, apparently unable to recognize its height value when it is being used for another purpose. And although chimps can use objects as tools, their preferred mode of action is usually more direct. Finally, chimps' tool use never has a social context; it never has a cumulative impact across individuals or across generations. In other words, the chimps don't demonstrate a historical culture.[2]

Where is the barrier? Why can the chimps only go so far in their problem solving? It is not a question of whether the chimps are able to think. Clearly they are, because they could not devise the solutions they use to obtain the fruit unless they are doing some sort of deliberate mental processing. Rather, the issue is the type of thought they are capable of demonstrating. In particular, their thought appears limited to their ability to mentally manipulate images that are within their perceptual field. To go further, they would need a different symbol system, one that allowed them to deal with objects outside of their sensory or motor awareness. They would need language. For Kohler and Vygotsky it was the absence of language in chimps and its presence in humans that differentiated the two phylogenetically.[3] The chimps did show the ability, at times even a creative ability, to invent tools, and in this sense they are no different from humans, but that's as far as it went. The tools are never used for the purpose of labor—that is, to intentionally alter the environment in a way that conforms to the needs of the individual or the group. And the reason that tools are never used by chimps for the purpose of labor but always are by humans is that humans have ways of representing and acting on their experiences that are not limited to what is in their perceptual field. We have language, and for Vygotsky, that changes everything.

> Thus, in the sphere of adaptation to nature, the absence of labor and, connected with it, control over nature distinguishes ape from man. In the ape, the process of adapting can be generally characterized as a manipulation of external natural conditions and passive adaptation to them. In the psychological sphere, it is again characteristic for the ape to lack self-control over behavior or, in other words, to be unable to control behavior with the use of artificial signs. This constitutes the essence of the cultural development of man's behavior. (Vygotsky & Luria, 1993, pp. 76–77)

Language is one type of artificial sign. Vygotsky believed that language evolves because humans are phylogenetically able to use tools for the purpose of labor (to change the environment to meet their needs). Labor requires some form of cooperative effort, and cooperative effort requires some form of communication. As humans we are able to do this because we have the ability to create and use artificial signs (language) to further our labor, and in so doing, we shift our development as a species from a primary emphasis on biological evolution to a primary emphasis on the historical evolution of cultures.

---

[2] It should be noted that more recent work with chimps has found evidence for the passing on of discovered tool use from one generation to another. Even so, Kohler's major conclusions have held up well.

[3] Here, too, its important to note that more recent research with chimps shows them to be capable of developing and using a significant number of American Sign Language signs. But even here, the use is at best at the level of a young child, is only acquired with much time and effort, and does not appear to become the preferred mode of communication.

Cultural Evolution—Primitive to Cultured   For Vygotsky the crucial difference between humans and apes was the use of language. The fact that apes appear to have little if any linguistic skill meant to Vygotsky that their problem solving would always be limited to what they could do with those objects within their perceptual field. That was their limitation. But language poses no such limitation. By virtue of its arbitrary structure, language offers virtually limitless possibilities. For Vygotsky perhaps the most important of these possibilities was the formation of culture and, with the formation of culture, the possibility of historical evolution across generations or cohorts. Vygotsky now turned from a comparative study of species, ape and human in particular, to a comparative study of cultures. Two important interpreters of Vygotsky's work, Van der Veer and Valsiner (1991), describe this distinction:

> Vygotsky argued that the way the introduction of signs—or stimulus means—changed the whole psychological structure resembled the way tools changed labor operations. Both tool and sign form an intermediate link between object and operation, between object and subject. Both labor operations and instrumental acts are mediated activities, that is, they involve a third element that comes between human beings and nature. The essential difference between instrumental psychological acts and labor operations is that signs are intended to control the psyche and behavior of others and the self, whereas tools are employed to master nature or material objects. Another difference is that stimuli, in contradistinction to tools (which are selected because of their material characteristics, such as flexibility or hardness) do not become signs because of their intrinsic properties; any stimulus can signify any other stimulus. (p. 220)

It is worth noting two things about Vygotsky's approach to the comparison of cultures, even though only one of these is favored by contemporary contextualists. As is true today, Vygotsky did not believe that the differences he noted between cultures were in any sense biological. Rather, they reflected the specifics of the particular sociohistorical contexts that defined each culture. All cultures are therefore capable of any of the accomplishments demonstrated by any one of them. Again, these differences reflect circumstance, not biology.

However, in contrast to current sociocultural theory, Vygotsky was quite comfortable in comparing cultures in terms of their respective levels of historical evolution. In fact, he went so far as to make comparisons between those cultures he described as *primitive* and those he described as *cultured*. Such comparisons were certainly consistent with the thinking of other scholars of his era, particularly Levy-Bruhl (1923, 1926) and Thurnwald (1922), on whose work Vygotsky drew heavily. He did not see such comparisons as in any way derogatory, because circumstance and not biology was the source of these differences. Given our more recent recognition of the great difficulty in or even impossibility of finding equally appropriate ways to compare cultures, we would be reluctant to make such comparisons. Instead, socioculturalists like Rogoff (1995) and Cole (1996a) are much more likely to consider each culture as a unique expression of its sociohistorical context.

Vygotsky focuses on three aspects of human behavior—memory, thought, and number—that he sees as strongly influenced by the historical evolution of cultures. In all three cases he describes a developmental sequence in which the functioning of individuals initially relies exclusively on their biological capacities. Then, gradually, cultures begin to invent *artificial signs,* which are used to shift the balance of power between humans and nature. Artificial signs allow humans to shift the evolutionary focus from phylogeny to history; they are ways to act on nature. They are, in effect, psychological tools and include such things as written and spoken language, number systems, maps, strategies for categorization, and methods of abstraction.

With respect to memory, for example, Vygotsky notes that although "primitives" have excellent memories, often better than those of more "cultured" individuals, their memory strategies are significantly different. Because memory is the only means that these "primitives" have of recording events, their memories tend to be concrete and highly detailed reproductions of actual events. They are, in effect, photographic or eidetic in nature. Furthermore, these memories are recorded holistically; no effort is made to act upon them in some way for the purpose of analysis or grouping. Such a rich oral tradition continues to be present in societies that do not use a written language.

At some point in a culture's evolution, however, a fundamental shift occurs. Artificial signs are invented as memory aids. Initially it might be the use of knots in a lace or notches on a piece of wood or the arrangement or shape of small objects. Later it becomes something resembling a pictogram. And eventually it becomes some type of written language. Vygotsky sees this shift as external development taking the place of internal development. That is, what the group is now able to collectively invent allows the individual to go beyond what he or she alone is biologically capable of.

Vygotsky says that it is essential to understand two points about this shift. First, the development and perfection of these artificial signs (i.e., psychological tools) is a social process, coming about through the interactions of individuals within a culture as they pursue their labor. Thus, what is initially intermental only later becomes intramental. Second, the artificial signs used by one culture are particular to that culture. There are no universal signs. Two or more cultures may invent signs that are *similar,* because their labor and therefore social organization is similar, but in no case are they *identical.* Anyone who has attempted to translate even between languages as similar as French and Italian and Spanish soon realizes that, even in these languages, which share a common root, no one-to-one correspondence in the full meaning of the words exists.

Vygotsky describes the historical development of language in a similar fashion. He depicts "primitive" language as detailed, concrete, and specific, "inundated by a large number of specific terms that precisely discern the individual features and distinctiveness of objects" (Vygotsky & Luria, 1993, p. 109). But what is missing are terms for concepts. Although there may be terms for each type of tree and bird, there is no generic word for either tree or bird. The grammar of these languages shows a similar pattern. Rather than using a generic verb (e.g., *to run*), which can be combined with any one of a number of other words to express a complete thought, these languages are more likely to have many different verbs to describe each instance in which someone or something in that culture might have reason to run.

As cultures continue to evolve and their labor becomes more integrated and complicated, Vygotsky notes that new language forms are invented to make group work more effective and efficient. He calls this second form of language *complexes* to distinguish them from a third form, *concepts*, which develops still later. A complex term is a way to refer to a group that does not rely on abstracting the generic or common properties of that group. Vygotsky gives the example of family names. A family name refers to a group and identifies members as belonging to a group. It is therefore more efficient to talk about the complex than each member of that complex. Concepts, however, are based on the defining properties of the objects belonging to that group. There is no way to tell by looking at a person whether she is a Goldhaber (a complex term), but it is certainly possible to tell by looking at a tall object with leaves that it is a tree (a conceptual term).

The evolution of socially mediated language forms is particularly important to Vygotsky because he sees language as the primary means through which thought is organized. As in the case of memory, what will become intramental starts out as intermental. Also as in the case of memory, language forms are socially mediated constructions and therefore specific to the cultural context in which they evolve.

The pattern for number is the same. What begins as a strategy for designating specific objects evolves, across generations, into a complex abstract notation system for designating concepts that often have no concrete referent. Numbering systems start out as little more than names for objects. They evolve into notations but are still limited by the number of things to be noted; for example, if asked to count 100 sheep, the individual would argue that it can't be done because no one owns 100 sheep. Only later does the culture invent strategies for dealing with quantities and relationships not literally present.

The advantage, as Vygotsky sees it, of the culturally mediated invention of artificial signs for language, thought, or number, or any other human activity for that matter, is that it allows the members of that culture to establish a collective domination over nature. It accomplishes this by enabling their labor to be better—to do more, to do it better, and therefore to better serve the needs of the members of the culture.

Vygotsky's first developmental analysis, phylogeny, focused on a sequence occurring over millions of years. Cultural evolution takes place much faster, over millennia. When Vygotsky turns to the child's development, he notes that the process occurs faster still. What took humans thousands and thousands of years to invent will take the child only a few years to acquire.

Ontogenetic Evolution—Child to Adult   For Vygotsky the primary developmental task for the child is to acquire the culturally mediated sign systems that have evolved over the historical evolution of that culture. Vygotsky depicts this acquisition process as occurring over a series of four stages. But unlike Piaget's stage description Vygotsky's is understandably more sketchy and more focused on the skill level typical of each stage rather than the actual psychological mechanisms regulating stage-based actions. In contrast to Piaget, Vygotsky's interest was the process through which these culturally mediated signs, especially language, were internalized rather than how they were processed once they were internalized.

The sequence roughly parallels the ones described for both phylogenetic and historical development, but as Vygotsky is quick to point out, this does not mean that each recapitulates the events of the other. Vygotsky notes, for example, in defending this nonrecapitulation argument that whereas development at the cultural level involves no biological changes (i.e., no further phylogenetic evolution over the historical evolution of cultures), those at the ontogenetic level involve biological as well as cultural mechanisms.

Vygotsky sees ontogenetic development as involving two processes—each initially independent of the other and only partially integrated during childhood. He refers to the first process as *natural* or *primitive*. It reflects the child's phylogenetic heritage and is seen as primarily regulating what others might refer to as maturational processes. The second process is *cultural*. Not surprisingly, it is this second process that held most of Vygotsky's interest because it is through this second process that what is first intermental (between people) eventually becomes intramental (within the child). As such, Vygotsky sees all higher psychological processes as first existing for the child as actual relations between individuals. Over time these social structures become internalized as psychological structures. The key element in these social interactions is the language structure of that culture.

Vygotsky's use of a four-step developmental sequence is meant to reflect the status of this progression from intermental to intramental. In describing the sequence, he is very specific that the progression is qualitative and nonreductionist in nature. Each step represents a unique dialectic between the child and the culture; each step a unique integration of the child's psychological processes. Let us first discuss the sequence in general and then examine some specific examples of children's level of functioning within each.

Vygotsky refers to his first developmental stage as a *natural* or *primitive stage*. This first stage corresponds roughly to the first two years of life, or until the child begins to use speech. He describes behavior during the stage as being regulated by *preverbal thought* and *preintellectual speech*. That is, both thought and speech are evident, but neither is reflective of the mediated forms within that culture. Rather, thought mechanisms are more or less analogous to those of the problem-solving chimps, and speech serves as an affective and social mechanism rather than as a regulator of thought. Not surprisingly, Vygotsky says little about development during this first stage.

Vygotsky's second stage is one of a *naive psychology* and characterizes behavior during the early childhood years and into the first part of middle childhood (approximately ages 2 to 7 or 8). The acquisition and use of the grammar and syntax of the culture now occupies much of the child's efforts. But even though the child is becoming adept at using language, it still does not serve the purpose of regulating thought. "The child may operate with subordinate clauses, with words like *because, if, when* and *but,* long before he really grasps causal, conditional, or temporal relations. He masters syntax of speech before he masters syntax of thought" (Vygotsky, 1962, p. 46).

During the school years the child makes a transition to a third stage, that of *external signs*. In this stage the child begins to use culturally mediated external signs as aids in internal problem solving, but only when the sign is provided or *scaffolded*. The child is not yet able to generate it for him- or herself.

Finally, if the historical level of the culture continues to support further development, the child, now well into adolescence, begins to demonstrate behaviors of the *ingrowth stage*. The culturally mediated sign systems such as language have been fully internalized and are available to the adolescent to use in problem solving, memory, concept formation, abstract thought, and so on.[4]

It may help to better appreciate Vygotsky's stage sequence by considering two of the research studies he and his colleagues reported as support for their arguments. The first deals with the development of children's memory strategies, and the second with concept formation. Because both studies illustrate the same developmental pattern, let us first look at the research designs and then explore their significance for Vygotsky.

In the memory experiment (Vygotsky, 1978) children and adults, ranging in age from 5 to 30, are presented with three different tasks. In the first task participants are asked a series of 18 questions each requiring a one-word answer. Of these 18, 7 concern colors (e.g., What color is your shirt? What color is the floor? What color can leaves be? etc.), and the others random topics (e.g., Do you have a friend? Can you write? Have you ever ridden on a train? etc.) The purpose of this first task is merely preparation for the remaining tasks. In the second task each person is again asked the same set of questions. But this time the participants also are told that they cannot use the names of two specific colors in their responses and can use a color name only once. In the third task each person once again is asked the same set of questions, but this time each is given a set of colored cards that can be used to help. The goal of the game is to not make a color-naming error.

The colored cards serve as a form of culturally mediated artificial sign, and the purpose of the experiment is to see how well different-aged individuals can make use of such signs. The findings are interesting. On task 2 (when no memory aids are available) there is a gradual but modest drop in the error rates from ages 5 through 13. In contrast, the adult sample does significantly better, with an error rate only about one third that of the young adolescents. The data from task 3 (when the colored cards are available as memory aids) shows a different pattern. The youngest group, ages 5 and 6, shows no improvement in performance from task 2. The 8- and 9-year-olds, however, do about twice as well, and both the 10- to 13-year-olds and young adults do even better. For these two last groups there is no difference in their problem-solving ability.

The second experiment is actually more of a task than an experiment, because only one condition is presented to every participant. The participants again range in age from preschool to early adulthood. Each person is presented with a random array of 22 wooden blocks. The blocks vary in color (5), shape (6), height (2), and size (2). On the underside of each block is a three-letter "nonsense word" such as "bik" or "cur" or "mur" or "lak." One word is on all the tall, large blocks; another, on all the tall, small blocks; another, on all the short, large blocks; and the fourth, on all the short, small blocks. The blocks also differ in color and shape, but there is no consistent relationship between the words and either of these two dimensions. The only consistent pattern is the pairing of a word with a particular height/size combination. Because

---

[4] You may have noticed by now the similarity of Vygotsky's stage sequence to that of Piaget. This is not solely coincidence; Vygotsky makes frequent reference to Piaget's work in his own writing (van der Veer, 1996). However, the similarity of the sequences and their timing should not be interpreted as reflecting a similarity in causal mechanisms. As will be discussed later, even though the two talked about the same issues, they saw them in a very different light.

there are only 22 blocks, not all of the possible combinations are represented. In effect, this adds a further complication to the task because the participants also must consider if the number of examples of each combination has something to do with figuring out the task. The number of examples does not have anything to do with the solution, but the words on the bottom of the blocks do. Specifically Vygotsky and his colleagues were interested in how well the different-aged participants are able to use the words (i.e., artificial signs) as a regulator of their behavior or, as Vygotsky would put it, as a tool of thought. As such, the words in the concept formation task serve the same purpose as the colored cards in the memory task.

The task begins with the experimenter picking up one of the blocks, showing it to the participant, and reading the name on its bottom. The participant is now asked to pick out all the blocks that she thinks belong to the same type. The participant makes her selection, and then the experimenter takes one of the incorrect blocks that has been selected and shows her that this block has a different word on it. Armed with this additional piece of information, she is again asked to identify the "correct" set of blocks. The process continues—she creating a set, the experimenter turning up an incorrect member of this new set—until she finally has all of the correct members of each of the four sets in their respective piles and none of the incorrect ones in any of the four piles. Vygotsky's interest was not so much whether participants solved the task (most eventually did) but rather the process each went through in doing so. The process was inferred from the succession of piles they each put together as they attempted to solve the task.

In both the color memory and concept formation studies, older children did better than younger ones. This was certainly expected and not of much interest to Vygotsky. He was more concerned with why the older ones did better, because the studies were designed to demonstrate the sequence through which individuals come to make use of culturally mediated sign systems such as language.

In the memory task, without the external aids only the adults do well. With the aids both the adolescents and the adults do well, the school-age children do significantly better, and only the youngest ones continue to have great difficulty with the task. Vygotsky notes that even when the use of the cards is explained to the 5- and 6-year-olds, they still can't make use of them. If anything, Vygotsky thinks that for some it may actually hinder their performance. That is, the sight of a particular colored card may make it more likely for some to say that color name more than once, a response contrary to the rules of the game. For those who do use the cards, two different strategies are evident. The school-age children are most likely to first put the "forbidden color" cards away, and then only after naming a color, selecting that card, and placing it face down. Notice that they turn to the card only after they make a response, not before. The teens and young adults also first put the forbidden colors away, but they do something different with the remaining colored cards, the ones that can only be named once. They select a card *before* they make their responses, not after. They are using the cards to determine their choices and, as such, to make sure they don't say the same color name twice.

Vygotsky's explanation is to the point. The youngest children's performance is not affected by the cards because they are still primarily using natural or nonmediated memory strategies. The adults do very well in both conditions because they are already using internalized mediated memory strategies. That is, they really don't benefit much from the cards because the intermental had already become the intramental; the external signs are therefore superfluous. But for the 8- to 13-year-olds, the external signs are very important, and they do significantly better with them than without them. They are at a developmental point at which they have not yet internalized culturally mediated signs. But they are able to make use of external ones when they are provided. Without the external signs their performance resembles that of the young children; with them their performance resembles that of the young adults.

What about the developmental sequence in the concept formation task? Vygotsky notes that the preschoolers have the greatest difficulty with the task, never really solving it. They tend to group objects in unorganized categories, or what Vygotsky graphically describes as "heaps"—a "vague syncretic conglomeration of individual objects" (Vygotsky, 1962, pp. 59–60). If there is a logic to these heaps, it is evident only to the child. But there probably isn't a logic even here, because the blocks in the heaps often change.

The concept formation strategies of the school-age children and young adolescents are different. The collections are no longer described as heaps, but now are seen as complexes. Vygotsky notes several examples of these. In one case the complex is formed by a strategy of adding blocks to the "correct" one by focusing on one attribute at a time of the correct block. In other words, if the correct block for a particular word is short and small, the child may add one block because it is short like the correct one, another block because it is red like the correct one, another because it is a square like the correct one, and so on. The resulting complex is not correct, but there is nevertheless a logic to the grouping that is no longer knowable only to the child. In other cases the child might combine blocks in terms of colors or shapes so that the resulting complex includes one of each color or one of each shape. In other words, the resulting complex is a complement to the correct block. Vygotsky sees such complementary complexes as reflecting thinking in complexes in the same way that we might group all the elements of a dinner place setting together. The objects do go together, but unlike a true concept they do not share a common defining property.

The defining characteristic of forming collections of objects as complexes is that the focus remains on the specific concrete attributes of the objects themselves. For Vygotsky, to move beyond this level, to truly function conceptually, it is necessary "*to abstract, to single out* elements, and to view the abstracted elements apart from the totality of the concrete experience in which they are embedded" (1962, p. 76). In at least this task, Vygotsky reports that there is not consistent evidence of true concepts until later adolescence or early adulthood. In other words, given the complexity of the task, it is not until this time that the participants can successfully view the blocks in terms of their individual attributes and, having done so, logically act on the various pairing in such a way as to finally recognize the defining properties of each of the four concepts (the four nonsense words) and then group the blocks accordingly.

For Vygotsky the significance of these two studies is not simply that adults do better than children. In fact, depending on the material, this may not even be true. Rather, it is the changing relationship of memory and thought evident in the data that is of developmental significance, because the change reflects the internalization process.

All these facts suggest that, from the point of view of psychological development, memory rather than abstract thought is the definitive characteristic of the early stages of cognitive development. However, in the course of development a transformation occurs, especially in adolescence. Investigations of memory at this age have shown that toward the end of childhood the interfunctional relations involving memory reverse their direction. *For the young child, to think means to recall; but for the adolescent, to recall means to think.* Her memory is so "logicalized" that remembering is reduced to establishing and finding logical relations; recognizing consists in discovering that element which the task indicates has to be found. (Vygotsky, 1978, pp. 50–51)

MAJOR THEMES OF VYGOTSKY'S THEORY   Because Vygotsky was never able to fully develop the specifics of his stage sequence, most interest in his work has focused instead on the more general principles that characterize his cultural-historical approach. Two have become particularly significant: (1) the internalization process and (2) the zone of proximal development.

The Internalization Process   The central component of Vygotsky's cultural-historical theory is the internalization mechanism through which culturally mediated sign systems—the intermental—come to be the intramental. Vygotsky's explanation of this process never came to be as detailed as, for example, Piaget's system of logical operations, but the essence of the process is well reflected in an example Vygotsky provides. This example, which concerns a young child's learning about the cultural significance of pointing, speaks to both how signs become culturally mediated and how they are then transmitted to children.

Vygotsky notes that children have a natural tendency to reach for and attempt to grasp an object that they desire. "His fingers make grasping movements. At this initial stage pointing is represented by the child's movement, which seems to be pointing at an object—that and nothing more" (Vygotsky, 1978, p. 56). A mother, observing her child's action, interprets it as a social sign and reacts accordingly. What started as an attempt by the child to get a reaction from the object by grasping it ends up instead as a reaction from another person. The mother has interpreted the child's action as a sign that has come to be interpreted in this culture as pointing. The child does not yet understand any of this, but with repeated experiences he gradually does come to understand the culturally mediated social meaning of his action. It is in this sense that Vygotsky argues that every function in the child's development occurs twice—first on the social level (the intermental) and then on the psychological level (the intramental). To Vygotsky the importance of this process cannot be overstated. "The internalization of socially rooted and historically developed activities is the distinguishing feature of human psychology, the basis of the qualitative leap from animal to human psychology" (1978, p. 57).

This particular example uses a gesture as a sign, but Vygotsky argues that the most significant culturally mediated human sign is *word meaning*. In fact, word meaning is so central to Vygotsky's theory that he defines it as the primary *unit of analysis* for the study of development, for three reasons. First, because word meaning embodies both speech and language, it links the social with the psychological—that is, communication with thought. Second, word meaning is a holistic concept that involves all psychological functions (i.e., memory, perception, cognition, etc.) simultaneously and in an integrated fashion. Attempting to reduce word meaning to smaller units (e.g., phonemes) reduces the unit of analysis to something that is no longer developmentally meaningful. That is, the focus of study would no longer be on the development of conscious action. Third, word meaning is the most flexible and adaptive of all sign systems. It allows the child to anticipate, plan, reflect, communicate, and engage in activities over extended periods of time. It frees the child from the immediacy of the perceptual world, a limit that chimps are unable to transcend.

The Zone of Proximal Development   Given Vygotsky's emphasis on development as a process of internalizing culturally mediated signs and the historical focus of the Russian Revolution on reeducating an entire nation, it is not surprising that much of Vygotsky's work concerns the process of education. The concept of a *zone of proximal development,* the defining element of this interest in education, arguably is the element of Vygotsky's theory that has received the most attention from developmentalists and educators (Berk & Winsler, 1995; Rogoff & Wertsch, 1984). Like many others, the concept behind a zone of proximal development was not original to Vygotsky, but as with many others, he did much to make the notion developmentally significant. And like most of Vygotsky's concepts, this one focuses on the internalization process. The concept of a zone of proximal development is also significant because it defines the relationship between development and learning. For Vygotsky development (a natural process) always lags behind learning (a culturally mediated process).

Vygotsky defines the zone of proximal development as "the distance between the actual developmental level as determined by independent problem solving and the level of potential development as determined through problem solving under adult supervision or in collaboration with more capable peers" (1978, p. 86). The actual developmental level in this sense is a measure of what the child has already accomplished. The potential developmental level is what the child is capable of if some sort of scaffold or support is provided. In the memory task mentioned previously, the colored cards serve as scaffolds, and the improved performance of the school-age children is presumed to be a reflection of the difference between their actual and potential levels of problem solving.

But simply providing a set of colored cards or other scaffold is not a guarantee that the child's potential problem-solving level will exceed her actual problem-solving level. Remember, for instance, that the colored cards did nothing to improve the youngest children's performance. In other words, for a scaffold to be a scaffold, the child must first be at a point in development at which she is able to benefit from the instruction or prop and second, a sense of *intersubjectivity* must be established between child and adult. The adult must find a way to communicate with the child so that the child can first intermentally participate in the activity and then eventually internalize the culturally mediated sign. This is exactly what had to happen in the example of the infant trying to grasp the object. For the infant to come to understand the gesture as a culturally mediated sign, the mother had to establish a level of intersubjectivity. Otherwise, the child would no more be able to comprehend the mother's actions than any of us could understand the meaning of someone speaking in a language very foreign to us.

There are three important implications of Vygotsky's concept of a zone of proximal development, each of which is as significant today as it was in Vygotsky's time. The first concerns the evaluation of children's competence, the second strategies for teaching, and the third strategies for studying the process of development.

Vygotsky was very critical of the techniques used to assess children's competence because most evaluations of children's competence are at best measures of their actual or current level of development. It doesn't matter if the test is a nationally normed standardized achievement test such as the SAT or the weekly spelling test given each Friday afternoon. In both cases the child works alone. Vygotsky argued that this information is useful, but from an educational standpoint the information is less useful than the child's potential level because the whole point of the educational process is to determine what the child is capable of doing, not what the child has already accomplished. Note that for Vygotsky a measure of what has been accomplished is not a measure of what can be accomplished because the child's potential is as much a function of the skill of the adult as it is the skill of the child. If we were to fully recognize the significance of Vygotsky's argument, our system of academic evaluation, at all levels, would change drastically. It might even be that a person's grade in a course might somehow be "handicapped" or "weighted" by the skill of the instructor teaching the course.

The second implication concerns the process of teaching. It highlights the fact that instruction can be effective only when a level of intersubjectivity is first established. For instruction to be effective, the teacher must understand where the child is developmentally and then present the new material in such a way that the child comes to be actively engaged intellectually in the learning process—that is, in the process of making intramental what is first intermental. If the instruction does not initially reflect the child's developmental level, it is of little value. Furthermore, because within any classroom children's developmental levels can vary significantly, instruction must be individualized to a large degree for it to be maximally effective.

Finally Vygotsky's idea about development occurring in a zone of proximal development is also a paradigm for the study of that development. The study of development should not focus on the static or, to use his word, fossilized forms of development—skills already obtained by the child—but rather on the process through which new forms or levels of development might emerge. In contrast to what he saw as the highly controlled research strategies of mechanism, Vygotsky's approach is more open-ended, more clinical than controlled. In such an approach the dependent variable can never be known ahead of time. Rather, it emerges as the process of development becomes apparent through the experimental manipulation.

Our approach to the study of these processes is to use what we call *the functional method of double stimulation*. The task facing the child in the experimental context is, as a rule, beyond his present capabilities and cannot be solved by existing skills. In such cases a neutral object is placed near the child, and frequently we are able to observe how the neutral stimulus is drawn into the situation and takes on the function of a sign. Thus, the child actively incorporates the neutral objects into the task of problem solving. We might say that when difficulties arise, neutral stimuli take on the function of a sign and from that point on the operation's structure assumes an essentially different character. (Vygotsky, 1978, p. 74)

One particularly interesting feature of this perspective on research is Vygotsky's belief that the findings from short-term experiments such as the color memory task and the concept formation task reflect or at least mimic the same developmental processes that longitudinal studies would reveal.

Vygotsky and Piaget Even though the relative merits of the theories of Vygotsky and Piaget cannot be directly tested, it is still instructive to compare the major arguments made by each, for three reasons. First, Vygotsky made frequent reference to Piaget's work in his writing. Second, comparisons between the two theorists are a frequent topic in the developmental literature (Bruner, 1997; Cole & Wertsch, 1996; Glassman, 1994; Kitchener, 1996; Nicolopoulou, 1993; Smith, 1996; Tryphon & Voneche, 1996; van der Veer, 1996). Third, such a comparison illustrates a point made previously—namely, that theories from different world views are best appreciated as complementing one another.

Vygotsky apparently was familiar with Piaget's work in the 1920s because he made frequent reference to it in his own writing. In *Thought and Language* (1962), for example, Vygotsky devotes an entire chapter to "Piaget's Theory of Child Language and Thought." Piaget, on the other hand, had little knowledge of Vygotsky's work. It was not until the early 1960s that Piaget reports that he had discovered "twenty-five years after its publication, the work of a fellow author who has died in the mean time, when that work contains so many points of immediate interest to him which should have been discussed personally and in detail" (Piaget, cited in van der Veer, 1996, p. 237).

The differences in the awareness levels of the two theorists is understandable. By the 1920s, Piaget's work was well known and well respected, having been translated into many languages. In much the same way that Freud's work served for a time as the frame of reference for all works on psychopathology, Piaget's served as the frame of reference for all developmental study. In contrast, Vygotsky's work was not well known outside of his circle of Russian developmentalists and educators. It had not yet been translated into other languages, and following his death, in 1934, his writing was suppressed for over 20 years by Stalin for being "anti-Soviet."

One of the ways to consider the relationship between the two is to ask if one theory is correct and the other incorrect. There are certainly enough points of contact between the two to consider the validity of such a direct comparison. Piaget envisions development as a universal process, reflecting an invariant stage sequence of cognitive operations and a set of functional invariant processes acting at all levels of development. Vygotsky envisions development as situated in a cultural-historical context, reflecting the internalization of culturally mediated sign systems unique to that context. Piaget sees peers as particularly instrumental in fostering development because peer interactions best enable the child's cognitive operations to construct new knowledge without being overwhelmed by the power of an adult's argument. Vygotsky sees adults as essential in fostering development because they are best able to support or scaffold the internalization of culturally mediated forms of knowledge. Piaget seems most interested in documenting the sequence of development. Vygotsky seems most interested in documenting the causal mechanisms functioning within the zone of proximal development. For Piaget the primary unit of analysis is the schema, an internally constructed representation. For Vygotsky the primary unit of analysis is word meaning, a socially constructed representation. As Jerome Bruner, the eminent interpreter of both theories and a major developmentalist in his own right, puts it, "So, if Piaget was preoccupied with the invariant order of mental development, Vygotsky was on his part preoccupied with how others provided the cultural patterning that makes the process of development possible" (1997, p. 69).

So, who is right—Piaget or Vygotsky? Is development best appreciated as a universal invariant sequence or as a process of cultural patterning? The answer is that this is the wrong question to ask. Consider Bruner's (1997) next sentence: "But please note that neither was blind to the other alternative—as with Vygotsky's belief that mental development moved from mastery of concrete particulars to higher mastery of the abstract, or in Piaget's belief that progress to the propositional stage required cultural support" (p. 69). Piaget and Vygotsky ask different questions. For Piaget the key question concerns those aspects of development that are seen as universal, that reflect qualities that define us as a species. He is asking an organismic question. For Vygotsky the key question concerns those aspects of development that are seen as particular to time and place, that define us each as members of a particular culture having a unique history. He is asking a contextualist question. But, as Bruner points out, neither denies the legitimacy of the other's question. Rather, for reasons particular to each, each pursued his own question. But at the same time each is aware that it was not the only question that needed to be answered if a full account of human development was ever to be obtained. Both recognized that there is, to use Vygotsky's terms, both a natural and a cultured line to development and that both lines are significant at all points of the life span. Piaget chose to pursue the natural line; Vygotsky, the cultured line.

Research and theory within each of the three world views complement rather than contradict each other. Each helps us move closer to understanding the contributions, limits, and boundaries of each. Each brings us closer to a time when we will be able to form a principled synthesis of the three and, in so doing, achieve a complete understanding of human development across the life span. We're not there yet, but most would argue that we are getting closer.

An Apprenticeship in Thinking

As you would expect from a theory within the contextualist world view, Vygotsky's theory serves as a foundation for much applied research and practice, particularly with respect to education (see, e.g., Moll, 1990). Much of this applied educational work has focused on the implication of the zone of proximal development for the development and education of children—that is, places where children "apprentice." One of the most significant programs of research on this topic is that of Barbara Rogoff (1990, 1993, 1997; Rogoff, Baker-Sennett, Lacasa, & Goldsmith, 1995; Rogoff, Mistry, Goncu, & Mosier, 1993; Rogoff, Radziszewska, & Masiello, 1995; Rogoff & Wertsch, 1984) and her colleagues. Appropriately enough, her best-known work is entitled *Apprenticeship in Thinking* (1990).

Rogoff's Theoretical Perspective

It is worthwhile to consider Rogoff's work because it is an excellent example of research built upon Vygotsky's sociocultural perspective. Consistent with the perspective, she views development as the progress children make as they attempt to acquire culturally defined ideals of mature thought and action. This progress involves the child's *appropriation* of culturally defined problems, intellectual tools, and social resources. "In their use of societal tools to reach goals and solve culturally defined problems, they also adapt to the traditions and agreements that constitute the institutions, norms, and technologies of their community. The picture is one of interdependent goal-directed activity" (Rogoff, 1990, p. 190).

An individual's *activity* becomes the unit of analysis in such an interdependent process of development because it is through a person's activity (i.e., engagement with others) that meaning is acquired. Each element in the activity or event defines and gives meaning to the others. Development from this perspective is truly interdependent because each element in the exchange defines and at the same time is defined by the other. The child influences the parent even as the parent influences the child. And the culture structures the individual even as the individual's actions redefine the culture.

Rogoff notes several theoretical and methodological implications of an activity-based perspective on development. The first is that, rather than conceptualizing a person's competence or skill as a collection of mental possessions such as memory or processing speed or logical operations, an activity-based approach defines skills in terms of what the individual is actually able to do within a given setting.

> Mental processes such as remembering, planning, contemplating, calculating or narrating a story generally occur in the service of accomplishing something, and cannot be dissected away from the goal to be accomplished and the practice and interpersonal (as well as intrapersonal) actions used. (Rogoff, 1993, p. 125)

If development therefore is reflected in what people actually do, rather than in what others think they can do, then the distinction between *competence* and *performance* made by both mechanists and organicists no longer has any meaning. In other words, from a contextual view, there can be no competence outside of performance. Rogoff argues that this same logic holds for the traditional separation between the study of the theoretical and the study of the applied. Just as there is no competence independent of performance, there is no level of theory outside of the level of application. The study of development *is* the study of what we are. And what we are depends on where we are—development is always situated in time and place. For Rogoff there is no generic development independent of actual communities and their practices (Rogoff, 1997).

The activity that is of most interest to a contextualist such as Rogoff is the activity that takes place within the zone of proximal development. One of Rogoff's more significant contributions to the sociocultural literature is her expansion on Vygotsky's original conceptualization of the events taking place in the zone.

For Rogoff activity within the zone reflects the inseparable influence of three levels of the sociocultural context. At the level of the community, activity within the zone reflects the concept of *apprenticeship*. The concept of apprenticeship emphasizes the fact that children's activity within the zone is directed toward the acquisition of culturally organized activities and forms of knowledge and discourse. It also reflects the fact that every society organizes experiences within the zone in such a way as to increase the likelihood that children will acquire these culturally mediated systems.

At the level of individual interactions, Rogoff (1993) describes the process as one of *guided participation*.

> The perspective of guided participation focuses attention on the system of interpersonal engagements and arrangements involved in participation in activities (promoting some involvements and restricting others) which is managed collaboratively by individuals and their social partners in face-to-face or other interaction as well as in adjustment of arrangements for each others' and their own activities. (p. 134)

Guided participation is an active two-way process as each participant deliberately tries to establish the intersubjectivity needed for true learning to take place. The less skilled person is deliberately trying to make sense out of the message of the more skilled participant. The more skilled participant is deliberately trying to tailor the message so that it is most meaningful and most likely to extend the skill level of the novice. These tailoring efforts often involve breaking down a large task into more manageable steps and making use of various scaffolding forms such as props, questions, observations, or assistance. Rogoff believes that guided participation is not limited to the academically oriented, face-to-face types of encounters discussed by Vygotsky but includes interactions involving more than two people and concerning all aspects of a child's life, not merely those related to schooling. Placing your finger on the knot so that the young child can make a bow is as much a form of scaffolding as is providing lecture outlines so that students can understand the relationships of the points in the lecture.

The ultimate goal of activity within the zone is for the child to acquire the sign and symbol systems of that culture. Vygotsky describes this level of the activity within the zone as a process of internalization; Rogoff prefers to see it as a process of appropriation.[5] Appropriation is an act of making something one's own. As an individual actively participates in some shared experience, he adopts, takes on, or recognizes the elements of that activity as belonging to him, as well as to the other participants. He

---

[5] Actually her decision has less to do with Vygotsky than with how the term is used in "information processing and learning accounts, where the term implies a separation between the person and the social context and assumes that learning and thinking involve the acquisition and retrieval of static concepts, memories, and so on" (Rogoff, 1993, p. 139).

feels a sense of ownership or entitlement to that process or skill or bit of knowledge. It is not, for Rogoff, a process of yours becoming mine. Rather it is a process of ours becoming mine. As she describes the process:

> People make a process their own through their (necessarily creative) efforts to understand and contribute to social activity, which by its very nature involves bridging between several ways of understanding a situation. Communication and shared endeavors always involve adjustments between participants to stretch their common knowledge to fit with new perspectives. Such stretching to fit several views together *is* development, and occurs in the process of communication and shared efforts. Appropriation is each participant's own change in understanding and skill in participation. (1993, p. 141)

Rogoff's Methodological Perspective

So what about the study of development? How does Rogoff's contextualist perspective translate into a contextualist methodology? As a way of thinking about this issue, consider Rogoff's take on the classic "pretest-intervention-posttest" research design common to mechanism. In a mechanistic research design the participant would first receive a pretest to measure her existing skill level, would next participate in some sort of experimental intervention, and would then be tested again. Any differences in the pretest/posttest scores would be presumed to be a reflection of the experimental intervention (when compared to the pretest/posttest difference for those in the control group).

For Rogoff the issue is not so clearcut. For her the posttest score (and by extension the pretest as well) is equally a reflection of the context in which it occurs. Rather than the posttest score being a "pure" assessment of the impact of the intervention, it reflects both the intervention and the context in which the posttest occurs. In other words, again, there are no assessments independent of context, and therefore there are no measures of universal competence. As Rogoff (1997) describes it:

> A posttest cannot be interpreted as revealing purely individual performance, in that posttests occur in interaction with experimenters in activities that are staged in particular cultural practices such as tests. The child in the posttest is working within the constraints and supports provided by the experimenter and by the research tradition and scholarly institutions that encompass the procedures and interpretations of posttests, according to a communicative contract that delineates the appropriate form of communication and resources available in responding to the problems posed by the experimenter. (p. 277)

Rogoff's alternative research strategy is *ethnographic* in nature. The initial focus is on obtaining as complete an understanding of the cultural context of the study as possible. Without such an understanding there is no way to make the participants' activity meaningful. The research samples are small rather than large; the experimenters are reasonably well known to the participants rather than strangers; and the settings are standardized in the sense that they are equally comfortable to each participant rather than identical for each participant. In doing sociocultural studies, this equality of comfort may mean that the actual settings are quite different in terms of who else is present, how the task is administered or the interview conducted, and in what setting the study actually takes place. The goal is not to seek a universal truth but rather to understand an activity in context. Coding of behavior is always relative to setting and sequence. As Rogoff (1993) explains, "A mother's question 'What do you think goes next?' means one thing if the child has just handled a similar problem with confidence but quite another if it follows a succession of errors" (p. 30). The search is for the patterns of interaction that give meaning to the activity. Issues of reliability and validity, which are solved by standardization of the treatment by the mechanist, are, for Rogoff, resolved in part by having the participant check the investigator's interpretations for accuracy. Also in contrast to more traditional research strategies, Rogoff's pattern analysis approach not only looks to identify significant outcomes but also is used even to identify the categories through which the data itself is interpreted. In more traditional designs the data analysis strategies are defined before the data is collected.

Perhaps the best way to fully understand this ethnographic approach is to see how Rogoff uses it in her research. One particularly good example (Rogoff et al., 1993) concerns the series of studies examining the cultural differences in how mothers and their toddlers go about engaging each other in the process of guided participation. The full study examines these interaction patterns in four different cultures; here we will discuss the patterns found in two of them.

Guided Participation in San Pedro and Salt Lake City

Rogoff's complete study looks at guided participation patterns between mothers and their toddlers in San Pedro, a rural Mayan Indian village in Guatemala; Salt Lake City, Utah; Dhol-Ki-Patti, a tribal village in India; and Kecioren, a middle-class urban neighborhood in Ankara, Turkey. But we will focus on the data from San Pedro and Salt Lake City.

In both San Pedro and Salt Lake City, mothers are presented with several objects that are new to the child and asked to get their child to use them. (A second part of the study also looked at interactions during dressing.) Each session is videotaped, and the analyses are based on the repeated viewing of the videotape, as well as interview information obtained from the parent about her child-rearing practices and goals, her child's daily routines, and her child's health.

Consistent with an ethnographic approach, Rogoff and her colleagues are most interested in the sequence of interactions occurring between mother and child. As Rogoff notes, "Such analyses are based on the idea that participants in social interaction usually provide explicit evidence to each other regarding the meaning of their actions, informing each other of their intentions through jointly created discourse and action and clarifying ambiguities" (1993, p. 31).

San Pedro and Salt Lake City are two very different cultural places. In an ethnographic analysis it is essential to understand the characteristics of each setting because these characteristics partially structure the nature of the activities within the zone. San Pedro is small and rural. Families live in extended family formats, often sharing a multiunit housing compound and a common water source. Electricity is available, but most houses have little more than lights and a radio. Each house is small, usually consisting of a kitchen and a combination living room/bedroom. Most residents have limited education. Typically fathers work in agriculture while mothers manage the house and do weaving to earn additional income. In contrast, Salt Lake City is a large, modern, prosperous American city. Families live in nuclear fashion in homes much larger than those of San Pedro. Unlike in San Pedro, children, including infants, sleep in their own room. Also unlike in San Pedro most mothers and fathers in the sample work outside of the home. Children of working parents are cared for by either a relative or a child care provider.

Given such differences in the structure of the two cultures, it is not surprising that there are also significant differences in how people function. Toddlers in San Pedro have greater exposure to the social and economic life of their community than do toddlers in Salt Lake City. They see both their mothers and others involved in all types of community endeavors. The toddlers in Salt Lake City see adults, whether their parents or someone else, function only in the role of child care. Salt Lake City parents are much more intentionally deliberate in advancing their children's development than are parents in San Pedro. The Salt Lake City parents are more concerned about their children's development being "on time." San Pedro parents feel that their children's development will happen when it happens, and although they take equal pride in and joy from their children, they are not very intentional in helping their children achieve milestones such as walking or toilet training or early language. But the children of San Pedro are expected to assume adult responsibilities much sooner than the children of Salt Lake City. Four-year-olds might help with meals or assist someone in the fields or even run errands. By age 10 the San Pedro children might have full responsibility for preparing a meal or caring for a child or even tending the crops. None of this is true for the Salt Lake City children.

How are these cultural differences reflected in the nature of the mother-child interactions? In analyzing the observation and interview transcripts, Rogoff notes that the two cultures (as is also true of the Indian and Turkish samples) do not differ in their guided participation in terms of what she describes as *creating bridges* and *structuring*. Creating bridges reflects the participants' efforts to establish a degree of intersubjectivity in the task, to ensure that the child and adult share the same purpose in the task. Structuring reflects how the participants shape or scaffold the toddlers' exploration of the novel objects. Mothers would adjust the position of the object, break the larger task into smaller pieces, and assist with difficult actions. Toddlers would request information, seek clarification, and ask for assistance. In others ways, however, mothers in the two cultures differ markedly in their guided participation, differences that reflect the distinctiveness of the two cultures.

There are significant differences in the role of verbal instruction between the two cultures. Salt Lake City mothers are much more likely to provide verbal information than are the San Pedro mothers. Appropriately enough, their children show the same pattern. But the San Pedro mothers are more likely to guide their toddlers' exploration through nonverbal means such as gesture, facial expression, posture, or timing of action. Again, the toddlers' nonverbal engagements mirror that of their mother's. The Salt Lake City mothers are much more likely to engage their children's exploration of the novel objects by acting in the role of playmate than are the San Pedro mothers.

This is reflected in their use of language and, more generally, in their efforts to establish a reciprocal give-and-take with their toddlers. San Pedro mothers are more comfortable supervising and offering assistance and instruction than actually playing with their children. Rogoff notes that the San Pedro mothers might invite an older sibling to play with the toddler as a strategy for getting the toddler to more fully explore the object, rather than getting directly involved themselves in the play. Salt Lake City mothers are much more deliberate and intentional in directing their toddler's exploration. San Pedro mothers are always available for assistance, but they seem more comfortable letting their children set the pace and direction of the play.

What is the relationship between the differences in the cultural contexts of San Pedro and Salt Lake City and the mother-toddler interaction patterns? Rogoff provides an extensive discussion of this issue, but two points are particularly worth noting because they help explain the data and because, more generally, they reflect the arguments of a sociocultural perspective. The major difference between the two cultures is the degree to which children are segregated from everyday adult activities. The greater the segregation, the more likely the pattern of deliberate, intentional, highly verbal instruction. In other words, because of the segregation, adults recognize the need to assume a greater responsibility to organize, motivate, and manage their children's development. But in a community like San Pedro, where children have virtually continuous access to all aspects of the social and economic roles of adults, learning is more likely to occur through observation and the responsive assistance of adults. Opportunities for learning culturally relevant skills don't need to be scheduled because they are always available. Perhaps because these opportunities are always available, adults seem comfortable granting children enough autonomy to learn the tasks in their own way, providing assistance only when the child requests it. Given a smaller "window of opportunity," the Salt Lake City parents seem to feel a greater need to ensure that the right things happen when there is the opportunity for them to take place. Put another way, there is no "take your kid to work day" in San Pedro because the kids are already there.

In summarizing her research Rogoff stresses that the purpose of such sociocultural investigations is not in some way to rank cultures. San Pedro and Salt Lake City, as well as the other settings she has explored, are each unique and distinct, but one is not "better" or "worse" than the other. Each is an integrated system whose characteristics are evident in terms of the ways the culture structures opportunities for apprenticeships, the patterns of guided participation, and the appropriation of culturally mediated sign and symbol systems. Rogoff's final point is that, rather than making claims about the superiority of one group over another, we should be spending our time exploring ways to better learn from one another.

Sociocultural Models in Perspective

It might seem strange that sociocultural theorists like Rogoff and Cole argue that this perspective is a new one, at least in the United States. After all, the Europeans have been talking about the role of culture for a long time, and certainly John Dewey (1916,

1938/1963) and others were making similar arguments in the United States many years ago. What happened? How is it that the sociocultural perspective seems to have disappeared and then recently reappeared in this country?[6]

Cole (1996a, 1997) offers an interesting explanation for how development came to be separated from culture. He argues that as academic disciplines grew, particularly after World War II, each, in effect, staked out its turf. The turf for psychology was the individual, for sociology the group, and for anthropology the culture. Furthermore, because the 1950s were perhaps the heyday of mechanism in psychology, the approach to the study of the individual became one of behavioral methodology. For the most part issues of culture were not pursued because such a broad concept was not easily controlled. And when such cross-cultural research was pursued, it was done from the perspective of comparisons across cultures. Culture in this sense was the independent variable, and behavior the dependent variable. The influence went in only one direction (culture to behavior), and the mechanisms were presumed to be universal. As such, it was possible to compare cultures directly.

The sociocultural perspective offers a different view on these issues. In this perspective all development is embedded in specific cultural matrices. Each cultural matrix has a unique history, which is reflected in the artifacts, procedures, and sign systems of that culture. This cultural matrix affects not only a person's outward behavior but the internal mental processes generating that behavior as well. The relationship of culture and person is not, however, unidirectional. Rather, it is bidirectional. At the same time that culture is shaping the individual, that individual's actions are changing the culture. Because of this interdependence, it is not possible to reduce the matrix to simple main effects, assigning one the role of independent variable and the other that of dependent variable. Behavior—or more correctly from this perspective, activity— must always be studied in context.

Sociocultural models challenge our notions of development. They challenge our beliefs as to what a scientific approach to the study of development really means. They challenge our beliefs as to how broadly we can make generalizations about the course of development. They challenge our beliefs about the appropriateness of the "hard sciences" as our source of theoretical inspiration; perhaps we should be talking more to the historian and less to the physicist. They even challenge our beliefs about how comfortable we ought to be in our sense of self vis-à-vis others. Maybe we aren't as advanced a culture as we think we are after all.

---

[6] This issue of disappearance and reappearance is only with reference to the study of life span development. Anthropologists, sociologists, and others have always been interested in the role of culture, but rarely from a developmental perspective.

15

Postmodern Perspectives

One way of thinking about the content of these past 14 chapters is that we have been moving from the ridiculous to the sublime, or perhaps the sublime to the ridiculous—it all depends on your perspective. In any case we have now reached the ridiculous or the sublime. Whatever your bias, no one would dispute the argument that the claims of the *postmodernists* are about as far as one can get from those of the mechanists and still be talking about the same species.

The structure of this chapter is different from most of the preceding ones. First, postmodernism is not specifically about human development. Its focus is much broader, and so this discussion will be as well. Second, there are no postmodern developmental theorists, at least not in the sense of a Skinner or a Bandura or a Piaget or even a Vygotsky. This is true both because the movement is relatively new and because many postmodernists eschew the very idea of a theory about individual behavior and development. Rather than theories, postmodernists interested in human development are more likely to offer critiques of theories found within both mechanism and organicism (Brannigan, 1997; Liu & Liu, 1997).

The theoretical perspectives presented in the previous two chapters—the life span cohort perspective and the sociocultural historical perspective—each make the point that broad, universal, absolute statements about human behavior and development must always be tempered by considerations of time and place, that is, by context. Such a tempering is the defining element of a contextualist world view. But even though the concept of variability is crucial to the views presented in Chapters 13 and 14, there is still the sense in these views that there is such a thing as a process of development, even if it might take different forms in different places and at different times. The theorists in the previous two chapters believe that it is still possible to argue that, within any given context, some forms of human expression are, as defined within that context, more advanced, mature, sophisticated, equilibrated, or whatever, than others.

Postmodern perspectives, in contrast, raise questions over even these contextualized and qualified images of the process of development. The questions reflect a concern with both how knowledge is acquired and what purposes it is put to. Let's get right to the heart of the matter:

354

We are defining a criticalist as a researcher or theorist who attempts to use his or her work as a form of social or cultural criticism and who accepts certain basic assumptions: that all thought is fundamentally mediated by power relations that are social and historically constituted; that facts can never be isolated from the domain of values or removed from some form of ideological inscription; that the relationship between concept and object and between signified and signifier is never stable or fixed and is often mediated by the social relations of capitalistic production and consumption; that language is central to the formation of subjectivity (conscious and unconscious awareness); that certain groups in any society are privileged over others and, although the reason for this privileging may vary widely, the oppression that characterizes contemporary societies is most forcefully reproduced when subordinates accept their social status as natural, necessary, or inevitable; that oppression has many faces and that focusing on only one at the expense of others (e.g., class oppression versus racism) often elides the interconnections among them; and, finally, that mainstream research practices are generally, although most often unwittingly, implicated in the reproduction of systems of class, race, and gender oppression. (Kincheloe & McLaren, 1994, pp. 139–140)

This quote, in essence, represents the postmodern view. It is a view whose adherents describe themselves through a variety of terms—*critical theorists, deconstructionists, social constructionists, feminist theorists,* and *contextualists*. There are important differences between the views reflective of each of these terms, but there is also significant overlap. It is at the level of overlap that this chapter will focus. To a large extent the issue of their differences reflects the degree to which each group agrees with all of the elements expressed in this quote and the relative priority each group gives to each element in the quote. The views reflected in this quote are fundamentally different— 180 degrees different—from those of the theories within either the mechanistic or organismic world view. The differences between mechanistic and organismic world views notwithstanding, both share a set of assumptions that place them within a modern, as opposed to a postmodern, approach to the acquisition of knowledge.

Modern vs. Postmodern Perspectives

The distinctions between modernism and postmodernism were discussed briefly in the opening text to Part IV. It is worthwhile now to look at these distinctions in more detail.

Modernism: A Belief in the Knowable

Modernism is largely a 20th-century phenomenon although its roots can be traced back to the Enlightenment and the writings of Locke, Hume, Newton, and Descartes, to name but a few. It emerged at a time when an earlier way of looking at the world, *romanticism,* was losing influence (Gergen, 1991b). According to Gergen, romanticism offered an image of the world as one of divine forces, unknowable urges and powers, and inherent qualities and characteristics, in which passion and emotion were seen as the dominant determinants of behavior. It was a time of heroes and geniuses. Gergen describes art during this period as emphasizing mythological themes and portraying images that challenge viewers to imagine the feelings of the subject rather than consider the artistry of the painter. In music Gergen sees the work of Richard Wagner as epitomizing the period, and he also views Freud's work as substantially reflecting romantic notions of inner impulses, forces, and often irrational drives and urges, all beyond the grasp of consciousness.

Romanticism offered a world that often seemed beyond comprehension and therefore beyond both control and change. Presumably one accepted things as they were because one had no capacity to make them otherwise. But as the impact of the Enlightenment continued to grow, so, too, did the notion that things were knowable if pursued in an objective, rigorous manner.

> Although romanticism furnished a rich resource for cultural life, little about its vision was practical or levelheaded. . . . At the same time, however, the sciences were bearing impressive fruits. Medicine and sanitation were improving life chances, better weapons invited new conquests and innovations in technology—electric lamps, washing machines, sewing machines, motion pictures, radio, motor cars and then airplanes—promised a utopia on earth. Science was antiromantic. It traced its lineage to the Enlightenment, to powers of reason and observation. In the same way that such powers had, it was said, lifted humankind above superstition and ignorance in the past, they were enabling scientists to do so in the present. The success of science rests, it was argued, upon the capacities of the scientist for systematic observation and rigorous reasoning. If these assumptions now seem mundanely commonsensical, this can be attributed to the power and pervasiveness of modernist thought. (Gergen, 1991b, p. 29)

Everything becomes knowable in the modern age. Now the belief was that things happen for a reason and that these reasons could be discovered through objective, rational observation and inference. Furthermore, scientific discoveries were leading many to argue that universal, potentially discoverable laws and principles governed all phenomena. Utopia was no longer a romantic but ultimately unobtainable state; now, with enough research it could be obtained. The quest for utopia was seen as the march of progress, and each experiment was seen as getting humanity just that much closer. And this notion was no mere pipe dream. Each of the discoveries in the basic sciences that led to each of the inventions mentioned by Gergen attested to the correctness of this view. What could easily be added were such medical advances as Banting's discovery of insulin, Fleming's discovery of penicillin, and Salk's discovery of the polio vaccine.

This sense of optimism about finally being able to fully understand the way things are was not limited to accomplishments in the physical and biological sciences. The advent of the modern era also marked the beginning of the social sciences as we know them. In fact, most of the professional organizations in the social sciences were founded around the beginning of the 20th century—for example, the American Psychological Association in 1892, the American Anthropological Association in 1902, and the American Sociological Association in 1905. The goals of these social scientists were no different—and are no different—than those of scientists in other domains (Smith, 1994).

Gergen notes that modernism's search for the truth was not limited to the sciences but was, and is, also evident in the arts and humanities. Music, art, dance, and architecture all moved in the direction of trying to discover the essence or core of their subject. Everything else was pared away, a relic of the romantic sensibility. Less became more. The arts became "pure."

Both mechanism and organicism evolved within this modern sensibility. Both shared a belief in universal, knowable forms. Both searched for what each saw as the core elements or laws regulating behavior and development. Mechanism emphasized following the same methodological strategies that were proving so successful within the physical sciences. The approach was rigorous and reductionist, and the influence of each variable was to be known independent of all others. Once all the variables were known, the individual could be "put together" in the same way the machine, mechanism's guiding metaphor, is assembled. So strong was the belief in the universality of these laws that major theorists such as Skinner spent most of their time studying not humans but mice and pigeons.

Whereas the mechanists placed their emphasis on the methodology of a modernist view, the organicists focused on modernism's core concept of progress. All organismic models envision the changes that occur over a person's lifetime as progressive. In fact, a failure to continue to progress—or even worse, to regress—is their defining characteristic of a failure to develop normally. From this perspective progress in the study of human development was seen as eventually making it possible to correct these problems and, even better, through a thorough understanding of factors such as the parent-child relationship, to prevent them from occurring in the first place.

If you asked the mechanist or the organicist how it is that we have come to know what we have come to know, each would likely argue that this is what there is to be known. That is, behaviorists would argue that we have found that positive reinforcement increases the frequency of occurrence of certain behaviors because that is the way it is. Behavior geneticists would say the same thing about their claims about the relative influence of heredity and environment; Gesell would say the same thing about why 4-year-olds act like 4-year-olds; and Piaget would argue that formal operational thought follows concrete operational thought because that is the way the mind develops.

Postmodernism: Deconstructing the Assumptions of Modernism

Postmodernists raise what to them are serious questions about these claims and others like them. They base their concerns on an examination, a *deconstruction* if you will, of the process by which such claims are made. In particular, the postmodernist asks why some questions are asked and not others. For the modernist the answer is that these are the questions that our search for the truth requires us to ask. It is the facts of the matter that are directing the search. But the postmodernist contends that there is no necessary truth out there, and therefore the reason some questions are asked rather than others is that these are the questions that the researchers find interesting to ask. And if interest is what motivates the researcher, then what determines why researchers find some questions interesting and others not?

Postmodernists argue that such questions need to be asked because they are skeptical about the assumptions supporting modernism (and by implication, the science that it generates). Their skepticism is rooted in a belief that modernism's claim of progress through objective research leading to the discovery of the truth and, theoretically at least, the achievement of utopia isn't well supported. These doubts fall into two general categories. The first is that every advancement, in fact, comes with one or more corollaries, which often negate or compromise the value of the advancement itself. Postmodernists point to such things as the greater pollution that has come with our remarkable industrial growth. They point to the suburban sprawl and the loss of our communities that has come with the evolution of the automobile and our extensive networks of highways. They point to the greater medical costs and ethical debates that have come with medical advances that, on the one hand, have allowed the smallest of premature infants a chance to live and, on the other, have allowed the very frail elderly to continue to linger through the use of "heroic" medical interventions. They point to recent medical evidence that even our "wonder drugs" are losing their potency as new, drug-resistant strains of microbes have evolved. It is important to recognize that postmodernists are not arguing that, for example, we should let premature infants and the elderly die. Clearly they are not. Rather, the issue is that every action has multiple consequences and that modernist arguments of progress have come about only because of a disregard for these collateral consequences.

The second category of doubt reflects postmodernists' concerns about who has received the benefits of progress. Postmodernists argue that these benefits, to the degree that they are benefits, have not been distributed equally. Within Western society these concerns have most frequently been voiced by women, the poor, and both racial and ethnic minorities (Gilligan, 1982; Goldberger, Tarule, Clinchy, & Belenky, 1996). On a global basis these concerns have been voiced by former colonies of the Western powers, by those in countries with limited industrial infrastructures but extensive natural resources, and by countries that see themselves as having little political influence in the global marketplace (Gergen, Gulerce, Lock, & Misra, 1996; Liu & Liu, 1997).

To the postmodernist the issue is not simply the need to take more things into consideration when making statements about progress, nor is it merely the importance of doing more research to find even more effective antibiotics, nor is it even the need to achieve social equity and justice. Rather, the issue is more fundamental; it is one of what knowledge is and how knowledge is constructed.

Postmodernists argue that it is impossible to even have an objective knowledge of the truth (i.e., reality). The issue is not whether such a thing as reality exists (a topic of considerable debate within some philosophical circles) but rather our ability to know this truth or reality. Modernists believe that their objective methodologies do provide such a window on reality. Postmodernists claim that there is no such window, no matter how many control groups are used in the experiment. For postmodernists method is never neutral; it can never be a mirror on reality. Rather, methodology, no matter what form it takes, no matter if it is mechanistic or organismic, is always based on a set of assumptions, either implicit or explicit. Furthermore, these assumptions reflect established norms of discourse among society in general and the members of the discipline pursuing the research in particular. These norms of discourse are what often pass for "common sense" or "givens." For modernists such givens are seen as factual reflections of reality; for postmodernists they are seen as a socially derived consensus. In other words, for postmodernists objectivity is nothing more than a *shared subjectivity*.

If, as argued by postmodernists, objectivity is nothing more than a shared subjectivity, then the focus shifts away from trying to know reality and toward trying to identify the social processes regulating this shared subjectivity. Who are the people participating in this "discussion"? What are the cultural, historical, economic, and interpersonal considerations that influence the discussion (Gergen, 1991a)? How many perspectives or shared subjectivities are there? Is there any way to order them? Who is influenced, and in what ways, from the consequences of these shared subjectivities? In particular, how are different people affected by the categorizations and criteria derived from this shared subjectivity? Fundamental concepts such as normality or intelligence or adaptation, concepts seen by modernists as proved through objective experimentation to exist in reality, are now seen by postmodernists as reflecting nothing more than the particulars of time and place. Consider, in this light, Gergen's critique of modernism's concept of individuality:

> To view knowledge as the possession of single minds is consistent with other propositions holding individuals to be the possessors of their own motives, emotions, or fundamental essences. Within this tradition, people are invited to see themselves as the center of their actions—the arbitrators of the true and the good. As it is argued, such beliefs not only favor a narcissistic or "me-first" disposition toward life, but cast others (along with the physical environment) into a secondary or instrumental role. Persons and environments are viewed primarily in terms of what they can do for oneself. Further, because of the sense of fundamental isolation ("me alone") bred by this orientation, human relationships are viewed as artificial contrivances virtually set against the natural state of independence. Most importantly, as peoples of the globe become increasingly interdependent, and as they gain the capabilities for mutual annihilation (either through arms or pollution) the ideology of self-contained individualism poses a major threat to human well-being. We are not then speaking of an abstract and arcane property of the academy but of a system of beliefs that the world's people can ill afford to maintain. (Gergen, 1995, p. 93)

For the modern scientist research is neutral—the facts are the facts, uninfluenced by the method used to obtain them. Furthermore, what becomes of these facts is not the primary concern of the scientist as scientist. The scientist's job is to probe his or her particular slice of reality. But for the postmodernist this separation of science and advocacy cannot exist. If there are always multiple perspectives, if the facts reflect the shared subjectivity that led to their pursuit as much as it does the object of study, then all science is political. All science is a process of advocacy. There can be no neutrality because there can be no objectivity.

At this point it might seem as if postmodernists are paranoid, that they see social scientists lurking in their labs hatching sinister plots. This really isn't the case. Post-modernists sees modernists as being just as honorable as the rest of us. But they also see them as being so convinced of the truthfulness of the assumptions supporting their work that they fail to recognize what to postmodernists is the most obvious of all facts —that our shared perspectives determine what we see, what we view as significant and worthy of study, and how we interpret our findings.[1] Postmodernists would ask, for example, why there are so many more studies about the effects of mother absence on child development than father absence. Or why issues of risk are much more likely to be associated with growing up in the inner city than other locales. Or why we are always trying to explain achievement test results that show black and Hispanic chil-dren doing more poorly than white children. The modernist would argue that we ask these questions because research has shown that mothers have more impact on the development of young children than fathers, that the inner city is a more dangerous place to grow up, and that, like it or not, blacks and Hispanics do score lower on achievement tests. The postmodernist would respond that, to the extent that these relationships hold at all, they reflect vested and often unrecognized biases in society. The real issue, they would say, is first to make the implicit explicit and then to decide if we want fathers to be as involved in the lives of their children as mothers, if we want to really recognize the advantages and disadvantages of growing up in any setting, and if we really want to consider the social structures that exist in a society that make it more likely that some children will score better on tests than others.

At this point it might also seem that for postmodernists anything goes. Get enough people to share a subjectivity that the world is flat, and the world becomes flat. The seemingly arbitrary nature of postmodern inquiry and analysis is a frequent charge leveled against postmodernists. They are accused of solipsism and of a form of tribalism in which every idea has equal weight with every other, with no way available to decide that some claims are more meritorious than others (Chandler, 1993; Mas-colo, Pollack, & Fischer, 1997; Smith, 1994).

Postmodernists counter these arguments by noting that most rational people are not about to claim that the earth is flat or to propose any other equally absurd notions. At the same time, however, they argue that their focus is more on the meaning that events come to hold for people than on the event itself. It could not be any other way, they would argue, because there is no independent, objective way to view reality. It is always viewed from a particular point of view. It is because their focus is on the mean-ing of events that perspective plays such a large role in the theorizing of postmod-ernists. And it is because their focus is on meaning that postmodernists pay particular

---

[1] For a more historical view of this issue, it is well worth reading Stephen Jay Gould's *Mismeasure of Man* (1996), a highly readable survey of what are now recognized as some of the more preposterous attempts to show that some groups in society are more capable than others. The studies Gould discusses were done in earnest by reputable social scientists of their day. Postmodernists point to Gould's findings as a good example of how unrecognized bias has influenced and continues to influence the study of why we are the way we are.

attention to the political implications of our shared subjectivities. The same event that is seen as an advantage to some may be seen as a disadvantage to others.

Let us try to make this admittedly abstract discussion somewhat more specific by discussing the differences in how gender has been viewed by modernists and post-modernists.

Different Voices on Gender

Postmodern feminist theory focuses on issues of gender. In particular, it is concerned with how women are portrayed in theories of human behavior and development. Debates about gender are not unique to postmodernism; they are certainly as common in both mechanism and organicism. What makes postmodern discussions of gender distinct is the fact that the topic is approached from a postmodern perspective. That is, rather than pursuing the topic in what postmodernists would claim is an attempt to establish objective, universal, dispassionate findings about the differences between males and females (i.e., the modern perspective), postmodern feminists are quite clear that their approach is "avowedly political" (Wilkinson, 1997).

It is avowedly political because postmodern feminists believe that modernist approaches to gender view women only as they exist in relationship to men, define women as less competent and less powerful when compared to men, and legitimate the claims that women's appropriate roles are domestic (Davis & Gergen, 1997; Gilligan, 1986; Thorne, 1997). Furthermore, postmodern feminists argue that the research upon which such conclusions are based is anything but neutral in that it serves as the basis for discriminatory practices and for rationalizing and justifying why women's situation is sometimes less favorable to men's.

For example, recent explanations of why women continue to earn less than men make reference to the fact that women "naturally" take time out from their careers to care for children. Therefore the seeming pay inequity is not, in fact, an institutional practice but rather reflects the choice of women to pursue their maternal roles. Postmodern feminists question the basis for claims about "natural" roles. And they further argue that social structures do indeed make it more likely that women rather than men will interrupt their careers because men are less likely to be socialized as nurturers and because the loss of income is less when women stay home—because of already existing institutional pay inequities.

> Women's (allegedly) limited achievements in the workplace are treated either as consequences of biological differences between the sexes, or as individual problems of social skills. The "solution" is either to accept those "differences" as givens (and not to expect women to perform as well as men in many domains) or to change women, through, for example, assertiveness training. This preoccupation with what is wrong with women in the workplace locates *women* as the problem and has nothing to say about organizational structure, policies, or procedures. It ignores the *social context* within which women (and men) work. The whole field of sex differences exhibits a

relentless focus on the individual and the internal at the expense of external circumstances and social systems. In giving precedence to individual and interpersonal explanations, mainstream psychology "explains" and justifies the structural oppression of women. (Wilkinson, 1997, pp. 253–254)

Although postmodern feminists share the concerns about how women have been portrayed within modern social science and about the need for science to be avowedly political, they do not necessarily agree as to the best way to portray gender from a postmodern perspective. In particular, they differ as to whether it is better to argue that women should be presented as having a distinct but equally valuable voice when compared to men or whether even defining behavior and development in terms of gender is a useful strategy in trying to understand why we are the way we are.

Gilligan's *In a Different Voice*

In a Different Voice is the title of Carol Gilligan's landmark 1982 book about gender differences. This book initiated a long-standing program of scholarship by her and her colleagues (Brown & Gilligan, 1992; Gilligan, 1986, 1988, 1996; Gilligan, Murphy, & Tappan, 1990; Gilligan, Ward, Taylor, & Bardige, 1988; Gilligan & Wiggins, 1988), as well as others sharing this perspective (Belenky, Bond, & Weinstock, 1997; Belenky, Clinchy, Goldberger, & Tarule, 1986; Goldberger et al., 1996), portraying women's voices not as they exist in relationship to men's but as they exist in their own right.

Gilligan's basic argument is that modernist images of development place women at a disadvantage because these images are too narrowly defined and reflect competencies growing out of socialization practices more often associated with the development of males than females. Consider, for example, Werner's orthogenetic principle, discussed in the Part III opening text. He argued that if development occurs, it does so in a particular direction. Specifically maturity is equated with increasing differentiation, articulation, and hierarchic integration. Piaget makes a similar argument when he states that one of the hallmarks of maturity is the ability to deal with the abstract and the hypothetical. In both cases psychological distance and differentiation are seen as more mature than being psychologically "embedded." To Gilligan both Werner and Piaget offer images of development that advantage men and disadvantage women. They advantage men because the types of socialization experiences more common in the lives of boys are the ones most likely to lead to such a differentiated view of the world. It is in the work of Lawrence Kohlberg (Kohlberg, 1984; Kohlberg & Ryncarz, 1990), however, that Gilligan sees the clearest example of this bias.

Kohlberg's work on moral development is organismic in orientation and offers a significant elaboration of Piaget's work on moral development—so significant that the work stands on its own right rather than simply being seen as neo-Piagetian. Although this is not the place for an extensive review of Kohlberg's stage sequence, it is necessary to understand the logic of the sequence to understand Gilligan's original critique.

Kohlberg envisions the development of moral reasoning as occurring in a stagelike sequence. Stages 1 and 2, which he refers to as *heteronomous* and *instrumental* morality, respectively, comprise a *preconventional* level of morality. Criteria for deciding what is right and what is wrong in these two stages, most evident in the behavior of young school-age children, is based solely on self-interest and the likelihood of reward and/or punishment. There is no fundamental moral code evident in the behavior of these children, one that reflects the perceived rightness or wrongness of certain actions. For these children right and wrong are specific to self-interest and personal consequence only.

By the time children approach adolescence, Kohlberg argues, they begin to demonstrate *principled moral reasoning*. Personal consequence is now replaced initially (stage 3, a good-child morality) by a belief essentially in the "golden rule." This notion of doing unto others as you would have them do unto you is, in turn, replaced by a fourth stage (a law-and-order morality) in which the golden rule principle is applied more abstractly to self-defining social systems instead of individuals.

For some adults moral development continues into a fifth (social contract reasoning) and, very rarely according to Kohlberg, even a sixth stage (universal ethical principles). In these last two stages individuals begin to develop a sense of moral reasoning that transcends social convention, interpersonal relationships, and even law. They begin instead to focus on what Kohlberg claims (consistent with a modern perspective) are universal moral principles of right and wrong. For example, even if the majority of people in a society agreed that legalized racial segregation were correct, individuals at stages 5 and 6 would still oppose such laws on the grounds that the higher principle of the dignity of all human beings demands that such laws be challenged. It is significant in this regard that the examples Kohlberg often uses of stage 6 individuals are Jesus Christ, Mahatma Gandhi, and Martin Luther King, Jr. In the most general sense Kohlberg describes a sequence in which higher levels of moral reasoning are equated with an absolute, abstract, universal perspective in which the consequences to self and others of one's actions take a back seat to the need to act in a manner consistent with a set of abstract principles.

For Gilligan the problem with Kohlberg's moral stage sequence in particular and organismic models in general is that, by defining maturity in terms of abstract principles and differentiation of self from others, Kohlberg frames an image of maturity more consistent with the developmental experiences of men than women. As such, Gilligan argues, the fact that women often score lower than men on measures of Kohlberg's moral sequence should not be interpreted to mean that they are less able or less likely to reason at a principled level of moral development. Rather, their principles are defined in different terms—in a different voice—than are males.[2] One is not inferior to the other; one does not imply a different potential for maturity. But as long as measures of maturity emphasize differentiation, then women are at a disadvantage.

The quality of embeddedness in social interaction and personal relationships that characterizes women's lives in contrast to men's, however, becomes not only a

---

[2] There is actually some question as to the degree to which women score lower on the Kohlberg scales when compared to men. Other studies (Galotti, 1989; Wark & Krebs, 1996) have not reported the same data as Gilligan. Nevertheless, Gilligan's larger issue—that there are fundamental differences in the socialization experiences of men and women that are reflected in different images of maturity—remains an important topic because it speaks to issues of bias and oppression.

descriptive difference but also a developmental liability when the milestones of child-hood and adolescent development in the psychological literature are markers of increasing separation. Women's failure to separate then becomes by definition a fail-ure to develop. (Gilligan, 1982, pp. 8–9)

For Gilligan the resolution to this bias involves two distinct measures of maturity, one more commonly found in the experiences of women and the other in those of men. These two images of maturity differ in that one, most common to men, empha-sizes an *ethic of justice,* and the other, most common to women, emphasizes an *ethic of caring.*

Gilligan argues that these distinct ethics evolve out of the differences in the devel-opmental experiences that characterize most men and women. In particular, she argues that the developmental experiences of men make equality synonymous with independence. As boys move through childhood and adolescence into adulthood, their notions of self as an adult are defined and reinforced in terms of separation. It is this distancing that is reflected in an ethic of justice, an ethic based on abstract princi-ples of right and wrong.

For women, Gilligan argues, the developmental pattern is quite different. Matu-rity and a sense of equality are defined by women not in terms of differentiation but in terms of a sense of connectedness. Rather than dependence being seen as the oppo-site of independence (and therefore as the opposite of maturity), it is seen as the oppo-site of isolation. In this alternative vision, dependence does not imply a sense of helplessness or a sense that one is not yet able to stand on his or her own two feet. Instead, it implies a recognition of the obligation of one person to care about another —that is, an ethic of caring.

> Being dependent, then, no longer means being helpless, powerless, and without con-trol, but rather signifies the knowledge that one is able to have an effect on others, as well as the recognition that the interdependence of attachment empowers both the self and the other, rather than one at the other's expense. The activities of care—being there, listening, the willingness to help, and the ability to understand—take on a moral dimension, reflecting the injunction to pay attention and not turn away from need. As the knowledge that others are capable of care renders them lovable rather than merely reliable, so the willingness and the ability to care becomes a standard for self-evaluation. (Gilligan, 1986, p. 50)

Moral reasoning based on an ethic of caring leads to different, and at times seem-ingly opposite, strategies for resolving moral dilemmas than moral reasoning based on an ethic of justice. Difficulties in resolving moral dilemmas because of difficulties in trying to decide how to act without hurting others is, from the perspective of an ethic of caring, a sign of moral maturity rather than a sign of a lack of moral principles.

When considered from a postmodern perspective, Gilligan's work highlights two distinct elements. First, she offers a "dual track" image of development to replace mod-ernism's (and in particular, organicism's) reliance on a universal developmental trajec-tory. There is more than one way to develop successfully. And although she does not pursue the issue, it is certainly consistent with her claim that similar arguments could as easily be made about the developmental patterns of other groups (in particular, individuals differing in terms of culture, race, and ethnicity). Members of these groups could argue that they have also been marginalized by a universal image of development, an image that allows for only one type of successful outcome. Second, Gilligan's work is avowedly political. Her interest has never been to present her arguments solely within the academic community. Rather, she uses these arguments as a basis to justify both a new image of women's development and changes in the social institutions that treat men and women differently. As significant as the impact of her work has been, however, it has not gone without criticism from other postmodern feminists. It is to this other postmodern feminist perspective that we now turn.

The Social Construction of Gender

Postmodern feminists working within a *social constructionist perspective* criticize Gilligan because, even though she offers an independent and unique image of women, one that provides a distinct path toward full development, it is nevertheless an analysis that rests on the assumption that gender is a legitimate basis on which to categorize people. Social constructionists[3] want to deconstruct the very notion of gender. Rather than talking about men and women, they want to talk about social institutions (Wilkinson, 1997).

> Shifting the level of analysis from the individual to social relations and from sex categories to the variable social organization and symbolic meanings of gender further unravels dichotomous constructions. When the topic is gender, there is no escaping the theme of difference. But the presence, significance, and meanings of differences are refocused when one asks about the social relations that construct differences—and diminish or undermine them. (Thorne, 1997, p. 191)

Deconstructing gender challenges one of our most seemingly obvious realities—that there are two distinct biological genders, and no matter how well or how poorly social systems treat men and women, the biological fact of their distinctiveness nevertheless remains. Social constructionists offer two responses to this seemingly obvious reality (Davis & Gergen, 1997).

The first is that, even at the biological level, gender is not so easily defined. Men are not clones of each other, and neither are women. There is as much variability within our constructions of male and female as there is between these two categories—if not more. Both men and women demonstrate the full range of behavioral expressions that are typically equated with one or the other gender. So we find nurturing males and nonnurturing females, aggressive females and nonaggressive males, and so on. Furthermore, our increasing understanding of the reality of gays, lesbians, and transgendered individuals suggests that gender and even genetically determined sex need not be the same (Brown, 1997). To parse this variability into two distinct groups,

---

[3] Be careful not to confuse the *social constructionists* with those Piagetians who refer to themselves as *constructivists*. The similarity between the terms is unfortunate, especially because they reflect different perspectives. But these are the names each group chooses to use, so we seem to be stuck with them.

at best, disregards much of the evidence. To do so, the social constructionists argue, creates two artificial categories. From a postmodern perspective the question then becomes, who is doing the parsing, and what are the consequences of such a dichotomization?

The second response social constructionists offer is that, at the social level, efforts to differentiate men and women are at best contextual in nature. As such, they primarily reflect the distribution of power within a social setting at a particular time and place. Most evidence indicates that prohibitions against women (or men for that matter) have no basis in fact other than serving as a self-fulfilling prophecy. That is, having identified the individual as male or female, the subsequent treatment of that child is a more likely determinant of his or her behavior than is the child's gender itself. The task, according to social constructionists, then becomes one of critically examining these social institutions, determining where the intended or unintended bias rests, and making the necessary changes so that questions of gender become irrelevant.

Such seemingly radical deconstructions are what modernists find so troubling about postmodernism. This is where modernists claim that the baby is being thrown out with the bath water, that postmodern notions are so relative as to make any consensus or conclusion (the hallmark of a science) virtually impossible (Chandler, 1993; Smith, 1994). Postmodernists counter that the "reality" of the matter is not the issue; what is at issue is how the raw data is interpreted, what meaning it is assigned (Bohan, 1997; Gavey, 1997; Wetherell, 1997). Or, more to the point, does dividing people into two groups—male and female—in any way advance our understanding of why we are the way we are? It is the very same line of reasoning that is used to question the legitimacy of racial or ethnic classifications or any other criteria that are used to place people into different categories (Collins, 1997). At the very least, given the history of how some groups have been privileged at the expense of others, it is a question worth asking.

This discussion about the status of gender as a relevant variable has a decidedly nondevelopmental tone to it. The focus has been on the more fundamental issue of how people should or should not be categorized. This has been the case because most social constructionists identify themselves as either social psychologists or sociologists, two groups that typically have been more interested in questions of status than questions of change. It has also been true because the basic assumptions of a postmodern perspective require one to ask if a concept such as development is any more useful to our understanding of why we are the way we are than does the concept of gender. To postmodernists development is no less a social construction than is gender. And as such, postmodernists who are interested in traditional developmental questions (i.e., those asked by mechanists and organicists) are primarily interested in their *deconstruction*.

Deconstructing Human Development

As Broughton (1987) notes, the discipline of human development segments, classifies, orders, and coordinates the phases of our growth. It defines what is and what is not development (as opposed to simply behavioral change), specifies the range of expression that is considered normal or typical, and therefore also defines what is abnormal or atypical. And, on the basis of this accumulated knowledge about the causes of development, the discipline of human development also makes claims as to what should and should not happen to improve the course of human development—claims that appear in popular as well as academic outlets.

But what is it that is being sorted, classified, and ordered? Is human development a natural or a constructed phenomenon? Is it, as modernists would argue, as natural an event as the orbit of the planets or, as the postmodernists would argue, a shared subjectivity situated in a particular sociohistorical context. Modernists argue that we are looking at a natural phenomena, one amenable to empirical analysis. Postmodernists argue that there is nothing natural about human development. Rather, human development is as we choose it to be. The postmodernists make this claim as a result of their deconstruction of the discipline of human development.[4]

Broughton (1987) is particularly pointed in his efforts to deconstruct the discipline. He argues that human development is so wedded to the concept of modernity and its keystone of progress that, rather than welcoming a critical analysis as a means to improve the discipline, the discipline is retreating into itself, creating concepts and findings that have meaning within the discipline but no relevance outside of it. To Broughton and other deconstructionists (Buck-Morss, 1987; Burman, 1994; Walkerdine, 1993), the discipline of human development has truly become "academic."

On what basis do postmodernists make these claims? What is it precisely that they deconstruct? Postmodernists are deconstructing the discipline of human development —that is, the practices, procedures, methods, and assumptions, both implicit and explicit, upon which, they argue, the discipline rests. Furthermore, they claim, such a deconstruction of the discipline reveals that developmentalists are far from being objective, neutral observers of a naturally occurring phenomenon. Developmentalists' subscription to a modern progressive view almost predetermines what questions they will ask and what answers they will find. The result is that what to postmodernists are statements of description become, for modernists, statements of prescription. Postmodernists are arguing that modernists have committed the logical sin of confusing "is" and "ought." The sin is not a trivial one. It is on the basis of this sin, postmodernists argue, that the modern social order is justified.

Again, a caveat is in order. Postmodernists are not claiming that modernists deliberately misrepresent data. Nor, for the most part, are postmodernists even arguing about the raw data itself. Rather, they are claiming that most developmentalists are so enmeshed in the concept of modernism that they are unable to recognize that, far from being a given, the concept of development is a presumption. Far from being the

---

[4] Most deconstructions of human development are actually focused more narrowly on a deconstruction of developmental psychology. As has been the practice throughout this text, I will continue to use the broader term *human development* rather than *developmental psychology*. Nevertheless, the issues raised about developmental psychology are for the most part equally appropriately asked of human development.

study of self-evident truths, it is a contextually situated process of meaning giving. Furthermore, postmodernists argue, it is a presumption that benefits some more than others, developmentalists included.

To clarify these issues, let us discuss how postmodernists deconstruct three fundamental aspects of the discipline of human development: (1) the origins of the discipline itself, (2) the manner in which the life span is segmented, and (3) the very question of what the basic needs of young children are.

Deconstructing Origins

Because postmodernists firmly believe that science of any sort is not distinct from politics but is part and parcel of it, an understanding of the origins of the discipline of human development requires an understanding of the social and political events that constructed it. The deconstructionists trace these events back to the 17th and 18th centuries—to the growth of democracy and the modern social state (Burman, 1994, 1996, 1997; Walkerdine, 1993), the replacement of religion by science (for many, not all) as the primary basis for explaining worldly events (Kessen, 1990), and the drastic social and economic transitions caused by the Industrial Revolution (Lichtman, 1987). To some degree these events occurred worldwide, but they were particularly evident in Europe and North America.

To say the least, these events changed everything. They challenged the assumption that one's "station in life" was permanent and reflected some "natural" order. For the first time the notion that people could "better" themselves became recognized as the concept of "equal opportunity" and was woven into the social fabric.[5] These changes also fueled the Industrial Revolution, which produced dramatic growth in urban areas as centralized factories required concentrations of workers and caused a shift from the family to the individual as the basic economic unit. Finally, all this centralization, this belief in the possibility of improving one's lot, this belief in science benefiting humanity led to the creation of what we now recognize as the modern bureaucratic political state or, as Burman (1997) refers to it, the body politic.

These changing social and political conditions created new problems, which required new strategies for solution, as well as new images of people. The switch from the family to the individual as the primary economic unit placed a greater emphasis on the individual than was ever the case before. Deconstructionists argue that human development as an academic discipline only became possible because of this shift toward the individual as the primary economic unit. Urbanization required new, more centralized strategies for maintaining social order and providing for the common good. And the increasing complexity of the products of the Industrial Revolution required more education for more people and some basis on which to decide who would benefit most from this increased instruction. Rather than being dispassionate observers and interpreters of the human condition, as postmodernists claim modern

---

[5] True, this sense of equal opportunity initially applied only to white males who owned property, but the very fact that the idea existed at all is the important thing to remember.

developmentalists view themselves, the postmodernists argue that the emergence of the discipline of developmentalism was very much tied to the social and political issues of the time. In fact, the argument goes, the discipline emerged specifically to address these issues. Notice that from this deconstructionist perspective the issues were defined not by the developmentalists but by the body politic. In particular, the discipline's first efforts were in terms of devising strategies for sorting and classifying individuals, a necessary practice in the modern bureaucratic state.

> Developmental psychology, while it currently functions as a separate subspecialty of psychology, is intimately connected with other areas of psychology. Indeed, it owes its origins to the domain of "individual psychology" emerging in the late nineteenth and early twentieth centuries. At that time, new nation states and empires of the West were consolidating their central and colonial power bases, and in need of techniques to classify and segregate individuals and populations. The topics of such classification ranged from mental ability to social adjustment, and the institutional arenas requiring such demarcation ranged from prisons, to mental asylums for the insane, to distinguishing educable children from ineducable (Ingleby, 1985; Rose, 1990). But first and foremost was the elaboration of criteria for the mental and physical fitness of recruits to fight colonial wars (Rose, 1985). (Burman, 1997, p. 138)

What could certainly be added to this list of early roles for developmentalists, especially in the United States, was the development and use of various intelligence measures that were used to justify the immigration quotas whereby some groups were preferred over others (Gould, 1996; Kamin, 1974). What is perhaps most telling about this practice, from a postmodern perspective, is that the groups have changed. Once, it was claimed, there was clear and convincing evidence why the English or the Germans should be given more immigration slots than the Irish or the Italians or the Poles. Today we no longer make such claims for these groups but continue to do so for others. The deconstructionist might ask if the Irish or the Italians or the Poles suddenly got smarter or if something else was going on?

Most modernists, mechanists and organicists alike, would not deny that our academic forefathers (and they were fathers) made mistakes and often confused political decisions for good science. Most would also suggest that this is no longer the case. Deconstructionists argue that this will always be the case and cite issues such as the seemingly ever-present debates about the competence of women vis-à-vis men and the competence of some racial groups vis-à-vis others. Ultimately it comes down to a question of whether good science, done well, can transcend existing social and political currents. Modernists say yes; postmodernists, no.

Deconstructing Stages

One of the primary endeavors of developmentalists is that of recognizing ways in which individuals may differ. Mechanists typically pursue this activity by making comparisons between groups of individuals. Organicists typically do it by segmenting the life spans of individuals. In either case there is the presumption that this process of sorting and classifying reflects some reasonably enduring quality of individuals and/or groups. To presume otherwise, they would argue, would be to suggest that these differences are so ephemeral as to be of little if any scientific and social significance.

But where do these differences come from? If people do differ from one another, or if any one individual differs in a meaningful way across the life span, how can we best explain these differences? Deconstructionists argue that, rather than reflecting some enduring quality of the individual, differences, where found, are really *epiphenomena*. That is, these differences actually reflect other factors. In particular, they reflect the same types of social and political forces that were discussed in the previous section.

Burman (1997), for example, notes that historical studies of children, especially those of Aries (1962), indicate that prior to the Industrial Revolution the life span was divided into at best two phases. The first was a period of infancy lasting from birth until approximately ages 5 to 8 and then a period of adulthood lasting for the rest of the life span. In other words, by the time individuals reached the age of 8, they were treated like any one else. Infants, as the term applied then, had few if any responsibilities; adults had many.

Burman argues that a further segmentation of the life span, one creating a distinct period of childhood, emerged only when the social and economic changes prompted by the Industrial Revolution required a "pliant and docile workforce, a workforce which would have been inculcated with the habits of industriousness." Creating such a work force led to compulsory school attendance laws. And school attendance laws led to the further segmentation of the life span, which, in turn, necessitated the study of how to deal with this heretofore unnatural grouping.

> What I am at pains to point out therefore is that developmental psychology is premised upon the construction of an object of study, "the developing child," and that very object is not real, not timeless but produced for particular purposes within very specific historical, social and political conditions. The argument is not about whether change and transformation happen throughout the life of a human subject, but how that change is understood and the effectivity of its discursive constitution. (Burman, 1997, pp. 453–454)

A similar argument can be made about our Western concept of adolescence. Teens hanging out at the mall is not a universal phenomenon, either cross-culturally or historically, even if we "correct" for what serves as the mall in other times and places. Rather, in other times and places, those in their teen years lead and led lives indistinguishable from their elders. Adolescence as we imagine it, as a distinct stage of the life span, is actually a relatively recent phenomenon resulting from two social trends. The first is that the continuing need for more education prompted by our continuing industrialization has led to more and more people staying in school longer. The second is that, as a result of improvements in diet, health care, and public sanitation, puberty for both boys and girls occurs earlier. At the end of the 19th century, puberty was an experience encountered in the late teens, not the early teens. In essence, our modern image of adolescence emerged when these two trends merged. That is, adolescence began when the age of puberty occurred before the age of leaving school. The result was a distinct group of individuals who were sexually mature like their elders but who remained in a social role similar to those who were younger (Goldhaber, 1986). Keniston (1971) has even argued for a further distinct stage of "youth." Youth in this sense is a time of the life span when one's education has been completed but before that person makes a full commitment to the adult roles of worker, parent, and intimate. The stage of youth is perhaps better know as the "postcollege singles scene." The fact that it's a post-college experience further illustrates the fact that many of the social and economic factors defining the segmentation of the life span for postmoderns have significant social class correlates.

The deconstructionist argument that developmental stages are epiphenomena is also well illustrated through Lichtman's (1987) treatment of old age. Lichtman argues that our modern image of old age first began to emerge at about the same time as our modern image of the "developing child." Both are seen as byproducts of the social, political, and economic changes of the Industrial Revolution and its aftermath.

Lichtman argues that the impact of the Industrial Revolution over the past century or two has been to replace what he refers to as *economies of use* with *economies of exchange.* Economies of use are based on barter or immediate consumption, and the family is usually the primary economic unit. As Lichtman describes it, these economies are oriented to human tasks and reflect both the physical and cultural conditions of their lives. In such economies time is not a constant but varies with the ebb and flow of the seasons, so that the working day is longer in some parts of the year than in others. Furthermore, because work is integrated into a cultural setting, there is less separation between it and other aspects of life. Work, play, and family fuse into a unique qualitative reality.

Economies of exchange are different. Factory work is less dependent on hours of sunlight than is farm work. Work now became coordinated and efficient, the individual replaced the family as the primary economic unit, an individual's worth was defined in terms of his or her productivity, and time became an abstraction rather than a reflection of human tasks and settings. The rhythms of life ceased being cyclical and became constant. But even though machines can function continuously with equal efficiency, people cannot. As people age, their capacity for sustained work declines. This age-related shift occurs equally in both economies of use and economies of exchange, but it has different consequences. Lichtman argues that economies of use, by virtue of being more organic to their particular setting, are better able to tolerate and even value age-related shifts in efficiency and productivity. In economies of exchange, however, declines in productivity are seen as wasteful, and so efforts are made to eliminate them. In other words, in Lichtman's deconstructionist analysis, the image of old age as a period of decline in ability and, more importantly, in value is not a natural part of life's cycle but a consequence of the social and economic changes whereby personal worth came to equated with economic value. For Lichtman (1987) the life span significance of economies of exchange is not limited to old age, however.

> When age is defined as dissolution we have a potent instance of a self-destroying prophecy. But it is not sufficiently noted in the traditional developmental literature that the anticipation of age casts a debilitating shadow over the middle years of life. If all one can look forward to is decline, the meaning of one's life as it proceeds will be marked by a deepening sense of despair. Retirement is most often a social exile, as the perversion of old age is mobilized for social control, for the threat of extinction that

reaches back into the middle years affects the alternatives and life priorities that precede it. Retiring people from work and making their later years dependent, devalued,
and debased encourages harder work at earlier periods and forces choices that would
not have been made if the later years of life could have been anticipated with seren-
ity. (pp. 135–136)

For deconstructionists like Burman and Lichtman, examinations of the situated
nature of the life span serve to challenge modernist presumptions of universal developmental laws and patterns—not so much our biology as our psychology. That is, they
are more concerned with the basis upon which we attribute meaning to the biologically related changes of the life span than they do those changes themselves. For
deconstructionists, being a certain age simply means that one has lived a particular
number of years. It says very little, if anything, about one's social worth or social roles,
about one's expectations or constructions of meaning or even competencies. It is
because postmodernists place less store in "what is" that they are so much more concerned with "what could be."

Deconstructing Motherhood

Most child development textbooks have a section entitled "Parent-Child Relations."
When deconstructionists examine the data that typically makes its way into these sections, they notice what to them are two interesting things. The first is that these sections should, in fact, really be called "Mother-Child Relations" because the study of
parenting within human development is almost exclusively the study of mothering.
The second is that, unlike in the discussion of the deconstruction of stages, in which at
least there appears to be a predictable pattern (i.e., an ever-increasing number of
stages), here there is no pattern—at least no pattern in a developmental sense (Burman, 1994; Singer, 1993). The issue, to postmodernists, that prompts such observations is the basis upon which we make claims about the role and structure of families,
about the importance of early experience in the development of children, and about
what are and are not appropriate ways of parenting (i.e., mothering). Because the
answers to these questions have a significant impact on social policy, this deconstruction is seen by postmodernists as essential.

> The model of the nuclear family, consisting of heterosexual couples with their genetic,
> "naturally" conceived children, with the man bringing home the wage and the
> woman keeping the house, is increasingly recognized to be a fiction. Over a third of
> children in Britain are born to single mothers, over a third of marriages end in divorce
> (more in the U.S.) and seventy percent of women are economically active (part-time
> or full-time) (Commission, 1991). As Robert Dingwall (1989) points out, over a quar-
> ter of a million children in Britain live in residential institutions (especially if we
> include young people in boarding schools). Yet the nuclear family continues to lie at
> the centre of social policy in terms of defining relationships and responsibilities (with
> women rendered economically dependent on men, and men emotionally and physi-
> cally serviced by women), and children treated as property of their parents. (Burman,
> 1994, p. 68)

So where does this "fiction" come from? On what do modernists base their claims about what constitutes a necessary environment for infants and young children? And on what basis do postmodernists argue that such claims say more about politics and economics than they do about science?

Most mother-child research within both mechanistic and organismic views stresses the importance of the bonding process. The infant must bond or attach with the mother so that a secure relationship will form. If this relationship is seen as giving the infant a sufficiently secure emotional base, he or she can begin to detach from the mother and explore his or her social and cognitive environment. If this attachment bond does not develop properly—that is, if the infant is overly attached or fails to attach at all—then subsequent development is compromised. The overly attached child remains so dependent on the mother that he or she is never able to engage the world. The "unattached" child, because of an absence of any emotional bonds, is seen as essentially asocial. This asocial child has no reluctance to engage the world but does so without the internal or interpersonal controls that emotional bonds are seen as providing. To put it in Freudian terms, such children are all ego and no superego.

Much of the modern attachment literature dates from the 1950s, first with the work of John Bowlby (1969) and then with the work of Mary Ainsworth (1982, 1989) and her students. The research has its origins in the discipline of *ethology*, the study of animal species. In those species that demonstrate any parenting, it is the mother that is the primary caregiver. Ethologists therefore argue that, given the evolutionary continuity across all species, including humans, mother care is a natural phenomenon. And, by extension, any actions contrary to this natural event will have negative consequences for the child.

The subsequent research by Ainsworth and others over the past 40 years has sought to identify the patterns of mothering that are most supportive of a healthy attachment—that is, an attachment that allows the child the emotional security to eventually become an autonomous individual. In the most general sense, Ainsworth found that children showed the strongest attachment when mothers were cooperative and not demanding, when available but not intrusive, when supportive but not directive. Ainsworth and others have also reported that such secure attachments are most likely to occur when the developmental history of the mother is free of stress and trauma and when mothers are generally available throughout the child's day. Comparative studies with infants and young children who spend a good portion of their day in child care settings (Belsky, 1988) and with infants and young children who remain at home but with mothers not demonstrating these qualities show, in each case, poorer attachment patterns (Hoff-Ginsburg & Tardif, 1995). The findings usually are presented as confirming the attachment argument.

Postmodernists offer several criticisms when they deconstruct this literature. Specifically, they raise questions about (1) the actual research design and (2) the assumptions upon which the research is based (Singer, 1993). The heart of the attachment literature is based on a research procedure known as the *strange situation setting*. In essence, a mother and child enter an unfamiliar room that has several toys in it. After a short period during which the child is assumed to get comfortable in the setting (usually measured by the child leaving the mother's lap and exploring the toys), a stranger enters the room. The stranger does not engage the mother-child pair but takes a seat between the mother and the door. The reaction of the child to the stranger is observed. After another short interval the mother leaves the room (the stranger remains but does not engage the child), and again the child's reaction is noted. Finally, after a brief absence, the mother returns, and again, the child's reaction is recorded.

Children who are said to demonstrate the most secure attachment engage the toys after a short period on the mother's lap when they first enter the room, act wary when the stranger enters the room, exhibit distress when the mother leaves, and show comfort when the mother returns. The attachment is said to be secure because the child clearly demonstrates an emotional tie to the mother, one strong enough that it allows the child to physically separate from the mother to engage the environment but also to express distress at her absence. In a sort of Goldilocks fashion, children are said to demonstrate poor attachment in the setting when they either are unable to physically separate from the mother and cannot calm themselves in her absence or when their behavior doesn't seem to be obviously affected by her presence or absence.

This procedure and others consistent with its logic are generally interpreted by their proponents as demonstrating the type of mother-child relationship necessary for healthy development—and, by extension, the types of family life most conducive to such behaviors. What bothers the deconstructionists is the claim that children who do not show a secure attachment pattern have a developmental deficit and that the families of these children are in some way inadequate. Deconstructionists note that it is just as reasonable to argue that children in child care would show different attachment patterns not because they were any less securely attached to their parents but because the nature of their relationships involve daily separations and reunions and, as such, are not experienced as an upsetting event (Singer, 1993). In other words, the child care children's less severe emotional response to the mother's absence can be seen as a sign not of a poor attachment but of an exceptionally strong attachment. Furthermore, the studies reporting attachment differences between home care and child care children in this country have not been replicated in other countries. As deconstructionists argue, this may say more about the often dismal quality of child care in the United States, especially for low-income families, than about the emotional development of infants and young children (Clarke-Stewart, 1993; Howes, Phillips, & Whitebook, 1992). Finally, deconstructionists note that, because the frequency of attachment patterns differs across cultures, maybe all that is being measured is the variability of family patterns within our own culture, particularly a middle-class, usually mother-present, culture. In terms of these traditional measures, Japanese children appear overly attached, and both Israeli kibbutz and German children seem emotionally distant (Grossman & Grossman, 1990; Miyake, Campos, Bradshaw, & Kagan, 1986; Sagi et al., 1985). Unless one wants to argue that some cultures are better at nurturing children than others, then, these attachment measures, deconstructionists claim, are at best relevant only to the culture in which they were developed.

To deconstructionists the attachment literature, when interpreted from a modernist perspective, has several negative and inappropriate consequences. First, it sets a single standard for appropriate child rearing, one that has little historical or cross-cultural validity. There may, in fact, be several ways to successfully raise developmentally healthy child. Second, by overemphasizing the importance of home care, the attachment literature has contributed (not necessarily intentionally) to a negative image of child care and therefore a reluctance at the political level to adequately support the provision of high-quality early childhood programs. Third, the attachment literature contributes to the argument that women's place is in the home, at least while young children are present. Thus, what modernists would view as good child-rearing advice based on sound empirical research, deconstructionists see as flawed research supporting social policies oppressing women.

Singer (1993) argues that a postmodern analysis of the parent-child relationship shows that there is no one right way to raise children. There are, in fact, many ways, each reflecting the limits and possibilities of the particular time and place. The real goal for a postmodern science of human development is to actively advocate for this position of relativity so that all children will not be judged against one common standard but against ones unique to their situation. In this regard, Singer goes on, research efforts should be directed toward a better understanding of (1) "how children organize their security" both in and out of the house, (2) "how children self-organize their social groups in child care settings," and (3) "how . . . parents and child care providers each meet children's emotional and moral needs."

> In the long run child psychology always involves a question of what "truth" and whose "judgment" counts the most—at once an ethical question and a question of power. Yet the truth of the psychologist should never be put, as a matter of course, above that of the parent—just as the truth of the parent should not be set above that of the child, or the truth of the man above that of the woman. The value of a scientific statement about children never depends on psychologists alone. As far as shared care is concerned, even greater modesty is required: as of now, developmental psychologists have no adequate way of understanding shared care. If the illusion of universal knowledge is broken, the social arrears of developmental psychological concepts come plainly into view. We really must have a major rethink! (Singer, 1993, pp. 445–446)

Postmodernism in Perspective

When I concluded the discussion on Freudian theory in Chapter 12, I began the last section by saying, "Say what you will about Freud . . .". I could just as easily start this section much the same way: Say what you will about postmodernism, their arguments are highly controversial. Organicists and mechanists criticize them as unscientific—and that's when they are being polite (Chandler, 1995). Their arguments are pictured as an "anything goes" philosophy that provides no basis to make judgments about the merits of competing arguments and offers such a situated image of human development that description becomes synonymous with explanation. Furthermore, modernists claim that postmodern arguments, lacking any reference point, ultimately regress into a form of tribalism, with every group competing with every other and each making claims of greater superiority and/or greater victimization. For modernists such an approach may or may not make for good politics, but it does not make for good science. Finally, modernists claim that all of the issues raised when postmodernists deconstruct modern social science are ones that can be effectively resolved within a modernist perspective, in terms of either a mechanistic or an organismic world view. Hence, we are back to the baby and the bath water.

Whatever the ultimate fate of the baby and the bath water, postmodernism raises some important claims about how we conduct a study of human development and to what purposes the information gained from such work is applied. In this last section let us again look at what these claims are.

The primary claim of a postmodern perspective is that there is no such thing as independent, objective knowledge. All knowledge is situated within a particular socio-historical context, and as such, what any group within a particular context believes to be an objective truth is, to postmodernists, no more—but also no less—than a shared subjectivity. To put it another way, common sense is just that—a shared subjectivity.

Given that all knowledge is situated, the second claim is that there is no theoretical justification for the study of the individual separate from his or her context. No individual is independent of context, and no reducible force or variable within the individual explains his or her actions. In essence, explanation does collapse into description.

Give this changing image of the individual, research strategies that postmodernists see as based on the concept of the individual as an independent unit of analysis must also change. Postmodernists view traditional modern research strategies, in which an experimenter in some way creates or observes a setting to see how the subject will react, as artificial and having little, if any, relevance to real life. For postmodernists the problem with such strategies is that they reflect the intentions of the experimenter rather than those of the subject. Only when the subject is able to define the experiment (including the setting) is it possible to understand what meaning the individual attributes to the setting and therefore understand the individual's actions within that setting.

Postmodernists argue that one consequence in this power shift from experimenter to subject is that it becomes possible to recognize a wider range of human experience as legitimate. This wider range represents the diversity of human existence rather than a core of normalcy surrounded by a sea of pathology (Walkerdine, 1993). Such an appreciation for diversity makes it much less likely that postmodernists will commit what they see as one of modernism's cardinal sins—confusing "is" and "ought." In this sense descriptions of developmental sequences, of patterns of parenting, of gender roles, and of strategies for "successful" aging are historically and socially situated statements of what some individuals and some groups do and have done; they are not statements of what all people ought to do.

If everything is situated, if there are no universals, if there is only "what is," what's left for science to do? The postmodern answer is that science serves the people by discovering the situated strategies that will lead to a better life for all. In this sense science is always both political and applied; it is always a servant of the shared subjectivities of the community.

Modernists—mechanist and organicist alike—reading these paragraphs might shake their heads in perplexity. They might ask, Aren't we trying to make a better life for all? Don't we recognize and value the diversity of human life? Haven't we included context in our models? Aren't these also the purpose of all of our work? Well, the answer is, yes and no; it depends on whom you ask.

Part IV—Summing Up

The contextual models discussed in Part IV challenge all that has been said previously. They challenge notions of universality; they challenge notions of objectivity; they even challenge the very notion that there is something that should be called human development. Unlike the organicists, who see the process of development as something to be discovered, the contextualists are much more inclined to view development as something invented. It is an invention unique to the place of its invention and, contextualists argue, perhaps even somewhat unique to its inventors as well.

To Elder, Rogoff, Gilligan, Gergen, and Vygotsky, this process of invention reflects the particulars of the sociohistorical context. It reflects a culture's level of technology, its division of labor, and its attitudes toward its citizens, both advantaged and disadvantaged. It reflects as well the degree of industrialization and urbanization of a culture, its literacy level, its form of government, and its processes for maintaining justice and social equality. Given this orientation, it should not surprise anyone that contextualists are avowedly political. If development is a situated phenomena and if both its structure and functions are a reflection (i.e., invention) of this setting, then certainly one would engage in the "body politic."

As true as this statement is for all contextualists, it is particularly so for those advocating a postmodern perspective. For these postmodernists a major focus is understanding (i.e., deconstructing) the social institutions that define a society and, in so doing, the behavior and development of the members of that society. These individuals see such an understanding as the first step in remedying the social injustices created by particular social structures.

How do contextualist theories reflect the four criteria of a good theory identified in Chapter 1? This question is easier to ask than to answer and again reflects the problem of using a common set of criteria to judge the merits of theories across different world views. Consider the first criterion, testability.

For mechanists testability means prediction, which, in turn, means replicability. For organicists testability is reflected in a theory's ability to explain (i.e., reveal) its deep structure. But neither is the case for contextualism. There is no expectation of prediction and replicability in a world view based on the "historical act," and there is no deep structure to discover. So what is left? For contextualism a measure of the testability of a theory is the degree to which it presents as accurate an image of the shared subjectivity as possible. This goal is reflected in the contextualist's interest in personal narrative, in letting participants of the experiment both participate in the design of the study and review the experimenter's findings for accuracy. It is equally evident in the importance placed on trying to obtain data from as many different perspectives as possible. The problem is always one of ensuring that every effort has been made to capture the historical act as fully and faithfully as possible.

Contextualist models are not highly organized in the sense that, say, Piaget's theory offers an organized explanatory system. They do provide highly organized images of the specific area of interest, but because these interests are always situated, so, too, would be the organizational schemata. Put another way, contextual models tend to be highly precise in their description of their focus of interest. Because there is no deep level to be uncovered, all efforts are directed at providing as detailed an understanding as possible of the social structures creating individuals' developmental status.

Contextualist models of human development are highly generative. Perhaps because they offer such a different perspective on why we are the way we are, they have been a source of much controversy and debate. As mentioned previously, these models force us to confront some of our most deeply held beliefs about social institutions, about the pursuit of science, about the status of individuals in different segments of society, and about our responsibility to make the world a better place for each of us.

So what does it mean to be a developmentalist within a contextualist world view? It means to be a chronicler of the human condition, to be sociologist and historian as well as psychologist, and to be avowedly political. It means recognizing that life span development is an invention of the settings in which it occurs.

Having completed all this, we are in a much better position to return to a discussion of the relationship among the three world views. The epilogue chapter adds further comment, interpretation, and information. Unfortunately the definition doesn't imply that epilogues necessarily follow greater events.

16

Epilogue

So, why are we the way we are? Having worked our way through three world views, many theorists and perspectives, and countless references, what conclusions can we draw about the human condition? And, more to the point, what are the chances of answering this question in a short epilogue? Erikson raised a similar concern at the start of his last chapter of *Childhood and Society* (1950) when he noted that, "Here I must concede that whatever message has not been conveyed by my description and discourse has but a slim chance of being furthered by a formal conclusion. I have nothing to offer except a way of looking at things" (p. 359). That's also all I hope to offer.

Reasonably Adequate World Views

If you will recall from the discussions in Part I, one of Pepper's (1961) main arguments about his world views approach is that each of the three world views—mechanism, organicism, and contextualism—offers a "reasonably adequate" explanation of human development. None alone is sufficient to explain all there is that needs to be explained. Furthermore, because each of the three is based on such fundamentally different root metaphors, direct evaluations of the relative merit of the theories in different world views is very difficult because methodology does not yet exist that would be equally acceptable to all three.

   Mechanism, consistent with its machine root metaphor, favors a reductionist, universalist model. It emphasizes efficient and material causes. It assumes that there are universal, lawful relationships that are best understood through the unraveling of complex behaviors so that each variable influencing that behavior can be examined independent of every other variable. Only once the influence of each is understood, mechanists argue, is it possible to begin to put them back together to see how they interact or influence one another. This teasing apart of variables is why I argue that the nature/nurture debate exists as a theoretical issue only within mechanism.

Organicism, consistent with its root metaphor of the living organism, is a syncretic, universal world view. Although it also recognizes efficient and material causes, it emphasizes formal and final causes. Isolated, independent variables have little meaning in organicism. It is the form of their association, their systemic relationships, that is the meaningful level of analysis. The research focus is on documenting and understanding what are conceptualized as unidirectional patterns of change over time. For organicists it is these patterns of change that are development.

Contextualism, consistent with its root metaphor of the historical act, is also syncretic but on a much larger scale. Rather than focusing on the individual as the integrated system, the context, including the individual, is the integrated system. Efficient, material, and formal causes are recognized, but because the meaning of each is always situated in time and place, no claims of universality are made. Furthermore, there appears to be no place in contextualism for final causes.

Given the fundamental differences in these basic assumptions and the methods that have developed consistent with each of the three world views, not surprisingly, Pepper argues that no one of these can be the judge of the other. To put it more concretely, if you and I argue over how tall a particular person is, we will be able to agree on a mutually acceptable strategy—a tape measure—as the most appropriate instrument to answer the question. Even if we each bring our own and yours happens to be in metric units and mine in English units, we can proceed because there is a way to fully translate one into the other. But this isn't the case with the three world views. There is no "tape measure" yet acceptable to all three because each world view's methodology reflects the basic assumptions unique to each.

So where does this leave us? We would seem to be at an impasse, especially given Pepper's insistence that the measure of a good theory is its *rational clarity*, or internal coherence. Is there no way to begin to think about some sort of synthesis or integration of the theories from the three different world views?

The theoretical work done within each has furthered our understanding of the human condition. Thus it would seem that if there was a way to pursue a principled integration of the three, we would be in an even better position to understand the human condition. Pepper was perhaps thinking the same thing, because in the same sentence that he talks about rational clarity, he also says something else, something seemingly almost contradictory to his own arguments. He says that, even though there does need to be rational clarity in theory, there also needs to be a "reasonable eclecticism in practice" (1961, p. 330).

Eclecticism in Practice

The notion of a reasonable eclecticism presumes that there is some practical way by which to consider each of the three world views in relationship to the others. As Pepper (1961) puts it:

> We wish in matters of serious discussion to have the benefit of all the available evidence and modes of collaboration. In practice, therefore, we shall want to be not

rational but reasonable, and to seek, on the matter in question, the judgment supplied from each of these relatively adequate world theories. (pp. 330–331)

The problem in seeking this "judgment supplied from each" is that each attempts to understand the human condition by asking different questions and by pursuing the answers at different levels of analysis. Therefore a first step in achieving such a practical eclecticism might be to consider the boundary conditions between the three world views.

Eclecticism in Topics of Analysis

Theories in each world view ask a different question about why we are the way we are. Mechanism asks a question about variability, about how we can best explain how we differ from each other. It may seek the answer to this question by looking at different schedules of reinforcement or different characteristics of the models we try to emulate or different gene frequencies or different short-term memory capacities. But in all these cases the questions are the same: How can we best explain why some people are different from other people? How can we explain why some people appear more skilled at some tasks than other tasks? How can we explain why some people appear more skilled than other people?

Organicism is asking the opposite question: How are we the same? The organicist is interested in those qualities that we have in common by virtue of being members of the same species. The search for pattern is a search for these universally shared, species-specific characteristics. It is ultimately the question of what it is that makes us human, that distinguishes us from other species. To the organicist it is of relatively less consequence that there is variability among us. It is the core or essence, which seems to be expressed in so many different ways, that is the primary focus. Thus it isn't merely some of us who need to form a sense of trust if we are to fully develop; it is all of us. It isn't merely some of us who must construct a sense of object permanence; it is all of us.

Contextualism asks a question that, at first blush, seems identical to mechanism's. Contextualists appear most interested in understanding the content of our lives—why some of us are more privileged than others, why some systems work better than others, how it is that categories and groups are formed. These questions do seem to be no different from those of the mechanist. Both focus on how we differ. But they are different in two fundamental ways. First, for the contextualist the focus is on description, on the actual situated content of our lives. For the mechanist it is on underlying processes, on such things as the laws of reinforcement or the mechanism by which a particular gene is said to account for some behavior. Second, for the contextualist the answers to these questions come from the lived experiences of people. The answers are given in their own voices as they attribute personal meaning to their unique contexts. For the mechanist the answer comes from what are seen as objective, observable, usually quantitative measures. Personal narrative is a rare dependent variable within mechanism.

So, which question is more important? Which provides better insight into the complexities of development across the life span? The scholarship prompted by each of the three questions has provided us with important insights into the human condition. We do have a better understanding of our shared sense of humanity. At the same time, we recognize that we are different from one another and that the meaning of these differences is not necessarily either obvious or universal. To argue, however, that one question is ultimately more important than another makes no sense. It is like arguing that hydrogen is more important in the formation of water than oxygen, or vice versa. Just as you don't get water unless you have both hydrogen and oxygen, you don't get a full understanding of life span human development unless you have answers to these three questions and, even more importantly, you know how the answer to any one relates to the answer to the others.

Eclecticism in Levels of Analysis

Given the fact that each world view asks a different question, not surprisingly, each seeks the answer to that question at a different level of analysis. Mechanism functions at a reductionist level of analysis. Its focus is on an examination of the discrete behaviors, genes, or processors of the individual. The goal is a full understanding of the relationship between each discrete efficient and/or material condition and the corresponding behavior(s). Organicism focuses at the level of the individual, who is conceptualized as a meaning-making system. In such a system discrete bits of data come to have meaning only when they become integrated into the system. Contextualism operates at the level of the sociohistorical context. Like organicism, contextualism's focus is systemic but at a broader level. Here the individual is no longer the focus; rather, it's the larger social context. How do the events at one level of analysis influence those at another? Do they even influence those at another? Is it possible that we actually have three independent levels, each with its own unique laws of operation?

This issue of levels of analysis is analogous to looking at a slide under a microscope at three different levels of magnification. Switch from one level of magnification to another, and the slide looks entirely different. Images present at one level of analysis disappear, only to be replaced by new images. If you didn't know that you were looking at the same slide, you could swear that you were looking at three different things.

The same may be true about the three world views. Each presents the same image under a different power of magnification. Is high power better than low power? Low power better than high power? You do see more detail under high power but at the cost of a smaller field. Go the other way, and you face the opposite problem. Clearly, although each power (i.e., level of analysis) may be most useful for answering certain questions, the full answer requires the understanding of things at all levels of analysis. More to the point, it requires an understanding of how what happens at one level of analysis influences what happens at another. What do gene frequencies have to do with personal narratives? What does a highly industrialized social system have to do with how children sort objects? What is the relationship between formal operational thought and schedules of reinforcement?

We don't yet know the answers to these questions about the relationship between events at different levels of analysis. Maybe the relationship is as simple as that of the odometer in a car. Each of the columns seems to change independent of the other until, every now and then, a change in one prompts a change in the one next to it. Maybe events at one level of analysis are relatively independent of one another until one reaches a particular level of magnitude or is present for a particular length of time. If this is the case, then we need to know more about the role both magnitude and duration play in defining the life course.

Ultimately a broad-based interdisciplinary perspective will be necessary if the study of life span human development is to move beyond the parochialism of distinct levels of analysis and questions specific to a world view. Although this point may not always be recognized, it is nevertheless an important point, one that has been made by other writers as well (Bronfenbrenner, 1993; Cairns, Elder, & Costello, 1996; Fiske & Shweder, 1986; Gottlieb, 1992; Hunt, 1961; Kegan, 1982; Lerner, 1993; Tudge, Shanahan, & Valsiner, 1997; Wohlwill, 1973).

As a practical matter perhaps the best place to begin the integration of these three levels and three questions is by asking a fourth question. Rather than structuring an investigation through the asking of one of these three questions, we should begin by asking the question, Why is this so? An answer to this broader question will, of necessity, lead to a consideration of the other three questions. The difference is that, rather than immediately looking at the topic of interest from the perspective of their differences or similarities, universalities, or situatedness, we will recognize that all three questions at all three levels of analysis are equally relevant to a full understanding of development across the life span. Always keeping the larger question in mind makes it much more likely that, irrespective of the answers to whichever of the three questions is eventually asked, the answer will always be couched in the recognition that it is only a partial answer. Keeping the fourth question in mind may help us better appreciate the boundaries that exist among the other three. It may also help us understand the degree to which a particular circumstance in one enhances or restricts the range of expression in the other two.

Ultimately the interplay among the answers to these three speaks to the issue of our potential as individuals and as members of a common species. Does each of us have the same potential? How can we best nurture this potential? Do we benefit equally from the same circumstances? How do we structure our schools and our governance so that each of us receives an equal measure of opportunity and social justice? How do we change an unjust system? What do we have in common with people from other places and times? Is it even possible (or desirable) for there to someday be universally accepted standards of action and accountability?

A Final Thought

The measure of a theory is how well it helps us understand our past, cope with our present, and shape our future. Each of the three world views we have examined has made significant contributions in each of these regards. But they are each still only "reasonably adequate." They need to be better integrated, in terms of both level of analysis and the questions each asks. Perhaps this is where you come in.

Bibliography

Aas, H., Klepp, K., Laberg, J. C., & Edvad, L. (1995). Predicting adolescents' intention to drink alcohol: Outcomes expectancies and self-efficacy. *Journal of Studies on Alcohol, 156*(3), 293–299.

Achenbach, T. M. (1978). *Research in developmental psychology: Concepts, strategies, methods.* New York: Free Press.

Ainsworth, M. D. S. (1982). Attachment: Retrospect and prospects. In C. M. Parkes & J. Stevenson-Hinde (Eds.), *The place of attachment in human behavior* (pp. 3–30). New York: Basic Books.

Ainsworth, M. D. S. (1989). Attachment beyond infancy. *American Psychologist, 44*, 709–716.

Ames, L. B. (1989). *Arnold Gesell—Themes of his work.* New York: Human Sciences Press.

Anastasi, A. (1958). Environment, heredity and the question "how?" *Psychological Review, 65*(4), 197–208.

Anderson, J. E. (1957). Dynamics of development: Systems in process. In D. B. Harris (Ed.), *The concept of development* (pp. 25–49). Minneapolis: University of Minnesota Press.

Archer, S. L. (1992). A feminist's approach to identity research. In G. R. Adams, T. P. Gullotta, & R. Montemayor (Eds.), *Adolescent identity formation* (pp. 25–49). Newbury Park, CA: Sage.

Aries, P. (1962). *Centuries of childhood: A social history of family life.* New York: Knopf.

Atkinson, R. C., & Shiffrin, R. M. (1968). Human memory: A proposed system and its control processes. In K. W. Spence & J. T. Spence (Eds.), *Advances in the psychology of learning and motivation* (Vol. 2). New York: Academic Press.

Attneave, F. (1959). *Applications of information theory to psychology.* New York: Holt, Rinehart & Winston.

Baer, D. M. (1970). An age-irrelevant concept of development. *Merrill-Palmer Quarterly, 16*, 238–245.

Baer, D. M. (1973). The control of developmental process: Why wait? In J. R. Nesselroade & H. W. Reese (Eds.), *Life-span developmental psychology: Methodological issues* (pp. 187–196). New York: Academic Press.

Baer, D. M. (1976). The organism as host. *Human Development, 19*, 87–98.

Baer, D. M., Wolf, M. M., & Risley, T. R. (1987). Some still current dimensions of applied behavioral analysis. *Journal of Applied Behavioral Analysis, 20*, 313–327.

Baltes, P. B. (1979). Life-span developmental psychology: Some converging observations on history and theory. In P. B. Baltes & O. G. J. Brim (Eds.), *Life-span development and behavior* (Vol. 2, pp. 255–279). New York: Academic Press.

Baltes, P. B. (1987). Theoretical propositions of life-span developmental psychology: On the dynamics of growth and decline. *Developmental Psychology, 23*(5), 611–626.

Baltes, P. B. (1997). On the incomplete architecture of human ontogeny. *American Psychologist, 52*(4), 366–380.

Baltes, P. B., Reese, H. W., & Nesselroade, J. R. (1977). *Life-span developmental psychology: Introduction to research methods.* Monterey, CA: Brooks/Cole.

Bandura, A. (1977). *Social learning theory.* Englewood Cliffs, NJ: Prentice-Hall.

Bandura, A. (1986). *Social foundations of thought and action: A social cognitive theory.* Englewood Cliffs, NJ: Prentice-Hall.

Bandura, A. (1988). Social cognitive theory of moral judgment and action. In W. M. Kurtines & J. L. Gewirtz (Eds.), *Moral behavior and development: Advances in theory, research, and applications* (Vol. 1). Hillsdale, NJ: Lawrence Erlbaum.

Bandura, A. (1989). Social cognitive theory. In R. Vasta (Ed.), *Annals of child development* (Vol. 6, pp. 1–60). Greenwich, CT: JAI Press.

Bandura, A., & Huston, A. C. (1961). Identification as a process of incidental learning. *Journal of Abnormal and Social Psychology, 63*(2), 311–318.

Bandura, A., & Kupers, C. J. (1964). Transmission of patterns of self-reinforcement through modeling. *Journal of Abnormal and Social Psychology, 69*(1), 1–9.

Bandura, A., & McDonald, F. J. (1963). The influence of social reinforcement and the behavior of models in shaping children's moral judgments. *Journal of Abnormal and Social Psychology, 67,* 274–281.

Bandura, A., Ross, D., & Ross, S. A. (1961). Transmission of aggression through imitation of aggressive models. *Journal of Abnormal and Social Psychology, 63*(3), 575–582.

Bandura, A., Ross, D., & Ross, S. A. (1963a). Imitation of film-mediated aggressive models. *Journal of Abnormal and Social Psychology, 66*(1), 3–11.

Bandura, A., Ross, D., & Ross, S. A. (1963b). Vicarious reinforcement and imitative learning. *Journal of Abnormal and Social Psychology, 67,* 601–607.

Bandura, A., & Walters, R. H. (1959). *Adolescent aggression.* New York: Ronald Press.

Bandura, A., & Walters, R. H. (1963). *Social learning and personality development.* New York: Holt, Rinehart & Winston.

Baumrind, D. (1993). The average expectable environment is not good enough: A response to Scarr. *Child Development, 64*(5), 1299–1317.

Bear, G. G., & Modlin, P. D. (1987). Gesell's developmental testing: What purpose does it serve? *Psychology in the Schools, 24*(1), 40–44.

Beilin, H. (1989). Piagetian theory. In R. Vasta (Ed.), *Annals of child development* (Vol. 6, pp. 85–132). Greenwich, CT: JAI Press.

Beilin, H. (1992). Piaget's new theory. In H. Beilin & P. Pufall (Eds.), *Piaget's theory: Prospects and possibilities* (pp. 1–20). Hillsdale, NJ: Lawrence Erlbaum.

Belenky, M. F., Bond, L. A., & Weinstock, J. S. (1997). *A tradition that has no name.* New York: Basic Books.

Belenky, M., Clinchy, B., Goldberger, N., & Tarule, J. (1986). *Women's ways of knowing.* New York: Basic Books.

Belsky, J. (1988). The "effects" of infants' day care reconsidered. *Early Childhood Research Quarterly, 3,* 235–272.

Bergenn, V. W., Dalton, T. C., & Lipsitt, L. P. (1992). Myrtle B. McGraw: A growth scientist. *Developmental Psychology, 28*(3), 381–395.

Berk, L. E., & Winsler, A. (1995). *Scaffolding children's learning: Vygotsky and early childhood education.* Washington, DC: National Association for the Education of Young Children.

Biddle, T. R., & Fischer, K. W. (1992). Beyond the stage debate: Action, structure and variability in Piagetian theory and research. In R. J. Sternberg & C. A. Berg (Eds.), *Intellectual development* (pp. 100–140). Cambridge: Cambridge University Press.

Bijou, S. W. (1979). Some clarifications on the meaning of a behavioral analysis of child development. *The Psychological Record, 29,* 3–13.

Bijou, S. W. (1989). Behavioral analysis. In R. Vasta (Ed.), *Annals of child development* (Vol. 6, pp. 61–84). Greenwich, CT: JAI Press.

Bijou, S. W., & Baer, D. M. (1978). *Behavioral analysis of child development.* Englewood Cliffs, NJ: Prentice-Hall.

Blank, T. O. (1989). Social psychology, contexts of aging, and a contextualist world view. *International Journal of Aging and Human Development, 29*(3), 225–239.

Bohan, J. S. (1997). Regarding gender: Essentialism, constructionism, and feminist psychology. In M. M. Gergen & S. N. Davis (Eds.), *Toward a new psychology of gender* (pp. 31–47). New York: Routledge.

Bouchard, T. J. J. (1994). Genes, environment and personality. *Science, 264,* 1700–1701.

Bower, T. G. R. (1979). *Human development.* San Francisco: Freeman.

Bowlby, J. (1969). *Attachment and loss: Vol 1. Attachment.* New York: Basic Books.

Brainerd, C. J. (1993). Cognitive development is abrupt (but not stage-like). *Monographs of the Society for Research in Child Development, 58*(9), 170–190.

Brannigan, A. (1997). The postmodern experiment: Science and ontology in experimental social psychology. *British Journal of Psychology, 48*(4), 594–610.

Broadbent, D. E. (1957). A mechanical model for human attention and immediate memory. *Psychological Review, 64,* 205–215.

Bronfenbrenner, U. (1989). Ecological systems theory. In R. Vasta (Ed.), *Annals of child development* (Vol. 6, pp. 187–250). Greenwich, CT: JAI Press.

Bronfenbrenner, U. (1993). The ecology of cognitive development: Research models and fugitive findings. In R. H. Wozniak & K. W. Fischer (Eds.), *Development in action: Acting and thinking in specific environments* (pp. 3–44). Hillsdale, NJ: Lawrence Erlbaum.

Broughton, J. M. (1987). An introduction to critical developmental theory. In J. M. Broughton (Ed.), *Critical theories of psychological development* (pp. 1–30). New York: Plenum Press.

Brown, L. M., & Gilligan, C. (1992). *Meeting at the crossroads: Women's psychology and girls' development.* Cambridge, MA: Harvard University Press.

Brown, L. S. (1997). New voices, new visions: Toward a lesbian/gay paradigm for psychology. In M. M. Gergen & S. N. Davis (Eds.), *Toward a new psychology of gender* (pp. 295–308). New York: Routledge.

Bruner, J. (1997). Celebrating divergence: Piaget and Vygotsky. *Human Development, 40*(2), 63–73.

Bryant, D. M. (1994). Family and classroom correlates of Head Start children's developmental outcomes. *Early Childhood Research Quarterly, 9,* 289–309.

Buck-Morss, S. (1987). Piaget, Adorno and dialectical operations. In J. M. Broughton (Ed.), *Critical theories of psychological development* (pp. 245–274). New York: Plenum Press.

Burman, E. (1994). *Deconstructing developmental psychology.* London: Routledge.

Burman, E. (1996). Continuities and discontinuities in interpretive and textual approaches in developmental psychology. *Human Development, 39,* 330–345.

Burman, E. (1997). Developmental psychology and its discontents. In D. Fox & I. Prilleltensky (Eds.), *Critical psychology: An introduction* (pp. 134–149). London: Sage.

Bussey, K., & Bandura, A. (1992). Self-regulatory mechanisms governing gender development. *Child Development, 63*(5), 1236–1250.

Cairns, R. B., Elder, G. H., & Costello, E. J. (Eds.). (1996). *Developmental science.* Cambridge: Cambridge University Press.

Cantor, J. H. (1986). Three decades of research on children's learning: Contributions of Charles C. Spiker. In L. P. Lipsitt & J. H. Cantor (Eds.), *Experimental child psychologist: Essays and experiments in honor of Charles C. Spiker* (pp. 67–96). Hillsdale, NJ: Lawrence Erlbaum.

Carter, N. (1992). Behavioral analysis and the primary prevention of occupational injuries. *Scandinavian Journal of Behavioral Therapy, 21*(2), 89–103.

Case, R. (1992). Neo-Piagetian theories of intellectual development. In H. Beilin & P. Pufall (Eds.), *Piaget's theory: Prospects and possibilities* (pp. 61–104). Hillsdale, NJ: Lawrence Erlbaum.

Cavanaugh, J. C. (1991). On the concept of development: Contextualism, relative time, and the role of dialectics. In P. van Geert & L. P. Mos (Eds.), *Annals of theoretical psychology* (Vol. 7, pp. 325–335). New York: Plenum Press.

Chandler, M. J. (1993). Contextualism and the post-modern condition: Learning from Las Vegas. In S. C. Hayes, L. J. Hayes, H. W. Reese, & T. R. Sarbin (Eds.), *Varieties of scientific contextualism*. Reno, NV: Context Press.

Chandler, M. J. (1995). Is this the end of "The Age of Development," or what? Or: wait a minute Mr. Post-man. *Genetic Epistomologist, 23*(1).

Chapman, M. (1988). *Constructive evolution: Origins and development of Piaget's thought.* New York: Cambridge University Press.

Chiszar, D. A., & Gollin, E. S. (1990). Additivity, interaction, and developmental good sense. *Behavioral and Brain Sciences, 13,* 124–125.

Chomsky, N. (1957). Review of Skinner's "verbal behavior." *Language, 35,* 26–58.

Clarke-Stewart, A. (1993). *Daycare* (Rev. ed.). Cambridge, MA: Harvard University Press.

Coghill, G. E. (1933). The neuroembryonic study of behavior: Principles, perspectives and aims. *Science, 78,* 131–138.

Coghill, G. E. (1936). Integration and the motivation of behavior. *Genetic Psychology, 48,* 3–19.

Cohler, B. J. (1982). Personal narrative and life course. In P. B. Baltes & O. G. J. Brim (Eds.), *Life-span development and behavior* (Vol. 4, pp. 206–241). New York: Academic Press.

Colby, A., & Damon, W. (1995). The development of extraordinary moral commitment. In M. Killen & D. Hart (Eds.), *Morality in everyday life: Developmental perspectives* (pp. 342–370). Cambridge: Cambridge University Press.

Cole, M. (1988). Cross-cultural research in the sociohistorical tradition. *Human Development, 31,* 137–157.

Cole, M. (1992). Context, modularity, and the cultural constitution of development. In L. T. Winegar & J. Valsiner (Eds.), *Children's development within social context* (Vol. 2, pp. 5–32). Hillsdale, NJ: Lawrence Erlbaum.

Cole, M. (1996a). *Cultural psychology: A once and future discipline.* Cambridge, MA: Harvard University Press.

Cole, M. (1996b). Interacting minds in a life-span perspective: A cultural-historical approach to culture and cognitive development. In P. B. Baltes & U. M. Staudinger (Eds.), *Interactive minds: Life-span perspectives on the social foundation of cognition* (pp. 59–86). Cambridge: Cambridge University Press.

Cole, M. (1997). Cultural mechanisms of cognitive development. In E. Amsel & K. A. Renninger (Eds.), *Change and development: Issues of theory, method, and application* (pp. 245–264). Mahwah, NJ: Lawrence Erlbaum.

Cole, M., & Wertsch, J. V. (1996). Beyond the individual-social antinomy in discussions of Piaget and Vygotsky. *Human Development, 39,* 250–256.

Coles, R. (1970). *Erik H. Erikson: The growth of his work.* Boston: Little, Brown.

Collins, P. H. (1997). The meaning of motherhood in Black culture and Black mother/daughter relationships. In M. M. Gergen & S. N. Davis (Eds.), *Toward a new psychology of gender* (pp. 325–340). New York: Routledge.

Cowan, P. A. (1978). *Piaget: With feeling.* New York: Holt, Rinehart & Winston.

Crick, F. (1981). *Life itself: Its origin and nature.* New York: Simon & Schuster.

Crow, J. F. (1990). How important is detecting interaction? *Behavioral and Brain Sciences, 13,* 126–127.

Dalton, T. C., & Bergenn, V. W. (Eds.). (1995). *Beyond heredity and environment: Myrtle McGraw and the maturation controversy.* Boulder, CO: Westview Press.

Damasio, R. (1994). *Descartes' error: Emotion, reason, and the human brain.* New York: Putnam.

Damon, W. (1977). *The social world of the child.* San Francisco: Jossey-Bass.

Damon, W. (1983). *Social and personality development.* New York: Norton.

Damon, W. (1984). Peer education: The untapped potential. *Journal of Applied Developmental Psychology, 5,* 331–343.

Damon, W. (1988). *The moral child.* New York: Free Press.

Damon, W. (1995). *Greater expectations: Overcoming the culture of indulgence in America's homes and schools.* New York: Free Press.

Damon, W. (1996). The lifelong transformation of moral goals through social influence. In P. B. Baltes & U. M. Staudinger (Eds.), *Interactive minds: Life-span perspectives on the social foundation of cognition* (pp. 198–220). Cambridge: Cambridge University Press.

Damon, W. (1997). *The youth charter: How communities can work together to raise standards for all children.* New York: Free Press.

Damon, W., & Colby, A. (1987). Social influence and moral change. In W. M. Kurtines & J. L. Gewirtz (Eds.), *Moral development through social interaction* (pp. 3–19). New York: Wiley.

Damon, W., & Hart, D. (1988). *Self-understanding in childhood and adolescence.* Cambridge: Cambridge University Press.

Dannefer, D. (1984). Adult development and social theory: A paradigmatic reappraisal. *American Sociological Review, 49,* 100–116.

Dannefer, D., & Perlmutter, M. (1990). Development as a multidimensional process: Individual and social constituents. *Human Development, 33,* 108–137.

Davidson, P., & Youniss, J. (1991). Which comes first, morality or identity? In W. M. Kurtines & J. L. Gewirtz (Eds.), *Handbook of moral behavior and development* (pp. 105–121). Hillsdale, NJ: Lawrence Erlbaum.

Davis, S. N., & Gergen, M. M. (1997). Toward a new psychology of gender: Opening conversations. In M. M. Gergen & S. N. Davis (Eds.), *Toward a new psychology of gender* (pp. 1–27). New York: Routledge.

Delprato, D. J., & Midgley, B. D. (1992). Some fundamentals of B. F. Skinner's behaviorism. *American Psychologist, 47*(11), 1507–1520.

DeMario, N. C., & Crowley, E. P. (1994). Using applied behavioral analysis procedures to change the behavior of students with visual disabilities: A research review. *Journal of Visual Impairment and Blindness, 88*(6), 532–543.

Dewey, J. (1916). *Human nature and experience.* New York: Holt.

Dewey, J. (1938/1963). *Experience and education.* New York: Macmillan.

Dingwall, R. (1989). Labeling children as abused or neglected. In W. S. Rogers, D. Hevey, & E. Ash (Eds.), *Child abuse and neglect: Facing the challenge.* London: Batsford.

Edelman, G. (1988). *Topobiology.* New York: Basic Books.

Edelman, G. M. (1992). *Bright air, brilliant fire.* New York: Basic Books.

Eichorn, D. H. (1973). The Berkeley longitudinal studies: Continuities and correlates of behavior. *Canadian Journal of Behavioral Science, 5*(4), 297–320.

Eichorn, D. H., Clausen, J. A., Haan, N., Honzik, M. P., & Mussen, P. H. (Eds.). (1981). *Present and past in middle life.* New York: Academic Press.

Elder, G. H. (1974). *Children of the great depression.* Chicago: University of Chicago Press.

Elder, G. H., (1986). Military times and turning points in men's lives. *Developmental Psychology, 22,* 233–245.

Elder, G. H. (1994). Time, human agency, and social change: Perspectives on the life course. *Social Psychology Quarterly, 57*(1), 4–15.

Elder, G. H. (1995). The life course paradigm: Social change and individual development. In P. Moen, G. H. J. Elder, & K. Luscher (Eds.), *Examining lives in context* (pp. 101–139). Washington, DC: American Psychological Association.

Elder, G. H. (1998). The life course as developmental theory. *Child Development, 69*(1), 1–13.

Elder, G. H., & Clipp, E. C. (1988). Wartime losses and social bonding: Influences over 40 years in men's lives. *Psychiatry, 51,* 177–198.

Elder, G. H., Eccles, J. S., Ardelt, M., & Lord, S. (1995). Inner-city parents under economic pressure: Perspectives on the strategies of parenting. *Journal of Marriage and the Family, 57,* 771–784.

Elder, G. H., & Hareven, T. K. (1993). Rising above life's disadvantage: From the great depression to war. In G. H. J. Elder, J. Modell, & R. D. Parke (Eds.), *Children in time and place: Developmental and historical insights* (pp. 47–72). Cambridge: Cambridge University Press.

Elder, G. H., King, V., & Conger, R. D. (1996). Intergenerational continuity and change in rural lives: Historical and developmental insights. *International Journal of Behavioral Development, 19*(2), 433–456.

Elder, G. H., Modell, J., & Parke, R. D. (Eds.). (1993). *Children in time and place: Developmental and historical insights.* Cambridge: Cambridge University Press.

Elder, G. H., & Rockwell, R. C. (1979). The life-course and human development: An ecological perspective. *International Journal of Behavioral Development, 2,* 1–21.

Emde, R. N. (1992). Individual meaning and increased complexity: Contributions of Sigmund Freud and Renee Spitz to developmental psychology. *Developmental Psychology, 28*(3), 347–359.

Enright, S. M., & Axelrod, S. (1995). Peer tutoring: Applied behavioral analysis working in the classroom. *School Psychology Quarterly, 10*(1), 29–40.

Equal Opportunity Commission (1991). *Some facts about women 1991.* Manchester, UK: EOC.

Erikson, E. (1997). *The life cycle completed.* New York: Norton.

Erikson, E. H. (1950). *Childhood and Society.* New York: Norton.

Erikson, E. H. (1958). *Young man Luther.* New York: Norton.

Erikson, E. H. (1964). *Insight and responsibility.* New York: Norton.

Erikson, E. H. (1968). *Identity: Youth and crisis.* London: Faber.

Erikson, E. H. (1969). *Gandhi's truth.* New York: Norton.

Erikson, E. H. (1977). *Toys and reasons: Stages in the ritualization of experience.* New York: Norton.

Erikson, E. H. (1980). *Identity and the life cycle.* New York: Norton.

Erikson, E. H. (1982). *The life cycle completed: A review.* New York: Norton.

Erikson, E. H., Erikson, J. M., & Kivnick, H. Q. (1986). *Vital involvement in old age.* New York: Norton.

Evans, R. I. (1967). *Dialogue with Erik Erikson.* New York: Dutton.

Evans, R. I. (1968). *B. F. Skinner: The man and his ideas.* New York: Dutton.

Evans, R. I. (1989). *Albert Bandura: The man and his ideas—A dialogue.* New York: Praeger.

Eysenck, M. W., & Keane, M. T. (1990). *Cognitive psychology: A student's handbook.* Hove, UK: Lawrence Erlbaum.

Featherman, D. L. (1983). Life-span perspectives in social science research. In P. B. Baltes & O. G. Brim (Eds.), *Life-span development and behavior* (Vol. 5, pp. 1–59). New York: Academic Press.

Featherman, D. L. (1985). Individual development and aging as a population process. In J. R. Nesselroade & A. Von Eye (Eds.), *Individual development and social change* (pp. 213–242). Orlando, FL: Academic Press.

Feldman, D. H. (1980). *Beyond universals in cognitive development.* Norwood, NJ: Ablex.

Ferster, C., & Skinner, B. F. (1957). *Schedules of reinforcement.* New York: Appleton-Century-Crofts.

Fischer, K. W., Bullock, D. H., Rotenberg, E. J., & Raya, P. (1993). The dynamics of competence: How content contributes directly to skill. In R. H. Wozniak & K. W. Fischer

(Eds.), *Development in action: Acting and thinking in specific environments* (pp. 93–117). Hillsdale: Lawrence Erlbaum.

Fischer, K. W., & Farrar, M. J. (1987). Generalizations about generalization: How a theory of skill development explains both generality and specificity. *International Journal of Psychology, 22,* 643–677.

Fischer, K. W., & Granott, N. (1995). Beyond one-dimensional change: Parallel, concurrent, socially distributed processes in learning and development. *Human Development, 38,* 302–314.

Fischer, K. W., Hand, H. H., & Russell, S. (1984). The development of abstractions in adolescence and adulthood. In M. L. Commons, F. A. Richards, & C. Armon (Eds.), *Beyond formal operations: Late adolescent and adult cognitive development* (pp. 43–73). New York: Praeger.

Fischer, K. W., Hand, H. H., Watson, M. W., Van Parys, M., & Tucker, J. (1984). Putting the child into socialization: The development of social categories in preschool children. In L. Katz (Ed.), *Current topics in early childhood socialization* (Vol. 5, pp. 27–72). Norwood, NJ: Ablex.

Fischer, K. W., Kenny, S. L., & Pipp, S. L. (1990). How cognitive processes and environmental conditions organize discontinuities in the development of abstractions. In C. N. Alexander & J. Langer (Eds.), *Higher stages of human development: Perspectives on adult growth* (pp. 162–190). New York: Oxford University Press.

Fischer, K. W., Knight, C. C., & Van Parys, M. (1993). Analyzing diversity in developmental pathways: Methods and concepts. In R. Case & W. Edelstein (Eds.), *The new structuralism in cognitive development: Theory and research on individual pathways* (Vol. 23, pp. 33–56). Basel, Switzerland: Karger.

Fischer, K. W., & Pipp, S. L. (1984). Processes of cognitive development: Optimal level and skill acquisition. In R. J. Sternberg (Ed.), *Mechanisms of cognitive development* (pp. 45–80). New York: Freeman.

Fischer, K. W., & Rose, S. P. (1994). Dynamic development of coordination of components in brain and behavior: A framework for theory and research. In G. Dawson & K. W. Fischer (Eds.), *Human behavior and the developing brain* (pp. 3–66). New York: Guilford Press.

Fischer, K. W., Shaver, P. R., & Carnochan, P. (1989). A skill approach to emotional development: From basic- to subordinate-category emotions. In W. Damon (Ed.), *Child development today and tomorrow* (pp. 107–136). San Francisco: Jossey-Bass.

Fischer, K. W., Shaver, P., & Carnochan, P. (1990b). How emotions develop and how they organize development. *Cognition and Emotion, 4,* 81–127.

Fiske, D. W., & Shweder, R. A. (Eds.). (1986). *Metatheory in social science: Pluralisms and subjectivities.* Chicago: University of Chicago Press.

Flavell, J. H. (1963). *The developmental psychology of Jean Piaget.* Princeton, NJ: Van Nostrand.

Flavell, J. H. (1992). Cognitive development: Past, present, and future. *Developmental Psychology, 28*(6), 998–1005.

Flavell, J. H., Miller, P. H., & Miller, S. A. (1993). *Cognitive development* (3rd ed.). Englewood Cliffs, NJ: Prentice-Hall.

Ford, D. H., & Lerner, R. M. (1992). *Developmental systems theory.* Newbury Park, CA: Sage.

Fraser, S. (Ed.). (1995). *The bell curve wars: Race, intelligence, and the future of America.* New York: Basic Books.

Freud, A. (1936). *The ego and the mechanisms of defense.* New York: International Universities Press.

Freud, A. (1958). Adolescence. *Psychoanalytic Study of the Child, 13,* 255–278.

Freud, S. (1900/1950). *The interpretation of dreams.* New York: Modern Library.

Freud, S. (1905). *Three essays on the theory of sexuality* (A. A. Brill, Trans.). New York: Modern Library.

Freud, S. (1951). *Civilization and its discontents.* New York: Norton.

Freud, S. (1975). *The future of an illusion.* New York: Norton.

Furth, H. G. (1987). *Knowledge as desire: An essay on Freud and Piaget.* New York: Columbia University Press.

Furth, H. G. (1969). *Piaget and knowledge: Theoretical foundations.* Englewood Cliffs, NJ: Prentice-Hall.

Gagne, R. M. (1968). Contributions of learning to human development. *Psychological Review, 75*(3), 177–191.

Gallistel, C. R., & Gelman, R. (1992). Preverbal and verbal counting and computation. Special issue: Numerical cognition. *Cognition, 44*(1-2), 43–74.

Galotti, K. M. (1989). Gender differences in self-reported moral reasoning: A review and new evidence. *Journal of Youth and Adolescence, 18*(5), 475–488.

Gavey, N. (1997). Feminist poststructuralism and discourse analysis. In M. M. Gergen & S. N. Davis (Eds.), *Toward a new psychology of gender* (pp. 49–64). New York: Routledge.

Gelman, R. (1972). Logical capacity of very young children: Number invariance rules. *Child Development, 43,* 75–90.

Gelman, R., Meck, E., & Markin, S. (1986). Young children's mathematical competence. *Cognitive Development, 1,* 1–29.

Gergen, K. J. (1977). Stability, change, and chance in understanding human development. In N. Datan & H. W. Reese (Eds.), *Life-span development psychology* (pp. 136–158). New York: Academic Press.

Gergen, K. J. (1980). The emerging crisis in life-span developmental theory. In P. B. Baltes & O. G. J. Brim (Eds.), *Life-span development and behavior* (Vol. 3, pp. 32–65). New York: Academic Press.

Gergen, K. J. (1985). The social constructionist movement in modern psychology. *American Psychologist, 40*(3), 266–275.

Gergen, K. J. (1991a). Emerging challenges for theory and psychology. *Theory & Psychology, 1*(1), 13–35.

Gergen, K. J. (1991b). *The saturated self.* New York: Basic Books.

Gergen, K. J. (1994). *Toward transformation in social knowledge* (2nd ed.). London: Sage.

Gergen, K. J. (1995). Social construction and the educational process. In L. P. Steffe & J. Gale (Eds.), *Constructivism in education* (pp. 17–40). Hillsdale, NJ: Lawrence Erlbaum.

Gergen, K. J., Gulerce, A., Lock, A., & Misra, G. (1996). Psychological science in cultural context. *American Psychologist, 51*(5), 496–503.

Gesell, A. (1940). *The first five years of life.* New York: Harper.

Gesell, A. (1948). *Studies in child development.* New York: Harper & Brothers.

Gesell, A. (1952). *Infant development: The embryology of early human behavior.* New York: Harper.

Gesell, A., & Ilg, F. L. (1943). *Infant and child in the culture of today.* New York: Harper.

Gesell, A., & Ilg, F. L. (1946). *The child from five to ten.* New York: Harper.

Gesell, A., & Ilg, F. L. (1949). *Child development.* New York: Harper & Row.

Gesell Institute. (1987). Developmental abuses of developmental screening and school readiness training: The Gesell Institute responds. *Young Children, 42*(2), 7–8.

Gewirtz, J. L., & Pelaez-Nogueras, M. (1992). B. F. Skinner's legacy to human infant behavior and development. *American Psychologist, 47*(11), 1411–1422.

Gholson, B., & Barker, P. (1985). Kuhn, Lakatos and Laudan. *American Psychologist, 40*(3), 755–769.

Gilligan, C. (1982). *In a different voice.* Cambridge, MA: Harvard University Press.

Gilligan, C. (1986). Remapping development: The power of divergent data. In L. Cirillo & S. Wapner (Eds.), *Value presuppositions in theories of human development* (pp. 37–53). Hillsdale, NJ: Lawrence Erlbaum.

Gilligan, C. (1988). Remapping the moral domain: New images of self in relationship. In C. Gilligan, J. V. Ward, & J. M. Taylor (Eds.), *Mapping the moral domain* (pp. 3–19). Cambridge, MA: Harvard University Press.

Gilligan, C. (1996). The centrality of relationship in human development: A puzzle, some evidence and a theory. In G. G. Noam & K. W. Fischer (Eds.), *Development and vulnerability in close relationships* (pp. 237–261). Mahwah, NJ: Lawrence Erlbaum.

Gilligan, C., Murphy, J. M., & Tappan, M. B. (1990). Moral development beyond adolescence. In C. N. Alexander & E. J. Langer (Eds.), *Higher stages of human development: Perspectives on adult growth* (pp. 208–228). New York: Oxford University Press.

Gilligan, C., Ward, J. V., Taylor, J. M., & Bardige, B. (Eds.). (1988). *Mapping the moral domain: A contribution of women's thinking to psychological thinking and education.* Cambridge, MA: Harvard University Press.

Gilligan, C., & Wiggins, G. (1988). The origins of morality in early childhood relations. In C. Gilligan, J. V. Ward, & J. M. Taylor (Eds.), *Mapping the moral domain* (pp. 111–138). Cambridge, MA: Harvard University Press.

Ginsburg, H., & Opper, S. (1969). *Piaget's theory of intellectual development: An introduction.* Englewood Cliffs, NJ: Prentice-Hall.

Glassman, M. (1994). All things being equal: The two roads of Piaget and Vygotsky. *Developmental Review, 14*(2), 186–214.

Goldberger, N., Tarule, J., Clinchy, B., & Belenky, M. (Eds.). (1996). *Knowledge, difference and power.* New York: Basic Books.

Goldhaber, D. E. (1979). Does the changing view of early experience imply a changing view of early development? In L. G. Katz (Ed.), *Current topics in early childhood education* (Vol. 2). Norwood, NJ: Ablex.

Goldhaber, D. E. (1981). *On asking the right question: A review and critique of research evaluating the concept of stages within the Piagetian model.* Paper presented at the annual meeting of the Jean Piaget Society, Philadelphia.

Goldhaber, D. E. (1982). The breadth of development: An alternative perspective on facilitating early development. In L. A. Bond & J. M. Joffe (Eds.), *Facilitating infant and early childhood development* (pp. 40–57). Hanover, NH: University Press of New England.

Goldhaber, D. E. (1986). *Life-span human development.* New York: Harcourt Brace Javonovich.

Goldsmith, H. H. (1993). Nature-nurture issues in behavioral genetic context: Overcoming barriers to communication. In R. Plomin & G. E. McClearn (Eds.), *Nature, nurture & psychology* (pp. 325–340). Washington, DC: American Psychological Association.

Goldsmith, H. H. (1994). The behavior genetic approach to development and experience: Contexts and constraints. *SRCD Newsletter, 16,* 10–11.

Gottesman, I. I. (1993). Origins of schizophrenia: Past as prologue. In R. Plomin & G. E. McClearn (Eds.), *Nature, nurture and psychology* (pp. 231–245). Washington, DC: American Psychological Association.

Gottlieb, G. (1983). The psychobiological approach to developmental issues. In P. H. Mussen (Ed.), *Handbook of child psychology* (Vol. 2, pp. 1–26). New York: Wiley.

Gottlieb, G. (1991). Experiential canalization of behavior development: Theory. *Developmental Psychology, 27*(1), 4–13.

Gottlieb, G. (1992). *Individual development and evolution.* New York: Oxford University Press.

Gottlieb, G. (1995). Some conceptual deficiencies in "developmental" behavior genetics. *Human Development, 38,* 131–141.

Gould, S. J. (1996). *The mismeasure of man: Revised and expanded.* New York: Norton.

Greenough, W. T., Black, J. E., & Wallace, C. S. (1987). Experience and brain development. *Child Development, 58,* 539–559.

Greenspan, S. I. (1979). *Intelligence and adaptation.* New York: International Universities Press.

Greenwood, C. R., Carta, J. J., Hart, B., Camps, D., et al. (1992). Out of the laboratory and into the community. *American Psychologist, 47*(11), 1464–1474.

Greenwood, C. R., Finney, R., Terry, B., & Arreaga-Mayer, C. (1993). Monitoring, improving, and maintaining quality implementation of the Classroom Peer Tutoring Program using behavioral and computer technology. *Education and Treatment of Children, 16*(1), 19–47.

Grossman, K. E., & Grossman, K. (1990). The wider concept of attachment in cross-cultural research. *Human Development, 33,* 31–47.

Gruber, H. E., & Voneche, J. J. (Eds.). (1996). *The essential Piaget* (100th Anniversary Edition). New York: Aronson.

Gutman, D. (1987). *Reclaimed powers: Toward a new psychology of men and women in later life.* New York: Basic Books.

Harris, B. (1979). Whatever happened to little Albert? *American Psychologist, 34,* 151–160.

Harris, P. (1997). Piaget in Paris: From "autisim" to logic. *Human Development, 40*(2), 109–123.

Helson, R., & Moane, G. (1987). Personality changes in women from college to midlife. *Journal of Personality and Social Psychology, 53,* 176–186.

Herrnstein, R. J. (1994). *The bell curve: Intelligence and class structure in American life.* New York: Free Press.

Hirsch, J. (1990). A nemesis for heritability estimation. *Behavioral and Brain Sciences, 13,* 137–138.

Hoff-Ginsburg, E., & Tardif, T. (1995). Socioeconomic status and parenting. In M. H. Bornstein (Ed.), *Handbook of parenting* (Vol. 1). Hillsdale, NJ: Lawrence Erlbaum.

Horowitz, F. D. (1987). *Exploring developmental theories: Toward a structural/behavioral model of development.* Hillsdale, NJ: Lawrence Erlbaum.

Horowitz, F. D. (1992). John B. Watson's legacy: Learning and environment. *Developmental Psychology, 28*(3), 360–367.

Houts, A. C. (1991). The contextualist turn in empirical social science: Epistomological issues, methodological implications, and adjusted expectations. In R. Cohen & A. W. Siegel (Eds.), *Context and development.* Hillsdale, NJ: Lawrence Erlbaum.

Howard, G. S. (1985). The role of values in the science of psychology. *American Psychologist, 40*(3), 255–265.

Howes, C., Phillips, D. A., & Whitebook, M. (1992). Thresholds of quality: Implications for the social development of children in center-based child care. *Child Development, 63,* 447–460.

Hull, C. L. (1943). *Principles of behavior.* New York: Appleton-Century-Crofts.

Hunt, J. M. (1961). *Intelligence and experience.* New York: Ronald Press.

Hunt, J. V., & Eichorn, D. H. (1972). Maternal and child behaviors: A review of data from the Berkeley growth study. *Seminars in Psychiatry, 4*(4), 367–381.

Huston, A. C., Wright, J. C., Alvarez, M., & Truglio, R. (1995). Perceived television reality and children's emotional and cognitive responses to its content. *Journal of Applied Developmental Psychology, 16*(2), 231–251.

Ingleby, D. (1985). Professionals as socializers: The "psy complex." *Research in Law, Deviance and Social Control, 7,* 79–109.

Ingleby, D. (1986). Development in social context. In M. Richards & P. Light (Eds.), *Children of social worlds* (pp. 297–317). Cambridge, MA: Harvard University Press.

Inhelder, B., & Piaget, J. (1958). *The growth of logical thinking from childhood to adolescence.* New York: Basic Books.

Inhelder, B., & Piaget, J. (1964). *The early growth of logic in the child: Classification and seriation.* New York: Norton.

Jackson, J. F. (1993). Human behavior genetics, Scarr's theory, and her views on intervention: A critical review and commentary on their implications for African American children. *Child Development, 64*(5), 1318–1332.

Jacob, F., & Monod, J. (1961). On the regulation of gene activity. *Cold Spring Harbor Symposia on Quantitative Biology, 26,* 193–209.

Jaeger, M. E., & Rosnow, R. L. (1988). Contextualism and its implications for psychological inquiry. *British Journal of Psychology, 79,* 63–75.

James, W. (1961/1892). *Psychology: The briefer course.* New York: Harper & Row.

Jencks, C. (1972). *Inequality.* New York: Basic Books.

Jensen, A. R. (1969). How much can we boost IQ and scholastic achievement? *Harvard Educational Review, 39,* 1–23.

Johnston, T. D. (1987). The persistence of dichotomies in the study of behavioral development. *Developmental Review, 7*(2), 149–182.

Jones, E. (1961). *The life and work of Sigmund Freud* (J. Trilling and S. Marcus, Eds.). New York: Basic Books.

Kail, R., & Bisanz, J. (1992). The information-processing perspective on cognitive development in childhood and adolescence. In R. J. Sternberg & C. A. Berg (Eds.), *Intellectual development* (pp. 229–260). Cambridge: Cambridge University Press.

Kail, R., & Pellegrino, J. W. (1985). *Human intelligence.* New York: Freeman.

Kamin, L. J. (1974). *The science and politics of I.Q.* Potomac, MD: Lawrence Erlbaum.

Kaplan, B. (1994). Paradigm, paraphrase, paralogia, paralysis: All in the name of progress. In P. V. Van Geert, L. P. Mos, & W. J. Baker (Eds.), *Annals of theoretical psychology* (Vol. 10, pp. 189–226). New York: Plenum Press.

Karmiloff-Smith, A. (1992). Nature, nurture and PDP: Preposterous developmental postulates? *Connection Science, 4*(3-4), 253–269.

Kegan, R. (1982). *The evolving self.* Cambridge, MA: Harvard University Press.

Kendler, H. H. (1992). Ethics and science: A psychological perspective. In W. M. Kurtines, M. Azmitia, & J. L. Gewirtz (Eds.), *The role of values in psychology and human development* (pp. 131–160). New York: Wiley.

Kendler, T. S. (1986). World views and the concept of development: A reply to Lerner and Kaufman. *Developmental Review, 6*(1), 80–95.

Kendler, T. S. (1995). *Levels of cognitive development.* Mahwah, NJ: Lawrence Erlbaum.

Keniston, K. (1971). Psychological development and historical change. *Journal of Interdisciplinary History, 2,* 329–345.

Kessen, W. (1990). *The rise and fall of development.* Worchester, MA: Clark University Press.

Kim, J. M., & Turiel, E. (1996). Korean and American children's concepts of adult and peer authority. *Social Development, 5*(3), 310–329.

Kincheloe, J. L., & McLaren, P. L. (1994). Rethinking critical theory and qualitative research. In N. K. Denzin & Y. S. Lincoln (Eds.), *Handbook of qualitative research* (pp. 138–157). Thousand Oaks, CA: Sage.

Kitchener, K. S., & King, P. M. (1981). Reflective judgment: Concepts of justification and their relationship to age and education. *Journal of Applied Developmental Psychology, 2,* 89–116.

Kitchener, K. S., King, P. M., Wood, P. K., & Davison, M. L. (1989). Consistency and sequentiality in the development of reflective judgment: A six year longitudinal study. *Journal of Applied Developmental Psychology, 10,* 73–95.

Kitchener, R. F. (1983). Changing conceptions of the philosophy of science and the foundations of developmental psychology. In D. Kuhn & J. A. Meacham (Eds.), *On the Development of Developmental Psychology* (Vol. 8, pp. 1–30). Basel, Switzerland: Karger.

Kitchener, R. F. (1996). The nature of the social for Piaget and Vygotsky. *Human Development, 36,* 243–249.

Klahr, D. (1980). Information-processing models of intellectual development. In R. H. Kluwe & H. Spada (Eds.), *Developmental models of thinking* (pp. 127–162). New York: Academic Press.

Klahr, D. (1989). Information-processing approaches. In R. Vasta (Ed.), *Annals of child development* (Vol. 6, pp. 133–186). Greenwich, CT: JAI Press.

Klahr, D., & Siegler, R. S. (1978). The representation of children's knowledge. In H. W. Reese & L. P. Lipsitt (Eds.), *Advances in child development.* New York: Academic Press.

Knapp, T. J. (1986). The emergence of cognitive psychology in the latter half of the twentieth century. In T. J. Knapp & L. C. Robertson (Eds.), *Approaches to cognition* (pp. 13–36). Hillsdale, NJ: Lawrence Erlbaum.

Kohlberg, L. (1984). *The psychology of moral development: The nature and validity of moral stages.* San Francisco: Harper & Row.

Kohlberg, L., & Ryncarz, R. A. (1990). Beyond justice reasoning: Moral development and consideration of a seventh stage. In C. N. Alexander & E. J. Langer (Eds.), *Higher stages of human development* (pp. 191–207). New York: Oxford University Press.

Kozol, J. (1991). *Savage inequalities.* New York: Crown.

Kozulin, A. (1990). *Vygotsky's psychology: A biography of ideas.* Cambridge, MA: Harvard University Press.

Kuenne, M. R. (1946). Experimental investigation of the relationship of language to the transposition behavior of young children. *Journal of Experimental Psychology, 35,* 471–490.

Kurtines, W. M., Azmitia, M., & Gewirtz, J. L. (1992). Science, values and rationality: Philosophy of science from a critical co-constructivist perspective. In W. M. Kurtines, M. Azmitia, & J. L. Gewirtz (Eds.), *The role of values in psychology and human development* (pp. 3–29). New York: Wiley.

Labouvie-Vief, G. (1980). Beyond formal observations: Uses and limits of pure logic in life-span development. *Human Development, 23,* 141–161.

Labouvie-Vief, G. (1992). A neo-Piagetian perspective on adult cognitive development. In R. J. Sternberg & C. A. Berg (Eds.), *Intellectual development* (pp. 197–228). Cambridge: Cambridge University Press.

Labouvie-Vief, G. (1994a). *Psyche and eros.* Cambridge: Cambridge University Press.

Labouvie-Vief, G. (1994b). Women's creativity and images of gender. In B. F. Turner & L. E. Troll (Eds.), *Women growing older: Psychological perspectives* (pp. 140–169). Thousand Oaks, CA: Sage.

Labouvie-Vief, G. (1996). Knowledge and the construction of women's development. In P. B. Baltes & U. M. Staudinger (Eds.), *Interactive minds: Life-span perspectives on the social foundation of cognition* (pp. 109–130). Cambridge: Cambridge University Press.

Labouvie-Vief, G., & Chandler, M. J. (1978). Cognitive development and life-span developmental theory: Idealistic versus contextual perspectives. In P. B. Baltes (Ed.), *Life-span development and behavior* (Vol. 1, pp. 182–210). New York: Academic Press.

Labouvie-Vief, G., Chiodo, L. M., Goguen, L. A., Diehl, M., & Orwoll, L. (1995). Representations of self across the life span. *Psychology and Aging, 10*(3), 404–415.

Labouvie-Vief, G., Diehl, M., Chiodo, L. M., & Coyle, N. (1995). Representations of self and parents across the life-span. *Journal of Adult Development, 2*(4), 207–223.

Labouvie-Vief, G., & Hakim-Larson, J. (1989). Developmental shifts in adult thought. In S. Hunter & M. Sundel (Eds.), *Midlife myths: Issues, findings and practical implications* (pp. 69–96). Newbury Park, CA: Sage.

Labouvie-Vief, G., Hakim-Larson, J., DeVoe, M., & Schoeberlein, S. (1989). Emotions and self-regulation: A life span view. *Human Development, 32*, 279–299.

Labouvie-Vief, G., & Lawrence, R. (1985). Object knowledge, personal knowledge, and the process of equilibration in adult cognition. *Human Development, 28*, 25–39.

Labouvie-Vief, G., Orwoll, L., & Manion, M. (1995). Narratives of mind, gender, and the life course. *Human Development, 38*, 239–257.

Laupa, M., Turiel, E., & Cowan, P. A. (1995). Obedience to authority in children and adults. In M. Killen & D. Hart (Eds.), *Morality in everyday life: Developmental perspectives* (pp. 131–165). New York: Cambridge University Press.

Leibert, R. M., Sparfkin, J. N., & Davidson, E. S. (1982). *The early window: Effects of television on children and youth* (2nd ed.). Elmsford, NY: Pergamon Press.

Lerner, R. M. (1993). A developmental contextual view of human development. In S. C. Hayes, L. J. Hayes, H. W. Reese, & T. R. Sarbin (Eds.), *Varieties of scientific contextualism.* Reno, NV: Context Press.

Lerner, R. M. (1996). Relative plasticity, integration, temporality, and diversity in human development. *Developmental Psychology, 32*(4), 781–786.

Lerner, R. M., & Kauffman, M. B. (1985). The concept of development in contextualism. *Developmental Review, 5*(4), 309–333.

Lerner, R. M., & Kauffman, M. B. (1986). On the metatheoretical relativism of analyses of metatheoretical analyses: A critique of Kendler's comments. *Developmental Review, 6*(1), 96–106.

Levy-Bruhl, L. (1923). *Primitive mentality.* New York: Macmillan.

Levy-Bruhl, L. (1926). *How natives think.* London: Allen & Unwin.

Lichtman, R. (1987). The illusion of maturation in an age of decline. In J. M. Broughton (Ed.), *Critical theories of psychological development* (pp. 127–148). New York: Plenum Press.

Lightfoot, C. (1992). Constructing self and peer culture: A narrative perspective on adolescent risk taking. In L. T. Winegar & J. Valsiner (Eds.), *Children's development within social context: Research and methodology* (Vol. 2, pp. 229–248). Hillsdale, NJ: Lawrence Erlbaum.

Liu, J. H., & Liu, S. (1997). Modernism, postmodernism, and neo-Confucian thinking: A critical history of paradigm shifts and values in academic psychology. *New Ideas in Psychology, 15*(2), 159–178.

Livson, F. B. (1981). Paths to psychological health in the middle years: Sex differences. In D. H. Eichorn, N. Haan, J. Clausen, M. Honzik, & P. Mussen (Eds.), *Present and past in middle life* (pp. 195–221). New York: Academic Press.

Luria, A. R. (1979). *The making of mind: A personal account of Soviet psychology.* Cambridge, MA: Harvard University Press.

Maas, H. S., & Kuypers, J. A. (1974). *From thirty to seventy.* San Francisco: Jossey-Bass.

Mann, C. (1994). Behavioral genetics in transition. *Science, 264*, 1686–1693.

Marcia, J. E. (1994). The empirical study of ego identity. In H. A. Bosma, T. L. G. Graafsma, H. D. Grotevant, & D. J. deLevita (Eds.), *Identity and development* (Vol. 179, pp. 67–80). Thousand Oaks, CA: Sage.

Mascolo, M. F., Pollack, R. D., & Fischer, K. W. (1997). Keeping the constructor in development: An epigenetic systems approach. *Journal of Constructivist Psychology, 10*, 25–49.

Massaro, D. W., & Cowan, N. (1993). Information processing models: Microscopes of the mind. In L. W. Porter & M. R. Rosenzweig (Eds.), *Annual review of psychology* (Vol. 44, pp. 383–425). Palo Alto, CA: Annual Reviews.

McCartney, K., Harris, M. J., & Bernieri, F. (1990). Growing up and growing apart: A developmental meta-analysis of twin studies. *Psychological Bulletin, 107*(2), 226–237.

McClannahan, L. E., & Krantz, P. J. (1993). On systems analysis in autism intervention programs. *Journal of Applied Behavioral Analysis, 26*(4), 589–596.

McClearn, G. E. (1993). Behavior genetics: The last century and the next. In R. Plomin & G. E. McClearn (Eds.), *Nature, nurture and psychology* (pp. 27–54). Washington, DC: American Psychological Association.

McClearn, G. E., Plomin, R., Gora-Mazlak, G., & Crabbe, J. C. (1991). The gene chase in behavioral science. *Psychological Science, 2*(4), 222–229.

McDougall, G. J. (1995). Memory self-efficacy and strategy use on successful elders. *Educational Gerontology, 21*, 357–373.

McGraw, M. B. (1935). *Growth: A study of Johnny and Jimmy.* New York: Appleton-Century.

McGraw, M. B. (1939). Later development of children specially trained during infancy. *Child Development, 10*, 1–19.

McGraw, M. B. (1940). Basic concepts and procedures in the study of behavior development. *Psychological Review, 47*, 79–89.

McGraw, M. B. (1942). *The neuromuscular maturation of the human infant.* New York: Columbia University Press.

McGraw, M. B. (1946). Maturation of behavior. In L. Carmichael (Ed.), *Manual of child psychology.* New York: Wiley.

McGuffin, P., & Katz, R. (1993). Genes, adversity, and depression. In R. Plomin & G. E. McClearn (Eds.), *Nature, nurture and psychology* (pp. 217–230). Washington, DC: American Psychological Association.

McShane, J. (1991). *Cognitive development: An information processing approach.* Oxford: Basil Blackwell.

Mead, G. H. (1934). *Mind, self and society.* Chicago: University of Chicago Press.

Meisels, S. (1987). Uses and abuses of developmental screening and school readiness testing. *Young Children, 42*(2), 68–73.

Michel, G. F., & Moore, C. L. (1995). *Developmental psychobiology.* Cambridge, MA: MIT Press.

Miller, P. J., & Goodnow, J. J. (1995). Cultural practices: Toward an integration of culture and development. *New Directions in Child Development, 67*, 5–16.

Miyake, K., Campos, J., Bradshaw, D. L., & Kagan, J. (1986). Issues in socioemotional development. In H. Stevenson, H. Azuma, & K. Hakuta (Eds.), *Child development and education in Japan.* New York: Freeman.

Moll, L. C. (Ed.). (1990). *Vygotsky and education.* Cambridge: Cambridge University Press.

Morss, J. R. (1992). Making waves: Deconstruction and developmental psychology. *Theory and Psychology, 2*(4), 445–465.

Muuss, R. E. (1996). *Theories of adolescence* (6th ed.). New York: McGraw-Hill.

Nelson, K. (1986). *Event knowledge: Structure and function in development.* Hillsdale, NJ: Lawrence Erlbaum.

Nelson, K. (1993a). Events, narratives, memory: What develops? In C. A. Nelson (Ed.), *Memory and affect in development: The Minnesota symposium on child psychology* (Vol. 26, pp. 1–24). Hillsdale, NJ: Lawrence Erlbaum.

Nelson, K. (1993b). Explaining the emergence of autobiographical memory in early childhood. In A. F. Collins, S. E. Gathercole, M. A. Conway, & P. E. Morris (Eds.), *Theories of memory* (pp. 355–386). Hove, UK: Lawrence Erlbaum.

Neugarten, B. L. (1975). The future and the young-old. *The Gerontologist, 15*, 4–9.

Newell, A., & Simon, H. A. (1972). *Human problem solving.* Englewood Cliffs, NJ: Prentice-Hall.

Newell, A., Shaw, J. C., & Simon, H. A. (1958). Elements of a theory of human problem solving. *Psychological Review, 65,* 151–166.

Nicolopoulou, A. (1993). Play, cognitive development, and the social world: Piaget, Vygotsky, and beyond. *Human Development, 36,* 1–23.

Nye, R. D. (1996). *Three psychologies: Perspectives from Freud, Skinner, Rogers.* Pacific Grove, CA: Brooks/Cole.

Overton, W. (1994). The arrow of time and the cycle of time: Concepts of change, cognition and embodiment. *Psychological Inquiry, 5*(3), 215–237.

Overton, W. F. (1984). World views and their influence on psychological theory and research: Kuhn-Lakatos-Laudan. In H. W. Reese (Ed.), *Advances in child development and behavior* (Vol. 18, pp. 194–226). San Diego: Academic Press.

Overton, W. F. (1985). Scientific methodologies and the competence-moderator-performance issue. In E. D. Neimark, R. DeLisi, & J. L. Newman (Eds.), *Moderators of Competence* (pp. 15–42). Hillsdale, NJ: Lawrence Erlbaum.

Overton, W. F. (1991). The structure of developmental theory. In H. W. Reese (Ed.), *Advances in child development and behavior* (Vol. 23, pp. 1–38). San Diego: Academic Press.

Overton, W. F., & Reese, H. W. (1973). Models of development: Methodological implications. In J. R. Nesselroade & H. W. Reese (Eds.), *Life-span developmental psychology: Methodological issues* (pp. 65–86). New York: Academic Press.

Oyama, S. (1985). *The ontogeny of information.* Cambridge: Cambridge University Press.

Palmer, S. E., & Kimchi, R. (1986). The information processing approach to cognition. In T. J. Knapp & L. C. Robertson (Eds.), *Approaches to cognition.* Hillsdale, NJ: Lawrence Erlbaum.

Papousek, H., & Papousek, M. (1984). Learning and cognition in the everyday life of human infants. In J. S. Rosenblatt, C. Beer, M. C. Busnel, & P. J. B. Slater (Eds.), *Advances in the study of behavior* (Vol. 14, pp. 127–163). New York: Academic Press.

Pastore, N. (1984). *The nature-nurture controversy.* New York: Garland.

Patterson, G. R. (1986). Maternal rejection: Determinant or product for deviant child behavior? In W. W. Hartup & Z. Rubin (Eds.), *Relationships and development* (pp. 73–94). Hillsdale, NJ: Lawrence Erlbaum.

Patton, M. Q. (1990). *Qualitative research and research methods* (2nd ed.). Newbury Park, CA: Sage.

Pavlov, I. P. (1927). *Conditioned reflexes: An investigation of the physiological activity of the cerebral cortex.* London: Oxford University Press.

Pepper, S. C. (1961). *World hypotheses: A study in evidence.* Los Angeles: University of California Press.

Perone, M. (1994). Single-subject designs and developmental psychology. In S. H. Cohen & H. W. Reese (Eds.), *Life-span developmental psychology: Methodological contributions* (pp. 95–118). Hillsdale, NJ: Lawrence Erlbaum.

Perry, W. G. (1970). *Forms of intellectual and ethical development in the college years: A scheme.* New York: Holt, Rinehart & Winston.

Piaget, J. (1952a). *The child's conception of number.* London: Humanities Press.

Piaget, J. (1952b). *The origins of intelligence in children.* New York: International Universities Press.

Piaget, J. (1954). *The construction of reality in the child.* New York: Basic Books.

Piaget, J. (1960). *The child's conception of physical causality.* Totowa, NJ: Littlefield, Adams.

Piaget, J. (1962). *Play, dreams and imitation in childhood.* New York: Norton.

Piaget, J. (1965). *The moral judgment of the child.* New York: Free Press.

Piaget, J. (1966). *Judgment and reasoning in the child.* Totowa, NJ: Littlefield, Adams.

Piaget, J. (1970). *Genetic epistomology.* New York: Columbia University Press.

Piaget, J. (1971a). *Biology and knowledge.* Chicago: University of Chicago Press.

Piaget, J. (1971b). *The child's conception of time.* New York: Ballantine Books.

Piaget, J. (1974a). *The development of physical quantities in the child: Conservation and atomism.* London: Routledge.

Piaget, J. (1974b). *The language and thought of the child.* New York: New American Library.

Piaget, J. (1976). *The grasp of consciousness.* Cambridge, MA: Harvard University Press.

Piaget, J. (1978). *Success and understanding.* London: Routledge.

Piaget, J. (1979). *The child's conception of the world.* Totowa, NJ: Littlefield, Adams.

Piaget, J. (1980a). *Adaptation and intelligence: Organic selection and phenocopy.* Chicago: University of Chicago Press.

Piaget, J. (1980b). *Experiments in contradiction.* Chicago: University of Chicago Press.

Piaget, J. (1985). *The equilibration of cognitive structures.* Chicago: University of Chicago Press.

Piaget, J., & Inhelder, B. (1956). *The child's conception of space.* London: Routledge.

Piaget, J., & Inhelder, B. (1969). *The psychology of the child.* New York: Basic Books.

Plomin, R. (1986). *Development, genetics and psychology.* Hillsdale, NJ: Lawrence Erlbaum.

Plomin, R. (1990). Trying to shoot the messenger for his message. *Behavioral and Brain Sciences, 13,* 144.

Plomin, R. (1993). Nature and nurture: Perspective and prospective. In R. Plomin & G. E. McClearn (Eds.), *Nature, nurture and psychology* (pp. 459–486). Washington, DC: American Psychological Association.

Plomin, R. (1994). *Genetics and experience: The interplay between nature and nurture* (Vol. 6). Thousand Oaks, CA: Sage.

Plomin, R., & Daniels, D. (1987). Why are children in the same family so different from one another? *Behavioral and brain sciences, 10,* 1–59.

Plomin, R., & DeFries, J. C. (1983). The Colorado Adoption Study. *Child Development, 54*(2), 276–290.

Plomin, R., Emde, R. N., Braungart, J. M., Campos, J., & Corley, R. (1993). Genetic change and continuity from fourteen to twenty months: The MacArthur Longitudinal Twin Study. *Child Development, 64*(5), 1354–1376.

Plomin, R., McClearn, G. E., Smith, D. L., Vignetti, S., Chorney, M. J., et al. (1994a). DNA markers associated with high versus low IQ: The IQ Quantitative Trait Loci (QTL) Project. *Behavior Genetics, 24*(2), 107–118.

Plomin, R., Owen, M. J., & McGuffin, P. (1994). The genetic basis of complex human behaviors. *Science, 264,* 1733–1739.

Plomin, R., Pedersen, N. L., Lichtenstein, P., & McClearn, G. E. (1994). Variability and stability in cognitive abilities are largely genetic later in life. *Behavior Genetics, 24*(3), 207–215.

Plomin, R., Reiss, D., Hetherington, E. M., & Howe, G. W. (1994). Nature and nurture: Contributions to measures of family environment. *Developmental Psychology, 30*(1), 32–43.

Plunkett, K., & Sinha, C. (1992). Connectionism and developmental psychology. *British Journal of Developmental Psychology, 10,* 209–254.

Podolefsky, A. (1994). Computer assisted qualitative date management: Some recent innovations in the management and analysis of field notes. In S. H. Cohen & H. W. Reese (Eds.), *Life-span developmental psychology: Methodological contributions* (pp. 171–186). Hillsdale, NJ: Lawrence Erlbaum.

Porwancher, D., & deLisi, R. (1993). Developmental placement of kindergarten children based on the Gesell School Readiness Test. *Early Childhood Research Quarterly, 8*(2), 149–166.

Reese, H. W. (1986). Behavioral and dialectical psychologies. In L. P. Lipsitt & J. H. Cantor (Eds.), *Experimental child psychologist: Essays and experiments in honor of Charles C. Spiker* (pp. 157–195). Hillsdale, NJ: Lawrence Erlbaum.

Reese, H. W. (1991). Contextualism and developmental psychology. In H. W. Reese (Ed.), *Advances in child development and behavior* (Vol. 23, pp. 188–232). San Diego: Academic Press.

Reese, H. W., & Overton, W. F. (1970). Models of development and theories of development. In L. R. Goulet & P. B. Baltes (Eds.), *Life-span developmental psychology* (pp. 116–145). New York: Academic Press.

Reiss, D. (1993). Genes and the environment: Siblings and synthesis. In R. Plomin & G. E. McClearn (Eds.), *Nature, nurture and psychology* (pp. 417–432). Washington, DC: American Psychological Association.

Richelle, M. N. (1993). *B. F. Skinner, a reappraisal.* Hillsdale NJ: Lawrence Erlbaum.

Rogoff, B. (1990). *Apprenticeship in thinking: Cognitive development in social context.* New York: Oxford University Press.

Rogoff, B. (1993). Children's guided participation and participatory appropriation in sociocultural activity. In R. H. Wozniak & K. W. Fischer (Eds.), *Development in action: Acting and thinking in specific environments* (pp. 121–154). Hillsdale, NJ: Lawrence Erlbaum.

Rogoff, B. (1997). Evaluating development in the process of participation: Theory, methods, and practice building on each other. In E. Amsel & K. A. Renniger (Eds.), *Change and development: Issues of theory, method and application* (pp. 265–285). Mahwah, NJ: Lawrence Erlbaum.

Rogoff, B., Baker-Sennett, J., Lacasa, P., & Goldsmith, D. (1995). Development through participation in sociocultural activity. In J. J. Goodnow & P. J. Miller (Eds.), *Cultural practices as contexts for development* (Vol. 67, pp. 45–65). San Francisco: Jossey-Bass.

Rogoff, B., & Chavajay, P. (1995). What's become of research on the cultural basis of cognitive development? *American Psychologist, 50*(10), 859–877.

Rogoff, B., Mistry, J., Goncu, A., & Mosier, C. (1993). *Guided participation in cultural activity by toddlers and caregivers* (Vol. 58). Chicago: University of Chicago Press.

Rogoff, B., Radziszewska, B., & Masiello, T. (1995). Analysis of developmental processes in sociocultural activity. In L. W. Martin & K. Nelson (Eds.), *Sociocultural psychology: Theory and practice of doing and knowing* (pp. 125–149). New York: Cambridge University Press.

Rogoff, B., & Wertsch, J. V. (Eds.). (1984). *Children's learning in the "Zone of Proximal Development."* San Francisco: Jossey-Bass.

Rose, N. (1990). *Governing the soul: The shaping of the private self.* London: Routledge.

Rose, R., J., Kaprio, J., Williams, C. J., Viken, R., & Obremski, K. (1990). Social contact and sibling similarity: Facts, issues and sibling similarity. *Behavior Genetics, 20,* 766–788.

Rotter, J. B. (1954). *Social learning and clinical psychology.* Englewood Cliffs, NJ: Prentice-Hall.

Rotter, J. B. (1966). Generalized expectancies for internal versus external control of reinforcement. *Genetic, Social, and General Psychology Monographs, 80,* 1–28.

Rotter, J. B. (1982). *The development and applications of social learning theory.* New York: Praeger.

Rowe, D. C. (1994). *The limits of family influence.* New York: Guilford Press.

Sagi, A., Lamb, M. E., Lewkowitz, K. S., Shoham, R., Dvir, R., & Estes, D. (1985). Security of infant-mother, -father, and metapelet attachments among kibbutz reared Israeli children. *Monographs of the Society for Research in Child Development, 50*(1-2, Serial No. 209).

Sameroff, A. (1975). Transactional models in early social relations. *Human Development, 18,* 65–79.

Sameroff, A. (1994). Developmental systems and developmental functioning. In R. P. Parke & S. G. Kellam (Eds.), *Exploring family relationships with other social contexts*. Hillsdale, NJ: Lawrence Erlbaum.

Sameroff, A. J. (1989). Commentary: General systems and the regulation of development. In M. R. Gunnar & E. Thelen (Eds.), *Systems and development: The Minnesota Symposium on Child Psychology* (Vol. 22, pp. 219–236). Hillsdale, NJ: Lawrence Erlbaum.

Scarr, S. (1991). Theoretical issues in investigating intellectual plasticity. In S. E. Brauth, W. S. Hall, & R. J. Dooling (Eds.), *Plasticity of development* (pp. 57–72). Cambridge, MA: MIT Press.

Scarr, S. (1992). Developmental theories for the 1990s: Developmental and individual differences. *Child Development, 63*(1), 1–19.

Scarr, S. (1993). Biological and cultural diversity: The legacy of Darwin for development. *Child Development, 64*(5), 1333–1353.

Scarr, S., & McCartney, K. (1983). How people make their own environments: A theory of genotype-environment effects. *Child Development, 54*(2), 424–435.

Scarr, S., & Ricciuti, A. (1991). What effects do parents have on their children. In L. Okagaki & R. J. Sternberg (Eds.), *Directors of development: Influences on the development of children's thinking* (pp. 3–23). Hillsdale, NJ: Lawrence Erlbaum.

Scarr, S., & Weinberg, R. A. (1983). The Minnesota Adoption Studies: Genetic differences and malleability. *Child Development, 54*(2), 260–268.

Scarr, S., & Weinberg, R. A. (1994). Educational and occupational achievements of brothers and sisters in adoptive and biologically related families. *Behavior Genetics, 24*(4), 301–325.

Schaie, K. W. (1965). A general model for the study of developmental problems. *Psychological Bulletin, 64*(2), 92–107.

Schaie, K. W. (1984). Historic time and cohort effects. In K. A. McCluskey & H. W. Reese (Eds.), *Life-span developmental psychology: Historical and generational effects* (pp. 1–16). Orlando, FL: Academic Press.

Schaie, K. W. (1994). Developmental designs revisited. In S. H. Cohen & H. W. Reese (Eds.), *Life-span developmental psychology: Methodological contributions* (pp. 45–64). Hillsdale, NJ: Lawrence Erlbaum.

Schaie, K. W., & Strother, C. R. (1968). A cross-sequential study of age changes in cognitive behavior. *Psychological Bulletin, 70*, 671–680.

Schank, R. C., & Abelson, R. P. (1977). *Scripts, plans, goals and understanding*. Hillsdale, NJ: Lawrence Erlbaum.

Scheibe, K. E. (1994). Cocaine careers: Historical and individual constructions. In T. R. Sarbin & J. I. Kitsuse (Eds.), *Constructing the social* (pp. 195–212). London: Sage.

Schneirla, T. C. (1957). The concept of development in comparative psychology. In D. B. Harris (Ed.), *The concept of development* (pp. 78–108). Minneapolis: University of Minnesota Press.

Schneirla, T. C. (1966). Behavioral development and comparative psychology. *Quarterly Review of Biology, 41*, 283–302.

Schorr, L. B. (1988). *Within our reach: Breaking the cycle of disadvantage*. New York: Anchor Press.

Scott, J. P. (1987). Why does human twin research not produce results consistent with those from nonhuman animals? *Behavioral and Brain Sciences, 10*(1), 46–47.

Sears, R. R., Maccoby, E. E., & Levin, H. (1957). *Patterns of child rearing*. Evanston, IL: Row, Peterson.

Selman, R. (1971). The relation of role taking to the development of moral judgment in children. *Child Development, 42*, 79–91.

Selman, R. L. (1990). *Making a friend in youth: Developmental theory and pair therapy.* Chicago: University of Chicago Press.

Sidman, M. (1960). *Tactics of scientific research.* New York: Basic Books.

Siegler, R. S. (1981). Developmental sequences within and between articles. *Monographs of the Society for Research in Child Development* (Vol. 46). Chicago: University of Chicago Press.

Siegler, R. S. (1983). Information processing approaches to development. In P. H. Mussen (Ed.), *Handbook of child psychology* (4th ed., Vol. 1, pp. 129–213). New York: Wiley.

Siegler, R. S. (1988a). Individual differences in strategy choices: Good students, not-so-good students and perfectionists. *Child Development, 59,* 833–851.

Siegler, R. S. (1988b). Strategy choice procedures and the development of multiplication skill. *Journal of Experimental Psychology: General, 116,* 250–264.

Siegler, R. S. (1989). How domain-general and domain-specific knowledge interact to produce strategy choice. *Merrill-Palmer Quarterly, 35*(1), 1–26.

Siegler, R. S. (1991). *Children's thinking* (2nd ed.). Englewood Cliffs, NJ: Prentice-Hall.

Siegler, R. S. (1995). How does change occur: A microgenetic study of number conservation. *Cognitive Psychology, 28*(3), 225–273.

Siegler, R. S. (1996). *Emerging minds: The process of change in children's thinking.* New York: Oxford University Press.

Siegler, R. S., & Crowley, K. (1991). The microgenetic method: A direct means for studying cognitive development. *American Psychologist, 46*(6), 606–620.

Siegler, R. S., & Crowley, K. (1994). Constraints on learning in nonprivileged domains. *Cognitive Psychology, 27*(2), 194–226.

Siegler, R. S., & Robinson, M. (1982). The development of numerical understandings. In H. Reese & L. P. Lipsitt (Eds.), *Advances in child development and behavior* (Vol. 16, pp. 241–312). New York: Academic Press.

Siegler, R. S., & Shipley, C. (1987). The role of learning in children's strategy choices. In L. S. Liben (Ed.), *Development and learning: Conflict or congruence?* (pp. 71–108). Hillsdale, NJ: Lawrence Erlbaum.

Singer, E. (1993). Shared care for children. *Theory & Psychology, 3*(4), 429–449.

Skinner, B. F. (1938). *The behavior of organisms: An experimental analysis.* New York: Appleton-Century-Crofts.

Skinner, B. F. (1948/1976). *Walden Two.* New York: Macmillan.

Skinner, B. F. (1953). *Science and human behavior.* New York: Free Press.

Skinner, B. F. (1971). *Beyond freedom and dignity.* New York: Knopf.

Skinner, B. F. (1974). *About behaviorism.* New York: Knopf.

Skinner, B. F. (1978). *Reflections on behaviorism and society.* Englewood Cliffs, NJ: Prentice-Hall.

Skinner, B. F. (1984). The shame of American education. *American Psychologist, 39,* 947–954.

Skinner, B. F. (1987). Whatever happened to psychology as the science of behavior? *American Psychologist, 42,* 780–786.

Skinner, B. F. (1989). *Recent issues in the analysis of behavior.* Columbus, OH: Merrill.

Smith, L. (1996). With knowledge in mind: Novel transformation of the learner or transformation of novel information. *Human Development, 39,* 257–263.

Smith, L. B., Sera, M., & Gattuso, B. (1988). The development of thinking. In R. J. Sternberg & E. E. Smith (Eds.), *The psychology of human thought* (pp. 366–391). Cambridge: Cambridge University Press.

Smith, M. B. (1994). Selfhood at risk. *American Psychologist, 49*(5), 405–411.

Solberg, V. S., Good, G. E., & Fischer, A. R. (1995). Career decision making and career search activities: Relative effects of career search self-efficacy and human agency. *Journal of Counseling Psychology, 42,* 448–455.

Spear-Swerling, L., & Sternberg, R. J. (1994). The road not taken: An integrative theoretical model of reading disability. *Journal of Learning Disabilities, 27*(2), 91–103, 122.

Spence, K. W. (1956). *Behavior theory and conditioning.* New Haven, CT: Yale University Press.

Spiker, C. C. (1966). The concept of development: Relevant and irrelevant issues. *Monographs of the Society for Research in Child Development, 31*(5), 40–54.

Spock, B. (1992). *Dr. Spock's baby and child care* (6th ed.). New York: Pocket Books.

Sporns, O., & Edelman, G. M. (1993). Solving Bernstein's problem: A proposal for the development of coordinated movement by selection. *Child Development, 64*(4), 960–981.

Sternberg, R. J. (1984). Mechanisms of cognitive development: A componential approach. In R. J. Sternberg (Ed.), *Mechanisms of cognitive development.* New York: Freeman.

Sternberg, R. J. (1985). *Beyond IQ: A triarchic theory of human intelligence.* Cambridge: Cambridge University Press.

Sternberg, R. J. (1988a). Intelligence. In R. J. Sternberg & E. E. Smith (Eds.), *The psychology of human thought* (pp. 267–308). Cambridge: Cambridge University Press.

Sternberg, R. J. (1988b). *The triarchic mind: A new theory of human intelligence.* New York: Viking Press.

Sternberg, R. J. (1989). Domain-generality versus domain-specificity: The life and impending death of a false dichotomy. *Merrill-Palmer Quarterly, 35*(1), 115–130.

Sternberg, R. J. (1990). *Metaphors of mind: Conceptions of the nature of intelligence.* New York: Cambridge University Press.

Sternberg, R. J., & Clinkenbeard, P. R. (1995). The triarchic mode applied to identifying, teaching, and assessing gifted children. *Roeper Review, 17*(4), 255–260.

Sternberg, R. J., & Zhang, L.F. (1995). What do we mean by giftedness? A pentagonal implicit theory. *Gifted Child Quarterly, 39*(2), 88–94.

Stevens, R. (1983a). *Erik Erikson: An introduction.* New York: St Martin's Press.

Stevens, R. (1983b). *Freud and psychoanalysis.* New York: St. Martin's Press.

Stevenson, H. W. (1983). How children learn—The quest for a theory. In P. H. Mussen (Ed.), *Handbook of child psychology* (Vol. 1, pp. 213–236). New York: Wiley.

Strachey, J. (Ed.). (1953–1966). *The standard edition of the complete psychological works of Sigmund Freud.* London: Hogarth Press.

Strecher, V. J., Seijts, G. H., Kok, G. J., & Latham, G. P. (1995). Goal setting as a strategy for health behavior change. *Health Education Quarterly, 22*(2), 190–200.

Teo, T. (1997). Developmental psychology and the relevance of a critical metatheoretical reflection. *Human Development, 40*(4), 195–210.

Thelen, E. (1989a). The (re)discovery of motor learning: Learning new things from an old field. *Developmental Psychology, 25*(6), 946–950.

Thelen, E. (1989b). Self-organization in developmental processes: Can systems approaches work. In M. R. Gunnar & E. Thelen (Eds.), *Systems and development* (Vol. 22). Hillsdale, NJ: Lawrence Erlbaum.

Thelen, E. (1995). Motor development: A new synthesis. *American Psychologist, 50*(2), 79–95.

Thelen, E., & Adolp, K. E. (1992). Arnold L. Gesell: The paradox of nature and nurture. *Developmental Psychology, 28*(3), 368–380.

Thelen, E., Kelso, J. A., & Fogel, A. (1987). Self-organizing systems and infant motor development. *Developmental Review, 7*(1), 39–66.

Thelen, E., & Smith, L. B. (1994). *A dynamic systems approach to the development of cognition and action.* Cambridge, MA: MIT Press.

Thelen, E., & Ulrich, B. D. (1991). Hidden skills. *Monographs of the Society for Research in Child Development, 56*(1), 1–99.

Thorne, B. (1997). Children and gender: Constructions of differences. In M. M. Gergen & S. N. Davis (Eds.), *Toward a new psychology of gender* (pp. 185–201). New York: Routledge.

Thurnwald, R. (1922). Psychologie des primitiven Menschen. In G. Kafka (Ed.), *Handbuch der vergleichenden Psychologie Band 1* (pp. 147–320). Munchen, Germany: Verlang von Ernst Reinhart.

Tobach, E., Aronson, L. R., & Shaw, E. (Eds.). (1971). *The biopsychology of development*. New York: Academic Press.

Todd, J. T., & Morris, E. K. (1992). Case histories in the great power of steady misrepresentation. *American Psychologist, 47*(11), 1441–1453.

Tryphon, A., & Voneche, J. (Eds.). (1996). *Piaget-Vygotsky: The social genesis of thought*. London: Psychology Press.

Tudge, J., Shanahan, M. J., & Valsiner, J. (Eds.). (1997). *Comparisons in human development: Understanding time and context*. Cambridge: Cambridge University Press.

Turiel, E. (1980). The development of social-conventional and moral concepts. In M. Windmiller (Ed.), *Moral development and socialization* (pp. 69–106). Boston: Allyn & Bacon.

Turkewitz, G., & Devenny, D. A. (Eds.). (1993). *Developmental time and timing*. Hillsdale, NJ: Lawrence Erlbaum.

van der Veer, R. (1996). Vygotsky and Piaget: A collective monologue. *Human Development, 36*, 237–242.

van der Veer, R., & Valsiner, J. (1991). *Understanding Vygotsky: A quest for synthesis*. Oxford: Blackwell.

Vygotsky, L. S. (1962). *Thought and language*. Cambridge, MA: MIT Press.

Vygotsky, L. S. (1978). *Mind in society*. Cambridge, MA: Harvard University Press.

Vygotsky, L. S. (1997). *Educational psychology*. Boca Raton, FL: St. Lucie Press.

Vygotsky, L. S., & Luria, A. R. (1993). *Studies on the history of behavior: Ape, primitive and child*. Hillsdale, NJ: Lawrence Erlbaum.

Wachs, T. D. (1983). The use and abuse of environment in behavior-genetic research. *Child Development, 54*(2), 396–407.

Wachs, T. D. (1992). *The nature of nurture*. Newbury Park, CA: Sage.

Wachs, T. D. (1993). The nature-nurture gap: What we have here is a failure to collaborate. In R. Plomin & G. E. McClearn (Eds.), *Nature, nurture and psychology* (pp. 375–394). Washington, DC: American Psychological Association.

Wadsworth, S. J., DeFries, J. C., Fulker, D. W., & Plomin, R. (1995). Cognitive ability and academic achievement in the Colorado Adoption Project: A multivariate analysis of parent-offspring and sibling data. *Behavior Genetics, 25*(1), 1–15.

Wahlsten, D. (1990). Insensitivity of the analysis of variance to heredity-environment interaction. *Behavioral and brain sciences, 13*, 109–161.

Walkerdine, V. (1993). Beyond developmentalism? *Theory and Psychology, 3*(4), 451–471.

Wark, G. R., & Krebs, D. L. (1996). Gender and dilemma differences in real-life moral judgment. *Developmental Psychology, 32*(2), 220–230.

Wartofsky, M. W. (1986). On the creation and transformation of norms of human development. In L. Cirillo & S. Wapner (Eds.), *Value presuppositions in theories of human development* (pp. 113–125). Hillsdale, NJ: Lawrence Erlbaum.

Waterman, A. S. (1994). Ethical considerations in interventions for promoting identity development. In S. L. Archer (Ed.), *Intervention for adolescent identity development* (Vol. 169, pp. 231–244). Thousand Oaks, CA: Sage.

Watson, J. B. (1913). Psychology as a behaviorist views it. *Psychological Review, 20*, 158–177.

Watson, J. B. (1914). *Behavior: An introduction to comparative psychology*. New York: Holt, Rinehart & Winston.

Watson, J. B. (1928). *Psychological care of the infant and child*. New York: Norton.

Watson, J. B. (1930). *Behaviorism*. Chicago: University of Chicago Press.

Watson, J. D. (1968). *The double helix: A personal account of the discovery of the structure of DNA*. New York: Atheneum.

Waung, M. (1995). The effects of self-regulatory coping orientation on newcomer adjustment and job survival. *Personnel Psychology, 48*(3), 633–650.

Werner, H. (1957). The concept of development from a comparative and organismic point of view. In D. B. Harris (Ed.), *The concept of development* (pp. 125–147). Minneapolis: University of Minnesota Press.

Wertsch, J. V. (1985). *Vygotsky and the social formation of mind*. Cambridge, MA: Harvard University Press.

Wertsch, J. V. (1991). *Voices of the mind: A sociocultural approach to mediated action*. Cambridge, MA: Harvard University Press.

Wertsch, J. V., & Kanner, B. G. (1992). A sociocultural approach to intellectual development. In R. J. Sternberg & C. A. Berg (Eds.), *Intellectual development* (pp. 328–349). Cambridge: Cambridge University Press.

Wertsch, J. V., Tulviste, P., & Hagstrom, F. (1993). A sociocultural approach to agency. In E. A. Forman, N. Minick, & C. A. Stone (Eds.), *Contexts for learning: Sociocultural dynamics in children's development* (pp. 336–356). New York: Oxford University Press.

Wetherell, M. (1997). Linguistic repetoires and literary criticism: New directions for a social psychology of gender. In M. M. Gergen & S. N. Davis (Eds.), *Toward a new psychology of gender* (pp. 149–167). New York: Routledge.

Wilkinson, S. (1997). Feminist Psychology. In D. Fox & I. Prilleltensky (Eds.), *Critical psychology: An introduction* (pp. 247–264). London: Sage.

Williams, W. M., & Sternberg, R. J. (1993). Seven lessons for helping children make the most of their abilities. *Educational Psychology, 13*(3-4), 317–331.

Wohlwill, J. F. (1973). *The study of behavioral development*. New York: Academic Press.

Wohlwill, J. F. (1991). Relations between method and theory in developmental research: A partial-isomorphism view. In P. van Geert & L. P. Mos (Eds.), *Annals of theoretical psychology* (Vol. 7, pp. 91–138). New York: Plenum Press.

Wolff, P. H. (1960). The developmental psychologies of Jean Piaget and psychoanalysis. *Psychological Issues, 2*(1), 5–183.

Wolman, B. B. (1981). *Contemporary theories and systems in psychology* (2nd ed.). New York: Plenum Press.

Youniss, J., & Damon, W. (1992). Social construction in Piaget's theory. In H. Beilin & P. B. Pufall (Eds.), *Piaget's theory: Prospects and possibilities* (pp. 267–286). Hillsdale, NJ: Lawrence Erlbaum.

Youniss, J., & Yates, M. (1997). *Community service and social responsibility in youth*. Chicago: University of Chicago Press.

Zimmerman, B. J., Bandura, A., & Martinez–Pons, M. (1995). Self-motivation for academic attainment: The role of self-efficacy beliefs and personal goal setting. *American Educational Research Journal, 29*, 663–676.

Zimmerman, R. S., Sprecher, S., Langer, L. M., & Holloway, C. D. (1995). Adolescents perceived ability to say "no" to unwanted sex. *Journal of Adolescent Research, 10*(3), 383–399.

Zuriff, G. E. (1985). *Behaviorism: A conceptual reconstruction*. New York: Columbia University Press.

Credits

Index